Beyond the Racial State

"The racial state" has become a familiar shorthand for the Third Reich, encapsulating its raison d'être, its ambitions, and the underlying logic of its genocidal violence. The Nazi racial state's agenda is generally understood as a fundamental reshaping of society based on a new hierarchy of racial value. However, this volume argues that it is time to reappraise what race really meant under Nazism, and to question and complicate its relationship to the Nazis' agenda, actions, and appeal. Based on a wealth of new research, the contributors show that racial knowledge and racial discourse in Nazi Germany were far more contradictory and disparate than we have come to assume. They shed new light on how racial policy worked and was understood, and consider race's function, content, and power in relation to society and nation, and above all in relation to the extraordinary violence unleashed by the Nazis.

DEVIN O. PENDAS is Associate Professor of History at Boston College. He received his BA from Carleton College and his MA and PhD from the University of Chicago. His research focuses on the history of Holocaust trials after World War II and the history of international law and mass violence. His publications include *The Frankfurt Auschwitz Trial, 1963–1965: Genocide, History, and the Limits of the Law* (2006) and *Political Trials in Theory and History* (co-edited, 2017).

MARK ROSEMAN is Pat M. Glazer Chair in Jewish Studies and Professor in History at Indiana University. Trained at Cambridge and Warwick universities in the UK, he has taught in the UK and the USA. His books include *The Past in Hiding* (2000), *The Villa, the Lake, the Meeting: Wannsee and the Final Solution* (2002), and *Jewish Responses to Persecution 1933–1946, Volume 1* (with Jürgen Matthäus, 2010).

RICHARD F. WETZELL is a Research Fellow at the German Historical Institute in Washington, D.C. Trained at Swarthmore College, Columbia University, and Stanford University, he was a Postdoctoral Fellow at Harvard and has taught at the University of Maryland, Georgetown University, and the Catholic University of America. His research focuses on the intersection of law, science, and politics in modern Germany. His publications include *Inventing the Criminal: A History of German Criminology, 1880–1945* (2000), *Engineering Society* (co-edited, 2012), and *Crime and Criminal Justice in Modern Germany* (2014).

Publications of the German Historical Institute

Edited by

Simone Lässig
with the assistance of David Lazar

The German Historical Institute is a center for advanced study and research whose purpose is to provide a permanent basis for scholarly cooperation among historians from the Federal Republic of Germany and the United States. The Institute conducts, promotes, and supports research into both American and German political, social, economic, and cultural history; into transatlantic migration, especially during the nineteenth and twentieth centuries; and into the history of international relations, with special emphasis on the roles played by the United States and Germany.

Recent Books in the Series

Anna von der Goltz and Britta Waldschmidt-Nelson, editors, *Inventing the Silent Majority in Western Europe and the United States*

Rebekka Habermas, *Thieves in Court: The Making of the German Legal System in the Nineteenth Century*

Eckart Conze, Martin Klimke, and Jeremy Varon, *Nuclear Threats, Nuclear Fear and the Cold War in the 1980s*

Jonas Scherner and Eugene White, *Paying for Hitler's War: The Consequences of Nazi Hegemony for Europe*

Adam T. Rosenbaum, *Bavarian Tourism and the Modern World, 1800–1950*

Hartmut Berghoff, Jürgen Kocka, and Dieter Ziegler, editors, *Business in the Age of Extremes: Essays in Modern German and Austrian Economic History*

Lars Maischak, *German Merchants in the Nineteenth-Century Atlantic*

Thomas W. Maulucci, Jr. and Detlef Junker, editors, *GIs in Germany: The Social, Economic, Cultural, and Political History of the American Military Presence*

Gerald D. Feldman, *Austrian Banks in the Period of National Socialism*

Eric C. Steinhart, *The Holocaust and the Germanization of Ukraine*

Alison Efford, *German Immigrants, Race, and Citizenship in the Civil War Era*

Cathryn Carson, *Heisenberg in the Atomic Age: Science and the Public Sphere*

Michaela Hoenicke Moore, *Know Your Enemy: The American Debate on Nazism, 1933–1945*

Yair Mintzker, *The Defortification of the German City, 1689–1866*

Astrid M. Eckert, *The Struggle for the Files: The Western Allies and the Return of German Archives after the Second World War*

Winson Chu, *The German Minority in Interwar Poland*

Hartmut Berghoff and Uta Andrea Balbier, editors, *The East German Economy, 1945–2010: Falling Behind or Catching Up?*

Roger Chickering and Stig Förster, editors, *War in an Age of Revolution, 1775–1815*

Monica Black, *Death in Berlin: From Weimar to Divided Germany*

J. R. McNeill and Corinna R. Unger, editors, *Environmental Histories of the Cold War*

Christof Mauch and Kiran Klaus Patel, editors, *The United States and Germany during the Twentieth Century: Competition and Convergence*

Beyond the Racial State

Rethinking Nazi Germany

xxx

Edited by
DEVIN O. PENDAS
Boston College

MARK ROSEMAN
Indiana University

and
RICHARD F. WETZELL
German Historical Institute
Washington, D.C.

GERMAN HISTORICAL INSTITUTE
Washington, D.C.
and
CAMBRIDGE
UNIVERSITY PRESS

CAMBRIDGE
UNIVERSITY PRESS

University Printing House, Cambridge CB2 8BS, United Kingdom

One Liberty Plaza, 20th Floor, New York, NY 10006, USA

477 Williamstown Road, Port Melbourne, VIC 3207, Australia

4843/24, 2nd Floor, Ansari Road, Daryaganj, Delhi – 110002, India

79 Anson Road, #06–04/06, Singapore 079906

Cambridge University Press is part of the University of Cambridge.

It furthers the University's mission by disseminating knowledge in the pursuit of
education, learning, and research at the highest international levels of excellence.

www.cambridge.org
Information on this title: www.cambridge.org/9781107165458
DOI: 10.1017/9781316691700

© Cambridge University Press 2017

First published 2017

Printed in the United States of America by Sheridan Books, Inc.

A catalogue record for this publication is available from the British Library.

Library of Congress Cataloging-in-Publication Data
NAMES: Pendas, Devin O. (Devin Owen), editor of compilation. | Roseman, Mark,
editor of compilation. | Wetzell, Richard F., editor of compilation.
TITLE: Beyond the racial state : rethinking Nazi Germany / edited by Devin O. Pendas,
Mark Roseman, and Richard F. Wetzell.
DESCRIPTION: First edition. | Washington, D.C. : German Historical Institute, 2017. |
Series: Publications of the German Historical Institute | Papers from a conference
held at Indiana University, Bloomington, October 23–25, 2009. |
Includes bibliographical references and index.
IDENTIFIERS: LCCN 2017009162| ISBN 9781107165458 (Hardback) |
ISBN 9781316616994 (Paperback)
SUBJECTS: LCSH: Germany–Race relations–Political aspects–History–20th century–Congresses. |
Germany–Politics and government–1933–1945–Congresses. | Germany–Social policy–Congresses. |
Racism–Political aspects–Germany–History–20th century–Congresses. | Ethnicity–Political aspects–
Germany–History–20th century–Congresses. | Antisemitism–Political aspects–Germany–History–20th
century–Congresses. | Group identity–Political aspects–Germany–History–20th century–Congresses. |
Minorities–Government policy–Germany–History–20th century–Congresses. | Women–Government
policy–Germany–History–20th century–Congresses. | National socialism and science–Congresses.
CLASSIFICATION: LCC DD256.7 .B48 2017 | DDC 943.086–DC23 LC record
available at https://lccn.loc.gov/2017009162

ISBN 978-1-107-16545-8 Hardback
ISBN 978-1-316-61699-4 Paperback

Contents

Contributors

Frank Bajohr, Center for Holocaust Studies, Institute for Contemporary History (IfZ), Munich

Donald Bloxham, School of History, Classics and Archaeology, University of Edinburgh

Herwig Czech, Medical University of Vienna

Christian Geulen, Institute for History, University of Konstanz-Landau

Pascal Grosse, Charité – Universitätsmedizin Berlin

Stefan Hördler, Mittelbau-Dora Concentration Camp Memorial Site, Nordhausen

Martina Kessel, Department of History, University of Bielefeld

Jürgen Matthäus, The Jack, Joseph, and Morten Mandel Center for Advanced Holocaust Studies, United States Holocaust Memorial Museum, Washington, DC

Regina Mühlhäuser, Institute for Social Research, Hamburg

Devin O. Pendas, Department of History, Boston College

Mark Roseman, Department of History and Borns Jewish Studies Program, Indiana University Bloomington

Dirk Rupnow, Institute for Contemporary History, University of Innsbruck

Nicholas Stargardt, History Faculty, University of Oxford

Richard Steigmann-Gall, Department of History, Kent State University

Dan Stone, Department of History and Holocaust Research Centre, Royal Holloway, University of London

Annette F. Timm, Department of History, University of Calgary

Richard F. Wetzell, German Historical Institute, Washington, DC

Michael Wildt, Department of History, Humboldt University Berlin

Gerhard Wolf, Department of History, University of Sussex

Acknowledgments

The present volume grew out of an academic conference co-organized by the three editors. The editors wish to express their gratitude to the Robert A. and Sandra S. Borns Jewish Studies Program and the Department of History at Indiana University, as well as the German Historical Institute Washington, for co-sponsoring the original conference. For additional financial support for the Bloomington conference we are grateful to the Fritz Thyssen Stiftung, the German Academic Exchange Service, the Center for Arts and Humanities at Indiana University, the West European Studies program at Indiana University, and the Office of the Vice President for International Affairs, Indiana University. Although this volume does not reflect the proceedings of the conference – about half of the chapters were not presented as papers at the conference and the rest have been significantly revised – the editors would like to thank all the participants of the original conference for contributing to stimulating discussions that have influenced the arguments developed in this volume. A special thank you goes to those colleagues who served as commentators at the conference: Doris Bergen, Edward Ross Dickinson, Marion Kaplan, Claudia Koonz, Michelle Moyd, and Julia Roos. Finally, we would like to thank the anonymous reviewers for their helpful comments and David Lazar, senior editor at the German Historical Institute, for editing the manuscript with consummate skill.

Introduction

Devin O. Pendas, Mark Roseman, and Richard F. Wetzell

As Eve Rosenhaft noted recently, over the past two decades the term "racial state" has become a "shorthand" explanation for understanding the Third Reich – a shorthand that presumes that the Nazis pursued a coherent and purposeful racial policy and that a widely disseminated and shared knowledge about race gave the different strands of their societal policy impetus and cohesion.[1] It is this shorthand, and concerns that the concept of the "racial state" is beginning to prove more of an obstacle than an aid to understanding Nazi Germany, that provided the impetus for the present collection, which explores racial ideology, racial policy, and Nazi rule.

BURLEIGH AND WIPPERMANN'S *THE RACIAL STATE*

While the label "racial state" is as old as the Nazi regime itself,[2] its present prominence is almost entirely due to Michael Burleigh and Wolfgang Wippermann's lucid and widely read 1991 synthesis, *The Racial State,* which helped to crystallize a new orthodoxy about the scope and character of Nazi policy.[3] Drawing on a wealth of new research that had been conducted in the 1980s, not least some remarkable and passionate scholarship conducted outside the universities, Burleigh and Wippermann argued that the Nazis had pursued a coherent racial policy. Their book advanced three main arguments. First, they situated the familiar story of anti-Jewish persecution in the larger context of an "all-pervasive racism of the Nazi state" that targeted all manner of German citizens and subjects.[4] Though now common knowledge, until the 1980s the degree to which the Nazis had targeted the mentally and physically handicapped, for example, had been shamefully neglected in research. Alongside the persecution and murder of the Jews, *The Racial State* captured in its spotlight the persecution and murder of Roma and Sinti, the sterilization of the "hereditarily ill" and of racially defined groups such as the offspring of French African troops and German mothers, and the "euthanasia" murder of the mentally and physically handicapped as well as the Nazi persecution of "asocials" and homosexuals. While there were "different specificities," all of these groups, Burleigh and Wippermann argued, "were persecuted for the same reasons."[5] The "Final Solution" to the Jewish question was thus presented as just one, albeit the most pressing, of a set of "answers" to an overarching question, namely, how to cleanse society of undesirable elements and create a racial utopia.

Second, Burleigh and Wippermann insisted that Nazi racial and social policy must be seen as "two sides of the same coin,"[6] because a racial utopia required not just the removal of undesirables but also the grooming and monitoring of the rest of the population. Just as striking as the range of victims Burleigh and Wippermann uncovered was their argument that the social policies directed at the mainstream population also had a significant racial component. Offering chapters on youth, women, and men, the authors showed, for example, the degree to which allocating state resources became tied to genealogical pedigree and racial quality. The Nazis, they maintained, sought to create a new racial hierarchy that would replace the class structure of German society. Through financial inducements and criminal sanctions, racially favored groups were induced to reproduce. The regime's social policies "struck at people whether they were rich or poor, bourgeois, peasants or workers"[7] – and indeed whether they were male or female, though women were particularly affected by state-organized racial reproduction policies. The whole population was thus affected by the reorganization of society along racial lines.

None of this would have been possible, the authors contended in their third major argument, without the remarkable and chilling involvement of elites and intellectuals, be it in state service, in the professions, or in a variety of research institutes and agencies. "Racial anthropologists, biologists and hygienicists, economists, geographers, historians and sociologists," they argued, "created the conceptual framework and the scientific legitimisation" for the regime's racial policy.[8] Many academic disciplines and professional groups experienced boom conditions under Nazi rule. Few areas of Nazi policy emerged without the active involvement of academics in providing content, momentum, and intellectual legitimacy.[9]

In Burleigh and Wippermann's hands, therefore, the older view of Nazi racism and anti-Semitism as the private fantasy of a narrow coterie of deranged cranks thus gave way to that of a comprehensive societal project aided and abetted by Germany's best and brightest.

THE HISTORIOGRAPHICAL CONTEXT

Burleigh and Wippermann's study was less an original statement than a synthesis that captured and contributed to a burgeoning consensus. But their book also had a polemical edge, in that the two authors saw one of their central tasks as refuting recent arguments about the modernity of the Third Reich.[10] On the one hand, they wanted to rebut a series of influential studies of the social history of the Third Reich, published in the 1960s and 1970s, by David Schoenbaum, Ralf Dahrendorf, and Tim Mason, who claimed that the Nazi regime's social policies had had a significant modernizing effect on German society, which Schoenbaum labeled "Hitler's social revolution."[11] Burleigh and Wippermann explicitly countered this interpretation because they saw it as ignoring the racial character of Nazi policies.

On the other hand, they argued that recent work that was more cognizant of the racial elements of Nazi policy had inappropriately labeled those elements as modern. In the chapter of his 1982 book *Volksgenossen und Gemeinschaftsfremde* entitled "Racism as Social Policy," Detlev Peukert had anticipated significant elements of *The Racial State* by arguing that the Nazi regime's

racism offered a model for a new order of society ... It rested on the racially legitimated removal of all elements that deviated from the norm, refractory youth, idlers, the asocial, prostitutes, homosexuals, people who were incompetent or failures at work, the disabled. National Socialist eugenics ... laid down criteria of assessment ... that were applicable to the population as a whole.

But he also advanced the thesis that National Socialism must not be seen as "an inexplicable, sudden appearance of 'medieval barbarism' in a progressive society" but on the contrary "demonstrated, with heightened clarity and murderous consistency, the pathologies and seismic fractures of the modern civilizing process."[12] Similarly, in 1985, a group of young historians, including Götz Aly and Karl Heinz Roth, began publishing the series *Beiträge zur nationalsozialistischen Gesundheits- und Sozialpolitik*, which presented pioneering research on the Nazi euthanasia program, eugenics, and racial and social policy, and focused on neglected victim groups, including the mentally ill, Roma and Sinti, asocials, and forced laborers.[13] Like Peukert, these authors saw Nazi social and racial policies as different sides of the same coin, but they went further than Peukert in three respects:[14] by arguing that the Nazi "concept of rule ... combined German population policy, economic policy, and social policy in order to attain the goal of a 'final solution of the social question'"; by positing a close connection between "extermination and modernization";[15] and by drawing attention to the "scientifically and economically rational" elements in National Socialism.[16]

Even though Burleigh and Wippermann agreed with these authors that Nazi racial and social policy were inextricably connected (and drew on the pioneering research published in the *Beiträge*), they vigorously disputed that Nazi racial policy was part of modernization. The fact that Peukert and the editors of the *Beiträge* had departed from classic modernization theory and earlier social historians of the Third Reich such as Schoenbaum and Dahrendorf by decoupling modernization from any notion of progress in order to call attention to modernization's dark side did not seem to matter to Burleigh and Wippermann, for their objection was essentially a moral one: in their view, interpreting National Socialism as a phenomenon of modernity or modernization was tantamount to relativizing its crimes. "Older titles like *Hitler's Social Revolution* are joined by *Modernity and the Holocaust*," they wrote, "as the unique horrors of the Third Reich disappear within the fog of relativizing sociological rhetoric. The fact of Nazi Germany's murder of millions of Jews, Sinti and Roma and others at a specific point in time is obscured by talk of general genocidal impulses allegedly latent beneath the thin civilized crust of all 'modern' societies."[17] Instead, Burleigh and Wippermann insisted that the Nazi regime was "novel and *sui generis*," "a singular regime without precedent or parallel."[18]

To be sure, "modernity" as such has generally proved an unhelpful category of analysis for historians of the Nazi era, not least because there is little consensus on what it stands for and because there are massive variations within the modern epoch between different temporal phases and societies.[19] But by limiting legitimate use of the term "modernity" to contexts where it connoted betterment, improvement, or progress, *The Racial State* had no concept left with which to describe shared characteristics of the industrialized world that are not benevolent.[20] Just as importantly, having rejected any association of National Socialism with modernity, Burleigh and Wippermann had to disconnect Nazism from modern science. This was not an easy case for the authors, given that they were so conscious of the contributions to Nazi policy made by Germany's intellectual elites; indeed, they showed that there "were few areas of Nazi racial policy which did not involve academics in its formulation and legitimization, and that many of the latter were culpably involved in its implementation."[21] To be sure, they acknowledged that many scientists involved were convinced of their objectivity and believed their work was essential for national progress. But although they argued that science had lent Nazism its specifically academic and scientific character, Burleigh and Wippermann characterized science under the Nazi regime as a "corrupt" and "inherently distorted" science.[22] *The Racial State* paid particular attention to the loss of moral judgments and also to such factors as professional animosities, careerism, and the myopic vision of the individual institution. Even though these tendencies were surely present, it is hard to see them as somehow extraneous to the normal functioning of modern science. As a result, most subsequent research has not accepted Burleigh and Wippermann's account of science under the Nazi regime as deviant science.

This collection of essays was not prompted by a desire to revisit the idiosyncratic elements of Burleigh and Wippermann's *The Racial State*. Instead, we seek to question the consensus over the power and coherence of Nazi racial ideology that established itself in the book's wake in order to tackle many of the kinds of questions about science, rationality, and more generic features of the modern world that exercised the earlier volume from a different angle.

While we may balk at Burleigh and Wippermann's emphatic claim that Nazi racial policy was *sui generis*, many of the contributions to this volume are informed by a central tension in thinking about Nazi Germany, namely the conflict between locating the regime in the wider world and maintaining a sense of the Third Reich's distinctiveness. On the one hand, we are mindful of a certain longstanding myopia in studies of Nazi Germany. Remember, for example, Jacob Robinson, who in his 1944 foreword to Jacoby's *Racial State* had confidently claimed that the Nazis were the first who "introduced the racial point of view in modern government" – a breathtaking claim given the formal and informal rules long operating in Europe's overseas empires and indeed in the United States.[23] Within scholarship on Nazi Germany, it was long forgotten that racial violence had been a commonplace under European rule and that racially based legal distinctions and administrative conventions were also profoundly constitutive of the United States. Likewise, many of the Nazis' ideas and practices found precedents, parallels, and eager emulators beyond Germany's borders. Yet at the same time, the planned nature, scale, and organization of Nazi violence, and the fact that it was the Nazis' own fellow citizens who were the first to be transformed into the objects of murderous social engineering, remain distinctive and horrifying historical problems that provide the vanishing point for any serious analysis of the origins, content, and function of Nazi racial thinking.

We should also note that "racial state" is used in this volume more as a kind of shorthand than as a precise term. For one thing, we follow Burleigh and Wippermann in not treating "state" narrowly. A good part of the apparatus of imagination and enforcement in Burleigh and Wippermann's analysis and in the essays in this volume lies outside the state proper. "Racial regime" might be a better description, but even that title would not capture the fact that we are as interested in the boundary lines between regime and society as in the regime's apparatus per se.

QUESTIONING THE CONSENSUS ABOUT NAZI RACIAL IDEOLOGY

In the years since the publication of *The Racial State*, many historians of the Third Reich have followed Burleigh and Wippermann in emphasizing racial ideology, racial policy, and racial engineering, as at least three historiographical developments make clear. First, the now quite extensive literature on the role of science, especially medicine and the life sciences, under the Nazi regime – much of it associated with the research program on the history of the Kaiser Wilhelm Institutes in the Nazi era – has more fully documented the involvement of medical doctors, human geneticists, and racial anthropologists in the racial policies and crimes of the Third Reich.[24] Second, a series of studies – including Ulrich Herbert's biography of Werner Best and Michael Wildt's study of the higher officials of the Reichssicherheitshauptamt – have focused on the central role of ideology for an elite group of academically trained Holocaust perpetrators who held leadership positions in the SS, police, and security apparatus.[25] While in the debate over the origins of the Holocaust the "intentionalists" had limited the question of ideology almost exclusively to that of Hitler's intentions and the "functionalists" had tried to explain the Holocaust through a process of "cumulative radicalization" at the Nazi regime's periphery without paying much attention to ideology,[26] these new studies in *Täterforschung* have modified the "functionalist" paradigm by examining the ideological factors that explain the readiness, even eagerness, of so many perpetrators to drive the process of cumulative radicalization forward in the direction of mass murder.[27] Finally, building on Detlev Peukert's aforementioned book *Volksgenossen und Gemeinschaftsfremde*, some of the recent studies that draw on the concept of the *Volksgemeinschaft* to examine German society in the Nazi era have stressed the key role of racial ideology in the larger society by focusing on the "dialectic of inclusion and exclusion" as a central element in the functioning of the *Volksgemeinschaft*.[28]

Concealed behind the common analytical language of race, however, are significant differences in the ways in which "race" is used and understood in these studies. Therefore, one of this volume's principal aims is to render visible the remarkable range of meanings and ambiguities inherent in using "race" and the "racial state" as analytical categories in the Nazi context. To take just one example, biology was clearly much more prominent in the debates about science and race than in those about the racializing of the *Volksgemeinschaft*. But the present volume also seeks to go further by challenging our assumptions about the relationship between racial ideology, race speech and policies, popular participation, and racial violence. Can we really see the spirit of science (particularly the biosciences) behind Nazi racial thinking and policy? Is it clear that the scientific exploration of race dovetailed with Nazi rhetoric, or that eugenic thinking and the murder of the handicapped were as closely connected as has been claimed? How coherent was the Nazis' overarching racial ideology and program? Have we perhaps lost sight of the fragmentary, instrumental, and performative character of Nazi racial discourse? What was the relationship between its overarching vision and the persecution of particular groups? How did the Nazis' racial policy connect to their other social objectives? Can we really encapsulate the mantra of "world Jewry" as the enemy under the mantle of "race thinking"? Did the Nazis draw on a "colonial archive" of racial theories, or was the ethnic violence in Europe's "rimlands" and "shatterzones" a more significant precedent?

As noted earlier, this volume defines the "state" in "racial state" very broadly. A central characteristic of the Nazi regime was, after all, the involvement in policy-making of a multitude of Party and para-state actors, who both infiltrated and competed with the inherited state bureaucracy. This competition and partial cooptation enhanced the regime's energy and reach, even if it often led to conflict and obstruction between agencies. Looking beyond the world of Party agencies, a vital source of the regime's power was the degree to which it enjoyed legitimacy and support among the population. A number of contributors thus question the nature of the relationship between racial thinking and racial policy and the allegiances that motivated and sustained the regime. Was the language of the *Volksgemeinschaft* in its popular reception really based on notions of biological inheritance, or was it closer to a form of nationalism with ethnic overtones?

In approaching these issues, the contributors do not share a single line, and a number would no doubt disagree with at least some of the propositions advanced by the editors in this introduction. All, however, agree that, despite the wealth of research on Nazi Germany, important facets of race and racial policy remain seriously underexplored, while others have been subject to the most varied and contradictory interpretations. The remainder of this introduction outlines the collection's structure and the individual essays before offering some concluding thoughts about future directions for research.

COMPARATIVE AND HISTORICAL PERSPECTIVES

If the major thrust of the present volume is to complicate the concept of the Nazi racial state, as a matter of ideology and as a matter of policy and everyday practice, another dimension is to situate this ideology and policy in a broader historical context. One central element in the racial state paradigm, certainly as first articulated by Burleigh and Wippermann, has been to argue that the Third Reich was highly unusual – perhaps unique – in its use of race as a category of social policy. We problematize this assumption in two respects. First, several chapters – those by Mark Roseman, Donald Bloxham, and Pascal Grosse – expand the temporal and spatial frame of reference by situating Nazi racial ideas and policies in a broader, European and colonial context. Second, a number of chapters, including Roseman's and Devin Pendas's, take a comparative approach, contrasting the Third Reich to other overtly racist and genocidal regimes.

Mark Roseman seeks to situate Nazi racial views in a longer perspective. He sees Nazi racism as part of a more diffuse, though potentially destructive, set of narratives of difference that one can broadly group under the label of radical nationalism, noting that the Nazis' "ruthless destruction of perceived enemies was more akin to the goals of radical nationalist regimes. To this they added a new style of 'postcolonial' imperialism, aiming at claiming land through settlement and expelling or even eliminating the original occupants. The language of race accompanied much of this, but did not drive it." Nazi racial language was far from coherent or homogeneous, comprising an admixture of scientific and cultural concepts that blurred the distinctions between race, ethnicity, and nation. Moreover, race competed with *Volk* as the central concept in Nazi ideology, and indeed, Roseman argues, it was the language of *Volk*, rather than race, that served a primary mobilizing function in the Third Reich. After World War I, *Volk* served as a language of patriotism and nationalism, a way of defining what it meant to be a true German that was far from biological.

Biological racism was the "hard edge" of this broader cultural nationalism that, Roseman argues, was at the heart of the Nazi project. In this light, he suggests it is necessary to differentiate what he terms "socially stratifying" and "nationally demarcating" racisms. He sees race as having a far more distinctive political function in those contexts where "race served to enforce the rules of unequal coexistence." But where race "marked the boundaries of the national community [it] was always ... a secondary attribute to nation." While stratifying racism can be extraordinarily violent in some segregationist contexts or in the case of slavery, Roseman suggests that demarcating racism may be more likely to lead to genocide and ethnic cleansing. This has less to do with biological-racial imperatives, however, than it does with demands for national exclusivity. In Roseman's view, genocide is as much (or more) an artifact of nationalism and nation-building as it is an outgrowth of biological-racial thinking.

Donald Bloxham argues that a transnational approach to the history of the Third Reich involves "thinking of continuums and interrelationships in the policies of different states." This is not so much a comparative project – contrasting racial policies in distinct, if more or less similar, contexts – as it is a way to trace the genealogy of Nazi ideas and policies to a much older, and much broader, European tradition. Bloxham suggests that Nazi genocide was a continuation by other, even more murderous, means of population-engineering and -transfer projects that dated back to the nineteenth century. These projects were not the exclusive purview of authoritarian or "totalitarian" states. The Final Solution, he argues, needs to be understood in "an age of wider European genocide and ethnic cleansing in which similar patterns can be discerned across very different states." In this sense, it constitutes "an only partly discrete episode in a wider European process of violent flux." From this vantage point, geopolitics loom as large as (or larger than) racial ideology in the history of European genocide. Of course, one might add that this is true only within a certain conceptual frame in which populations themselves could be construed as "problems" and "resources," an aspect perhaps of what Zygmunt Baumann famously called the "gardening state."[29] In Bloxham's analysis, there is thus a marked continuity from the ethnic (or ethnoreligious) cleansing of Muslims from the newly independent territories of the receding Ottoman empire in Southeastern Europe in the last third of the nineteenth century, through the reciprocal expulsions of Bulgarians, Hungarians, Romanians, Poles, Ukrainians, and others across the shifting borders of Eastern Europe in the first third of the twentieth century, to the Nazi genocide of the Jews. Seen in this light, the Holocaust becomes a particularly acute moment in what Bloxham has elsewhere called the "unweaving of Europe."[30]

Like Bloxham, Grosse argues for a longer-term perspective on Nazi racism and racial policy. His context, however, is not European population transfer but rather the rise of eugenics and the history of German colonialism. He argues that "eugenics bore a complex intellectual matrix in the context of German colonialism" and, as a result, "territorial expansion became intertwined with racial politics." In this sense, Grosse argues, there is an ineluctable tension between racism – with its colonial sense of space – and the bourgeois nation-state, which gave the Third Reich its characteristic dynamism. Starting in the late nineteenth century, the earlier European tradition of typologizing peoples according to physical and phenotypical characteristics gave way to a Darwinian and eugenic emphasis on "descent." It was this understanding of race as a form of genealogy, Grosse maintains, that held Nazi racial policies together. This shift from typology to genealogy had profound practical implications. "Politically, a genealogical approach to race supersedes territorial boundaries defined by nation-states, as genealogies intrinsically reach across frontiers." In contrast to Roseman, Grosse argues that Nazi racism was "incongruent with existing nation-states." In this sense, race was always a deeply *colonial* concept. The key element here, according to Grosse, was the fact that this genealogical, eugenic understanding of race was future-oriented. The question was how Germans could conquer racially "other" spaces, such as the tropics (or later Eastern Europe), while remaining "white" and "German/Aryan." The answer was a eugenic consensus, one with several key implications: "the nexus between race and space was redrawn, racialized notions of citizenship emerged, and finally, traditional boundaries between the civil and military spheres were erased."

If one way of reframing the context for understanding Nazi racism and genocide is to treat it as part of a longstanding framework of European imperialism, another is to compare it to other regimes in distinct historical contexts. Clearly, the Nazi state was neither the first nor the last in world history for which race was a useful category of social analysis and policy formulation. The value of such comparative analysis is that it highlights both similarities and differences and can thus illuminate aspects of the Third Reich that are less obvious when viewed from within a purely national frame. In this respect, Pendas contends that the Nazis shared with several other regimes – including European colonial empires, the Jim Crow South, and apartheid-era South Africa – a desire to differentiate dominant and subordinate groups on the basis of often loosely defined racial categories. Across a number of domains of social life – sexual relations, labor relations, and citizenship – these states all adopted related policies. At the same time, Pendas argues, there was a fundamental difference between states whose racial policies operated along the global color-line and the Third Reich, which sought to constitute racial difference entirely among Europeans, all on the "white" side of the color-line. This difference, he suggests, may help account for the rather more violent character of Nazi racism. Because Jews could collectively "pass" for "Aryan," they were perceived as a particularly dangerous threat, one that demanded some kind of permanent solution – a solution that ultimately took the form of genocide.

Burleigh and Wippermann developed the racial state paradigm in part out of a desire to argue that the Third Reich must not be understood as a variant of welfare-state modernity. Nazism was not, they insisted, one version of some more general phenomenon but a specific, indeed unique, political form, distinguished by its use of race as *the* organizing category for social policy. According to Burleigh and Wipperman, the Nazi racial state was both more comprehensive than other racist regimes and – *as a consequence* – also more murderous. The utopian quality of Nazi racism, on this reading, points to a thoroughgoing reorganization of *German* society on racial lines, and also to the radical, and ultimately final, exclusion of racially undesirable elements. In other words, Burleigh and Wippermann argue that the Third Reich was both uniquely racist and as a result uniquely violent. The essays in the first section of this volume all challenge aspects of this view, though not necessarily the same ones. Grosse and Pendas reject the claim that Nazi racism was unique or unprecedented. They each present a broader comparative and transnational history of race and racism that refutes the notion that the Nazis had a uniquely comprehensive or coherent racial vision, without gainsaying the extraordinary violence and global aspirations of the Nazis' policies. Both accept that Nazi genocide had a racial dimension. Bloxham and Roseman, on the other hand, challenge the intrinsic connection that Burleigh and Wippermann drew between racism and genocide. Drawing on a comparative and transnational history of violence, they argue that religion could be quite as murderous as race, and that it was radical nationalism, not racism, that was the common ingredient in European genocides. For all their differences, these four essays share a common goal of widening the context in which the history of the Third Reich is considered and linking it to broader European trends.

RACE, SCIENCE, AND NAZI BIOPOLITICS

As noted above, Burleigh and Wippermann's *The Racial State* drew on a wave of pioneering research on the history of medicine in Nazi Germany, especially on eugenics and the "euthanasia" program, published in the 1980s. One of the book's central arguments was that German doctors, academics, and scientists "voluntarily and enthusiastically put their skills at the service of the regime" in order to "create . . . the conceptual framework and scientific legitimization for the implementation of Nazi racial policy."[31] While German doctors' and scientists' complicity with the Nazi regime, confirmed by all subsequent research, is beyond dispute, the essays in this section take issue with Burleigh and Wippermann's implication that Nazi-era eugenics, anthropology, and *Rassenforschung* created a coherent scientific framework for Nazi eugenic and racial policy. In addition to probing the incoherence, heterogeneity, and contradictions of racial science in the Third Reich, some of the essays also question Burleigh and Wippermann's claim that science under the Nazi regime was "inherently distorted," asking whether it was not, in many respects, "normal science." Finally, some of the essays challenge Detlev Peukert's thesis that the final solution resulted from a "fatal racist dynamic in the human sciences"; that thesis, although it differs from Burleigh and Wippermann's views, is also part of the "racial state paradigm" in the larger historiographical sense.[32]

The section opens with Richard Wetzell's contribution, which argues that we must distinguish the question of the complicity of German racial scientists – including eugenicists, anthropologists, human geneticists, and *Rassenforscher* – in Nazi eugenic and racial policy from the question of what influence these scientists had on the shaping of Nazi eugenic and racial policy. While the bioscientists' widespread complicity is now well documented, Wetzell challenges the claims that Nazi racial science "created the conceptual framework" for Nazi racial policy (Burleigh and Wippermann) or that Nazi racial policy was propelled by a "fatal racist dynamic" in the biosciences (Peukert). Racial science could not have provided a coherent conceptual framework because the field was characterized by competing conceptions of race and heredity, which frequently led to controversies and conflicts, three of which are examined in the first part of Wetzell's chapter. In assessing racial science's influence on policy, Wetzell argues, one has to differentiate between different scientific fields and different areas of Nazi policy. Whereas key figures in the eugenics movement were indeed eager to cooperate with the Nazi regime in order to implement their eugenic agenda and actively sought to radicalize Nazi eugenic policy, German anthropologists and *Rassenforscher* certainly contributed to and participated in Nazi racial policy but did not shape or radicalize it to nearly the same extent as eugenicists did in the case of Nazi eugenic policy. Instead of using "race" as an analytical category for understanding the Third Reich, Wetzell contends, we must recognize that "race" was a diffuse concept whose competing and contested meanings in the Third Reich are in need of historical analysis. A careful examination of the interaction of racial science with the Nazi regime, he argues, should elucidate how both scientists and Nazi officials deployed competing conceptions of race for various strategic purposes at different points in the development of the Nazi regime.

The essays by Dan Stone and Christian Geulen both grapple with the incoherence of Nazi racial thinking, but come up with quite different solutions to the historical question this raises. Stone calls for distinguishing two different "registers" of racial thinking: "race science" and "race mysticism." He argues that Nazi anti-Semitism, the identification of the Jews as a dangerous and polluting race, derived not from race science but from "mystical race thinking"; race science was then drafted to lend legitimacy and placed at the service of "a fundamentally mystical or non-rational idea," a kind of "Aryan salvation history." Building on this distinction, Stone criticizes interpretations that assign racial science a central role in Nazi Germany and draw a straight line from the sterilization law to the euthanasia program and on to the Holocaust. Furthermore, he argues that researchers focusing on the history of science have fallen victim to a "methodological fallacy": their focus on scientific sources has made it appear as if Nazi racial legislation and the Holocaust were the result of the activities of racial scientists, whereas in reality, all the key decisions regarding eugenic and racial policy, the euthanasia murders of the mentally ill, and the mass murder of the European Jews were made by the Nazi leadership. In Nazi Germany, Stone contends, race was "too important to be left to the race scientists"; the scientists needed the regime more than the regime needed the scientists. Placing Holocaust historiography in a comparative context, Stone concludes by arguing that recent genocide studies have been characterized by two key mistakes: taking "race thinking" to be synonymous with "race science" and downplaying the circumstances in which race theory is mobilized.

Christian Geulen's chapter begins with an analysis of the "rules of racial conduct" that Goebbels's Ministry of Propaganda issued in 1935. The document's use of the term *Volk* leads him to explicate a turn-of-the-century semantic shift in the German concepts of *Volk* and *Nation*, by which the formerly political term *Volk* became a marker of the nation. By the post-World War I period, he argues, *völkisch* notions of Germanness no longer functioned as references to a prehistoric racial nation but rather as an impetus to artificially reconstruct the nation through "technologies of race building." For the Nazi era, Geulen stresses the incoherence of Nazi racial thinking, arguing that the Nazis intertwined "the mythical and the biological meaning of race" and "did not really care" whether their racial politics was "scientifically valid." Given the incoherence of Nazi racial thinking, Geulen asks what function it served in the Nazi regime. His answer is that racial thinking in the Third Reich was not a "belief system determining politics and society"; it did not provide a "racial master plan" and did not serve to define racial superiority and inferiority. Instead, the "inner logic of racial thinking" served a "more limited" function, namely, to give plausibility to the notion that all social and political life was a Darwinian struggle for existence and thus to strengthen the imperative to "enforce the racial struggle as such."

The section's final chapter, by Herwig Czech, examines the connection between Nazi eugenics and the euthanasia murders of the mentally ill. According to Czech, the euthanasia killings followed an economic rather than a eugenic logic because the primary criterion for selection was the inability to perform productive work, rather than hereditary illness. While the almost complete irrelevance of eugenic criteria in the euthanasia program has led others to conclude that the murder of the mentally ill cannot be explained as the logical outcome of Nazi eugenic thinking, Czech, by contrast, argues that Nazi eugenics and the euthanasia murders were "based on the same logic" because, to a considerable extent, Nazi "health and welfare" policy also used socio-economic rather than genetic criteria. In a detailed examination of the activities of "public health offices," Czech argues that both their hereditary health surveys and their implementation of positive and negative eugenics, including forced sterilization, showed "a strong bias toward social diagnostics" rather than "genetic pathologies in the strict sense." In conclusion, he suggests broadening the concept of racism in order to integrate the role that social and economic factors played in Nazi eugenics, euthanasia, and racial policy.

ANTI-SEMITISM BEYOND RACE

The essays in this section all examine the relationship between anti-Semitic speech and policy, on the one hand, and explicitly biological or racial thinking on the other. Within the racial state paradigm, anti-Semitic policy was simply the most prominent element of an increasingly murderous assault on non-German races. It drew on a biologized and racialized rewriting of an older anti-Semitism. But in different ways, each of the contributors in this section show that speech acts, policy, and violence toward Jews were far from being simply a component of a broader racial program, and often bore only an oblique relationship to biological understanding of race.

Jürgen Matthäus argues that historians have spent far too much time focusing on the mindset or ideology of the practitioners and far too little exploring the complex history of the policy process. As he demonstrates, political policies in the Third Reich were very far from being simply "ideas turned into action," and the complicated relationship between measures against Jews and other racial policies has been barely explored. Focusing on the regime's early years and highlighting the central role of the Reich Interior Ministry, Matthäus reveals that while there was a striking commitment among senior civil servants to pursue both eugenic and anti-Semitic measures as part of a comprehensive racial agenda, their efforts led to quite different legislative outcomes. Anti-Jewish measures were initially constrained by economic and diplomatic concerns, in contrast to the quite radical sterilization policies adopted against Aryans of supposed inferior biological quality. As the regime consolidated its position, however, the balance between domestic pressures, economic restraints, and diplomatic concerns shifted. By 1935, Jews could be legislatively targeted as such in the Nuremberg Laws, but the all-encompassing language targeting non-Aryans that had appeared in some 1933 legislation was now dropped to avoid offending potential non-Aryan allies abroad. The Four Year Plan of 1936 would change the rules of the game again, creating a new economic impetus to target Jewish assets and also bring new players onto the scene, though in the ensuring turf wars the Interior Ministry would continue to play a more significant role than has often been acknowledged.

Richard Steigmann-Gall argues that race's role and content in Nazi Germany has been surprisingly under-theorized. He notes, for example, that the mosaic of Nazi victims consisted almost exclusively of outgroups that had been subject to discrimination long before biological language emerged. As he argues, many leading Nazis acknowledged the cultural and spiritual components in the definition and formation of race. Hitler himself argued that a "spiritual" race was more durable than a "natural" one, whatever that meant, and Jews in particular were seen by many Nazis as something other than a biological entity. From this starting point, Steigmann-Gall goes on to explore the remarkable degree to which Christian ideas and imagery remained at the core of Nazi anti-Semitism. These factors lead Steigmann-Gall to see biological thinking less as the source of determinative logic in Nazi policy and more as a discursive edifice superimposed on older cultural and religious prejudices and oppositions.

In similar vein, Dirk Rupnow examines the place, function, and content of Nazi academic research into "the Jewish question." After the Nazis came to power, the advocates of research on Jews sought to make it into a discipline in its own right for the first time. A striking range of institutional players was involved, not just in Germany but also during the war in the occupied territories. Their claim to scientific objectivity was belied by the notion of "fighting scholarship," and in reality a powerfully anti-Jewish line united the competing practitioners. All were agreed on assigning the Jewish question centrality in German history. Despite the lip-service paid to biological ideas, Rupnow argues that research into Jews was not primarily based on racial biology or physical anthropology; instead, the "Jewish spirit" and "Jewish mind" figured heavily in Nazi *Judenforschung*. There was nevertheless considerable cross-referencing between the historical and social research into the Jewish spirit, and medical research by racial scientists of the stamp of Otmar von Verschuer. Humanists and racial biologists referred to each other's work to try to compensate for the lack of any consistent evidence for Jews' racial character. The practitioners of *Judenforschung* not only provided broad legitimation for Nazi anti-Jewish policies as a whole but also were directly implicated in advisory decisions on the Jewish character of specific sub-groups.

RACE AND SOCIETY

If the "racial state" has established itself as shorthand for the Nazi regime, the "racial society" has not enjoyed similar currency as a way of describing German society under Nazi rule. True, recent work has emphasized the Nazis' ability racially to groom the population, the success and appeal of their notion of *Volksgemeinschaft*, and even their success in fostering a sense of common identity in relation to genocide. But no one is claiming that, in the short period of Nazi rule, the German population was or ever could have been transformed into a *Rassengesellschaft*, however defined. Whatever German society was in 1933 or 1939 or 1945 was clearly messy, multifaceted, and characterized by a mixture of continuity and change. In that sense, the essays in this section are not confronting a clear-cut paradigm but rather offering new ways of thinking about the place of racial ideology in Germany society, the impact of racial policies on the population, and popular involvement in developing a racial regime. Two of the essays, from Michael Wildt and Annette Timm, are conceptual or methodological, inviting us to think about race's evolving significance for German identities, relationships, and behavior. Frank Bajohr offers a distinctive and intriguing vantage point from which to observe German society. Martina Kessel and Nicholas Stargardt engage more directly with popular attitudes and behavior, focusing, respectively, on humor in Nazi Germany and popular attitudes during the war.

Michael Wildt has written some the most influential recent studies of the power of the *Volksgemeinschaft* as slogan, vision, and experience of identity in Nazi Germany. In his contribution here, he approaches the topic from a new angle, showing how the concept evolved from its origins in Imperial Germany through to the Nazi era. The term took on particular significance in the wake of the Kaiser's speech on the eve of World War I, when the Kaiser declared, to much applause, that he no longer recognized political parties and saw only Germans. In this rhetorical move, *Volksgemeinschaft* could coexist with social and political divisions while also transcending them in common loyalty to Germany. During the 1920s, as Wildt shows, the term was often used to prescribe a desirable societal goal of a social community that transcended class division. But there was also a racial-nationalist variant that predicated the unity of the people on the exclusion of "foreign" races, above all Jews. Building on this eclectic history, Wildt convincingly demonstrates that the appeal of the *Volksgemeinschaft* under Nazi rule drew on the fact that it was not prima facie a racist concept, even if the populace increasingly accepted the exclusionary elements that were integral parts of the Nazi vision. According to Wildt, the utility of the term as an analytical category is thus not that the Third Reich ever *created* a *Volksgemeinschaft*, whatever that might mean, but rather that it alerts us to a project – to the performance and enactment of community by the Nazis, and to its complicated reception by the population. The image of the *Volksgemeinschaft* became an important part of popular experience, but what different groups understood under the term varied considerably.

One of the major contributions of the racial state paradigm was that it incorporated official policies toward women into the "grand narrative" of the history of the Third Reich. The question of women's relationship to the regime, however, was, as Annette Timm reminds us, always contentious, and it became even more complex once the paradigm of gender replaced an older generation of women's history (although it remains the case that gendered analysis of women is still far more common than analyses of masculinity in Nazi Germany). Older standoffs over women as perpetrators or victims have been replaced by new arguments about the scope for agency and self-assertion. In addition to offering a wide-ranging account of the place of race in gendered approaches to the history of Nazi Germany, Timm's particular contribution is to ask how thinking about the history of emotions might transform our understanding of race. She argues that assessing women's relation to the Nazi regime in terms of "hot emotions," such as love, desire, or even anger, helps reveal the ways in which the "rewards of belonging" helped secure the loyalty of everyday citizens, and obscured their growing complicity in the regime's genocidal policies.

Frank Bajohr examines perceptions of the Third Reich among foreign diplomats who served in Germany between 1933 and 1945. He notes that these often highly perceptive outside observers anticipated most of the historiographical interpretations of the Nazi regime offered after the war – with the notable exception of the racial state paradigm. They variously characterized it as a strong or weak dictatorship, as repressive or popular, as conservative or radical. But none of them characterized it as a racial regime. It is not that they failed to perceive the Nazis' racism – how could they? – but they did not attribute to it any general significance as a descriptor of the regime. He explains this in part with reference to the necessary focus in these diplomatic observations on matters of foreign policy. At the same time, however, he argues that their views reveal the striking plasticity of the regime, its constantly shifting policies and priorities, which the diplomats characterized as a radical unpredictability.

These contemporary foreign observers saw nothing of the coherence implied in the concept of a racial state.

In older scholarship on Nazi Germany, jokes from the period were often cited as a way of showing the population's distance from the regime and its skepticism about Nazi leaders, Nazi slogans, and the Nazis' ability to deliver on their promises. By contrast, Martina Kessel reads the (largely unfunny) Nazi joke as collusion with the regime and as consciously or unconsciously performing social exclusion of the unwanted, above all of Jews. Not only was this humor thus not an act of covert opposition but in fact, she argues, it became part of an agreed and almost required communication style, by which acceptance of the exclusionary terms of community was signaled through anti-Jewish jokes. This kind of humor drew on and transformed older traditions of anti-Semitic German jokes. Such jokes, she argues, were not racist in the sense of being based on ideas about biological difference but were a form of "cultural performance" of Germanness. Racist jokes both articulated and created cultural-racial differences, and signaled inclusion for the joke-teller at the same time as they enforced the exclusion of the object of the joke.

Of all the contributors to this section, it is Nicholas Stargardt who most explicitly questions the degree to which the population bought into the Nazis' racial ideology. While recognizing the value of recent discussions of the *Volksgemeinschaft*, Stargardt argues in his essay that the concept has often been deployed in a crudely functional way, taking the regime's murderous energy as the measure of popular acceptance of its ideas. Instead, Stargardt seeks to uncover the complexity of the German people's views during the war, and the way radicalization of attitudes could go hand in hand with a loss of trust in the regime. The war, he shows, was no plebiscite on Nazi ideology, even if it did at times help to forge a sense of national solidarity on the home front. The real shared sentiment was of the need to defend a beleaguered nation – a powerful defensive-aggressive nationalism that long predated the Nazis, and on which the regime drew to the end. The legitimacy of the war thus went unquestioned even as the regime lost support. Yet Germans had, willy-nilly, to accommodate to the war the Nazis imposed on them, and at different times and in this context the discourse of *Volksgemeinschaft* could be deployed to different ends. Many Germans accepted the premise that this was a "Jewish" war and that world Jewry was somehow coordinating the opposition, even while they began to worry that Allied bombing represented just retribution for Germany's crimes against the Jews.

RACE WAR? GERMANS AND NON-GERMANS IN WARTIME

Much of the literature discussing the Third Reich as a racial state focuses on the prewar period, when the Nazi regime sought ways to implement social policy in accordance with its ideological predilections. Yet the Third Reich spent fully half of its brief, terrible existence at war. Given that one of the ironic consequences of Germany's initial military successes was to massively expand the foreign populations under German control, the crucial question becomes: To what extent and in what ways did race inform Nazi policies in occupied territories or regarding "undesirable" peoples?

The racial state paradigm would lead one to assume this was, for the Nazis, viewed exclusively as a problem to be solved by means of violent exclusion and mass murder. The war itself is cast, on this view, as a straightforward race war, an understanding nicely captured in Lucy Dawidowicz's description of the Holocaust as a "war against the Jews."[33] Yet, as historians have long recognized, there was in fact a great deal of vacillation in Nazi occupation policy, and even anti-Jewish measures did not simply proceed on a linear path from discrimination to genocide. Often, this is presented as a concession to practicality on the part of a regime whose preferences were for ideological purity. The essays in this section take a different tack. First, they demonstrate that since race was such an ambiguous and ill-defined concept, Nazi bureaucrats were often able to give it whatever content suited their local needs at a given point in time. Second, they show that competing logics – economic and patriarchal – were not secondary considerations that at times trumped primary, racial ideological constructs for pragmatic reasons. Rather, they were themselves primary ideological categories for the regime – ones which at times complemented and at other times supplanted racial concepts, not for pragmatic but for ideological reasons.

Gerhard Wolf examines Nazi Germanization policies in occupied Poland, where procedures were put in place for determining which members of the local population were suitable for German citizenship. What is striking in this instance is that in the initial policy as formulated by the Reich Interior Ministry, it was *völkisch* rather than racial criteria that mattered. Here it was ethnic rather than biological markers that were key. As a ministry decree put it, "language, education, culture, etc." were what indicated membership in the German *Volk* among Christian Poles and *Volksdeutsche*. (Jews were perforce excluded.) It was not even necessary to prove that one had German ancestors in order to prove German ethnicity; it was far more important that one declare one's belonging to the German people. This implied a very expansive and largely voluntarist understanding of Germandom. Himmler and the SS challenged this expansive view, pushing for a more restrictive, racialized policy, and even though this view won out in the bureaucratic tussle, in the end the "racial screenings" proposed by the SS amounted to little. This was because the racial language imposed by the SS was exploited by the Interior Ministry to create a more inclusive policy in practice than Himmler seemed to have envisaged in theory. Less than 10 percent of the population ended up undergoing racial screenings. According to Wolf, this indicates that

If some aspects of Nazi ideology, such as race, proved to be dysfunctional by, for example, interfering with the need of formulating a coherent occupation policy ... and thus threatening the reproduction of the political system itself, even hardcore Nazis cared little for Hitler's writing but instead turned into ideological entrepreneurs, themselves co-contributing to what in any case was the incoherent corpus constituting Nazi ideology.

Ideology did not dictate policy but functioned rather as a resource to be mobilized and redefined in the internal disputes over the proper course of action. Race was a moving target, subject to constant redefinition; it could be used as a label that was applied to policies of very different sorts, deployed for purposes of inclusion as much as exclusion.

If Wolf reveals that, during the war, racial ideology did not preordain a more radical, exclusionary, murderous policy, Regina Mühlhäuser and Stefan Hördler each demonstrate, in distinct ways, that race could work in tandem with – and even be trumped by – alternate logics. Mühlhäuser examines wartime sexual encounters on the eastern front and Wehrmacht and SS efforts to police them. Nazi racism, like its counterparts elsewhere, tended to focus on miscegenation as a particularly grave threat. This would seem to require draconian policies against fraternization with the racially inferior Slavs whom the Germans encountered on the eastern front. Yet this racial logic ran counter to another potent ideological construct: male sexual prerogative. As Mühlhäuser puts it, "a large number of men acted on the assumption that they were entitled to almost unlimited access to women's bodies." The result of these conflicting imperatives – racial purity and sexual privilege – was a weak and inconsistently enforced policy of prohibition on sexual encounters – consensual or coerced, hetero- and homosexual – between German troops and local residents. According to Mühlhäuser, this inconsistency reveals not just the power of patriarchal attitudes to trump racist commitments but also the internal limitations of racism itself, as both individual soldiers and Nazi authorities "harbored contradictory ideas" about the racial value of the Soviets they encountered. For instance, race rarely factored into rape prosecutions, which focused on the harm done to the Wehrmacht's reputation and military discipline. Mühlhäuser concludes that for individual German soldiers and SS men, their degree of commitment to Nazi ideology did not necessarily influence their sexual choices in a direct way. At the eastern front, many soldiers and SS men who were more or less enthusiastic Nazis breached the racial laws without assuming they had in any way violated the German idea. When there was a contradiction between competing ideological imperatives, ordinary German soldiers and SS men were able to, in effect, pick and choose between them as circumstances dictated, without necessarily seeing any significant inconsistency.

If it is striking that the eastern front, the *locus classicus* of a war of extermination, opened up a space for alternative ideological priorities, it is perhaps even more surprising that the same is true of the concentration camps. Stefan Hördler argues that as the war progressed, the camps became ever more multi-ethnic, both in terms of the inmate population *and* in terms of the guards, who themselves met the proper racial criteria for the SS in decreasing numbers. According to Hördler, as manpower needs became ever more acute, the camps were increasingly staffed by whoever was available and distinctions between "old" SS men, ethnic Germans, and foreign auxiliaries began to disappear. In this context, ideology no longer served as a driver of criminal behavior and mass murder but at most as a "frame of reference" that could serve to either legitimate violent activities or be deployed instrumentally as a means to an end. Hördler argues that the same was beginning to apply to the inmate population. "Above all in the final years of the war, the racial hierarchy among the inmates was incrementally levelled out." The manifest need to increase arms production led not just representatives of the army or industry, but even party stalwarts, including Himmler, to prioritize the exploitation of prisoner labor over the murder of racial enemies, culminating in the *Vernichtungsstop* at Auschwitz in November 1944. Although this did little to improve living conditions for the inmates, it did change the criteria for murder. In the final phase of the war, "selections and mass killings were directed above all at those inmates who were viewed, according to the SS three-tier selection system, as unsuitable because of illness or general physical exhaustion. There is no evidence for a primarily racially motivated selection." In the end, genocide was subsumed into a more utilitarian, though no less brutal, policy of exploitation.

The war exacerbated inconsistencies and contradictions within Nazi racial ideology that had already been apparent before 1939. It opened up a space for race to be reinterpreted by entrepreneurial bureaucrats. This could – and often did – lead to a dynamic of "cumulative radicalization," but it also could, and did, lead to contradictory impulses, toward greater inclusion of "Germanized" non-Germans, toward the exploitation of labor and sexual opportunity, even when the targets were racially inferior. The war, in other words, made a complicated conceptual and policy landscape even more complex. This means that any adequate characterization of the Third Reich at war needs to consider multiple conceptual frameworks, divergent policy impulses, and the changing fortunes of war.

CONCLUDING REFLECTIONS

Book titles that claim to be "beyond" reveal two things: first, that the book in question is defined by a critique of the phenomenon or concept that it seeks to transcend, but second, that what is transcended – the thing the book is "beyond" – is easier to define than the book's ultimate destination. Certainly the present volume has no simple substitute to offer for the "racial state." Indeed, Grosse and perhaps also Wildt would seem to be reemphasizing the centrality of race in Nazi ideology and policy while challenging received views of its genealogy. Other critiques of the racial state are partial, for example, Rupnow's and Steigmann-Gall's demonstrations that Nazi anti-Semitism cannot easily be subsumed under the rubric of race, or Matthäus's evidence of the contingencies and political considerations that helped to shape the evolution of Nazi policy. No one is denying that the Nazis constructed an elaborate set of racial policies or launched a barrage of racial rhetoric.

The broadest critique of the racial state paradigm can be found in the contributions from Bloxham, Roseman, and others that attribute Nazi violence not to the demands of racial thought in particular but to the intersection between a much broader set of modern vocabularies of difference (in which some notion of the nation often acted as the core anchor for distinguishing between "them" and "us," on the one hand, and the state broadly defined, on the other). Here, international competition in the circumstances of the late nineteenth century and interwar Europe, coupled with an increasingly biopolitical conception of population quality as a source of national strength, were instrumental in giving rise to violent and sometimes genocidal projects. Race thinking was, as Bloxham argues, merely one element on a much broader continuum, and religio-ethnic difference could be just as explosive. The central thrust of this critique is thus to reject the idea that racial ideas and racial bureaucracy (whose existence is not in question) constituted the decisive locus of explanation for Nazi violence and murder. That same critique can be found in Pendas's comparative framing, which shows the parallels between the Nazi and other racial states while noting the massive differences in their trajectories.

Another of the volume's core positions, exemplified by contributions from Czech, Stone, Wetzell, and others, is that the "science" of race – whether understood as biological science or just as professionally conducted *Wissenschaft*, which could also be social science – did not provide the knowledge or conclusions that motivated Nazi policy. Contributions from Hördler, Mühlberger, and Wolfe show that, even when loosely defined, racial distinctions were often a poor guide to important elements of Nazi policy. No single line emerges from the volume on race's place in Nazi society – either in terms of Nazi social policy or in society's response to the regime – though Bajohr, Kessel, Stargardt, and Timm each bring innovative methodological lenses to the question. All these essays invite further study to locate race's place in the evolving economies of sentiment, loyalty, and identity in peace and war under Nazi rule.

One possibility opened up by the volume is to shift attention from racial knowledge and theory to racial discourse. The very vagueness of that discourse may have been the key to its versatility and utility – even if it also meant that racial discourse was more the servant than the agent of policy. In different ways, Stone's and particularly Geulen's contributions open up this possibility and suggest the need for careful charting of the continuum from the policy-directing imperatives of thought, at one end, to the more diffuse legitimating and mobilizing functions of rhetoric, at the other.

Ultimately, our aim was to remind ourselves just how multifaceted, complex and elusive is the relationship between "race," state, and Nazism. We certainly did not aspire to have the last word. We thank our contributors, and the other participants of the original conference on which this volume drew, for their innovative and imaginative approaches to this conversation. And we hope that readers will be inspired to revisit and rethink the shorthand of the racial state.

Notes

1 Eve Rosenhaft, "Blacks and gypsies in Nazi Germany: the limits of the 'racial state,'"*History Workshop Journal* 72 (2011), 161.

2 Gerhard Jacoby, *Racial State: The German Nationalities Policy in the Protectorate of Bohemia-Moravia* (New York, 1944).

3 Michael Burleigh and Wolfgang Wippermann, *The Racial State: Germany, 1933–1945* (Cambridge, 1991).

4 Ibid., 73.

5 Ibid., 305.

6 Ibid., 2.

7 Ibid., 305.

8 Ibid., 51.

9 Ibid., 56.

10 Ibid., 1.

11 David Schoenbaum, *Hitler's Social Revolution: Class and Status in Germany 1933–1939* (New York, 1966); Ralf Dahrendorf, *Society and Democracy in Germany* (New York, 1967); Tim Mason, *Sozialpolitik im Dritten Reich: Arbeiterklasse und Volksgemeinschaft* (Opladen, 1977), translated as *Social Policy in the Third Reich*, ed. Jane Caplan (Providence, 1993).

12 Detlev Peukert, *Volksgenossen und Gemeinschaftsfremde* (Cologne, 1982), 246, 279, 296; translated as *Inside the Third Reich* (New Haven: Yale University Press, 1987), 208, 234–5, 248. Peukert's essay "The genesis of the 'Final Solution' from the spirit of science," which connects this argument more closely to the role of the modern sciences in the Nazi regime, was first published (in German) in 1989 and had probably not been read by Burleigh and Wippermann when they wrote the book; it is not cited in their footnotes. Detlev Peukert, "Die Genesis der 'Endlösung' aus dem Geist der Wissenschaft"in D. Peukert, *Max Webers Diagnose der Moderne* (Göttingen, 1989), 102–21; published in English as Detlev Peukert, "The genesis of the 'Final Solution' from the spirit of science," in David F. Crew (ed.), *Nazism and German Society, 1933–1945: Rewriting Histories* (London, 1994), 274–99.

13 *Beiträge zur nationalsozialistischen Gesundheits- und Sozialpolitik* (1985–). In particular, the first six volumes (1985–7) contained pioneering and influential essays on racial and social policy, euthanasia, and eugenics.

14 The reference here is to Peukert's *Volksgenossen und Gemeinschaftsfremde*; Peukert later advanced more radical arguments in his 1989 essay "Die Genesis der 'Endlösung'."

15 "Editorial" in Götz Aly, Angelika Ebbinghaus, Matthias Hamann, Friedmann Pfäfflin, and Gerd Preissler, *Aussonderung und Tod: Die klinische Hinrichtung der Unbrauchbaren*, vol. 1 of Beiträge zur nationalsozialistischen Gesundheits- und Sozialpolitik (Berlin, 1985), 7–8, here 7; Burleigh and Wippermann, *The Racial State*, 4.

16 "Editorial" in Götz Aly, Karl Friedrich Masuhr, Maria Lehmann, Karl Heinz Roth, and Ulrich Schultz, *Reform und Gewissen: 'Euthanasie' im Dienst des Fortschritts*, vol. 2 of Beiträge zur nationalsozialistischen Gesundheits- und Sozialpolitik (Berlin, 1985), 7–8, here 7.

17 Burleigh and Wippermann, *The Racial State*, p. 2; for a similar argument, see ibid., 304. *Modernity and the Holocaust* was almost certainly a reference to Zygmunt Baumann's 1989 book of the same title, which Burleigh and Wippermann did not explicitly cite. The important work of Michael Prinz and Rainer Zitelmann on Nazism and modernization appeared only in 1991, the same year that *The Racial State* was published, and is not cited anywhere in the book; see Michael Prinz and Rainer Zitelmann, *Nationalsozialismus und Modernisierung* (Darmstadt, 1991); Rainer Zitelmann, *Hitler, Selbstverständnis eines Revolutionärs*, 3rd edn. (Stuttgart, 1990); Rainer Zitelmann, "Die totalitäre Seite der Moderne" in Michael Prinz and Rainer Zitelmann (eds.), *Nationalsozialismus und Modernisierung* (Darmstadt, 1991), 1–20.

18 Burleigh and Wippermann, *The Racial State*, 306–7.

19 Mark Roseman, "National Socialism and the end of modernity," *American Historical Review* 116 (2011), 688–701.

20 Burleigh and Wippermann, *The Racial State*, 2, 17.

21 Ibid., 56.

22 Ibid., 56.

23 Jacob Robinson, foreword to Gerhard Jacoby, *Racial State: The German Nationalities Policy in the Protectorate of Bohemia-Moravia* (New York, 1944), v–viii, here v–vi.

24 For an introduction to the vast literature on this subject, see Margit Szöllösi-Janze, *Science in the Third Reich* (Oxford, 2001); Doris Kaufmann (ed.), *Geschichte der Kaiser-Wilhelm-Gesellschaft im Nationalsozialismus: Bestandsaufnahme und Perspektiven der Forschung*, 2 vols. (Göttingen, 2000); Christopher Hutton, *Race and the Third Reich: Linguistics, Racial Anthropology and Genetics in the Dialectic of Volk* (Cambridge, 2005); Susanne Heim, Carola Sachse, and Mark Walker (eds.), *The Kaiser Wilhelm Society under National Socialism* (New York, 2009); Sheila Faith Weiss, *The Nazi Symbiosis: Human Genetics and Politics in the Third Reich* (Chicago, 2010).

25 Ulrich Herbert, *Best: Biographische Studien über Radikalismus, Weltanschauung und Vernunft, 1903–1989* (Bonn, 1996); Michael Wildt, *Generation des Unbedingten: Das Führungskorps des Reichssicherheitshauptamtes* (Hamburg, 2002), translated as *An Uncompromising Generation* (Madison, 2010); Lutz Hachtmeister, *Der Gegnerforscher: Die Karriere des SS-Führers Franz Alfred Six* (Munich, 1998); Christian Ingrao, *Believe and Destroy: Intellectuals in the SS War Machine* (Cambridge, 2013).

26 On the debate of intentionalists versus functionalists, see Ian Kershaw, *The Nazi Dictatorship: Problems and Perspectives of Interpretation*, 4th edn. (London, 2000), 69–92; Mark Roseman, "Beyond conviction? Perpetrators, ideas, and action in the Holocaust in historiographical perspective" in Frank Biess, Mark Roseman, and Hanna Schissler (eds.), *Conflict, Catastrophe and Continuity: Essays on Modern German History* (New York, 2007), 83–103.

27 Ulrich Herbert, "Vernichtungspolitik" in U. Herbert (ed.), *Nationalsozialistische Vernichtungspolitik* (Frankfurt, 1998), 9–66, esp. 44–5; see also Michael Wildt, *Geschichte des Nationalsozialismus* (Göttingen, 2008), 13, 171–2; Kershaw, *Nazi Dictatorship*, 263–4; Roseman, "Beyond conviction."

28 Janosch Steuwer, "Was meint und nützt das Sprechen über 'Volksge-meinschaft,'" *Archiv für Sozialgeschichte*, 53 (2013), 487–534, esp. 520–5; Michael Wildt, "'Volksgemeinschaft' – Eine Zwischenbilanz" in Dietmar von Reeken and Malte Thießen (eds.), *Volkgemeinschaftals soziale Praxis* (Pader-born, 2013), 355–69, esp. 362ff.; Martina Steber and Bernhard Gotto, "*Volksgemeinschaft*: writing the history of the Nazi regime" in M. Steber and B. Gotto (eds.), *Visions of Community in Nazi Germany: Social Engin-eering and Private Lives* (Oxford, 2014).

29 Zygmunt Bauman, *Modernity and the Holocaust* (Ithaca, 1989), 13.

30 Donald Bloxham, *Genocide, the World Wars and the Unweaving of Europe* (London, 2008).

31 Burleigh and Wippermann, *The Racial State*, 51.

32 Peukert, "Die Genesis der 'Endlösung," 104.

33 Lucy Dawidowicz, *The War Against the Jews, 1933–1945* (New York, 1986).

PART I

COMPARATIVE AND HISTORICAL PERSPECTIVES

Racial Discourse, Nazi Violence, and the Limits of the Racial State Model

Mark Roseman

It seems obvious that the Nazi regime was a racial state. The Nazis spoke a great deal about racial purity and racial difference. They identified racial enemies and murdered them. They devoted considerable attention to the health of their own "race," offering significant incentives for marriage and reproduction of desirable Aryans, and eliminating undesirable groups. While some forms of population eugenics were common in the interwar period, the sheer range of Nazi initiatives, coupled with the Nazis' willingness to kill citizens they deemed physically or mentally substandard, was unique. "Racial state" seems not only a powerful shorthand for a regime that prioritized racial-biological imperatives but also above all a pithy and plausible explanatory model, establishing a strong causal link between racial thinking, on the one hand, and murderous population policy and genocide, on the other.

There is nothing wrong with attaching "racial state" as a descriptive label to the Nazi regime. It successfully connotes a regime that both spoke a great deal about race and acted in the name of race. It enables us to see the links between a broad set of different population measures, some positively discriminatory, some murderously eliminatory. It reminds us how strongly the Nazis believed that maximizing national power depended on managing the health and quality of the population. The problem lies rather with "racial state" as an explanatory category that provides the key to Nazi actions and their appeal.

I would like to thank Donald Bloxham, Alon Confino, Robert Pergher, Miriam Rürup, and my fellow editors, as well as our anonymous readers, for their helpful comments.

This essay seeks to sketch the broad contours of an argument that race thinking, while pervasive, was not as coherent, distinct, or purposeful as the model suggests; the roots of Nazi thought were far too eclectic to be subsumed under the label of biological racism. Second, it argues that, even when more loosely defined, racism does not explain Nazi violence. The sources of the Nazis' inclination and capacity for massive violence lay elsewhere. As part of this argument, this essay challenges the idea that a distinctively racial (as against, say, ethnically inflected nationalist) ideology was the primary cement bonding the population to the regime or the force that unleashed popular energy.

In offering an introductory survey of these themes, this essay has two goals. It seeks to capture important elements of discourse and policy in the Third Reich, and to question on a more general level the distinction between a racial state, on the one hand, and the radical nationalist policing and elimination of difference, on the other. It believes that racial discourse has a more distinctive and determinative political and social role when it is not merely adding an edge to radical nationalism but has the prime function of maintaining societal inequality, as in, say, the Jim Crow South or apartheid regimes. It is because of the legacy of that function that "race" continues to be such a powerful analytical tool in North American academia. By contrast, Nazi racial policy aimed to reinforce the unity and exclusivity of the German people. The Nazis did not want to create an enduringly segregated society by racial classification. "Others" would be present only as a temporary expedient. Even when they conquered new territory and thus engaged in what might look like a colonial endeavor, they in fact aimed at Germanizing land through settlement and expelling or eliminating the original occupants. The language of race accompanied the Nazis' domestic and expansionary policies, but those policies resemble closely the radical nationalist pursuit of unity and world power by (biopolitically minded) regimes that did not primarily speak the language of race. Where Nazi policies were distinctive, as in the Holocaust, it is not clear that racial ideas account for the difference.

Given the limited space available here, this essay can make only a few first moves toward teasing apart the strings holding the racial state model together. After some preliminary observations about language, the first three sections discuss the content of race-thinking before and during Nazi rule. They show that Nazi racial ideology was far more heterogeneous and far less rooted in (pseudo-)scientific knowledge about race than we have been wont to assume. The essay turns first to the character of racial science and racial hygiene; then to the cultural assumptions that continued to blur the boundaries between racial, ethnic, and national thinking; and finally to the peculiar characteristics of Nazi anti-Semitism, which cannot be subsumed under the idea of race. It then moves to consider another central idea that competed with, and often sat uneasily alongside, race in Nazi discourse, namely the idea of the *Volk*. That idea, the framing and connotations of which cannot be reduced to an ideology of race, was critical for the Nazis' ability to mobilize their following. The final section takes a more comparative and more functional approach, considering the Nazi state in relation to other "racial states" and other modern genocides, and identifying a diffuse ethnic nationalism as the common core ideology of ethnic cleansing and genocides.

RACE TO REIFICATION

If it is true, as is argued here, that in recent years we have overemphasized the strength and cohesion of past discourse and ideologies of race, this is the paradoxical result of our lack of belief in them. From our twenty-first century perspective, biological racial theory is so obviously based on bogus assumptions that we find it difficult to make sense of past generations who believed in it.[1] Our difficulty is compounded in the Nazi case by the regime's utterly murderous actions in the name of this chimera. It is not surprising that after the war, European intellectuals rapidly moved to disavow the whole apparatus of race-thinking. Eugenics virtually disappeared from the intellectual and political scene. The Nazis' pursuit of racial policies was consigned to a chamber of horrors and seen as the product of Hitler's own manic obsessions – obsessions that were tragically translated into action by cadres mesmerized by the Führer or opportunistically pursuing their own careers. In the 1980s, however, the rediscovery that many experts and scientists had been centrally involved in race and eugenic thinking on both sides of the Atlantic meant that racial politics could no longer be consigned to the fantasies of a Hitler or a Himmler. Shocked by this new knowledge but even more doubtful of any real substance to biological race thinking, we switched from marginalizing a crazy coterie of cranks to emphasizing the disturbing wrong-headedness of an intellectual generation, foregrounding the sincerity and intellectual coherence of a much larger body of experts and power holders. But in doing so, we reified racial language and lost sight of its flexibility, heterogeneity, multifunctionality, and instrumental character.

In the conversation between English language and German scholarship on Nazi policy, this problem of determining race's reality has been exacerbated by two problems of translation: *Volk* as used in interwar Germany has connotations that are not immediately transparent in the English "people"; "race" as used now in English-language scholarship no longer easily translates to *Rasse*. Richard Evans' magisterial survey of Nazi Germany, for example, translates the title of the Nazi newspaper as the "Racial Observer."[2] We can see why the translator went there: there's something about *Völkischer Beobachter* that "The People's Observer" doesn't catch. "*Racial* Observer" reminds us that the Nazis did not accept everyone as part of the people's community and that *völkisch* conveyed both representation and program, both being *of* the people and advocating a particular definition of who *belonged to* the people. But in the translation to "racial" something has flipped; the national-popular element has gone, and with it crucial elements of what gave the Third Reich its cohesion and élan. In a small way, this renaming reflects some of the conceptual costs of the racial state paradigm, which lie above all in the obscuring of the popular, the national, and the social by the biological.

By contrast, contemporary Anglo-American use of race blunts our ability to analyze race's coherence as a biological theory and its difference from other taxonomies of human difference. When David Theo Goldberg, for instance, dubs *all* modern states racial states, this does not imply that all states are run by people who believe in race as a biological category or that all states preside over societies whose subjects have that belief.[3] It does not even imply a claim about discourse in such cases, that is, that all states are run by people who use the term "race" or that explicit talk about race is present in the societies over which they preside. Goldberg is instead making a claim about the state's central involvement in generating or reproducing *difference* on the basis of national origins, religion, or ethnicity; for Goldberg and for analysts of the contemporary United States such as Michael Omi and Howard Winant, these differences of origin and communal identity are seen as having played a central role in shaping the character of the state itself.[4] They use race as a catch-all phrase to capture all of them.

This flexible usage of race can be useful in the North American context because it highlights awareness of the continuing reality of inequality even when the overt terminology or legal framework of race has gone. But as a category of analysis, race in this modern sense cannot clearly establish the distinctive character and implications of, say, religious difference as against tension between groups of different national origins, by contrast with more biological views of different groups of people. In relation to interpreting the Nazi state it thus elides key distinctions, above all the question of whether Nazi eliminatory violence arises from a coherent and particular set of racial theories as against, say, resentments against other national minorities or hatred of other religious groups. Moreover, if every state is a racial state, the term loses any explanatory value for the Nazis' distinctive violence. In fact, as will be argued below, when considered comparatively, race performed such a different function for Nazi Germany than, say, for the US that we wonder whether the racial state provides a useful and apt explanatory model to understand the Third Reich at all.

RACE SCIENCES

Recent research has demonstrated the striking degree to which racial science enjoyed acceptance both inside and outside Germany in the early part of the twentieth century. A broad array of scientific experts talked of race as a biological fact. It is clear that it will not do to discount this simply as bogus science, even if it was based on assumptions that are no longer tenable.[5] For one thing, much that was discussed under the heading of race connected with the growing knowledge of and interest in genetic inheritance.[6] Unaware of the disastrous potential implications, contemporaries perhaps understandably believed that genetic selection would provide the key to engineering healthier populations in the future. Starting with its 1910 edition, the *Encyclopedia Britannica*'s entry for "Civilization" declared that the future of humanity would probably be ruled by the "biological improvement of the race"[7] and by man applying "whatever laws of heredity he knows or may acquire in the interests of his own species, as he has long applied them in the case of domesticated animals."[8] Unsurprisingly, this text was quietly deleted from the 1945 edition.

In Germany, eugenics, often practiced under the title of *Rassenhygiene*,[9] was advocated by many who hoped to protect the health and enhance the quality of the German race or races. Yet even here, as Richard Wetzell's piece in this volume argues at much greater length, we will not find easy foundations for the Nazi project. For one thing, when racial biology was given what has been dubbed its "second chance"[10] at scientific status – as a result of developments in evolutionary biology at the end of the nineteenth century – some of the classic assumptions that had characterized biological racism's earlier incarnations were no longer tenable. For example, empirical observation of variety within species and, above all, Mendel's observations that a variety of genes might present in any given case against a backdrop of underlying potentiality overturned the platonic notion that races had a simple and characteristic appearance.[11] As Pascal Grosse notes elsewhere in this volume, racial experts were increasingly of the view that establishing descent was the only reliable way to identify racial belonging. Yet this collided with the claims about enduring and stable racial difference that were a staple feature of Nazi rhetoric and propaganda.

The "racial" in "racial hygiene" also often did not refer to a distinctive German race but was the term used by scientists to describe the given population whose genetic pool was subject to study and policy (the *Vitalrasse*) or sometimes humanity as a whole, as in the *Encyclopedia Britannica* entry cited above.[12] In that sense, race was a bio-buzz word that did not necessarily imply a hierarchical ranking of different human races.[13] Moreover, serious scientists who did believe in the notion of discrete races argued that modern societies were characterized by complex racial mixtures, and indeed many scientists thought that mixtures were the source of social health.[14] This was true even of the founder of *Rassenhygiene*, Alfred Ploetz, and certainly of an important research figure in the Third Reich, Eugen Fischer.[15] (Fischer did however believe that it was harmful to interbreed races that were too far apart.)

André Pichot has found similarly that of the thousands of articles published in the four major German anthropological periodicals between 1890 and 1914, there are only six on the subject of Jews – five written by Jews and the sixth a critique of anti-Semitism.[16] This does not mean that there were not anti-Semitic subtexts. In the Weimar era, racial scientists sometimes trimmed their sails to the prevailing demands of Weimar funding bodies; hence Eugen Fischer's support for a 1930 proposal to change the Berlin Racial Hygiene Society's name to Eugenics Society.[17] So the absence of overt anti-Semitism or anthropological racism in the 1920s is not always a reliable guide to underlying beliefs. Even so, it is significant that while Fritz Lenz praised Hitler's program in Ploetz's *Archiv* in 1931, "he was embarrassed by Hitler's racial antisemitism which he blamed on pseudo-scientific ideologues such as Chamberlain and Fritsch."[18] Paul Weindling has demonstrated the complex and ambivalent relationship between the Nazis and eugenicists and racial scientists that resulted.[19] As Richard Wetzell reminds us in this volume, shortly after the Nazis assumed power, even Eugen Fischer ridiculed current expressions of racial anti-Semitism, a fact that almost cost him his position as director of the Kaiser Wilhelm Institute in Berlin. Perhaps even more striking, by the time the Nazis came to power, serious racial scientists had discarded the notion of an Aryan race.[20]

Thus the key protagonists of racial hygiene stood at some remove from many of the popular claims made by the Nazis, and the Nazis themselves held extraordinarily varied views on race. Populist ideologues were influential, such as Hans F. K. Günther, whose two volumes *Humanitas* and *Platon als Hüter des Lebens* could be found on many bookshelves. Günther offered up an aesthetic image of racial purity that racial scientists had largely discarded. In the hands of a "Rassengünther" or a Rosenberg, race became almost a spiritual quality.[21] It certainly mattered, however, that Fischer, Lenz, and others actively supported the new regime and opportunistically embraced its rhetoric. From one point of view, they were, in Benno Müller Hill's words, "useful idiots"; from another, they were canny and unprincipled opportunists.[22] Despite his earlier criticism of racial anti-Semitism, Fischer was willing to provide hundreds of expert racial opinions on individuals' Jewish descent in race-related court cases.[23] Arguably the most sinister cooperation between science and the regime lay in scientists' use of living or dead tissue taken from victims of Nazi murder policy. This ruthless discounting of the rights of others could be based on a notion of differential racial quality, but it did not need to be. It simply depended on the acceptance that the state had made some lives dispensable and put them at the researchers' disposal. And as Christopher Hutton has shown, once the Jewish question had been largely "solved" within Germany through deportation and murder, racial scientists lost interest in much of the anthropological racism they had opportunistically embraced in the early years of Nazi rule.

In other words, Nazi ideas and policy were not driven forward by a concerted and coherent body of knowledge that was understood as racial science. Indeed, as Herwig Czech shows elsewhere in this volume, Nazi euthanasia was not tied to contemporary notions of genetic conditions; instead, it was above all those who were unable to work who were murdered. This was a form of lethal biopolitics to be sure, prioritizing collective needs over individual rights, but it was at most loosely legitimated by contemporary understanding of race. The paradigm of a racial state thus does not explain these policies.

RACE CULTURES

> Since race is not a mere word, but an organic living thing, it follows as a matter of course that it never remains stationary; it is ennobled or it degenerates, it develops in this or that direction and lets this or that quality decay. This is a law of all individual life. But the firm national union is the surest way to protect against going astray; it signifies common memory, common hope, common intellectual nourishment; it fixes firmly the existing bond of blood and impels us to make it ever closer.
>
> Houston Stewart Chamberlain[24]

Like the previous one, this section is principally concerned with the ideas that helped give energy and momentum to the Nazi project. If the previous section argued that the science of race as it developed in the early twentieth century was not particularly helpful for the Nazis, this one argues that their language of race was as much about performing nation as turning biological knowledge into action. In *The Origins of Nazi Violence*, Enzo Traverso, echoing Roger Chartier's dictum that the French Revolution had invented the Enlightenment, argues that Auschwitz "invented" anti-Semitism. Auschwitz had conferred "the appearance of a coherent, cumulative, and linear process on a body of discourse and practices that, before Nazism, had been perceived in the various European countries as discordant, heterogeneous and in many cases decidedly archaic."[25] An analogous line of argument could be made that Auschwitz or, more broadly, Nazi racial laws and practice "invented" our view of biological racism. In the short term, the Nazis made overt racism utterly unrespectable in Western Europe and allowed much of its prewar pervasiveness to disappear from view. Yet when scholars began to knit this web of knowledge back together in the 1980s, it was easy to overemphasize the coherence of contemporary expert knowledge and forget just how diffuse, multifaceted, and rhetorical race-thinking had been. It is remarkable, in fact, just how far even many of the influential classics of racial thought were from what we would see as a narrowly biological approach – indeed, how the very historical function they ascribed to race often militated against a narrowly biological understanding of its character and formation, and blurred into notions of national culture.

The distinction between ethnic (as pertaining to different cultural groups) and biological ways of understanding difference was made in English only in 1935, and "ethnicity" as a noun was coined only in 1950.[26] Julian Huxley's explicitly cultural deployment of the adjective "ethnic" in 1935 was in response to what he saw as the Nazi biologization of the race concept.[27] To that extent, Huxley affirms the idea that the Nazis were departing from common ground and advocating a distinctively biological concept of race. Yet the fact remains that in the discourse of the day that provided Nazi Germany with its vocabulary and plausibility, the language of race did not connote by definition a repudiation of cultural notions of ethnicity, even if ideas of blood were present too. British interwar discourse was full of pronouncements like that of Arthur Keith, president of the Royal Anthropological Institute, who in 1919 linked a strongly racial view to the cultural proposition that, in the case of Britain, "statesmanship has succeeded in raising up in the minds of all the inhabitants of the British Isles – all save a greater part of Ireland – a new and wider sense of nationality, a spirit of British nationality."[28]

To be sure, German discourse about race differed from its British counterpart. Yet classic German racial texts often emphasized culture over biology every bit as much as Arthur Keith had. Eugen Dühring, in some senses the father of racial anti-Semitism, had anything but a clearly defined concept of race. As Shulamit Volkov has pointed out, he used the terms people, nation, race, and culture interchangeably. *Judenhaftigkeit* was deployed to refer to non-Jews behaving like Jews; those "Jewish" in style and conduct but not in race were, according to Dühring, just as abhorrent as Jews.[29] Dühring was in any case a marginal figure – but that is a point about the history of anti-Semitism to which I must return. As indicated by the quotation with which this section opens, Houston Stewart Chamberlain saw races as constantly changing. The Germanic world, or *Germanentum*, was for Chamberlain absolutely not a clearly delineated tribe or grouping. In forging that world, two elements were at work: "social processes" and "ideas." The Germans had not defeated the French by being the true Germanic people; their victory had made them such. In the words of Christian Geulen, this was "a kind of Renanian plebiscite: the 'assertion' of race through the deeds of the nation."[30] The key task for the nation-state was precisely to give the race an enduring self-consciousness.

If the term "ethnicity" emerged in the English language to wrest culture away from race's shoulders only in 1950, it is equally noteworthy that the concept of sociology entered the German language in the context of racial theory via Ludwig Gumplowicz's *Der Rassenkampf: Soziologische Untersuchungen* (1883).[31] For Gumplowicz, race could not be purely an anthropological concept but also had a historical dimension. "Race as a unit has emerged in the course of history through social development. Its origins lie in the world of the spirit (language, religion, ethics, law, culture, etc.) and only then does race find its way to the powerful physical forces, the veritable glue, the unity of blood, that holds it together."[32] Here again, just as for Keith and for Chamberlain, race was the product of long years of collective interaction via religion and language; here again, the state and politics had a key role in cementing ethnic consciousness.

Many historians, while conceding the plasticity of race-speak for the pre-World War I period, have identified a change in the interwar years. The cauldron of war, defeat, and postwar chaos served to melt, reforge, and rework Wilhelmine discourse and politics. Though the German student movement, to take just one example, was already characterized by mounting anti-Semitism in the prewar period, its stance on German descent rapidly hardened thereafter.[33] Two strands of *völkisch* nationalism initially competed within the new Deutsche Hochschulring; it was the more biological wing, with its unrelenting belief in the incompatibility of Germans and Jews, that won out in the end. As Ulrich Herbert and Michael Wildt have shown, this intellectual climate created a body of like-minded figures that would help to police the racial state in the 1930s. Werner Best, after all, was one of the Hochschulring's hard men.[34]

Yet this transformation, vital as it was, is not quite what it seems. For one thing, most members of the *völkisch* movement eschewed or downgraded the language of *Rasse*. There was, according to Herbert, a widely shared awareness that science and anthropology had not come up with any convincing evidence for the existence of races.[35] This awareness was to persist and in part to deepen in the 1930s as intensive research failed to deliver the goods.[36] The language of race could still be heard, but often in the shadows of the discourse of *Volk* and *völkisch*. *Völkisch* was an interesting term because it simultaneously presented itself as the mere adjectival counterpart to the given entity, the *Volk*, and yet knew itself to be much more than that. It contained a specific set of assumptions and values challenging Weimar's state form, the inclusive character of its citizenship, the postwar borders, and the primacy of representational democracy as a way of establishing national will. In other words, its power lay in its ability to carry the national with it even while adding exclusions and political emphases. It was a power that vastly exceeded the language of race.

What is important about this process is, moreover, the particular national and international political constellation that gave the emphasis on the *Volk* its meaning. *Völkisch* ideology was a clarion call for a patriotism that stayed loyal to Germandom while rejecting the responsibility of loyalty to the new Reich authorities. To be *völkisch* meant to be anti-Versailles and anti-Weimar. Ernst von Salomon captured the subtle separation of *völkisch* nationalism from the existing national framework in a 1929 article for the *NS Monatshefte*:

Yes we were patriotic, and it seemed to us self-evident to be so.

Until even we began to make fun of such grand notions as "Fatherland" and "loyalty to the Kaiser. Until even we – and we above all – turned away from the banner-carrying and drum-beating, from the hero's courage and the field of honor … By then the word "Fatherland" had taken on a deeper meaning for us, by then we sensed that it belonged to us, and to us only.[37]

As this quotation implies, what it was to be *völkisch* was defined as much in competition with other groups within Germany – the competition between Germans and *true* Germans – as it was distinguishing between what was German and what was foreign. *Völkisch* nationalism, seemingly the language of national unity, was in fact the language of political conflict.[38] It is within that context that we should understand the unseemly scramble among the student corporations to fly the *völkisch* flag and prove themselves more German than the next – a scramble that, as Michael Wildt has shown, had only one target.[39] One could establish a claim to true Germandom, as against the mere superficial citizenship identity of Weimar, by calling for the exclusion of one, and only one, group. That group was the Jews. I want to return later to anti-Semitism's defining place, which far more than in the pre-World War I period became the touchstone differentiating the *völkisch* from the *Volk*.[40] But even ignoring that for a moment, it is clear that, rather than biological thinking driving the debate, biological racism was the kind of demonstrable hard-edge – the cultural code, in fact – for laying claim to true nationalism.[41] Both *Volk* and *Rasse* were narratives of origins, as Alon Confino has argued, but the foregrounding of *Volk* showed that what was at stake was establishing true nationalism.[42] The acceptance of biological language reflected a belief less in the proven biological character of race than in the performative value of demanding purity in order to demonstrate one's national credentials. And, as noted above, the idea that making this kind of demand would strengthen national consciousness in fact fitted well with the surprisingly culturalistic account of the state's role in creating race that was offered by theorists of the stamp of Houston Stewart Chamberlain.

The vehement assertion of biological difference thus often reflected in the first instance less a deep-seated belief in race science than confidence in the binding and strengthening power for the *Volksgemeinschaft* of enforcing and policing ethnic exclusion. It is hard, of course, always to distinguish the bioracial speech act made from straightforward belief in race's power from the one made, or assented to, because of belief in the cultural efficacy of bioracial language and enforcement. Yet something of the latter can be found in Claudia Koonz's account of the early years of Nazi Germany, as intellectuals and officials made sense of the new regime. When Interior Minister Wilhelm Frick proposed an ambitious program to evaluate "'our *Volkskörper* according to its genetic value,'" he did so explicitly "as one dimension of a comprehensive moral revolution that would revive communal values."[43] A memorandum from Frick's subordinate, Arthur Gütt, operates on similar terrain, if adding a spiritual dimension: "A person practicing racial hygiene and racial science is religious, and a religious person must practice racial hygiene and strive towards ennobling his race."[44] Indeed, the remarkable lack of consensus in the Ministry of Interior over the simplest terminological or scientific racial questions makes the participants look utterly unprincipled unless we ascribe to them belief in the cultural value of biopolitics. This helps too to explain Justice Minister Gürtner's emphasis on the importance of not moving too fast for the people. At stake was less the resistance that a nonconsensual race policy might engender than the basic point that one of race policy's prime functions was to cement the national spirit.

ANTI-SEMITISM, RACE, AND PEOPLE

For many Germans in the pre- and post-World War I period – and indeed for large parts of the *völkisch* movement, including large sections of the Nazi party – the issue of racial purity or ethnic homogeneity was reducible to a single relationship: Germans and Jews. For Weimar's right, the defining issue in discussions of the *Volksgemeinschaft* was who did not belong to it, and the answer was first and foremost: the Jews. The term *Volksgemeinschaft* surfaces in Hitler's rhetoric for the first time in his speech "Why we are anti-Semites."[45]

Yet if Jews figured heavily in thinking about *Volk* and *Rasse*, neither before nor during the Third Reich could anti-Semitism itself be reduced to the question of race. In the late nineteenth century, as Peter Pulzer has observed, "Historians of racism tend to yield to the temptation of overestimating its importance in the general development of anti-Semitism, simply because it was such a central component of National Socialism and the *Shoah*."[46] Avowedly racial anti-Semites such as Dühring, as we have seen, had shown anything but a clearly biological understanding of race. Moreover, they were far from the mainstream in a broad cultural movement that combined nationalist, Christian, and more narrowly economic components.[47]

True enough, racial anti-Semitism grew in significance as movements such as the Pan-German League radicalized during the war. Concepts from colonial racial policy were self-consciously applied to Jews, as would be evident in the Nazi policies against Jewish *Mischlinge*.[48] The furor about the "black shame" on the Rhine would spill over into right-wing protests against mixed marriages between Aryans and Jews.[49] Racialized black caricatures in advertising and popular culture helped to prepare the way for the racialized images of Jews that circulated in the 1920s.[50] Yet despite these racist trappings, important though they were, the immediate postwar constellation makes us question whether the Jewish question can really be designated a racial one.[51] War, revolution, and postwar treaties together contrived to produce a dramatic confluence of Jewish issues just as new political identities were being formed in Germany's postwar crisis. So much came together. The strains of war exacerbated tensions against the outsider, while the shortages in many cities added bitterness against the speculator.[52] The huge exodus of Jews from Russia before and during the war, coupled with the unfamiliar image of Eastern European refugees in every European capital, produced in the postwar world a sense of global Jewry as never before.[53] The wartime competition between London and Berlin for Russian Jewish support had, among other things, helped give rise to the Balfour Declaration. After the war, Jews were nominally the beneficiaries of the minority rights elements in the postwar treaties, toothless though they often really were.[54] All this reinforced the view that Jews had become a global force capable of manipulating international policy. The overrepresentation of Jewish leaders among the left-wing revolutionary movements lent credence and color to the idea of Jews as fomenters of internal sedition. The visibility, global character, and intersection with class conflict (with Jews cast now as capitalist, now as revolutionary leaders) of the Jewish question was thus remarkable. Brigitte Hamann concluded that it was not prewar Vienna but postwar Munich that made Hitler's anti-Semitism existential.[55] The striking global prevalence of anti-Semitic conspiracy theories in the aftermath of World War I shows how distinctive this epochal moment was. In the second half of the 1920s, true enough, conditions changed. Global anti-Semitism subsided, at least until the slump hit hard. But by then, political movements had been forged for which the Jewish question was central.

Of crucial importance in Germany was not just Jewish hypervisibility but the distinctive ways in which Jews could be seen as opposed to the nation. Be it in revolutionary St. Petersburg or the Paris of Allied deliberations, Jews appeared to be influential actors wherever there was an international stage that could affect life in Berlin. Zionism's newfound prominence suggested Jews' loyalties lay overseas, while success in extracting the Balfour Declaration pointed to their ability to influence foreign Cabinets.[56] The resonance from Dearborn to London to Bern to Grahamstown of the *Protocols of the Elders of Zion* suggests that this discovery of Jewish internationalism was no German invention.[57] For the

Nazis and other members of the radical right, another peculiarity of the time reinforced the sense of Jews as the antithesis of the *Volksgemeinschaft*. The unity of the *Volksgemeinschaft* sought by the right, after all, was a weapon in, and designed to supersede, the bitter internecine conflict of class war. Jews, uniquely and peculiarly to this moment, could be linked both with wartime profiteering and with international Marxism. For the radical right, to be national was thus to be anti-Semitic in every sense. To be sure, Hitler's explanation for Jewish predilections was couched in racial language. Thanks to their blood, they could do no different. But the power of his *j'accuse* lay in the ostensible evidence of an organized international conspiracy against the German *Volk*.

In the racial language after 1933, Jews, as we know, were lumped with many other "parasites" and "bacteria" to be removed from the bloodstream of the body politic.[58] The handicapped were sterilized, the asocials and other misfits interned and segregated, and Sinti and Roma became subject to their own "Nuremberg Laws" and brutal harassments. But already in the boycott campaign in April 1933 and with increasing vehemence in the second half of the 1930s, the Jewish danger was construed differently from the others. The danger was less one of substandard individuals threatening the health of the *Volk* than of an international conspiracy, one now with its capital in Moscow, now operating through intermediaries in London and Washington. Initially, this fantasized international web of Jewish power gave the Nazis reason to be somewhat cautious in the Jewish question. As Hitler grew more confident and allowed the assault on the Jews to mount, so the perceived reasons for linking Jews to foreign enemies strengthened too. There was, of course, an element of self-fulfilling prophecy about this, as influential Jews in London, Washington, and Hollywood did indeed – though often with little result – urge their governments to be aware of the German threat. It is striking how little energy the Nazis expended in the 1930s on imagining international conspiracy on the part of any expatriate groups on German soil. The country embraced a surge in foreign tourism with seemingly no anxiety that spies were sneaking from the Black Forest to Berlin.[59] It was only Jews who inspired paranoia about links between inner insurgency and outer international machinations. Though the language continued to be racial, the real core of the argument was that Jews constituted an insidious foreign power.[60]

It may well be argued that Hitler's anti-Semitism had still deeper roots. Saul Friedländer famously highlighted Nazi anti-Semitism's distinctively redemptive character.[61] Philippe Burrin has recently cogently emphasized the inherited power of Christian anti-Semitism, though here fused with the idea of national defense and racism.[62] The transmogrification of an older Christian Manichean image is plausible. Alon Confino has shown how early and clearly the Nazis imagined a world without Jews, and how many older cultural tropes were refashioned and deployed in the Nazis' violent practices in the 1930s.[63] Race-thinking provided some kind of formal language to describe this religious group's prescriptive ills (though with the previous section of this essay in mind, the ascription of enduring evil fitted poorly with racial theorists' emphasis on racial evolution – a contradiction already present in Chamberlain's own writings.) Yet, as Richard Steigmann-Gall reminds us, there were widely held doubts about whether the Jews really were a race.[64] Jews were attacked as an organized conspiracy, a transnational community that threatened the integrity of the nation.

THE PEOPLE'S COMMUNITY

"The enduring popularity of the Nazis rested on the idea of the *Volksgemeinschaft*, the people's community. It was not a Nazi idea and it was not perceived as something imposed or something strange."[65] Thus Peter Fritzsche, who notes, too, that many of the Nazis' achievements were cherished by Germans who did not identify with Nazis. The heart of the Nazis' appeal, and the reason they could be construed as being a "dictatorship by acclamation" (*Zustimmungsdiktatur*),[66] lay in the ethnically inflected national community they invoked.[67] Space prevents me from doing justice to this issue, and this section can do little more than pencil in the briefest of points. National community meant in the first instance dissolving class divisions in the balm of nation (and crushing the communists with its hammer). In 1933, national unity meant the triumph of order over the threat of Bolshevism. It meant surmounting the party divisions of a faltering democracy and establishing strong unified leadership. It meant finding common purpose to overcome the ravages of the depression. It meant bringing youthful energy and traditional values together.

To be sure, this pride went hand in hand in many people's minds with some kind of downgrading of Jews' place. Even on this point, though, the evidence is contradictory. A case can be made that anti-Semitism played a relatively limited role in the Nazis' electoral success before 1933.[68] The Nazis were also more than disappointed with the resonance of their April boycott.[69] It is true that the imagined people's community was an ethnic

one, in that the sense of Germanness reached beyond the boundaries of
the existing nation-state and excluded some current citizens – above all
the Jews. Yet much of the pride was old-fashioned pride in the nation-
state, its order, its resurgence, its growing international prestige. National
unity, national strength, and national revival were key. More than almost
any other event in these years, the power of Potsdam Day and May Day
speaks through the diaries Fritzsche examines in his study of the popular
appeal of Nazism.[70]

The evidence of how responsive Germans were to racial grooming
following the Nazi seizure of power is contradictory. Where Nazis
reinforced existing prejudices – as in attacks on asocials, Sinti and Roma,
homosexuals – they did well. In other areas, the regime was less convincing. As Claudia Koonz reminds us, because of public concern, the Nazis
rapidly learned to suppress the statistics regarding forced sterilization.
Save for those of some youngsters at school and Hitler Youth, the diaries
Fritzsche uses are often not very revealing here, whereas their responses
on national triumphs are unambiguous. National spectacle and foreign
policy success continued to touch the hearts of even those alienated from
the regime. The German-Jewish patriot and passionate Zionist Willy
Cohn, who was murdered in Kovno in 1941, noted in his diary on March
14, 1938:

You have to admire the forceful way all this was accomplished. It is going to be
difficult for the Jews heavily concentrated in Vienna who were – as so often –
backing the wrong horse and convinced that a union with the clerics' party
[*Klerikalen*] would bring them salvation . . . Perhaps we Jews in Germany should
not join in this welling up of national emotion, but one does so nevertheless, and
anyone with feelings for his country can relate to this!

He added, "We Jews should be just as unified."[71]

In any case, whatever successes the Nazis had in racial grooming, the
six-year period before the war was not long enough to change hearts and
minds. When war broke out, security, power, and prestige were again the
dominant emotions, with popular responses oscillating between fear of
war, relief at success, and pride in grandeur. Again, despite exhaustive
new studies, a surprising lack of clarity and agreement remains about the
degree to which Germans bought into the Holocaust.[72] There is no doubt
that the population knew of atrocities and feared reprisals. To that extent,
as Nicholas Stargardt argues in his contribution to this volume, perceptions of national survival became linked to the Jewish question. Yet this
implied the acceptance less of a racial concept than of the political idea of

international Jewish power. No doubt fear of this international force was magnified for many by inner unease at the knowledge of having so excluded other nations' interests from the national vision.

It is noteworthy that the first attempt to describe the "racial state" in relation to Nazi rule did not believe Nazi Germany itself qualified for this title. Gerhard Jacoby's *Racial State*, published in 1944, was about the "Protectorate" Germany established in the Czech lands, not about the Third Reich per se.[73] As Jacob Robinson explained in the foreword, it was the Protectorate that constituted the first racial state because it was there that for the first time three stable racial classes were created and administered by the state. Nazi Germany itself was not a racial state because it had so rapidly sidelined and expelled its in any case tiny Jewish population and thus did not preside over a racially divided society. Robinson, of course, suffered from the myopia of his age: describing Nazi-ruled Bohemia and Moravia as the first racial state meant completely disregarding European colonial rule![74] But he does lead us to an important insight: that Nazi Germany lacked an element normally integral to definitions of a racial state, namely, the administration of a racially stratified society.

For many racial theorists, such as Gobineau, Gustav Klemm, or the sociologist Ludwig Gumplowicz, modern European states were "racial" in that they owed their origins or development to racial struggles.[75] More common now are definitions that assume states are "racial" when they administer, and interact with, racially stratified societies. Thus David Goldberg's comparative study *The Racial State* and also recent scholarship by Moon-Kie Jung, Michael Omi, and Howard Wynant characterizing the United States as a racial state.[76] All of these authors take the existence of races (or of social groups that are the legacies of race-thinking) for granted; the racial state presides over and interacts with this stratified or conflicted society. It might be argued that Burleigh and Wippermann are talking about such a relationship between state and society in its infancy. The "races" were not yet there, but they were being created by the state out of the preexisting clay of religions and classes. In fact, however, the Nazis were clearly not tolerant of multiple races. Jews and Gypsies were being stigmatized and demarcated as the prelude to exclusion. Foreign forced labor was disciplined and regulated during the war as the price for the unpleasant and temporary fact that it needed to be employed on German home soil.[77] Even in imperial zones to the east, the more seriously the Nazis envisaged German population settlement, the more provisional became the right of non-Germans to live there.[78]

This underlying intolerance of racial difference alerts us in turn to an important distinction in race's relationship to nation. We have become very aware over the past few decades that racial "knowledge" and ideology was transnational, and that metropolitan societies drew from and deposited ideas in the "colonial archive."[79] But we have perhaps not always remembered that race's function varied quite markedly. In many contexts, racism performed the function of social stratification, often buttressing massive economic inequality, including slavery; in others, it emerged as an effort to capture the quintessence of national identity. In the context of social stratification, race served to enforce the rules of unequal coexistence; as hyper-nationalist ideology, it marked the boundaries of the national community and was always in that sense a secondary attribute to nation.[80] This distinction between socially stratifying racism and nationally demarcating racism does not equate to the difference between domestic and international conflict. The dividing line of racial social stratification could be global, as in the global color-line, but it did not run along national boundaries. By the same token, the national line of identity – as between "Germans" and "Jews" – could exist within the boundaries of the state if, as in the German case, the line of exclusion was being drawn between those who had "true" national identity and those "aliens" who had somehow managed to be citizens.

The distinction I am drawing here is similar in some respects to Pierre-André Taguieff's notions of *hétéroracisation* and *autoracisation*.[81] Taguieff sees the search for exclusivity that characterizes the latter as the extreme form of racism.[82] The ethnoracism of national exclusiveness is, however, very often far less brutal and destructive than the oppressive, segregating violence of an apartheid system. Taguieff may well be right that, of the two, it is the racism seeking to achieve national exclusivity that is more likely to result in ethnic cleansing and genocide. But as Mark Levene and others have shown, this is because of a goal of national exclusivity that can be equally lethal in the absence of biological or racial language (e.g., in the many cases of lethal violence targeting minorities who differ from the mainstream in both ethnicity and religion, such as the Turks' targeting of the Armenians), and not because of the specific dictates of the racial-biological, or indeed of any explicitly racial language.[83] We will return to this in a moment.

Seen with these distinctions in mind, Nazi Germany's outlook was ironically as much a symptom of Germany's "post-racial" condition as it was that of a racial state. Until the end of World War I, Germany had been a participant in the European domination of the world and, as a latecomer to the world scene, keenly conscious of sharing in white superiority. In 1918, however, it was kicked out of the colonial system. As Hitler's thinking about world power concretized, it became clear, as Gerhard Wolf writes in this volume, that Nazi rule would not in fact tolerate the coexistence of races that had characterized the major colonial empires, albeit under unequal and segregated conditions. Instead, a new kind of national land-settlement policy and ethnic *Flurbereinigung* (reordering) was to be the *Bodenpolitik* (territorial policy) of the future.[84] The Nazis were not seeking to recreate a racially stratified society.

The reader who has accepted the difference posited here between nationally demarcating and socially stratifying racism might nevertheless argue that Nazi Germany should still be seen as a racial state because its racialized construction of German national identity was an essential prerequisite of its murderous policies. We have already raised doubts that the lethal nature of Nazi anti-Semitism can really be designated as racial. But the widely shared view that it took the Nazi biological vision to perpetrate the Holocaust can be tackled on a more general level too. For Zygmunt Bauman, the Holocaust was unthinkable without the confluence of three modern forces usually flowing in different riverbeds: race thinking, medical thinking, and an engineering approach to society.[85] The argument is powerful, as is the claim that it took the racial component to make anti-Semitism so murderous. It is striking when we look more closely at Bauman's argument, though, that the issue of Nazism's relationship to other genocides, which did not necessarily involve race-thinking, is fudged. "No doubt the Holocaust was another episode in the long series of attempted mass murders and the not much shorter series of accomplished ones," he writes: "It also bore features that it did not share with any of the past cases of genocide. It is these features which deserve special attention. They had a distinct modern flavor. Their presence suggests that modernity contributed to the Holocaust more directly than through its own weakness and ineptitude."[86] Despite his avowed commitment to comparison, Baumann quickly buries the issue under a comparison between the Holocaust and its "alleged pre-modern equivalents."[87] Bauman makes the Holocaust thus stand out as the "modern" case without explicitly making the comparison with other recent genocides.

In fact, as Michael Mann, Norman Naimark, Donald Bloxham, Mark
Levene, and others have shown, in the modern era murderous population
policies were often pursued by nations thinking nationally, without any
very clear biologization of their identity beyond, perhaps, some strong
narrative of descent. The Turks pursued the Armenians with a religious-
cultural sense of their separateness and malevolence. This antagonism had
long been reinforced by the great powers' pro-Christian diplomatic maneuverings, which had turned minorities such as the Armenians into an
excuse for encroaching on the sovereign prerogatives of the Ottoman
Sultanate. Now it was exacerbated by wartime worries that the Armenians represented a fifth column. The mass killings in the Balkans before
and after World War I saw similar religious-cultural-ethnic identities
at stake. For Michael Mann, who looks at Armenia and Nazi Germany
as well as Rwanda and post-1989 Yugoslavia, if there was a common
ideological theme to many of the killings he surveyed, it was a more
diffuse kind of organicist nationalism, a nationalism intolerant of difference.[88] Norman Naimark's study of ethnic cleansing begins with some
warm but rather careless citations from Bauman but proceeds to describe
an eclectic set of ethnicist ideologies and concludes by using the vocabulary of integral nationalism.[89] Donald Bloxham, one of the most careful
and historically precise of these authors, shows that that one did not need
a racial theory "in order to treat other peoples as collectively dangerous
or disposable. As a legitimation for genocide, biological racism is only
at the extreme of a continuum of exclusionary beliefs that have the
potential to attribute malign characteristics to all members of another
group."[90] Often these exclusionary beliefs constituted the "cultural
inheritance of collective identity bequeathed by religion and woven in
the modern period into newer forms of political identity, whether extant
or desired."[91] Often, too, the explosions of violence took place in time of
war or acute international stress, when ethnic minorities became tainted
(often without real justification) by association with the interests and
machinations of foreign powers.

Identifying such patterns does not preclude a specific Nazi commitment
to biological thinking or deny that the Holocaust still commands a special
horror, even when arrayed against the other contestants in this grisly
league table. All the authors cited in the previous paragraph recognize
features that distinguish the Nazis from other murderous regimes. Mann
in particular has difficulty fitting the Holocaust into some of the generic
features of his model, notably his observation that the danger zone in
ethnic cleansing is reached when two old ethnic groups lay claim to the

same state.[92] Yet it must give us pause that biological racism is not necessary for such wholesale ethnocide. It prompts us to look anew at the national-popular roots both of Nazi ideology and of the murderous energy the Nazis mobilized. Moreover, though again there is no space to explore this here, the Nazis' remarkable propensity for violence, which was evident already in their war with the Communists in the 1920s, and the energy and reach that they brought to their murderous projects, which had to do with their harnessing of the resources of an advanced state and military and their ability to mobilize popular commitment to defending a beleaguered nation, were clearly not a function of racial ideology.

CONCLUSION

For the victims of racial policy, it probably made little difference what the protagonists believed. Whether used performatively, instrumentally, or sincerely, the biological language of race took on a life of its own. Those stamped as of lesser value were left with the puzzle of trying to make sense of ideas and practices that marked them out as less than human. (As we have seen, many of these policies and practices were not founded in any racial doctrine.) For the perpetrators too, believers in "race" were valorized, and others learned to use the code. Yet for us, seeking to understand the advocates and participants, it surely matters that even many leading Nazis remained unsure how sincerely that code was being used. Walter Gross, the head of the Office for Racial Policy, certainly worried about it and suspected that many of the ambitious young physicians applying to his institute to carry out race projects did not really believe. At a deeper level, he was not sure of the reality of race himself.[93] This is not to belittle the importance of rhetoric and codes, or to return the historiography to the de-ideologized categories of obedience and ambition characteristic of the older intentionalist-functionalist debates. But we do need to think in more complex, differentiated, and performative terms about policies, speech acts, and participatory gestures in Nazi Germany.

Moreover, instead of locating Nazi violence and genocide in a world of early twentieth-century biological knowledge (even of biological knowledge twisted and skewed by the aggressive ambitions of a radical regime in a hurry), we should be thinking of a broader context of violent state projects. This is not to say that this essay is offering a single paradigm to replace the racial state; indeed, it is clear that no single paradigm will capture the different impulses at work in the Third Reich. It inherited radical nationalist ideas of unity and exclusivity that evolved before and in the aftermath of World War I. As Roberta Pergher has pointed out, the interwar epoch added distinctive ingredients, discrediting conventional imperialism and prompting the Nazis, like their Italian and Japanese counterparts, to reconcile the desires for inner homogeneity and outer growth by pursing a new kind of settler-colonialism-cum-national expansion.[94] And, more than any other powerful regime before or since, the Nazis allowed the Jewish question and global Jewry to become the touchstone symbols of internal and external threats and obstacles. In all of this, "race" played rhetorical functions, reinforcing national difference and superiority, and helping to legitimate and focus the cleansing, classification, exploitation, and expunging of different population groups. Yet not race science, nor broader biological race thinking, nor even more diffuse race knowledge or race mysticism provided the foundation or the driving impetus for Nazi expansionism and Nazi violence.

Notes

1 This is of course not to deny that today's scientists identify certain genetic differences between broad population groups. See Charmaine Royal and Georgia Dunston, "Changing the paradigm from 'race' to human genome variation," *Nature Genetics* 36 (2004), S5–S7.

2 Richard J. Evans, *The Coming of the Third Reich* (New York, 2004), 178.

3 David Theo Goldberg, *The Racial State* (Malden, 2002).

4 Michael Omi and Howard Winant, *Racial Formation in the United States: From the 1960s to the 1990s* (New York, 1994).

5 Sheila Faith Weiss, *The Nazi Symbiosis: Human Genetics and Politics in the Third Reich* (Chicago, 2010), 6–8.

6 Veronika Lipphardt, "Isolates and crosses in human population genetics; or, a contextualization of German race science," *Current Anthropology* 53(S5) (2012), S69–S82.

7 *Encyclopaedia Britannica*, 11th edn., *s.v.* "civilizaton."

8 Ibid.

9 At times, the two labels *Rassenhygiene* and *Eugenik* had distinct connotations, as is clear below in the discussion of Fischer's name-change proposal.

10 Christopher Hutton, *Race and the Third Reich: Linguistics, Racial Anthropology and Genetics in the Dialectic of Volk* (Cambridge, 2005), 25.

11 Simona Forti, "The biopolitics of souls: racism, Nazism, and Plato," *Political Theory*, 34(1) (2006), 9–32.

12 Hutton, *Race and the Third Reich*, 17, 30; Lipphardt, "Isolates and crosses."

13 Weiss, *The Nazi Symbiosis*, 153; Wulf D. Hund, *Rassismus: die soziale Konstruktion natürlicher Ungleichheit* (Münster, 1999), 98.

14 Lipphardt, "Isolates and crosses."

15 Hutton, *Race and the Third Reich*, 30.

16 André Pichot, *The Pure Society: From Darwin to Hitler* (London, 2009), 313.

17 On anti-Semitic subtexts, Helga Satzinger, "Racial purity, stable genes, and sex difference: gender in the making of genetic concepts by Richard Gold-schmidt and Fritz Lens, 1916 to 1936" in Susanne Heim, Carola Sachse, and Mark Walker (eds.), *The Kaiser Wilhelm Society under National Socialism* (New York, 2009), 145–70, 149. On Fischer's support for the renaming pro-posal, Paul Weindling, *Health, Race, and German Politics between National Unification and Nazism, 1870–1945* (Cambridge, 1989), 482.

18 Weindling, *Health, Race, and German Politics*, 477.

19 Ibid., 470.

20 Hutton, *Race and the Third Reich*, 3.

21 Forti, "The biopolitics of souls," 17–18.

22 On Benno Müller Hill's discussion of useful idiots, see Pichot, *The Pure Society*, 315.

23 Alexandra Przyrembel, *Rassenschande: Reinheitsmythos und Vernichtungsle-gitimation im Nationalsozialismus* (Göttingen, 2003), 113.

24 Houston Stewart Chamberlain, as quoted in Paul Gilroy, *Against Race: Imagin-ing Political Culture Beyond the Color Line* (Cambridge, MA, 2000), 9.

25 Enzo Traverso, *The Origins of Nazi Violence* (New York, 2003), 6.

26 Verena Stolcke, "Is sex to gender as race is to ethnicity?" in Teresa del Valle (ed.), *Gendered Anthropology* (London, 1993), 17–37, particularly 24.

27 Julian Huxley, Alfred C. Haddon, and A. M. Carr-Saunders, *We Europeans: A Survey of "Racial" Problems* (New York, 1936).

28 Arthur Keith, cited in Paul Rich, "The long Victorian sunset: anthropology, eugenics and race in Britain, c1900–48," *Patterns of Prejudice* 18(3) (1984), 3–17, 5.

29 Shulamit Volkov, *Germans, Jews, and Antisemites: Trials in Emancipation* (Cambridge, 2006), 77.

30 "*Eine Art Renansches Plebizit: die 'Behauptung' der Rasse durch die Tat der Nation*": Christian Geulen, *Wahlverwandte: Rassendiskurs und Nationalis-mus im späten 19. Jahrhundert* (Hamburg, 2004), 178.

31 Ibid., 157.

32 Cited in ibid., 160.

33 On the prewar period, Norbert Kampe, *Studenten und "Judenfrage" im Deutschen Kaiserreich: die Entstehung einer akademischen Trägerschicht des Antisemitismus* (Göttingen, 1988).

34 Ulrich Herbert, *Best: biographische Studien über Radikalismus, Weltanschau-ung und Vernunft, 1903–1989* (Bonn, 1996), 51–69.

35 Ibid., 60–1.

36 Claudia Koonz, *The Nazi Conscience* (Cambridge, MA, 2003), 175.

37 "Ja, wir waren patriotisch und es erschien uns als selbstverständlich, dass wir es waren. Bis auch wir, auch wir anfingen, über die großen Worte von 'Vaterland' und 'Kaisertreue' zu spötteln, bis wir, auch wir und gerade wir uns abwandten vom Fahnenrauschen und Blechmusik und Heldenmut und Feld der Ehre … Schon hatte das Wort 'Vaterland' für uns einen tieferen Sinn, schon ahnten wir, daß es bei uns war und nur bei uns." Cited in Ulrich Bielefeld, *Nation und Gesellschaft: Selbstthematisierungen in Frankreich und Deutschland* (Hamburg, 2003), 282.

38 Helge Matthiesen, "Von der Massenbewegung zur Partei. Der Nationalsozialismus in der deutschen Gesellschaft der Zwischenkriegszeit," *Geschichte in Wissenschaft und Unterricht* 48(5–6) (1997), 316–29.

39 In addition to Herbert, *Best*, see now Michael Wildt, *Volksgemeinschaft als Selbstermächtigung: Gewalt gegen Juden in der deutschen Provinz 1919 bis 1939* (Hamburg, 2007), 63–8.

40 For much of the pre-World War I period, Polish nationalism was probably just as important in shaping approaches to German identity politics. On this, see Rogers Brubaker, *Citizenship and Nationhood in France and Germany* (Cambridge, MA, 1992), 126–32; Dieter Gosewinkel, "Citizenship in Germany and France at the turn of the twentieth century: some new observations on an old comparison" in Geoff Eley and Jan Palmowski (eds.), *Citizenship and National Identity in Twentieth-Century Germany* (Stanford, 2008), 27–39, particularly 34–5.

41 The reference in this sentence is to Shulamit Volkov, "Anti-Semitism as a cultural code," *Leo Baeck Institute Year Book*, 23 (1978), 25–45.

42 Alon Confino, *A World Without Jews: The Nazi Imagination from Persecution to Genocide* (New Haven, 2014), 58.

43 Koonz, *The Nazi Conscience*, 103.

44 "Wer Rassenhygiene und Rassenkunde treibt, ist religiös und wer Religion hat, muß auch Rassenhygiene treiben und eine Veredlung seiner Rasse anstreben": quoted from Cornelia Essner, *Die "Nürnberger Gesetze," oder, Die Verwaltung des Rassenwahns 1933–1945* (Paderborn, 2002), 145. See also Jürgen Matthäus' chapter in this volume.

45 Wildt, *Volksgemeinschaft*, 64–5.

46 Peter Pulzer, "Third thoughts on German and Austrian antisemitism," *Journal of Modern Jewish Studies*, 4(2) (2005), 137–78, 160.

47 Klaus Holz, *Nationaler Antisemitismus: Wissenssoziologie einer Weltanschauung* (Hamburg, 2001); Helmut Walser Smith, *The Butcher's Tale: Murder and Anti-Semitism in a German Town* (New York, 2002); Helmut Walser Smith, *The Continuities of German History: Nation, Religion, and Race across the Long Nineteenth Century* (Cambridge, 2008).

48 Christian S. Davis, *Colonialism, Antisemitism, and Germans of Jewish Descent in Imperial Germany* (Ann Arbor, 2012).

49 Przyrembel, *Rassenschande*, 62ff.

50 David Ciarlo, *Advertising Empire: Race and Visual Culture in Imperial Germany* (Cambridge, MA, 2011), 323.

51 Cited in Saul Friedländer, "Political transformations during the war and their effect on the Jewish question" in Herbert Arthur Strauss (ed.), *Hostages of Modernization: Studies on Modern Antisemitism, 1870–1933/39* (Berlin, 1993), 150–64, 158.

52 Ibid.

53 Yuri Slezkine, *The Jewish Century* (Princeton, 2004).

54 Carole Fink, *Defending the Rights of Others: The Great Powers, the Jews, and International Minority Protection, 1878–1938* (Cambridge, 2004); David Engel, "Fighting expulsion in the diplomatic arena: the case of Galician-Jewish refugees in Vienna, 1919–1923," unpublished paper presented at the 2006 annual meeting of the American Historical Association.

55 Brigitte Hamann, *Hitler's Vienna: A Dictator's Apprenticeship* (New York, 1999).
56 Fink, *Defending the Rights of Others*, is excellent on this.
57 On the *Protocols*, see B. W. Segel and Richard S. Levy, *A Lie and a Libel: The History of the Protocols of the Elders of Zion* (Lincoln, 1995). Dearborn was of course the home of Henry Ford's *Dearborn Independent*, while the London *Times* briefly also believed in the forgery. Bern and Grahamstown both saw spectacular trials in which advocates of the genuineness of the *Protocols* were successfully able to defend their position.
58 Philippe Burrin, *Nazi Anti-Semitism: From Prejudice to the Holocaust* (New York, 2005), 55.
59 On the growth of foreign tourism, see among others Hans Dieter Schäfer, *Das gespaltene Bewusstsein: über deutsche Kultur und Lebenswirklichkeit, 1933–1945* (Munich, 1982).
60 On all this, see now Jeffrey Herf, *The Jewish Enemy: Nazi Propaganda during World War II and the Holocaust* (Cambridge, MA, 2006).
61 Saul Friedländer, *Nazi Germany and the Jews* (New York, 1997).
62 Burrin, *Nazi Anti-Semitism*, 46ff.
63 Confino, *A World Without Jews*.
64 See Adolf Hitler, *Politisches Testament: Die Bormann-Diktate vom Februar und April 1945* (Hamburg, 1981), 68–69, cited in Richard Steigmann-Gall, "Aryan and Semite, Christ and Antichrist: rethinking religion and modernity in Nazi Antisemitism," paper presented at the conference "Rethinking German Modernity," Toronto, 2005. And see Steigmann-Gall's essay in this volume.
65 Peter Fritzsche, *Life and Death in the Third Reich* (Cambridge, MA, 2008), 38.
66 Frank Bajohr, "Die Zustimmungsdiktatur: Grundzüge nationalsozialistischer Herrschaft in Hamburg" in Josef Schmid (ed.), *Hamburg im "Dritten Reich"* (Göttingen, 2005), 69–131.
67 See Moritz Föllmer, "The problem of national solidarity in interwar Germany," *German History* 23(2) (2005), 202–31. Even more than they espoused the language of the "people's community" per se, the population welcomed the emphasis on placing the national good above that of the individual (provided of course that they as individuals were doing all right too). On the striking lack of reference to *Volksgemeinschaft* amid continuing powerful patriotism in German POW conversations, see Sönke Neitzel and Harald Welzer, *Soldaten: Protokolle vom Kämpfen, Töten und Sterben* (Frankfurt, 2011).
68 Oded Heilbronner, "The role of Nazi antisemitism in the Nazi party's activity and propaganda," *Leo Baeck Institute Year Book* 35 (1990), 397–439; Michael Mayer, *NSDAP und Antisemitismus: 1919–1933* (Munich, 2002).
69 See the documents in Jürgen Matthäus and Mark Roseman, *Jewish Responses to Persecution, 1933–1946* (Lanham, 2009).
70 Fritzsche, *Life and Death in the Third Reich*, 44.
71 Translated from Willy Cohn and Norbert Conrads, *Kein Recht, nirgends: Tagebuch vom Untergang des Breslauer Judentums, 1933–1941* (Cologne, 2006).

72 Bernward Dörner, *Die Deutschen und der Holocaust: was niemand wissen wollte, aber jeder wissen konnte* (Berlin, 2007); Herf, *The Jewish Enemy*; Peter Longerich, *"Davon haben wir nichts gewusst!": die Deutschen und die Juden-verfolgung 1933–1945* (Munich, 2006): Michael Wildt, "Sammelrez: Die Deutschen und der Holocaust," H-Soz-u-Kult / Rezensionen / Bücher," http://hsozkult.geschichte.hu-berlin.de/rezensionen/2008-1-200.

73 Gerhard Jacoby, *Racial State: The German Nationalities Policy in the Pro-tectorate of Bohemia-Moravia* (New York, 1944), v–viii.

74 See A. Dirk Moses, "Empire, colony, genocide: keywords and the philosophy of history" in A. Dirk Moses (ed.), *Empire, Colony, Genocide: Conquest, Occupation, and Subaltern Resistance in World History* (New York, 2008), 3–55.

75 See Eric Voegelin's still under-appreciated *Rasse und Staat* (Tübingen, 1933), 167–81.

76 Moon-Kie Jung, "Constituting the US empire-state and white supremacy" in Moon-Kie Jung, Joäo H. Costa Vargas, and Eduardo Bonilla-Silva (eds.), *State of White Supremacy: Racism, Governance, and the United States* (Stanford, 2011), 1–27, 1. Jung echoes Omi and Winant, *Racial Formation in the United States*, 5.

77 On this dynamic relationship, Ulrich Herbert, *Fremdarbeiter: Politik und Praxis des "Ausländer-Einsatzes" in der Kriegswirtschaft des Dritten Reiches* (Berlin, 1985).

78 On the relationship between Holocaust and imperialism, see now the recent roundtable: Roberta Pergher, Mark Roseman, Jürgen Zimmerer, Shelley Baranowski, Doris L. Bergen, and Zygmunt Bauman, "Scholarly forum on the Holocaust and genocide," *Dapim: Studies on the Holocaust* 27 (2013), 1, 40–73.

79 Antoinette M. Burton, *Archive Stories: Facts, Fictions, and the Writing of History* (Durham, 2005); Antoinette M. Burton, *Empire in Question: Read-ing, Writing, and Teaching British Imperialism* (Durham, 2011).

80 Here I would part ways with Heide Fehrenbach and Rita Chin's otherwise admirable attempt to situate Nazi racism in longer-term continuities of German racial thinking. They see parallels between anti-Semitism's and anti-black racism's functions as consolidating the nation-state. I do not think this is true of anti-black racism. Being anti-black was about establishing one's place in *society* but not in *nation*. Rita C. K. Chin and Heide Fehrenbach, "Introduction" in Rita C. K. Chin, Heide Fehrenbach, Geoff Eley, and Atina Grossmann (eds.), *After the Nazi Racial State: Difference and Democracy in Germany and Europe* (Ann Arbor, 2009), 1–29, 11.

81 Pierre-André Taguieff, *The Force of Prejudice: On Racism and Its Doubles* (Minneapolis, 2001), here 120–3.

82 For a discussion of Taguieff, see Robert Miles and Malcolm Brown, *Racism* (London, 2003), 85.

83 Mark Levene, *The Meaning of Genocide* (London, 2005), 204. See also below p.19 [will need to change this cross-reference in page proofs].

84 Cited in Gerhard Wolf, *Ideologie und Herrschaftsrationalität: Nationalsozia-listische Germanisierungspolitik in Westpolen* (Hamburg, 2012), 11.

85 Zygmunt Bauman, *Modernity and the Holocaust* (Ithaca, 1989), 85.

86 Ibid., 88.

87 Ibid., 89.

88 Michael Mann, *The Dark Side of Democracy: Explaining Ethnic Cleansing* (New York, 2005), 61–8.

89 Norman M. Naimark, *Fires of Hatred: Ethnic Cleansing in Twentieth-Century Europe* (Cambridge, MA, 2001), 7–8, 198.

90 Donald Bloxham, *The Final Solution: A Genocide* (Oxford, 2009), 6.

91 Ibid., 4.

92 Mann, *The Dark Side of Democracy*, 6.

93 Koonz, *The Nazi Conscience*, 115, 28.

94 These ideas are influenced by the work of Roberta Pergher, including a paper given at the original "Beyond the Racial State" conference.

2

The Murder of European Jewry

Nazi Genocide in Continental Perspective

Donald Bloxham

The Holocaust provides either one of the strongest arguments for Nazi Germany as a radically different state bent on racial utopia or an argument for continuity, given Europe's deep and recent history of violent intolerance of Jews. With alternating Nazi perceptions of Jews as a race, a non-race, and an anti-race, it is certainly plausible to understand their depiction of the ultimate "other" as an updated version of occidental Jew-hatred for an Enlightened age in which many Jews had secularized and assimilated. There is no need to make the dichotomy so sharp; besides, as the editors of this volume recognize, it would be wrong to react too strongly against a racial state paradigm, not least because that itself emerged in reaction to a historiography paying insufficient attention to the peculiarities and centrality within Nazi ideology of Nazi doctrines of inclusion and exclusion. If this volume is seeking to move the dialectic along, thinking of continuums and interrelationships in the policies of different states will help. Ongoing scholarship has rightly suggested the extent to which the murder of the Jews was related to other Nazi population policies, even while of course having its own specific character and dynamics. I want to argue here for a still wider context, extending conceptually beyond the crimes of the "totalitarian" states, chronologic-ally beyond the era of World War II and even the "European civil war" of c.1914–1945, and geographically beyond the rather narrow definition that tends to be given to "Europe" in the continent's historiography.

I thank Mark Roseman, Devin Pendas, Jürgen Matthäus, and Raz Segal for feedback on this essay – in Jürgen's case, for comments on two drafts. I thank Ahmet Efiloğlu for statistics on Ottoman "Greeks" deported in the World War I era.

The Holocaust was a European crime as well as a Nazi German crime, and the "Final Solution" occurred in an age of wider European genocide and ethnic cleansing in which related patterns can be discerned across very different states. Consider correlates at the ideological level. As Gerhard Wolf's contribution to this volume shows, in areas of Nazi policy, such as Germanization, where biological-racial considerations should have been at their purest (that is, free of the sometimes quasi-theological rhetoric about the "Jewish threat"), there were pronounced frayed edges in policy. This suggests that racism is not categorically different from ethnonationalism, with its contested cultural boundaries, but further along a continuum of spurious essentialisms whose proponents cannot quite create reality as they wish it, nor identify a consistent idiom to divide up the world of human variety as they see it.

Nazi racism was always contaminated, as it were, with categories of *Volk*, nation, and even *Kultur*, just as cultural and "national" categories were often expressed by other European nationalists in the idiom of "blood." As with Bulgaria, with its differing attitudes to "Turks," Islamized Slavs ("Pomaks"), and ethnic Bulgarians; or as with sometime Polish state attitudes to Jews, Ukrainians, and ethnic Poles; or as with Turkish attitudes to Christians, non-Turkic Muslims (especially Kurds), and ethnic Turks, there was a sort of demographic triage in which peoples were divided into (i) the unassimilable, (ii) the potentially assimilable, and (iii) the desirable – with the greatest fluctuations in thought and policy regarding the relationship between groups (ii) and (iii) but no absolutely hard and fast boundaries between any of them, even (i) and (iii). Note the arbitrary delineation at the fringes of the *Mischling* categorization. The term "triage" had some contemporary resonance in the form of the French *commissions de triage* used during and immediately after World War I to divide the population of Alsace Lorraine along a combination of ethnic, national, linguistic, and political lines. One of the results of such classificatory suspicion was the expulsion or "encouraged" emigration of about 100,000 people of German origin between 1918 and 1921.[1]

The idea of a continuum between states cuts both ways, bringing other polities and their policies helpfully into view while providing an important context for Nazi ideology and practice. The connections and parallels on which we might focus inhere not just in high concepts like "modernity" but in concrete actions and institutions: there are indeed symmetries between, on the one hand, the SS's central offices for immigration and emigration that moved Germans, Poles, and Jews around Poland, and, on the other, the late Ottoman state's Directorate for the Settlement of Tribes and Immigrants, which simultaneously housed and strategically settled Muslim refugees from the Balkan conflicts of 1912–13 and marshaled the murderous deportations of Armenians during World War I. Both have similarities with Romania's State Under Secretariat of Colonization and Evacuated Populations, established in 1940 to manage a Romanian-Bulgarian population exchange around Dobruja and also tasked with Aryanization and the general Romanization of the state. In each of these cases, territorial gain or loss, the consolidation of trustworthy ethnic brethren and the removal of the untrustworthy, and the redistribution of property were part of one and the same ethnopolitical project.

I wish to ask simultaneously what light European history sheds on the Final Solution at a particular conjuncture of ideological and geopolitical reconfiguration and, in turn, what light the Final Solution sheds on European history.[2] This is more than a comparative endeavor. In line with what has been called "the new international history," I wish to integrate interstate relations with transnational cultural and socio-economic trends and to transcend a sharp heuristic division between the external relations of states and their internal politics. To an extent, some of this thinking is already in the common sense of Holocaust historiography, given its attention to the impact of one sort of interstate interaction – the course of the German-Soviet War – on the Nazis' Jewish policy. I depict the Holocaust here as an only partly discrete episode in a wider European process of violent flux – and an episode that can itself be partly disaggregated into national and regional components. The geopolitical, economic, and demographic agendas of a range of European states and ethnonationalist elites created a remarkably conducive atmosphere for genocide in the early war years, though that would change later in the conflict.

Naturally, I cannot hope to be exhaustive of the instances of violence in the spatiotemporal sphere under examination. In particular, the vast crimes of the USSR receive no mention here.[3] I do not consider the full range of Nazi crimes and victim groups. There is always a trade-off between breadth and depth of coverage, and like any work of history this essay has an arbitrary element to the delineation of its boundaries. I am concerned with specific lineages, morphologies, and connections of mass violence. I move from the broader consideration of general patterns in late modern Europe to a closer consideration of the dynamics of Nazi ideology, policy, and power, and then back again to the broader European level in order to elucidate the continental expansion, patterns, and in some instances even limitations of the murder of the Jews. I do this with reference to the influence of a wide range of national and sub-national actors and a number of related ethnocentric ideologies and agendas.

Clearly, many aspects of the Final Solution can only be explained with reference to Nazi German specificity, yet, as the comparativist would say, it is only in the light of comparison that specificities are detectable. The same point can also be expressed through the idiom of "historicization," which has become an especially fraught term in Holocaust historiography. Historicization in the way I intend it is not some attempt to render the Holocaust safe through distancing. I take my lead from Wilhelm Dilthey, for whom the particular at once shed light on the general and was only perceptible as particular in light of the general. I do not ignore the structure and content of Nazi ideology here, but other chapters in this volume give it the greater attention it merits as a complex of ideas. Crucial in terms of particular dynamics is the "postliberal" nature of the Nazi regime. The dictatorship differed from the right-wing authoritarian regimes of East-Central and Southeastern Europe in that it grew in a state with an advanced infrastructure, a civil society, traditions and channels of expressing public opinion, and the experience of parliamentary rule, where the conflicting interests of well-organized social classes were given expression. It was impossible not to take account of these factors or ignore the need for symbols of political legitimacy in such a state. The relationship between regime and people, while highly unequal, was not unidirectional. And although the rhetoric of a *Volksgemeinschaft* of racial equals often remained just rhetoric when measured against the socio-economic evidence as a whole, some of the new Nazi-inspired organizations that fused themselves onto the existing state machinery did actually provide avenues of social mobility based on the *Leistungsprinzip* (principle of achievement). They created structures of self-expression that were anything but traditionally hierarchical. The vanguard organizations of persecution and genocide, especially within the SS, were among those most institutionally expressive of Nazism as a movement and an ideology; they were products of the same modernization process that had also produced the "Jewish question," so it is scarcely surprising that they were at the forefront of "answering" the question. This ideological movement had the machinery of a major European power with which to work, which was why it could actualize its criminal ambitions across a huge territorial empire.

THE GREATER EUROPEAN BACKGROUND

My spatiotemporal framework encapsulates some particular characteristics of Europe's experience of late modernity. At the end of the nineteenth century, the greater Europe that is my concern was composed of the multinational dynastic empires to the center, east, and southeast (the Romanov, Habsburg, and Ottoman) and more ethnically homogeneous nation-states in the north and northwest, with the status of great power applied to some of each. The broad narrative of the European crisis begins with the demise of the dynastic empires under the pressures of modernization that stemmed from and exacerbated international competition. The narrative continues with the establishment, in the geopolitical spaces created by imperial decline, of a number of insecure new nation-states, in the Balkans and Eastern and Central Europe. These states were fearful of the greater powers to their east and west (Russia/ the USSR and Germany), determined to hold on to recent territorial gains or to redress losses, and suspicious of internal minorities who were perceived as sources of weakness at best, treachery at worst. In particular, these new states feared the subversive links between these internal minorities and external powers. The next part of the narrative is the competitive intrusion into those spaces of three new imperial forms with new ideologies that turned two of them against the third: the USSR; Italy, as it sought a Mediterranean empire; and Nazi Germany.

The contested spaces from the Baltic to the Black Sea and the eastern Mediterranean and between the changing eastern and western borders of Germany and Russia, respectively, provided the area where, for the most part, genocide happened during World War II. It had also been the site of much other mass anti-civilian violence in the quest for land and ethnic or ethnoreligious supremacy over the preceding three generations. Though the German case obviously has primacy here, the Italian one merits greater attention than it has yet received in the debate about continuities between European colonialism overseas and Nazi colonialism in Europe. Italy shared with Germany continuities between pre-fascist and fascist times regarding some of the spatial goals of imperialism: parts of North Africa in the Italian case; parts of Poland, the Baltic, and Ukraine in the German case. Moreover, Mussolini's imperialism, as with pre-fascist aspirations, looked partly within and partly outside Europe: it was based partly on the annexation of lands contiguous to Italy and partly on lands separated by water. Accordingly, it blended aspects of the tradition of European land empires in the center, southeast, and east of the continent with aspects of the maritime empires of the north and northwest. It also provided the template for a Mediterranean successor to the Ottoman Empire that could perform the same function as that empire of joining Europe to wider landmasses – the Middle East and North Africa – offering a reminder that Europe cannot be easily demarcated.

Finally in this connection, the burgeoning, fruitful debate about (settler-)*colonial* continuities has in important respects obscured some of the *imperial* connections across time and place. First, not all imperial considerations, even in lands of direct rule, are connected with settler-colonialism: British India shows how exploitative, racist, and security considerations ran together in a situation of white minority rule over a vast non-white majority that was very different to the land-theft and extermination of the indigenous peoples in the settler regimes of Australasia and North America. Second, whatever their particular ideological inflections, the USSR, Nazi Germany, and Fascist Italy often acted like traditional great powers with spheres of interest and strained and reciprocally manipulative, if unequal, relations with lesser powers. Along with other deep elements of European political culture, geopolitical considerations, the nature of imperial rule in a range of situations, economic relations, and high diplomacy remain necessary elements in explaining genocide, even if they are not sufficient elements.

The Ottoman Empire provides a conceptual point of departure. It was the weakest link in the European great power system – the first of the older dynastic empires to crumble under the weight of industrial modernity and heightened international competition elsewhere on the continent and, relatedly, of the development of nationalism among its subject peoples. The Eastern Crisis of 1875–1878 is a chronological point of departure. It was the greatest single step toward the removal of the Ottoman Empire from mainland Europe, and the violence of the process as new Slavic states appeared on the map foreshadowed the violence of the end of Romanov and Habsburg empires and the contested disposition of their lands in World Wars I and II. Ethnic cleansing and mass murder in pursuit of land and supremacy; minorities treaties that did as much to arouse hostility and suspicion toward minorities as to protect them; population transfers around newly established borders: all of these things occurred in the Ottoman Empire's prolonged terminal phase from *c.*1875 to the outbreak of World War I before they were generalized in the coming generations to much wider swathes of Europe. Starting shortly after the Eastern Crisis, Europe began to export its great power competition in earnest, notably via the murderous scramble for Africa. The United States joined in with its brutal occupation of the Philippines. The return of inter-occidental competition to Europe's interior is no trivial context for the World Wars.

Another advantage in starting with the Ottoman case and the Eastern Crisis – and here I and other contributors to this volume depart from most recent analyses of European violence – is that it highlights the enduring significance of religion in many places as a still relevant metaphysical system, and yet more as a source of identity. This greater Europe was the meeting point of the three great monotheistic religions, and it is a frequently overlooked aspect of the period that many of the most outright murderous intergroup dynamics were superimposed on religious cleavages. This was as true for the different Christian sects in Polish-Ukrainian, Magyar-Ukrainian, and Croat-Serb conflicts as for the Muslim-Christian-Jewish dynamic. If the Protestant-Catholic dynamic did not prove as murderous as that between Protestants and Catholics on the one hand and Orthodox Christians on the other (or between Roman Catholics and "Eastern" Catholics), that likely has to do with the modus vivendi worked out after the earlier wave of intra-Christian violence that marked the post-Reformation wars of religion.

Even if one was not governed by religious categories, the idea of other peoples being so governed could reinforce a belief that they were subject to a sort of metaphysical groupthink as well as a supranational loyalty. Here was the potential for especially virulent conspiracy theories. The idea of an Islamic conspiracy had occupied British colonial thought since the 1857 Indian rising, while French fears of the same had been ignited in the preceding decades in the face of resistance to the conquest of Algeria. Conspiratorial Islam was also a spurious explanation for the 1915 revolt in the Upper Volta region of France's African empire. The huge violence of French military repression saw some 30,000 insurgents killed in battle, but there were also confirmed cases of slaughter of the defeated, the use of women and children as hostages, and the deliberate destruction of the agricultural and pastoral basis of life for entire communities, with obvious consequences for substantially greater mortality.[4]

Because of relative Ottoman weakness, the greatest violence of the later nineteenth century and up to about 1913 had Muslims as its victims, as czarist Russia expanded its borders in the Crimea and the Caucasus partly at the expense of the Ottomans and expelled many millions of Muslims in the process, and the Christian nationalists of new Balkan states evicted Muslims, who were associated with historic Ottoman dominance. The death toll of Muslims in these sequences totals several hundreds of thousands at least. Then, in the era of World War I, it was the turn of the Ottoman Christians to constitute the largest civilian victim group of extreme violence at the hands of a state whose new, exclusivist rulers were obsessed with the idea of a conspiratorial inner enemy-outer enemy link. From the late nineteenth century, the Armenians suffered waves of massacre culminating in outright genocide – which also included so-called Assyrian Christians – and a death toll in seven digits during World War I. Greek Orthodox Ottomans from sensitive coastal regions were expelled (around 200,000) and internally deported (around 300,000) at the end of the Balkan wars and during World War I, prior to their near complete eructation from Anatolia by murder and expulsion during and after the Greco-Turkish war of 1921–1922.

Continuing with the ethnoreligious theme, czarist and White Russian violence against Jews in the turmoil of World War I and especially during the Russian civil war was a particularly pronounced feature of the general mass anti-civilian violence in the wide western marches of the Romanov empire. More extreme than any other czarist wartime violence against civilians was the Russian killing of perhaps 100,000 members of the Kyrgyz and Kazakh Dungan populations of the Semireche region in Central Asia in 1916. The World War I era came to a close with the internationally sponsored ethnic cleansing of "Turks" and "Greeks," that is, of hundreds of thousands of Greek Muslims and more than one million Orthodox Christians, as part of the peace dispensation after the Greco-Turkish war. That was the last such post-Ottoman violence on "mainland Europe" until the attacks on and evictions of Balkan Muslims both during and after World War II, in particular the murder of tens of thousands of Bosnian Muslims, primarily by Serbian Četniks, and the Bulgarian expulsion of Muslims in 1950–1952. The final phase (to date) in the Yugoslav sequence came with the murder and ethnic cleansing of Bosnian and Kosovan Muslims after the Cold War.

Europe's Jews became a particularly common target as the European crisis spread northwards from the Ottoman lands. Part of the reason for this was terrible fortune, given that the majority of the continent's Jews happened to live squarely in the territory most affected by repeated war, migration, revolution, and changing state boundaries in the first half of the twentieth century: the territory in and around the Pale of Settlement. The larger part of the reason was the interaction of culture with economic and political conditions stemming from urbanization, industrialization, and the tensions between elite and mass politics. As with Christians in the Ottoman state, pre-existing cultural stereotypes regarding Jews, based particularly on commercial specialisms and transnational diasporic affiliation, provided a template into which new nationalist and racist conceptions of their purportedly exploitative or disloyal otherness could fit. Both Ottoman Christians and European Jews ultimately suffered more than ever before with the advent of a secularizing capitalistic modernity that first promised to empower them through emancipation, but ended up inducing accusations that they were using their new status for nefarious purposes.

The depressions of the 1870s–1890s contributed to the traumas of modernization and a backlash against liberalism. Rural anti-Semitism increased with rural poverty. In an update of the old usury stereotype, Jews were a target for those who had lost money on the stock market or who feared the doom of their "organic" communities in the face of a burgeoning, interconnected international economy. Some of the same blame associations were at work in the interwar depression. Industrial countries – including, obviously, Germany – were the primary casualties, and international – "Jewish" – finance was often held responsible. Reactions to the Bolshevik revolution fitted into a pre-existing set of perceptions that Jews were beneficiaries of industrial-commercial-cultural modernity. The ruptures in Europe's social order that began with the egalitarian, secular rhetoric of the French Revolution and found contemporary political expression through the rise of liberalism and the European left, as well as the minorities treaties imposed on the lesser European powers in 1878 and 1918–1923 as they emerged from the shells of the dynastic empires, were seen as the work of Jews seeking to benefit from the decline of Europe's Old Regime.

The Bolshevik revolution was only the most potent recent indicator of the alleged rise to power of the Jews in modernity. Like the moral panic and conspiracy theories thrown up by the French Revolution (especially targeted at freemasonry), 1917 produced a sense of established (Christian) verities assailed by hidden forces. Right across the continent, and indeed the occident, the Russian Revolution stimulated particularly virulent expressions of anti-Semitism. If Napoleon had been the antichrist to the rulers of the German principalities, *Zhydo-Bolshevyzm*, as it was in the Ukrainian, was invoked across the occident. Such anti-Semitic evocations were particularly effective in those places that were reconquered by the USSR after briefly gaining independence from Russian rule in the civil war years or even, as with the Baltic states, for the whole interwar period. Without the newly stoked indigenous anti-Semitism that, along with other factors, prompted tens of thousands of Latvians, Lithuanians, Ukrainians, and, to a lesser extent, Belarussians to collaborate with German forces in the Soviet territories, the Final Solution could not have achieved the dimensions it did in the region. Without the anti-Semitism present in some of those independent states that had emerged uncertain into a hostile Europe from the shatter zones of the empires, Germany would not have been able to internationalize the Final Solution to anything like the degree it did.

There was an element of contingency to Germany's leading the European assault on the Jews (in the rise to power there of a particularly virulent and aggressive ethnonationalist movement), but it is much less surprising that much of the continent as a whole turned upon the Jews at this time.

Nazism was both product and shaper of continental history. As with the persecution of Muslims in earlier decades, transnational violence against Jews – and Sinti and Roma, at least 200,000 of whom were murdered during World War II – was facilitated by the fact that they were targets on whom many European chauvinists could agree without fear of contradiction by relevant international co-participants. Jews, Sinti, and Roma were the victims of a particularly channeled international persecution at a time when alliance politics and German preferences inhibited violence against certain other minorities, say Ukrainians or Hungarians in Romanian territory, or ethnic Germans anywhere outside of territory still ruled by the Soviet Union. And this even where other ethnic dynamics had greater local political immediacy than the Jewish–non-Jewish one—as with the Ukrainian nationalists who were primarily anti-Russian/Soviet and anti-Polish yet spent much of 1941–1942 slaughtering Volhynian Jews under German command. The constellation of alliance factors could also moderate violence via the established precedent of "population exchange," which was deployed between ethnic Romanians and Bulgarians, and would likely have provided the solution to the Transylvanian question in the strained Romanian-Hungarian alliance in the event of an Axis victory. But it bears emphasizing that of the ethnic conflicts not involving Jews in the period, some of the most vicious and unrestrained were either enacted as Germany was losing control (mutual Polish-Ukrainian massacres) or in the face of sometime German opposition, given Berlin's concern for stability (Croat-on-Serb massacres).[5]

The extent to which each set of state and proto-state actors within the German orbit participated in genocide on their own account varied. This can partly be attributed to the patterns of intergroup action and stereotype that preceded the war. Insofar as former Ottoman subjects such as Greeks, Serbs, Albanians, and Bulgarians proved less inclined to participate on their own initiative in the murder of the Jews than some of the other groups in the German sphere of influence, this is less because of any particular benevolence than because the Muslim-Jewish dynamic was historically much less important than its Muslim-Christian counterpart, and (relatedly) because there were simply fewer Jews living among them. Nevertheless, when the matter was of Jewish-Muslim competition at the level of land and statehood, as looked likely to be the case in Palestine, the

Grand Mufti of Jerusalem showed that some Muslim nationalists in
former Ottomania were willing to align themselves strategically with the
goals of the (ostensibly) coming great power, Germany.

Palestine tells us something about the dynamics of the greater Europe to
which it seemed marginal. In the last Ottoman decades, it was the theatre
of early Zionist immigration. Amid the general anti-minority violence of
the World War I era, the Jews of the region escaped relatively lightly when
compared to the subjects of other Ottoman demographic policies or the
Jews residing in or around the Pale of Settlement. Palestine then figured
both in British and – for a while in the early 1930s – Nazi German visions
of the future as an extra-European area in which Jews could find a national
home of sorts, one in which, judging by the visions of people as different as
Winston Churchill and the denizens of the SS's Security Service, they
would be territorialized and thus in some sense "normalized." It is interesting that Palestine's Jewish population was not mentioned at the infamous Wannsee Conference. Despite the convenor's intention to solve the
Jewish question "irrespective of geographical boundaries," he was nevertheless bound by borders of cultural convention, for at the same time he
talked of solving the Jewish question in "Europe." Only the European part
of Turkey, not the "Asiatic" one, was listed as a target – and, contrary to
periodic speculation by historians, the Jews of French North Africa were
not included as targets in the exaggerated number of French Jews depicted
by Eichmann in the conference's minutes.[6] The situation changed early in
1942 as the Nazis' murderous ambitions spread even beyond "Europe"
with the establishment of the Einsatzkommando Ägypten (Operations
Detail Egypt), abortively tasked with murdering the Jews of the Yishuv.
That the Einsatzkommando did not carry out that particular mission of
slaughter was down to British victories in North Africa in the second half
of the year. From the end of 1942, Palestine was again to appear as a
possible refuge for a few Balkan Jews; many Jewish migrants and refugees
came after the war, by which time the nascent Israeli state was embroiled
in its own successful battle for land and supremacy with the Arab military
and civilian population of the area.

WAR, NATIONAL CONSOLIDATION PROJECTS, AND GENOCIDE IN HARMONY

Nazi Germany's agenda as a great power included playing on ethnic fears
and antagonisms as a way of fracturing the 1918 peace settlement, as in
Czechoslovakia and Yugoslavia. The German government's explicitly

anti-Semitic policies also helped legitimate radical elements in Eastern and Southeastern Europe, by extension inviting the more established conservative right to move further rightward, and ultimately influencing the adoption of anti-Semitic legislation beyond Germany in the later 1930s through 1941. But Germany could only encourage what was already there, and furthermore the independent states concerned only went as far as they perceived to be in their own interests. Germany was especially successful at gaining the allegiance of states that had emerged from World War I with territorial losses. As Germany divided up Eastern and Southeastern Europe in sometime partnership with the USSR in 1938–1941, it was in a position to reverse a number of the post-World War I boundary awards: Hungary and Bulgaria gained territory at the expense of Romania, Czechoslovakia, Yugoslavia, and Greece; Romania also lost Bessarabia and Bukovina to the adjoining USSR.

As territory changed hands, any conceptually "foreign" populations dwelling in it were in particular danger from their new masters. They were in danger because they were seen as potential grounds for future irredentist claims by the recently dispossessed state; because as non-co-nationals they were simply distrusted; because they increased the overall number of members of the non-titular ethnic group within the state's borders; and because they had little claim to citizenship or even residual compassion as a result of the change in territorial control. Bulgaria followed up its acquisition of Dobruja from Romania with the exchange of Bulgarians and Romanians between the two states, and it was later prepared to allow Germany to murder Jews from the Macedonian and Thracian territories acquired from Greece and Yugoslavia, as well as to expel hundreds of thousands of Greeks. From June 1941, Hungary evicted into Ukraine and eastern Galicia "foreign" and "stateless" Jews (many of whom were neither) from the areas it acquired from Czechoslovakia as well as many Jewish refugees who had fled Poland. Romania followed suit. The desire to regain the territory it had just lost led it to join the German alliance under a more radical leadership. As it regained Bessarabia and Bukovina from the USSR on the German invasion of summer 1941, Romania expelled and murdered or let die most of the Jews of the two regions, along with scores of thousands of the Jews of Transnistria, which it gained at the end of August and which also became a reception point for the refugees from Bessarabia and Bukovina. In the eyes of the Romanian leadership as of that moment, these expulsions and murders were only the first phase in a more general program of ethnic cleansing that would be targeted at a range of non-ethnic Romanians, especially Jews, in the short to medium term.

Two of Germany's allies were prepared to act quickly against the entirety of their Jewish populations regardless of where they lived, namely Slovakia and Croatia. These states look like the exception rather than the rule when their records are compared with the proportions of Jews surrendered by other states allied with Germany. The new governing regimes, while both Catholic in confessional orientation and both owing their very existence as states to Germany (and in Croatia's case to Italy and Hungary too), were otherwise different in outlook and stability. The differences shaped the fact that whereas the Ustaša murdered 20,000–25,000 Jews on its own account – out of a total of about 40,000 under its jurisdiction – and handed over another 7,000 Jews for murder at Auschwitz from August 1942, in the Slovakian case almost all the killing was done by Germany. The vast majority of Slovakian Jews were delivered to German hands in 1942 from March onwards, whence most were murdered or worked to death in Lublin and later at Auschwitz. But the fact that the Tiso regime let Germany do the dirty work should not conceal its desire to "cleanse" the economy and ultimately the society in the name of "Christianization." Surrender into German hands was an easy way to fulfill a social goal that might otherwise have been hindered by reluctant recipient states and to remove a people who were considered a burden precisely because of the Slovak state's measures of enforced impoverishment. The SS, which oversaw the deportations, had not forcefully imposed the design on Slovakia; it had prompted and facilitated, and it had received distinct reciprocal encouragement from the Slovak regime starting the previous autumn. This was a genocidal synergy.[7]

Why did Slovakia and Croatia kill or surrender such a high proportion of their Jews? The salient similarity was not special obedience: though the Slovak regime was dependent on Germany in many ways, it still had considerable freedom of action, and the Ustaša could scarcely be considered obedient to anyone. The general extremity of the Ustaša certainly helps account for their violence, even though in terms of anti-Semitism they tended to see Jews not as puppet masters but as servants of the Serbs, whom they murdered in even larger numbers. (Such notions about Jewish loyalties were not uncommon in former territories of the Dual Monarchy. Increased Slovak-regime anti-Semitism was certainly spurred by the loss of territory to Hungary in 1938–1939, given the earlier Magyar-Jewish symbiosis under the Habsburgs, even as territorial losses by Hungary after World War I ironically increased Magyar anti-Semitism.) In relation to the territorial issue, I speculate that part of the explanation for the degree of Croatian and Slovakian complicity is that each, as an entirely new state on the map, with no legitimacy in the eyes of the world beyond the Axis powers, was of the mind to seize the moment and create an ethnic fait accompli where and when it could. Starting from scratch, they sought maximum consolidation in a state system where ethnic homogeneity and the associated creation of a "national economy" seemed an ordained goal. In an important sense, the whole of the territory of each state presented the same sort of special license for innovation – a sort of experimental ground to create a tabula rasa – as did the "regained" parts of Romania, Hungary, and Bulgaria. Even when Jews were not the primary targets of ethnonationalist spleen, they could nevertheless be excised from the national body easily (and with economic benefit to the excisers) because of the relatively small size of their communities, and because Germany was all too ready to take them.

There were other ways in which German and non-German anti-Semitic agendas could coalesce in genocide. The first of the SS Einsatzgruppen to progress to the murder of Soviet Jews of all ages and both sexes (Einsatzgruppe A) did so in the context of much local collaboration in killing in the occupied Baltic. And independent states could take the lead. On August 18, 1941, Hitler not only suggested that Europe was presenting a "united front" against the Jews, he also implied that Antonescu was showing the way by being more radical than Germany had been so far. By this, Hitler was obviously referring to Romania's killings in Bessarabia and Bukovina, which were greater in number at that point than the SS Police murders in neighboring German-occupied Ukraine.[8]

Barely a week after Hitler's reflections on the Romanian situation, another tributary modality of murderous radicalization manifested itself. If groups of indigenous activists added impetus in the Baltic, and Romania had shown what other states could do on their own account, there were also inadvertent but important interactions between the demographic policies of different Axis states. At the end of August, what Klaus-Michael Mallmann calls a "qualitative leap" occurred in the murder of Ukrainian Jewry when a massacre of about 23,600 people at Kamenets Podolsky carried out by forces under the regional Higher SS and Police Leader (HSSPF) Friedrich Jeckeln more than doubled the entire death toll inflicted by all SS police agencies in the region to that point. The "problem" of overcrowding and people-management that they sought to solve by massacre had been partly created by Hungary: many of the Jews had been expelled from Hungary's formerly Czechoslovakian acquisitions.[9] Later, in mid-October, the Jews who had been forced back into eastern Galicia by Hungarian forces compounded overcrowding in the

ghettos of that district, and so contributed to the proximate reasons by
which the local SS and Police Leader Friedrich Katzmann ordered the
killing of the "superfluous" at Stanislavow. This massacre of around
10,000 people was the first on anything like its scale in the Government
General, to which eastern Galicia had been annexed after the invasion of
the USSR.[10]

Eastern Galicia acted as a sort of bridge of policy radicalization
between the USSR and Poland. At almost exactly the same time as the
Stanislavow massacre, the decision was made for the establishment of
the extermination center Belzec under the authority of Himmler's most
radical Polish SS and police leader, Odilo Globocnik. Located on the
border of the Lublin district and eastern Galicia, the camp was primarily
to murder the Jews from southeastern Poland on either side of the former
Nazi-Soviet demarcation line. If Belzec's construction had nothing to do
with external relations, there is some evidence to suggest that its sister
camp, Sobibor (further north in Lublin on the demarcation line), was
conceived later in October partly because of the live prospect at that time
of receiving Jews from an increasingly ruthless Slovakia.[11]

Germany's expanding ambition of eastward deportations into the
killing zones of the new Nazi empire was influenced by yet another
modality of interaction between states. From the end of October 1941,
the German Foreign Office approached three of the states recently
mentioned – Romania, Croatia, and Slovakia – about the possibility of
deporting Jews of their citizenship who happened to be living in the
Reich. This would help fill deportation quotas of German Jews bound
for Poland, and in retrospect it set a precedent for later, more extensive
deportations from some of those states themselves. The three agreed in
principle (subject to Slovakia's concerns about securing the wealth of
these Jews for itself). This was still near the height of the Axis alliance's
military success, around the time of what Christopher Browning has
termed Germany's second point of victory "euphoria," when these
minor allies could not have cared less about these Jews.

Hitler deployed the "European" idiom again at this expansive
moment. On November 28, 1941, he revealed to the Grand Mufti that
"Germany has resolved, step by step, to ask one European nation after the
other to solve its Jewish problem, and at the proper time, direct a similar
appeal to non-European nations as well."[12] The minister for the occupied
Soviet territories, Alfred Rosenberg, had made a similar distinction
ten days earlier – one which he had also made previously – when he
proclaimed that "the Jewish question is solved for Germany only when

the last Jew has left German territory, and for Europe when not a single Jew lives on the European continent up to the Urals."[13] The language is instructive, alluding to a more global "solution" as the aggregate of a number of individual national "solutions." Of course, by this time Germany's own internal "Jewish problem" had expanded in proportion to the growth of the Nazi empire. Germany applied to that entire space of directly ruled territory the most radical version of the philosophy and consolidation that nationalist elites in other states applied to new border areas and/or extant interiors.

"CLEANSING" GERMANY'S EMPIRE, DESTROYING EASTERN JEWRY

The c.6.2 million victims of the Holocaust can be divided into three groups of ascending size. The first category comprised "full" citizens surrendered freely by independent or semi-independent states. The second category comprised Jews surrendered by independent or semi-independent states who were either not citizens or who held second-class status, whether citizenship was judged on normal grounds of naturalization, as in France or Belgium, or hinged on place of dwelling, as in the Balkan – and, as we shall see, Hungarian – examples. The third and by far the largest comprised Jews living under direct German control in the expanded Reich, including the Austrian, Czech, French, Luxembourgian, Slovenian, and Polish areas annexed in 1937–1941, and also those places scheduled for full annexation to the Reich (notably the Netherlands) and/or put under full civil administration (the Protectorate); the eastern territories ruled as imperial civilian satrapies (Poland, Ukraine, the Baltic states, and other areas conquered from the USSR); and the southeastern areas (Serbia, Greece) that came more contingently under direct military rule of a sort altogether more ruthless than that obtaining in northern France and Belgium. Within this third category, the vast majority of victims were erstwhile citizens of Poland or the USSR and were killed in or near the places of their prewar residence within or proximate to the old czarist Pale of Settlement. As indeed with the vast majority of non-Jewish civilian (and POW) victims of Nazism, it was not just that they were murdered in Poland and the Soviet lands but that they came from those places. The co-incidence of Eastern European Jewish demography and the Nazi empire means that, whatever else must be said, it makes little sense to consider the Holocaust without considering the imperial context.

As with other states, Germany's expansion entailed a sort of self-radicalization as new populations were acquired with different "racial" and political relationships to the center and as vanguard Nazi organizations gained particular influence on virgin territories, turning them into experimental chambers for manipulation or expropriation and expulsion, and finally mass murder. The addition of part of Upper Silesia in 1937 and Austria and the Sudetenland in 1938 also fit a European pattern of border-obsessed pan-national expansionism. With the acquisition of the Protectorate early in 1939 and the conquest of Poland later that year, irredentist border enlargement fused with imperialism. The occupation of the USSR from 1941 fell entirely into the latter category, with the added factor that, like Poland, the USSR contained a huge Jewish population that axiomatically had no place in the New Order. Once Hitler had set his imperial sights on Eastern Europe, the future was incredibly bleak for the Jews there. Unlike the German Jewish population, which was relatively small and, ceteris paribus, might have been removed by forced flight, no such option was available for the eastern Jews. Unlike the Muslims earlier expelled from the Balkans and the Caucasus, there was nowhere for the Jews to be expelled to.

Though by the end of 1941 Germany ruled vast swathes of Europe directly, administrative subdivisions were manifestly important, and many of these also represented cultural boundaries. Obviously important was the distinction between the eastern borders of the Reich and the Slavic dominions beyond. Once the envisioned "territorial solution" had gradually morphed into a solution of increasingly accelerated and expanded murder, events on the ground in the occupied East show differences in the ease with which the Germans embarked on the murder of Jews from different places and of different "sorts."

Himmler's censorious reaction to the murder of 1,000 German Jews in Riga at the end of November 1941 suggests he feared a negative response within Germany to any leaked information about the murder of German citizens, some of whom may have had non-Jewish family members. Eastern Jews could be more freely murdered because no consideration whatsoever was given to the sentiments of non-Jewish Slavs. But the attitudes of some occupation officials and even SS shooters who regarded German Jews as more cultured than eastern Jews suggests a perception that murdering German Jews and other Central European Jews represented yet another step of radicalization because the Jews were of different "types."[14] It was only from late spring 1942 that the policy was entrenched of routine mass murder of the Central European Jews who were deported into the space created by the horrific murder of Soviet and Polish Jewry that had begun months earlier in the Polish case and many months earlier in the Soviet case.[15] (Many of these Central European deportees would soon be sent to Auschwitz along with Western and Southeastern European Jews.) It was the routinization of the murder of eastern Jewry that made imaginable the murder of the Jews of the Reich and the Protectorate – the first Central European Jews deported eastwards, from October 15, 1941, onwards – and then the indiscriminate murder of the Jews of states beyond the German empire as they were deported from March 1942, beginning with Slovakia and select Jews from occupied France.

Some distinctions can also be made from the Nazi perspective between the Jews of Poland and those of the USSR, but these can largely be explained with reference to the specifics of the German-Soviet war of ideologies. Mass murder of adult male Soviet Jews began immediately on the invasion and rapidly achieved colossal dimensions. The initial intention was not to kill all Jews, and subsequent escalations were not planned from the outset. The aim had been to decapitate the Jewish community and the "Judeo-Bolshevik" state and thereby pre-empt potential resistance. It is noteworthy that the mass murder of Jews was at this stage largely restricted to Jews living in areas that had been Soviet rather than Polish before 1939 – the key distinction did not involve the demarcation line established in the Molotov-Ribbentrop pact. Almost simultaneously, the German military authorities in occupied Serbia also used Jewish and Romani men as hostages and murdered them in reprisal for partisan action. These paranoid, racist security policies were intrinsically unstable and susceptible to radicalization but were in accordance with the widespread view of the "Jewish enemy."[16] In the USSR, the circle of victims rapidly expanded, owing as much to the radical ethos of the SS police forces and their open-ended remit as to central initiatives, although SS chief Himmler frequently toured the occupied east to exhort his men to greater extremes – and sometimes to instill circumspection.[17]

The non-realization of the plan for swift victory over the USSR contributed to the yet greater escalation of killing, which was starting to spread back westward into Poland, in part via eastern Galicia. Again, the dynamic often entailed regional initiatives by regional officials and SS leaders that were tacitly or explicitly approved at the central level and then replicated elsewhere. The background to these developments comprised the containment policy of the ghettoization of most Polish Jews, which occurred over several months from the conquest in September

1939, at which point the "final aim" of Jewish policy had involved some notion of future spatial removal, contingent on military success. With the failure to knock Britain out of the war, the Madagascar deportation plan was shelved. With preparations for the invasion of the USSR from spring 1941, the tentative intention was that, given the planned summary victory, Europe's Jews plus the Jews of the conquered USSR would be pushed over the Ural "border" between Europe and Asia, and/or to the unforgiving lands around the Arctic Sea to the north.[18] As the war unfolded in reality, autumn 1941 saw the beginning of a series of regional initiatives in Poland to establish murder facilities using gas to dispose of indigenous Jews who were too ill, young, or old to work and were seen as burdens, especially in the face of incoming transports of Jews deported from the Reich that would further overcrowd often deliberately under-sized ghettos. Those capable of work were kept alive until they were no longer physically useful. Two such technological initiatives were Belzec and Sobibor. Another materialized on the other side of Poland: Chelmno was established in the Reichsgau Wartheland, the western region annexed to Germany, which was also the site of the most intensive population engineering involving Poles and ethnic Germans, conducted in the interests of borderland homogenization.[19]

If proximate causes for growing mass murder included demographic engineering, ghetto overcrowding, disease, the ideological-cum-"pragmatic" refusal to feed the imprisoned and otherwise marginalized Polish and Soviet Jews adequately, the radicalized security policy of the Soviet war, and the diminishing prospect of deportation to the Soviet interior given the state of the war, then there was also a very significant ideological rationale for the targeting of the *Ostjuden* specifically even within the broader context of Nazi anti-Semitism. The westward migration of eastern Jews since the late nineteenth century had reminded many of the "real" face of Jewry behind its assimilated western façade. The idea that these Jews were "half-Asian," an epithet derived from an ultimately sympathetic 1876 book by (the Jewish) Karl Emil Franzos, had been seized upon by anti-Semites and had entered the German cultural lexicon long before the advent of Nazism, ultimately becoming a code for all Jews. Stereotypes of the squalor and backwardness of the *Ostjuden* were reinforced by Germany's experience in occupying parts of Eastern Europe during World War I and the growing population of *Ostjuden* in Germany as a result of refugee flows and labor programs. On the eve of the Nazi takeover, one conservative had mooted the full integration of German Jewry, to be complemented by the sealing off of "the German cultural community" against "half-Asia" and the eastern Jews who, inter alia, were seen as importing the virus of revolution from the USSR.[20] Steven Aschheim writes that in the Weimar period the literary critic Adolf Bartels "asserted that external differences merely camouflaged inner unity ... Jews remained ineradicably Jewish regardless of the culture to which they purportedly belonged. The great danger was that Eastern Jews would come to Germany and in the superficial sense be rapidly assimilated by their western brothers." Aschheim adds that "[t]his perception, that Ostjudentum functioned as a massive reservoir for the continual revitalization and strengthening of Western Jewry, was voiced repeatedly." The reservoir notion went at least back to Heinrich von Treitschke, with his 1880 depiction of Poland as the "inexhaustible cradle" of west-bound Jewry.[21] At the Nazi seizure of power, the first Jews to be denaturalized, as of July 1933, were the eastern Jews who had entered Germany after World War I; the *Ostjuden* also provided one of the easiest stereotypes for Nazi propaganda.[22]

Bogdan Musial describes how, on the German return to Poland in 1939, the confrontation with unprecedentedly large numbers of "eastern Jews" greatly reinforced the anti-Semitic stereotypes already held by soldiers, policemen, and occupation officials.[23] Dan Michman's study of Nazi ghettoization policy in Poland points to the culturally imbued determination to "quarantine" eastern Jewry" to prevent further "contamination."[24] Shortly before the defeat of France in June 1940, a German Foreign Office official suggested a policy differentiating *Ostjuden* and more westerly Jews. He proposed three alternative courses of action as regards the European Jews. The first was simply to remove all Jews from Europe to an unspecified destination. The third was a Jewish national home in Palestine (bringing "the danger of a 2nd Rome!"), which clearly built on the SS's earlier encouragement of emigration to the Middle East. The second proposal entailed dividing eastern and western Jewry. Western Jewry would be removed from Europe to a place such as formerly French Madagascar. Eastern Jewry, which provided "fecund and Talmudically faithful recruits for the militant Jewish intelligentsia," should be kept in the east, for instance in the Lublin district, there to stand as hostages in order to "paralyze" (*lahmlegen*) American Jewry in its fight against Germany.[25]

Though, as we have seen, the tentative Madagascar Plan was ruled out, not long afterwards the SS Reich Security Head Office (RSHA) used an identical differentiation. In November 1940, Jewish emigration was banned from the Government General because it further reduced the already diminished opportunities for emigration from the Reich and the Protectorate and because

The continued emigration of Jews from Eastern Europe [to the west] spells a continued spiritual regeneration of world Jewry, as it is mainly the Eastern Jews who supply a large proportion of the rabbis, Talmud teachers, etc., owing to their Orthodox-religious beliefs, and they are urgently needed by Jewish organizations active in the United States, according to their own statements. Further, every Orthodox Jew from Eastern Europe spells a valuable addition for these Jewish organizations in the United States in their constant efforts for the spiritual renewal of United States Jewry and its unification.[26]

Now this regulation was issued a year before the much more infamous emigration ban for Reich Jews of October 23, 1941. In terms of the sheer number of human beings for whom it was effective confirmation of a death sentence, however, it was far more significant. From well before the beginning of systematic mass murder of Jews, the very best that the *Ostjuden* could hope for was effectively imprisonment in isolation where they were, or targeted deportation to some utterly inhospitable region where genocide by attrition was at least as large a probability.

Even with the onset of the Soviet war, the distinctions between Eastern European Jewish populations and Western and Central European ones remained salient, given that emigration remained theoretically possible for German Jews until into October. SS Unterführer Krumbach was a member of the state police station in Tilsit involved in the murder of 214 men and one woman in Kretinga, in the Lithuanian border area, on June 25, 1941 – one of the earliest massacres of Jews (alongside communists) of Operation Barbarossa. During a postwar investigation, Krumbach claimed his superiors had told him of a Hitler order to the effect that "the whole of eastern Jewry had to be exterminated so that there would no longer be Jewish blood available there to maintain a world Jewry, thus bringing about the decisive destruction of world Jewry. This affirmation was by itself not new at the time and was rooted in the ideology of the Party."[27]

In a remarkably similar vein to Krumbach, the erstwhile commandant of Auschwitz recalled after the war that he had been commissioned by Himmler to "obliterate the biological basis of Jewry" and that

Eichmann was absolutely convinced that if he could succeed in destroying the biological basis of Jewry in the East by complete extermination, then Jewry as a whole would never recover from the blow. The assimilated Jews of the West, including America, would, in his opinion, be in no position (and would have no desire) to make up this enormous loss of blood.[28]

The difficulties of exegesis from postwar testimony are well known, but Höß and Krumbach had nothing to gain from these particular elements of their claims; moreover, the claims chime with some of the foregoing wartime documents. And while it is unlikely that the design was encapsulated in a specific Hitler order, we have more than enough evidence already to accept the idea that the destruction of *Ostjudentum* was an important element in Nazi discourse as what Krumbach called an "affirmation ... rooted in the ideology of the Party."[29] In terms of continuities speaking to specific, actionable visions of destruction prior to the full Europeanization of the Final Solution from late 1941, the evidence here comprises as strong a chain as anything else that has been propounded in the scholarship. It is a discourse that has been rather obscured by a historiography that either works with a chronology following the persecution of German Jews from 1933 or takes Wannsee's continental ambition as its telos (or both).

One should not overplay the distinction between eastern and non-eastern Jews within the ideological firmament because "the Jew," irrespective of adjective, was the central target of Nazi racism, as is abundantly clear in the drive to make Germany itself *judenfrei*, and because vituperation against eastern Jews frequently functioned as vituperation against all Jews. But there was not just one anti-Semitic discourse, nor, as I will elaborate in the next section, was there just one corresponding policy stream. One of the significances of the particular discourse on *Ostjudentum* is how it reconciles longstanding Nazi preoccupations not just with German or European Jewry but with world Jewry, with the inevitable limitations on Germany's reach. Equally, the discourse reconciles the biological, cultural, and political idioms within which Jewish enmity was variously cast: destruction of the seedbed was at once destruction of the biological and cultural core without which the political machinations of world Jewry would have no locus of inspiration, loyalty, or purpose. If international Jewry really was a collective body, then it could be "crippled," to use a term of genocidal art coined by Raphael Lemkin, by a sufficiently large assault on its nerve center.[30]

However far the Final Solution was to extend beyond the Polish and Soviet areas of the Nazi empire, the murder of the people in and proximate to the old Pale of Settlement was the largest and the core task. It was also almost completely successful. Here, in territories under direct and supposedly permanent German sovereign control, the expansion and intensification of genocide was a matter of the interplay of tactical concerns only. Considerations of wartime economics did come into play, especially (as concerns food supply) in the acceleration of genocide in the east from spring 1942, and labor concerns were never entirely irrelevant for certain Jewish workers. But there were none of the strategic or diplomatic concerns that pertained in dealings with other states.

THE EUROPEANIZATION OF GENOCIDE: DYNAMICS OF "INTENT"

From autumn 1941 through most of the rest of the war, Germany clearly tried, with some success, to reach beyond its empire and to induce other states to deport their Jewish populations to camps and ghettos in German-held territory. If, in Hitler's terms of late autumn 1941, the solution of Europe's and Germany's Jewish questions were fusing as an administrative project, the merger had occurred by the time of the Wannsee Conference, when every country in Europe was listed as a target. Whatever the issue of absolute numbers in different categories of Jewish victims, the full Europeanization of the Final Solution rightly highlights the exceptionally murderous ambition of Nazism. Where the tentative aim had once been of expelling Jewry from Europe (to Madagascar, beyond the Urals), now the aim was to bring Jews from across Europe to the interior of Germany's eastern empire, there to work them to death or to kill them outright. RSHA chief Reinhard Heydrich was perhaps aware of the bitter irony of bringing Jews "back" to the Pale-lands to murder them: as he said at Wannsee, the "possible final remnant" of deported Jews would have to be dealt with appropriately, "since it will undoubtedly consist of the most resistant portion," as a "product of natural selection" that would, "if released, act as the seed [or germ-cell, or nucleus: *Keimzelle*] of a new Jewish revival (see the experience of history)."[31]

So why did Germany ultimately seek not just to facilitate the destruction of other countries' Jewish populations, as with Slovakia but to drive that process so determinedly? Any sensible answer cannot elide the significance of ideology, or rather ideologies, as Nazism was scarcely monolithic. Yet the history of Jewish policy from 1933 to 1941 shows that even the most phobic and Manichean ideology could legitimate different goals from continent-wide murder. What was conceivable, what desirable, what legitimate, and what possible changed over time, and even when one or more of those conditions was fulfilled, the others by no means necessarily were. There is a "logic of ideas," but there is no law of history ruling that ideas have to find their logical fulfillment. Every tradition of politics suggests that they are unlikely to because of the friction of changing contexts and the fact that different bearers of ideas carry them in different fashions and with different levels of vision or priority. Nor does there seem much heuristic value in shifting the explanatory burden from "ideology" to "intent" because "intent" lacked ontological stability as well. Intent had no one consistent, all-determining locus and nature, whatever the role of Hitler in providing ultimate sanction for the genocide. We can talk only of intents in the plural and, at least as important, trace their evolution in events that actually occurred in order that we can distinguish intent in the causal (and legal) sense, of an attempt to actualize desire, from "mere" aspiration.

Breaking down the idea of a monolithic intent is the necessary complement to explaining the very extremity of Nazi Jewish policy in the first place; they are two sides of the same coin. Nazism was both a cluster of ideas and a power system functioning in changing institutional and international contexts, and neither ideas nor system can be extricated from the other. The special destructive power of Nazi rule resided in its nature as a responsive, dynamic, innovative, flexible, multipart, multibrain system underpinned by precepts of competitive self-empowerment, rather than as the expression of one "will" that was either realized or thwarted: therein lies one central importance of Nazism's postliberal modernity. The momentum and initiative created within such a system was not just vital in arbitrating the horrific extent of the Final Solution but obtained in other areas of ethnopolitics too, whether in the ever greater extension of "euthanasia" killing to the elderly and infirm in the last war year or the murder by staff at the Bavarian state hospital of Kaufbeuren of a four-year-old boy some twenty-one days after Germany's unconditional surrender.[32]

Some of the part-competing, part-collaborating organizations had more to gain than others by capitalizing on the opportunities for the full "Europeanization" of genocide that came into view later in 1941.[33] Across the Nazi German imperium as a whole, the heavy bias of interests among regional administrators – from SS officials on the ground, with their regional remits, to the German Gauleiter and the civil administrations in the east – lay in the direction of getting their own delineated area of territorial jurisdiction "free of Jews." Things were different for the RSHA and the Foreign Office.

The initial diplomatic success with Slovakia, Romania, and Croatia in autumn 1941, along with Romania's independent murder program, helps explain the optimism of Heydrich and the Foreign Office representative Martin Luther. At Wannsee, Luther said he foresaw no great difficulties in getting the western and southeastern states to surrender their Jews.[34] In any event, the identity of the two organizations – the RSHA and the Foreign Office – explains something important about the full Europeanization of the Final Solution, about why Germany ultimately sought not just to facilitate the destruction of other countries' Jewish populations but to drive that process. The explanation pertains to the most important quotidian pressure of organizational life: the desire for relevance and power, which Browning has illustrated so clearly in relationship to the "Jewish desk" within the Foreign Office's Abteilung Deutschland. The two organizations were, after all, those whose influence in Jewish policy was most heavily invested in the extension of Jewish policy beyond Germany's imperium. This is obviously true for the Foreign Ministry, but it is also true of the RSHA despite Heydrich's earlier leadership in emigration policy and then murder policy at the outset of the invasion of the USSR.

Far from a unitary organization, the SS police was a conglomerate of different agencies with cross-cutting remits. All SS police units cooperated with each other in killing, as did the civilian authorities; competition for power over Jewish policy took place within the framework of ideological collaboration and so only accelerated the development of genocide – except when the particular circumstances of labor shortage intervened. Since the early weeks of the invasion, the much larger SS police bodies, namely the Waffen-SS and the Ordnungspolizei (Order Police), had driven Jewish policy at least as murderously in the Soviet Union as had Heydrich's Einsatzgruppen, thus compromising Heydrich's leadership. The HSSPFs were particularly prominent as the leadership of killing operations requiring combined forces. So influential was HSSPF Jeckeln in the developing murder process in the southern USSR, for instance, that in October 1941 a unit of Einsatzgruppe C – Einsatzkommando 4a – assured Berlin that it too had taken part in killings in the area and that the killings were not the achievement of the HSSPF alone.[35] Meanwhile, civil authorities, private industrialists, and the military had incorporated many surviving Jews into work projects in Poland and the USSR and the administration of the Government General in particular contested the SS's jurisdiction in aspects of Jewish policy, and the Reich Ministry for the Occupied Eastern Territories (i.e. Rosenberg's ministry) likely also played a greater role than has hitherto been estimated in the expansion of genocide beyond the USSR. For leadership on the Jewish question, Heydrich would have to look away from the occupied east. Indeed, he would have to look to many of those places that were not occupied at all.[36]

To the invitations to Wannsee, Heydrich appended Hermann Göring's July 31, 1941, commission for Heydrich "to make all the necessary organizational, technical and material preparations for a general solution of the Jewish question throughout the German sphere of influence in Europe." At Wannsee, however, Heydrich claimed the authority for the "final solution of the Jewish question in Europe" simpliciter.[37] He preemptively and successfully laid claim to Jewish policy in as many places as possible at a point of international anti-Semitic confluence that gave great encouragement to the most ambitiously murderous designs.

WAR AND GENOCIDE IN TENSION AT THE EUROPEAN LEVEL

Heydrich's and Luther's confidence about expanding genocide to a fully continental level did not, however, result in complete success. With Axis setbacks after mid-1942 (defeat at Alamein and Midway, Soviet resistance against the German summer offensive, the Anglo-American bombing campaign, and, in the connection of the Final Solution, even Heydrich's death in June) and especially after the Stalingrad defeat at the turn of 1942–1943, the earlier "multiplier effect" of genocidal synergies was cancelled out, as a burgeoning continental consensus on the most radical Jewish policy was fractured.

From later 1942 onwards, with the exception of Croatia, Germany's major and lesser allies competed not to mimic Nazi racial laws or to supply the murder machine, as earlier but rather to justify their own diminishing collaboration. These states became more aware of their increased leverage over Germany as the United States, the USSR, and Britain increasingly looked to be the likely arbiters of the peace. Jews without full citizenship status were sometimes still used as disposable pawns in this changing dynamic, both to rid the states concerned of a "foreigner problem" and to placate Germany. Like Vichy France, which willingly turned Jews without French citizenship over to the Germans, Romania was pleased to murder and let die the Jews of Bessarabia, Bukovina, and Transnistria; but the great majority of Jews of "old Romania," Moldavia, and Wallachia were neither murdered, nor expelled to Transnistria, nor surrendered to German custody. Bulgaria was prepared to allow the deportation unto death of the Jews of newly acquired Macedonia and Thrace (in March 1943), but it surrendered no Jew from "old Bulgaria." To be sure, Romania and Bulgaria, like Hungary, still felt they had a Jewish question to solve, but they variously sought to alleviate it in ways that would not attract Allied criticism and might even gain Allied favor. Antonescu felt that "emigration," as opposed to deportation, was now an appropriate solution. Evacuation to Palestine was one option in this direction. Internal deportation, meanwhile, could also fulfill a function for such states, if obviously not for Germany: when 20,000 Jews were internally deported from Sofia, it was a useful way of appropriating the capital of Jews forced to move – generally from the cities to the provinces.

Regional geopolitics could function as a restraint, just as they had earlier functioned to exacerbate genocide. Romania cooled toward the Reich not just because of the changing war situation and its own military sacrifices but also because of its frustration over a desired resolution of the Transylvanian question. Fear of the economic consequences was also an important factor in the decision to delay any eviction of the Jews of the Regat.[38] Even Croatia used the Jewish question to play Germany off against Italy. Resentful of Italian imperialism in the former Yugoslav lands and happy to surrender all its Jews from August 1942, the Croatian government nevertheless suggested that Germany prioritize the deportation of Croatian Jews within the Italian occupation zone.[39]

Italy, with its less pronounced anti-Semitism, was a particular obstacle to German designs because it had a supranational jurisdiction and, as the second Axis power in Europe, set an example to the lesser allies and provided them with a point of reference about sovereign prerogatives vis-à-vis Germany.[40] In October 1942, the Hungarian government invoked alliance parity with Germany's major alliance partner Italy in forming its policy toward Hungarian Jews in German-controlled territory, demanding that in every facet of the Jewish question it be treated according to the established diplomatic most-favored-nation principle; this shows the importance of amour propre over sovereignty issues within the Axis alliance.[41]

I posit that it is important to conceive of Germany the state – as opposed to Hitler the anti-Semite or the RSHA as the forward echelon of Germany's uninhibited generation – less as a racial polity with an implacable desire for genocide on principle, and more as an utterly ruthless great power concerned with the control and solidity of its sphere of interest in the form of its wartime alliance. In terms of the German state's overall war agenda, using the complicity of other states in genocide as a way of binding them to the German war effort was at least as important as the principle of expanding genocide per se outside the sphere of direct German control. (This was roughly analogous to the way in which information about the Final Solution was increasingly leaked to the domestic German population in the attempt to create a "community of fate.") But matters could not be pushed too hard with allies on whom Germany was relying materially and/or militarily. Thus on April 5, 1943, the German legation in Sofia concluded that "under the circumstances," the deportation of the 11,343 Jews of Thrace and Macedonia "must be considered satisfactory."[42] With Bulgaria as with Hungary and Romania: the Foreign Office and RSHA spent a deal of energy in 1943 opposing evacuations of Jews to Palestine, and was more successful in that than in pressuring these states to deport their citizens to German control. The concern, as over Italy, was to maintain the impression of Axis unity or at least to minimize the impression of disunity, especially given that the possibility of defection to the Allies was now live.[43]

Outside the areas of direct German rule, the only thing that could alter the deportation situation was changes in the war situation, and the Allied invasion of Italy brought precisely that. The Italian armistice with the Allies in September 1943 triggered the German occupation of northern Italy and the foreign territories occupied by Italy. Deportations of Jews swiftly began, too, from the new puppet republic in the north and from the former Italian zones of Greece and Yugoslavia.

The events of late 1943 remind us that the Nazi German state sought to destroy any Jewish community it could lay its hands on; it was not, however, prepared to take any means necessary to lay its hands on Jews not yet under its control. This distinction, which may sound like a minor qualification, gains its significance from reflection on the way in which German extermination policy was often synergistic with, rather than unilaterally imposed on, its allies and less intensively occupied states. Here, as in explaining historical causation generally, we need to look to conjunctions of factors rather than master determinants. What I mean is this. On one hand, it took German hegemonic power and the particularity of Nazi anti-Semitism to translate a series of individual national ethnic cleansing campaigns into outright, continent-wide genocide. On the other, had many of those countries not already had the latent preparedness or self-actualizing desire for such "cleansing," the Final Solution would have been very largely restricted to the territories under direct German rule. I take all this less as a comment on Nazi Germany, for which indeed no comment is adequate, than on the (Christian) Europe that produced Nazi Germany and with which Nazi Germany interacted.

Nazi Germany could also bear to let small numbers of Jews slip from its grasp in the interests of stability of alliance and control, and even some conventional diplomatic concerns. Putting aside the abortive Jewish exchange programs for some Allied and "privileged" Jews, we might recall that over many months in 1943, Germany repeatedly provided opportunities for several neutral and German-allied states to repatriate Jews of their citizenship who dwelt in German-ruled territory instead of having them deported.[44] This flexibility at the margins had even existed at the ostensible height of genocidal hubris, Wannsee. Heydrich recognized the absence of significant Nordic anti-Semitism and allowed that deportations might be deferred from Scandinavian states given the small number of Jews involved. The actual policy outcomes were variable. In late 1942 and early 1943, 770 Norwegian Jews were taken by Germany, whereas 930 – a high proportion in the extraordinarily murderous context of the Final Solution – escaped to Sweden. The light-touch German administration in Denmark meant that when the Security Police did try to round up the Danish Jews in autumn 1943, escape was relatively easy and perhaps something of a convenience for the SS man and chief civilian administrator, Werner Best, who remained concerned with securing Danish cooperation in the war effort. As Best pointed out, Germany had wanted Denmark rendered "free of Jews'" and that had been achieved – albeit by flight to Sweden.[45]

THE COMPLETION OF GENOCIDE WITHIN THE GERMAN EMPIRE

As it happens, immediately after the Danish exodus, on October 4, 1943, Himmler made a notorious speech to a group of SS leaders in Posen. The part about the murder (the "evacuation") of the Jews was delivered in the past tense.[46] Himmler repeated the message about the Jewish question a few days later at another speech addressing Gauleiter and Reichsleiter. After discussing the "necessity" of murdering Jewish women and children at this major, set-piece event, he observed that the task of removing the Jewish people from the earth had been accomplished, with no reference to restricted geographical location. He then stated that the Jewish question would be solved in the countries under German occupation by the end of the calendar year and implicitly acknowledged that the presence of Jews in genuinely important war industries and the questions of some "half-Jews" and Jews in mixed marriages might linger before resolution.[47] The later reference to the direct German sphere of rule (or "occupation") as opposed to "the earth" was not a qualification of his claim to general success and was made with no qualification of the difference between German-occupied Europe and Europe as a whole. Well into 1944, he made similar boasts about having solved the Jewish question. Some of these claims had no specific territorial reference, while others did, as in a mention of "Juden in unserem Bereich" (Jews in our domain).[48]

It may seem puzzling to anyone acquainted with what was still to come in the Holocaust that the Reichsführer-SS would be congratulating himself in the autumn of 1943, as far in excess of a million Jews remained alive in Axis and Axis-dominated lands from Hungary, Romania, and Bulgaria to France. There may have been an opportunistic element to his slight ambiguity and to his focus on what had been done as opposed to what had not fully been achieved, but we might equally say that there were a number of slightly different strands within the discourse of Nazi genocidal ambition from which he was free to choose, as revealed previously in this chapter. As the prime empire-builder in the east, Himmler was certainly concerned with the "integrity" and purity of a specific territory, albeit territory of a far larger scale than that ruled by the average Gauleiter. Moreover, the justification that Himmler used for the celebration of his achievement was not uncommon in the wider history of genocide. In his October 4 speech, the justification for celebration was one shared with the likes of the Young Turks as they substantially eliminated the Armenian presence from Anatolia: it was the annihilation of an inner enemy, an enemy within one's borders. Thus: "we know how difficult we would have made it for ourselves, if, on top of the bombing raids, the burdens and the deprivations of war, we still had Jews today in every town as secret saboteurs, agitators and troublemakers. We would now probably have reached the 1916–17 stage" – the point at which the German *Volksgemeinschaft* started to show major internal divisions in World War I.[49]

In any case, many nearly complete destruction programs from the end of 1943 could be accommodated within the spirit of Himmler's pronouncements. Consider, for instance, the murder through late summer 1944 of the remaining Jews of Theresienstadt and the numerous last workers of the Lodz ghetto, plus most of the surviving Jewish workers in the occupied Soviet territories and the General Government.[50] Alongside relentless mass murder within Germany's eastern empire, the SS had succeeded in forcing most of the surviving Jews into SS-run labor-concentration camps where they could reinforce the growing SS economic empire while not compromising the SS's remit for enforcing racial security and purity. Accordingly, from the perspective of there and then, early October 1943 remained an apposite moment. The disappearance of the Danish Jewish population over the preceding few days had rendered yet another part of the German sphere *judenrein*, even if by somewhat – by the standards of 1942–1943 – unorthodox methods. The Reinhard death camps of Treblinka and Sobibor had each received their final transportations of Jews in August and September and were shortly to be completely dismantled; Belzec already had been. The time from March 1943 and again from September had witnessed the murder of most of Greek Jewry. The vast majority of Reich and Czech Jews had been deported and killed. More than 80 percent of the 102,000 Dutch Jews who would be murdered had been murdered by the beginning of October. Early in November, the final major massacre related to Aktion Reinhard took place when 42,000 Jews were murdered in "Operation Harvest Festival." The victims comprised most of the remaining laborers in the Lublin district.

The day after "Harvest Festival" – November 4 – the anti-Semitic newspaper *Der Stürmer* made a pronouncement in a now familiar idiom that was complementary, though not identical, to Himmler's, and picked up on another of the strands of genocidal discourse. The editor, Julius Streicher, was still close to Hitler and made it his business to be regularly informed about developments in Eastern Europe. After quoting an earlier article from the Swiss *Israelitisches Wochenblatt* to the effect that the Jews had virtually disappeared from Europe, he commented: "this is not a Jewish lie." "It is really true," he continued, "that the Jews have, so to speak, disappeared from Europe and that the Jewish 'Reservoir of the East' from which the Jewish pestilence has for centuries beset the peoples of Europe has ceased to exist."[51] He went on to emphasize the ongoing hostility of "world Jewry" in order to stiffen German backs in the war effort, and the specter he invoked could in that sense be held to have great functional utility, as indeed it did for explaining so many of Germany's "misfortunes" – as Tim Mason once put it, the regime thrived "upon the supposed threat from the enemies which it persecuted so implacably."[52] But by the logic – happily, faulty – of Streicher's words, world Jewry could not long survive without its vital reservoir.

HUNGARY 1944: BALKAN GEOPOLITICS AND GENOCIDE

From the perspective of autumn 1943, the genocide of Hungarian Jewry in 1944 was not predictable, even though a glance at Hungarian history in the years immediately prior to 1944 shows the political desire for some form of national "cleansing" of various populations deemed foreign. The Hungarian deportations hinged in their inception and conclusion on Europe's geopolitical dynamics; the attitudes of Hungary's political elites to national "purification," as they differed slightly according to different categories of the Jewish population; and Germany's contingent calculus about the relationship between fighting the war and murdering the Jews.

After the German invasion of Hungary in March 1944, in a six-week period starting in mid-May 1944, 438,000 human beings were deported, most to Auschwitz. Around 108,000 were used for slave labor, the rest murdered more or less immediately. The prospect of deporting Jews was not, however, a significant factor in the decision to go into Hungary. The Allied push into Italy the previous autumn and the continuing Soviet advance through Ukraine had led the Hungarian leadership to consider Allied peace overtures. From Germany's perspective, that would have meant the loss of an important ally along with its raw materials. This is not to say, of course, that the fate of Hungarian Jewry was an irrelevance to the German actors – it was of central importance to the RSHA and many others – but rather that in this situation the most ardent Jew-hunters found that their agenda was again congruent for a while with the German state's war effort and alliance politics.

Despite the occupation, the issue of different categories of Hungarian Jews was not rendered immaterial; nor was the cooperation of a large number of willing Hungarian ethnic cleansers guaranteed under all circumstances. The Hungarian conservative elite tended to see the large Jewish population of the Budapest area as constituting a separate and slightly less undesirable group. The country was divided into different deportation zones. The first and largest deportations to take place were from the Carpatho-Ruthenian region taken from Czechoslovakia, and from northern Transylvania, taken from Romania in 1940. Around 290,000 of the *c.*438,000 May-June deportees came from those regions. Some 16,000 Jews from the areas Hungary had taken from Yugoslavia (the Backa and Baranja regions) were handed over to German police at the border of the Government General. Of the 255,000 Jews (according to the problematic Nazi racial criteria) who survived the Holocaust, some 190,000 had been citizens of Hungary within its 1920 borders.[53]

The deportations ended before Hungary was made to disgorge even all of the Jewish citizens of Trianon Hungary because the balance of alliance politics was about to shift again with Romania's defection to the Allied side on August 23, 1944. Now that Hungary had missed the opportunity for defection, it re-emphasized its alliance commitment. It now saw the opportunity to gain territory at Romania's expense during the war and, by the same token, defend its own earlier gains against a revisionist Romania. On August 25, as Hungary had seemingly decisively bound itself to Germany in the war effort once again, and in knowledge of Hungarian apprehension about protests from the outside world and the regime's attitude to Budapest Jewry and belief that internal deportation of the remaining Jews was the way forward, Himmler forbade further deportations. Notwithstanding some horrific aftermaths from October both under the fascist Arrow Cross within Hungary and in murderous forced-march deportations of Hungarian Jews for slave labor in the Reich, which brought tens of thousands more Jewish deaths, the centralized genocide of the Hungarian Jews was not brought to completion.[54]

CONCLUSIONS AND CODA

The Hungarian story shows that some of the shared characteristics of "Europe" – the priorities of its state system, its geopolitics, and its system of greater and lesser powers – could be a decelerator of genocide, just as they and other shared characteristics – cultural phobias, the desire for ethnically homogenous populations, and "national economies" – had constituted an accelerator. At one point in European history, material and ideological components came together in a way that was neither inevitable, as can be seen by their later divergence, nor purely fortuitous, as can be seen by the common choice of target: Jews, though very often Roma and Sinti too.

In 1945, a different window of opportunity temporarily opened for the pursuit of ethnonationalist agendas by Magyars and others. Receiving a green light from the victorious Allies, a range of states recently either conquered by or allied to Germany turned their attention to that newly vulnerable Eastern and East-Central European diaspora population: ethnic Germans. Some of the selfsame Hungarian officials who had previously targeted Jews adopted their persecutory expertise to the expulsion of Hungary's share of 12–15 million more people.

Notes

1 Joseph Schmauch, "Les services d'Alsace-Lorraine face à la réintégration des départements de l'Est (1914–1919)," Ph.D. thesis, École des Chartes, Sorbonne (2004), part II, ch. 2, http://theses.enc.sorbonne.fr/2004/schmauch. For the estimate of numbers, see Volker Prott, "International concepts and practices of borders: experts, ethnicity, and the Paris system in the early interwar period," Ph.D. thesis, European University Institute, Florence (2013).

2 For stimulating pointers as to the content of a temporal historicization of the Third Reich, see the conclusion to Mark Roseman, "National Socialism and the end of modernity," *American Historical Review* 116 (2011), 688–701.

3 For the Nazi-Soviet connections here, see Timothy Snyder, *Bloodlands: Eastern Europe Between Hitler and Stalin* (New York, 2010).

4 Mahir Şaul and Patrick Royer, *West African Challenge to Empire: Culture and History in the Volta-Bani Anticolonial War* (Athens, OH, 2001).

5 On Ustaša conflicts with German agendas, see Alexander Korb, *Im Schatten des Weltkriegs: Massengewalt der Ustaša gegen Serben, Juden und Roma in Kroatien, 1941–45* (Hamburg, 2013).

6 Dan Michman, "Waren die Juden Nordafrikas im Visier der Planungen zur 'Endlösung'? Die 'Schoah' und die Zahl 700.000 in Eichmanns Tabelle am 20. Januar 1942" in Norbert Kampe and Peter Klein (eds.), *Die Wannsee-Konferenz am 20. Januar 1942. Dokumente, Forschungsstand, Kontroversen* (Cologne, 2013), 379–97.

7 Tatjana Tönsmeyer, *Das Dritte Reich und die Slowakei 1939–1945: Politischer Alltag zwischen Kooperation und Eigensinn* (Paderborn, 2003), 137–62. See also the special section on the Holocaust in Slovakia in *Jahrbuch für Antisemitismusforschung* 7 (1992), 13–102.

8 Joseph Goebbels, *Die Tagebücher von Joseph Goebbels,* ed. Elke Fröhlich (Munich, 1998), part II, vol. 1, 269. On the comparative scale of massacres, see Alexander V. Prusin, The Lands Between: *Conflict in the East European Borderlands, 1870–1992* (Oxford, 2010), 152–3.

9 Klaus-Michael Mallmann, "Der qualitative Sprung im Vernichtungsprozeß. Das Massaker von Kamenez-Podolsk Ende August 1941," *Jahrbuch für Antisemitismusforschung,* 10 (2001), 239–64; Christopher R. Browning with Jürgen Matthäus, *The Origins of the Final Solution: The Evolution of Nazi Jewish Policy, 1939–1942* (Lincoln, 2004), 291.

10 Dieter Pohl, *Nationalsozialistische Judenverfolgung in Ostgalizien: Organisation und Durchführung eines staatlichen Massenverbrechens* (Munich, 1997).

11 Peter Klein, "Die Rolle der Vernichtungslager Kulmhof (Chełmno), Belzec (Bełżec) und Auschwitz-Birkenau in den frühen Deportationsvorbereitungen" in Dittmar Dahlmann and Gerhard Hirschfeld (eds.), *Lager, Zwangsarbeit, Vertreibung und Deportation* (Essen, 1999), 459–81, here 474, 478; Peter Longerich, *Holocaust: The Nazi Persecution and Murder of the Jews* (Oxford, 2010), 295–6. See also Livia Rothkirchen, "Czechoslovakia" in David S. Wyman and Charles H. Rosenzweig (eds.), *The World Reacts to the Holocaust* (Baltimore, 1996), 156–99, here 169; Stanislav J. Kirschbaum, *A History of Slovakia: The Struggle for Survival* (London, 1995), 198.

12 Browning and Matthäus, *Origins,* 379, 406.

13 Browning and Matthäus, *Origins,* 404. This pronouncement had a number of precursors: see, e.g., *Völkischer Beobachter,* March 29, 1941. The editors of Alfred Rosenberg's diary also address the evolution of Rosenberg's demand to render first Germany, then Europe, "free of Jews": Jürgen Matthäus and Frank Bajohr (eds.), *The Political Diary of Alfred Rosenberg and the Onset of the Holocaust* (Lanham, 2015). The Nov. 18, 1941, speech is printed as document 13, 385–9.

14 Richard Breitman, *The Architect of Genocide: Himmler and the Final Solution* (New York, 1991), 220.

15 Bogdan Musial, *Deutsche Zivilverwaltung und Judenverfolgung im General-gouvernement. Eine Fallstudie zum Distrikt Lublin 1939–1944* (Leipzig, 1999).

16 Christoph Dieckmann, "The war and the killing of the Lithuanian Jews" in Ulrich Herbert (ed.), *National Socialist Extermination Policies: Contemporary German Perceptions and Controversies* (New York, 2000), 240–75; Ralf Oggoreck, *Die Einsatzgruppen und die "Genesis der Endlösung"* (Berlin, 1996).

17 Michael Wildt, *Generation des Unbedingten: Das Führungskorps des Reichssicherheitshauptamtes* (Hamburg, 2003); Jürgen Matthäus, "Controlled escalation: Himmler's men in the summer of 1941 and the Holocaust in the occupied Soviet territories," *Holocaust and Genocide Studies* 21 (2007), 218–42.

18 Götz Aly, "'Jewish resettlement': reflections on the political prehistory of the Holocaust" in Herbert, *National Socialist Extermination Policies*, 53–82.

19 See Gerhard Wolf's chapter in this volume.

20 Steven Aschheim, *Brothers and Strangers: The East European Jew in German and German-Jewish Consciousness, 1800–1923* (Madison, 1999), 32, 233 and passim. (Franzos's book was entitled *Aus Halbasien*.)

21 Ibid., 235, 79.

22 Musial, *Deutsche Zivilverwaltung*, 183.

23 Ibid., 183–8.

24 Dan Michman, *The Emergence of Jewish Ghettos During the Holocaust* (Cambridge, 2011).

25 Magnus Brechtken, *"Madagaskar für die Juden": Antisemitische Idee und politische Praxis 1885–1945* (Munich, 1997), 228.

26 Regulation for the Ban on Jewish Emigration from the Government-General, November 1940, doc. 99 in Yitzhak Arad et al. (eds.), *Documents on the Holocaust* (Lincoln, 1999), 219–20.

27 Dieckmann, "The war and the killing of the Lithuanian Jews," 246.

28 Rudolf Hoess, *Commandant of Auschwitz: The Autobiography of Rudolf Hoess* (London, 1961), 206–8, 214–15.

29 A point confirmed by Dan Michman in his unpublished paper "The Jewish dimension of the Holocaust in dire straits: current challenges of interpretation and scope." I thank Prof. Michman for sharing the text with me.

30 Raphael Lemkin, "Genocide as a crime under international law," *American Journal of International Law*, 41 (1947), 145–51, here 147.

31 Kurt Pätzold and Erika Schwarz (eds.), *Tagesordnung Judenmord. Die Wannsee-Konferenz am 20. Januar 1942. Eine Dokumentation zur Organisation der "Endlösung"* (Berlin: Metropol, 1992), doc. 24.

32 On the case of the boy, Richard Jenne, see Henry Friedlander, *The Origins of Nazi Genocide: From Euthanasia to the Final Solution* (Chapel Hill, 1995), 162–3. On the other killings mentioned here, see Götz Aly, "Medizin gegen Unbrauchbare" in G. Aly (ed.), *Aussonderung und Tod Die klinische Hinrichtung der Unbrauchbaren* (Berlin, 1985), 9–74.

33 The arguments in the following paragraphs stem substantially from chapter 6 of Donald Bloxham, *The Final Solution: A Genocide* (Oxford, 2011).

34 Pätzold and Schwarz, *Tagesordnung Judenmord*, doc. 24.

35 Ruth Bettina Birn, *Die Höheren SS-und Polizeiführer. Himmlers Vertreter im Reich und in den besetzten Gebieten* (Düsseldorf, 1991), 171–2.

36 Further argumentation and substantiation along these lines can be found in Bloxham, *The Final Solution*, chap. 6. On the relationship with civil authorities and Heydrich's Wannsee motives, see Yehoshua Büchler, "Document: a preparatory document for the Wannsee 'Conference,'" *Holocaust and Genocide Studies*, 9 (1995), 121–9. On relations between Heydrich and other SS Police leaders and organizations, see "Guidelines by Heydrich for Higher SS and Police Leaders in the Occupied Territories of the Soviet Union," July 2, 1941, in Arad et al. (eds.), *Documents on the Holocaust*, 377–8; Richard Breitman, *Official Secrets: What the Nazis Planned, What the British and Americans Knew* (New York, 1998), 73–4 and passim. Most recently on Heydrich's agenda at Wannsee, see Gerhard Wolf, "The Wannsee Conference in 1942 and the National Socialist living space dystopia," *Journal of Genocide Research*, 17(2) (2015), 153–75. As to the arguments for the under-appreciated significance of Rosenberg's ministry, see Matthäus and Bajohr (eds.), The *Political Diary of Alfred Rosenberg*, which inter alia points out that it was the only institution (other than the SS/police) represented with two staff at the Wannsee Conference.

37 Emphases added. Documents in Pätzold and Schwarz, *Tagesordnung Judenmord.*

38 Jean Ancel, "The German-Romanian relationship and the Final Solution," *Holocaust and Genocide Studies* 19 (2005), 252–75; Holly Case, *Between States: The Transylvanian Question and the European Idea During World War II* (Stanford, 2009); Martin Broszat, "Das dritte Reich und die rumänische Judenpolitik," *Gutachten des Instituts für Zeitgeschichte* 1 (1958), 102–83. I thank Raz Segal very much for discussions on these points.

39 Luther, to Feldquartier Feldmark, August 21, 1942, *Akten zur deutschen auswärtigen Politik 1918–1945* (hereafter *ADAP*), Series E., vol. III, (Göttingen, 1974), 353–60, point 7. Generally on Germany's dealings with these states, see Christopher Browning, *The Final Solution and the German Foreign Office: A Study of Referat D III of Abteilung Deutschland, 1940–43* (New York, 1978), chaps. 6 and 7.

40 See RSHA to Foreign Office, February 25, 1943, betr. "Endlösung der europäischen Judenfrage unter besonderer Berücksichtigung der Haltung Italiens zu dem Gesamtproblem," reproduced in Tuviah Friedman (ed.), *Die drei verantwortlichen SS-Führer für die Durchführung der Endlösung der Judenfrage in Europa waren: Heydrich – Eichmann – Müller* (Haifa, 1993). For the Foreign Office's similar position, see the documents – especially document 5 (Luther to Ribbentrop, October 22, 1942) – reproduced in the appendix to Liliana Picciotto Fargion, "Italian citizens in Nazi-occupied Europe: documents from the files of the German Foreign Office, 1941–1943," *Simon Wiesenthal Center Annual* 7 (1990), 93–141.

41 Unterstaatssekretär Luther, Auswärtiges Amt, Vortragsnotiz, 6. Oktober 1942. *ADAP*, Series E., vol. IV (Göttingen, 1975), 22–7.

42 Cited in Robert Bideleux and Ian Jeffries, *The Balkans: A Post-Communist History* (London, 2006), 82.

43 See Martin Luther to Bucharest Embassy, January 9, 1943, Nuremberg Document NG-2200. On Italy, see the document taken from Friedman in note 40

above and the RSHA communiqué in the same note, specifically the part citing Himmler to Ribbentrop, January 29, 1943.

44 Longerich, *Holocaust*, 389–90.

45 Best to Foreign Office, October 2, 1943, reproduced in Siegfried Matlock (ed.), *Dänemark in Hitlers Hand* (Husum, 1988), 302 . Norwegian statistics from Longerich, *Holocaust*, 372–3.

46 Reproduced in Jeremy Noakes and Geoffrey Pridham (eds.), *Nazism 1919–1945, vol. 3: Foreign Policy, War and Racial Extermination* (Exeter, 1988), 1199–200.

47 Bradley F. Smith and Agnes F. Peterson (eds.), *Heinrich Himmler. Geheimreden 1933 bis 1945* (Frankfurt, 1974), 169–70.

48 See, e.g., the speeches of January 26, May 5, May 24, and June 21, 1944, in Smith and Peterson (eds.), *Heinrich Himmler Geheimreden*, 201, 202, 203 (quote from June 21 speech).

49 Ibid.

50 On Himmler's relationship to the "liquidation" of the Lodz ghetto after becoming Reich Interior Minister in August 1943, see Peter Klein, *Die 'Gettoverwaltung Litzmannstadt' 1940–1944: Eine Dienststelle im Spannungsfeld von Kommunalbürokratie und staatlicher Verfolgungspolitik* (Hamburg, 2009).

51 *Der Stürmer*, November 4, 1943.

52 Tim Mason, "The Third Reich and the German Left: persecution and resistance" in Hedley Bull (ed.), *The Challenge of the Third Reich* (Oxford, 1986), 100.

53 The narrative detail here is taken from Christian Gerlach and Götz Aly, *Das letzte Kapitel: Der Mord an den ungarischen Juden* (Stuttgart, 2002), and to a lesser degree from Randolph L. Braham, *The Politics of Genocide: The Holocaust in Hungary* (New York, 1994).

54 The events of October can be incorporated within the logic of my interpretation since they occurred only after Horthy did try to withdraw from the Axis and was imprisoned by Germany.

3

Meanings of Race and Biopolitics in Historical Perspective

Pascal Grosse

It seems that historical scholarship had a long road to travel before it was able to appropriately identify the uniqueness of National Socialist rule in Germany and Europe. In 2000, Ian Kershaw concluded, in the fourth edition of his survey of the historiography of National Socialism: "historical research on the Third Reich has, therefore, finally come to focus on the heart of Nazi rule: extermination policy, the killing of an intended 11 million Jews and the remodeling of Europe on race lines following a war of planned barbarity to establish race dominance and the brutal subjugation – in some cases eradication – of 'inferior' peoples."[1] Thus, according to Kershaw, the ultimate goal of Nazism was to establish a new socio-political order under a racially defined German hegemony in Europe, which was to be accomplished by means that went beyond previous understandings of the limits of "civilized" behavior on the part of states.

Essentializing National Socialism in this way does not entirely disregard other historical perspectives on this period of German history. However, one key implication of Kershaw's statement is that if other fields of historical research – such as diplomatic history, economic history, social history, or cultural history – were to dismiss racial politics altogether, the quintessential aspect of what defines the uniqueness of National Socialism would be missing. This logic is based upon the assumption that all spheres of life – politics, the economy, society, culture – became racialized in some way under Nazi rule. That assumption, which is supported by much evidence, is summed up in Burleigh and Wippermann's phrase "the racial state." In Germany, as they note, "racial ideologies enjoyed the widest currency and the greatest political salience: the Third Reich became the first state in world history whose dogma and practice was racism."[2] The underlying claim, obviously, is that Nazi Germany was not just a dictatorship like so many others elsewhere before and after. Nazi Germany's exceptionalism as a dictatorship, it seems, was that the political and social body was defined by rules of inclusion and exclusion related to – perhaps – rather vague notions of "race."

Burleigh and Wippermann's catchphrase from the early 1990s reflects an important intellectual move. It suggests that Nazi racial politics were more than an addendum to other political agendas. With some exceptions, historians had previously viewed Nazi racial policy as a separate sphere of social policy that concerned only particular groups within the population, not the entire German citizenry. But what has since come to the fore is that Nazi racial policy comprehensively infiltrated spheres of political and social life at least on the normative – that is, legal and cultural – level. The notion of the racial state thus also overcame the traditional reductionist equation of Nazi racial policy with the Holocaust alone. To recognize that the racialization of German politics and society took place at a normative level, however, does not necessarily imply that racial policy became a consistent social and cultural practice at all levels of political and social action. It is nothing more than a truism that everyday policies during National Socialism were mostly erratic and borne out of a polycratic administration. Why then should racial policies have been implemented more consistently than any other policy? There is no reason why racial policies could not be strategically useful in political debates and social confrontations while at the same time representing a genuine political goal.

Burleigh and Wippermann's understanding of Nazi Germany as a racial state might be misleading because they understate the tensions inherent in the Nazis' attempt to transform German society into a racialized political and social body. As the catchphrase suggests, they identify the state as the key agent in the implementation of a preconceived racial ideology. Historians have conclusively shown that the state, in the sense of a coherent political and administrative body, did not exist in Germany under the Nazis.[3] In light of this, Burleigh and Wippermann's contention that racial policies were administered in synchronized fashion by a monolithic state might not accurately reflect the intricacies of Nazi racial politics. Hannah Arendt's understanding of Nazism as a constant movement in opposition to and ultimately destroying the state counters such an assumption of coherent state operations.[4] As the Nazi party was not a traditional political party that merely implemented its political manifesto once in power, Arendt's concept of constant movement captures the operations of racial politics in Nazi Germany better than a working model that sees the state as the center of gravity. It would thus perhaps make sense to substitute the phrase "racial state" with "racial order."

In the end, what Burleigh and Wippermann's book provides is a comprehensive study of what the Nazis understood by their own racial politics, that is, the persecution of groups singled out on supposedly racial grounds. What the two authors do not offer, however, is an analysis of what race and its underpinnings meant at the different levels of discourse and politics. They consider racial policy to be the implementation of an ideology that supposedly became a state doctrine in Germany after 1933.[5] More importantly, because the two authors analyze each persecuted group separately, they lose sight of one of the essential points addressed by Kershaw: that Nazi racial politics cannot be decoupled from the territorial expansion the Nazi regime pursued after 1938 because Nazi racial politics inherently aimed to create a racially ordered German empire in Europe.

That point deserves closer examination as it opens up new historiographical perspectives. Traditionally, World War II, the Holocaust, and the persecution of particular groups under the Nazis have been examined independently of each other. The link between expansionism and racial politics has, however, recently come under closer scrutiny, less from historians of National Socialism than from scholars studying European colonialism and genocides in colonial settings.[6] The so-called colonial turn in the historiography of National Socialism should be understood,[7] though, less as a fundamental reinterpretation of National Socialism than as a means to pinpoint some conceptual shortcomings in prior narratives of National Socialism. Some scholars have proposed that European colonialism in the late nineteenth and early twentieth centuries should be regarded as the immediate historical precursor to the extreme violence of Nazi warfare in Eastern Europe after 1939. In this reading, the genocidal experience of European colonialism – some scholars stress German colonialism alone, suggesting German exceptionalism in colonial politics – provides *the* template for the extermination policies implemented by the Nazis during World War II.[8] Other historians have strongly disputed the idea of direct continuity from "Windhoek to Auschwitz" and point to the fact that phenomenological similarities may develop in very distinct historical settings and therefore bear no explanatory authority.[9] The most persuasive point made in this debate is the assertion that the Nazis' war in Eastern and Southeastern Europe should be conceptualized as a colonial war rather than as a traditional conflict between rival European powers that would eventually end with a peace treaty and a divvying up of booty.

With this perspective in mind, I would argue that in trying to look beyond the racial state paradigm, it is probably not productive to linger on traditional issues, such as the discrepancy between the Nazis' ideological rhetoric of race and the racial policies they enacted. Such discrepancies are obvious and are ultimately inherent in any transformative political and social processes driven by an agenda, be it ideologically grounded or not. Nor will older historiographical controversies over intentionalism vs. structuralism, or the dispute over the ambivalent "modernity" of the Nazi regime, help us to better understand its racial policies. After all, what distinguishes German expansionism under the Nazis from, for instance, British or French expansionism is that the Nazis' ultimate goal was not to create an extended German nation-state in Europe and overseas. Rather, the goal was to shape a comprehensive racially connoted political and social body – a new German Empire – that that would depart from many aspects of the bourgeois nation-state model of the nineteenth century. The Nazis' vision of racial order propelled a metanational concept of order that eventually supplanted the bourgeois nation-state. It was Hannah Arendt who pointed out that the concept of race ultimately undermines key notions of the classical nation-state.[10] Unfortunately, this crucial observation has been largely ignored by historians of National Socialism.

In what follows, I will flesh out Arendt's observation to suggest a perspective that might take us beyond the racial state. To this end, I shall explore three interrelated dimensions of race as a biopolitical category. First, I will investigate the inner logic of race as a biopolitical category and its potential connections to racial politics during National Socialism. Second, I want to demonstrate how race bore a complex intellectual matrix in the context of German colonialism immediately prior to World War I. I offer this case study as an example of how territorial expansionism became intertwined with racial politics at multiple layers. My key argument here is that although there were no direct continuities in racial politics from German colonial rule to the Nazis, colonialism provided the first opportunity in German history to test models for establishing a racial order. Last, I will briefly revisit a few aspects of the discourse on National Socialist racial politics after World War II that finally remapped former understandings of the biological and cultural underpinnings of race. My general contention is that racial discourses and the politics they have engendered since the eighteenth century should not be viewed as a stable set of ideas condensed into a coherent ideology, but rather as an intellectual matrix of varying biocultural interpretations of the human condition. Given the variety of meanings that have been attributed to race, a uniform racial politics is hardly to be expected. My more specific contention, however, is that the German discourse on race in the nineteenth and twentieth centuries, in contrast to those in most other Western countries, had very deeply rooted biological underpinnings, which is why the biological implications of what race stood for are taken very seriously in what follows.

RACE AS A BIOPOLITICAL CATEGORY

Race is a biopolitical category because race has organized power (political, social, and cultural) around specific material, namely the corporeal aspects of the human existence. At their outset in the eighteenth century, racial discourses did not distinguish between cultural and biological interpretations of race; rather, the concept of race fused human biology and human culture into one single overarching dimension of the human condition. It was not the mere bodily materiality that was decisive in the formation of biopolitical discourses and practices centered on race and races. The biological body was just a measurable representation that was thought to correspond to each human being's mental disposition because mental faculties are what supposedly produce specific human cultures. After World War II, Fritz Lenz, one of the founding fathers of German eugenics, offered perhaps the best explanation of the supposed synthesis of body, mind, and culture conveyed by the notion of race: "every attempt to restrict racial differences to physical differences is both arbitrary and scientifically unjustifiable," he maintained, because "psychical hereditary differences are much more important than physical differences."[11] By implication, mental characteristics are as much racial traits as complexion, skull shape, or other physical features. Lenz also contested the notion that "the history of cultural experience," which he equates with the term "traditions," explains the development of human culture and the emergence of different cultures. He argues rather that culture is determined by biology: "it seems ... that there is very strong evidence to show that genetic differences are a 'major factor' in producing differences between cultural groups."[12]

Lenz's comprehensive understanding of race had its origins in eighteenth-century philosophical materialism, which first gave currency to the idea of using bodily markers as a means to subdivide humankind.[13]

During this age of taxonomy, when all of nature was inventoried and its animate and inanimate constituents were classified according to morphology (*Gestalt*), it was only logical that mankind, as one element of natural history (*Naturgeschichte*), would also be subject to morphological classification. To explain why different morphological types within humanity exist was relatively simple for monogenist anthropologists.[14] Humans adapt to their physical environment, which is shaped most decisively by climate, in order to increase their chances of survival and well-being. In other words, the physical environment exerts a formative influence on human biology. Such geographical determinism asserted that each race optimizes its existence in a specific geographic area through adaptive biological changes. The prevailing dogma, which saw biology and culture as two sides of the same coin, thus insisted that cultural practices are also shaped by the environment and represent the necessary adaptations to the environment. The logic behind these assumptions is straightforward: people must differ bodily from one region of the world to another because of their exposure to different physical environments. In this view, human biology and human culture are interchangeable; both are synthetic expressions of how the geographical environment shapes individuals.[15] Notions of race in the eighteenth century, in short, carried inextricable biological and cultural implications: race always referred to the literal and figurative embodiment of an adaptive biocultural synthesis. From this perspective, race appears to be a neutral, secular, and scientific concept.[16]

Nevertheless, taxonomic anthropology in the eighteenth century set up an inherently contradictory agenda in organizing the similarities and differences among humans. On the one hand, biologizing the totality of the human condition implied an egalitarian and incorruptible empirical concept to corroborate the unity of mankind: every single human being was subject to universally applicable natural laws. On the other hand, the internal logic of such biologism leads to the assumption that every difference between humans, as expressed, for example, in the categories of race, class, or gender, must have biological correlates. Whether such biological differences are the product of a transformative geography or are tied to genetic variables is not relevant given the assumption that social and cultural difference is represented in the material body. Such a biology of difference implicitly calls the notion of a biologically based egalitarianism into question. Such have been the intellectual tensions by which variable notions of race have operated, making race a highly multivalent biopolitical category that has borne many different meanings since the eighteenth century.

The question now is whether this working model of the original meaning of race has bearing on the interpretation of racial politics under the Nazi regime. Most historians since the 1960s have indeed identified the (scientific) discourse on race that originated in the eighteenth century in Europe and the Americas as the intellectual precursor to Nazi racial politics.[17] Those authors contested previous axioms that had detached National Socialist racial discourse and policies from earlier racial discourse in Germany and the Western world. More recent scholarship, by contrast, has focused on identifying such intellectual continuities in order to make Nazi racial politics intelligible to at least a certain extent. In particular, this approach rejects interpretations that identify National Socialist racial politics as a form of psychopathology, that invoke a *Rassenwahn* (racial frenzy).

However, there are some simple reasons for doubting whether there were in fact linear intellectual continuities between racial politics under the Nazis and its supposed discursive precursors starting in the eighteenth century. Although there is no question that numerous discourses referencing race existed, it is difficult, if not impossible, to prove any intellectual consistency in these discourses from the eighteenth century through to the Nazi era. The only clear overarching intellectual principle in these centuries was the understanding of race as a comprehensive biocultural concept. This extremely vague concept was more a philosophical hypothesis than a scientific principle backed by evidence. At all levels, intellectual confusion rather than order prevails.[18] In Burleigh and Wippermann's work, the complex intellectual landscape of racial sciences is reduced to what they call "racial ideology." Such a reductionist approach makes little sense in light of the many diverse interpretations of what race stood for. Other historians have tried to identify dominant intellectual lines in the "maze of racial logic." One example is Cornelia Essner's attempt to distinguish between "contagionist" and "Nordic-eugenic" approaches to the purification of the "Aryan" race.[19] Contagionist thinking, as the core of *völkisch* anti-Semitism, centered on the belief that any sexual contact between an Aryan and an individual who is not fully Aryan would leave the former forever contaminated by the latter and thus incapable of producing healthy offspring thereafter, even through subsequent sexual intercourse with a pure Aryan. Conversely, eugenic Nordicism was based on contemporary scientific principles claiming that races could be purified over several generations by fostering race-selective reproduction.

The example of Essner's detailed analysis of two models within the spectrum of discourse on race highlights some of the limitations inherent in attempts to systematize that discourse. Certainly, the distinction Essner makes helps us better understand some of the fierce debates that took place among various factions within the Nazi administration during the preparation of the Nuremberg Laws. Also, such distinctions clarify some of the underpinnings of early twentieth-century anti-Semitism and the way such sentiments could become operational at the bureaucratic level. However, the differences Essner outlines present an explanation for one issue, namely the Nazi bureaucracy's treatment of people of mixed racial decent, most prominently, of course, the "Jewish *Mischlinge*." Conversely, the distinction between *völkisch* anti-Semitism and Nordic eugenics does not answer the question of why Jews were even considered to be a separate race, nor does it address the specificity of other groups targeted by Nazi racial policies. Nor, contrary to Essner's claims, is that distinction relevant to efforts to understand the Holocaust. Ultimately, there is no single dominant and comprehensive racial discourse that can explain the complex workings of racial policy during National Socialism. Rather, racial discourses in general should be viewed as multifaceted intellectual matrices encompassing all dimensions of human life, and National Socialist racial discourse was no exception. Instead of trying to crystallize dominant lines of thought in mostly inconsistent racial assumptions, I therefore propose to recenter the debate on the meaning of race in National Socialist Germany by looking at how race became functional at the operational level. Such an approach might perhaps disclose more consistency. From this perspective, the most important development in the transition from the nineteenth century to the twentieth was the move away from a static cataloguing of humankind according to physical, psychological, or cultural traits and toward a dynamic view of human life that ascribed a decisive role to genetics. This paradigmatic transition shifted interest away from defining biologically defined classes toward analyzing trends in human reproduction and their potential consequences. The individual human being is in effect doubled in this outlook: an individual exists as a real living being in the present and, at the same time, harbors a hidden genetic potential that will shape the makeup of entire populations in the future. Genetics and eugenics aimed to anticipate future genealogies, and one product of this change of paradigms was a eugenic program of selective human breeding – and, eventually, of selective elimination as well.

I would contend that race, understood in terms of eugenics as detailed above, was perhaps what held National Socialist racial policies together. For instance, it is well known that physical anthropologists never established reliable criteria to determine whether an individual was a Jew.

The decision whether a person was Jewish was made at registration offices or was based on ecclesiastical records. Anthropological expertise was not required in determining whether an individual was Jewish: Jewishness was conceptualized by the Nazis as a question solely of descent.[20] Eugen Fischer, the key figure in German eugenics, summarized the apparent limitations of his own field in 1934 by stating that "the assignment of the race is to be decided by asking: from where does he descend, who is his father, who is his grandfather, his mother and grandmother? ... I am not seeing a way by which doctors would be in the capacity in a few years to decide whether an individual belongs to an alien race or not."[21] In other words, race was operationalized as the sum of an individual's ancestry

I give this example in order to clarify one point: racial assignments were made on the basis of descent, that is, genealogy, not on the grounds of bodily markers. Some physical anthropologists might have wished they had the necessary tools to make accurate anthropological diagnoses, but in fact such diagnoses were not necessary according to the logic of eugenics because the genealogical approach had a stronger internal logic than first appearances suggested. Different ancestries represent different sets of gene pools (in today's parlance) and, in the logic of genetics, different genetic potentials. How an individual was categorized anthropologically was thus of less importance for future generations than the genetic potential that he/she represented. While it appears at first glance that the absence of biological standards was a conceptual weakness in the selection process used to classify populations on racial grounds, I would argue that there was no need for such standards because genealogy could be used more easily in classifying the population. Race was a concept that established genealogies, and the assessment of physical traits was only one of the tools employed to do so. Paul Weindling is certainly right when he states that physical anthropology emerged in the eighteenth century as a bourgeois project to radically challenge aristocratic privileges by biologizing more archaic notions of race tied up with "good breeding" and "good blood."[22] But the modern and "scientific" bourgeois enterprise of racial sciences rested on the very same principles as its aristocratic predecessor, as both rested on tracing and creating pedigrees.

COLONIAL RACIAL POLITICS IN GERMANY

The concept of race as a eugenic principle had implications beyond the constructions of new races – such as the "Jewish," "Aryan," and "Nordic" races – that supposedly represented some common and "pure" ancestry.

Politically, race supersedes territorial boundaries defined by nation-states, as races intrinsically reach across arbitrarily drawn frontiers. Race thus defies the paradigmatic unity of territory, culture, and language held together by a state bureaucracy that roughly defined the bourgeois nation-state model in the nineteenth century. Race is an inherently transnational category and, by implication, incongruent with existing nation-states. Over the course of the nineteenth century, that incongruity between race and the nation-state became effective in various historical instances, most obviously in colonial settings. During the nineteenth century, colonies provided emerging European nation-states with an opportunity to experiment with racialized political concepts free of the territorial limitations they faced at home, because colonial holdings were not defined by an imagined territorial, cultural, and linguistic unity. The case of German colonialism offers an outstanding opportunity to study the tensions between concepts of the nation and concepts of race at the end of the nineteenth century and the beginning of the twentieth – tensions that were to have wide repercussions over the course of the twentieth century. German colonialism magnifies one of the core problems in the constitution of the modern nation-state, namely, defining citizenship and, in turn, determining who is eligible for citizenship. The German response in the colonies was to establish a racialized order with a strong biological emphasis.

It should be noted from the outset that the racialization of the German colonial state operated on two different levels. The first level ordered the multi-ethnic population living in the colonies and assigned legal status on the basis of physical traits. The second, future-oriented level focused on securing the political, socioeconomic, and cultural hegemony of one race – the white one – over all other groups. Those prospective reflections brought in a dynamic perspective that envisaged the future composition of the demographic inventory of a colony. Together, the two levels laid the groundwork for a doubling of the German nation-state and its citizenry: to be German also meant to be white and, in turn, colonial subjects were non-whites.

How did such an equation between citizenship and biological traits come about at the normative level? When Germany became a colonial power in 1884/1885, the German government immediately established a racial order at the judicial level. The Colonial Law (*Schutzgebietsgesetz*) of 1886 organized political, social, judicial, and economic relations on the basis of the distinction between "citizens" (*Reichsangehörige*) and "natives" (*Eingeborene*). This fundamental distinction was of twofold importance. The Colonial Law protected the civil rights of white Europeans living in in faraway colonies. It also allowed the German authorities to enact special legislation over the natives and relegate them to the legal status of colonial "subjects" (*Untertanen*). German authorities deployed the concept of native to mean "all coloreds who reside in the colony" and to distinguish them from German citizens and "members of other civilized nations" (*Angehörige anderer zivilisierter Staaten*).[23] From the outset, the German colonial rulers dismissed concurrent concepts of ethnicity in multi-ethnic colonial settings in favor of an overarching racialized white-colored dichotomy. Racial difference structured all aspects of public and private life in the colonies, and the German government legally codified inequality on the basis of biological and ethnic differences.

The racialized foundations of the early German colonial state did not, however, take into account future demographic developments. The adoption of eugenicist perspectives in German colonial racial policy began to gain momentum only after the turn of the century and peaked just before World War I. In essence, eugenics sought to supplant political, social, and cultural questions about the constitution and preservation of power with the institutionalization of selective biocultural reproduction. Geoff Eley coined the phrase "eugenic consensus" in the early 1990s to describe what he saw as the most innovative force in German politics prior to World War I.[24] This supposed consensus did not represent the agenda of a particular political party or political movement. Rather, eugenics was part of the intellectual matrix of the German bourgeoisie and encompassed the entire political spectrum. More importantly, eugenics should not be understood as an attempt at social engineering that sought to translate theory into administrative practice. Many advocates of eugenic policies were not even aware that their views were in line intellectually with the eugenics movement. Perhaps it is this lack of awareness, which bordered on nescience, that defines consensual politics as a cultural practice.

In the beginning of the twentieth century, eugenics offered the prospect of an efficient racial order based on the idea of selective, "pure," racial reproduction – with particular relevance in colonial settings. Eugenics reinforced the concept of "white rule" in the colonies, and the logic of eugenics ultimately shaped and racialized the German nation-state as a whole. The eugenicist perspective in German colonial policy resulted in some remarkable epistemological turns in racial politics generally. One major epistemological turn came about as a result of the remapping of the impact of the natural environment on humans. Would a white population living outside the temperate regions retain its characteristic biological traits or would it "turn native"? Naïve as it may seem, this line of inquiry posed the most fundamental question of modern colonialism from the viewpoint of theoretical anthropology. At the heart of the problem lay an intellectual paradox. European overseas expansion was justified on the grounds of the supposed superiority of the white race. But according to the geographic determinism of the eighteenth century, Europeans, as whites, would have to adapt to the natural environments of the colonies if they were to survive. In other words, to survive in the tropics, whites would have to lose the biocultural traits that defined them as white. This paradox obviously put substantial epistemological pressure on claims of white supremacy. Logically, an exclusively male colonial ruling class could not ensure the biological reproduction of a truly white population in colonial societies. White supremacy presumed that the "white family" was the biological foundation for "racial purity." Consequently, by the end of the nineteenth century, the settlement of white women in Africa and Asia emerged as one of the decisive concerns of German colonial policy. Because European women had long been considered incapable of surviving in the tropics on account of their very nature as women, not simply because they belonged to the white race, their inclusion in colonial societies represented a decisive turn in thinking about how the "white race" was to survive in different natural habitats. The locus of whiteness was effectively bound to the presence of white women and their biological reproductive capacity.

Another epistemological turn in German colonialism linked citizenship to race. Notions of racialized citizenship rested on a set of negotiations over how to achieve a legal framework for a racially structured system of German citizenship. Among other problems,[25] one key issue stemmed from the fact that native women could become German citizens by marrying German men, and children born in wedlock to German fathers were automatically German, their racial make-up notwithstanding. Consequently, some German colonial administrations issued bans on mixed marriages. As racially mixed descendants of German fathers were gradually barred from claiming German citizenship, the concept of racialized citizenship took a more distinct shape. The colonial administration explicitly called for the limitation of German citizenship to white individuals. Radical nationalist lobbies echoed such efforts and went so far as to agitate for a law prohibiting "white-colored" miscegenation (*Reichs-mischlingsgesetz*). That call went beyond the issue of mixed-race marriages in the colonies and demanded an overarching framework for the German state as a whole that would anchor German citizenship in race regardless of place of residency. The fervent discussions about race and citizenship that took place among civil servants, scientists, and politicians did not so much reflect an actual state of affairs, but rather were the expression of inflated concerns over potential future demographics and the scenario of impending racial "decline" as a result of miscegenation in the colonies. Even though truly eugenicist legislation to establish racialized citizenship was not formally enacted before World War I, the efforts to bring about such policy change challenged one fundamental principle of the traditional nation-state model: racial categories to implement "pure" racial reproduction would clearly defy the principle on which the very idea of the nation-state rested, namely the principle of patriarchal lineage.[26] The "German family" presided over by the *Hausvater* as the core unit of the nation-state became contested as the concept of the "racially pure German family," which imposed sexual restrictions on the *Hausvater*, gained currency.

A third epistemological turn ensuing from colonial eugenics can perhaps be identified in the dissolution of traditional boundaries between the civil and military spheres. It is most likely not a mere coincidence that the eugenic shift in German colonial racial politics – and in German politics in general – really came into full swing only in the years just prior to World War I. In contrast to scholars who see eugenics prior to World War I narrowly as the emergence of a scientific concept of social engineering,[27] I would suggest that in Germany, the eugenic shift, at its core, bridged traditional boundaries between the military and civic spheres in very new ways, making the two spheres interchangeable against the backdrop of an impending global war.[28] As a result, the human body was conceived of as a potential weapon, which in turn necessitated the development of selection criteria to determine which Germans could realize that potential. Such selection could be made according to the territorial limitations of the nation-state or by establishing transnational, racial genealogies that contested the boundaries of the nation-state.

In the years after 1911, the "birth question," virtually unheard of previously in Germany, became the focus of a debate on population policy that involved virtually every sector of society. This passionate public debate can be viewed as a gender-specific counterpart to the concurrent debates on the male military service. Through the birth question, German women were mobilized in the militarization of German society and could thereby be symbolically integrated into the German *Wehrgemeinschaft* (defense community) without the legal equality of full citizenship being conferred upon them.

The call for a rapprochement between the civil and military spheres was also expressed in the revision of German citizenship laws, which was completed in 1913 and based on the slogan "keine Volksgemeinschaft, keine Wehrgemeinschaft" (No *Volk* community, no defense community). The equation of the "*Volk* community" with the "military community" reflected a dimension of militarism in Germany at a time when the military claimed to be the central institution that structured German society. Bourgeois militarists attempted to explicitly integrate the category of race into their militarized vision of citizenship. According to the bourgeois militarists' transnational understanding of citizenship, for instance, the so-called *Auslandsdeutschen* (ethnic Germans living outside the Reich) should be allowed to serve in the German armed forces although they were citizens of another country, while the status of Prussian Poles and German Jews was open to debate even though they held German citizenship. The same was true of colonial subjects. The Pan-German League agitated to exclude colonial subjects from service in the Prussian army.[29] However, what seems at first glance to be a racialized concept of military participation through military service and procreation in fact contributes to the foundation of a racial order because participation in the military sphere conferred citizenship. And, as seen above, citizenship was gradually conceptualized in racial terms. In the end, bourgeois militarists and radical nationalists failed in their attempts to formally include ethnicity or race in the equation of military service and civic citizenship. Nevertheless, through their efforts, a new model of a militarized *and* racialized citizenship emerged in German political discourse. The emerging concept of a racialized and militarized citizenship provided the foundation for a new set of criteria for deciding whether individuals as well as ethnocultural groups were to be included in the German nation-state.

This very condensed analysis of a few key elements of German colonial racial politics should be understood as a template for how, in a specific historical setting, race can become operational as a eugenicist principle in more than one way. Correspondences between German colonial racial politics and National Socialist racial politics seem to be only too obvious: an expansionist and militarized setting; the segregation of biologically defined social groups; the militarization of society at all levels, leading to the eventual fusion of the military and the civic spheres; and, perhaps most importantly, the implementation of anthropo-legal practices that barred selected individuals from citizenship, in both legal and socio-cultural terms, and even deprived some individuals of the citizenship they held. The eugenicist perspective was not, however, fully translated into policy in either Germany or the German colonies before World War I. Eugenicist proposals should be seen rather as fluid thought experiments. But I would argue that these thought experiments are of importance because some radical nationalist segments of the German bourgeoisie made race the basic concept by which they sought to revise the nation-state. From this radical nationalist perspective, the traditional nation-state model apparently did not suffice as a judicial and social framework because it did not allow for territorial and cultural expansion on grounds of the German-white claim to racial superiority. Just prior to World War I, radical German nationalists articulated racialized versions of the nation-state that effectively undermined previous understandings of the nation-state. If one wishes to identify lines of continuity between German colonialism and National Socialism, it is perhaps most promising to look into such novel and distinctive discursive configurations. These configurations do not make German colonialism a precursor to National Socialism but rather suggest that the last phase of German colonialism created the intellectual matrix from which new notions of racialized empire-formation emerged.

(NOT) COMING TO TERMS WITH NATIONAL SOCIALIST RACIAL POLITICS

Perhaps one of the greatest achievements in scholarship on National Socialist racial policy since the 1960s has been the systematic contextualization of the period between 1933 and 1945 within a larger historical framework. The reconceptualization of National Socialist racial policy entailed a reassessment of the seemingly scientific underpinnings of racial policy under Nazism and of the role of the sciences, medicine, and technology in society more generally. In order to allow for critical interrogations of Nazi racial policy, it was necessary—as an intellectual precondition—to disentangle science, medicine, and technology from the idea of progress. Disentangling science from notions of progress removed basic intellectual obstacles associated with the role of science and technology in society, and should thus be viewed as a true paradigmatic shift in the history of science in the Western world after World War II. One result of this effort was that the sciences and scientists were divested of a notion of absolute objectivity and impartiality. From this perspective, scientists are political actors and, moreover, science and technology are spheres of political activity.

Racial politics are obviously not a peculiarity of German history. A problem arises, however, in trying to place Nazi racial politics in broader context or comparative perspective. If we denounce the Nazis' introduction of race as a principle for ordering, we call into question the validity of race as a scientific category. There have been two responses to this problem. One has been to dismiss the racial sciences deployed under the Nazis as "pseudoscience"; the other has been to reject race as a scientific category altogether.

Natural scientists and social scientists have systematically pursued both of these lines of argument since 1945. The most significant turn in the effort to come to terms with different notions of race was channeled through the institutional platform of UNESCO in the late 1940s, when an eminent group of scientists from around the world and from multiple disciplines sought to solve the "racial problem" scientifically.[30] The question of whether Nazi racial sciences could be dismissed as pseudoscientific was hotly debated – and it remains a matter of contention today. This line of inquiry does not question race as a scientific concept; the paradox thus remains that the majority of scientists (and many politicians) claim to be solving the racial problem with the tools of science. In other words, the social pathologies surrounding the concept of race that the racial sciences themselves had created are to be remedied with the intellectual instruments of those very sciences. However, other perspectives on the political implications of race shifted radically. Dismissing race as a scientific concept applicable to a specific set of social problems, such perspectives identify the concept of race to be in fact the problem.

Since the 1950s, the concept of race has disintegrated epistemologically and has been relegated to two separate arenas of investigation. Race continues to exist as a concept in the sciences, reduced solely to its biological meanings; the traditional biocultural understanding of race has been abandoned. The separation of biology from culture resulted from the concession that culture cannot be studied through scientific methods, as scientists had once asserted. Although some scholars still claim that human biology determines human culture, such research now risks being labeled as "pseudoscience" and dismissed for lacking truly scientific evidence. On the other hand, race and racial politics have become the object of socio-political investigations that ultimately reject race as a scientific category and focus instead on race as a socio-political construct. These two approaches have little in common. They are separated from each other not only methodologically but also along the dichotomy of biologism vs. culturalism, which is precisely the divide that conceptions of race had initially bridged in the eighteenth century.

It has become a highly problematic task to identify the appropriate historical contexts in which to understand National Socialist racial politics, given the multiple meanings the concept of race carries today. This new challenge stems in part from the assumption that, as a scientific category, the concept of race is stable and remains unchanged over time. Such an understanding is inherent to the sciences, as they deal with supposedly universally applicable natural laws that never change. And precisely because racial scientists operated with an understanding of race as a stable category, historians can easily get caught in a trap and inadvertently accept the postulates of racial scientists. If historians go solely by the writings and working of racial scientists, they unavoidably establish questionable historical continuities and causal connections because they are dealing with a matter that is supposedly unchangeable. But the crucial question is what relevance and explanatory power these continuities possess in specific historical constellations. To contextualize National Socialist racial politics historically, I would therefore suggest that one must take into account the discrepancy between the assumedly stable category of race and the dynamic historical constellations in which this category became operational. And perhaps it is even more important to understand how race, with all of its scientific, social, political, and cultural meanings, operated in specific, complex historical settings rather than to establish genealogical continuities that seem to converge in racial politics under the Nazis.

* * *

There is extensive evidence to support the assumptions that there was a complex interaction between the racial sciences and National Socialist racial politics and, in turn, that racial scientists participated in the implementation of the regime's racial policies. Under the Nazis, race operated as a multivalent biopolitical category that could entail discrimination in everyday life, displacement, or racialized killing. However, the question remains: Does a dictatorial regime need scientific authority if it intends to annihilate parts of its own population and other peoples elsewhere? One would be tempted to answer "No": history offers too many examples of regimes that carried out racialized or ethnized mass murder without attempting to offer scientific justification for their actions. However, what seems to be peculiar to racialized mass murder under the Nazis is precisely the fusion of a racial discourse cast in scientific terms with racial politics. Accordingly, some historians assert that the Nazis employed the sciences and their proponents to legitimize racial politics to the German population. Indeed, at first glance that seems to have been the case to a certain extent. Many racial scientists were able to inflate their importance after 1933 because the regime provided political and social settings in which their work was disproportionately magnified. Furthermore, scientific and medical experts helped to shape and execute racial policies. The scientism in Nazi racial politics would thus seem to be nothing more than a legitimizing masquerade.

Although I agree with the assertion that scientific racism is not required for racialized murder, I would also argue that scientific racism is culturally formative when it comes to what distinguishes some of the forms of racialized murder carried out under National Socialism from other forms of racialized killings. If we view the racialized killings carried out under the Nazis as medicalized killings following a scientific logic, we might perhaps grasp more of what characterizes the mass murder during National Socialism. In this sense, scientific racism is perhaps less of a legitimizing doctrine and much more of a cultural practice for which the sciences and medicine provide the intellectual and technological logistics. In his 1976 lectures, Foucault suggested that all notions of "race" intrinsically imply the killing of other humans.[31] I would contend that such a reductionist view of the meanings of "race" is historically misleading. Rather, any attempt to make racialized killings somewhat intelligible should also necessitate an effort to understand racialized killings in their own historical complexity across time.

Notes

1 Ian Kershaw, *The Nazi Dictatorship: Problems and Perspectives of Interpretation*, 4th edn. (London, 2000), 269.
2 Michael Burleigh and Wolfgang Wippermann, *The Racial State: Germany 1933–1945* (Cambridge, 1991), 23.
3 Martin Broszat, *Der Staat Hitlers. Grundlegung und Entwicklung seiner inneren Verfassung* (Munich, 1969); Kershaw, *The Nazi Dictatorship*, 69–92.
4 "Duplication of offices and division of authority, the co-existence of real and ostensible power, are sufficient to create confusion but not to explain the 'shapelessness' of the whole structure. One should not forget that only a building can have a structure, but that a movement – if the word is to be taken

as seriously and as literally as the Nazis meant it – can have only a direction, and that any form of legal or governmental structure can only be a handicap to a movement which is being propelled with increasing speed in a certain direction ... Therefore, judged by our conceptions of government and state structure, these movements, so long as they find themselves physically still limited to a specific territory, necessarily must try to destroy all structure, and for this willful destruction a mere duplication of all offices into party and state institutions would not be sufficient." Hannah Arendt, *The Origins of Totalitarianism*, new edn. with added prefaces (San Diego, 1994; originally published 1951), 398.

5 Burleigh and Wippermann, *The Racial State*, 23–43.
6 See Robert Gerwarth and Stephan Malinowski, "Hannah Arendt's ghosts: reflections on the disputable path from Windhoek to Auschwitz," *Central European History* 42 (2009), 279–300; Matthew P. Fitzpatrick, "The prehistory of the Holocaust? The Sonderweg and Historikerstreit debates and the abject colonial past," *Central European History* 41 (2008), 477–503; Edward Ross Dickinson, "The German Empire: an empire?" *History Workshop Journal* 66 (2008), 129–62.
7 For the "colonial turn" see Gerwarth and Malinowski, "Arendt's ghosts," 297.
8 For German colonialism see Jürgen Zimmerer, "Holocaust und Kolonialismus. Beitrag zu einer Archäologie des genozidalen Gedankens," *Zeitschrift für Geschichtswissenschaft* 51 (2003), 1098–119; Jürgen Zimmerer, "Die Geburt des 'Ostlandes' aus dem Geiste des Kolonialismus. Ein postkolonialer Blick auf die NS-Eroberungs- und Vernichtungspolitik," *Sozial. Geschichte. Zeitschrift für die historische Analyse des 20. und 21. Jahrhunderts* 1 (2004), 10–43; Jürgen Zimmerer, *Von Windhuk nach Auschwitz. Beiträge zum Verhältnis von Kolonialismus und Holocaust* (Münster, 2007); Benjamin Madley, "From Africa to Auschwitz: how German South West Africa included ideas and methods adopted and developed by the Nazis in Eastern Europe," *European History Quarterly* 33 (2005), 429–64.
9 Birthe Kundrus, "Kontinuitäten, Parallelen, Rezeptionen. Überlegungen zur 'Kolonialisierung' des Nationalsozialismus," *Werkstatt Geschichte* 43 (2006), 45–62; Birthe Kundrus, "Von den Herero zum Holocaust? Einige Bemerkungen zur aktuellen Debatte," *Mittelweg 36* (2005), 82–91; Pascal Grosse, "What does German colonialism have to do with National Socialism? A conceptual framework" in Eric Ames, Marcia Klotz, and Lora Wildenthal (eds.), *Germany's Colonial Pasts* (Lincoln, 2005), 115–34.
10 Pascal Grosse, "From colonialism to National Socialism to postcolonialism: Hannah Arendt's 'Origins of Totalitarianism,'" *Postcolonial Studies* 9 (2006), 35–52, here 41–5.
11 UNESCO, *The Race Concept: Results of an Inquiry* (Westport, 1952), 46. As early as the 1920s, Lenz stressed that all racial studies essentially dealt with the study of mental faculties and that bodily variations were at the most surrogate measures of differing mental faculties in the absence of better measurements.
12 Ibid., 61.
13 Nevertheless, it should be noted that "race" could also mean mankind in general as opposed to animals and plants. That sense of the word has never

had much resonance in German, in contrast to English (the human race) or French (*la race humaine*).

14 The monogenists contended that all humans shared a common ancestry; the polygenists, by contrast, claimed that the various races had evolved independently of one another in different parts of the world.

15 David N. Livingston, "Human acclimatization: perspectives on a contested field of inquiry in science, medicine and geography," *History of Science* 25 (1987), 359–94; Michael A. Osborne, *Nature, the Exotic and the Science of French Colonialism* (Bloomington, 1994); Warwick Anderson, "Climates of opinion: acclimatization in nineteenth-century France and England," *Victorian Studies*, 35 (1992), 135–57. The writings of Georges-Louis Leclerc de Bouffon, Denis Diderot, Georg Forster, Johann Friedrich Blumenbach, and Samuel Thomas Sömmering stand out among the many works on the subject published in their time.

16 It should perhaps be stressed that conceptually, "race" followed early modern philosophical paradigms which tightly entangled the "political body" (culture) with the "natural body" (nature) as the foundation of the (nation-) state, an outlook best exemplified in Hobbes' *Leviathan*. See, for instance, Kenneth Robert Olwig, *Landscape, Nature, and the Body Politic. From Britain's Renaissance to America's New World* (Madison, 2002).

17 Hans-Günther Zmarzlik, "Der Sozialdarwinismus in Deutschland," *Vierteljahreshefte zur Zeitgeschichte* 11 (1963), 243–75; Gunter Mann, "Medizinisch-biologische Ideen und Modelle in der Gesellschaftslehre des 19. Jahrhunderts," *Medizinhistorisches Journal* 4 (1969), 1–23; Gunter Mann, "Dekadenz-Degeneration-Untergangsangst im Lichte der Biologie des 19. Jahrhunderts," *Medizinhistorisches Journal* 20 (1985), 6–35; Patrick von zur Mühlen, *Rassenideologien. Geschichte und Hintergründe* (Bonn, 1977); George L. Mosse, *Towards the Final Solution* (New York, 1978); Peter Weingart, Jürgen Kroll, and Kurt Bayertz, *Rasse, Blut und Gene. Geschichte der Eugenik und Rassenhygiene in Deutschland* (Frankfurt, 1988); Peter Emil Becker, *Zur Geschichte der Rassenhygiene. Wege ins Dritte Reich* (Stuttgart, 1988); Sheila Faith Weiss, *Racial Hygiene and National Efficiency: The Eugenics of Wilhelm Schallmayer* (Berkeley, 1987); Paul Weindling, *Health, Race and German Politics between National Unification and Nazism* (Cambridge, 1989).

18 For instance, the terms "race" (with its many variations, such as *Vitalrasse* and *Systemrasse*), *Volk* (with its many derivatives), and nation were often used interchangeably into the twentieth century. The establishment of new scholarly and scientific fields that made reference to race – anthropobiology, anthroposociology, *Gesellschaftsbiologie*, *Vererbungswissenschaften*, racial hygiene, eugenics, racial biology, just to mention a few – points to the very unclear allocation of subject matter in discourses on race. And whereas race could mean the entirety of humankind in some languages (e.g., English, French, Spanish), the German analog, "*die menschliche Rasse*," was less common than terms such as "*die Menschheit*" or "*das Menschengeschlecht*."

19 Cornelia Essner, *Die "Nürnberger Gesetze" oder Die Verwaltung des Rassenwahns* (Paderborn, 2002), 32–49.

20 Similarly, when the so-called *Rheinlandbastarde*, the offspring of white German mothers and French colonial troops stationed in the occupied Rhineland following World War I, were to be sterilized in 1937, anthropological standards were not used in the selection of individuals for sterilization even though anthropologists were involved in the process. The selection guidelines stipulated that the children of German mothers and French colonial soldiers were to be sterilized only if it could be reliably documented that the father had in fact been an "occupation Negro" (*Besatzungsneger*): Bundesarchiv Berlin-Lichterfelde R22/1933,102. Niederschrift über die Sitzung der Arbeitsgemeinschaft II des Sachverständigenbeirats für Bevölkerungs – und Rassenpolitik am 11.3.1935. In the case of Sinti and Roma, racial categorization was based on both bodily markers and genealogical records. See Michael Zimmermann, *Rassenutopie und Genozid. Die nationalsozialistische "Lösung der Zigeunerfrage"* (Hamburg, 1996).

21 Quoted from Essner, *Die "Nürnberger Gesetze,"* 102.

22 Weindling, *Health, Race, and German Politics*, 49.

23 Paul Laband, *Das Staatsrecht der Deutschen Reiches*, 5th edn., vol. 2 (Tübingen, 1911), 287–9.

24 Geoff Eley, "Die deutsche Geschichte und die Widersprüche der Moderne. Das Beispiel des Kaiserreiches" in Frank Bajohr (ed.), *Zivilisation und Barbarei: Die widersprüchlichen Potentiale der Moderne* (Hamburg, 1991), 17–65, here 54f.

25 Another important and often overlooked issue was the fear among colonial administrators that some "white" emigrants would devolve into a "poor white" segment of the colonial society and eventually lose their distinctiveness as "whites" vis-à-vis non-white communities. After 1900, colonial administrations therefore imposed a series of restrictions on whites, including German citizens, who might eventually become wage-dependent. See Robbie Aitkin, *Exclusion and Inclusion: Gradations of Whiteness and Socio-Economic Engineering in German Southwest Africa, 1884–1914* (Oxford, 2007).

26 Lora Wildenthal, "Race, gender and citizenship in the German colonial empire" in Frederick Cooper and Ann Laura Stoler (eds.), *Tensions of Empire: Colonial Cultures in a Bourgeois World* (Berkeley, 1997), 263–83.

27 Weingart et al., *Rasse, Blut und Gene*; Weindling, *Health, Race, and German Politics*.

28 For a more detailed discussion on the relation between eugenics and German military policy prior to World War I, see Pascal Grosse, *Kolonialismus, Eugenik und bürgerliche Gesellschaft in Deutschland* (Frankfurt, 2000), 193ff.

29 "Sitzungsbericht über den Alldeutschen Verbandstag in Erfurt 1912," *Alldeutsche Blätter* 22 (1912), *Deutsche Tageszeitung* (1909), cited in P. Martin, *Schwarze Teufel-Edle Mohren. Afrikaner im Bewußtsein und Geschichte der Deutschen* (Hamburg, 1993), 126.

30 UNESCO, *The Race Concept*, 5.

31 Michel Foucault, *Society Must Be Defended: Lectures at the Collège de France 1975–1976* (New York, 2003), 254ff.

4

Racial States in Comparative Perspective

Devin O. Pendas

The point of this volume is to complicate our understanding of the Nazi state as a racial state. This does not necessarily mean dismissing the term altogether. The heuristic value of the concept remains substantial, so long as one recognizes that no racial state is ever complete. Racism is always a partial and internally contradictory ideology. Consequently, even in those states most deeply committed in principle to a racial ideology, social policy is formulated according to multiple logics in which race can only ever be one factor among others. Clearly, the Nazi regime was deeply racist and sought to include racial considerations in the formulation of a wide range of social policies. Yet the regime also operated according to other logics – ethnonationalist, economic, geostrategic – alongside racial categories, and Nazi racism was (like all racisms) self-contradictory and internally inconsistent. In this sense, as I will suggest in this essay, it may be more useful to think of the Third Reich and other states driven by racist ideology as racializing but never fully racial in character.

Part of the problem is that the very terminology "racial state" creates an artificially monolithic image. Obviously, the noun "state" implies a discrete, purposive institution that is too easily confused for a unitary, volitional entity. States are not unified apparatuses. They are always marked by internal dispute and differences of opinion about policy goals and implementation. This is certainly true of the Third Reich. Despite research reaching back to the 1940s on the internally contested and fragmented character of the Third Reich, the return to analyses of Nazism

I would like to thank my colleagues Heather Cox Richardson and Cynthia Lyerly, as well as my two coeditors, all of whom provided invaluable feedback on this essay.

focused on ideology in the 1990s risked effacing this polycratic structure.[1] In their field-defining analysis of the Nazi racial state, Burleigh and Wipperman certainly tended to fall into this trap, even though their own arguments regarding the role of intellectual elites belied an overly narrow focus on the state as such. In other words, state agents in the strict sense were never the only, and often not even the most important, proponents of racial policy. Intellectuals, scientists, corporate executives, and ordinary Germans were often deeply implicated in articulating, motivating, and implementing racial ideas and policies. As we pointed out in the introduction, it might for this reason be better to refer to racializing regimes rather than states.

The adjective "racial" is no less potentially reifying. The core claim of racism is that races are "real," that is that they are natural entities to be discovered in the world, whose innate characteristics determine subjective human attributes. This understanding may be rooted in scientific ideas about human biology and evolution, or it may be grounded in more intuitive, aesthetic, moral, or religious principles. Often, as with Nazi ideology, racism represents an admixture of all these elements. In addition, at least for historically minded racists like Hitler, racial difference – which invariably means racial conflict – drives world history. The logic of racism thus asserts the discrete, unitary, and homogeneous quality of each race, and the unavoidable moral and political differences between them. Taken at face value, this would imply that racial regimes ought to pursue racial policies that are at least internally coherent and consistent.

Yet, as this volume shows, neither the Nazi state nor Nazi racial ideology was anything like as coherent or unitary as this reified understanding would suggest. To a greater extent even than most states, the Third Reich was characterized by internal fragmentation and contestation, with overlapping jurisdictions and a dispersal of authority at various levels of the hierarchy. To be sure, as Ian Kershaw and others have shown, ideology did serve to provide a degree of coherence to this unstable institutional formation, albeit indirectly, as the multiple power centers of the regime all competed within the same conceptual frame by "working toward the Führer."[2] The bonds between subordinates and their leader were personal, and "charismatic," but the goals toward which they worked were framed as ideology. Action therefore became less a matter of the personal values of individual mid- and low-level Nazis than a structure of loyalty embedded in an overarching conceptual framework. Yet that framework – Nazi ideology – was no more consistent or homogeneous than Nazi institutions. There were multiple intellectual strands at work within the broad stream of Nazi ideology, not all of them mutually compatible. To give but one example, the continuities with Christian thought that Richard Steigmann-Gall has identified in Nazi ideology co-existed uneasily with strains of both panetheism and neo-paganism.[3]

More fundamentally, though, to the extent that Hitler and other major ideological figures within the NSDAP sought to use race to coalesce these diverse strands into a unified account of the world, they came up against the inherent limitations of race-thinking. Because racism presupposes that races are real, rather than social categories constituted and made real by racial ideologies, it is constantly disappointed by external reality's failure to live up (or down) to its expectations. Since races do not exist independent of racisms, the presumptive homogeneity of races at the heart of racism must be constantly reasserted in a futile quest to create the reality that purportedly lies outside the ideological frame. The unreality of race means that racist policy is always less than fully consistent or coherent, even on its own terms, shot through with definitional conundrums and genealogical paradoxes. To resolve these, racism must have recourse to other logics outside those of race.

This does not mean, however, that all racial regimes have been identical in the challenges they face in making race real or in how they have sought to meet these. To take only the most obvious difference between the Third Reich and the other "overtly racist regimes" – the Jim Crow South and Apartheid-era South Africa – the primary targets of Nazi racial policy were other "white" Europeans.[4] Most modern racializing regimes operated along what Du Bois called the "global color line." There was a long history of European thinking about the "colored races," which the Nazis could and did draw upon. This was the racism of imperial anthropology.[5] But the core genealogy of Nazi racism, from Gobineau and Chamberlin to Hitler himself, was strikingly obsessed with intra-European racial difference not easily reduced to phenotypic differences of skin color.[6] The Nazis themselves concentrated their racial animus on their fellow Europeans – Jews most obviously but also Slavs and Sinti and Roma. This was partially for the obvious geopolitical reason that Germany no longer had overseas colonies. Yet there were other important reasons as well. The Nazis stood in the tradition of those thinkers who felt that racial differences on the "white" side of the color-line were more insidious and dangerous than the seemingly more manifest, and more manifestly imperial, difference of color itself. The fact that racially inferior Europeans like Jews could collectively "pass" for their racial betters was part of what made them so particularly dangerous, according to anti-Semitic lore.

This is not to say that the phenotypically based racism of the color-line was more reality-based than the Nazi variant.[7] After all, the color-line was always an uncertain, fragile marker of difference. The phenomenon of passing was a problem for phenotypic racisms as well, one that could produce enormous anxiety on both sides. It could encompass everyone from Catholic bishops to American fascists to, ironically, celebrity scientists passing for black.[8] Moreover, the so-called one-drop rule meant that many individuals with no phenotypic markers of African ancestry were considered "black" for legal purposes in the United States.[9] So skin color only ever offered a partial solution to the problem of identifying racial others. Nevertheless, by targeting Europeans for racial categorizations and anxieties more typically directed at non-Europeans, the Nazis (and other anti-Semites as well) faced rather distinct difficulties.

Because the color-line mapped fairly neatly onto the geopolitics of European and Euro-American global dominance, it seemed (to Europeans) to have more self-evident political implications, in the form of colonialism.[10] And in the postbellum American context, the need to reconstitute a commercial agricultural sector on the basis of nominally free labor led to a similar (white) consensus about the political implications of racial difference. It was relatively easy to construct a racist consensus among the dominant racial groups in these contexts. In Nazi Germany, more work needed to be done to naturalize the politics of race, where the trend had been rather in the opposite direction for the better part of a hundred years or more. After all, in the nineteenth century, the German state had been busy tamping down popular anti-Semitic violence, not implementing it.[11] To be sure, anti-Semitism had a long history in Germany, even if it had never been uncontested, but *political* anti-Semitism had for the most part been an oppositional movement outside the bounds of state policy.[12] This is not to deny Peter Pulzer's claim that "there had always been a wide spread right-wing anti-Semitic consensus that would enable much of German society to adapt painlessly to a system of 'post-liberal' *apartheid*."[13] Rather, it is to suggest that that system of apartheid, and eventually genocide, had to be constructed against a history of emancipation and assimilation rather than by extending a legacy of segregation or slavery. In other words, in the United States or South Africa, racial policy was intent on preserving political-racial differences that were already in place, whereas in the Third Reich, the Nazis were seeking to reinstate differences that had been on the decline and to radicalize their significance far beyond what had previously been typical. Germans in the Third Reich had to learn to think in racial terms to a degree unprecedented in German history.[14] This was less true in the other overtly racist regimes.

Yet for all that the Nazis confronted distinct challenges in trying to apply racial categories to white Europeans rather than colonized peoples on the other side of the color-line, it would be a mistake to see the Nazi racializing regime as unique, as the first and only racial state in world history. If one mistakenly views Nazi racial ideology as more coherent and consistent than it was, as more directly applicable to real-world situations without the mediating impact of alternate logics, then perhaps a claim to uniqueness has some plausibility. This seems to have been the guiding principle behind Burleigh and Wippermann's assertion that the Nazi regime's "objects were novel and *sui generis*" and that the Third Reich could not properly be understood in terms of broader theoretical constructs, such as modernization or fascism.[15] So while they nowhere considered explicitly the racial goals or policies of other states, their argument is that the Third Reich was more or less unique in being a racial state. It was, they insist, a "singular regime without precedent or parallel."[16] What was unique about the Third Reich, according to Burleigh and Wipperman, was not its racial ideology as such, which they acknowledge was not exclusive to Germany. Rather, it was the consequential implementation of that ideology that marked the Nazi regime as unprecedented, at the very least. "The Third Reich became the first state in world history whose dogma and practice was racism."[17]

The plausibility of this claim rests on the authors' reading of Nazi social policy as being consistently and thoroughly racialized. It is the great contribution of their work to be among the first to point in a systematic manner to the ways in which disparate areas of Nazi policy – from negative measures against Jews, Sinti and Roma, asocials, and others, to positive measures to promote the welfare of racially desirable elements – could be viewed as designed to implement a comprehensive, racist social vision. This effort to implement racial ideology reached its murderous apex in the genocide of the Jews:

Notwithstanding attempts to construct elaborate psychological explanations for those who carried out these barbaric policies, let alone attempts to displace responsibility on to tendencies allegedly latent in all modern industrial societies, the bleak truth of the matter is that the self-appointed elite were intoxicated by the idea of actions which were secret, racially therapeutic, and which took them beyond what they regarded as an obsolete morality.[18]

In this volume, we have in various ways tried to show that this vision of a coherent, ideologically consistent racial policy, pointing teleologically toward genocide and mass murder, is overly simplistic. This creates another challenge for Burleigh and Wipperman's account. Their claim that the Third Reich was *the*, rather than *a*, racial state hardly bears scrutiny unless one believes, as they apparently do, that the Nazi regime was more thoroughly and consistently racist than other states. When Burleigh and Wipperman argue that racism became "dogma and practice" in the Third Reich, unlike in other states, this can only be plausible if one takes it as a matter of degree. For the Third Reich to have been unique as a racial state, it must have been more dogmatic in its racism and more comprehensive in its racial practice than other regimes. It is an open question as to when this quantitative distinction would become qualitative. In this volume, we have sought to show that the Nazi state was neither so consistently dogmatic nor so practically efficacious as all that. But it is also true that other states have been equally dogmatic and policy-oriented in their racism.

Whether one considers the history of European overseas colonialism or that of segregationist states like the Jim Crow South and apartheid-era South Africa, one discovers the presence of elaborate racist ideologies and wide-ranging racial policies.[19] It thus appears that the difference between the Third Reich and many other modern states was more a difference of degree than of kind. Before turning to the ways in which the Third Reich differed from other racializing regimes, it is worth emphasizing the substantial similarities first. Charles Mills has argued that "we live in a world which has been foundationally shaped for the past five hundred years by the realities of European domination and the gradual consolidation of global white supremacy."[20] Already in 1903, W. E. B. Du Bois could declare that "the problem of the twentieth century is the problem of the color-line,—the relations of the darker to the lighter races of men in Asia and Africa, in America and the islands of the sea."[21] For Du Bois, the problem of race and racial domination was ubiquitous, simultaneously American and global. Certainly there can be no doubt that the "global color line" constituted a major element in world history throughout the twentieth century, drawn and defended by "racial knowledge and technologies ... [and] strategies of exclusion, deportation and segregation, in particular, the deployment of those state-based instruments of surveillance, the census, the passport and the literacy test."[22] The centrality of race to world history in the modern period is clearly linked closely to the history of European imperialism.[23] As recent research has revealed the extent to which the Nazi expansion in Eastern Europe shared crucial features with the larger European imperial project, the parallels between Nazi and imperial racism have become more salient as well.[24]

From its earliest origins, European overseas imperialism was confronted with questions of difference in a new key. Prior to 1492, it had been relatively easy to subsume virtually all "others," including Africans (heavily Islamized in the areas encountered by Europeans), under the category of "infidels."[25] But Indians, who quickly converted to Christianity in large numbers, eluded such categorization. While it would be an oversimplification to equate the *sociedad de castas* (society of breeds) of the Spanish New World with modern racializing regimes, it was nevertheless a "system of socioracial stratification."[26] While all early modern colonies were marked by high levels of interracial contact due to low levels of European settlement, even under such circumstances, "the Spanish attempted to maintain categorical distinctions for whites and between Indians and the rest."[27] There were formal legal categories for Indians, while most Africans were slaves. Free blacks occupied a more ambiguous position; not legally defined as an administrative category, as were Indians and slaves, they nonetheless occupied a lower position in the social (and economic) hierarchy than whites and Indians, above only their enslaved compatriots. Even opponents of Spanish colonial brutality began to take racial formulations for granted. In his famous debate with Juan Ginés de Sepúlveda, Bartolomé de Las Casas argued that, contrary to Sepúlveda's contention that Indians were "homunculil," Indians were indeed fully human. Yet part of Las Casas's universalizing argument was cast in terms of racial aesthetics. He emphasized not just the "goodness" and "simplicity" of the Indians but also their "color and beauty," implicitly imbuing phenotypic characteristics with moral value.[28] This aestheticization helps to account for why it took Las Casas so long to realize that his logic of human universalism applied to Africans as well as Indians.[29]

Of all early modern imperial institutions, none was more obviously racial than slavery. While ancient slavery had been primarily an economic institution, in the course of the Middle Ages it became mainly a religious one centered on the Mediterranean. "The general premise, on both sides of the religious line, was that the followers of Christ and Muhammed did not enslave their own believers."[30] The establishment of plantation economies in the New World, especially in parts of South America, in the Caribbean, and in the southern colonies of North America, gradually expanded the scale of slavery. This initially focused heavily on indigenous populations, but as these died out from disease, malnutrition, and over-work, replacements were sought, mainly from Africa.[31] The transatlantic enslavement of Africans was "something noticeably new" in that it gave slavery a "stark racial character" for the first time.[32] With the help of the so-called Hametic hypothesis, Aristotelian arguments about "natural slavery" were radicalized, racialized, and given divine sanction.[33]

If racial (or at least proto-racial) categories were thus present in European imperialism from the outset, they only increased in significance with the passage of time. Virtually all early modern colonies tolerated and sometimes even legitimized (literally) interracial sexual relations, particularly between European men and indigenous women. There were obvious pragmatic reasons for this, given the relative scarcity of European settlers in the early years, especially women. But it also reflected a broader permeability of racial categories in what were at that point still primarily trading empires, where indigenous knowledge remained economically valuable.[34] In the course of the nineteenth century, this changed dramatically. The racial boundaries between colonizer and colonized increasingly came to be seen as in principle impermeable, and any transgression a cause for concern. Ann Stoler has pointed out that, for all their political and economic differences, French, British, and Dutch colonial racial policies all shared "similar discourses" concerning *métissage*. "Conceived as a dangerous source of subversion, it was seen as a threat to white prestige, an embodiment of European degeneration and moral decay."[35] These fears led to both increased policing of miscegenation and, frequently, a reconceptualization of the problem in explicitly racial (rather than religious) terms. In the Dutch East Indies, for instance, mixed marriages between Christians and non-Christians had been barred since 1617. With the new Civil Code of 1848, these were recast to regulate marriage between "Europeans" and "natives," forcing a woman to adopt the legal status of her husband.[36]

At the same time, most colonial regimes were often reluctant to simply criminalize interracial sex, as the Nazis would do. As Lora Wildenthal has argued, there was a "tension between colonial racial hierarchy and masculine sexual prerogatives over African and Pacific Islander women."[37] This led to mixed systems of regulation, police harassment, social and cultural pressure, and administrative discrimination. As a consequence, "the older pattern of marriage, long-term cohabitation, public liaisons, and rape was replaced by the new system of prostitution, secret liaisons, and rape."[38] In other words, attempts to limit miscegenation by state policy did not "rule out sexual relationships with indigenous women, but it relegated them to more clandestine ones."[39] Recent research has revealed that much the same could be said of Nazi efforts to prohibit "mixed-race" sexual encounters in occupied Eastern Europe.[40]

Modes of colonial labor organization and discipline also changed considerably in the nineteenth century. The abolition of slavery over the course of the nineteenth century marked the most dramatic transformation in labor regimes. It did not, however, lead to a deracialization of colonial labor relations; if anything, it reinforced racial boundaries. As communities of free blacks emerged in the new world, even before emancipation, creole elites sought to buttress racial categories.[41] Indeed, it was not uncommon for freed blacks to be subject to more virulent racism than slaves since their formal (and sometimes largely nominal) legal emancipation seemed to threaten European and white supremacy. Once slave status was no longer available as a marker of subordination, substitutes had to be found. Racial discrimination and violence were well suited to this task. One might think here of lynching and Ku Klux Klan terror in the American South.[42] Some of these practices of racial subordination were not state policies but rather cultural practices encouraged or at least tolerated by the state. Whether they would qualify as elements in a racial state could perhaps be debated, but it is worth recalling that they usually occurred in tandem with more official forms of racial discrimination and subordination. Moreover, if one moves from considering states to broader, social and political regimes, the distinction between official policy and customary practice becomes less consequential.

The abolition of slavery also led to the need to find alternate labor supplies, a process that reinscribed in a new vein formal legal inequality on racial lines. After the abolition of the slave trade, it quickly became apparent that replacement sources of labor would have to be found. In the British Caribbean, for example, the number of enslaved persons fell by 14 percent in the years between the abolition of the slave trade and the abolition of slavery itself. This decrease resulted from the gender imbalance in the slave population and, more fundamentally, from murderous working conditions on the sugar plantations that led to catastrophic mortality rates.[43] As a consequence, sugar production in the British Caribbean stagnated in the first decades of the nineteenth century.[44] Emancipation exacerbated these problems, since "staying clear of the hated plantation was a high priority for many persons liberated from a lifetime of forced labor."[45] Whenever possible, former slaves preferred subsistence agriculture to wage labor in the sugar-cane fields. As a result, "slave emancipation jolted the British colonial sugar industry, leading to a universal decline in sugar production."[46] If the industry was to recover and become profitable again, sugar planters needed to find an alternative source of labor. Given the preference for subsistence agriculture among former slaves, the presumption (never questioned at the time) was that higher wages would not attract workers back to the cane fields for long, but merely allow them to buy small individual plots of land sooner.[47]

In response, the colonial powers turned to indentured labor, overwhelmingly from East and especially South Asia. Although a small number of poor Europeans were recruited for indentured labor on the plantations of the British and French Caribbean, the overwhelming majority were Indians and Chinese. Of the 529,404 indentured migrants to the British Caribbean between 1831 and 1920, just under 41,000 were Europeans (all recruited in the 1840s and 1850s). In the French Caribbean, the number of Europeans numbered only 1,000 out of 100,798 indentured migrants.[48] These figures point to the distinctly racial quality to indentured labor in the nineteenth century. As the British counsel in Paramaribo noted in 1884, "the Surinam planters ... found in the meek Hindu a ready substitution for the negro slave he had lost."[49] While the labor conditions for indentured workers varied substantially, they were frequently almost as harsh as those of their slave predecessors, and any violation of their terms of indenture was treated as a criminal, not a civil, infraction. As a system of effectively unfree labor, the indentured labor system of the nineteenth century showed its roots in the slave trade.

Indeed, in some cases, the parallels with slavery were even more precise. Indentured laborers destined for the French island colony of Réunion in the 1850s were in fact purchased from African slave traders, "manumitted," made to sign indenture contracts, and then loaded onto ships for the island. The Réunionese claimed that in doing this, they were "liberators, we who come to save niggers from sacrifice and death, we, who bring them to our plantations after having freed them."[50] The ideological underpinnings of slavery – that blacks were "natural" slaves, that only coercion could effectively motivate them to work, that whites could and should benefit from the coerced labor of racial inferiors – here revealed themselves to have survived emancipation largely intact.

If European colonies thus show distinct characteristics of having turned race into a category of social practice and government policy, there are two other examples that reveal even more striking parallels with the Nazi racializing regime. These are the Jim Crow South and apartheid-era South Africa. As soon as the Civil War ended, white Southerners had deployed terror and economic pressure to try to reconstitute a racial hierarchy based on white privilege, a project that gained steam after the Democrats regained control of the South in the late 1870s. In the ensuing decades (and accelerating toward the end of the nineteenth century), white Southerners created a comprehensive system of formal and informal racial domination, known simply as "Jim Crow," so called after the well-known minstrel character.

Jim Crow was, as historians have recently noted, a "precarious balancing act, pulled in all directions by class, gender, and racial tensions." African Americans were not passive victims but active interlocutors of Jim Crow throughout its existence. Nevertheless, as these same historians insisted, it was "not the logical or inevitable culmination of the civil war and emancipation, but rather the result of a calculated campaign by white elites to circumscribe all possibility of African American political, economic, and social power."[51] As such, for all that Jim Crow was contested and varied regionally across the South, it is fair to speak of it as a "system," albeit an evolving one that developed gradually in the later part of the nineteenth century.[52]

The Jim Crow system had several major elements. The first and most obvious was a comprehensive structure of racial segregation. Public transportation, public facilities and spaces, lodgings, most private businesses, and virtually any possible space or social context in which whites might come into contact with African Americans were segregated into separate black and white areas. The most consequential area of segregation was in schooling, where racially segregated schools produced radically differential outcomes, with black students taught only remedial skills aimed to qualify them solely for menial labor. Based on formal legislation at both the state and local levels, segregation laws "constituted the most elaborate and formal expression of sovereign white opinion," as C. Vann Woodward put it in his classic study.[53]

The oddity of Jim Crow as a racial system is that, unlike the Nazi racial regime, it was based on a fiction of formal equality.[54] The Fourteenth Amendment to the US Constitution had made any man born in the US, including former slaves (although excluding certain Indians), a citizen and declared that all citizens should have "equal protection of the laws." Consequently, any system of overt racial discrimination would seem to be unconstitutional. This had been the intent of the amendment in the first place.[55] Yet, in a series of crucial decisions, mainly in the 1880s and 1890s, the United States Supreme Court upheld segregation and the disenfranchisement of blacks, sweeping away the last vestiges of Reconstruction-era civil rights.[56] The most important of these were the

1883 Civil Rights Cases (190 US 3), which held that Congress did not have the authority to enforce the provisions of the Fourteenth Amendment against private individuals or groups, and a series of rulings in the 1890s (*Louisville, New Orleans, and Texas Railroad* v. *Mississippi, Plessy* v. *Ferguson,* and *Williams* v. *Mississippi*) that upheld formal legal segregation. Already in 1875, in *Minor* v. *Happersett* (88 US 162), the Supreme Court had separated voting from citizenship with respect to women, which paved the way for the subsequent bevy of pro-segregation rulings that disaggregated civil rights from citizenship status. To circumvent the equal protection provisions of the Fourteenth Amendment, the Supreme Court declared that legally distinguishing races, which it held were already differentiated by nature in any case, did nothing to affect their (purported) legal equality:

A statute which implies merely a legal distinction between the white and colored races – a distinction which is founded in the color of the two races and which must always exist so long as white men are distinguished from the other race by color – has no tendency to destroy the legal equality of the two races, or reestablish a state of involuntary servitude.[57]

"Distinctions based on physical differences" derived from "racial instincts" were held not to violate the civil equality of individuals. The Supreme Court thus paved the way for a comprehensive system of state-enacted racial segregation and white supremacy.

In the political realm, the Jim Crow South was also somewhat different from the Third Reich in that the Southern states were formal democracies with nominally multiparty elections, the fact of Democratic Party dominance notwithstanding. Given the large numbers of African Americans resident in the Southern states, the only way to successfully achieve and maintain white domination was to systematically disenfranchise black voters. This was accomplished through a number of measures: the poll tax, the literacy test, and the white primary. Poll taxes imposed financial burdens for voting that most blacks could not meet. Literacy tests precluded yet more African Americans from voting, given the segregated school systems. And because primaries were organized by political parties and not by the state as such, federal law was held not to apply to them. Blacks could therefore be prohibited from voting in primaries without this violating the Fourteenth Amendment. Given that after 1877 most Southern states were effectively under one-party rule, this was a particularly effective strategy for disenfranchisement.[58] Many of these legal measures were cleverly designed to appear race-neutral, yet their point was overtly and explicitly racial domination. As James K. Vardaman, one of the most zealous of the first-generation segregationists, declared, "There is no use to equivocate or lie about the matter. Mississippi's constitutional convention [enacting literacy requirements] was held for no other purpose than to eliminate the nigger from politics; not the ignorant – but the nigger."[59]

As with segregation, the US Supreme Court legalized these discriminatory measures, holding in *Williams* v. *Mississippi* (1898) that since literacy tests do not, "on their face, discriminate between the white and negro races" they did not violate the Equal Protection Clause.[60] Of course, because the point of these measures of disenfranchisement was racial domination, they all contained "loopholes ... through which only white men could squeeze" in order to accommodate poor or illiterate whites.[61] This fact was held by the Supreme Court to show not "that their actual administration was evil, but only that evil was possible under them" and thus did not affect their constitutionality.[62] With the Supreme Court's approval, the disenfranchisement of blacks under the nominally democratic political system of the Southern states was nearly total.[63]

This system of comprehensive legal segregation and disenfranchisement was complemented by less formal mechanisms of racial domination. Racially discriminatory enforcement of criminal law, combined with a system for leasing prisoner labor, created a de facto system of forced labor throughout much of the South.[64] At its peak, as many as 30,000 African Americans a year were working in hard-labor prison-lease camps, some 25 percent of whom were children.[65] More fundamentally, the entire system of Jim Crow was sustained by the widespread deployment of terror and violence. Throughout the 1890s and early 1900s, more than 100 African American men and women were lynched each year.[66] More significant than the number of blacks killed was the extreme, highly ritualized violence that accompanied these murders, often widely publicized.[67] Though not officially authorized by the state, the racial violence of the Jim Crow South was de facto state-sanctioned. It was universally tolerated and frequently perpetrated by members of local law enforcement.

As in the Jim Crow South, racial policy in South Africa developed over time into a comprehensive system of racial rule. Even before the institution of a full regime of apartheid, South Africa was marked by strong policies of segregation.[68] The purpose of this system was to deprive Africans of land and alternative sources of livelihood, thus drawing them into the broader economy as cheap labor, while simultaneously protecting white privilege.[69] The Mines and Work Act (1911), the Natives Labour

Regulation Act (1911), the Natives' Land Act (1913), and the Industrial Conciliation Act (1924) formed the cornerstone of this segregation regime. Together, these laws relegated Africans to menial labor, deprived them of land, regulated their access to employment and urban areas, and prohibited them from labor organizing. Politically, the separation and disenfranchisement of Africans began before apartheid as well. The Native Administration Act (1927) placed the Department of Native Affairs in charge of all policies regarding Africans. "Under this Act, the government ruled by decree rather than law in the African rural areas."[70] Voter rolls were purged of most eligible Africans in the 1930s.

This same desire to separate and exclude Africans while simultaneously exploiting their labor governed the dynamics of apartheid as well. In this respect, apartheid merely radicalized trends already apparent in the system of segregation. As with Jim Crow, the system of apartheid that developed starting in the late 1940s sought to encompass virtually all aspects of African life, thus creating a "more rigid and thorough-going system of racial domination than had existed to date."[71] The ultimate goal was a territorial solution that, in principle, would separate whites from Africans entirely and eventually repatriate Asians. Such an approach, of course, was utterly impracticable not only because whites represented a very small and decreasing minority of the South African population in the postwar period but also, as importantly, because without African labor, the South African economy would have collapsed. Thus Hendrik F. Verwoerd, the architect of "grand apartheid," argued in the mid-1950s that "total territorial segregation . . . is the ideal and in the process of achieving that – and it will take a long time – each generation should formulate its own attainable policy and state what it wants to do."[72] If territorial separation was the ultimate goal, internal segregation, disenfranchisement, and coercion were the interim policies upon which the South African government settled until the perpetually deferred day of total racial exclusion could arrive.

The "linchpin" of apartheid was regulated by the Population Registration Act (No. 30) of 1950 that required the registration of South Africans by race, as white, colored, or native/Bantu.[73] (Indians were later included in 1959 as "Asians.") Even prior to the institution of apartheid, African men had been required to carry passes in order to enter urban areas reserved for whites, which they had to do in order to secure employment. Under apartheid, this pass system was greatly extended (and included women for the first time) and centralized under the Native Laws Amendment Act (No. 54) and the Abolition of Passes and Co-Ordination of

Documents Act (No. 67).[74] Sexual relations between whites and Africans had already been criminalized in 1927, but in 1950 the prohibition was extended to prohibit sexual relations between whites and all non-whites. The final key element in the physical segregation of Africans was the Group Areas Act, which provided for the "comprehensive residential and business segregation of the different colour groups in every city, town and village."[75] The Bantu Education Act (No. 47) of 1953 created segregated and deliberately inferior schools for Africans. Finally, "coloured" people were disenfranchised in the 1950s; Africans had been already been largely disenfranchised with the creation of the Union in 1910 and by purges of the vote rolls in the 1930s. The upshot of all this racial legislation was that

every aspect of South African life was determined under law by race. From the most basic rights of citizenship to the most personal choices of association, life in South Africa was dictated by race laws. These laws not only aimed at separating whites and blacks, they also instituted the legal principles that whites should be treated more favorably than blacks, that separate facilities need not be equal, and that the state should exercise the power deemed necessary to deal with any opposition.[76]

In both the Jim Crow South and South Africa, then, we see fully developed and elaborated racial regimes in which principles of racial difference and hierarchy permeated every aspect of both social life and state policy. These racial regimes were no more successful than the Third Reich in seamlessly defining and consistently applying race as a political and legal category. Though both American and South African racism focused more strongly on phenotypic differences – skin color above all – than did the Nazis, this did little to solve the problem of defining racial others. The amount of "black blood" required to render an individual black and thus subject to discriminatory legislation was a source of never-ending debate. The conflict between fears over race-mixing and the desire to protect male sexual privilege persisted. (In New Orleans's notorious red-light district, Storyville, only white men were allowed to enter as customers, frequenting both white and black prostitutes. A smaller district was later established for black men, with only black prostitutes allowed.)[77] No racial state is entirely and only racial, the Third Reich no more than the segregated South, or South Africa, or European overseas colonies.

One of the key similarities among all these racializing regimes, including the Third Reich, was the stress on the unity of the white community that segregation and racial discrimination would foster, a kind of white "people's community" freed from internal divisions of class and politics by their shared racial identity. The Southern educator Thomas P. Bailey declared, "in fine, disfranchisement of the negroes has been concomitant with the growth of political and social solidarity among the whites."[78] South African Prime Minister J. G. Strijdom asserted:

If the European loses his colour sense, he cannot remain a white man ... On the basis of unity you cannot retain your sense of colour if there is no apartheid in the everyday social life, in the political sphere ... and if there is no residential separation ... South Africa can only remain a white country if we continue to see that the Europeans remain the dominant nation.[79]

This sense of race as a unifying force within the privileged community, fed by the exclusion and political suppression of the subordinated racial groups, appears to be a common feature of racial regimes.

Given these parallels, it should hardly be surprising that there were some elements of mutual admiration and reciprocal learning among the Jim Crow South, the Third Reich, and apartheid-era South Africa. Jim Crow laws were one of the few things the Nazis would admit to admiring about the United States.[80] If white Southerners were reluctant to return the favor, this had more to do with the anxieties provoked by Hitler's foreign policy and a hypocritical critique of Nazi racial "excesses" than it did with any fundamental disagreement over race.[81] More directly influential for the Nazis than Jim Crow segregation was the example of US continental expansion into the "open" territories of the West.[82] The lines of influence were also open and explicit in the case of South Africa, where South African Nazis had a significant impact on the development of Afrikaner nationalism. According to Patrick Furlong, each of the major elements of the apartheid system – racial purity laws, segregation laws, and measures for police repression – "in its own way reflected ... the years of involvement with Radical Right philosophy."[83]

Clearly, then, there are good reasons to think that the Third Reich was far from the only regime in world history to raise racism to the level of "dogma and practice." But how generalized is this phenomenon? It can be argued that the modern nation-state inclines strongly toward a racial character. This argument has been made most forcefully by David Theo Goldberg: "the *modern* state has always conceived of itself as racially configured. The modern state, in short, is nothing less than a racial state."[84] Goldberg's argument is complex, but consists of two key elements. The first is that the state, or rather the modern state, "founds itself not just on exclusions ... but on the internalization of exclusions."[85]

By this, he means simply that the state's capacity to include depends on its capacity to exclude; insiders depend on the definition of outsiders. "Exclusions accordingly become internal to the possibility of inclusions, the latter predicated upon the realization of the former."[86] Since inclusion is the criterion through which the state both fosters identity and distributes resources, the ineluctable linkage between inclusion and exclusions means, according to Goldberg, that all modern states must be exclusionary in some degree.

Second, this function of the state as a mechanism for inclusion and exclusion is mobilized specifically to deal with the challenge of heterogeneity in modernity. Goldberg's historical argument is that, beginning in the early modern period, increases in global mobility led to tremendous increases in the internal heterogeneity of states, exacerbated by colonial conquest as European powers in effect annexed heterogeneous spaces and peoples. States responded to this situation with a drive for homogeneity, with nationalism and liberalism both serving this function in different ways. "Heterogeneity may be read as a challenge or threat, opportunity or potential problem. For modernity generally, and in the nineteenth century in particular, heterogeneity was interpreted very much in the latter vein, taken to inject into the safety and stability of the known, predictable, and controllable worlds elements of the unknown, the unpredictable, the uncontrollable."[87] Race was the modern state's way of attempting to "know" and "control" the difference of heterogeneity, to rein it in and dominate it. The paradox is that racializing difference magnifies the danger it poses because "race," unlike other potential ways of defining difference, defines it as necessarily a threat. Race "reifies" and "renders real" the abstract threat posed by heterogeneity, gives it concrete form. This, according to Goldberg, is why racial states tend to be so repressive and extravagantly violent.[88]

Goldberg clearly overstates his case. There are multiple categories of difference besides race that modern states can deploy in their drive for homogeneity, gender being only the most obvious. Moreover, the homogenizing tendencies of states clearly vary across time and space. It may be true that no modern state is ever fully comfortable with the full range of heterogeneity among its constituent populations, but there are clearly more or less "open" and "closed" polities, whether one considers this in terms of citizenship regimes, cultural cosmopolitanism, intermarriage, or any number of other measures of plurality. Finally, Goldberg's analysis tends to needlessly homogenize and reify racial states in precisely those ways we seek to avoid in this volume.

Still, one need not go so far as Goldberg to see that racializing regimes are commonplace in the modern era. However, the widespread use of race as an organizing principle for modern states in no way obviates the fact of significant differences among racial regimes, which have varied in their degree of formality (from elaborate legal regimes to informal discrimination), the structure of the regime (from authoritarian to democratic), the rigidity of their racial categories (from unyielding to permeable), the ideological characterizations of race (scientific, cultural, historicist, or mostly some combination of all of these), and their levels of violence toward racial others (from police brutality, to lynching and pogroms, to genocide). Clearly, not all racializing regimes are the same. At the same time, it seems mistaken to claim that the Third Reich represented some unique outlier in its use of race as a social category. Race is among the salient categories of social classification in the modern era and the Third Reich needs to be understood as lying on a continuum of racializing regimes – none of them ever fully racial, but all of them using race alongside other conceptual categories to formulate policy.

To understand the full range of ways in which race has been deployed by modern states, it is important to specify some of the key policy differences between the Third Reich and other racializing regimes. Here, two aspects stand out. First, the Third Reich was more intense and extravagant in its violence. With the exception of certain settler-colonies, most of the other modern racializing regimes did not engage in full-fledged genocide. Second, the Nazis evinced a striking and unusual willingness to extend the logic of racism to those considered racially desirable and not just to racial inferiors, as both positive and negative eugenic measures were applied to so-called Aryans.

In neither the American South nor South Africa did racial violence, terrible as it often was, rise to the level of genocide. To be sure, in both cases, genocidal fantasies could sometimes be found among the more rabid white supremacists. For instance, a Georgia congressman declared, "the ultimate extermination of a race is inexpressibly sad, yet if its existence endangers the welfare of mankind, it is fitting that it should be swept away."[89] But no matter how much murderous violence they engaged in, neither the Jim Crow South nor South Africa sought the extermination of blacks. Indeed, in both cases, the dominant racist ideology was marked by a strong degree of delusional paternalism. South African Prime Minister Hendrik Verwoerd justified the creation of African tribal homelands by promising that they constituted the "key to the true progress of the Bantu community" and a way to avoid "a struggle for equality in a joint territory." The homelands would serve as the "spring-board from which the Bantu in a natural way, by enlisting the help of dynamic elements in it, can increasingly rise to a higher level of culture and self-government on a foundation suitable to his own inherent charac-ter."[90] Though still deeply racist and in no small measure hypocritical (given that the white minority constituting less than 20 percent of the population had laid claim to more than 80 percent of South Africa's land), this ideological justification for radical separation of the races was not a recipe for extermination.

If the paternalism of Southern and South African racism was one limiting factor in restraining the level of racial violence, the more signifi-cant factor was dependency on black labor. In both regimes, black workers formed the linchpin of the most crucial economic sectors: agri-culture and, in South Africa, mining. Indeed, it is one of the ironies of both Jim Crow and apartheid that, for all that the dominant white population wanted to be separated from their black compatriots, they could ill afford for Africans or African Americans to actually leave the area. Indeed, during the "Great Migration" of African Americans to Northern states in the 1910s and 1920s, Southern localities undertook numerous measures to try to prevent "their" blacks from leaving. These included legal regulations on Northern labor agents, ranging from pro-hibitively high licensing fees of up to $1,000 in Jacksonville, Florida, to criminal penalties, such as the $500 fine levied in Mississippi.[91] They also included less formal measures. Southern railroads refused to honor prepaid tickets issued by Northern railroads. Blacks were forcibly evicted from railroad stations to prevent them from boarding north-bound trains and "at Summit, Mississippi, local officials simply closed the railroad ticket office and had the trains pass through without stopping."[92] The same kinds of legal and quasi-legal harassment used to keep African Americans segregated and disenfranchised were thus deployed, with less success, to prevent them from leaving the South.

The situation, of course, was rather different in the major settler-colonies in the Americas and the Antipodes, where large-scale European immigration created enormous pressure to seize indigenous lands. This led to long-term campaigns of ethnic cleansing that not infrequently assumed genocidal dimensions.[93] Here there are clear parallels to Nazi genocidal policies in Eastern Europe, for example, *Generalplanost*, which envisioned a substantial depopulation of what Timothy Snyder has termed Europe's "bloodlands" to make way for German settlement.[94] This differs, however, from the Holocaust, which, whatever its underlying logic, was not a land-grab.[95] Regardless of whether one privileges ideological or structural causes for the Holocaust, it differed from settler genocides in that, once the decision was taken to move from a territorial to a "final" solution, the mass murder of Jews was detached from the incorporation of territory.

If one major axis of difference between the Third Reich and other racializing regimes concerns the extent and nature of the racial violence they practiced, the other concerns their relations with their "racially desirable" citizens; in other words, the eugenic cultivation of "good blood." Obviously, eugenic thinking was in no way the unique preserve of the Nazis. Eugenic ideas enjoyed widespread acceptance throughout Europe, North America, and the antipodes in the early twentieth century.[96] They were, for instance, a major determinate of US immigration policy with the Restriction Act of 1924. Some thirty US states passed compulsory sterilization laws in the early twentieth century, with more than 60,000 individuals being sterilized between 1907 and 1963.[97] More generally, though, eugenics that focused on desirable populations, for instance healthy whites, remained the province mainly of civil society organizations, which promoted high birth rates, "better babies," and "fitter families."[98] Racialized cultural encouragement to propagate – for example, with the founding of Mother's Day in 1914 – was hardly of a piece with the "positive" eugenic measures undertaken by the Nazis, which included state-provided financial incentives alongside widespread propaganda.[99] And where other states did support such strong pronatalist policies, as did France in the interwar years, they were typically justified on security rather than eugenic grounds.[100] The Nazis were in this respect different, viewing Aryans as well as undesirables as major objects of bioracial manipulation by the state.

The policy difference between the Third Reich and other racializing regimes are to be found on either end of the spectrum – greater violence against racial undesirables, on the one hand, and greater eugenic intervention in the lives of racially desirable elements through racial hygiene and pro-natalist measures, on the other. One way to account for these manifest differences between the Third Reich and other overtly racist regimes is to deny their core similarities – to claim, as Burleigh and Wipperman did, that the Third Reich was the one and only racial state. As I have shown, this claim is untenable.

Rather, we must understand that the Third Reich was neither the only racial state, nor was it ever purely racial; it remained a racializing regime, not a racial state. Like all racial regimes, the Nazis sought to impose racial categories upon a heterogeneous social reality that resisted such easy categorization. Hence the perpetual need to supplement racial categories and policies with alternatives – religious, ethnic, or economic. Unlike other racializing regimes, however, the Nazis could not fall back on the illusory obviousness of physical differences to disguise this incompleteness. Nazi policy-makers sought to construct a racial regime without the aid of the color-line. Without recourse to phenotypic markers of difference, the inherently incomplete nature of race as a social category was more overtly manifest than in situations where it could be more easily disguised by visual markers. And herein lies the key to understanding the greater radicalism of the Nazi racializing project.

Constituting intra-European racism necessitated more extreme policies. The Nazis saw Jews as the most dangerous racial enemy because they were the least visible, neither readily identifiable by phenotype nor geographically fixed. The uncanny character of the Jews, according to Nazi ideology, as simultaneously sub-human and super-powered – their protean capacity to embody seemingly contradictory forces of evil, like finance capitalism and communism – is linked to their "invisibility."[101] The history of Jewish emancipation and assimilation was understood by the Nazis as a kind of collective passing for white and Aryan on the part of Jews, which was a major source of their threat. Unlike most racial others, the Jews evaded ready identification. Hitler famously claimed that his conversion to anti-Semitism began when he first encountered a "real," unassimilated Orthodox Jew who, unlike the assimilated Jews in the Linz of his childhood, looked noticeably foreign.[102] And in his historical account of the Jews, he asserted that the moment of emancipation marked a decisive change, for Jews, already pernicious in their influence, no longer acknowledged their foreignness as in previous eras:

> In the course of more than a thousand years he [the Jew] has learned the language of the host people to such an extent that he can venture in future to emphasize his Judaism less and place his "Germanism" more in the foreground; for ridiculous, nay, insane, as it may seem at first, he nevertheless has the effrontery to turn "Germanic," in this case a "German." With this begins one of the most infamous deceptions that anyone could conceive of.[103]

As a consequence of this "deception," more typical mechanisms for subordinating racial others – segregation and political repression – were deemed insufficient in the long run to address the threat of the hidden enemy. Since the Jews were similarly without a defined territory, established practices of ethnic cleansing – even genocidal ethnic cleansing – could not adequately combat such a geographically dispersed foe. Nor was

Jewish labor deemed indispensable (at least until late in the war, after the major period of extermination), and hence they were not shielded by the non-racial considerations that offered minimal protections to Africans and African Americans in South Africa and the American South. The Jewish threat derived from their parasitical, disguised intrusion into the heart of the German/Aryan people. This could not be fought by traditional means. Nazi racism was more radical because its target was different.

Notes

1 This is the downside of what Neil Gregor has termed the "voluntarist turn" in the historiography of the Third Reich. Neil Gregor, "Nazism – a political religion? Rethinking the voluntarist turn" in N. Gregor (ed.), *Nazism, War and Genocide: Essays in Honour of Jeremy Noakes* (Exeter, 2005).

2 Ian Kershaw, *Hitler, 1889–1936: Hubris* (New York, 1998), 529–31.

3 Richard Steigmann-Gall, *The Holy Reich: Nazi Conceptions of Christianity, 1919–1945* (Cambridge, 2003). For countervailing positions, see, for instance, Robert Cecil, *The Myth of the Master Race: Alfred Rosenberg and Nazi Ideology* (New York, 1972); Robert Poise, *National Socialism and the Religion of Nature* (New York, 1986); or, more recently, Karla Poewe, *New Religions and the Nazis* (New York, 2006). In this respect, the debate over just how Christian the Nazis were is a bit like the proverbial blind men and the elephant; the answer depends heavily on which aspect of the regime one examines. For the debate, see Doris Bergen, Manfred Gailus, Ernst Piper, and Irving Hexham, "Reviews of Steigmann-Gall, *The Holy Reich*," *The Journal of Contemporary History* 42 (January 2007), 35–78. Steigmann-Gall's response can be found as "Christianity and the Nazi movement: a response," *The Journal of Contemporary History* 42 (April 2007), 185–211.

4 The phrase comes from George M. Frederickson, *Racism: A Short History* (Princeton, 2003), 1. Other European states confronted analogous challenges regarding Jews as well, and adopted related – though less murderous – policies in response. See William W. Hagen, "Before the 'final solution': toward a comparative analysis of political anti-semitism in interwar Germany and Poland," *Journal of Modern History* 68 (1996), 351–81.

5 George W. Stocking Jr., *Race, Culture, and Evolution: Essays in the History of Anthropology* (Chicago, 1982); Larry Wolff and Marco Cipolloni (eds.), *The Anthropology of the Enlightenment* (Palo Alto, 2007).

6 George Mosse, *Toward the Final Solution: A History of European Racism* (New York, 1985).

7 The definitive debunking of race as a biological category began with Richard Lewontin's influential work in the 1970s. See, e.g., Lewontin, "The apportionment of human diversity," *Evolutionary Biology* 6 (1972), 391–98. The human genome project produced definitive evidence that "race" is meaningless as a biological category in the early 2000s. See Ian Tattersall and Rob DeSalle,

Race? Debunking a Scientific Myth (College Station, 2011) and Sheldon
Krimsky and Kathleen Sloan (eds.), *Race and the Genetic Revolution: Science, Myth, and Culture* (New York, 2011). Nicholas Wade has recently tried
to revive the idea that race is a meaningful biological category, an endeavor
which has been rejected by the very geneticists whose work he appropriates.
See Nicholas Wade, *A Troublesome Inheritance: Genes, Race and Human
History* (New York, 2014). For a repudiation of his work by many of the
scientists whom he cites, see the open letter at http://cehg.stanford.edu/letter-from-population-geneticists/.

8 Gerald Horn, *The Color of Fascism: Lawrence Dennis, Racial Passing, and
the Rise of Right-Wing Extremism in the United States* (New York, 2009);
James M. O'Toole, *Passing for White: Race, Religion, and the Healey Family,
1820–1920* (Amherst, 2003); Martha A. Sandweiss, *Passing Strange:
A Gilded Age Tale of Love and Deception across the Color Line* (New York,
2010). More generally, see Allyson Hobbs, *A Chosen Exile: A History of
Racial Passing in American Life* (Cambridge, MA, 2014).

9 Erica Faye Cooper, "One 'speck' of imperfection – invisible blackness and
the 'One-Drop Rule': an interdisciplinary approach to examining *Plessy* v.
Ferguson and *Jane Doe* v. *State of Louisiana*," Ph.D. thesis, Indiana University (2008).

10 John Darwin, *After Tamerlane: The Rise and Fall of Global Empires,
1400–2000* (London, 2009), 342–3.

11 Helmut Walser Smith, *The Butcher's Tale: Murder and Anti-Semitism in a
German Town* (New York, 2002).

12 This was less true in Austria, where overt anti-Semites such as Vienna Mayor
Karl Lueger were closer to the levers of power. See John W. Boyer, *Culture
and Political Crisis in Vienna: Christian Socialism in Power, 1897–1918*
(Chicago, 1998).

13 Peter Pulzer, *The Rise of Political Anti-Semitism in German and Austria*, rev.
edn. (Cambridge, MA, 1988 [1964]), xiv.

14 This is one of the main points made by two important studies: Peter Fritsche,
Germans into Nazis (Cambridge, MA, 1999), and Claudia Koonz, *The Nazi
Conscience* (Cambridge, MA, 2005).

15 Michael Burleigh and Wolfgang Wippermann, *The Racial State: Germany
1933–1945* (Cambridge, 1991), 306.

16 Ibid., 307.

17 Ibid., 23.

18 Ibid., 107.

19 On colonialism, see Jan Breman (ed.), *Imperial Monkey Business: Racial
Supremacy in Social Darwinist Theory and Colonial Practice* (Amsterdam,
1990). On South Africa, see Nancy L. Clark and William H. Worger, *South
Africa: The Rise and Fall of Apartheid*, 2nd edn. (London, 2011); Jens
Meierhenrich, *The Legacies of Law: Long-Run Consequences of Legal Development in South Africa* (Cambridge, 2010); Deborah Posel, *The Making of
Apartheid, 1948–1961: Conflict and Compromise* (Oxford, 1991); David
Welsh, *The Rise and Fall of Apartheid* (Charlottesville, 2009). For the Jim
Crow South, the classic remains C. Vann Woodward, *The Strange Career of*

Jim Crow (Oxford, 2001 [1955]). See also Jerrold M. Packard, *American Nightmare: The History of Jim Crow* (New York, 2003) and Richard Wormser, *The Rise and Fall of Jim Crow* (New York, 2003).

20 Charles W. Mills, *The Racial Contract* (Ithaca, 1997), 20.

21 W. E. B. Du Bois, *The Souls of Black Folk* (Oxford, 2007 [1903]), 8.

22 Marilyn Lake and Henry Reynolds, *Drawing the Global Colour Line: White Men's Countries and the International Challenge of Racial Equality* (Cambridge, 2008), 4.

23 Jane Samson, *Race and Empire* (London, 2005).

24 Shelley Baranowski, *Nazi Empire: German Colonialism and Imperialism from Bismarck to Hitler* (Cambridge, 2011); Wendy Lower, *Nazi Empire-Building and the Holocaust in the Ukraine* (Chapel Hill, 2007); Mark Mazower, *Hitler's Empire: How the Nazis Ruled Europe* (New York, 2008).

25 A. C. de C. M. Saunders, *A Social History of Black Slaves and Freedmen in Portugal, 1441–1555* (Cambridge, 1982), 37–8.

26 Peter Wade, *Race and Ethnicity in Latin America* (London, 1997), 29.

27 Ibid., 28.

28 Diego A. von Vacano, *The Color of Citizenship: Race, Modernity and Latin American/Hispanic Political Thought* (Oxford, 2012), 46.

29 Ibid., 51.

30 Seymour Drescher, *Abolition: A History of Slavery and Antislavery* (Cambridge, 2009), 11. Indeed, Drescher argues that Mediterranean slavery remained largely multiracial until well into the eighteenth century (36).

31 Robin Blackburn, *The Making of New World Slavery: From the Baroque to the Modern, 1492–1800*, 2nd edn. (London, 2010).

32 Robin Blackburn, "The old world background to European colonial slavery," *The William and Mary Quarterly* 54 (1997), 66.

33 Benjamin Braude, "The sons of Noah and the construction of ethnic and geographical identities in the medieval and early modern periods," *The William and Mary Quarterly* 45 (1997), 103–42.

34 See, e.g., Jennifer S. H. Brown, *Strangers in Blood: Fur Trade Company Families in Indian Country* (Vancouver, 1980).

35 Ann Stoler, "Sexual affronts and racial frontiers: European identities and the cultural politics of exclusion in colonial Southeast Asia," *Comparative Studies in Society and History* 34 (1992), 515.

36 Ibid., 540.

37 Lora Wildenthal, *German Women for Empire, 1884–1945* (Durham, 2001), 79.

38 Ibid., 105–6.

39 Samson, *Race and Empire*, 66.

40 Regina Mühlhäuser, *Eroberungen: Sexuelle Gewalttaten und intime Beziehungen deutscher soldaten in der Sowjetunion 1941–1945* (Hamburg, 2010).

41 Yvvan Debbasch, *Coleur et Liberté: Le Jeu de Critère ethnique dans un Ordre Juridique Esclavagiste* (Paris, 1967).

42 Michael J. Pfeifer, *Rough Justice: Lynching and American Society, 1874–1947* (Urbana, 2004); Allen W. Trelease, *White Terror: The Ku Klux Klan Conspiracy and Southern Reconstruction* (New York, 1971).

43 Vivid and disturbing descriptions can be found in Adam Hochschild, *Bury the Chains: Prophets and Rebels in the Fight to Free an Empire's Slaves* (New York, 2005).

44 David Northrup, *Indentured Labor in the Age of Imperialism, 1834–1922* (Cambridge, 1995), 18.

45 Ibid., 19.

46 M. D. North-Coombes, "From slavery to indenture: forced labour in the political economy of Mauritius 1834–1867" in Kay Saunders (ed.), *Indentured Labour in the British Empire 1834–1920* (London, 1984), 79.

47 Northrup, *Indentured Labor*, 21–2.

48 Ibid., 159.

49 Cited in P. C. Emmer, "The meek Hindu: the recruitment of Indian indentured labourers for service overseas, 1870–1916" in P. C. Emmer (ed.), *Colonialism and Migration: Indentured Labour before and after Slavery* (Dordrecht, 1986), 187.

50 Hubert Gerbeau, "Engagees and coolies on Réunion Island: slavery's masks and freedom's constraints" in Emmer (ed.), *Colonization and Migration*, 220.

51 Jane Daily, Glenda Elisabeth Gilmore, and Bryant Simon, "Introduction" in Daily, Gilmore, and Simon (eds.), *Jumpin' Jim Crow: Southern Politics from Civil War to Civil Rights* (Princeton, 2000), 3–6.

52 There is a significant debate concerning the degree of racial openness and fluidity in the immediate aftermath of the Civil War, and consequently, the degree to which Jim Crow marked a reimposition of racial hierarchies that had been seriously undermined by emancipation. C. Vann Woodward stressed the degree to which Jim Crow marked a transformation of the more open situation of reconstruction. See C. Vann Woodward, *The Strange Career of Jim Crow*, 3rd rev. edn. (New York, 1974). Howard Rabinowitz, on the other hand, argued that race relations in the South ossified very quickly after the war and that informal white supremacy was already in place well before formal Jim Crow laws. See Howard Rabinowitz, *Race Relations in the Urban South, 1865–1890* (Oxford, 1978). For an overview of the debate, see Michael J. Pfeifer, "Review of Woodward, C. Vann, *The Strange Career of Jim Crow: A Commemorative Edition*. H-South, H-Net Reviews. May, 2003": www.h-net.org/reviews/showrev.php?id=7561 (April 20, 2016).

53 Woodward, *Strange Career*, 7.

54 For attempts at broader comparisons between German and American racial history that extend well beyond the Third Reich/Jim Crow South, see the essays in Larry Eugene Jones, *Crossing Boundaries: The Exclusion and Inclusion of Minorities in Germany and America* (New York, 2001).

55 Garret Epps, *Democracy Reborn: The Fourteenth Amendment and the Fight for Equal Rights in Post-Civil War America* (New York, 2007).

56 For an overview, see Lawrence Goldstone, *Inherently Unequal: The Betrayal of Equal Rights by the Supreme Court, 1865–1903* (New York, 2011).

57 *Plessy* v. *Ferguson* 163 U.S. 552 (1896).

58 This is not to deny that in some regions, African Americans continued to vote and shape Southern politics until the end of the nineteenth century before their final disenfranchisement around 1900. See J. Morgan Kousser, *The Shaping of*

Southern Politics: Suffrage Restriction and the Establishment of the One-Party South, 1880–1910 (New Haven, 1974).

59 Cited in Richard Wormser, *The Rise and Fall of Jim Crow* (New York, 2003), 70.

60 *Williams* v. *Mississippi* 170 U.S. 214 (1898).

61 Woodward, *Strange Career*, 84.

62 *Williams* v. *Mississippi* 170 U.S. 214 (1898).

63 In Louisiana, for instance, between 1896 and 1904 the number of registered African American voters decreased from 130,334 to 1,342. Woodward, *Strange Career*, 85.

64 David M. Oshinsky, *Worse than Slavery: Parchman Farm and the Ordeal of Jim Crow Justice* (New York, 1997).

65 Wormser, *Rise and Fall of Jim Crow*, 57.

66 Ibid., 74.

67 Amy Louise Wood, *Lynching and Spectacle: Witnessing Racial Violence in America, 1890–1940* (Chapel Hill, 2011).

68 Bernard Magubane, *The Making of a Racist State: British Imperialism and the Union of South Africa 1875–1910* (Trenton, 1996).

69 Harold Wolpe, "Capitalism and cheap labour power in South Africa: from segregation to apartheid" in William Beinart and Saul Dubow (eds.), *Segregation and Apartheid in Twentieth Century South Africa* (London, 1995), 60–90.

70 Nancy L. Clark and William H. Worger, *South Africa: The Rise and Fall of Apartheid*, 2nd edn. (Harlow, 2011), 23.

71 Posel, *The Making of Apartheid*, 1.

72 Cited in ibid., 68.

73 Welsh, *The Rise and Fall of Apartheid*, 54.

74 Clark and Worger, *South Africa*, 49.

75 Welsh, *The Rise and Fall of Apartheid*, 55.

76 Clark and Worger, *South Africa*, 48.

77 Melissa Hope Ditmore (ed.), *Encyclopedia of Prostitution and Sex Work*, vol. 1 (Westport, 2006), 329.

78 Woodward, *Strange Career*, 92.

79 Cited in Hermann Giliomee, "The growth of Afrikaner identity" in Beinart and Dubow, *Segregation and Apartheid*, 189–205, here 201.

80 Johnpeter Horst Grill and Robert L. Jenkins, "The Nazis and the American South in the 1930s: a mirror image?" *Journal of Southern History* 58 (1992), 667–94.

81 "It is remarkable how often editorials in southern papers attacked German racism and prejudice while defending white supremacy and segregation in the South." Ibid., 688.

82 Carroll P. Kakel, III, *The American West and the Nazi East: A Comparative and Interpretive Perspective* (Houndsmills, 2011); Alan E. Steinweis, "Eastern Europe and the notion of the 'frontier' in Germany to 1945," *Yearbook of European Studies*, 13 (1999), 56–90.

83 Patrick J. Furlong, *Between Crown and Swastika: The Impact of the Radical Right on the Afrikaner Nationalist Movement in the Fascist Era* (Hanover, 1991).

84 David Theo Goldberg, *The Racial State* (London, 2002), 2.

85 Ibid., 9.

86 Ibid., 9–10.

87 Ibid., 23.

88 Ibid., 131–2.

89 Wormer, *Rise and Fall of Jim Crow*, 77.

90 Welsh, *The Rise and Fall of Apartheid*, 63.

91 James R. Grossman, *Land of Hope: Chicago, Black Southerners, and the Great Migration* (Chicago, 1989), 46.

92 Ibid., 48.

93 For global perspectives, see A. Dirk Moses (ed.), *Empire, Colony, Genocide: Conquest, Occupation, and Subaltern Resistance in World History* (New York, 2009) and A. Dirk Moses and Dan Stone (eds.), *Colonialism and Genocide* (London, 2006). On North American instances where violence, rather than disease, was unambiguously the major culprit in the destruction of native communities, see John Grenier, *The First Way of War: American War Making on the Frontier, 1607–1814* (New York, 2008) and Brendan C. Lindsay, *Murder State: California's Native American Genocide, 1846–1873* (Lincoln, 2012). For an argument that most of the mistreatment of Native Americans should be considered ethnic cleansing, not genocide, see Gary Clayton Anderson, *Ethnic Cleansing and the Indians: The Crime That Should Haunt America* (Norman, 2014). For the contrary argument, see most recently Alexander Laban Hinton, Andrew Woolford, and Jeff Benvenuto (eds.), *Colonial Genocide in Indigenous North America* (Durham, 2014). A nuanced compromise can be found in Alex Alvarez, *Native America and the Question of Genocide* (Lanham, 2014).

94 Timothy Snyder, *Bloodlands: Europe between Hitler and Stalin* (New York, 2010). For an example of the genocidal dimensions of the German occupation policy, see Christian Gehrlach, *Kalkulierte Mord. Die Deutsche Wirtschafts- und Vernichtungspolitik in Weißrußland, 1941–1944* (Hamburg, 2008). On *Generalplan Ost*, see Mechtild Rössler and Sabine Schleiermacher (eds.), *Der "Generalplan Ost." Hauptlinien der nationalsozialistischen Plannungs- und Vernichtungspolitik* (Berlin, 1993).

95 This is not necessarily to embrace a "uniqueness" interpretation, just to point to areas of difference alongside elements of similarity. For the uniqueness debate, see Ron S. Rosenbaum, *Is the Holocaust Unique? Perspectives on Comparative Genocide*, 3rd edn. (Boulder, 2008). For perhaps the most sophisticated attempt to resolve this problem, see A. Dirk Moses, "Conceptual blockages and definitional dilemmas in the 'Racial Century': genocides of indigenous peoples and the Holocaust," *Patterns of Prejudice*, 36(4) (2002), 7–36.

96 For a broad overview, see Alison Bashford and Phillipa Levine (eds.), *The Oxford Handbook of the History of Eugenics* (Oxford, 2012).

97 Alexandra Minna Stern, "From legislation to lived experience: eugenic sterilization in California and Indiana, 1907–79" in Paul Lombardo (ed.), *A Century of Eugenics in America: From the Indiana Experiment to the Human Genome Era* (Bloomington, 2011), 96.

98 Steven Selden, "Transforming better babies into fitter families: archival resources and the history of the American eugenics movement, 1908–1930," *Proceedings of the American Philosophical Society*, 149(2) (2005), 199–225.

99 Claudia Koonz, *Mothers in the Fatherland: Women, the Family, and Nazi Politics* (New York, 1988).

100 Mary Louise Roberts, *Civilization Without Sexes: Reconstructing Gender in Postwar France, 1917–1927* (Chicago, 1994), 98–119.

101 Jeffrey Herf, *The Jewish Enemy: Nazi Propaganda during World War II and the Holocaust* (Cambridge, MA, 2008).

102 Adolf Hitler, *Mein Kampf*, trans. Ralph Manheim (Boston, 1943), 56.

103 Ibid., 312.

PART II

RACE, SCIENCE, AND NAZI BIOPOLITICS

5

Eugenics, Racial Science, and Nazi Biopolitics

*Was There a Genesis of the "Final Solution"
from the Spirit of Science?*

Richard F. Wetzell

Most historical research of the past twenty-five years on the history of eugenics and racial science under the Nazi regime has followed the interpretive paradigms laid out in Burleigh and Wippermann's *The Racial State* (1991) and Detlev Peukert's article "The genesis of the 'Final Solution' from the spirit of science" (1989) by demonstrating the pervasive complicity of German medical doctors (especially psychiatrists), human geneticists, and anthropologists in Nazi biopolitics.[1] The term "biopolitics" will be used here in its broad sense: to refer to the complex of ideas, policies, and practices that are concerned with the regulation of bodies, both at the individual level and at the collective level of the national population; a complex that, in the case of the Nazi regime, ranged from public health to eugenic and racial policy, including the Holocaust.[2]

The historical evidence of the complicity of German physicians and biomedical scientists in Nazi eugenic and racial policy is overwhelming. Prominent academics advised the Nazi government on eugenic policy; Ernst Rüdin, for instance, who headed Germany's most prestigious institute of psychiatric research, participated in drafting the 1933 Nazi sterilization law. Most medical doctors were willing to report patients to the authorities for compulsory sterilization, and hundreds of medical doctors as well as leading academics in psychiatry and anthropology served as medical judges on the Hereditary Health Courts, which ordered compulsory sterilizations.[3] Leading anthropologists, including Eugen Fischer and Otmar von Verschuer, supplied *Rassegutachten* (racial expert opinions) to the Nazi authorities.[4] Several key Kaiser Wilhelm institutes, including Fischer's Kaiser Wilhelm Institute (KWI) for Anthropology, Human Genetics and Eugenics, trained SS officers in "racial science."[5] Some academic anthropologists, such as Otto Reche, participated in implementing racial policy in the Eastern territories occupied during the war.[6] The racial classification of "Gypsies" conducted by the *Zigeunerforscher* Robert Ritter was closely connected to the deportation of Sinti and Roma to concentration camps.[7] Psychiatrists working in mental hospitals participated in the "euthanasia" murders of handicapped and mentally ill patients.[8] Medical doctors closely associated with leading research institutes, such as Josef Mengele, performed inhuman medical experiments on concentration camp inmates, and a number of researchers at these institutes used "human material" obtained from murdered concentration camp inmates.[9]

All this evidence of widespread complicity has definitively refuted the apologetic accounts of science and medicine under the Nazi regime that dominated the West German public sphere until they were challenged in the 1980s. Today no serious student of the subject can deny that a large number of Germany's physicians and biomedical scientists – including leading academics in the related fields of anthropology, eugenics, human genetics, and *Rassenforschung* (racial science) – were complicit in the eugenic and racial policies of the Nazi regime that culminated in the Holocaust. While the issue of complicity has been definitively settled, this essay proposes that several other questions about the relationship between the biosciences and the Nazi regime are still worth asking. The first thing to note here is that Burleigh and Wippermann went well beyond the mere claim of complicity by asserting that medical doctors, racial anthropologists, and other bioscientists "created the conceptual framework and scientific legitimization for the implementation of Nazi racial policy." Detlev Peukert advanced an even more ambitious thesis by arguing that the "Final Solution" resulted from a "fatal racist dynamic in the human sciences."[10] As this essay will argue, even though research since the 1980s has provided incontrovertible evidence of widespread complicity, the implications of this research for a series of further questions about the relationship between the biosciences and Nazism – including the question whether racial science did indeed provide a "conceptual framework" that the Nazi regime translated into racial policy – are more complex and worth closer examination.

Burleigh and Wippermann's claim that German bioscientists created the conceptual framework for Nazi racial policy rests on their understanding of racial science under the Nazis as a cohesive field of science. In reality, the broad field that came to be known as racial science – including eugenics, human genetics, and physical anthropology – was characterized by several competing conceptual frameworks, just as there were competing visions of Nazi racial policy. Even though much of the research on science under the Nazi regime has focused on demonstrating the complicity of particular scientists and institutions, its detailed examinations of scientific research and practice have also revealed the complexity, incoherence, and diversity of the scientific fields that came to be known as racial science during the Nazi era. In fact, competing conceptions of race and human heredity resulted in a remarkable number of conflicts and controversies. To demonstrate just how contested the terrain of eugenics and racial science was, this essay will begin with a discussion of three such conflicts. In the essay's second half, we will turn to a series of broader questions about the relationship between racial science and Nazi biopolitics: whether racial science under the Nazis should be characterized as science or pseudoscience; how the fields of science and politics interacted in a polycratic regime; to what extent one can support the claim that Nazi racial policy and the Holocaust resulted from a "fatal racist dynamic in the human sciences"; and whether racial science became radicalized under the Nazi regime.

CONFLICTS OVER STERILIZATION POLICY

Sterilization policy, a key arena of Nazi biopolitics, was far more contested than the racial state paradigm has suggested. The two key players in Nazi sterilization policy were Arthur Gütt, the Nazi-appointed chief of the Division of Public Health (Abteilung Volksgesundheit) at the Interior Ministry, who was the driving force behind the drafting of the sterilization law of July 1933, and Ernst Rüdin, director of the renowned Deutsche Forschungsanstalt für Psychiatrie (German Research Institute for Psychiatry) in Munich, who closely advised Gütt during the drafting of the law and thereafter as a member of the Ministry's Expert Advisory Council on Population and Racial Policy (Sachverständigenbeirat für Bevölkerungs- und Rassenpolitik).[11] Together with the lawyer Falk Ruttke, Gütt and Rüdin co-authored the influential semi-official commentary on the law, which advocated an aggressive interpretation of the law in order to sterilize a maximum of people.[12] This attempt to implement a maximalist sterilization program came under attack from two different directions. On the one hand, the Gütt-Rüdin-Ruttke commentary was criticized for expanding the definition of congenital feeblemindedness (*angeborener Schwachsinn*), on which the majority of sterilizations were based, beyond what was scientifically warranted. In German psychiatric

terminology of the era, "feeblemindedness" referred to intelligence
defects, whereas defects in the realm of emotion, will, or character fell
under the diagnosis of *Psychopathie* (psychopathy), which was not
among the diagnoses listed in the sterilization law.[13] Ignoring this well-
established diagnostic distinction, Gütt and Rüdin's commentary
expanded the law's target group by broadening the definition of feeblemindedness to include persons who suffered from "disturbances in emotions, will, drives, or ethical sentiments" even if their intelligence was not
significantly impaired.[14] This expansion of the diagnosis of feeblemindedness was criticized in a number of published articles by psychiatrists
and jurists.[15] More importantly, a number of sterilization court decisions
that were based on this expanded definition were reversed by the Superior
Hereditary Health Courts in some districts. Thus in 1935 the Superior
Hereditary Health Court of Kiel ruled that a recidivist criminal with
fourteen previous convictions should not be sterilized because the term
feeblemindedness only referred to intelligence defects, whereas psychopaths had been "intentionally left out of the sterilization law."[16] In short,
the attempt by eugenic hardliners such as Gütt and Rüdin to target
so-called asocials and criminals for sterilization on the basis of supposed
defects in will, character, or "ethical sentiments" met with resistance from
psychiatrists and hereditary health courts who insisted on a narrow
interpretation of the law.

On the other hand, the aggressive sterilization policy promoted by Gütt
and Rüdin was also criticized by Reichsärzteführer (Reich Leader of
German Doctors) Gerhard Wagner, who framed his criticism in a completely different way. For Wagner, the errors of sterilization policy were
due not to eugenic hardliners *straying* from science, but rather to the
extremist influence of *volksfremde Wissenschaft* (science that has been
alienated from the people). In 1936, Wagner, who headed the Nazi
Doctor's League and the Nazi Party's Public Health Department (Haupt-
dienstleiter für Volksgesundheit in der Reichsleitung der NSDAP),
launched a frontal assault on Gütt and Rüdin and their nefarious influence on sterilization policy. Apparently reacting to complaints from party
members and others who (or whose relatives) had been targeted for
sterilization, Wagner delivered a speech in October 1936 at the annual
meeting of the Westphalian Doctor's Association (Westfälischer Ärzte-
tag), in which he criticized the sterilization courts' schematic use of intelligence tests for diagnoses of feeblemindedness. To guard against such
abuses, he demanded that representatives of the Nazi Party be included
on the sterilization courts. This speech was only the first public salvo in

a sustained campaign to rein in the sterilization policies pursued by the Ministry of the Interior under Gütt's leadership. In 1937, Wagner elaborated his complaints in a *Denkschrift,* presented to Hitler, in which he attacked Gütt as a "health bureaucrat who has gone off the rails" (*verwaltungsmedizinischer Schwärmer*) and Rüdin as an "eugenics fanatic," and accused them of turning sterilization policy into a "playground for ... a science removed from reality and from the people" (*Tummelplatz ... wirklichkeits- und letztlich volksfremder Wissenschaft*).[17] In a 1938 letter to Himmler, Wagner warned that "the handling of the sterilization law and the constant search for any kind of supposed biological defect [*Minderwertigkeitsschnüffelei*] on the part of our eugenicists [*Rassenhygieniker*] runs the risk of destroying the public's trust in our entire population policy."[18] Wagner's campaign, which lasted until his death (and Gütt's retirement) in 1939, led to a series of high-level meetings all the way up to Hitler and the Chancellor's Office (Reichskanzlei). Although Wagner did not succeed in getting Nazi Party representatives included in the sterilization courts, there is evidence that his complaints did not go unheeded and that by 1937 there was some pressure on sterilization courts to be more careful in making diagnoses of feeblemindedness.[19] As these two sets of attacks on sterilization policy demonstrate, both German eugenics as a scientific field and Nazi eugenic policy were far more contested than has often been assumed.

THE FISCHER CONTROVERSY

If key areas in eugenics remained subject to discussion and disagreement, the same was true to an even greater extent of the field of German physical anthropology, which also became known as *Rassenforschung* (racial science) during the Nazi period. German physical anthropology had long been characterized by a diversity of approaches to the concept of race. At the outset of the Nazi regime, these approaches ranged from the Nordic racial theories of Hans F. K. Günther, whose *Rassenkunde des deutschen Volkes* (Racial guide to the German people) had been published in 1922 and quickly became influential in *völkisch* circles,[20] to the dynamic conceptions of race propounded by Karl Saller and Friedrich Merkenschlager, who argued that races were malleable and subject to constant transformation.[21] Ironically, the first anthropologist who got into trouble with Nazi authorities was a scholar who occupied a moderate position in the middle of this spectrum of racial theories: Eugen Fischer, professor of anthropology at the University of Berlin and founding

director, since 1927, of Germany's most important anthropological institute, the Kaiser-Wilhelm-Institut für Anthropologie, menschliche Erblehre
und Eugenik (KWI for Anthropology, Human Genetics, and Eugenics) in
Berlin-Dahlem. Although, like Günther, Fischer subscribed to a static
conception of race, he did not define races by physical or psychological
characteristics, but by their genetic traits.[22] At the beginning of the Nazi
regime, Fischer and Rüdin were the two most powerful academics in
the field of eugenics and racial anthropology. Whereas Rüdin's radical
eugenic agenda was almost perfectly aligned with that of the key Nazi
official in charge of eugenic policy (Gütt), Fischer's case was more complicated, for two reasons. First, although Fischer was politically conservative
and had on occasion signaled his agreement with Nordicist racial theories, as the head of a publicly funded research institute he had generally
kept a studied distance from such theories during the later Weimar years
in order to position his institute as engaged in value-free theoretical
science. Second, Fischer's views on racial mixing were more complex
and nuanced than those of the Nazis – a difference of opinion that was
to cause conflict in the very first days of the Nazi regime.

Two days after Hitler's seizure of power, on February 1, 1933, Fischer
delivered a long-scheduled public lecture on "Racial Mixing and Mental
Aptitude" (*Rassenkreuzung und geistige Leistung*), in which he argued
that the mixing of races (*Kreuzung*) generally had a beneficial effect on
offspring; high cultures were usually the product of a mixing of races, not
of their purity. The flowering of culture in Central Europe from the
Renaissance on, he explained, took place in a *Mischzone* (mixing zone)
in which the Nordic race had mixed with the Alpine and Dinaric races.
Fischer also explicitly addressed the question of race-mixing between the
Nordic races and Jews. Making a biological distinction between long-
resident German-Jewish families and recently arrived *Ostjuden,* he argued
that the mixing of Nordic races with the former was unproblematic, while
mixing with the *Ostjuden* was not. Since Fischer made this argument in a
public lecture attended by journalists two days after Hitler had come to
power, we may assume that he fully intended his comments to have a
political effect, namely, to advise the Hitler government to take a moderate line in discriminating against Jews.[23]

Because the lecture was widely reported in the press, Fischer did not
have to wait long for reactions; he soon found out that he had transgressed the limits of acceptable discourse on racial policy under the Nazi
regime. In fact, he found himself the target of a sustained campaign of
denunciation, lasting well into 1934, that was orchestrated by Richard

Walther Darré, chief of the SS Office of Race and Settlement (SS Rasse- and Siedlungsamt, later Hauptamt), Reich Minister of Food and Agriculture (after June 1933), and one of the major proponents of Nordic racial theory. Several of Darré's associates, including the racial anthropologist Bruno Kurt Schultz, editor of the journal *Volk und Rasse*, and the maverick physician Lothar Tirala, who succeeded Fritz Lenz as professor of racial hygiene at the University of Munich in 1933, mounted a series of public attacks that posed a serious threat to Fischer's career. Fischer was vigorously defended, however, by Arthur Gütt at the Ministry of Interior, who argued in a letter to Darré that Fischer's international academic reputation in racial anthropology made him indispensable for the regime: "A dispute between [Fischer] and official authorities would easily create the impression in Germany and abroad that Professor Fischer disapproves of the path that the government has taken in racial policy and that the government's measures contradict the findings of science."[24]

No doubt in response to pressure from Gütt, Fischer decided to adjust his views in a way that the historian Hans-Walter Schmuhl has described as a "dirty trick": Although Fischer refused to label the Jewish race as inferior, he described the Jews as an *andersartige Rasse* (a race different in kind) that had to be excluded from race-mixing with Nordic races. Although it took a while for the campaign against Fischer to subside, this concession, together with Fischer's willingness to purge his institute of the Catholic eugenicist Hermann Muckermann and to offer ten-month training courses at the institute for SS doctors selected by Darré's Race and Settlement Office, allowed Fischer to retain control of the Dahlem institute and become "the undisputed academic spokesman for racial science under the swastika." By contrast, his adversary Lothar Tirala, who saw himself as a guardian of true National Socialist ideology, was removed from his university professorship for incompetence in 1936.[25]

In contrast to Rüdin, Fischer cannot be described as a racial scientist who was glad that the new political regime would finally allow him to translate his scientific ideas into official policy. His initial clash with the regime led to a negotiation in which, in Mitchell Ash's terms, science and politics were resources for one another.[26] In this negotiation, Fischer sought the support of the regime in order to finance his institute's research and to defend his own academic position of influence; conversely, Gütt at the Interior Ministry defended Fischer so that the internationally renowned anthropologist would lend Nazi racial policies scientific respectability. Although Fischer found out that there were clear boundaries to acceptable discourse on race under the new regime, there was some room for him to negotiate a compromise position on race-mixing, precisely because academic and public discourse on race during the early years of the Nazi regime remained surprisingly diverse and the question of "official" racial theory remained unsettled. Although Fischer's case demonstrates the powerful reach of the Nazi regime into the realm of academic research as well as the willingness of key scientists to cave in to the regime's demands, it also shows that the claim that racial scientists created the conceptual framework for Nazi racial policy – a key element of what we might call the "racial state" paradigm – does not stand up to empirical scrutiny as a general characterization of racial scientists' relationship to the regime.

THE CONTROVERSY OVER THE NOTION OF A "GERMAN RACE"

A second, no less revealing controversy over racial theory during the early years of the Nazi regime concerned the notion of a "German race" put forward by the anthropologist Karl Saller and the botanical geneticist Friedrich Merkenschlager. According to Saller and Merkenschlager, races could not be defined as fixed types characterized by specific physiological, genetic, or psychological traits because races were malleable and in constant transformation. All one could say is that the average distribution of certain physical and mental characteristics differed from one race to another; but this was a matter of statistical distribution, not individual characteristics. Races, they insisted, were affected by both genetic and environmental factors and therefore never something absolute, but always "states of equilibrium" reflecting the influences of heredity and environment. Because races were malleable, Saller and Merkenschlager thought it made sense to speak of a "German race" that was in the process of being formed. In making the case for their notion of a German race, both engaged in sharp attacks against Günther's theory of Nordic superiority and his idea that one could *entmischen* (literally: unmix) the races – that is, gradually "undo" the racial mixtures in the German population and thereby bring about the "re-creation of the original Nordic race."[27]

After military service in the First World War, Merkenschlager had briefly served in a freecorps, joined the Nazi Party in 1920, and been an active SA member until the attempted Beer Hall Putsch of 1923; when the NSDAP was re-founded after Hitler's release from prison and Merkenschlager moved to northern Germany in 1925, he let his membership in the party and SA lapse, for by the mid-1920s he had become sharply critical of the Nordic racial theories promoted by the Nazi Party. Shortly after he became head of the Botanical Laboratory of the Biologische Reichsanstalt für Land- und Forstwirtschaft (Biological Reich Institute for Agriculture and Forestry) in Berlin-Dahlem in 1927, he published a scathing critique of Hans F. K. Günther's racial theories.[28] In 1928, he came into contact with the young anthropologist Karl Saller, a *Privatdozent* at the Anatomical Institute of the University of Göttingen who had written his 1927 *Habilitationsschrift* on the topic "Die Entstehung der nordischen Rasse" (The origins of the Nordic race), in which he came to the conclusion that Günther's theory of Nordic superiority was untenable.[29]

After Hitler came to power, Merkenschlager was the first of the two scholars to feel the wrath of the new regime. In October 1933, he was fired from his tenured civil service position as Regierungsrat at the Biologische Reichsanstalt under article 4 (political unreliability) of the cynically titled Law for the Restoration of the Civil Service. Since the Reichsanstalt was part of the Ministry of Agriculture, the Minister in charge was now none other than the Nordicist racial fanatic Darré.[30] Nevertheless, far from becoming more cautious after the Nazi seizure of power, Saller and Merkenschlager unfolded prodigious publishing and speaking activities in order to propagate and popularize their dynamic conception of a "German race," clearly making a bid to influence official racial policy. Thus in 1933 Merkenschlager published *Rassensonderung, Rassenmischung, Rassenwandlung* (The separation, mixing, and transformation of races), while Saller published *Der Weg der deutschen Rasse* (The path of the German race), and in 1934 they co-wrote two books, *Ofnet – Wanderungen zu den Mälern am Wege der deutschen Rasse* (Ofnet: Wanderings to the landmarks on the path of the German race) and *Vineta – eine deutsche Biologie, von Osten her geschrieben* (Vineta: a German biology written from the East).

The reception of Saller and Merkenschlager's concept of a "German race" among Nazi officials was sharply divided. While Nordicists like Darré were fiercely opposed, the notion of a German race met with considerable assent in other quarters. For not only did the notion of a German *Volksrasse* reflecting the unity of *Volk* and *Rasse* have considerable appeal for those steeped in *völkisch* thought. Support for the notion of a German race also derived from a concern that the Nordicists might advocate a racial policy that would introduce invidious distinctions of "racial value" within the German population, perhaps even calling for racial-eugenic measures of "nordification" (*Aufnordung*) directed against those deemed insufficiently Nordic, and the fear that such a policy of Nordic superiority would threaten the cohesion of the *Volksge-meinschaft* and undermine the legitimacy of Nazi racial ideology.

Among the major players in racial policy, the strongest advocate of the notion of a German race was Achim Gercke, the Expert for Racial Research at the Interior Ministry (Sachverständiger für Rassenforschung beim Reichministerium des Innern), who advocated a "Hochzüchtung der deutschen Rasse" (breeding of the German race). Another prominent supporter of the concept of a German race was Fritz Bartels, who held three key positions in party and state. He was simultaneously a Nazi-appointed senior official (Ministerialrat) in the Ministry of the Interior, the Deputy of Reichsärzteführer Gerhard Wagner, and, from June 1934, the head (Reichsamtsleiter) of the Nazi Party's Office of Public Health (Hauptamt für Volksgesundheit). Some Nazi newspapers, such as the *Hessische Landeszeitung*, also published reviews and articles that were sympathetic to the dynamic notion of a German race rather than Günther's Nordicism.[31]

The Nazi official who decided to quash the debate between Nordicists and advocates of a German race was Walter Groß, head of the Nazi Party's Rassenpolitisches Amt (Office of Racial Policy), who was emerging as the most important player in the realm of controlling official and academic discourses on race. A physician who had been working in the Public Health section of NSDAP national headquarters since 1932, Groß took the initiative right after the Nazi seizure of power to create the Aufklärungsamt für Bevölkerungspolitik und Rassenpflege (Office for Education in Population and Racial Policy), nominally under the auspices of the Nazi Doctors' Association, which in May 1934 became the Rassenpolitisches Amt (Office of Racial Policy) of the NSDAP, reporting directly to the Führer's Deputy, Rudolf Heß. Under Groß's energetic leadership, the Rassenpolitisches Amt gradually managed to assert control not only over all racial propaganda and training but also over relations between the regime and academic researchers on race, and also established its right to approve all publications on racial matters.[32]

In an October 1934 circular (*Rundschreiben*) to all the Rassenbeauftragte (officials in charge of racial matters) at the Gauleitungen, Groß launched a major attack on the notion of a German race, arguing that this conception derived from the Jewish and Catholic intellectual milieu and was a camouflaged attempt to remove the factor of race and call for harmony among the German *Volk*. "Whoever speaks of a German race is leaving the foundation of the factual. There is a German language, a German *Volk* ... racially, however, Germany, is a racial mixture

[*Rassengemisch*]." Groß also warned that the notion of a German race might lead to the inclusion of Jews and Gypsies in the "German race."[33] His attack was flanked by critical book reviews in the press and by an outright ban on certain publications.[34] Despite Groß's effort to declare an official ban on the notion of a German race, however, a December 1934 meeting of party and state officials revealed that key party officials in the area of racial policy – including Reichsärzteführer Gerhard Wagner, his deputy Fritz Bartels, and the Expert on Racial Research at the Interior Ministry, Achim Gercke – supported the concept of a German race.[35]

Alarmed that the notion of a German race might be gaining political support, Groß now decided to take decisive action against Saller, who was still teaching at the University of Göttingen, even though he had already been prohibited from delivering public lectures outside the university and two of his books had been banned. In January 1935, undoubtedly at Groß's behest, the Reich Minister of Research and Education revoked Saller's teaching credentials (*venia legendi*) and barred him from teaching based on the charge that he had "harmed the reputation of the university." Both the *Völkischer Beobachter* and the journal *Volk and Rasse* carried official denunciations of Saller's research and teaching prepared by Groß's Rassenpolitisches Amt.[36] When Saller, deprived of his academic career, decided to practice medicine, he was denied the *Kassenapprobation* (recognition by state insurance) that was necessary to practice. He ended up practicing homeopathic and *naturheilkundlich* medicine in a private sanatorium until he was drafted into the military as a medic during the war. Friedrich Merkenschlager was briefly interned in a concentration camp for alleged oppositional activity in 1937.[37]

It would be wrong, however, to conclude that the silencing of the academic advocates of the dynamic notion of a German race was synonymous with the triumph of Nordicist racial theory. Although it may have seemed that way for a while, Christopher Hutton has argued that Walter Groß and the Rassenpolitisches Amt eventually turned against Nordicism as well.[38] This development is reflected in a later conflict involving the founder of *Rassenseelenkunde*, Ludwig Ferdinand Clauss, who found himself the subject of a secret trial in front of the Oberstes Parteigericht (Supreme Party Court) of the Nazi Party in 1941/1942. Although the legal proceedings had begun with Clauss bringing a complaint against Walter Groß for obstructing his work and harming his academic reputation, in the course of the trial the roles were reversed, and Clauss became a defendant facing expulsion from the party. Although the case against Clauss included the charge that his primary academic collaborator was Jewish, it also included the accusation, pressed by Groß with the help of academic expert opinions, that Clauss's *Rassenseelenforschung* was scientifically and politically suspect. Once more Groß prevailed, and the trial ended with Clauss's expulsion from the Nazi party and the loss of his academic position in 1942.[39]

While the Fischer and Saller/Merkenschlager controversies took place in the early years of the Nazi regime, Wagner's sustained attacks on sterilization policy in the years 1936–1939 and Clauss's trial in 1941/42 show that conflicts over eugenics and racial science continued in the regime's later years. In fact, evidence of disagreement and conflict over racial policy can be found in wartime occupation policy. As Gerhard Wolf's essay in this volume demonstrates, the polycratic Nazi regime continued to witness significant disagreements over who should count as a German and who should count as a Pole in occupied Poland, which reflected differing conceptions of *Rasse* and *Volk*.

Even though the conflicts we have examined demonstrate the power that key Nazi officials could exert over academic research, they also show that racial science was characterized by competing conceptions of race and therefore could not have supplied the conceptual framework for Nazi racial policy, as the racial state paradigm has suggested. This finding does not diminish the incontrovertible and widespread complicity of racial scientists in Nazi racial policy. But by jettisoning the misleading notion that the Nazi regime translated the precepts of racial science into practice, we can embark on a more differentiated analysis of the relationship between racial science and Nazi biopolitics and, in particular, of the question of what exactly the influence of racial science on Nazi eugenic and racial policy was.

SCIENCE IN NAZI GERMANY: SCIENCE OR PSEUDOSCIENCE?

Any analysis of the role of science under the Nazi regime is haunted by the debate whether science in the Third Reich should be regarded as "normal science" or "pseudoscience."[40] Interestingly, Burleigh and Wippermann's *The Racial State* was characterized by an unresolved tension in this regard, for even though the authors stressed that Nazism drew on the support of *mainstream* medicine and bioscience, they also maintained that: "Contrary to the notion that Nazism somehow corrupted and distorted the temples of learning – which of course it did – one could argue that a corrupt and inherently distorted science lent Nazism its specifically 'academic' and 'scientific' character."[41] In this formulation, the blame for the corruption of science was shifted from the Nazi regime to the scientists themselves, but the fact of corruption remained. The historiography of the past twenty-five years has generally abandoned this ambivalence. Keenly aware that postwar apologists often sought to deny the complicity of mainstream science by arguing that only a small coterie of "pseudoscientists" had cooperated with the Nazis, most studies have decisively rejected the notion that science under the Nazi regime should be regarded as pseudoscience and have, instead, emphasized the complicity of mainstream, "normal" science with the Nazi regime.[42] This historiographical trend reflects the fact that most historians of science have adopted a sociological definition of science. Thus, according to Robert Proctor, "science is what scientists do";[43] or, in Sheila Faith Weiss's formulation, "science is what is accepted as science in peer-reviewed journals and funded by scientific agencies."[44] In short, the consensus among historians of science is that we should not impose an anachronistic litmus test of what qualifies as science. If Nazi racial science used scientific forms, methods, and terminologies and was practiced in scientific institutions and recognized by other scientists, then we, as historians, should treat it as science.

Although this near-consensus among historians of science has largely banished the term "pseudoscience" from more recent studies on science under the Third Reich, the pseudoscience debate still occasionally flares up, as it did in a 2012 exchange between Sheila Faith Weiss and Eric Ehrenreich. Taking issue with Weiss's analysis of Nazi racial science as "science" (rather than pseudoscience) in her book *The Nazi Symbiosis*, Ehrenreich argued that Otmar von Verschuer, director of the Institut für Erbbiologie und Rassenhygiene in Frankfurt from 1935 to 1942 and thereafter Fischer's successor as head of the Kaiser Wilhelm Institute in Dahlem, had bent his scientific standards when he wrote about anti-Semitism. Whereas most of Verschuer's research in human genetics qualified as "science," Ehrenreich insisted, his anti-Semitic pronouncements ought to be labeled "pseudoscience."[45]

The exchange illuminates both sides of the debate. On the one hand, the pseudoscience position in this debate has become untenable because historians of science have adopted a sociological definition of science that rejects ex post facto distinctions between science and pseudoscience. They have done so at least in part because of a recognition that science always operates in a political context. Moreover, in the case of Nazi Germany,

distinctions between pseudoscience and science are tainted by the fact that
postwar scientists used this distinction to deny the complicity of mainstream science with the Nazi regime. On the other hand, Ehrenreich's
sense that Verschuer's anti-Semitic publications do not reflect the same
scientific rigor that can be found in his research on human genetics is
undoubtedly correct. Therefore, even if we agree with the near-consensus
among historians of science that it does not make sense to draw distinctions between science and pseudoscience, we are still left with the challenge
of interpreting the difference – in tone, method, and content – between
Fischer's and Verschuer's research in human genetics and their statements
on the "Jewish question." This kind of interpretive challenge can only be
met by moving beyond the finding that mainstream scientists were compli-
cit with the Nazi regime in order to analyze the relationship between the
biosciences and the Nazi regime in greater detail.

SCIENCE AND POLITICS IN A POLYCRATIC REGIME

In a seminal essay, Mitchell Ash has proposed that the relationship
between science and politics is best analyzed by conceiving of science
and politics as "resources for one another."[46] What makes this interpretive model especially useful for an analysis of science in Nazi Germany is
that it helps us to move beyond longstanding tropes by which science was
"instrumentalized" or even "abused" by the Nazi regime. Instead, the
resource model insists that the relationship between science and politics is
based on a two-way interaction, in which scientists and political actors
negotiate with one another, with each side offering certain resources in
order to obtain resources controlled by the other side. In short, both
scientists and political actors have agency and room for maneuver. If we
apply this model to the biosciences in Nazi Germany, we can say that the
key resource that eugenicists and anthropologists could offer the regime
was the scientific legitimation of Nazi biopolitics, especially eugenic and
racial policy, while the key resource offered by the state was financial
support for research.[47] As we saw, the controversy over Eugen Fischer's
lecture on racial mixing revealed this kind of calculus with exceptional
clarity.

At times of political change, Ash argues, scientists can adopt two
different rhetorical strategies in conducting negotiations over resources
with the new political regime: a rhetorical strategy proposing an "instrumental relationship" between their scientific field and the regime or a
rhetorical strategy establishing "ideological coherence" between their

scientific field and the new regime.[48] Whereas fields such as nuclear physics or rocketry proposed *instrumental* relationships to the Third Reich, eugenicists such as Rüdin and anthropologists such as Fischer clearly adopted a strategy of stressing their *ideological* affinity with the Nazi regime. While it is easy to see which elements of eugenic thinking a right-wing eugenicist such as Rüdin was able to draw on for this purpose – the concern with the health of the *Volkskörper* (the body of the *Volk*) as well as the distinction between genetically inferior and superior individuals – we must remember that the case for ideological coherence with the regime was a rhetorical strategy and not a reflection of natural affinities. In fact, as recent research has shown, German eugenics before 1933 drew support from across the political spectrum and thus had no more affinity with National Socialism than with other political movements.[49] Although physical anthropology presents a more complicated case, it too cannot be said to have had an inherent affinity for the Nazi movement. The key issue here is that of Nazi anti-Semitism. Although both the eugenics movement and the field of physical anthropology had no shortage of anti-Semites, anti-Semitism was not an intrinsic part of either eugenics or anthropology.[50] As we have seen in the case of Fischer, at the outset of the Nazi regime, even the views of anthropologists who were undoubtedly anti-Semitic were not in line with the radical anti-Semitism of the Nazi party. In short, despite a *rhetoric* of ideological affinity, there were real tensions between Nazi ideology and the scientific fields of eugenics, anthropology, and racial science.

While Ash's model of science and politics as resources for one another provides a general framework for analyzing how these tensions were negotiated, the polycratic character of the Nazi regime meant that individual scientists had to negotiate with a multitude of state and party agencies that often worked at cross-purposes. Especially in the early years of the Third Reich multiple agencies sought to control eugenic and racial policy, and the balance of power between these agencies changed over time. Although this led to a complicated and changing set of conflicts and controversies, we can identify some central lines of conflict. From 1933 to 1939, there was an ongoing battle over the control of Nazi biopolitics (ranging from public health to eugenic and racial policy) between Arthur Gütt, the Nazi-appointed state official in charge of public health at the Ministry of the Interior, and Reichsärzteführer Gerhard Wagner, the party official in charge of the NSDAP Department of Public Health (Hauptamt für Volksgesundheit). Wagner's attacks on sterilization policy, which included severe criticisms of Rüdin, must be seen in the context of this larger battle, in which Gütt generally prevailed. When, after Wagner's death and Gütt's health-related retirement in 1939, Leonardo Conti was appointed to both positions, this conflict between state and party was temporarily resolved, but it reemerged in 1942 when Karl Brandt was appointed as Bevollmächtigter des Führers für das Sanitäts- und Gesundheitswesen (Führer's Representative for Public Health).[51]

Despite the salience of this party vs. state conflict, it must be remembered that there was a third player, the SS. In the regime's early years, the SS Race and Settlement Office (Rasse- und Siedlungshauptamt), led by Darré until 1938, found itself outmaneuvered by Gütt, who managed to establish control over eugenic and racial legislation, and Walter Groß, who succeeded in establishing control over propaganda and education in matters of racial policy. As a result, in the prewar period the role of Darré's office was limited to racial selection and indoctrination within the SS. After the outbreak of the war, however, the situation changed, and the SS became the most important agency in setting and executing racial policy in occupied Eastern Europe and then in Germany as well.[52]

Both Fischer and Rüdin found it easiest to work with Gütt, who shielded them from attacks mounted by Darré (who sought to have Fischer removed from his directorship) and Wagner (who criticized Rüdin and other academics as part of his attack on sterilization policy). Cooperation with the SS was more difficult; during the war Rüdin, who had turned to the SS for additional funding, ran into serious trouble with SS members of his institute who tried to oust him.[53] Other racial scientists, however, saw the SS's control over racial policy in the occupied East as a welcome opportunity to offer their services to the SS.[54]

The compromises that scientists made with different Nazi officials and agencies are often described as "Faustian bargains."[55] The problem with this analogy is that scientists who decided to cooperate with the Nazi regime in its early years, such as Fischer and Rüdin, could not have foreseen the radicalization of racial policy that culminated in the Holocaust. Even though it can certainly be argued that even these early cooperations compromised these scholars' scientific integrity and therefore amounted to Faustian bargains, the radicalization of Nazi racial policy effectively exacted an ever higher price from the scientists who had agreed to the bargain. Any analysis of the relationship between science and politics under the Nazi regime must therefore ask not only why prominent scientists were willing to cooperate with the regime early on, but why they *continued* to cooperate and to lend scientific legitimacy to Nazi racial policy after it became a program of mass murder.

While there most certainly were racial scientists – such as Otto Reche, professor of anthropology at the University of Leipzig – who were "true believers" in a radical anti-Semitism fully in line with Nazi ideology and who therefore jumped at the chance of participating in implementing racial policy in the occupied East,[56] other representatives of racial science, including Eugen Fischer and Otmar von Verschuer, were not "true believers" in this sense. Thus, even if we reject Ehrenreich's distinction between science and pseudoscience for the heuristic reasons sketched above, his contention that the anti-Semitic writings of Verschuer did not meet the same methodological standards as his publications on human genetics calls attention to important differences between different sub-fields of racial science under the Nazi regime and to the fact that the costs exacted by these Faustian bargains kept increasing.

It can, of course, be argued that the eugenics movement was never purely scientific and always reflected ideological imperatives: hereditarian assumptions and eugenic convictions led eugenicists to recommend sterilization even though many of them admitted that the scientific evidence was still lacking. But the anti-Semitic statements made by Fischer and Verschuer fall into a different category. In Fischer's case, the controversy over his 1933 lecture on racial mixing demonstrates that he changed his views as a result of political pressure. By 1938, he delivered a lecture on the "Jewish question" that endorsed the crudest of anti-Semitic stereotypes. In this instance, it is hard to believe that Fischer was not conscious of compromising his scholarly integrity in order to maintain his position as head of the KWI and to gain resources for this institute.[57]

WAS THERE A "GENESIS OF THE 'FINAL SOLUTION' FROM THE SPIRIT OF SCIENCE"?

So far, we have focused on the legitimating function of racial science under the Nazi regime. But in his seminal 1989 article on the "genesis of the 'Final Solution' from the spirit of science," Detlev Peukert made a claim that went considerably further, namely that the "red thread in the causal nexus" that led to the Holocaust was a "fatal racist dynamic in the human sciences."[58] Similar claims can be found in the more recent literature, in slightly different formulations. Thus, Benoit Massin concludes an important 2004 essay on racial science under the Nazi regime with the sentence: "Racial anthropologists and medical geneticists intervened in almost every aspect of Nazi racial policy ... Not only did these scientists help the regime, sometimes they directly inspired its murderous policies."[59] In the conclusion of her magisterial study of human genetics and politics in the Third Reich, Sheila Faith Weiss writes: "If there was anything uniquely 'Nazi' about human heredity and eugenics in the Third Reich, it pertains to the particular way in which human genetics interfaced with National Socialist politics, and how these served as resources for one another. The symbiosis that ensued between human heredity and the broad political context of Nazism served to radicalize them both."[60]

The claims that racial scientists "directly inspired" policies of mass murder or helped to "radicalize" Nazi racial policy deserve careful scrutiny. On the question whether the biomedical sciences influenced or even radicalized Nazi policies, I would argue that we have to make careful distinctions between Nazi eugenic policy (targeting "genetically defective" individuals within the German *Volksgemeinschaft*) and different aspects of Nazi racial policy (targeting racially defined groups, such as Jews, Roma and Sinti, and Slavic peoples).

In the realm of eugenic policy, eugenicists such as Rüdin were certainly keen on implementing both negative and positive eugenic measures on the general population. Here, especially in the early years of the Third Reich, the agenda of radical, right-wing eugenicists was largely congruent with that of the Nazi officials in charge of "hereditary health" policy. The *völkisch* wing of the German eugenics movement saw the Nazi regime as offering a welcome opportunity, and figures such as Rüdin played an active role in shaping Nazi eugenic policy, especially sterilization policy. Because they saw eugenics as not just addressing medical pathologies but also as a way of solving social problems, including crime, vagrancy, and "asocial" behavior, their participation in eugenic policy-making was also a way of expanding the medical profession's influence into the realm of social policy. Rüdin and other eugenicists such as Fritz Lenz did indeed seek to radicalize Nazi policy, and they succeeded in certain respects. The drastic expansion of the criteria for sterilization through the influential, semi-official Gütt-Rüdin-Ruttke commentary on the law is a prominent example. Even though, as we saw, the eugenic hardliners also met with opposition, key figures in the German eugenics movement – most importantly Ernst Rüdin – most certainly had a direct causal role in shaping and radicalizing Nazi eugenic policy in the early years of the regime.

The systematic murder of the handicapped and mentally ill that began in 1939 is a different matter that cannot be examined in any detail here. Suffice it to say that even though most psychiatrists went along with the murder of the mentally ill in their care and a substantial number participated in the selection process, recent research has stressed the economic as opposed to eugenic motivations behind the euthanasia killings, weakening the argument that there was some sort of logical progression from eugenics to the murder of the mentally ill and handicapped.[61]

The role of racial scientists in the area of racial (rather than eugenic) policy – that is, policies targeting groups who were excluded from the German *Volksgemeinschaft* on the basis of their supposed race rather than policies targeting individuals within the German *Volksgemeinschaft* on the basis of supposed genetic defects – presents a more complicated picture. Racial scientists did play a key role in the persecution and murder of the Roma and Sinti. Because Roma and Sinti were perceived as asocial and criminal, they were targeted by sterilization policy through diagnoses of feeblemindedness; there also were discussions about specifically targeting all "Gypsies" (regardless of supposed feeblemindedness) for sterilization, but these were overtaken by the turn to mass murder; most importantly, racial research on Gypsies conducted by Robert Ritter and others had a direct influence on the course of Nazi racial policy toward the Sinti and Roma which culminated in mass murder.[62]

By contrast, the role of racial scientists in Nazi anti-Semitic policy was more limited. German racial scientists were deeply complicit in the implementation of Nazi anti-Semitism and the Holocaust. But there is little evidence that they played any significant role in the shaping and radicalization of Nazi anti-Semitic policy. Although most German *Rassenhygieniker* and anthropologists were anti-Semites (Fischer and Rüdin clearly were), their role in drawing up specific anti-Semitic measures and policies seems to have been extremely limited. Neither the passage of the Nuremberg Laws – for which racial science failed to deliver any biological criteria – nor the turn toward the mass murder of the Jews can be attributed to the influence of scientists; the initiative clearly came from the Nazi leadership. Dan Stone, pointing to a growing body of research, has argued that "leading Nazis rather than the race scientists were the prime movers in the creation and implementation of *Judenpolitik*."[63] This does not diminish the complicity of anthropologists, eugenicists, and *Rassenforscher*, who lent scientific legitimacy to anti-Semitism, provided racial expert opinions, or performed medical experiments on concentration camp inmates. But in the area of anti-Semitic policy (as opposed to eugenic policy and the persecution of Sinti and Roma) their role was that of supporting the implementation of Nazi policy – not that of shaping or radicalizing it.

The role of racial scientists in the "racial screening" of the populations of Nazi-occupied Eastern Europe and the "resettlement" policies adopted there was significant. The anthropologist Otto Reche, for instance, sought to exert a radicalizing influence on Nazi racial policies toward Poles. At the same time, Gerhard Wolf's recent study of Nazi Germanization policy in Poland provides an example of how Nazi officials who favored a highly inclusive policy of Germanization could also draw on racial science to defend their position against more restrictive policy proposals. Albert Forster, Gauleiter of Danzig-West Prussia, convinced Hans F. K. Günther to visit his Gau for a ten-day field study in order to obtain his "expert opinion" on the racial composition of the population. Although Günther noted that the local population represented an "inextricable mixture of races," he argued that the key question was whether their "offspring would represent a welcome addition to the German population" and answered this question in the affirmative, noting that the majority of the local Polish population was "racially not too far removed from the German population of east-central Germany." Thus Forster obtained the scientific legitimation of his more inclusive Germanization policy, which stood in stark contrast to the more radical, that is, restrictive policies promoted by Himmler and the SS.[64]

DID RACIAL SCIENCE BECOME RADICALIZED UNDER THE NAZI REGIME?

After critically examining the thesis that German racial science radicalized Nazi biopolitics, I shall now turn to probing the converse thesis, also found in the literature, that the Nazi regime radicalized racial science. The impact of the Nazi regime on the development of the biomedical sciences was certainly greater than these sciences' impact on the regime. Nevertheless, the thesis that Nazism *radicalized* the biomedical sciences conveys only a partial picture.

To be sure, one can identify processes of radicalization, above all the willingness of racial scientists to support and legitimize the regime's racial policy in a myriad of ways, such as providing racial expert opinions, delivering anti-Semitic lectures and publications, training SS personnel at KWI research institutes, and participating in the implementation of racial policy in the occupied East. What is more, some racial scientists conducted anthropological, genetic, and medical research on concentration camp inmates – including Jews, Sinti and Roma, and Soviet prisoners of war – that violated fundamental ethical principles, including the principle of informed consent, while others, including Verschuer, conducted laboratory research using "human material" sent to them from

Auschwitz.[65] This transgression of ethical boundaries, sometimes referred to as an *Entgrenzung* or *Grenzüberschreitung* (removal of boundaries, crossing of boundaries) in German-language studies, can most certainly be described as a radicalization. But it is important to note that this ethical transgression was a crime of opportunity that was not connected to a radicalization of the *content and research paradigms* of racial science. As Hans-Walter Schmuhl has shown, the research projects for which Otmar von Verschuer and others at the KWI for Anthropology in Dahlem used the "human material" sent to them from Auschwitz were conceived within the new paradigm of *Phänogenetik* (pheno-genetics), which broke with the genetic determinism of older models of racial science.[66]

Indeed, one of the most remarkable developments in the field of racial science under the Nazis was that research at the KWI for Anthropology (directed by Fischer until 1942, when Verschuer assumed the director-ship) began to reflect international research trends by moving in the direction of population genetics, which undermined the simplistic hered-itarian assumptions of Mendelian genetics. Although researchers at the KWI were not themselves engaged in population or experimental genetics, they began to draw on these developments in their research, which was increasingly shifting to the new paradigm of *Phänogenetik* after about 1938.[67] As Veronika Lipphardt has demonstrated, "[w]ith regard to its theoretical groundings, research problems, research designs, methods, practices, results, and interpretations, German race science was far more embedded in contemporary research on human diversity around the world than is generally assumed."[68] In some important respects, research at Nazi Germany's premier research institute in racial science was thus becoming increasingly disconnected from Nazi racial policy. As Peter Weingart, Jürgen Kroll, and Kurt Bayertz have argued, this development could not have been lost on Eugen Fischer, who "must have been con-scious of a growing gulf between an ever more radical Nazi racial policy and the direction of the development of his own science."[69] More gener-ally, the turn to the new genetics was beginning to sideline traditional racial anthropology in Nazi Germany.[70]

This development brings us to the central paradox of racial science under the Nazi regime: even as racial scientists became ever more compli-cit in Nazi racial policy, they were adopting new research paradigms that undermined the deterministic understandings of heredity and race that undergirded this racial policy. This paradox leads to two further reflec-tions. First, the egregious violations of medical ethics involved in the KWI's harvesting of "human material" from concentration camp inmates took place in the context of "normal science" in line with international developments; it is therefore clear that even the most sophisticated paradigms of contemporary genetics provided (and provide) no inherent protection against such violations. Second, Fischer, Verschuer, and other leading racial scientists were well informed about scientific developments that undermined the hereditarian determinism and the static notion of race that provided the foundation for Nazi racial policy. They participated in Nazi racial policy despite this knowledge and hence against their better judgment. This surely increases their culpability.

CONCLUSION

In this essay, I have sought to distinguish the question of German racial scientists' complicity in Nazi eugenic and racial policy from the question of what influence they had on the shaping of those policies. While their widespread complicity is now well documented in depressing detail, claims that Nazi racial science "created the conceptual framework" for Nazi racial policy (Burleigh and Wippermann) or that Nazi racial policy was propelled by a "fatal racist dynamic" in the biosciences (Peukert) are problematic. In assessing the influence of racial science on Nazi biopolitics, one has to distinguish between different scientific fields and different areas of Nazi policy. While one can indeed make a strong case that Ernst Rüdin influenced Nazi sterilization policy and that the *Zigeunerforscher* Robert Ritter influenced the murderous Nazi policy toward Roma and Sinti, there is little evidence that research in racial science exerted any influence on the radicalization of Nazi anti-Semitic policy and the turn to mass murder. Neither does the historical evidence bear out the general assertion that the Nazi regime exerted a radicalizing influence on the field of racial science. While there were racial scientists who adopted more radical positions as Nazi racial policy became radicalized, others – including the researchers at the Dahlem KWI, Nazi Germany's leading research institute in racial science – were adopting research paradigms that undermined the genetic determinism on which Nazi racism was based, thus widening the gulf between their academic research and Nazi racial policies.

The racial-state paradigm that Burleigh and Wippermann formulated in *The Racial State* has made two crucial contributions to the historiography by, first, calling attention to the complicity of doctors and racial scientists in Nazi crimes and, second, demonstrating that Nazi anti-Semitism and the Holocaust were part of a larger biopolitical agenda targeting a range of groups and individuals that were labeled as racially inferior (including Sinti and Roma, Poles, and other Slavic peoples) or biologically defective (including the handicapped and mentally ill, homosexuals, and so-called asocials). For these reasons, the racial-state paradigm rightly remains influential. What is problematic is the paradigm's claim that racial science provided a conceptual blueprint for Nazi racial policy that the regime then translated into practice.

Without denying the central role of race in the Third Reich, I have tried to argue here that instead of using "race" as an analytical category for understanding the Nazi regime, we must recognize that "race" was a diffuse concept whose competing and contested meanings during the Nazi era are in need of historical analysis. A careful examination of the interaction of racial scientists with different parts of the Nazi regime might help us understand the Third Reich better by elucidating how both scientists and Nazi officials deployed competing conceptions of race for strategic purposes at different points in the regime's development.

Notes

1 Michael Burleigh and Wolfgang Wippermann, *The Racial State: Germany 1933–1945* (Cambridge, 1991); Detlev Peukert, "Die Genesis der 'Endlösung' aus dem Geist der Wissenschaft," in Peukert, *Max Webers Diagnose der Moderne* (Göttingen, 1989), 102–21 – an English version was published as "The genesis of the 'Final Solution' from the spirit of science" in Thomas Childers and Jane Caplan (eds.), *Reevaluating the Third Reich* (New York, 1993), 234–52. Quotations from Peukert's essay in this chapter are my own translations from the German original. Because Burleigh and Wippermann as well as Peukert based their interpretations on a first wave of historical studies on eugenics and racial science published in the 1980s, the research of the past two-and-a-half decades can also be said to have broadened and deepened the key findings of these pioneering early studies, including: Ernst Klee, *Euthanasie im NS-Staat* (Frankfurt, 1983); Benno Müller-Hill, *Tödliche Wissenschaft* (Reinbek, 1984); the series *Beiträge zur nationalsozialistischen Gesundheits- und Sozialpolitik* (1985–), edited by Götz Aly, Karl Heinz Roth, et al.; Gisela Bock, *Zwangssterilisation im Nationalsozialismus: Studien zur Rassenpolitik und Frauenpolitik* (Opladen, 1986); Peter Weingart, Jürgen Kroll, and Kurt Bayertz, *Rasse, Blut und Gene: Geschichte der Eugenik und Rassenhygiene in Deutschland* (Frankfurt, 1988); Robert Proctor, *Racial Hygiene: Medicine under the Nazis* (Cambridge, MA, 1988); Paul Weindling, *Health, Race, and German Politics between National Unification and Nazism, 1870–1945* (Cambridge, 1989).

2 On biopolitics in modern German history see Edward Ross Dickinson, "Biopolitics, fascism, democracy: some reflections on our discourse about 'modernity'," *Central European History* 37 (2004): 1–48; on biopolitics as an analytical concept, including its Foucauldian version, see Thomas Lemke, *Biopolitik zur Einführung* (Hamburg, 2007).

3 On the current state of historical research on German eugenics, see Hans-Walter Schmuhl, "Eugenik und Rassenanthropologie," in Robert Jütte et al. (eds.), *Medizin und Nationalsozialismus: Bilanz und Perspektiven der Forschung* (Göttingen, 2011), 24–38. On Rüdin and his institute, see Sheila Faith Weiss, *The Nazi Symbiosis: Human Genetics and Politics in the Third Reich* (Chicago, 2010), 121–83; Matthias Weber, *Ernst Rüdin* (Berlin, 1993); Volker Roelcke, "Psychiatrische Wissenschaft im Kontext nationalsozialistischer Politik und 'Euthanasie': Zur Rolle von Ernst Rüdin und der Deutschen Forschungsanstalt für Psychiatrie/Kaiser-Wilhelm-Institut" in Doris Kaufmann (ed.), *Geschichte der Kaiser-Wilhelm-Gesellschaft im Nationalsozialismus* (Göttingen, 2000), vol. 1, 112–50.

4 Hans-Walter Schmuhl, *Grenzüberschreitungen: Das Kaiser-Wilhelm-Institut für Anthropologie, menschliche Erblehre und Eugenik, 1927–1945* (Göttingen, 2005), 268–69; translated as *The Kaiser Wilhelm Institute for Anthropology, Human Heredity and Eugenics, 1927–1945* (Dordrecht, 2008); Weiss, *Nazi Symbiosis*, 99–102; for a detailed analysis of von Verschuer's *Erb- und Rassegutachten*, see Sheila Faith Weiss, "The loyal genetic doctor, Otmar Freiherr von Verschuer, and the Institut für Erbbiologie und Rassenhygiene: origins, controversy and political practice," *Central European History* 45 (2012), 631–68.

5 Schmuhl, *Grenzüberschreitungen*, 264–8; Weiss, *Nazi Symbiosis*, 105–7.

6 On Reche, see Isabel Heinemann, "Defining '(un)wanted population addition': anthropology, racist ideology, and mass murder in the occupied East" in Anton Weiss-Wendt and Rory Yeomans (eds.), *Racial Science in Hitler's New Europe* (Lincoln, 2013), 39–42; Katja Geisenhainer, *"Rasse ist Schicksal": Otto Reche (1879–1966) – ein Leben als Anthropologe und Völkerkundler* (Leipzig, 2002); Weindling, *Health, Race, and German Politics*, 540–1; Weingart, Kroll, and Bayertz, *Rasse, Blut und Gene*, 401–3.

7 See Karola Fings, "Die Gutachtlichen Äusserungen der Rassenhygienischen Forschungsstelle und ihr Einfluss auf die nationalsozialistische Zigeunerpolitik" in Michael Zimmermann (ed.), *Zwischen Erziehung und Vernichtung: Zigeunerpolitik und Zigeunerforschung im Europe des 20. Jahrhunderts* (Stuttgart, 2007), 425–59 and other chapters in that volume; also the standard work: Michael Zimmermann, *Rassenutopie und Genozid: Die nationalsozialistische "Lösung der Zigeunerfrage"* (Hamburg, 1996).

8 For the most recent research on the murder of the mentally ill and handicapped, see Gerrit Hohendorf, *Der Tod als Erlösung vom Leiden: Geschichte und Ethik der Sterbehilfe seit dem Ende des 19. Jahrhunderts in Deutschland* (Göttingen, 2013), 64–131; Götz Aly, *Die Belasteten: "Euthanasie" 1939–1945* (Frankfurt, 2013); Maike Rotzoll, Gerrit Hohendorf, et al. (eds.), *Die nationalsozialistische "Euthanasie"-Aktion "T4" und ihre Opfer* (Paderborn, 2010). See also the pioneering studies: Ernst Klee, *"Euthanasie" im NS-Staat* (Frankfurt, 1983); Hans-Walter Schmuhl, *Rassenhygiene, Nationalsozialismus, Euthanasie* (Göttingen, 1987; 2nd rev. edn. 1992); Michael Burleigh, *Death and Deliverance: Euthanasia in Germany, 1900–1945* (Cambridge, 1994); Henry Friedlander, *The Origins of Nazi Genocide: From Euthanasia to the Final Solution* (Chapel Hill, 1995).

9 Schmuhl, *Grenzüberschreitungen*, 532–3, 423–530; Carola Sachse (ed.), *Die Verbindung nach Auschwitz: Biowissenschaften und Menschenversuche an Kaiser-Wilhelm-Instituten* (Göttingen, 2003).

10 Burleigh and Wippermann, *Racial State*, 51; Peukert, "Die Genesis," 104.

11 Historians differ on Rüdin's role. In his biography of Rüdin, Matthias Weber argues that Rüdin did not participate in drafting the law, but only in writing the published commentary (Weber, *Ernst Rüdin*, 181–3). By contrast, Gisela Bock (*Zwangssterilisation*, 84), Paul Weindling (*Health, Race and German Politics*, 524) and Joachim Müller (*Sterilisation und Gesetzgebung*, 106) maintain that Rüdin participated in drafting the law. Whether or not Rüdin participated in the initial stages of preparation (Müller), his prominent role in the *Sachverständigenbeirat* strongly suggests that he played a part in drafting the law. See also A. Ploetz and Ernst Rüdin, "Ministerialdirektor Dr. Arthur Gütt: 5 Jahre Leiter der Abteilung für Volksgesundheit im Reichs- und Preussischen Ministerium des Inneren," *Archiv für Rassen- und Gesellschaftsbiologie* [hereafter *ARGB*] 33 (1939), 89; Ernst Rüdin, "Die Bedeutung Arthur Gütt's für die Erb- und Rassenforschung und deren praktische Anwendung," *Der öffentliche Gesundheitsdienst*, 4 (1938/39), 897–9; Alfred Ploetz, "Der Sachverständigenbeirat für Bevölkerungs- und Rassenpolitik," *ARGB* 27 (1933), 419.

12 *Gesetz zur Verhütung erbkranken Nachwuchses*, bearbeitet und erläutert von Arthur Gütt, Ernst Rüdin, Falk Ruttke, 1st edn. (Munich, 1934), 56.

13 Oswald Bumke, *Lehrbuch der Geisteskrankheiten*, 3rd edn. (Munich, 1929), 188; quoted in Hans Fickert, *Rassenhygienische Verbrechensbekämpfung* (Leipzig, 1938), 41, which also gives other references confirming this psychiatric consensus.

14 Gütt, Rüdin, and Ruttke, *Gesetz*, 94.

15 Hans Luxenburger, "Review of: Gütt, Rüdin, and Ruttke, *Gesetz zur Verhütung erbkranken Nachwuchses* [2nd edn., 1936]," *ARGB* 30 (1936), 422–3; for the same criticism, see also Robert Müller, "Zum Schwachsinnsbegriff in der Praxis der Erbgesundheitsgerichte," *Der Erbarzt* 5 (1938), 49.

16 Verdict of the Erbgesundheitsobergericht [hereafter EOG], Kiel, 14 February 1935, in: *Juristische Wochenschrift* [hereafter *JW*] 64 (1935): 2143. See also the following court decisions: EOG Kiel, 14 February 1935, *JW* 64 (1935): 2143; EOG Jena, 21 March 1935, ibid., 1869; EOG Kassel, 28 March 1935, ibid., 3111; EOG Darmstadt, 8 April 1935, ibid., 1867; EOG Berlin, 18 Mai 1935, ibid., 2149; for an overview, see Fickert, *Rassenhygienische Verbrechensbekämpfung*, 47–8. On the German efforts and debates regarding the application of eugenic measures to criminals during the Weimar and Nazi era, see Richard Wetzell, *Inventing the Criminal: A History of German Criminology, 1880–1945* (Chapel Hill, 2000), 233–94.

17 Christian Ganssmüller, *Die Erbgesundheitspolitik des Dritten Reiches* (Cologne, 1987), 100–15, quote 104; Weiss, *The Nazi Symbiosis*, 160–2; Proctor, *Racial Hygiene*, 114–17; Matthias Weber, *Ernst Rüdin* (Berlin, 1993), 254–7.

18 Letter from Wagner to Himmler, Janruary 24, 1938, Bundesarchiv Berlin-Lichterfelde, NS 19, file 3434, Bl. 71.

19 Weiss, *Nazi Symbiosis*, 161.

20 On Günther, see Hutton, *Race and the Third Reich*, 35–63, 168–9; Uwe Hoßfeld, *Geschichte der biologischen Anthropologie in Deutschland* (Stuttgart, 2005), 220–9; Uwe Hoßfeld, "Die Jenaer Jahre des 'Rasse Günther' von 1930 bis 1935," *Medizinhistorisches Journal* 34 (1999), 47–103; Hans-Jürgen Lutzhöft, *Der nordische Gedanke in Deutschland, 1920–1940* (Stuttgart, 1971), esp. 390–402.

21 See the literature and sources on Saller and Merkenschlager cited in the next section.

22 On Fischer and his institute, see Schmuhl, *Grenzüberschreitungen*; Niels Lösch, *Rasse als Konstrukt: Leben und Werk Eugen Fischers* (Frankfurt, 1997); Weiss, *Nazi Symbiosis*, 69–120; Benoit Massin, "Rasse und Vererbung als Beruf," in Hans-Walter Schmuhl (ed.), *Rassenforschung an Kaiser-Wilhelm-Instituten vor und nach 1933* (Göttingen, 2003), 190–244; Weingart, Kroll, and Bayertz, *Rasse, Blut und Gene*, 239–46, 407–24; quote from Fischer in Saller, *Rassenlehre*, 37.

23 Memo from Eugen Fischer to Gütt, April 30, 1934, Bundesarchiv Berlin, R 1501, file 126245, Bl. 219–235; Schmuhl, *Grenzüberschreitungen*, 157–61, 176–83; Lösch, *Rasse als Konstrukt*, 231–3; Weiss, *Nazi Symbiosis*, 85–9; Hutton, *Race and the Third Reich*, 143–9.

24 Letter from Gütt to Walter Darré, Reichsminister für Ernährung und Landwirtschaft, May 23, 1934, Bundesarchiv Berlin, R 1501, file 126245, 218-19.

25 Schmuhl, *Grenzüberschreitungen*, 156–83, quote 176; Weiss, *Nazi Symbiosis*, 85–93, 111; Lösch, *Rasse als Konstrukt*, 234–53; Hutton, *Race and the Third Reich*, 143–9; Lothar Gottlieb Tirala, "Rassenmischung," *Volk und Rasse* 9 (1934), 185–8; Eugen Fischer, "Rassenkreuzung," *Volk und Rasse* 9 (1934), 247–51; Tirala, "Rassenhygiene oder Eugenik," *Volk und Rasse* 9 (1934), 353–7. On Tirala, see Helmut Heiber, *Universität unterm Hakenkreuz*, Teil 1, *Der Professor im Dritten Reich* (Munich, 1991), 445–60; Ernst Klee, *Das Personenlexikon zum Dritten Reich*, rev. edn. (Frankfurt, 2005), 625; Weingart, Kroll, and Bayertz, *Rasse, Blut und Gene*, 541.

26 See Mitchell Ash, "Wissenschaft und Politik als Ressourcen füreinander" in Rüdiger vom Bruch and Brigitte Kaderas (eds.), *Wissenschaften und Wissenschaftspolitik* (Stuttgart, 2002), 32–51.

27 On Saller and Merkenschlager, see Karl Saller, *Die Rassenlehre des Nationalsozialismus in Wissenschaft und Propaganda* (Darmstadt, 1961); Andreas Lüddecke, *Der "Fall Saller" und die Rassenhygiene: Eine Göttinger Fallstudie zu den Widersprüchen sozialbiologistischer Ideologiebildung* (Marburg, 1995); Hutton, *Race and the Third Reich*, 150–7; Cornelia Essner, *Die "Nürnberger Gesetze" oder die Verwaltung des Rassenwahns 1933–1945* (Paderborn, 2002), 61–9; Gerd Berghofer, *Friedrich Merkenschlager: Ein Wissenschaftler trotzt den Rassegedanken der Nazis* (Treuchtlingen, 2010), Karl Saller, "Friedrich Merkenschlager" in Willi Ulsamer (ed.), *100 Jahre Landkreis Schwabach (1862–1962): Ein Heimatbuch* (Schwabach, 1964), 287–96.

28 Berghofer, *Merkenschlager*, 44–73.

29 Lüddecke, Der "Fall Saller," 59–60.

30 Berghofer, *Merkenschlager*, 107–110.

31 Essner, *Die "Nürnberger Gesetze,"* 64–9; Saller, *Die Rassenlehre,* 87–8 and passim.

32 On Groß and the *Rassenpolitisches Amt,* see Claudia Koonz, *The Nazi Conscience* (Cambridge, MA, 2003), esp. 103–30; Weingart, Kroll, and Bayertz, *Rasse, Blut und Gene,* 376, 402–6, 558–61; Hutton, *Race and the Third Reich,* 154–7; Roger Uhle, *Neues Volk und reine Rasse: Walter Gross und das Rassenpolitische Amt der NSDAP (RPA) 1934–1945* (Garmisch-Partenkirchen, 1999).

33 Rassenpolitisches Amt, Rundschreiben Nr. 37, 24. Oktober 1934, reprinted in Leon Poliakov and Josef Wulf, *Das Dritte Reich und seine Denker: Dokumente,* rev. edn. (Munich, 1978), 411ff. and in Saller, *Die Rassenlehre,* 84–5.

34 Saller, *Die Rassenlehre,* 86–91; L. Leonhardt, "Deutsche Rasse oder nordische Rasse im deutschen Volk," *Volk und Rasse* 9 (1934), 188–90 (review of Saller's book *Der Weg der deutschen Rasse*); Kurt Holler, "Deutsche Rasse," *Rasse: Monatsschrift der nordischen Bewegung* 2 (1935), 31–2.

35 Essner, *Die "Nürnberger Gesetze,"* 69–71.

36 Saller, *Die Rassenlehre,* esp. 33–49; Weingart, Kroll, and Bayertz, *Rasse, Blut und Gene,* 317–19, 539–41, Saller quote 539; Andreas Lüddecke, *Der "Fall Saller"*; Hutton, *Race and the Third Reich,* 15–54.

37 Hutton, *Race and the Third Reich,* 151–7; Saller, *Die Rassenlehre,* 43; Lüddecke, *Der "Fall Saller."*

38 Hutton, *Race and the Third Reich,* 128–9, 138–9, 160–1, 166–9.

39 On Clauss, see Peter Weingart, *Doppel-Leben. Ludwig Ferdinand Clauss: Zwischen Rassenforschung und Widerstand* (Frankfurt, 1995), which reconstructs the party trial in detail – see esp. 81–91, 144–8; Heiber, *Universität unterm Hakenkreuz,* Teil 1, *Der Professor,* 481–91; Hutton, *Race and the Third Reich,* 183–6; Hans-Christian Harten, Uwe Neirich, and Matthias Schwerendt, *Rassenhygiene als Erziehungsideologie des Dritten Reichs* (Berlin, 2006), 144–50.

40 On the concept of pseudoscience, see Dirk Rupnow et al. (eds.), *Pseudowissenschaft* (Frankfurt, 2008) and Michael Gordin, *The Pseudoscience Wars: Immanuel Velikovsky and the Birth of the Modern Fringe* (Chicago, 2012).

41 Burleigh and Wippermann, *The Racial State,* 56.

42 For an excellent overview, see Margit Szöllösi-Janze, "National Socialism and science" in M. Szöllösi-Janze (ed.), *Science in the Third Reich* (Oxford, 2001), 1–35.

43 Proctor, *Racial Hygiene,* 9.

44 Weiss, "The loyal genetic doctor," 656.

45 See Ehrenreich's book review and letters to the editor in *American Historical Review [AHR]* 116 (2011), 1587–8; *AHR* 117 (2012), 321–2 and 661–2. See also Eric Ehrenreich, "Otmar von Verschuer and the 'scientific' legitimization of Nazi anti-Jewish policy," *Holocaust and Genocide Studies* 21 (2007), 55–72; Weiss, "The loyal genetic doctor."

46 Ash, "Wissenschaft und Politik als Ressourcen für einander."

47 For an application of Ash's model to Nazi Germany, see also Sheila Weiss, "Human genetics and politics as mutually beneficial resources: the case of the Kaiser Wilhelm Institute for Anthropology, Human Heredity and Eugenics during the Third Reich," *Journal of the History of Biology* 39 (2006), 41–88.

48 Ash, "Wissenschaft und Politik als Ressourcen für einander," 40; see also Mitchell Ash, "Scientific changes in Germany 1933, 1945, 1990: towards a comparison," *Minerva* 37 (1999), 329–54, esp. 345–6.

49 For an overview of the current state of research on German eugenics, see Hans-Walter Schmuhl, "Eugenik und Rassenanthropologie" in Robert Jütte et al. (eds.), *Medizin und Nationalsozialismus: Bilanz und Perspektiven der Forschung* (Göttingen, 2011), 24–38; on the wide range of support for eugenics, see Regina Wecker et al. (eds.), *Wie nationalsozialistisch ist die Eugenik?* (Wien, 2009); Stefan Kühl, *Die Internationale der Rassisten* (Frankfurt, 1997); Marius Turda, *Modernism and Eugenics* (Houndmills, 2010).

50 See Veronica Lipphardt, "'Jüdische Eugenik'?" in Wecker et al. (eds.), *Wie nationalsozialistisch ist die Eugenik?,* 151–63; Lipphardt, *Biologie der Juden* (Göttingen, 2008); Raphael Falk, "Eugenics and the Jews" in Alison Bashford and Philippa Levine (eds.), *Oxford Handbook of the History of Eugenics* (Oxford, 2010), 462–76.

51 See Weindling, *Health, Race, and German Politics,* esp. 493–7, 542; Alfon Labisch and Florian Tennstedt, *Der Weg zum 'Gesetz über die Vereinheitlichung des Gesundheitswesens'vom 3. Juli 1934* (Düsseldorf, 1985).

52 On the Rasse- und Siedlungsamt, especially its wartime role, see Isabel Heinemann, *"Rasse, Siedlung, deutsches Blut": Das Rasse- und Siedlungshauptamt der SS und die rassenpolitische Neuordnung Europas* (Göttingen, 2003).

53 Weiss, *Nazi Symbiosis,* 162–83.

54 See Heinemann, "Defining '(un)wanted population addition.'"

55 Weindling, *Health, Race, and German Politics,* 497; Weiss, *Nazi Symbiosis,* 85, 110, 303, passim; Schmuhl, *Grenzüberschreitungen,* 155, passim.

56 On Reche, see Heinemann, "Defining '(un)wanted population addition,'" 39–42.

57 Schmuhl, *Grenzüberschreitungen,* 303–12; Weiss, *Nazi Symbiosis,* 102–4; Lösch, *Rasse als Konstrukt,* 278–97.

58 Peukert, "Die Genesis der 'Endlösung,'" 104.

59 Benoit Massin, "The 'Science of Race'" in United States Holocaust Memorial Museum (ed.), *Deadly Medicine: Creating the Master Race* (Chapel Hill, 2004), 89–125, 125.

60 Weiss, *Nazi Symbiosis,* 306.

61 See Rotzoll, Hohendorf et al. (eds.), *Die nationalsozialistische "Euthanasie"-Aktion "T4"*; Hohendorf, *Der Tod als Erlösung vom Leiden,* 64–131; see also Herwig Czech's chapter in this volume.

62 See, for instance, Fings, "Die 'Gutachtlichen Äusserungen," along with other chapters in Zimmermann (ed.), *Zwischen Erziehung und Vernichtung*; also the standard work, Zimmermann, *Rassenutopie und Genozid.*

63 Stone, *Histories of the Holocaust,* 201; see also Stone's chapter in this volume.

64 Gerhard Wolf, *Ideologie und Herrschaftsrationalität: Nationalsozialistische Germanisierungspolitik in Polen* (Hamburg, 2012), 329–31; see also Wolf's chapter in this volume.

65 Schmuhl, *Grenzüberschreitungen,* 532–3, 423–530; Carola Sachse (ed.), *Die Verbindung nach Auschwitz: Biowissenschaften und Menschenversuche an Kaiser-Wilhelm-Instituten* (Göttingen, 2003).

66 Schmuhl, *Grenzüberschreitungen*, 510, 533–5, 313–27.

67 Massin, "Rasse und Vererbung als Beruf"; Schmuhl, *Grenzüberschreitungen*, 313–27; Weingart, Kroll, and Bayertz, *Rasse, Blut und Gene*, 418–19. The argument that racial science under the Nazi regime was involved in international trends in human genetics was first advanced by Karl Heinz Roth, "Schöner neuer Mensch: Der Paradigmenwechsel der klassischen Genetik und seine Auswirkungen auf die Bevölkerungsbiologie des 'Dritten Reichs'" in Heidrun Kaupen-Haas (ed.), *Der Griff nach der Bevölkerung* (Nördlingen, 1986), 11–63, reprinted in Heidrun Kaupen-Haas and Christian Saller (eds.), *Wissenschaftlicher Rassismus* (Frankfurt, 1999), 346–424. Roth's provocative claim that Nazi racial policy demonstrated the radicalizing implications of the new genetics has not been borne out by subsequent research (see Schmuhl, *Grenzüberschreitungen*, passim).

68 Veronika Lipphardt, "Isolates and crosses in human population genetics: or a contextualization of German race science," *Current Anthropology* 53(5) (April 2012), S69–S82.

69 Weingart, Kroll, and Bayertz, *Rasse, Blut und Gene*, 416.

70 Anne Cottebrune, *Der planbare Mensch: Die Deutsche Forschungsgemeinschaft und die menschliche Vererbungswissenschaft, 1920–1970* (Stuttgart, 2008), 209–13; Andrea Adams, *Psychopathologie und "Rasse": Verhandlungen "rassischer" Differenz in der Erforschung psychischer Leiden (1890–1933)* (Bielefeld, 2013), 269–71.

6

Race Science, Race Mysticism, and the Racial State

Dan Stone

The Third Reich was a racial state, of that there is no doubt. But of what sort? The dominant historiographical paradigm of the past two decades – since the gradual displacement of the structuralist explanation – has been the "return of ideology" to the study of Nazism and the Holocaust. This paradigm has had spectacular results, reminding us that ideology was no secondary concern for the Nazis, to be espoused merely for rhetorical effect or to facilitate social mobilization. Rather, the seriousness with which the Nazis dedicated themselves to building their new *Volksgemeinschaft* (racial community) and the eagerness with which many Germans subscribed to the project have been all too clearly illuminated by this research. We have seen that in the case of the war in Poland and, especially, in the Soviet Union, the ideology of the "war of annihilation" was the necessary counterpart to the *Volksgemeinschaft*, for the killing of the Reich's enemies in "the East" went hand in hand with the creation of a comfortable feeling of belonging at home.[1] Whether one looks at SS indoctrination programs, regional studies of the Holocaust, the history of ghettos and ghettoization, Nazi culture, the internal structure of the Third Reich, local and regional administration, the development of the concentration camp system, education and schooling under Nazism, racial science and *Judenforschung* (research into the Jews, a significant academic field in the Third Reich), or *Täterforschung* (perpetrator

This essay builds on my arguments in *Histories of the Holocaust* (Oxford, 2010), especially chapter 4, "Race science: the basis of the Nazi world view?" I'm grateful to the editors of this volume for their invitation to contribute to it and for their detailed comments on earlier drafts.

research) broadly conceived – to name just some of the many flourishing research areas – ideology is now widely regarded as central to any explanation of the nature of the Third Reich and its crimes.

To be sure, there are some objections. Some historians challenge the so-called voluntaristic turn, which conceives of the Third Reich less as a terror state and more as a consensus dictatorship, for overlooking the spheres of German society which Nazism found it hard to penetrate and for downplaying the role of terror.[2] (Few would dispute, however, that recent scholarship on popular adherence and allegiance has exploded some of the myths of duress or mere fellow-travelership prevalent in the postwar Germanies). In the case of the recent literature on the *Volksgemeinschaft*, much of which has yet to find its way into English, the concept's ability to contribute to historical understanding is also being questioned. Historians do not object to the argument that the Nazis wanted to create such an ethnic community, which would overcome the cleavages of class, religion, and region among Germans, but they do think it is important not to exaggerate the extent to which the Nazis actually achieved this goal. Ian Kershaw, for example, suggests that when talking of the Nazis' *Volksgemeinschaft*, great care must be taken not to lend the regime a coherence that in actuality it lacked, for this would be to fall prey to Nazi propaganda and Nazi dreams and visions.[3] Citing well-known, representative memoirs, such as Melita Maschmann's, on the appeal of the racial community should not obscure the fact that the *Volksgemeinschaft* never existed in the way she and others dreamed of.[4] Still, there is no going back to the comforting vision of a terrorized German population brutalized by a vicious, conspiratorial elite with the aid of their ubiquitous and single-minded Gestapo secret police network. Too many historians writing in too many different ways – whether from the standpoint of German moral life or the linking of mass murder and home front comforts – have brought to light the true extent of popular support for the Reich and its ambition to create a *Volksgemeinschaft*.[5] Even when we acknowledge that the Nazis could not entirely overcome existing class and religious divisions, or that some sections of the population remained more or less impervious to the attractions of the *Volksgemeinschaft*, or, most pertinent to this discussion, the fact that racial science and *völkisch* thought were far from synonymous, the general picture of a willing population is clear.

No topic better illustrates the gains and limitations of the "return of ideology" paradigm than the literature on "race." Thanks to the sorts of studies mentioned above, scholars now paint a picture of the Third Reich as a society imbued with racial thinking, in which every area of life, from schooling to sport, from charity and leisure, from religion to the army, was dominated by race-thinking and reorganized along racial lines. The very notion of the *Volksgemeinschaft* presupposes a definition of the *Volk* to which people could willingly subscribe. And this implies that some variety of race-thinking – but not necessarily one based on science – lay at the heart of the Third Reich.

The starting point for this essay is a recognition of the gains that have been made by understanding the Third Reich in racial terms. Even with all the scholarship of the past two decades, the vast amount of racially inspired literature and research produced by the Third Reich is still being uncovered, whether (e.g.) with respect to academic historians' complicity with the regime or the ways in which art exhibitions, music, or poetry were supposed to represent the revivified, authentic Germanic impulse.[6] But I will go on to suggest that one result of all this scholarship is that the limits of the racial paradigm are now clear. In particular, I will suggest that while it remains imperative to see the Third Reich as a "racial state," we need to distinguish two different registers of race-thinking: race science on the one hand and race mysticism or simply "race-thinking" on the other. The emphasis on the former in the literature results from the notion of Nazism as "modern" and the assumption that race mysticism is somehow atavistic, when in fact it too is a symptom of modernity. That emphasis on racial science has the consequence too of making the Nazi regime and its intellectual legitimizers appear far more coherent and consistent than was actually the case. Furthermore, by drawing this distinction between race science and race mysticism we can see that in each case, race on its own is insufficient as an explanation for the crimes committed by the Third Reich or, by extension (as I discuss in the second part of the essay), for genocide elsewhere. Irrespective of the extent to which actions and policies are driven by race-thinking – and the Third Reich is the clearest example of this phenomenon – neither race science nor race mysticism operates in a vacuum. They must be set to work and made intelligible by their advocates in particular historical contexts.

Race science may be intrinsically fascinating as a historical phenomenon, but as an explanation of the internal structure of the Third Reich – not to say of the Holocaust – it is too neat and tidy. Where the modernity argument associated with Götz Aly, Susanne Heim, Detlev Peukert, or Zygmunt Bauman was originally the more politically radical (with its implied attack on the "surveillant" or "disciplinary" state; by contrast, the earlier, Nuremberg-inspired "Nazism as aberration" thesis suggested a need for more Enlightenment, and restricted the spread of guilt in Germany to the Nazi leadership), over time it has become more conservative in its implications: Nazism as a form of or mutated version of Darwinism or of modern science becomes an indictment of biological science or Enlightenment aspirations per se and/or potentially a defense of counter-rational thinking. This is a worrying trend because the sources of Nazism ultimately lay in non-rational fantasies about the world, which took on a modern flavor because of the ways in which they were mixed up with and legitimized by a scientific vocabulary and, more significantly, the collaboration of scientists with the Nazi regime. In particular, the notion that Nazi racism followed logically from Darwinism stems from a very presentist concern that genetic engineering is "playing God" and implies that the dangers thrown up by twenty-first-century genetics far outweigh any potential medical benefits. Hitler undoubtedly drew on social Darwinism to support his beliefs in racial struggle and the need for selection to maintain and improve the Aryan race, but the genocide of the Jews was less an expression of evolutionary ethics – the pursuit of evolutionary progress in biological terms understood as the elimination of a racially polluting enemy – than the attempt to rescue the Aryan race from the political threat of the international Jewish conspiracy. This conspiracy involved the use, as the Nazis saw it, of miscegenation and the promotion of anything that furthered Aryan racial degeneration (such as jazz or modern art), but the belief in that conspiracy, whatever may have been the means with which it was combated, did not derive from science in the strict sense.[7] Raphael Gross, for example, argues that many authors have pointed out that "the essence of National Socialist ideology lay in its attempt to biologize the social"; but, he adds, an explanation of the fact that these biological concepts are bound up with moral categories, and that this is how they acquire their aggressive character, is seldom offered.[8]

What these points add up to is a need to distinguish between race science and race mysticism. Both registers were at work in Nazi Germany, and the former was ultimately dependent upon the existence of the latter. The Third Reich was a racial state, but one that was not driven primarily by "rational" scientific calculations about racial belonging or the (mis) application of vulgar Darwinian notions of struggle and selection, except in the loosest (metaphorical) sense. Rather, Nazi race science was placed at the service of a fundamentally mystical or "non-rational" idea, one that really owed nothing to science: the idea of an Aryan salvation history that understood History as the clash of Aryan and non-Aryan forces. This sort of vulgar Nazism, as Mark Roseman reminds us in relation to Nazi views of the Jewish threat, is not reducible to the question of race: "Though the language continued to be racial, the real force of the argument was of a particularly insidious foreign power."[9] Besides, Nazi race theorists and other scientists often condemned Darwinism for being intellectual, mechanistic, and too far removed from the life of the *Volk*. The botanist Ernst Bergdolt, for example, "accused Darwinism of liberal and Jewish influences."[10] As Christopher Hutton states in his detailed survey of the links and differences between racial science, genetics, linguistics, and psychology under the Third Reich and the Nazi regime, "The fact that Nazi ideology made foundational use of Darwinism should not be understood as implying any simplistic equation of the two."[11]

Very helpful articles by David Lindenfeld and Alan Beyerchen make the point clearly and in a way that will guide this essay. "To be sure," writes Lindenfeld, "the execution of the Holocaust required massive amounts of planning and organization on the parts of the state and parts of the private sector as well. But this was pursuant to decisions that had been made by other, nonrational means."[12] Or, as Beyerchen notes, "Means were certainly open to suggestions, measures of efficiency, and participation by specialists, professionals, academics, and other rationally motivated experts," but this indictment of Germany's professional elite for their complicity with Nazi genocide should not obscure the fact that they were not the ones who decided on *ends*. These were the products of the leading Nazis' "aesthetic-cultic" vision of Aryan salvation through the two-pronged strategy of eliminating racial enemies, especially the Jews, and the creation of a *Volksgemeinschaft*.[13] I suggest, following Lindenfeld and Beyerchen, that historians need to re-place race mysticism at the heart of Nazism and the Third Reich instead of race science; doing so, I suggest, maintains the significance of "race" as a category for understanding the Third Reich but does not succumb to the danger, identified by Mark Roseman, of "obscuring the popular, the national and the social by the biological."[14] Making this distinction also allows us to see more clearly that because race was not as coherent as the Nazis wanted it to be, it cannot function for us as an explanation *sui generis* for Nazi genocide; rather, for all its power, race in Nazi Germany needed a wider set of social, political, and institutional backers to make it popular, seductive, and powerful. Among these broader settings we could include varieties of group thinking other than racial – nationalist, ethnic, or religious, all of which mobilized Germans just as powerfully as did race.

A few examples will suffice to show that "race" and *Volk* were different, that race science and race mysticism did not add up to a coherent and logical body of thought, and that non-biological varieties of group thinking played a role at least as significant as race in Nazi Germany. Perhaps the most famous and best loved of the popularizers of race science was Hans F. K. Günther (known as "der Rassen-Günther" to distinguish him from the many others with the same common surname). In his *Kleine Rassenkunde des deutschen Volkes* (first edition 1929), Günther plainly stated that all Western nations were racially mixed and that what distinguished them was "not the race as such, but the proportion in which the races are mixed." He then went on, apparently without seeing any contradiction, to explain in detail the racial characteristics of the Nordic race, a combination of noble physical and moral features, not least "a pronouncedly heroic disposition" and "a transcendent leadership in statesmanship or creativity in technology, science and art."[15] Walter Gross, the head of the NSDAP's Rassenpolitisches Amt, provided guidance in a circular of October 24, 1934 to regional racial-political offices, stressing the need for consistency in racial thinking when dealing with outsiders who question Nazi racial thinking. Interesting here is his remark in a speech to *alte Kämpfer* who had little time for academic debate that "Even though the rightness of our racial ideas is absolutely clear to us without additional scientific proof, such proof is indispensable in our struggle against those who oppose racial values." That is to say, proof of racial theory would only be required for nay-sayers, not for those who already believed. What Gross stressed in this instance was the need not to use the term "German race" because, as Günther had established, the Germans were racially mixed. Instead, one should use the term "German *Volk*."[16] Gross saw his role as mediating between the world of "science" and that of "ideology" and understood the education of the German people to be the best way of bringing about a practical reconciliation between the scientists' understanding of genetics and the Nazis' *Weltanschauung*.[17] From the party's point of view, as long as that did not threaten the dominance of Nazi ideology, this approach was acceptable. Where applied science could serve the regime best by adhering to and performing well according to international norms, the "disciplines of Volk" would be "under the tutelage of the NSDAP."[18] Hence, once it became clear that there was no scientific proof of Jewishness – once, as Koonz puts it, "No blood type, odor, foot- or fingerprint pattern, skull size, ear lobe or nose shape, or any other physiological marker of Jewishness withstood scrutiny" – the party focused instead on Jews' cultural traits – which were supposedly racially given – in its propaganda, and encouraged race theorists to focus as much on *intuition* as on *observation*.[19] Intuition, of course, is not a recognized scientific method.

Naturally, one can reasonably argue that because these two examples come from popularizers of race science, they do not represent the contribution of race scientists to the Nazi regime. But precisely their status as popularizers is what is important here. As Hutton notes of Günther, while his "aestheticizing racial anthropology" was "fundamental to Nazi images at the level of propaganda, it was inadequate as a basis for a science of race." Racial anthropology as practiced by academic scientists separated from "popular race propaganda," with writers such as Günther and Gross acting as mediators.[20] Besides, when one examines race science, one quickly runs up against a similar fundamental problem: for all the genuine scientific research and for all that the race scientists were located in prestigious, world-famous institutions such as the Kaiser Wilhelm Society's various institutes, there is a gulf between the way in which their research was conducted and the presuppositions that underpinned it. Certainly genetic, biometric, and physical anthropological experiments and measurements were carried out in order to try and establish the racial origins of different population groups under Nazi control. But these were underpinned by a non-rational belief in the existence of and the possibility of distinguishing between races, in particular the possibility of isolating and defining scientifically a Jewish race. That race had already been separated by a moral outlook that decreed "the Jew" was a menace to "the Aryan." Otmar Freiherr von Verschuer, for example, one of Nazi Germany's foremost geneticists and race scientists, may have been held in high regard across the world for his work on, among other things, hereditary disposition to tuberculosis, but his rabid Jew-hatred was not based on scientific methodology or research. As Eric Ehrenreich demonstrates, "there is compelling evidence that the theories that proponents used to rationalize Nazi racial, and especially anti-Jewish, policies were clearly not 'scientific' in any meaningful sense, even as the term was then understood."[21] Indeed, like Eugen Fischer and his student Josef Mengele, and like Günther, Gross, and many others, Verschuer had to abandon scientific methodology in order to make his claims about Jews' racial characteristics, for these were not supported by scientific evidence.

I draw this distinction between race science and race mysticism in order to show that the coherent image of the Third Reich painted by scholars who focus solely on one or the other is unwarranted. Especially in the historiography of race science, there is a tendency for scholars to assume that the internal coherence of the race scientists' world corresponded seamlessly with the norms underpinning wider society. If one examines race science and the dominance of a Social Darwinist standpoint under Nazism, it seems logical that there was a straight line running from the sterilization law of July 1933 to the Nuremberg Laws of September 1935 and thence to the T4 euthanasia program of 1939–1940 and to the murder of asylum inmates in occupied Poland and the USSR, and finally to the murder of the Jews in what has become known as the Holocaust. The latter is then seen as the logical conclusion of the Nazis' eugenic vision; beginning with the removal of racially degenerate Aryans and the attempt to encourage the racially fit to breed, the eugenic logic of the cleansing program became more and more radical – particularly under war conditions – and culminated in the elimination of racial enemies: Roma and Sinti, Poles, Soviet POWs, and especially Jews.[22]

But this image is false. There is first of all a methodological fallacy at work: studying the sources relating to race science gives the impression that the Nazi racial legislation and the Holocaust emerged logically from the writings and activities of race scientists and physical anthropolo-gists.[23] The latter most certainly had a major impact on the Nazi regime, helping to spread the word through advising "hereditary courts," creating propaganda films, and offering medical advice about the cost to the *Volksgemeinschaft* of supporting the disabled, for example, and thus justifying their "removal." More importantly, their activities helped to create a community of Aryans who complied with the regime's require-ment that they acquire an *Ahnenpass* (an ID card showing "ancestral proof") in order to access state services and, in general, to document their membership in the *Volksgemeinschaft*.[24] Yet the sources, without wider contextualization, might not provide the whole story. Informative though such research into racial science often is, it cannot even account for the murder of the disabled, which might appear prima facie to have derived from racial science; nor can it account for the genocide of the Jews.[25] The decision-making process for those programs cannot be reconstructed from the works of the race scientists alone. They served the Nazi state, but they did not direct it. As Robert Proctor notes, "The Nazis supported anthropology – but perhaps only because so many anthropologists were so eager and willing to support the Nazis."[26] It was not necessary to be an anthropologist or physician to send women, children, and old people to the gas chambers in Birkenau.[27] And most crucially, while the anthro-pologists and doctors certainly threw their lot in with the Nazi regime most enthusiastically – what is said here is in no sense meant to white-wash their crimes – the key decisions regarding the murder of asylum patients and Jews were made by Hitler, Himmler, Heydrich, other leading Nazis, and the SS, a fact that is inexplicably often overlooked in much of the literature on race science in the Third Reich.

What these various claims suggest is that the monolithic ubiquity of the racial state paradigm needs to be unpacked. The point is not that race was unimportant to the Third Reich, but that it was too important to be left to the race scientists. Like anti-Semitism, which has been described as a "moving target," race was a floating signifier, a master concept that could be used in any number of different ways depending on the context.[28] Hence the Nazi regime valued simplicity; academics who spent too much time trying to ascertain the percentage of Dinaric, Alpine, or Mediterra-nean stock that contributed to the German *Volk's* racial make-up were likely to find themselves not the recipients of research funding but at best ignored, and at worst ordered to cease their research. The Nazi regime – as opposed to individual Nazis, many of whom took a "philosophical" interest in such matters – was not interested in academic racial scientists' attempts to provide scientifically precise definitions of race but wanted the race scientists to confirm the regime's basic, simple, repeatable point about the supremacy and vitality of the German *Volk*.[29] Race, then, meant political paranoia as much as it meant skull shape and blood groups. The persecution of the Jews, though certainly framed in racial terms, resulted less from the diagnosis of the Jews as an inferior or degenerate race, and more from their identification as a dangerous, pol-luting race, whose deviousness threatened the purity and success of the Aryans. Jews' characteristics were racialized, that is, understood as immutable and hereditary; combating them was a duty understood by the Nazis in social Darwinist terms as the struggle of the fittest to survive. But the identification of the Jews as a racial group and the belief in the need to fight their supposedly deleterious influence stemmed not from race science, but from a mystical race thinking that postulated the Jewish conspiracy to overthrow Aryan purity, whether through capitalism, com-munism, degenerate art and music, the liberal press and the arts, humanist ethics, or race mixing.[30] Race science was drafted in to lend this prepos-terous theory credibility, not the other way round. Hence we need to go beyond the notion of the racial state understood as a coherent monolith dominated and directed by racial science and to replace it with a more complex view of a society mixing long-established norms and moral values with revolutionary aspects of the Nazi worldview, in which new institutions co-existed uneasily with older ones, and in which the language of race and racial struggle gradually seeped into every area of life, but in a promiscuous, fast-shifting, and mobile way.

*

These claims can best be understood by situating the Third Reich in a wider context. It is obviously the case that, as a racial state, the Third Reich was more radical than other European states, for nowhere else was race made the basis of state policy in the same, all-embracing way. However, this fact did not preclude the successful rise to prominence of *völkisch*, ultranationalist, racist movements elsewhere in Europe, and it certainly did not prevent many other states from participating in national "cleansing" projects. In particular, many states tied themselves into or made themselves indispensable to the Nazis' murder of the Jews, and some, under the umbrella of Nazi-directed criminality, also used the opportunity to eradicate national minorities and other traditional "enemies," such as Romanies and Serbs in the Yugoslav territories under control of the Independent State of Croatia.[31] But race in these instances was rarely the main driving force, and race science specifically was of limited import. A more diffuse notion of race-thinking, however, certainly has some purchase here. And more important still are non-biological varieties of exclusivist group identities; if in Nazi Germany, where race-thinking was ubiquitous, one has to take account of *völkisch*, nationalist, and other forms of group belonging instead of just seeing everything as being situated in the domain of race science, so in other genocidal contexts we see very clearly that even where social distinctions were racialized, non-biological group distinctions played a greater role in energizing eliminatory ambitions than did race in the narrow sense of race science or a biologization of the social. What recent research shows is that race-thinking needs to be seen as but one part of radical nationalist (and sometimes transnationalist) thinking in which the articulation and performance of racial thought is driven by factors and forces that have little to do with the inner logics of race-thinking itself.[32]

Although comparative history is hardly a recent invention, and although the notion of the Holocaust's uniqueness is no longer the subject of heated debate in academia in the way it was in the West German *Historikerstreit* of the mid-1980s, the attempt to situate Nazism in general and the Holocaust in particular in a broader context has, of late, become newly controversial. This time, in the different setting of the discipline of "genocide studies," scholars have set out to show that Nazism emerged in the context of the collapse of the European empires and the violence that characterized the successor states of Central Europe, and that the Holocaust should not be understood only as an internal problem of the Third Reich but, on the one hand, as part of a Euro-Asian history of ethnic and nationalist violence that dates back at least fifty years prior to Hitler's accession to power, and, on the other (to the extent that these strands are separable), as related to the history of the violence that accompanied European overseas colonialism and imperialism.[33]

In this narrative of the widespread turn to violence in modern European history, race-thinking is only one explanatory strand. On the one hand, the argument suggests a less prominent role for race-thinking than might be the case if one examines Nazi Germany on its own or if one's focus is solely on an institutional history of race-science institutions, publications, or ideas. On the other hand, the widespread complicity of scientists with ethnonationalist projects has emerged more clearly. We know now that race scientists accompanied and encouraged national cleansing projects throughout Europe.[34] Thus, even if the idea of the racial state is too simplistic for understanding the turn to authoritarian ethnocracies across Europe in the interwar years, a transnational race-thinking that posited a more mystical notion of racial struggle and national renewal as intertwined played a significant role in fueling this process.

Like fascism, then, race-thinking and particular related manifestations of it, such as the eugenics movement, should be seen as transnational movements.[35] To give one example: in Romania in the early twentieth century, "race" in a rather diffuse sense played a role in spreading a "revolutionary ethos" against "modern" institutions and liberal ethics, and in contributing to nationalists' advocacy of the elimination of non-Romanian, especially Jewish, elements in the population.[36] Romanian race scientists often found themselves at odds with these ethnonationalist accounts of Romania's Dacian roots.[37] Nevertheless, when it came to eugenic sterilization, such measures could be justified both in terms of the scientific campaign against "undesirables" and in terms of the political discourse that aimed at "the political engineering of a biologically defined community."[38] During World War II, the eugenicist Iordache Făcăoaru, following his mentor Iuliu Moldovan at the Institute of Hygiene and Public Health in Cluj, advocated compulsory sterilizations based not on notions of Romanian racial purity (which they rejected) but on reversing the putative threat of racial degeneration.[39] In Transnistria, the area of Ukraine occupied by (though not fully incorporated into) Romania during the war (including the city of Odessa), anthropologists sought to identify the Romanian essence of the population and took part in the Holocaust in the process. As Marius Turda puts it, there was a clear connection "between eugenic discourses of national purification and ideas of ethnic homogeneity" in Transnistria.[40] Although there was neither always nor necessarily a direct correlation between eugenic discourse and radical-right politics,[41] the point here is to show that the racial state that was being created in various forms throughout interwar and wartime Europe – not just the German *Volksgemeinschaft* – was a product not only of science but of far broader political presuppositions and aspirations.[42]

Race-thinking, then, was clearly key to the process of creating ethnocracies in interwar and wartime Europe. But that race-thinking should be seen as part of a broader social, cultural, and above all political process that emerged out of the great changes in European life that followed World War I. Race here was a social and political driver that could be expressed in scientific terms but that gained purchase the more it was conjoined to political processes that contributed to the forging of new nation-states, such as the eradication of minorities from civil services, universities, and the worlds of trade and culture; the creation of ethnically homogeneous middle classes; and the enforcement of linguistic conformity. Focusing only on Germany has tended to encourage overlooking these wider processes. By widening the picture, we see that race-thinking was by no means confined to Germany but also that race only took effect as an idea when it furthered social and political change.

*

If the racial state approach has overstated the coherence of the race idea to the internal social history of the Third Reich, what then accounts for the current centrality of race in the historiography not only of the Third Reich but of the modern world in general, including the histories of eugenics and genocide? The answer is not only a matter of presentist concerns, for, as I have argued, race-thinking of a certain variety was indeed one element of the makeup of the Nazi state and of others besides. But today, a combination of identity politics, human rights awareness, and the prevailing definition of genocide has made "race" in the sense of racial science loom larger in the historical imagination than is warranted by the diversity of factors that contributed to the nature of the Third Reich. By focusing on race at the expense of non-biological forms of group identity such as nationalism, it is also easier to assume that "we" in the civilized world are immune from such "crazy" ways of thinking.

Although Holocaust historiography and genocide studies are sometimes perceived as at odds with one another – particular versus universal, or specific versus typologizing – in fact, the centrality of race to genocide studies, which has increased since a new generation of historians began developing the earlier work of political scientists, means that genocide studies is confirming the new consensus within Holocaust history.[43] This again brings up the question of whether race is a determining factor of genocide. While no one would gainsay the role played by racialization (in the broad sense of the biologization of the social or more narrowly in the narrowing of identity options) in recent cases of genocide, such as in Cambodia, Bosnia, or Rwanda, the notion that either genocidal regimes or whole populations were mobilized solely on the basis of race-thinking is somewhat fanciful. What the historiography of Nazi Germany that goes beyond the racial paradigm reveals is that far from being united by race, in fact modern genocides, including the Holocaust, all have exactly the opposite in common: they are all characterized to a greater or lesser extent by race-thinking, but it is not this race-thinking per se that is significant. Rather, what is noteworthy is that this race-thinking is articulated and mobilized when it meshes with the concerns of other varieties of radical, exclusivist group-thinking.

In Cambodia, the Khmer Rouge sought to build Democratic Kampuchea on the basis of a range of ideological imperatives, most clearly expressed by Kiernan as the four factors that for him characterize genocide in general: race, religion, expansion, and cultivation.[44] While certain minority ethnic groups in Cambodia were targeted, especially the Muslim Chams, the Vietnamese, and the Chinese, the Khmer Rouge were motivated more by a Social Darwinist, ultra-peasantist Maoism than by racial science, which, if they knew of it at all – from Pol Pot's student days in France, for example – was put through the rice-growing mangle and made the agent of ultra-radical social reorganization. In Bosnia, as John Mueller has shown, the violence was directed by a small, radical leadership and executed by paramilitaries and gangs of violent thugs and common criminals, who were able to exercise a role in society at a moment of crisis that they would normally be unable to enjoy. Mueller may himself understate the role played by longer-term factors in the Wars of Yugoslav Succession, especially competing memories of World War II, which were keenly exploited by all sides. But his basic point, that ethnic warfare derives from "banalities" rather than highfalutin racial theory, is surely right.[45] Even in Rwanda, which is the example in which longstanding racial theories and stereotypes, derived from colonial anthropology, played the most obvious role in directing the genocide,[46] the radical fracture between Hutus and Tutsis that occurred between the Rwandan Patriotic Front's (RPF) invasion of 1990 and the genocide of 1994 was one that had been turned from a social to an "ethnic" question over many decades but that reached crisis point only in the context of other factors. The civil war that consumed Rwanda was itself a long-term consequence of the 1959 revolution, which left several generations of Tutsi refugees outside of Rwanda, so this conflict was a "racial" one from the start. But racial politics needed other crises to become effective, and these occurred in the late 1980s and early 1990s, in the context of Rwandan economic decline and constitutional confusion over the introduction of a more democratic polity, and the civil war engendered by the collapse of power sharing and the RPF invasion.

Nevertheless, for most scholars it is axiomatic that race is central to understanding genocide. This understanding has two important consequences. First, the circumstances in which race theory is mobilized are downplayed, so that race-thinking is taken as both a necessary and a sufficient explanation for the occurrence of genocide. Second, race-thinking is taken to be synonymous with racial science. But are we really thinking of racial science when we call to mind powerful organic notions of the *Volk*, of Angkar, or of Hutu Power? Did not these notions, with their calls to organic purity,[47] rely far less on science – though science was welcome to back them up where it could do so – than on a desire for their ethnopolitical visions and fantasies to become true? Could it be that scholars' and other commentators' determination to find racial motives where thuggish ones exist relies too heavily on the perpetrators' own categories? And, more worryingly, does this procedure of taking the perpetrators literally help to make the perpetration of atrocities easier and persuade the international community that intervention is impossible? John Mueller thinks so:

The mistaken – even racist – notion that an entire ethnic group is devotedly out to destroy another ethnic group can in such cases shatter any ability to perceive nuance and variety, and it can be taken to suggest that efforts to foster elite accommodation are essentially irrelevant and therefore bound to prove futile. Further, the all-against-all image can discourage policing because it implies that the entire ethnic group – rather than just a small, opportunistic, and often cowardly subgroup – must be brought under control.[48]

One cannot simply assume that Mueller's argument is right even though his description of a radical genocidal regime backed by armed thugs is an accurate account of Bosnia or Rwanda, and even though it has received the backing of scholars who stress that for genocide to occur one needs not (or not at first) large social movements but a determined leadership group.[49] Yet there are many reasons why "race" in the sense of race science is overemphasized in the scholarly literature. One is the science of victimhood that has emerged since the 1960s and the rise of the civil rights movement in the US. For all its shortcomings – its tendency toward conspiracy theory, most notably – Peter Novick's explanation of the rise of "Holocaust consciousness" in the US compellingly shows how an interest in the Holocaust among Jews was inculcated by community organizations, and how that interest gradually spread more widely across the American population. Second is the emerging human rights agenda, which has developed rapidly since 1968.[50] But most important for the scholarly analysis of genocide, the UN Genocide Convention (UNGC) famously specifies that for genocide to occur, there must be the "intent to destroy, in whole or in part, a national, ethnical, racial or religious group, as such." Given that the international legal regime on genocide has developed so quickly and influentially since 1999, with the establishment of the International Criminal Court and the first judgments of the International Criminal Tribunal for Rwanda and the International Criminal Tribunal for the Former Yugoslavia, it is no surprise that scholars have tended toward the "racialization" of their subjects in order for them to meet the criteria of the "crime of crimes."[51]

None of this is meant to suggest that race per se is unimportant to the perpetration or understanding of genocide. Nor is it meant to suggest that science in general in the Third Reich was nothing other than "pseudoscience"; a glance at microscope technology, new data technologies, cancer research, or the activities of engineers and aircraft designers during the Nazi regime immediately scotches such a claim.[52] But the assumption that "race" and "race science" were synonymous in the twentieth century means that a far too coherent vision of race has been applied to cases of genocide and ethnic cleansing – one that dissociates race from society, or at best assumes that social consequences are driven ideologically by regimes subscribing to scientific (or "pseudoscientific") ideas. In fact, the type of race-thinking that is key to genocide is the more mystical one of social and national regeneration, which is a more generally held "modernist" view for the rebuilding of the nation in a time of supposed threat or degeneration. In this understanding, race is just one of the terms – articulated more or less scientifically, depending on the context – that contributes to sustaining and developing national stereotypes. This is why so much of race science merely confirmed existing norms, which had been derived from folklore, hearsay, or cultural stereotypes. It is also why the Third Reich was more of a racial state than anywhere else: there, the mystical fantasies of race that were so important to the regime were mobilized in the absence of genuine conflict, as occurred in other cases of genocide, where the element of fantasy thinking required was one that necessitated jumping from a certain, usually low-level threat (e.g., from Armenian nationalist groups) to mass murder of all members of the putatively threatening group. In Nazi Germany, the language of race permeated all spheres of life, but it hardly added up to a coherent and orderly scientific system; it was, rather, an ontologically articulated *Weltanschauung* that postulated – in the absence of evidence, or rather with the absence of evidence being taken as proof of the conspiracy – a *Lebenskampf* (or *Todeskampf*) between Aryan and non-Aryan.

As the Third Reich collapsed, Hitler dictated the following words to Martin Bormann in the bunker: "Out of the sacrifice of our soldiers and out of my own close ties with them unto death, the seed will one day germinate in German history one way or another, and give rise to a glorious rebirth of the National Socialist movement, and thus to the realization of a true racial community [*Volksgemeinschaft*]." As Bernd Wegner notes of this passage, it reveals that "it was not Social Darwinism that ultimately prevailed, but *völkisch* romanticism."[53] At the moment of self-destruction that Hitler here perversely celebrated, the central element of the Nazi *Weltanschauung* became clear: not race *science*, but the mystical communion of the *Volk*.

Notes

1 An argument stated most clearly and controversially by Thomas Kühne, *Belonging and Genocide: Hitler's Community, 1918–1945* (New Haven, 2010). But see also Michael Wildt, *Volksgemeinschaft als Selbstermächtigung: Gewalt gegen Juden in der deutschen Provinz 1919 bis 1939* (Hamburg, 2007); Frank Bajohr and Michael Wildt (eds.), *Volksgemeinschaft: Neue Forschungen zur Gesellschaft des Nationalsozialismus* (Frankfurt am Main, 2009); Boaz Neumann, *Die Weltanschauung des Nazismus: Raum, Körper, Sprache* (Göttingen, 2010); Peter Fritzsche, *Life and Death in the Third Reich* (Cambridge, MA, 2008); Peter Fritzsche and Jochen Hellbeck, "The new man in Stalinist Russia and Nazi Germany" in Michael Geyer and Sheila Fitzpatrick (eds.), *Beyond Totalitarianism: Stalinism and Nazism Compared* (New York, 2009), 302–41.

2 For warnings to avoid getting too carried away by the voluntaristic turn, see
   Geoff Eley, "Hitler's silent majority? Conformity and resistance under the
   Third Reich," *Michigan Quarterly Review* 42(2) (2003), 550–83 (part 1) and
   42(3) (2003), 389–425 (part 2); Neil Gregor, "Nazism – a political religion?
   Rethinking the voluntarist turn" in N. Gregor (ed.), *Nazism, War and Geno-*
   cide: Essays in Honour of Jeremy Noakes (Exeter, 2005), 1–21; Richard Evans,
   "Coercion and consent in Nazi Germany," *Proceedings of the British Academy*,
   151 (2007), 53–81. It should be noted that the voluntaristic turn is not coter-
   minous with an emphasis on ideology. Götz Aly's recent work, for example, has
   placed far more emphasis on the Third Reich as a "welfare dictatorship" than
   on the power of ideas. See his *Hitler's Beneficiaries: Plunder, Racial War, and*
   the Nazi Welfare State (New York, 2006).

3 Ian Kershaw, "'Volksgemeinschaft': Potenzial und Grenzen eines neuen For-
   schungskonzepts," *Vierteljahrshefte für Zeitgeschichte*, 59(1) (2011), 1–17.

4 Melita Maschmann, *Fazit: Mein Weg in die Hitler-Jugend* (Munich, 1981); on
   Maschmann and the way in which her text has been incorporated into text-
   books on the Third Reich, see Joanne Sayner, "'Man muß die bunten Blüten
   abreißen': Melita Maschmann's autobiographical memories of Nazism,"
   Forum of Modern Language Studies 41(2) (2005), 213–25.

5 Raphael Gross, *Anständig geblieben: Nationalsozialistische Moral* (Frankfurt
   am Main, 2010); Frank Bajohr, *"Aryanization" in Hamburg: The Economic*
   Exclusion of Jews and the Confiscation of Their Property in Nazi Germany
   (New York, 2002); and the controversial Aly, *Hitler's Beneficiaries*.

6 For example: Konrad H. Jarausch, "Unasked questions: the controversy about
   Nazi collaboration among German historians" in Jeffrey M. Diefendorf (ed.),
   Lessons and Legacies, Vol. VI: New Currents in Holocaust Research (Evan-
   ston, 2004), 190–208; Alan E. Steinweis, "Nazi historical scholarship on the
   'Jewish question,'" in Wolfgang Bialas and Anson Rabinbach (eds.), *Nazi*
   Germany and the Humanities (Oxford, 2007), 399–412; Alan E. Steinweis,
   Studying the Jew: Scholarly Antisemitism in Nazi Germany (Cambridge, MA,
   2006); Dirk Rupnow, *Judenforschung im Dritten Reich: Wissenschaft zwischen*
   Politik, Propaganda und Ideologie (Baden-Baden, 2011); Joan L. Clinefelter,
   Artists for the Reich: Culture and Race from Weimar to Nazi Germany
   (Oxford, 2005); Jay W. Baird, *Hitler's War Poets: Literature and Politics in*
   the Third Reich (Cambridge, 2008).

7 Cf. Richard Weikart, *Hitler's Ethic: The Nazi Pursuit of Evolutionary Progress*
   (New York, 2009). Weikart writes, for example, that "In Hitler's view, whatever promoted the health and vitality of the human species was morally good.
   Conversely, anything contributing to biological degeneration or decline he
   deemed immoral" (5). So far, so good, for Hitler's beliefs here have nothing
   to do with the findings of race science, but rather with assumptions that have
   been common since antiquity. But when Weikart goes further, the argument is
   less persuasive: "Hitler's evolutionary ethic was the guiding principle behind
   many important policies, including eugenics, population growth, killing the
   disabled, expansionist warfare, racial struggle, and killing the Jews" (15). In
   explaining the Holocaust, or even the ubiquity of race-thinking in the Third
   Reich, one runs up against nonrational beliefs at every turn, such as "the Jews

are an inferior race" – according to what scientific criteria? Hitler's Social Darwinism – the emphasis on life as racial struggle – is more appropriately understood as race mysticism than race science. See also *Hitler's Ethic*, chapter 4, where the two categories merge. In general, Weikart ascribes far too great a sense of coherence and consistency to Nazi racial thinking.

8 Gross, *Anständig geblieben*, 8. See also Neumann, *Die Weltanschauung des Nazismus*, 24. For Neumann, Nazism should be understood not as an ideology but as a *Weltanschauung*; that is to say, not as a way of thinking that is restricted to a political program but as a way of life. "Wir hoffen," as Goebbels said in a speech of 1935, "daß einmal die Zeit kommt, daß man über den Nationalsozialismus nicht mehr zu sprechen braucht, sondern daß er die Luft ist, in der wir atmen!" (cited in Neumann, 24). Nazism, in Neumann's understanding, is based on a pure "ontology of life" (34).

9 See Mark Roseman's chapter in this volume.

10 Thomas Junker and Uwe Hoßfeld, "The architects of the evolutionary synthesis in National Socialist Germany: science and politics," *Biology and Philosophy*, 17(2) (2002), 223–49, here 242. For another example, see Paul Brohmer, *Biologieunterricht und völkische Erziehung* (Frankfurt am Main, 1933), extracted in George L. Mosse (ed.), *Nazi Culture: Intellectual, Cultural and Social Life in the Third Reich* (Madison, 1966), 81–90.

11 Christopher M. Hutton, *Race and the Third Reich: Linguistics, Racial Anthropology and Genetics in the Dialectic of Volk* (Cambridge, 2005), 198.

12 David Lindenfeld, "The prevalence of irrational thinking in the Third Reich: notes toward the reconstruction of modern value rationality," *Central European History* 30(3) (1997), 376–7.

13 Alan Beyerchen, "Rational means and irrational ends: thoughts on the technology of racism in the Third Reich," *Central European History* 30(3) (1997), 390–2.

14 Roseman, this volume, 34.

15 Günther, *Kleine Rassenkunde des deutschen Volkes* (edition of 1933), extracted in Mosse, *Nazi Culture*, 63–5.

16 Gross, cited in Claudia Koonz, *The Nazi Conscience* (Cambridge, MA, 2003), 197. For the original, see Walter Gross, "Deutsche Rasse" (October 24, 1934) in Léon Poliakov and Joseph Wulf (eds.), *Das Dritte Reich und seine Denker* (Frankfurt am Main, 1983), 411–13.

17 Hutton, *Race and the Third Reich*, 181–3.

18 Ibid., 194.

19 Koonz, *The Nazi Conscience*, 197.

20 Hutton, *Race and the Third Reich*, 208.

21 Eric Ehrenreich, "Otmar von Verschuer and the 'scientific' legitimization of Nazi anti-Jewish policy," *Holocaust and Genocide Studies* 21(2) (2007), 55–72, here 56.

22 For further discussion, see A. Dirk Moses and Dan Stone, "Eugenics and genocide" in Alison Bashford and Philippa Levine (eds.), *The Oxford Handbook of the History of Eugenics* (New York, 2010), 192–209.

23 Detlev J. K. Peukert, "The genesis of the 'Final Solution' from the spirit of science" in David F. Crew (ed.), *Nazism and German Society, 1933–1945* (London, 1994), 274–99.

24 Eric Ehrenreich, *The Nazi Ancestral Proof: Genealogy, Racial Science, and the Final Solution* (Bloomington, 2007). For another example of scientists' service to the Nazi state, see Sheila Faith Weiss, "'The sword of our science' as a foreign policy weapon: the political function of German geneticists in the international arena during the Third Reich," *Ergebnisse: Vorabdrucke aus dem Forschungsprogramm "Geschichte der Kaiser-Wilhelm-Gesellschaft im Nationalsozialismus,"* 22 (2005), and Weiss, *The Nazi Symbiosis: Human Genetics and Politics in the Third Reich* (Chicago, 2010).

25 See, for example, the excellent exhibition catalogue, *Deadly Medicine: Creating the Master Race* (Washington, DC, 2004).

26 Robert Proctor, "From *Anthropologie* to *Rassenkunde* in the German anthropological tradition" in George W. Stocking (ed.), *Bones, Bodies, Behavior: Essays on Physical Anthropology* (Madison, 1988), 138–79, here 166.

27 Henry Friedlander, *The Origins of Nazi Genocide: From Euthanasia to the Final Solution* (Chapel Hill, 1995), 302.

28 "Moving target" is Peter Pulzer's term, cited in Gross, *Anständig geblieben*, 18.

29 See Hutton, *Race and the Third Reich*. As Hutton notes, the *völkisch* movement contained strongly anti-Darwinist elements, such as Julius Langbehn, Ludwig Klages, and Oswald Spengler (177–8).

30 Theodor Fritsch's highly influential *Handbuch der Judenfrage* (49th edn., Leipzig, 1944 [1887]) detailed the supposed activities of the Jews in some fifteen spheres of German cultural life, from the stock exchange to the theatre.

31 For fuller discussion of the pan-European dimension of the Holocaust, see my *Histories of the Holocaust*, chapter 1.

32 My thanks to Mark Roseman for this formulation.

33 Donald Bloxham and Robert Gerwarth (eds.), *Political Violence in Twentieth-Century Europe* (Cambridge, 2011); Cathie Carmichael, *Genocide before the Holocaust* (New Haven, 2009); Benjamin Liebermann, *Terrible Fate: Ethnic Cleansing in the Making of Modern Europe* (Chicago, 2006); Bloxham, "Europe, the Final Solution and the dynamics of intent," *Patterns of Prejudice* 44(4) (2010), 317–35; Bloxham, *The Final Solution: A Genocide* (Oxford, 2009); Jürgen Zimmerer, *Von Windhuk nach Auschwitz? Beiträge zum Verhältnis von Kolonialismus und Holocaust* (Münster, 2009); Stone, *Histories of the Holocaust*, chapter 5; Geoff Eley, *Nazism as Fascism* (London, 2013), chapter 5. See especially the forum on Bloxham's *The Final Solution: A Genocide* in the *Journal of Genocide Research* 13(1–2) (2011), 107–52.

34 For example, see the essays in Marius Turda and Paul J. Weindling (eds.), *Blood and Homeland: Eugenics and Racial Nationalism in Central and Southeast Europe 1900–1940* (Budapest, 2007). See also Ingo Haar and Michael Fahlbusch (eds.), *German Scholars and Ethnic Cleansing, 1919–1945* (New York, 2005).

35 For example: Federico Finchelstein, *Transatlantic Fascism: Ideology, Violence, and the Sacred in Argentina and Italy, 1919–1945* (Durham, 2010); Marius Turda, *Modernism and Eugenics* (Basingstoke, 2010); Weiss, *The Nazi Symbiosis*, chapter 1.

36 Răzvan Pârâianu, "Culturalist nationalism and anti-semitism in fin-de-siècle Romania" in Turda and Weindling (eds.), *Blood and Homeland*, 354–6.

37 Richard McMahon, "On the margins of international science and national discourse: national identity narratives in Romanian race anthropology," *European Review of History* 16(1) (2009), 101–23.

38 Marius Turda, "'To end the degeneration of a nation': debates on eugenic sterilization in inter-war Romania," *Medical History* 53 (2009), 77–104, here 78.

39 Ibid., 92–3.

40 Ibid., 103. See also Vladimir Solonari, "Patterns of violence: local populations and the mass murder of Jews in Bessarabia and Northern Bukovina, July-August 1941," *Kritika: Explorations in Russian and Eurasian History*, 8(4) (2007), 749–87, which shows that genocide was driven primarily by a program of nation-building.

41 Maria Bucur, "Eugenics in Eastern Europe, 1870s–1945," in Bashford and Levine (eds.), *Oxford Handbook of the History of Eugenics*, 398–412, here 403.

42 See also Richard McMahon, "Anthropological race psychology 1820–1945: a common European system of ethnic identity narratives," *Nations and Nationalism*, 15(4) (2009), 575–96 on the role of race science in legitimizing national-racial stereotypes, and their contribution to geopolitical identity narratives.

43 A. Dirk Moses, "The Holocaust and genocide" in Dan Stone (ed.), *The Historiography of the Holocaust* (Basingstoke, 2004), 533–55.

44 Ben Kiernan, "Twentieth-century genocides: underlying ideological themes from Armenia to East Timor" in Robert Gellately and Ben Kiernan (eds.), *The Specter of Genocide: Mass Murder in Historical Perspective* (New York, 2003), 29–51. See also Kiernan, *Blood and Soil: A World History of Genocide and Extermination from Sparta to Darfur* (New Haven, 2007).

45 John Mueller, "The banality of 'ethnic war,'" *International Security* 25(1) (2000), 42–70. See also Mart Bax, "Warlords, priests and the politics of ethnic cleansing: a case-study from rural Bosnia-Hercegovina," *Ethnic and Racial Studies*, 23(1) (2000), 16–36.

46 Mahmood Mamdani, *When Victims Become Killers: Colonialism, Nativism, and the Genocide in Rwanda* (Princeton, 2001).

47 Scott Straus, "Organic purity and the role of anthropology in Cambodia and Rwanda," *Patterns of Prejudice* 35(2) (2001), 47–62.

48 Mueller, "The banality of 'ethnic war,'" 70. Besides, Mueller is not making a point about race but about the identification of wider society with the perpetrators, which need not be (and probably is not) made on the basis of race.

49 Benjamin A. Valentino, *Final Solutions: Mass Killing and Genocide in the 20th Century* (Ithaca, 2004).

50 Samuel Moyn, *The Last Utopia: Human Rights in History* (Cambridge, MA, 2010).

51 Jeffrey S. Morton and Neil Vijay Singh, "The international legal regime on genocide," *Journal of Genocide Research* 5(1) (2003), 47–69; Alex Obote-Odora, "Genocide on trial: normative effects of the Rwanda Tribunal's jurisprudence," *Development Dialogue*, 55 (2011), 125–51.

52 Robert Proctor, "Nazi science and Nazi medical ethics: some myths and misconceptions," *Perspectives in Biology and Medicine* 43(3) (2000), 335–46.

Cf. Volker R. Remmert, "What's Nazi about Nazi science? Recent trends in the history of science in Nazi Germany," *Perspectives on Science*, 12(4) (2004), 454–75; Volker Roelcke, "Medicine during the Nazi period: historical facts and some implications for teaching medical ethics and professionalism" in Sheldon Rubenfeld (ed.), *Medicine after the Holocaust: From the Master Race to the Human Genome and Beyond* (New York, 2010), 17–28.

53 Bernd Wegner, "The ideology of self-destruction: Hitler and the choreography of defeat," *Bulletin of the German Historical Institute London* 26(2) (2004), 18–33, here 33. For the context, see Hans Mommsen, "The Indian summer and the collapse of the Third Reich: the last act" in Hans Mommsen (ed.), *The Third Reich between Vision and Reality: New Perspectives on German History, 1918–1945* (Oxford, 2001), 109–27, and Michael Geyer, "*Endkampf* 1918 and 1945: German nationalism, annihilation, and self-destruction" in Alf Lüdtke and Bernd Weisbrod (eds.), *No Man's Land of Violence: Extreme Wars in the 20th Century* (Göttingen, 2006), 35–67.

7

Ideology's Logic

The Evolution of Racial Thought in Germany from the *Völkisch* Movement to the Third Reich

Christian Geulen

In 1935, the German Ministry of Propaganda published a leaflet that presented the twelve essential rules of National Socialist racial theory in easy-to-remember terms.[1] The final rule was the famous and often quoted slogan: "Be proud to be a German," printed in capital letters and punctuated with an exclamation mark. Although presented as the most important racial law of all, this concluding exhortation made no reference to the biological framework of racial thinking. Instead, it referred to a very traditional and classic feature of modern nationalism. Politicians, revolutionaries, and intellectuals across the globe had been calling for citizens to take pride in their nation ever since the modern idea of the nation was born in the eighteenth century. In Nazi propaganda, however, national self-esteem was no longer regarded as a basis for the regeneration of the nation and the shaping of a new "national community" (*Volksgemeinschaft*). The twelfth rule suggests, by contrast, that national pride was seen as the result or final quintessence of orderly racialist conduct. More precisely: to be proud of being a German, one had to behave in accordance with the laws of racial theory. Obviously, this placed the category of race above that of the nation. However, it also reduced the idea of race to an instrument by which the political and in themselves non-biological goals of the National Socialist "new order" were to be achieved. Such observations lead us to question the assumption that we know all there is to know about the role of racial thinking in the Third Reich. This chapter starts from the premise that the meaning and function of racial discourse within the Nazi system is still not fully understood and must be investigated further. For, as will be argued in this essay, the Nazis did not derive their political agenda from a theory of race; rather, they used an abstract, non-empirical notion of race to rationalize their political actions.

Before developing this point further, a closer look at the Ministry of Propaganda leaflet can illuminate some other aspects of the issue at hand. The first rule listed in the leaflet demanded: "Secure the eternal life of your nation [*Volk*] through an abundance of children in your family." Once again, this exhortation shared very little with contemporary racial theory, which demanded very careful control of reproduction ever since it was observed that the less desired groups within a given nation tended to reproduce at a higher rate than the desired groups. To any informed and up-to-date racial theorist, such a general call for more sexual reproduction so as to ensure the eternal perpetuation of the nation must have sounded completely outdated. Similarly, the second rule seems too undiscriminating to be part of a program of racial improvement: "German man, respect and protect in every woman the mother of German children." The reference to "every woman" instead of "your wife" or "every *German* woman" indicates the extent to which the Nazis conceived of *Volksgemeinschaft* as a unity beyond the family. The ideal was a community as strictly separated from any outsiders as it was undifferentiated within. Accordingly, the third rule read: "German woman, never forget your highest purpose: to be the guardian of the German stock [*Art*]." As mothers of the nation, it was women's responsibility to watch over the boundary separating the German *Volk* from non-German outsiders. In contrast to the German man, who, as the second rule suggests, could father a purely German child with "every woman," the German woman had to be very careful when choosing a mate. This obviously gendered concept of collective reproduction was again decades behind what racial theory taught about the gender-independent perils to racial purity.

The next four rules, addressed to the German woman, simply underlined the responsibility introduced in the third:

4. Protect your children from the fate of the half-breed [*Mischling*].
5. Keep the German blood pure.
6. Everybody who is not of German blood is of foreign blood.
7. Preserve your honor and your stock [*Art*] when you encounter *Volksfremde* [foreigners, those who don't belong to the *Volk*].

Step by step, the focus shifted from the woman's responsibility for the German nation to the most important way of fulfilling this responsibility:

stay clear of outsiders. *Volksfremde* were defined negatively: anyone not of German blood. Consequently, the eighth rule offered the assurance: "German girls: Your reserve toward *Volksfremde* is not an insult. On the contrary, every respectable foreigner will honor you for this." This is perhaps the most interesting of the "racial laws" set out in the ministry's leaflet. With the turn from German women to German girls, the focus shifted from motherhood to sexual contact in general, including contact not necessarily bound to reproduction. The Nuremberg Laws had declared any sexual contact with non-Germans, even if conception did not occur, to be an act of "racial defilement" (*Rassenschande*) punishable by law.[2] The scientific legitimization of this law drew upon very traditional, pre-Darwinian theories of evolution such as Lamarckism and telegony. Those theories had claimed that sexual experiences leave a hereditary footprint in women, whose later children (fathered by somebody else) might still carry traits of their former lovers.[3] The German biologist August Weismann had disproven such assumptions decades earlier, but the Nazis had to rely on them to establish a link between non-reproductive sex and racialist ideas of purity. Moreover, the racialist advice to German girls to keep away from *Volksfremde* was based on the claim that the preservation of purity was not only a German necessity but a general biopolitical law upheld and obeyed by all nations. In other words, the Nazis argued, not without basis, that radical-nationalist ideas of biological self-preservation enjoyed wide international appeal and used this apparent international legitimacy to dignify their call for sexual abstinence toward outsiders at home.

The next two laws given in the leaflet emphasized the universal validity of racial principles:

9. The protection of one's own blood does not mean contempt for other nations.
10. Maintaining purity of blood is in the interest of all valuable races.

Here, for the first and only time, the term "race" (*Rasse*) was used, introducing the universal importance and objective dimension of racialist behavior as a primary law of nature, underpinning and informing all other laws of racial conduct. Only in the two concluding rules was this universal dimension reunited with the idea of Germanness:

11. The purity of blood is not a private matter but a natural obligation of every German [*deutscher Mensch*] to his nation [*Volk*].
12. Be proud to be a German![4]

THE SEMANTICS OF NATION, *VOLK*, AND *RASSE*

The way we interpret the 1935 leaflet will depend to a large extent on how we translate the German term *Volk*. In this essay, it is translated as "nation" – a decision that may surprise some readers. Historians have long tended to place the meaning of *Volk* in the context of the discourse of the *völkisch* and Nazi movements, assigning it a meaning closer to "race" than to "nation." A glance at the history of the terms concerned indicates, however, that, throughout the "long nineteenth century," *Volk* was a political term meaning *Staatsvolk*, a group of people constituting a political or state community. By contrast, *Nation* in German designated a group linked by a shared past, a common language and culture, or a common ancestry. Even in 1906, when the *völkisch* movement was at its peak, a standard German encyclopedia emphasized that the German terms *Nation* and *Volk* had different meanings than the English and French concepts of nation/*nation* and people/*peuple*. Nation, in both English and French, designated the political concept and people/*peuple* the pre-political concept. In German, the idea of *Nation* had to be understood pre-politically as a *Völkerschaft* with a common history, language, and culture, whereas *Volk* was the political community made up by the citizens of a state. Accordingly, the 1906 encyclopedia article stated that, whereas it was possible to speak of a German *Volk* as well as of a German *Nation*, one could speak only of an Austrian *Volk* and not of an Austrian *Nation* – because the Austrians were Germans by nation but belonged politically to a multinational *Volk*.[5]

The *völkisch* movement desperately tried to dispense with the purely political meaning of *Volk* by racializing it and making it synonymous with the term *Nation*. It is interesting to note how much effort this required. The very invention of the awkward adjective *völkisch* illustrates how conscious these movements were of the size of the task involved in redefining and restructuring contemporary political language. In their writings, most authors of the *völkisch* movement preferred to speak of *das Völkische* or directly of "race" rather than of *das Volk* in an attempt to refer to some deeper unity that transcended the boundaries of state or nation. It was not just radical groups, however, that tended to obscure the difference between *Volk* and *Nation*. The terms became ever more similar in the development of political semantics during the long transition from the nineteenth century to the twentieth. Already in the 1860s, for example, liberals in Germany had begun to develop a theory of the *Nationalitätenprinzip* (literally, principle of nationality). It postulated that every nation had a natural right to create its own state, that is, "to become a *Volk*."[6] This "principle" became less persuasive during the era of high imperialism but was revived after World War I with Woodrow Wilson's declaration that the reconstruction of Europe should be based on national self-determination.[7] Both the *Nationalitätenprinzip* and the principle of national self-determination envisioned a world in which the historical boundaries between cultures would be turned into political and state boundaries, thus suggesting a universal order of nation-states.[8] Despite the globalizing forces of imperialism, capitalism, and transnational migration, twentieth-century politics upheld this principle for a long time – even though the problems of population transfer, deportation, and mass violence, nourished by the underlying idea of national homogeneity, became all too obvious, especially in Eastern and Southeastern Europe during the war and in the early postwar years.

These international developments and radical nationalists' success in popularizing *völkisch* notions of belonging contributed to the semantic shift that the German concepts of *Volk* and *Nation* went through during the early twentieth century. Whereas the terms *Nation* and *national* became signifiers of a political principle based upon the rather abstract idea of loving one's fatherland, the formerly political term *Volk* now referred to what had previously been markers of the nation: history, culture, and ethnicity. In the 1920s, right-wing groups such as the Nazis, racial theorists, and eugenicists went even further in stripping the term *Volk* of its traditional meaning. In direct opposition to the idea that the ultimate realization of a nation was its own state, the idea of the national (now *Volk*, *völkisch* in German) was linked to concepts of a sub-national, naturally or biologically given body politic: population, race, *Volkskörper*, and finally *Volksgemeinschaft* in the Nazi sense. It is very important to understand that these concepts did not automatically imply a pre-existing or defined community. They referred rather to an undefined site at which a culture, a nation, and eventually a nation-state could emerge. Population or race was understood as something like the natural cradle of nations, but also as a natural battlefield on which the fate and future of the nation would be decided.

The political philosopher Eric Voegelin analyzed this most lucidly in his book *Rasse und Staat*, published in the fateful year 1933.[9] Working from a close study of racial theory from Gobineau to H. F. K. Günther, Voegelin reconstructed how the concept of race had been transformed into a new and modern political *Leibidee* (body-idea). It promised access not so much to the natural basis of a given group or community but to the very roots of all group-building – be it social, national, or cultural. The nineteenth century, Voegelin argued, had witnessed the collapse of the aristocracy, the rise of the bourgeoisie, and the emergence of a proletarian class all at the same time. The European social order was shaken and altered to such a degree that it appeared to have become "transparent," with the underlying energies and powers on which it had been based now rendered visible. And "race," in its mythical or biological meaning, was one of the names given to the underlying force that was believed to make culture-, nation-, and state-building possible.

Just as the modern sciences of economics, sociology, and psychology attempted to uncover the driving mechanisms and guiding laws of social evolution, racial theory was concerned with discovering the biopolitical principles required to *create* forms of collective belonging and racially derived types of community. That is why the category of race, especially in the German language, could be applied to virtually any kind of particularity: local, regional, social, religious, gendered, cultural, national, or even transnational (as in the "Aryan" myth and in the imperial context). This was largely a matter of imagination for the early *völkisch* movement, which invented a Germanic race in dire need of protection, improvement, and space to expand and called for a German nation that would satisfy the demands of the Germanic race. After World War I, however, racial thinking in Germany became much more concrete, pragmatic, and political. Defeat, revolution, reconstruction, and the political violence of the early Weimar years had taught that social evolution was not simply a matter of slowly evolving natural bloodlines but could also be strongly determined by short-term political actions.

To many contemporaries, such as Max Weber, Germany's experience of defeat and upheaval rendered notions of racial development and visions of a racially determined political order obsolete.[10] Others, however, managed to integrate historical contingency into a racial worldview. Some interpreted recent events, in the manner of Oswald Spengler, as signs of a much broader, long-term period of decay that was transforming Western civilization on a fundamental level. Others, especially those interested in eugenic forms of racial engineering, easily interpreted war, violence, and economic depression as "evolution at work," as race-building forces that exposed the nation to the ever-cleansing struggle for existence.

Consequently, the more stable the Weimar Republic became in the years after 1923, the more eugenicists and racial theorists called for new approaches to reviving the nation. An important feature of the eugenic discourse in Germany at this time was that ideas of race, racial origin, or racial history, though still used and worshipped, no longer provided a sense of security and stability. They ceased to function as identity-builders and instead became markers of a lost unity in need of regeneration. They signified the dream of a state of the nation still to come. In accordance with the Darwinian principles of evolution, racial development was regarded as being governed by forces at work on a *daily* basis. Reproduction, natural selection, struggle, and survival – these elements of evolution were no longer considered part of gradual natural change, but seen rather as aspects of everyday behavior and as a political matter.[11]

The pre-1914 debate on whether the laws of evolution still applied to humankind was decided – or, better, abandoned – in favor of the position that modern societies should use the principles of evolution to create a social world in accordance with the demands of nature. It was this engineering principle that dominated racial thinking in Germany prior to 1933.[12] The *völkisch* ideas of Germanness figured within this framework no longer as references to an original prehistoric racial state of the nation but as something that could be artificially reconstructed. The technology of race-building, making use of the Darwinian forces at work daily, became more important than the vision of what was to be accomplished. For a while, this engineering principle was so detached from traditional notions of long-lasting races and racial differences that Jewish bioscientists felt safe to fight traditional anti-Semitism from within the dynamic new field of racial biology. And, indeed, many non-Jewish biologists had to admit by the late 1920s that much of the traditional racial view on Jews was nothing but an irrational myth lacking any empirical foundation. This attempt to fight racial anti-Semitism from within failed utterly, however, when the proponents of the science of racial biology very willingly committed themselves in 1933 to the National Socialist vision of a racial order without Jews.[13]

RACE AS IDEOLOGY

Looking at the Ministry of Propaganda leaflet quoted at the outset of this essay or at the Nuremberg Laws, it is clear that the Nazis did not really care whether their racial policies were scientifically valid or state-of-the-art. In schoolbooks and popular scientific works, for example, they carelessly intertwined the mythical and the biological meanings of race, often simply identifying the concept with terms such as *Volk*, *Volksgemeinschaft*, nation, or population. The term "race" was omnipresent in

National Socialist rhetoric, but it carried many different meanings. Racial discourse and racist policies are thus not necessarily evidence that the Nazis had a coherent ideological program aimed at creating a racial state or even a racial world order. The existence of such a program would suggest that the Nazis' vision originated in and relied on a clear-cut conception of race that would be the exclusive criterion in distinguishing between the members of the *Volksgemeinschaft* they had set out to build and the outsiders, the *Gemeinschaftsfremde*, who were to be excluded. Indeed, the concept of race as used in the 1930s could not provide a blueprint for the creation of a racial state. The Nazis' ideology drew upon virtually every racial theory developed in the nineteenth and early twentieth centuries, combining not entirely compatible mythical, evolutionary, and eugenic ideas: it is simply impossible to reconstruct a specific National Socialist concept or theory of race. The Nazis used the notion of race to rationalize virtually every form of political action, but it was not the cornerstone on which their political program rested. The question, then, is: How are we to understand the ideological role the notion of race played in the Third Reich?

In 1951, Hannah Arendt suggested a way to interpret the role of racial thinking within National Socialism that, despite the revival of interest in Arendt among historians, has long been ignored. Citing the work of Voegelin and early analyses of the Third Reich such as Franz Neumann's *Behemoth*, she focused on the nature and function of the concept of race rather than its part in utopian visions of a new political order.[14] The nomological laws proposed by totalitarian regimes, Arendt argued, should not mistakenly be seen as a stabilizing factor to regulate life, define boundaries, and determine a given order. All laws in totalitarian regimes, she contends, "have become laws of movement" to set society in motion toward a higher goal and toward a *new* society. Law under totalitarianism no longer defines the space in which people can act freely and make their own history; rather, it signifies a much larger process in which individuals and the state have predetermined roles to play. It was this new idea of lawfulness, Arendt said, that Nazi racial discourse expressed and rationalized: "underlying the Nazi's belief in race laws as the expression of the law of nature in man is Darwin's idea of man as the product of a natural development which does not necessarily stop with the present species of human beings."[15]

This observation suggests an answer to the question of what function the Nazis' internally inconsistent and incoherent racial thinking assumed within their ideological system. The concept of race might have been more important as an indicator of a natural process, of movement in a predetermined direction, than as a means of establishing identity, of fostering a stabilizing sense of belonging, or of identifying enemies. In short, racial discourse may have been less important for supporting the Nazis' ideological goals than for making those goals appear to be logical steps in a naturally determined course of action, namely the radical transformation of Germany and the world around it.

In arguing along these lines, it is important to briefly consider possible misunderstandings. Arendt's study has often been misread as putting National Socialism and Stalinism on equal footing or as subsuming them under the broader concept of totalitarianism, or even seeing them as identical, under the heading of a generalizing notion of totalitarianism. Arendt tried to uncover the historical circumstances behind the fusion of ideology and terror in the twentieth century; she regarded Nazism and Stalinism as two separate and distinct examples of this phenomena. Her references to Darwin, as in the passage quoted earlier, certainly do not imply that his ideas were in any way responsible for the ways in which the concept of race was understood in Nazi Germany or that the secret of Nazi racism was simply evolutionism. In Arendt's view, Darwin had merely articulated logical mechanisms explaining natural change, just as Marx had set out the mechanism explaining historical change. It was the various attempts to turn these explanatory mechanisms into guidelines for controlling natural and historical processes that introduced the idea that political action aimed at such a control had to be brought in line with those abstract mechanisms or "laws of movement." In that context, scientific theory became ideology. In the case of racial thinking, this meant that, regardless of its particular form, a desired racial order could be realized only by actively harnessing the driving factors of evolution: struggle, selection, survival, and extinction. The supposed validity of such "laws," however remote from the real world, was, according to Arendt, the central element of a totalitarian ideology: the "emancipation of thought from experience." In the end, racial myths and the political claims of racial theory and racial politics became secondary to the prime imperative of enforcing the racial struggle as such. Accordingly, totalitarian terror is the one and only form of politics in accordance with such an aimless project and capable of rendering it logical and lawful. For terror simply executes the laws of nature: "Wo gehobelt wird, da fallen Späne" – or, as the saying in English goes, "You can't make an omelet without breaking eggs."[16]

Second, it is important to note that an ideology such as racism cannot function without the support of historical or scientific claims about the greatness of one's own race or the threat posed by enemy races and the need to put an end to them. This is why Arendt carefully distinguished between imperialism and anti-Semitism as factors in the rise of totalitarianism, and at the same time acknowledged both the general violent potential of modernity and the very specific role the Jews and anti-Jewish sentiment played in this context. Although Nazi racism encompassed a number of "undesirable" groups, it was first and foremost hatred of the Jews that gave form and purpose to Nazi racial politics. In turn, the totalitarian logic of racial ideology served as rationalization for taking racial politics to a genocidal extreme.

This point was already noted by Eric Voegelin in 1933. He argued that the way in which the concept of race had developed into an abstract name for the natural and fundamental precondition of group-building made the idea of a "counter-race" (*Gegenrasse*) necessary. A *Gegenrasse* is not just any other race regarded as an enemy. Rather, it is the one race that contradicts, declines, neglects, or even negates and counteracts the very rules and laws of racial development; it contradicts and denies precisely what racial theorists desperately tried to establish as the one and only path to national renewal. The mere existence of such a race threatens to disprove racial laws, and for that reason, Voegelin argues, a *Gegenrassse* is the ultimate racial enemy. In the late nineteenth and twentieth centuries, the Jews increasingly figured in German racial theory as a non-race, a counter-race, a race that, according to racial science, should not exist.

Indeed, one hallmark of early twentieth-century anti-Semitism was its preoccupation with the question of how the Jews – who had never been a warrior people, who lived widely dispersed around the world, and who had long mingled with other races – had managed to survive as a race. The fixation with that question touches on an important, often overlooked aspect of racial thinking, namely its inherent universalist promise. Racial theorists at the time saw their ideas not just as helping to define their own collective belonging or to define specific enemies. For most of them, racial theory provided a worldview that explained the past, present, and future of the world through universal and ever-valid laws of nature. In this view, racial belonging as such was a principle uniting humanity and was expressed in the presumed desire of *every* race to preserve itself. As the Ministry of Propaganda's 1935 leaflet noted, "The purity of blood is in the interest of all valuable races." This is why, during World War I and even earlier, the idea of racial betrayal (*Rassenverrat*) associated, for instance, with the imperial practice of recruiting non-European soldiers to fight European wars was deemed a betrayal both of one's own race and of the racial principles in general.[17] By virtue of the centuries-long experience of the Diaspora, the Jews stood as the fundamental exception to the laws of racial theory and were thus by definition a non-valuable race – indeed, a non-race.

It was the supposed universal validity of racial laws that placed the Jews outside the racial continuum and transformed them from a race made up of real people with a history, culture, and even physiology into a counter-race, an abstract counter-principle that had to be fought regardless of the concrete lives of the actual human beings representing it. The workings of this ideological logic can be observed in the ways in which Jewish life in Germany changed under the Nazis. Initially, as historians have frequently noted, many German Jews did not experience direct hostility and persecution but rather saw their social networks dissolve as non-Jewish Germans increasingly distanced themselves from their Jewish friends, neighbors, and colleagues.[18] This social detachment, one could argue, mirrored the ideological gap within racial thinking that had opened up between the Jews as a living people and *Judentum* (Jewry) as a counter-race that threatened to undermine the basis of German racial self-understanding. In other words, the growing distance separating non-Jewish and Jewish Germans in the wake of Hitler's rise to power mirrored the gap between experience and theory. With the onset of Nazi rule, Jews were merely a theoretical notion.

Arendt's view on racism as a totalizing ideology goes even further. Racism, she argues, spurred the translation of theory into action: what the laws of nature demanded was brought about through terror, and experience was rendered irrelevant. This concept of ideology turns the classic Marxist notion on its head. For Arendt, ideology is primarily driven by the logic of its ideas. It is detached from experience and replaces experience. Material interests, which, according to Marx, underpin all ideas, merely provide the framework for the realization of the ideas behind any given ideology. Applying this view not only to the early phase of the Third Reich but to the genesis of the "Final Solution" brings the Goldhagen debate to mind, as well as the question of how to explain the willingness of so many Germans (and non-Germans) to support and participate in the systematic murder of an entire race.[19] Although Goldhagen's argument that most Germans were driven by an "eliminationist anti-Semitism" has been largely rejected by other scholars, he articulated an impressive critique of the structural, psychological, and sociological models that have been put forward to explain the manifest willingness of so many individuals to participate in mass murder. In one way or another, all such models refer to ahistorical mechanisms that were undoubtedly at work in the realization of the Holocaust – as well as in a whole range of other incidents of mass destruction in history. Those models thus cannot fully explain the particular – and, in the eyes of many, singular – case of the Holocaust.

Arendt's notion of totalitarianism does not provide a fully sufficient alternative. However, I would argue that it does point to the important fact that structural forms of behavior, psychological mechanisms, and certain types of rationalization have their own history. They are not simply ex post facto explanations applied by historians. Precisely because they appear to have performed so efficiently in helping the Nazis to achieve their murderous goals, their rationality must at least in part have played a motivational role then and perhaps even have been learned in the years before. That is not to say that our understanding of the perpetrators' motives is identical to the perpetrators' own ideas about their motives. But there is one common factor: the detachment of thought from experience – resulting in forms of violent action that look mechanical to us but apparently seemed rational and necessary to those carrying out the actions. And one way to learn to give oneself up to a rationality detached from reality and freed from experience was certainly to learn the laws and logic of racism. Goldhagen's "willingness" and Arendt's "lawfulness" might thus turn out to be two sides of the same coin. Many Germans might have willingly participated in the Nazi crimes because doing so seemed like a rational course of action in line with natural laws of movement.

Again, this does not mean that the idea of race was more important than anything else in the Third Reich. Arendt's only vaguely developed observations on the logic of ideology lead to a somewhat Foucauldian question: If the perpetrators were able to do what was demanded of them and to commit crimes willingly and almost mechanically, what made this particular kind of discipline and/or willingness possible? What kind of rationality was the precondition for this synchronization, coupling, or identification of presumably objective processes with willful actions? What kind of knowledge made it plausible to regard any form of conscious action as just another step in a natural process? More simply put: Which ideology declared that only those who survive and outlive others will evolve and develop?

These questions make sense only if we re-evaluate our understanding of racism and the role it played in the Nazi system. Instead of regarding it as an ever-present, all-encompassing belief system resting on very specific ideas of superiority/inferiority and dedicated to the creation of a purely Germanic racial state, we could ask if the impact of racism was in fact much more limited and, for that reason, all the more fatal. Perhaps racism's most important contribution to the Nazi system was not that it provided a foundation for claims of German superiority or for the idea of racially defined *Volksgemeinschaft*, but rather that it made plausible the idea that all facets of social and political life were subordinate to the natural process of the struggle for existence. That struggle was seen as independent of social and historical reality because that reality was itself subject to the evolutionary struggle's laws of movement. Consider Nazi-era schoolbooks that warned of the perils of allowing too many "asocial" and disabled individuals to live in a society, or the ever more radical persecution of the Jews, or the Nazis' claim that Germany was entitled to an empire in Eastern Europe: the common factor in these examples is not a clearly outlined racial theory or model of racial politics but rather the idea of an unceasing natural struggle for survival.[20] If there is a core element of Nazi racism, it is certainly not a clearly defined notion of race but rather an abstract bio-political logic of "life through death." That logic did not favor one particular group over the other, but denied particularity as such. This logic might be described as Social Darwinian but not in the metaphorical sense in which the term had been applied to economic and political ideologies of competition. Rather, Nazi racism was Darwinian in a very literal sense: struggle, survival, and selection – they all lost their metaphorical implications and became, in their literal biological sense, the laws of the Nazi system.

Such a Darwinian racism, precisely because it no longer reflected the interests and particular perspectives of one specific group and relied instead on abstract laws and universal principles, required what Voegelin called a *Gegenrasse*. Only within the framework of such a bipolar structure could a radically Darwinian racism serve the function of identity-building and create an artificial sense of belonging. This sense of belonging remains unstable, however, and requires the control and testing of one's own race and the persecution of the enemy. For only the continuous application of the universal laws of nature guarantees the experience of particularity.

As Hitler awaited the downfall of the Third Reich in his Berlin bunker in April 1945, he insisted, according to Joachim Fest, that the German *Volk* would prove itself "unworthy" if it betrayed its Führer and did indeed lose the war.[21] This can be read not only as an expression of bitterness uttered by a failed emperor before killing himself but also as a reaffirmation of the logic that was at the center of the fascist experiment from the outset: the only way for a *Volk* to realize its superiority is to actively engage in the struggle for survival – and to prevail. That is one of the few common elements among the vast variety of racial theories developed in the wake of Darwin's discovery that the driving mechanism of evolution is to be found not in the past but in the present, in the daily process of natural selection that decides who lives and who dies. For it is not the fittest who survives, but the survivor who proves to be the fittest.

   This interpretation of the role and function of racism in Nazi Germany allows us to focus analysis on the inner rationalities and motivations that were conveyed by the notion of race and to dismiss the idea that everything the Nazis said about the issue of race somehow fit into an overall racial masterplan. It seems unwise to interpret the Nazi system exclusively within the framework of its own self-descriptions. Looking at the inner logic of racial thinking rather than the legitimizing stories it produced opens a perspective onto aspects of racism and its effects that have not yet been adequately addressed. Moreover, focusing on racism from this perspective can also help us to rediscover elements of the Third Reich that have been overshadowed in recent research guided by the racial state paradigm, such as anti-Semitism, nationalism, or Germans' reactions to the experience of World War I. One thing seems certain: the logic of ideologies can be understood only through analysis of their development over the long term.

Notes

1 Deutsches Historisches Museum (DHM), Berlin, Do 77/342.1II.
2 See Cornelia Essner, *Die "Nürnberger Gesetze" oder die Verwaltung des Rassenwahns 1933–1945* (Paderborn, 2002); Alexandra Przyrembel, *"Rassenschande." Reinheitsmythos und Vernichtungslegitimation im Nationalsozialismus* (Göttingen, 2003).
3 See Franz K. Stanzel, *Telegonie – Fernzeugung* (Cologne, 2008).
4 The German text of the twelve rules of racial conduct reads: "Sichere die Ewigkeit Deines Volkes durch den Kinderreichtum Deiner Familie. / Deutscher Mann, achte und schütze in jeder Frau die Mutter deutscher Kinder. / Deutsche Frau, vergiß nie Deine höchste Aufgabe, Hüterin deutscher Art zu sein. / Schütze deine Kinder vor dem Schicksal des Mischlings. / Halte das deutsche Blut rein. / Jeder, der nicht deutschen Blutes ist, ist fremdblütig. /Wahre Deine Ehre und Deine Art bei Begegnung mit Volksfremden. / Deutsches Mädchen, Deine Zurückhaltung gegenüber Volksfremden ist keine Beleidigung. Im Gegenteil: Jeder anständige Ausländer wird Dich deswegen besonders achten. / Der Schutz des eigenen Blutes bedeutet keine Verachtung der anderen Völker. / Die Reinhaltung des Blutes liegt im Interesse aller wertvollen Rassen. / Die

Reinhaltung des Blutes ist keine Privatangelegenheit, sondern eine selbstverständliche Pflicht jedes deutschen Menschen gegenüber seinem Volke. SEI STOLZ, DASS DU EIN DEUTSCHER BIST!"

5 *Meyers Lexikon*, vol. 6 (1906), p442. See also the entry "Volk, Nation, Nationalismus, Masse" in Otto Brunner, Werner Conze, and Reinhart Koselleck (eds.), *Geschichtliche Grundbegriffe. Historisches Lexikon zur politisch-sozialen Sprache in Deutschland* (Stuttgart, 1972–97).

6 Johann C. Bluntschli, "Nation und Volk, Nationalitätsprinzip" in J. C. Bluntschli and Karl L. T. Brater (eds.), *Deutsches Staatswörterbuch* (Stuttgart, 1862).

7 See Erez Manela, *The Wilsonian Moment: Self-Determination and the International Origins of Anti-Colonial Nationalism* (Oxford, 2007).

8 Interestingly, scientists and intellectuals active in the international peace movement before 1914 had articulated very similar egalitarian ideas about self-determination based not on the concept of nation but on that of race. The Universal Races Congress held in London in 1911, for instance, was dedicated to creating global harmony among the races through their conscious, scientifically controlled self-improvement. Convinced that races were not fixed but growing and plastic entities, many prominent participants in the congress demanded, on the basis of the scientifically proven plasticity of race, an egalitarian and open approach to the rising races of the non-European continents. See Gustav Spiller (ed.), *Inter-Racial Problems. Papers from the First Universal Races Congress held in London in 1911* (Boston, 1911; reprint edn., ed. Herbert Aptheker, New York, 1970). See also Christian Geulen, "The common grounds of conflict: racial visions of world order 1880–1940" in Sebastian Conrad and Dominic Sachsenmaier (eds.), *Competing Visions of World Order: Global Moments and Movements, 1880s–1930s* (New York, 2007), 69–96.

9 Eric Voegelin, *Rasse und Staat* (Tübingen, 1933). Unlike his later interpretation of National Socialism as a "political religion," this early work on the ideological origins of the German fascist movement and its racial ideas is largely forgotten. But it was Voegelin's analysis that informed Hannah Arendt's interpretation of the role of ideology in the twentieth century's politics of terror and violence. See Hannah Arendt, *Elemente und Ursprünge totaler Herrschaft*, 3rd edn. (Munich, 1993: first published in 1951), 268, 703–30.

10 See Hans-Walter Schmuhl, "Max Weber und das Rassenproblem" in Manfred Hettling, Claudia Huerkamp, Paul Nolte, and Walter Schmuhl (eds.), *Was ist Gesellschaftsgeschichte? Positionen, Themen, Analysen* (Munich, 1991), 331–42.

11 The developments of racial and eugenic thought emphasized here are those most important for understanding the origins of National Socialist ideas of race. However, a wide range of other ideas and perceptions shaped German and international discourse on race and racial development in the first decades of the twentieth century, including an optimistic vision of a harmonious and tolerant world order built upon on the scientific basis of racial theory. See Geulen, "The common grounds of conflict."

12 See Thomas Etzemüller (ed.), *Die Ordnung der Moderne. Social Engineering im 20. Jahrhundert* (Bielefeld, 2009).

13 Veronika Lipphardt, *Die Biologie der Juden. Jüdische Wissenschaftler über Rasse und Vererbung 1900–1935* (Göttingen, 2008).

14 As is well known, Arendt wrote the original version of her book in English and later translated it herself into German, in the process rewriting and sometimes substantially changing certain paragraphs. The passages referred to here, from the concluding chapter on "Ideology and terror," can be fully understood only by consulting both the English and the German versions. Although the latter leaves out many of the direct references to the Bolshevism and the Soviet system, speaking instead more generally about historical materialism, it goes into more detail than the English original and clarifies Arendt's observations on the "lawfulness" of totalitarianism. Arendt changed the term "totalitarianism" in the title to "*totale Herrschaft,*" signaling a slight, but not unimportant, change of perspective.

15 Hannah Arendt, *The Origins of Totalitarianism*, 2nd edn. (Cleveland, 1958), 463.

16 Arendt, *Elemente und Ursprünge totaler Herrschaft,* 712. This German saying is left out in the English version of the text. A more direct translation would be "Where wood is planed, shavings will fall."

17 For a more detailed analysis of this issue, see Christian Geulen, *Wahlverwandte. Rassendiskurs undNationalismus im späten 19. jarhundert* (Hamburg, 2004), 354–67.

18 See Marion Kaplan, *Between Dignity and Despair: Jewish Life in Nazi Germany* (New York, 1998).

19 Jonah Goldhagen, *Hitler's Willing Executioners: Ordinary Germans and the Holocaust* (New York, 1996).

20 The subject of *Ostraum-Politik* (eastern policy) raises the issue of Nazi racism directed against the Slavs. Even though this issue cannot be explored here, it seems that the Slavs represented a different kind of "counter-race" than the Jews. They figured in Nazi ideology not so much as an abstract, eternal counter-principle, as was the perception of the Jews, but rather as a concrete enemy race occupying the space needed to insure the creation and survival of a new German *Volk*. Tracing the historical origins of this spatial notion of "survival" would probably lead back to the imperial and colonial versions of racism and Social Darwinism that emerged in the late nineteenth century.

21 Joachim Fest, *Der Untergang. Hitlers und das Ende des Dritten Reiches. Eine historische Skizze* (Berlin, 2002), 87–101.

8

Nazi Medical Crimes, Eugenics, and the Limits of the Racial State Paradigm

Herwig Czech

Although the medical crimes against the allegedly biologically "unfit" under National Socialist rule have received increased attention during the past two decades, their exact relationship to the regime's broader objectives in terms of racial policy remains in large part an open question. This is not to say that race has not been addressed in this context. On the contrary, race and racism are at the core of a number of canonical studies of Nazi health policy. Therein, "racism" is often used in a broad sense to include the diverse racial-hygiene measures that were directed against individuals considered members of the German *Volk*. In this context, we are still far from a consensus on how to address the relationship between eugenics, medical crimes, and racism in a conceptually coherent way.

The aim of this essay is thus to clarify the relevance of "race" and "racism" in explaining the motivations for acts of discrimination, persecution, and mass murder in a medical context in Nazi Germany, and to explore how race and economics are related in this context. After a short review of important contributions to this area of research, I will focus upon the limitations of this approach and conclude with some suggestions for an alternative interpretation that integrates the racist and socio-economic aspects of medicine and racial hygiene under National Socialism.[1] Racism and economic considerations have been offered as competing ways of accounting for Nazi medical crimes; the aim of this essay, by contrast, is to explore the possibility of integrating the two in a more unified theoretical model.

I would like to thank the editors for numerous helpful suggestions during the various stages of writing, and Matthew Feldman for proofreading an earlier version of this chapter.

One possible approach is to take Michael Foucault's concept of bio-politics as a point of departure.[2] By defining biopolitics as an "economy of life forces," racism can be understood as a technology of power concerned with the strengthening of a biological entity for the "struggle for survival" that was at the heart of the Nazi worldview. Nazi biopolitics aimed above all to achieve not "purity" but "fitness," even if the two sometimes seem interchangeable. A working definition of racism that would be in keeping with Foucault's approach while retaining enough flexibility to reconcile his bird's-eye view of history with Nazism's rela-tively short *durée* would therefore focus on its strategic function rather than its ideological content. That function could be best described as the reification of certain traits of individuals as markers of a fundamental biological difference believed to be transmitted from one generation to the next. Such differences can rest on the assumption of radical otherness (racism in the narrower anthropological sense of the term) or of illness, unfitness, or other biological deficiencies.

With this in mind, I will try to address several important questions about the relationship between race, eugenics, and economics under National Socialist rule. Most importantly: Was eugenics – which, prior to the Nazis' ascent to power, had adherents of diverse political creeds across Europe and beyond – inherently racist, or was there merely a certain affinity with racial thinking? Second, what was the link between racial hygiene and the Nazis' so-called euthanasia program? Lastly, how were racist and economic motivations connected and what role did race play in shaping National Socialist policies in the realm of public health?

Scholars have taken a variety of approaches to answering these interlinked questions. I will start with a short overview of the literature and the respective roles ascribed to racism and economic arguments in attempting to make sense of the Nazis' euthanasia campaigns. I will then consider the practical implementation of racial-hygiene measures in the public health system. The guiding question is whether racial hygiene policies, exemplified by forced sterilization, and the euthanasia killings were linked by a common logic and, if that was the case, how best to describe it.

THE NAZI EUTHANASIA KILLINGS: BEYOND THE RACIAL STATE PARADIGM?

The first and most important issue to consider in attempting to define the role of medicine under National Socialism is the euthanasia program.

A number of authors put these killings squarely in the context of the Nazi "racial state." Recently, however, the argument that economic motives were paramount in the euthanasia program has gained the upper hand. This has important implications, especially with regard to the question of continuity between Nazi racial hygiene policies before 1939 and the euthanasia killings.

The most important statement of the racial state paradigm is Michael Burleigh and Wolfgang Wippermann's 1991 study of Nazi biopolitics, *The Racial State: Germany 1933–1945*. As the title of their book suggests, race and racism occupy a central place in Burleigh and Wippermann's argument. Nonetheless, *The Racial State* is at best vague in attempting to define and to analyze these elusive concepts. Throughout the book, the term "Nazi racial policy" is employed as an umbrella term to cover the persecution and extermination not only of Jews and Roma and Sinti but also of the "hereditarily ill," the mentally ill, the disabled, "asocials," criminals, and homosexuals. Burleigh and Wippermann do concede that criteria other than "racial purity" also played a part in the Nazis' conception of social policy: "The 'National community' itself was categorized in accordance with racial criteria. The criteria included not merely 'racial purity,' but also biological health and socio-economic performance."[3] They fail, however, to address this apparent contradiction. In what follows, I will put forward a closer reading of the relationship between racial/biological and socio-economic rationales behind the Nazi euthanasia killings.

In his *Rassenhygiene, Nationalsozialismus, Euthanasie* (1987), Hans-Walter Schmuhl argued that the racial hygiene movement in interwar Germany was a direct precursor to the Nazis' euthanasia program. Schmuhl came close to declaring euthanasia in Germany an "inevitable development" (*zwangsläufige Entwicklung*) given the polycratic structure of the Third Reich and its inherent tendency towards radicalization.[4] Answering the criticism of Michael Schwartz,[5] Schmuhl later conceded that he had underestimated the political diversity of the eugenics movement in the interwar years, but nevertheless insisted that racial hygiene/eugenics and the Nazi euthanasia program had common roots in Social Darwinism and shared several basic premises. Both presumed that one human life could be judged more or less valuable than another; both gave collective entities such as *Volk* and race priority over individuals; and both devalued basic human rights. Moreover, after 1933, there was frequent overlap between the implementation of racial-hygiene policies and the euthanasia program in terms of discourse, institutions, and protagonists.[6] Given the now well-documented economic factors at work in the development of the Nazi euthanasia program, this totalizing view seems outdated. There appears to be a sharp contrast between the economic motivations behind the killing of psychiatric patients, on the one hand, and, on the other, the biologistic aims of Nazi eugenics.

Another important study links the euthanasia killings to racism, more specifically anti-Semitism, and thereby extends the traditional understanding of the Holocaust: Henry Friedlander's *The Origins of Nazi Genocide* (1995).[7] Although his argument focuses on the organizational connections between T4 – the euthanasia program initiated in the autumn of 1939 – and the "Aktion Reinhardt" – the systematic murder of Jews in occupied Poland – Friedlander leaves no doubt about where he stands on the issue of race vs. economics: "Nor were these patients murdered to free hospital space or to save money; the killers were motivated by an ideological obsession to create a homogenous and robust nation based on race ... Heredity determined the selection of the victims."[8] For Friedlander, the Holocaust encompassed three "hereditary" groups: Jews, Roma and Sinti, and the disabled. His reading squarely placed the Nazis' T4 program within a broadened understanding of National Socialist genocide.

Influential as these books have been, none established a consensus among scholars as to the centrality of race and racism as explanatory concepts for medicalized killings under the Nazis. That was due in part to competition from arguments – put forward by, among others, Götz Aly, Karl Heinz Roth, and Klaus Dörner – that strongly emphasized the dominance of economic factors.[9] Although many of these authors' conclusions remain controversial – in the case of Aly and Roth, for instance, largely due to their apodictic rhetoric and their occasionally over-simplifying conclusions – economic arguments seem to have gained ground on those foregrounding ideological factors, particularly racism.

It is interesting to note that in his study of euthanasia, *Death and Deliverance* (1994), Burleigh seems to step away from the position taken a few years earlier in *The Racial State*, even if the "racial paradigm" is partially retained: "Mentally and physically disabled people were killed to save money and resources, or to create physical space for ethnic German repatriates and/or civilian and military casualties ... Nazi Germany was unique in attempting to exterminate the chronically mentally ill and physically disabled in the interests of economy and racial fitness."[10] In this study, Burleigh recognizes that economic factors were considerations in the T4 program, but it remains unclear if or how economics related to racial conceptions of health.

Attesting even more clearly to a conceptual shift in the scholarship on euthanasia, Hans-Walter Schmuhl, in a 2010 review of theories on the genesis of the Nazi euthanasia program, identifies six main interpretative currents, none of which postulates "race" or "racism" as a driving element.[11]

A critical factor eroding the credibility of racial paradigms is their connection to "intentionalist" interpretations of Nazi persecution, which have increasingly fallen into disrepute among scholars. Insofar as racism is most commonly understood as an ideology that becomes effective by shaping the worldview of individual actors, the assumption that race was a causal factor in the genesis of the Nazi euthanasia program sits uneasily with "structuralist" or "functionalist" interpretations that stress contingency and the role of bureaucracy and competition between elites, along with improvisation and incremental ad hoc radicalization from the bottom up, as central features of the Third Reich's polycratic power structures.[12] This is not to say that ideology as a concept has been dropped by historians of Nazism; indeed, as other contributors to this volume emphasize, it has enjoyed something of a revival. But the more extreme versions of intentionalism, according to which the destructive dynamic of National Socialism is best explained as the systematic application of a stable and pre-existing set of ideological beliefs held by Hitler and his immediate followers, seem hopelessly inadequate today. Applied to the subject of Nazi medical crimes, an intentionalist interpretation would posit that the pursuit of racial purity was an end in itself and was the driving force behind the implementation of the racial-hygiene and euthanasia programs. Ideology plays a far more limited role, by contrast, when the emphasis is placed on institutional dynamics driven by ad hoc solutions against the background of an ever-escalating war effort. Today, most scholars would agree that both institutional dynamics and individual agency need to be taken into account. A closer analysis of both the institutional dynamics and the arguments used by the perpetrators involved at the different levels of the euthanasia program seems to confirm the primacy of economic motives.

A few examples may suffice to underline this point. I should note that, although in later sections of this essay I will widen the definition of "racial criteria," I use the term at this point to mean criteria that conform to the paradigm of racial hygiene, that is, selection on the basis of hereditary pathology aimed at improving the genetic quality of future generations.

Following his arrest by Soviet authorities in 1945, Erwin Jekelius, coordinator of the T4 organization in Vienna (and for a time the lover of Hitler's sister Paula), told his NKVD interrogators about his recruitment into the euthanasia program. Viktor Brack, he said, had personally explained to him that the mentally sick were a burden on the *Volk* and useless to the state and should therefore be exterminated. Jekelius also reported that Herbert Linden of the Reich Ministry of the Interior had used the same argument to explain Hitler's murderous plan to a group of doctors who had been called to Berlin as potential recruits for the T4 operation.[13]

In autumn 1940, Richard Günther, a doctor at the Am Steinhof psychiatric hospital in Vienna, wrote to Alfred Dubitscher of the Reich Health Office in Berlin to share some observations on the deportation of nearly 3,200 of the hospital's patients. Clearly aware that patients were being killed, Günter explained that "patient material" was being sent to "less attractive institutions" in order to free beds for military personnel. He also pointed out that during the selection process – which was carried out by a commission of doctors and aides, and was based solely on case files – the question of work performance (*Arbeitsleistung*) was given special attention. Günther explicitly supported the euthanasia killings, but he heavily criticized the selection procedure, which had sent patients "who through their work had rendered valuable services to the hospital" to the Hartheim gas chamber.[14]

Jürgen Peiffer provides further examples from closer to the top of the T4 hierarchy. On April 3, 1940, the leaders of the T4 program informed the Deutscher Gemeindetag, the association of municipal governments, of the imminent start of the killing campaign: the reasons given to justify the program were exclusively economic. The same was true when the heads of the state superior courts (*Oberlandesgerichte*) and attorney generals (*Generalstaatsanwälte*) were briefed on the details of the program. According to the testimonies of Hans Heinrich Lammers and Prinz Philipp von Hessen, even Hitler used this line of argument.[15]

Further evidence can be found in documents such as the infamous "Hartheimer Statistik," which contains detailed listings of purported savings on food and other expenses achieved by the killing of more than

70,000 people.[16] The T4 organization also painstakingly registered the number of hospital beds it had "freed" for other purposes.[17] Karl Brandt and Philipp Bouhler, the two recipients of Hitler's euthanasia order of October 1939, defined the aim of the killing campaign in March 1941 as the "elimination of all those unable to perform productive work even if institutionalized, therefore not only of the mentally dead."[18]

Looking beyond the discourse of the perpetrators, scholars have given increased attention to the selection process used to determine who was to be murdered. Much of this research, carried out by a team led by Maike Rotzoll, Gerrit Hohendorf, and Petra Fuchs, is based on the medical files of some 30,000 T4 victims. After the war, these files were secretly retained by the East German Ministry for State Security, and it was only after German unification that they were rediscovered and made accessible to researchers.[19] More than 3,000 of these files were examined by the research group.[20]

Their research clearly disproves the contention that heredity and racial hygiene played an important role in the euthanasia killings – at least as far as T4 is concerned. One of the group's most important findings is that among the criteria influencing the probability that a given patient would be selected for gassing, by far the most important was his or her ability to work. Among the victims, 46.3 percent had not been working, 26.9 percent had been classified as slightly productive (*wenig produktiv*) and had performed only mechanical tasks, 15.8 had been rated as average, and only 10.9 percent were deemed productive workers. In the sample of surviving patients, the opposite is the case: 43.5 percent were deemed productive workers, 26.5 percent were rated as average, 15.2 percent were described as slightly productive, and only 14.8 percent had not been working.[21] Interestingly, the importance of productivity-related criteria varied greatly between the different killing centers. Among victims killed at Hartheim, 7.3 percent were deemed "productive" according to their files, and 60.1 percent had not been working. Among the victims at Sonnenstein, by contrast, the numbers are 16.7 percent and 36.7 percent, respectively.[22] Besides productivity, several other criteria influenced the selection process, although to a much more limited extent. Behavior in the hospital, "cleanliness," and gender (women were at a greater risk of being selected than men) were the most important.[23] The biggest surprise is that the criterion of heredity did not play a statistically significant role in the selection of patients to be killed. Of the files analyzed, 44 percent contained no information about the hereditary background of the patient's condition. Of the remaining cases, roughly equal numbers of survivors and victims were suspected to have been suffering conditions in which heredity was a factor. In other words, a patient believed to have a hereditary disorder was no more likely to be killed than one whose condition was not attributed to hereditary factors.[24]

But what about the other euthanasia programs besides T4? In the case of the "decentralized" killings that took place after Hitler stopped T4 in August 1941, it is difficult to reach definite conclusions because the circumstances differed greatly from region to region and even from institution to institution. There is little reason, however, to assume that the selection criteria after August 1941 were much different from those used by T4. Ernst Gelny, one of the main perpetrators of decentralized euthanasia in Austria, boasted in a 1944 letter to the Gauhauptmann of Lower Austria that he had personally killed close to 400 incurable patients "who in the present situation constituted a heavy burden to the state" in the psychiatric hospital in Gugging.[25] The only patients in Gugging to survive the war were those deemed capable of productive work in the institution's fields, stables, or workshops.[26] Michael Wunder came to a similar conclusion in his study of the Langenhorn institution in Hamburg: "The selection process 1944 in Langenhorn was efficient, highly differentiated and rational in the sense of a radical emphasis on the work productivity of the patients."[27]

The situation was similar with so-called child euthanasia (*Kindereuthanasie*). Initially aimed at newborns and infants up to the age of three, child euthanasia stood midway between the eugenic prevention of unwanted births and the killing of primarily adult patients in the T4 program. Again, there was one overriding criterion for selection: "educability" (*Bildungsfähigkeit*). This term implied a prognosis whether a given child could be expected to earn a living as an adult. *Bildungsfähigkeit* in children was analogous to *Arbeitsfähigkeit* (ability to work) in adults. Children diagnosed as uneducable would likely be killed by medical personnel regardless of whether their condition was considered hereditary.[28]

To sum up, it seems that the overarching logic guiding the euthanasia killings was an economic one, resulting in the murder of those deemed "unproductive." Contrary to what has long been assumed in the scholarly literature, the various euthanasia campaigns were not based on the paradigm of racial hygiene, that is, on the principle of selection according to inheritable traits aimed at improving the genetic quality of future generations. Although there was common ground between the euthanasia program and the Nazi regime's racial hygiene policies, the aims they were intended to serve were nonetheless different. I will come back to this point in the conclusion in order to discuss how such an economic understanding of Nazi medical crimes may be usefully reconciled with the concepts of race and racism. But first it is necessary to turn to the field of Nazi welfare policy, more specifically to the practical implementation of racial hygiene in the public health system, in order to better elucidate the relationship between euthanasia, eugenics, race, and economics under Nazi rule.

HEREDITY, RACE, AND ECONOMICS IN NAZI HEALTH AND WELFARE POLICY

Because the economic argument sketched out above is sometimes used to draw a too clear-cut dichotomy between "economic rationality" and "racialist ideology," I propose to now take a closer look at the relation between heredity and economics in the field of racial hygiene. If we accept that the euthanasia killings were predominantly motivated by economic factors, does this necessarily mean that these crimes were in no way the result of a radicalization of the regime's racial hygiene policies? Or, to reframe the question, might it still be possible to argue for a direct connection between forced sterilizations (as well as the regime's other eugenic measures) and the euthanasia killings not on the basis of ideology or institutional continuities but rather on the basis of the concept of biopolitics? And if that is the case, how does racism in the classical, anthropological sense come into play?

With the 1934 Law for the Consolidation of the Health System (*Gesetz zur Vereinheitlichung des Gesundheitswesens*), the Nazi regime undertook a complete overhaul of the public health system in Germany. This reform created a unified, centrally controlled nationwide system of public health offices. Endowed with far-reaching powers, these offices were the regime's main instrument for implementing its biopolitical agenda within the sphere of public health. Unlike the Nazi party's health organizations, the state's public health administration possessed both the authority and the means to put racial-hygiene measures into practice efficiently and on a broad scale. The regime thus created an effective biopolitical instrument that allowed for the comprehensive medical policing of the entire population.[29]

Racial hygiene policies were implemented under the rubric *Erb- und Rassenpflege* (hereditary and racial care). Of cardinal importance in the formation of *Erb- und Rassenpflege* as a field of scientific research and biopolitical intervention in the Third Reich was the reference work *Menschliche Erblichkeitslehre und Rassenhygiene*, commonly called Baur-Fischer-Lenz after its lead authors. Five editions of the book were published between 1921 and 1940.[30] It provided a detailed overview of the state of knowledge on human heredity and genetic pathology while at the same time advocating measures such as marriage interdictions and mass sterilizations (of 10 percent or more of the population) and propagating a worldview dominated by a scientistic Nordic racism.[31] The importance of this work can hardly be overstated: it provided a scientifically respectable – and ideologically acceptable – template for the Nazi party's initially vaguely conceived public health policies. Reichsgesundheits- and Reichsärzteführer Leonardo Conti, the head of the German health system, attested to the importance of Baur-Fischer-Lenz in the shaping of Nazi health policies in a speech to a group of Nazi doctors in April 1942: "We want to acknowledge that we have taken and continue to take the larger part of our knowledge and therefore of the tools of our discipline from this work."[32]

The newly established field of *Erb- und Rassenpflege* provided the official basis for the activities of the public health offices after 1933. In keeping with its dual character, *Erb- und Rassenpflege* encompassed eugenic measures in the strict sense of the term as well as policies directed against racially defined minorities. Even if the former took up more of public health officers' time, the latter were clearly also important.

In the case of so-called positive measures aimed at encouraging the "valuable" and "fit" to increase procreation, "race," in the anthropological sense, was used within a binary logic of inclusion or exclusion. For German Jews, this was deployed according to the criteria established by the 1935 Nuremberg Laws. Members of other racially defined minorities, such as Roma and Sinti, were also excluded from benefits such as child allowances and marriage loans. To carry out their new tasks in the field of racial policy (meant here in the narrower sense of *Rassenpolitik*), special anthropological departments were established in public health offices that were responsible for determining the fate of people whose "racial origin" was unclear or undocumented.[33] One indicator of public health offices' role in racial policy is the importance attached to collecting information that could be relevant only in this context. The Viennese public health office, to give one example, systematically collected information on Jews, so-called *Mischlinge* ("mixed-race" individuals), Roma and Sinti, and a host of other ethnic minorities living in Vienna at the time. This may not come as a complete surprise: enforcing the "Law for the Protection of the Blood" (*Blutschutzgesetz*), the provision of the Nuremberg Laws against marriages between Jews and non-Jews, fell within the jurisdiction of the public health offices.

Forced sterilizations were carried out on the basis of the Law for the Prevention of Hereditarily Diseased Offspring (*Gesetz zur Verhütung erbkranken Nachwuchses*, 1933/1934). This law was directed against people considered biologically or hereditarily unfit and was never applied to those considered racial outsiders.[34] In addition to legally enforced sterilizations, however, extra-legal sterilizations were carried out on so-called Rhenish bastards (*Rheinlandbastarde*), the children of German women and (predominately) African members of the French occupation forces in the Rhineland between 1918 and 1929.[35]

The practical implementation of racial hygiene under the Nazi regime was clearly double-faced, combining eugenic measures and acts of discrimination and persecution on racial grounds in the narrower sense of the term. Even if we accept the primacy of socio-economic factors in the euthanasia killings, the question arises whether a conceptual framework stressing biological thinking rather than socio-economic factors can provide a convincing common denominator for the fields of eugenics and racial policy (*Rassenpolitik*). Gisela Bock argued for such a reading in the seminal study of forced sterilizations that she published in 1986.[36] To account for the double character of *Erb- und Rassenpflege*, she coined the twin terms "anthropological racism" and "eugenic (or hygienic) racism." "Racial hygiene/eugenics," she noted, "was a vital part of occidental racism and cannot be separated from racism towards ethnic minorities."[37] The disciplines of racial anthropology and of racial hygiene, she argues, were closely interconnected, directly influenced each other on many levels, and were based on two concepts of race that were not mutually exclusive. The common denominator between the two disciplines was the assumption that a hierarchy of races could be established based on putatively scientific criteria. Employed in this way, racism designates an ideology that puts the interests of a biologically defined collective above those of individuals on the basis of scientist assumptions about genetic determinism. Even where the term "race" is not used explicitly, Bock argues, the notion of "heredity value" is in and of itself racist.[38]

Compelling as this argument is – especially as the double term *Erb- und Rassenpflege* strongly suggests a binary yet unifying concept of racism – the problems of such an approach should not be overlooked. First, such a reading can hardly account for the great diversity of political positions taken by eugenicists across Europe in the interwar period, not least within Germany.[39] Similarly, it is hard to see how viewing eugenics as intrinsically racist and tying it by implication to the Nazi activities in this field can help in understanding eugenic practices after 1945 and, in some instances, into the present. In short, there is a certain danger that explanations centered on the concept of racism will miss the particularities of Nazi policies in pursuit of "purity" and "fitness." Nevertheless, I would argue that subsuming the thinking behind much of Nazi biopolitics under the juxtaposition of eugenic racism and anthropological racism can be a useful theoretical construct. But it is important that its pitfalls not be overlooked, especially the temptation to use the concept of these two forms of racism as a basis for claims of continuity or inevitability that are not necessarily grounded in historical reality. Also, structural similarities do not in and by themselves mean moral equivalence.

Furthermore, it is unclear where the euthanasia killings fit into this picture. As discussed above, the explanation that racism was the motivation behind them is contradicted by the abundant evidence of the role played by economic considerations. One obvious conclusion would be to draw a line between racial hygiene and euthanasia and to consider them as conceptually and ideologically separate entities. By so doing, the assumption that racial hygiene was principally about implementing a racist social order could be upheld while acknowledging the overwhelming evidence pointing toward economic motives behind the medical killings.

But what if *Erb- und Rassenpflege* was also guided to a large extent by economic (and social) motives? That would sit rather uneasily with the idea that the primary goal in this area was the pursuit of biological purity. In what follows, I will show that economic considerations were indeed of paramount importance, and I will argue that a comprehensive concept of racism capable of grappling with the totality of issues posed by the Nazis' racial hygiene policies will therefore have to integrate socio-economic motives.

One cornerstone of the Nazis' "hereditary health policy" (*Erbgesundheitspolitik*), for example, was the compilation of a census according to criteria of racial hygiene. This "hereditary inventory" was supposed to serve as a kind of biological register of the German *Volkskörper*. The ultimate goal was to collect information on the entire population; initially, however, the focus was on identifying the "genetically unfit" (*erbbiologisch Minderwertige*). Physical, psychological, and social deviations or abnormalities were registered and used to determine whether individuals and their families carried a "hereditary burden" (*erbliche Belastung*). That information, in turn, served as a basis for systematic discrimination and persecution. Vienna, to take the example of Germany's second largest city after the annexation of Austria, had a leading position in what amounted to a competition to register more and more of the population. By 1944, public health offices had compiled a registry with information on 767,000 individuals. What role did the criterion of heredity play in this context? In theory, the whole enterprise was carried out under the rubric of "hereditary biology." But in taking a closer look at the kind of information collected, we find that documentation of genetic defects in the stricter sense was practically absent. Most entries focused instead on psychiatric conditions and behavior deemed socially deviant. The largest group of registry entries was based on information gathered from case files on psychiatric patients, pupils with learning disabilities, youth welfare clients, and individuals who had been treated for venereal diseases. The registry also drew on police records on alcoholics and women suspected of engaging in prostitution or of having multiple sexual partners. Approximately 6 percent of the entries compiled by July 1939 were based on files on Jews, *Mischlinge*, and other "racial aliens" (*Fremdrassige*).[40]

The information collected was used in enforcing the Law for the Protection of the Hereditary Health of the German People, commonly called the Marriage Health Law, enacted at the same time as the Nuremberg Laws. This law gave public health offices, in collaboration with the civil registry offices, jurisdiction over all intended marriages. As of October 1935, a certificate of "medical fitness" (*Ehetauglichkeitszeugnis*) was a prerequisite for marriage. All engaged couples were screened based on the information collected in the hereditary inventory. If doubts arose, a couple would be required to undergo a medical examination. Certificates were conferred upon prospective couples only if they were likely to produce genetically desirable offspring. Contagious illnesses (especially tuberculosis and venereal diseases), mental deficiencies, hereditary diseases, and psychological disorders – all of which were supposed to pose a threat to the well-being of the *Volksgemeinschaft* – were possible legal impediments to marriage.[41] As we have seen, the nature of the information collected in the hereditary registry introduced a strong bias toward social diagnostics and away from genetic pathologies in the strict sense.

Another important area in which public health offices cooperated with police, the Nazi party, and other institutions was the tracking down and persecution of so-called asocials. Aside from the hereditary inventory, the most important instrument in this endeavor was the small army of social workers (*Volkspflegerinnen*) who were instructed to identify families with a history of criminality, unwillingness to work (*Arbeitsscheue*, literally "work-shyness"), prostitution, other antisocial behavior, feeblemindedness, hereditary diseases, or alcoholism. Reports were to include detailed information on the family's financial situation, the education of the children, and the appearance of the household.[42] Deeply imbedded in the persecution of allegedly antisocial behavior were gendered criteria of social conformity. In the case of men, "work-shyness" and failure to comply with rigid workplace rules were by far the most important reasons for commitment to "labor reeducation camps" (*Arbeitserziehungslager*), such as the one operated by the Gestapo in Oberlanzendorf, near Vienna. The persecution of women and girls as asocials took a more medicalized form and frequently relied on existing institutional arrangements to control venereal disease and prostitution as well as on disciplinary institutions that combined features of the workhouse and the hospital. Institutions in the youth welfare sector, ranging from workhouses to concentration camps for youths, also played an important role in the suppression of behavior considered undesirable. In none of these institutional contexts, which were all to varying degrees under the control of public health authorities, did hereditary pathology play much of a role beyond providing political and scientific legitimacy.[43]

One could argue that the focus on socially deviant behavior rather than hereditary pathology was due to the sketchy nature of genetic knowledge at the time. Social criteria were taken into account because it was assumed that they pointed toward as yet unknown genetic defects that could be eradicated by preventing those apparently afflicted from procreating. This argument cannot be easily dismissed in favor of a one-sided explanation emphasizing social diagnostics alone. Rather, I would argue that social, economic, and biological criteria were intertwined to a degree that makes it impossible to wholly dismiss one explanation in favor of the other, which makes a synthetic approach necessary.

That said, socio-economic criteria were clearly not just used as substitutes for as yet unidentified genetic defects. Despite the rhetoric of biological and racial fitness, Nazi authorities were well aware that actual hereditary pathology played only a marginal role in the ideologically charged field of *Erb- und Rassenpflege*. In 1940, the Reich Ministry of the Interior issued "Guidelines on the Evaluation of Hereditary Health" (*Richtlinien zur Beurteilung der Erbgesundheit*). According to the guidelines, "The hereditary fitness [*Erbtüchtigkeit*] of a person depends on his own health status and the quality of his family [*Sippe*]. Both their general value for the community in view of skills and gifts and existing hereditary diseases have to be taken into account."[44] This definition explicitly opened the way for consideration of social and economic criteria in the implementation of *Erb- und Rassenpflege* measures. What is more, the ministry made it clear that these criteria should be not be used merely as a complementary diagnostic tool; they were applied to redefine the very meaning of "hereditary." "Hereditary diseases are not only those listed in the 'Law for the Prevention of Hereditarily Diseased Offspring' plus severe alcoholism, but all hereditary diseases and character traits [*Eigenschaften*] that affect the value of a person for the *Volksgemeinschaft*." Consequently, the guidelines continue, "In selection according to eugenic criteria, the evaluation of personal productivity must be of decisive importance." At the same time, the importance of hereditary defects for judging the eugenic value of socially well-adapted individuals and families was systematically downplayed: "A gifted and productive family will have to be considered valuable to the *Volksgemeinschaft* even if isolated cases of hereditary defects, etc. have occurred." In the case of families of little value to the community, the public health authorities were instructed to take limited socio-economic performance as an indicator of "hereditary unfitness" even in the absence of proven hereditary diseases.[45] The gender bias inherent in Nazi *Erb- und Rassenpflege* is highlighted by the fact that women with illegitimate children by different fathers were to be considered ipso facto "hereditarily undesirable" (*erbbiologisch unerwünscht*).

Throughout these guidelines, the language of "performance" and "value" is inextricably intertwined with the language of biological or genetic "fitness." The Interior Ministry guidelines exemplify the contradictions between the racial and economic paradigms operating at the very heart of Nazi healthcare policies. Moreover, this is a key document insofar as the Ministry's definition of "hereditary health" was binding on the agencies under its jurisdiction, including the public health services. Genetic pathology was completely marginal in this mechanism of bureaucratic stigmatization, which was firmly based instead on productivity and conformity to the Nazi social model.

The forced sterilizations carried out on the basis of the Law for the Prevention of Hereditarily Diseased Offspring (*Gesetz zur Verhütung erbkranken Nachwuchses*), which was issued in July 1933 and took effect on January 1, 1934, provide another important case in point. Gisela Bock estimated that some 400,000 individuals were sterilized under the law between 1934 and 1945.[46] Some race hygienists deemed the law too moderate in scope because it was limited to conditions that experts generally agreed were hereditary and did not explicitly include conditions such as "antisocial behavior" and "feeblemindedness."[47] On closer inspection, however, a series of questions arise.

The following disorders were defined as grounds for sterilization: congenital feeblemindedness, schizophrenia, manic-depressive disorders, hereditary epilepsy, Huntington's chorea, hereditary deafness or blindness, severe physical deformations, and severe alcoholism. The role of heredity in this context was ambiguous, to say the least. Of these disorders, only Huntington's chorea was known at that time to be a genetic disease in the strict sense of the term. Statistically, Huntington's chorea was insignificant. A study of 1,320 cases considered by the hereditary health courts in Vienna found that of the 1,223 cases in which the courts ordered individuals to be sterilized, only five involved diagnoses of Huntington's chorea.[48] In the case of epilepsy, blindness, and deafness, the law mandated that the court had to establish whether the condition was hereditary. In the absence of unequivocal and irrefutable proof of exogenous causation, the hereditary character was considered established; the burden of proof was thus placed entirely on the "defendant." The doctors serving on such courts had broad discretion in deciding what they would admit as proof, tilting the process further against the victims.[49] Epilepsy accounted for 201 of the 1,320 cases studied (15.2 percent). Deafness (twenty-four cases) and blindness (eight) together accounted for 2.4 percent of the cases.[50] As for schizophrenia and manic-depressive disorders, the law did not stipulate that the hereditary character of the condition had to be established because it was considered established *ipso facto* with the diagnosis.[51] Schizophrenia accounted for 29.6 percent of the diagnoses in the Viennese sample, manic-depressive disorders for 3.25 percent.[52]

The most frequent diagnosis by far was "congenital feeblemindedness," a term so broad that a wide range of "socially undesirable behavior" could be subsumed under it. In Vienna, this category accounted for 42.9 percent of all cases.[53] As the official commentary on the law pointed out, the word "congenital" was used in the law rather than "hereditary" in order to facilitate the case for sterilization. Although the authors had to concede that the hereditary mechanism was not fully understood and that no "systematic empirical hereditary prognostic studies" (*systematische empirische Erbprognoseuntersuchungen*) existed, they nevertheless insisted that the majority of cases were caused by hereditary factors. Once again, the burden of proof in demonstrating exogenous causation fell on the defendant; in cases where the cause was unclear, the defendant was to be sterilized.[54] The commentary also explained that intelligence was not the sole criterion in defining feeblemindedness. "Asocials," "antisocials," troubled (*schwer erziehbar*) youth, and "severe psychopaths" were to be considered candidates for sterilization "even if they are not far behind in their intellectual development." In addition to intelligence, factors such as character, attitude toward the law, and ability to function in everyday life were to be taken into consideration. The way would thus be open for the state to sterilize "many psychopaths, hysterics, criminals, prostitutes, and so on" under the law. The same was to apply to pupils in special education schools (*Hilfsschüler*).[55]

Perhaps more clearly than elsewhere, the comments on the category "severe physical malformations" highlight the paradoxical relationship between biological/heredity criteria and social criteria.[56] On one hand, the authors insisted that the decision whether to sterilize a person had to take into account the defect in its "natural state" – how it would have developed without medical or surgical intervention. This was of course in keeping with the stated eugenic goal of eliminating genetic defects from the gene pool, regardless of whether the resulting malformation could be treated or not.[57] On the other hand, the distinction between acceptable defects and those to be eradicated was based on social criteria. The decisive question, the commentary advised, should be whether the defect rendered the individual incapable of "extraordinary life accomplishments" (*außergewöhnliche Leistungen des Lebens*), such as, for example, "moderate or above average accomplishments in sports, in life, in war, in surviving dangers."[58]

Interestingly, the law did not explicitly refer to heredity in connection with "severe alcoholism," which was the diagnosis in 3 percent of the sterilizations in Vienna. The authors of the official commentary on the law struggled to define the condition in a medically coherent way. Although they conceded that alcoholism could not be considered a medical condition per se, they nevertheless insisted that "according to the experience of medical science," it was rooted "almost without exception" in constitutional traits that were genetically determined. And again following a familiar pattern, the actual definition of the condition was outlined in mainly social terms. A severe alcoholic was someone who continued to drink despite the negative consequences that had already become manifest. These included a decline in performance (*Leistungsfähigkeit*), the loss of the ability to take care of one's affairs, becoming a burden to others, harassing or causing injury to others, neglecting oneself, or generally "moving down the social ladder."[59]

If anything, the bias toward social diagnostics that was inherent in the sterilization law from the beginning deepened in the years following its introduction. The second edition of the official commentary stated that if somebody was not able "to earn their own living through an orderly professional life" or to "integrate socially," the cause lay "with the highest probability" in feeblemindedness, even if "sometimes intelligence defects were barely detectable."[60] *Lebensbewährung* (roughly "the test of everyday life") became a key concept. It opened the way for social norms to supplant the ostensibly unbiased measurement of intelligence as the basis for deciding whether a person should be sterilized. Perhaps not surprisingly, the norms applied to men were very different from those applied to women. In the case of men, the courts usually based their decisions on the ability and willingness to work; in the case of women, the additional criteria of compliance with traditional gender norms regarding sexual behavior, mothering, and housekeeping were also taken into consideration.

The implementation of the sterilization law varied greatly among "hereditary health courts" (*Erbgesundheitsgerichte*) and over time, particularly in the standard of certainty they demanded in deciding whether a condition was hereditary. Gisela Bock documented numerous cases of forced sterilizations on grounds of "moral feeblemindedness" or "antisocial behavior" that were based purely on the moral judgments of medical experts and judges.[61] In Hamburg, the boundaries of the law were pushed in order to include cases of behavior deemed socially undesirable under the rubric of "moral insanity."[62] However, many experts considered that an invalid interpretation of the law, which in their view did not, perhaps regrettably, allow for forced sterilization solely on grounds of antisocial behavior.[63] In Vienna, where the sterilization campaign started much later than elsewhere in the Reich and with many war-related restrictions, some sterilization decisions were rejected on appeal because of lack of evidence that a condition was hereditary.[64] Even if generalizations should therefore be avoided, there is little doubt that even in this apparent core area of eugenically applied hereditary pathology, social criteria entered the picture on many different levels.

It is perhaps time to restate the central question of this essay: How can we explain the predominance of socio-economic criteria in the implementation of many Nazi racial-hygiene policies? And where does this leave us with regard to race as an explanatory concept? Although, as I have shown, explanations of Nazi medicine based on the ideological primacy of "race" have been losing ground in recent years in the context of Nazi medicine – especially when it comes to explaining the euthanasia killings – there are noteworthy exceptions. Winfried Süß, referring to Gisela Bock and Detlef Peukert, has insisted on the importance of racism as driving and providing legitimacy for Nazi policy. According to Süß, racism is an appropriate concept that covers discrimination on eugenic, racist, and economic grounds. In his view, this better explains the translation of ideology into practice. He distinguishes between three main ideas at the core of racism: the notion that the subjects of history are not individuals or social classes but communities of a common biological origin; the belief that social conditions are based upon biological causes; and finally, the conviction that individuals and collectives have unequal worth on account of genetic endowment.[65] From this perspective, racism is seen as an ideology in and of itself, a term essentially equivalent to "biologism." Economic criteria are meant to be included in the concept, yet it remains unclear exactly how. One possibility is to differentiate the paradigms along a temporal axis. Süß notes a shift from genetics and hereditary pathology toward criteria of social conformity and productivity over time. Nazi health policy, he claims, was dominated by the racial hygiene paradigm only from 1933 to 1941. Especially after the invasion of the Soviet Union, the imperatives of a medical war economy came to the fore.[66] There is certainly something to this argument, especially if the focus is limited to the *Altreich* (i.e. Germany in its 1937 borders) and the implementation of racial hygiene is seen solely through the lens of forced sterilizations. But in the case of Austria, for example, it is clear that *Erb- und Rassenpflege* measures were implemented on a broad scale after 1941 despite the war. Again, it is not so much that race hygiene was restrained by economic imperatives; rather, the field itself was, to a large extent, governed by them. In my view, the economic, social, and racial dimensions of Nazi racial hygiene cannot be understood separately because they derived their meaning from each other. Instead of opposing economic and racial explanations, therefore, it might be more useful to understand them as inextricably intertwined in a process aiming at the establishment of an economy of life itself.

TOWARD A POLITICAL ECONOMY OF POPULATION AND RACE?

Even if racism can hardly be dismissed as a unifying ideological factor and an essential semantic source of legitimacy in Nazi Germany, its precise content, meaning, and function remain highly controversial. Two questions stand at the center of this essay: What role did race play in Nazi eugenics and racial hygiene? What was the connection between these policies and the so-called euthanasia killings? In my view, to answer these questions, it is necessary to broaden the concept of race and racism to take into account the predominant role played by socio-economic considerations in Nazi racial-hygienic practices at all levels. It is possible to speak of "anthropological" and "eugenic" forms of racism. Taken together, the eugenic and anthropological measures implemented in the context of Nazi racial hygiene can be understood as an applied economy of the "forces of life" of the German people. The euthanasia killings, although not a eugenic measure in the strict sense of the term, can be seen as having been based on the same logic: they were intended to strengthen the *Volkskörper*, the phantasmal source of eternal life that was engaged in the equally phantasmal struggle with other races for survival.

What follows from the arguments laid out so far, therefore, is not so much that race should be dismissed or that economy trumped race, but rather that some of the implicit assumptions behind the opposition of race/biology and socio-economic motives need to be questioned. As I have suggested, one possibility for moving beyond this opposition is to turn to Michel Foucault's concept of biopolitics. In contrast to his equally influential idea of governmentality, biopolitics is not generally associated with socio-economic categories. That is the case, however, with Giorgio Agamben's application of the concept. Drawing on the philosophy of law, Agamben focuses on the opposition between inclusion and exclusion. From this perspective, biopower is the power to distinguish between those forming part of the body politic and those excluded from it. This is how so-called "bare life" is constituted. In Agamben's theory of biopolitics, the term refers to a life that can be taken without sanction: the victims of the medical experiments carried out in the concentration camps stand as the paradigmatic example.[67] Such a binary concept of biopower may be adequate for describing the selection of victims in the euthanasia programs, but it cannot account for the innumerable techniques of stigmatization, discrimination, and control that were characteristic of Nazi racial hygiene, welfare, and healthcare policies. Furthermore, this approach also tends to obscure the economic principles underpinning *Erb- und Rassenpflege* as a social technology.

Instead, it might be more promising to focus on what Foucault defined as racism's primary strategic function, namely, the drawing of dividing lines between different human groups in order to create points of contact for biopolitical strategies to increase the productivity of individual bodies and the population as a whole.[68] This conception of racism gives the idea of biopolitics a decidedly economic twist. In his famous seminar on racism in March 1976, Foucault indicated how economics and biopower could be brought together: "racism justifies the death-function in the economy of biopower by appealing to the principle that the death of others makes one biologically stronger insofar as one is a member of a race or a population, insofar as one is an element in a unitary living plurality."[69] Surprisingly, he never made the question of economics and biopolitics the object of systematic inquiry. It remains a promising avenue of research. Ulrich Bröckling has suggested that a stronger emphasis on economic categories be introduced into the concept of biopolitics to allow for an analysis of the "political economy of the population" that examines "the intersection between the politicization and the economization of life."[70] Such an approach could extend the analysis of racism to consider it as a technology of power, which, in turn, would open the way for the integration of biological and economic factors. Such an integration is necessary because, as the examples in this essay (many more could doubtlessly be found) demonstrate, neither of these two poles can supersede or be reduced to the other.

Such an approach would also allow for the integration of both eugenic and anthropological elements within a larger concept of racism. Racism might then be examined with greater attention to its effects instead of its epistemological status (as a system of prejudices, as an ideology, or as a "pseudo-science"). Considering race as a strategically employed (bio-) political technology might also allow us to account for its flexibility; from this perspective, its lack of coherence would not be a weakness but rather a factor contributing to its destructive capacity. As a technology, race can easily be combined with other ideas, discourses, and programs, often to radicalizing effect. Nazi medicine could then be integrated into a broader history of modern biopolitics. In this context, it is important to note that the dualism of economics and biology is not unique to Nazi racial hygiene, but rather has been a defining feature of Darwinian thinking since its inception. Last, such an approach would also open new ways of making sense of the National Socialist regime's paradoxical "modern" character.

Some doubts remain, however. While the concept of biopolitics facilitates the construction of a coherent history of how human life became an object (and the primary justification) of modern power, it remains unclear if this approach is truly able to explain the unique historical character of National Socialist (medical) crimes. Foucault's writings are hardly of much help when it comes to developing his theoretical assumptions into falsifiable hypotheses on the genesis of Nazi euthanasia and other problems in this field. Ultimately, the best theory can guide, but never replace, careful analysis of the forces and motives at work in a specific historical situation.

Notes

1 Where I use the term "race hygiene," I refer to the specific Nazi version within the vast array of eugenic programs brought forward during the first half of the twentieth century. "Race" and "racism" are either used in the commonly accepted sense of these terms (where I discuss their use in the scholarly literature) or in the more specific Foucauldian sense outlined in the introduction.

2 Among a variety of works in which Foucault addressed biopolitics, a seminar held in March 1976 at the Collège de France is the most useful for our purposes: Michel Foucault, *"Society Must Be Defended": Lectures at the Collège de France, 1975–76* (New York, 2003), 239–63.

3 Michael Burleigh and Wolfgang Wippermann, *The Racial State: Germany 1933–1945* (Cambridge, 1991), 306.

4 Hans-Walter Schmuhl, *Rassenhygiene, Nationalsozialismus, Euthanasie. Von der Verhütung zur Vernichtung "lebensunwerten Lebens" 1890–1945* (Göttingen, 1987), 18–20.

5 Michael Schwartz, ""Rassenhygiene, Nationalsozialismus, Euthanasie"? Kritische Anfragen an eine These Hans-Walter Schmuhls," *Westfälische Forschungen* 46 (1996), 604–22.

6 Hans-Walter Schmuhl, "Eugenik und "Euthanasie" – Zwei Paar Schuhe? Eine Antwort auf Michael Schwartz," *Westfälische Forschungen* 47 (1997), 757–62.

7 Henry Friedlander, *The Origins of Nazi Genocide: From Euthanasia to the Final Solution* (Chapel Hill, 1995).

8 Ibid., xi–xii.

9 Götz Aly, "Medizin gegen Unbrauchbare. Soziale Minderwertigkeit als "Euthanasie"-Grund" in Götz Aly, Angelika Ebbinghaus, and Matthias Hammen (eds.), *Aussonderung und Tod. Die klinische Hinrichtung der Unbrauchbaren* (Berlin, 1985), 9–74; Karl Heinz Roth, ""Auslese' und "Ausmerze'. Familien- und Bevölkerungspolitik unter der Gewalt der nationalsozialistischen 'Gesundheitsfürsorge'" in Gerhard Baader and Ulrich Schultz (eds.), *Medizin und Nationalsozialismus*, 3rd edn. (Frankfurt, 1987), 152–64; Klaus Dörner, *Tödliches Mitleid. Zur Frage der Unerträglichkeit des Lebens oder: die Soziale Frage: Entstehung, Medizinisierung, NS-Endlösung heute, morgen* (Gütersloh, 1988).

10 Michael Burleigh, *Death and Deliverance. "Euthanasia" in Germany 1900–1945* (New York, 1994), 4, 7.

11 Hans-Walter Schmuhl, "Die Genesis der 'Euthanasie.' Interpretationsansätze" in Maike Rotzoll, Gerrit Hohendorf, Petra Fuchs, Christoph Mundt, and Wolfgang Eckart (eds.), *Die nationalsozialistische "Aktion T4" und ihre Opfer. Von den historischen Bedingungen bis zu den ethischen Konsequenzen für die Gegenwart* (Paderborn, 2010), 66–73.

12 Winfried Süß's study of Nazi health policy owes much to this model, but he insists nevertheless on the importance of race: Winfried Süß, *Der "Volkskörper" im Krieg. Gesundheitspolitik, Gesundheitsverhältnisse und Krankenmord im nationalsozialistischen Deutschland 1939–1945* (Munich, 2003).

13 USSR Ministry for State Security, transcript of the interrogation of Erwin Jekelius, July 9, 1948, page 42/5 f.: copy and German translation, Dokumentationsarchiv des österreichischen Widerstandes, Vienna (hereafter DÖW) 51401.

14 Richard Günther to Alfred Dubitscher, October 29, 1940, DÖW 22796.

15 Jürgen Peiffer, "Wissenschaftliches Erkenntnisstreben als Tötungsmotiv. Zur Kennzeichnung von Opfern auf deren Krankenakten und zur Organisation und Unterscheidung von Kinder-'Euthanasie' und T4-Aktion" in Susanne Heim (ed.), *Ergebnisse. Vorabdruck aus dem Forschungsprogramm "Geschichte der Kaiser-Wilhelm-Gesellschaft im Nationalsozialismus"* (Berlin, 2005), 45; www.mpiwg-berlin.mpg.de/KWG/Ergebnisse/Ergebnisse23.pdf (May 17, 2016).

16 For a detailed analysis of this document, see Andrea Kammerhofer, "'Bis zum 1. September 1941 wurden desinfiziert: Personen: 70.273'. Die 'Hartheimer Statistik'"in Brigitte Kepplinger, Gerhart Marckgott, and Hartmut Reese (eds.), *Tötungsanstalt Hartheim* (Linz, 2008), 117–30.

17 Bundesarchiv Berlin, All. Proz. 7/111, FC 1806; microfilm copy, DÖW, Hartheim Collection, No. 599.

18 "Decisions of the euthanasia commissioners concerning the selection," quoted in Ernst Klee, *Dokumente zur "Euthanasie"* (Frankfurt, 1985), 100.

19 Volker Roelcke and Gerrit Hohendorf, "'Akten der Euthanasie'-Aktion T4 gefunden," *Vierteljahreshefte für Zeitgeschichte* 41 (1993), 479–81; Peter Sandner, "Schlüsseldokumente zur Überlieferungsgeschichte der NS-'Euthanasie'-Akten gefunden," *Vierteljahreshefte für Zeitgeschichte* 51 (2003), 285–90.

20 Maike Rotzoll, "Wahnsinn und Kalkül. Einige kollektivbiografische Charakteristika erwachsener Opfer der 'Aktion T4'" in Maike Rotzoll et al., *Die nationalsozialistische "Aktion T4,"* 272–83, here 274.

21 Gerrit Hohendorf, "Die Selektion der Opfer zwischen rassenhygienischer "Ausmerze," ökonomischer Brauchbarkeit und medizinischem Erlösungsideal" in Rotzoll et al., *Die nationalsozialistische "Aktion T4,"* 310–24, here 318. It has to be noted, however, that many Jewish patients were sent to the T4 gas chambers on "racial" rather than "medical" grounds. In my view, the group's publications thus far do not take sufficient account of this fact; the reason might be that the records of Jewish patients are apparently strongly under-represented in the euthanasia files at the Bundesarchiv (only 75 out of a total of 30,000 according to Annette Hinz-Wessels, "Jüdische Opfer der 'Aktion T4' im Spiegel der überlieferten 'Euthanasie'-Krankenakten im

Bundesarchiv" in Rotzoll et al., *Die nationalsozialistische "Aktion T4,"* 143–6, here 143.

22 Gerrit Hohendorf, Maike Rotzoll, Petra Fuchs, Annette Hinz-Wessels, and Paul Richter, "Die Opfer der nationalsozialistischen 'Euthanasie'-Aktion T4 in der Tötungsanstalt Hadamar" in Uta George and Georg Lilienthal (eds.), *Hadamar: Heilstätte, Tötungsanstalt, Therapiezentrum* (Marburg: Jonas Verlag, 2006), 176–89, 184.

23 Hohendorf, "Die Selektion der Opfer," p. 321; Rotzoll, "Wahnsinn und Kalkül," 275.

24 Hohendorf, "Die Selektion der Opfer," 315.

25 Landesgericht Wien, Vg 8a Vr 455/46, Trial of Dr. Emil Gelny and associates, letter from Gelny to Gauhauptmann Josef Mayer, February 6, 1944; copy, DÖW 18.860/7.

26 Herwig Czech, "From 'Action T4' to 'decentralized euthanasia' in Lower Austria: the psychiatirc hospitals of Gugging, Mauer-Öhling and Abbs" (2016), www.memorialguging.at/pds/Czech_Gugging_e.pdf.

27 Michael Wunder, *Euthanasie in den letzten Kriegsjahren. Die Jahre 1944 und 1945 in der Heil- und Pflegeanstalt Hamburg-Langenhorn* (Husum, 1992), 144.

28 See, for example, the medical files of the victims of the Viennese Spiegelgrund clinic: Wiener Stadt- und Landesarchiv (hereafter WStLA), 1.3.2.209.10, Wiener städtische Nervenklinik für Kinder. In the T4 program, children were selected according to the same criteria; see Petra Fuchs, "Zur Selektion von Kindern und Jugendlichen nach dem Kriterium der 'Bildungsunfähigkeit'"in Rotzoll et al. (eds.), *Die nationalsozialistische "Aktion T4,"* 287–96.

29 See Alfons Labisch and Florian Tennstedt, *Der Weg zum "Gesetz über die Vereinheitlichung des Gesundheitswesens" vom 3. Juli 1934. Entwicklungslinien und -momente des staatlichen und kommunalen Gesundheitswesens in Deutschland* (Düsseldorf, 1985).

30 See H. Fangerau and I. Müller, "Das Standardwerk der Rassenhygiene von Erwin Baur, Eugen Fischer und Fritz Lenz im Urteil der Psychiatrie und Neurologie 1921–1940," *Der Nervenarzt* 73 (2002), 1039–46.

31 Erwin Baur, Fritz Lenz, and Eugen Fischer, *Menschliche Erblichkeitslehre und Rassenhygiene*, 2 vols. (Munich, 1932); sterilization of 10 percent of the population, 273.

32 Leonardo Conti, "Der Arzt im Kampf um das deutsche Volksschicksal. Rede des Reichsgesundheitsführers Dr. Conti auf der Sitzung des NSD-Ärztebundes, Gau Berlin und der Berliner Medizinischen Gesellschaft am 24. April 1942," *Ärzteblatt für die deutsche Ostmark* 5 (1942), 131–7, here 134. Conti also referred to Baur-Fischer-Lenz as "the reference work of our theory of hereditary health" in a programmatic speech held on the occasion of the tenth anniversary of Hitler being named chancellor: Leonardo Conti, "Arzt und Nationalsozialismus. Zum 30. Jänner 1943," *Deutsches Ärzteblatt. Ausgabe Alpen- und Donaureichsgaue* 6 (1943), 31–2, here 31.

33 See, e.g., Herwig Czech, *Erfassung, Selektion und "Ausmerze." Das Wiener Gesundheitsamt und die Umsetzung der nationalsozialistischen "Erbgesundheitspolitik" 1938 bis 1945* (Vienna, 2003), 27–30.

34 "Gesetz zur Verhütung erbkranken Nachwuchses vom 14.7.1933," *Reichsgesetzblatt* 1933, part 1, 529. Kamila Uzarczyk has shown how in Silesia

forced sterilization was not used against the Polish minority, contrary to what Polish historians have assumed for many years: Kamila Uzarczyk, "'Rassen-politik' und 'Erbgesundheit'. Die nationalsozialistische Rassenhygiene und die polnische Minderheit in Schlesien" in Axel Hüntelmann, Johannes Vossen, and Herwig Czech (eds.), *Gesundheit und Staat. Studien zur Geschichte der Gesundheitsämter in Deutschland, 1870–1950* (Husum, 2007), 221–36.

35 See Reiner Pommerin, "The fate of mixed blood children in Germany," *German Studies Review*, 5 (1982), 315–23; Reiner Pommerin, "Die Sterilisier-ung der 'Rheinlandbastarde'" in Peter Martin and Christine Alonzo (eds.), *Zwischen Charleston und Stechschritt. Schwarze im Nationalsozialismus* (Munich, 2004), 532–47.

36 Gisela Bock, *Zwangssterilisation im Nationalsozialismus. Studien zur Rassen-politik und Frauenpolitik* (Opladen, 1986), 59–76.

37 Ibid., 60.

38 Ibid., 61.

39 For a detailed analysis, see Paul Weindling, *Health, Race, and German Politics between National Unification and Nazism, 1870–1945*, 3rd edn. (Cambridge, 1993).

40 WStLA, 1.3.2.212.A7.7 "Bericht der Abteilung Erb- und Rassenpflege über die bisher geleistete Arbeit," July 28, 1939.

41 Johannes Vossen, *Gesundheitsämter im Nationalsozialismus. Rassenhygiene und offene Gesundheitsfürsorge in Westfalen 1900/1950* (Essen, 2001), p. 327.

42 WStLA, 1.3.2.212.A7.7 Gundel to District Health Offices, November 20, 1941; copy DÖW 20.486/5.

43 For the case of Vienna, see Czech, *Erfassung, Selektion und "Ausmerze."*

44 WStLA, M.Abt. 121, A 7/7, "Richtlinien für die Beurteilung der Erbgesund-heit," circular issued by the Reich Minister of the Interior, July 18, 1940, IV b 1446/40-1072c.

45 Ibid.

46 Bock, *Zwangssterilisation im Nationalsozialismus*, 238.

47 Arthur Gütt, Ernst Rüdin, and Falk Alfred Ruttke, *Gesetz zur Verhütung erbkranken Nachwuchses vom 14. Juli 1933* (Munich, 1934), 61; Otto Pötzl, "Psychiatrisch-neurologische Probleme zur Verhütung erbkranken Nach-wuchses," *Wiener klinische Wochenschrift*, 51 (1938), 1205–9; Karl Ludwig Lechler, "Erkennung und Ausmerze der Gemeinschaftsunfähigen," *Deutsches Ärzteblatt* 70 (1940), 293–7.

48 Claudia Spring, *Zwischen Krieg und Euthanasie: Zwangssterilisationen in Wien 1940–1945* (Vienna, 2009), 198.

49 Gütt et al., *Gesetz zur Verhütung erbkranken Nachwuchse*, 105, 107, 114.

50 Spring, *Zwischen Krieg und Euthanasie*, 198–9.

51 Gütt et al., *Gesetz zur Verhütung erbkranken Nachwuchses*, 97–104.

52 Spring, *Zwischen Krieg und Euthanasie*, 199.

53 Ibid.

54 Gütt et al., *Gesetz zur Verhütung erbkranken Nachwuchses*, 91–3.

55 Ibid., 94. For a detailed discussion of the controversies around the imple-mentation of the sterilization policy, see Richard F. Wetzell, *Inventing the Criminal: A History of German Criminology 1880–1945* (Chapel Hill, 2000), 254–94.

56 This category accounted for 3 percent of the cases in Vienna: Spring, *Zwischen Krieg und Euthanasie*, 199.

57 Gütt et al., *Gesetz zur Verhütung erbkranken Nachwuchses*, 116.

58 Ibid., 123.

59 Gütt et al., *Gesetz zur Verhütung erbkranken Nachwuchses*, 127–8.

60 Gütt et al., *Gesetz zur Verhütung erbkranken Nachwuchses*, 2nd edn. (Munich, 1936), 125.

61 Bock, *Zwangssterilisation im Nationalsozialismus*.

62 Andrea Brücks and Christiane Rothmaler, "'In dubio pro Volksgemeinschaft'. Das 'Gesetz zur Verhütung erbkranken Nachwuchses' in Hamburg" in Angelika Ebbinghaus, Heidrun Kaupen-Haas, and Karl-Heinz Roth (eds.), *Heilen und Vernichten im Mustergau Hamburg* (Hamburg, 1984), 30–6.

63 Ibid., 35.

64 Spring, *Zwischen Krieg und Euthanasie*.

65 Süß, *Der "Volkskörper" im Krieg*, 20.

66 Ibid., 49, 51, 406.

67 Giorgio Agamben, *Homo Sacer. Le pouvoir souverain et la vie nue* (Paris, 1995).

68 Foucault, *"Society Must Be Defended,"* 239–63.

69 Ibid., 258.

70 Ulrich Bröckling, "Menschenökonomie, Humankapital. Eine Kritik der biopolitischen Ökonomie," *Mittelweg 36* (2003), 3–22.

PART III

ANTI-SEMITISM BEYOND RACE

9

"The axis around which National Socialist ideology turns"

State Bureaucracy, the Reich Ministry of the Interior, and Racial Policy in the First Years of the Third Reich

Jürgen Matthäus

I

Over the past two decades, scholars have produced a massive body of publications on the Third Reich's "final solution to the Jewish question," shedding new light on the course and outcomes of German anti-Jewish policy, including and beyond the actions of perpetrators, victims, and bystanders. Irrespective of differences in interpretation, historians as much as the broader public have come to understand the Holocaust as the essence of Nazism – a perceptual revolution with inbuilt problems due to its tendency to overstress the obsessively genocidal, monomaniacal, or otherwise irrational aspects of Nazi Germany's *Judenpolitik*. The prevailing focus of recent scholarship has been the role of ideology during the Holocaust; much less energy has been invested in exploring the interests and mechanics that helped transform racial prejudice into bureaucratic action and facilitate systematic policy. To put it differently: the colossus of the racial state has not yet been fully turned from its head onto its feet.

Studies on the early war years – especially what Christopher Browning calls the "crucial months" in the second half of 1941 – that reconstruct the interplay between ideology, interest, and implementation, between periphery and center, in the emergence of the Holocaust have provided significant

The opinions presented here are those of the author, not of the United States Holocaust Memorial Museum. I thank Donald Bloxham, Devin Pendas, and Mark Roseman for their comments and suggestions.

insights into the unfolding process, its driving forces, and the importance of
Nazi designs for the redrawing of the ethnic map in Europe.[1] Despite the
general upsurge in research since the 1990s, there have been neither com-
parable analyses of racial policy between 1933 and 1945 as a whole nor
studies that focus on the formative stages in the process as opposed to the
war years and their genocidal dynamic. Still, crucial findings abound in
earlier works by a range of scholars. From Raul Hilberg's monumental
Destruction of the European Jews, via Karl Schleunes's *Twisted Road to
Auschwitz* and Uwe Adam's outstanding yet today largely ignored monograph on German anti-Jewish policy, to books by Gisela Bock, Götz Aly,
Ernst Klee, Henry Friedlander, Michael Zimmermann, and others on
forced sterilizations, "euthanasia" killings, and the persecution of non-
Jewish outgroups such as "gypsies," "asocials," and homosexuals, historiography has paid attention to the broader aspects of what Michael Burleigh
and Wolfgang Wippermann termed the German "racial state."[2] At the
same time, scholars such as Claudia Koonz, Saul Friedländer, and Michael
Wildt have stressed the key importance of anti-Semitic discrimination for
the Nazi system's destructivity: the "Nazi conscience," "redemptive" anti-
Semitism, and "Volksgemeinschaft als Selbstermächtigung" (people's community as self-empowerment) have been invoked to explain the moral
orientation of Germans involved in the murder of the Jews.[3] Why is it,
then, that more recently we have seen few in-depth studies about the
interconnections between different strands of Nazi racial policy as practical
applications of ideology? To be sure, the new documentation that has come
to light since the 1990s has not only offered new insights into Holocaust
perpetration and the role of the periphery but has also revealed how
the Berlin center controlled and directed the dynamic toward genocide.
The more historians have focused on the anti-Jewish mindset as an
explanatory factor for the "Final Solution," it seems, the less inclined they
have been to ask how the concept of race was transformed into policy and
what this meant for the overall process of persecution. Consequently, the
hope expressed by Ulrich Herbert in the late 1990s that research will
"expose the regime's racist policy as a unified entity and trace its traditions
in German history" – and, one might add, its postwar ramifications –
remains largely unfulfilled.[4]

   Although the need for an integrated approach is widely accepted when
it comes to combining perpetrator and victim perspectives of the Holocaust, scholars have not yet applied the concept of integration to the study
of Nazi racial policy, with its broad range of target groups, institutional
agents, and interlocking implementation processes. The fact that current

historiography tends to reduce the issue of perpetration to personal intent and genocidal mentality exemplifies the uneven development of Holocaust scholarship and points to a degree of persistence of intentionalism that is surprisingly inconsistent with the prevalence of multicausal interpretations. No doubt, the question of what motivated Germans and their helpers to kill innocent Jewish men, women, and children is as central as it is vexing; yet it should not be overlooked that the quest to reconstruct individual motivation – in addition to its inherent methodological problems, especially for historians – promotes prioritizing ideological dispositions as key causal factors. Simultaneously, "ideology" and "racism" have become mere synonyms for "anti-Semitism," while "race science" is being studied as a topic of academic discourse and a means of legitimizing violence, not as applied state policy.[5]

In a historiographic climate dominated by the primacy of the ideological, scant attention is paid to structures and processes, be they administrative, societal, or systemic. The unbroken productivity and expansion of Holocaust studies measurable in publications, conferences, and media coverage increases the risk that what earlier scholars found out about the workings of the Nazi state and its legacy will be forgotten.[6] In the United States, Western Europe, and, increasingly, other parts of the world, the Holocaust is firmly integrated in collective memory – even if, in a growing number of countries, such as Hungary and Latvia, negatively; other Nazi measures against racially defined outgroups are not, even where these measures form part of a continuum extending far beyond the World War period. How else, to name but one example, would it be possible that in West Germany, attempts at "making good" (*Wiedergutmachung*) for Jewish Holocaust survivors became enshrined in national policy in the early 1950s, while compensation payments to the victims and families of Nazi-era forced sterilizations and "euthanasia" murders occurred extremely late? Only in 1998 did the Bundestag label forced sterilizations a crime, and it would take another ten years beyond that for the Law for the Prevention of Hereditarily Ill Offspring (*Gesetz zur Verhütung erbkranken Nachwuchses*, GzVeN) enacted in July 1933, which had facilitated these and other proto-genocidal measures, to finally be declared null and void.[7]

This essay argues for a conceptualist interpretation, as suggested by the late Michael Zimmermann, that links the analysis of intention with that of the role of institutions and the "polycentric dynamic" triggered by their interaction.[8] I focus on a small yet decisive part of the overall process: the shaping of racial policy between early 1933 and the decision for the Four-Year Plan in 1936, a time period in which the "interplay between will of the Volk and state leaders (Wechselspiel von Volkswillen und Staatsführung)"[9] created the building blocks of the "racial state." The question addressed here is not whether Hitler, to use Burleigh's and Wippermann's terminology, had a "comprehensive programme for a racial new order"[10]; instead, I try to explore how, by whom, and in which factors racial planning took shape as a "policy of the State" during the first years of Nazi rule. My aim is to complement the findings of earlier scholarship by integrating anti-Jewish legislative and administrative measures into the broader context of the Third Reich's early racial policy, and to provide stimulus for further study into areas passed by since historiography's "ideological turn."

II

From the vantage point of the twenty-first century, the destruction of the European Jews appears as a foregone conclusion to, if not the necessary consequence of, anti-Semitic fanaticism. Pre-1933 propaganda and early anti-Jewish actions such as the April 1, 1933, boycott seem to indicate the regime's determination to bring about a "final solution to the Jewish question" once Hitler was appointed Reich Chancellor. Yet if this were so, why did it take the Nazi regime more than two and a half years to enact a law that fulfilled the promise of racial segregation included not only in the NSDAP party program but also in the demands of *völkisch* extremists since the turn of the century? Why did a definition of "Jew" to replace the earlier, much broader, and less focused "non-Aryan" not become fully enshrined in law until the enactment of the Nuremberg Laws in September 1935? If the passing of the Nuremberg Laws was "no surprise" in light of everything the Nazi party stood for,[11] the same cannot be said about the Nazi state's relative lack of focus during the preceding period.

This time lag can no doubt be explained by the regime's need to gain a firm hold on power before it could make headway in the direction of implementing its main ideological aspiration. But there are limits to this argument. First, by mid-1934 Hitler was well enough established that his government could have moved ahead on one of the key goals of Nazi ideology. Many anti-Jewish activists did not wait for the passing of a law before striking against Jewish shop-owners, lawyers, or others, thus increasing the demand for workable regulations and definitions, especially when embarking on uncharted administrative terrain. Second, at a time when the "Jewish question" remained marginal in the field of state legislation, other laws were passed, some almost immediately after Hitler's coming to power, that showed his government's urge to push ahead on the issue of race, both in its discriminatory, negative meaning as well as in setting the stage for what were understood as "positive" measures to improve the hereditary health of the *Volk*.

When seeing the Third Reich's history through the lens of the Holocaust, we tend to overlook that in Germany, as in many Western countries during the late nineteenth and early twentieth centuries, racial policy was widely understood as a two-pronged means to an integrated end: excluding those groups deemed inferior, deviant, or otherwise defective and at the same time helping the in-group sustain, foster, and develop its potential in order to increase the biological vitality of the national body.[12] Nazi Party officials borrowed their propaganda ammunition from the arsenals of the *völkisch* and eugenics movements; the latter was part of a strong international current in science and politics toward understanding and addressing social problems in biological terms.[13] The borderlines between in- and out-group were precariously fluid in the early years of Nazi rule, depending on personal preference, ideological orientation, and political interest. Hitler's well-known retroactive fantasy of gassing 12–15,000 Jews during World War I as "Hebraic offenders against the *Volk*" (*hebräischen Volksverbrecher*) has a forward-looking, less frequently quoted analogy in his idea of "eliminating" (*beseitigen*) 700–800,000 of Germany's weakest newborns in order to improve the strength of the Volk in the long term.[14] In *Mein Kampf*, Hitler called for the "reduction of the fertility of the physically degenerate" (*Verhinderung der Zeugungsfähigkeit und Zeugungsmöglichkeit seitens körperlich Degenerierter*) and the abandonment of the artificial "humanism of the individual" in favor of the "humanism of nature," according to which the weak would be allowed to wither so the strong could prevail.[15]

The latter aspect of racial policy, namely the gradual eradication of those among the *Volksgenossen* who seemed unfit or degenerate, dovetailed with the Nazi take on the "Jewish question." As a historic precursor and basic ingredient of racism, Christian anti-Semitism shaped Nazi propaganda in many ways, perhaps most outspokenly in Hitler's notorious claim that he was "fighting the Lord's cause" in defending the nation against "the Jew."[16] Just as unoriginally, Nazi rhetoric also relied heavily on biologistic notions that stigmatized Jews as carriers of disease and agents of degeneration. To achieve the desired "removal of the Jews," the old-style *Radauantisemitismus* (loosely, rabble-rousing anti-Semitism),

with its erratic bouts of violence – as useful as it seemed in neutralizing
bottled-up activist energies and legitimizing anti-Jewish state intervention
under the pretext of "restoring order" – had to be replaced with a
systematic process driven by rational considerations. This implied that,
no matter how great Hitler's skepticism about bureaucrats embracing the
goals of the party, the regime needed procedures that were defined and
administered by experts in the German civil service. As Gisela Bock has
pointed out, the transformation of utopian racial ideas into reality
depended on their institutionalization; it was the merging of ideology,
societal support, administrative practice, and dynamic radicalization
that turned racial policy into the emblematic element of the Nazi system
after 1933.[17]

Especially within bourgeois circles, among public servants and busi-
nessmen with a fixation on order, a preference for the political right, and
long-held concerns about undue Jewish influence or the racial dangers
inherent in the Jewish question,[18] Hitler's promise of an *Antisemitismus
der Vernunft* (rational anti-Semitism) had a much greater appeal than
rabid displays of anti-Jewish violence by the SA or other parts of his
movement. Whether and how far Hitler and his closest supporters were
guided in their actions by deep convictions or by opportunistic and other
considerations is a question no easier to answer than whether German
society supported or rejected the Nazi Party despite or because of its racial
program.[19] Yet if we look at racial policy in its broader meanings and
concrete manifestations, leaders and followers appear to have been united
in their belief that the goal of improving the collective health of the nation
transcended ideological divisions and was the morally right, politically
wise, and scientifically advisable thing to do.

Younger bureaucrats in particular, whether party members or not, saw
the Nazi "revolution" as a welcome chance to purge the public service as
well as the nation as a whole of the "aberrations" of the Weimar democratic system. In the early years of the Nazi regime, the key parameters in
this direction were set less by the party, which already then presented
itself as a disparate body integrated primarily by the undisputed authority
of the Führer, than by the state apparatus, with its professional staff
of established career bureaucrats and ambitious newcomers. Given the
regime's polycratic structures and improvised decision-making processes,
it is important to identify where the center of political gravity was located
during each phase of the Third Reich's history. Between 1933 and 1936,
no other government institution provided as much stimulus and direction
to racial policy as the Reich Interior Ministry (RIM) under Wilhelm Frick.[20]

One of only three Nazi party members in Hitler's original cabinet, Frick could point to a degree of administrative experience as civil servant (in Bavaria) and minister (in Thuringia) that was unique among his peers. Countering the influence of vociferous race fanatics like Franconian Gauleiter and *Stürmer* editor Julius Streicher or Gerhard Wagner (since 1932 leader of the Nazi doctors' association and later, until his death in 1939, Reichsärzteführer) as well as others in the NSDAP, Frick strove to establish and maintain his ministry's prerogative in setting racial policy.

Frick had staked his claim as a leader in matters of racial policy most visibly when, during his tenure as Thuringian interior minister in 1930/1931, he had helped install the famous race theoretician Hans Günther ("Rasse-Günther") in a chair at Jena University. The fact that this was not a mere propagandistic stunt but an expression of conviction can be seen from Frick's motion submitted to the Reichstag in 1924, as leader of the Nazi Party caucus, to place "all members of the Jewish race under special law" and his introduction of a bill in the Reichstag in early 1930 that called for outlawing racial intermixture.[21] Among Frick's team of experienced administrators and race propagandists were State Secretary Hans Pfundtner, a World War I veteran and lawyer who had joined the Nazi Party in 1932; Hanns Seel, a senior advisor on civil service law (Referent für Beamtenrechtsfragen) who had been acquainted with Frick since his time in the Bavarian civil service; the RIM's first Rassereferent, Bernhard Lösener, a career bureaucrat and party member since 1930 who would later work closely with Hans Globke; Arthur Gütt, a physician, Nazi Party member since 1932, and SS officer, who took over the RIM's *Volksgesundheit* department; Herbert Linden, another doctor, who joined the RIM in late 1933 to work in Gütt's department and later co-authored with Gütt an influential commentary on the Nuremberg Laws; Helmut Nicolai, a lawyer and civil servant who had worked for the Nazi Party central office (NSDAP-Reichsleitung) before he joined the RIM in early 1934; and, from February 1935, the highly energetic and determined successor to State Secretary Grauert, Wilhelm Stuckart, a gifted operator of the new system that propelled him to become, among other things, SS-Obergruppenführer.[22]

Frick's team included devout anti-Semites, long-time eugenicists, and social policy reformers, all of whom were eager to address both negative and positive racial policy. Among the most radical thinkers and experienced administrators in the group was Nicolai. Dismissed from public service in the Weimar era due to his Nazi party membership, he published *Die rassengesetzliche Rechtslehre. Grundzüge einer nationalsozialistischen*

Rechtsphilosophie in 1932 and, one year later, offered his vision for the Third Reich's constitutional order in his *Grundlagen der kommenden Verfassung*. Insisting that is was necessary to determine "once and for all *who belongs to the German Volk and who does not*," he argued that the constitution must enshrine the "divine order given by nature, which it would be a heinous crime to offend against." Germanness, Nicolai argued, was determined by "blood, race, and ancestry." "A German is anyone of German ancestry," he wrote, "to which, to eradicate any doubt, we can add, 'whereby blood (race) is decisive.'" To ensure a clear differentiation between "us" and "them," Nicolai proposed new legislation that drew heavily on ideas long favored within the *völkisch* movement: "German blood" was to be cleansed by the exclusion of "aliens," primarily Jews and Poles, who would be subject to special laws; marriages and relations between Germans and "aliens" were to be regulated by a "racial protection law" (*Rassenschutzgesetz*) designed to prevent the "infiltration of alien blood into the body of the German Volk and protect it from further bastardization."[23]

Whereas Nicolai stressed the need for restrictive measures targeting "aliens," Arthur Gütt gave priority to a radical reform of social policy to serve "race preservation." An energetic "population and racial policy" (*Bevölkerungs- und Rassenpolitik*) could not only save the German nation but also prevent "the racial and cultural decline of all European peoples."[24] Gütt's warnings about the effects of demographic change (decline of the birth rate, over-aging) – still today standard items on the lists of populist propagandists in Europe – were meant to highlight the possibilities for holistic policies, both negative and positive, created by the Nazi takeover. An understanding of race as broad as Gütt's did not require invoking the "Jewish question" or any other specific outgroup: those blocking the path to the "preservation of the species and race" (*Art- und Rassenerhaltung*) were to be prevented from procreating, and everything possible had to be done to foster the multiplication of the racially healthy and valuable population. This, he declared, was true "service to the race" and the greatest task the Nazi state had to fulfill.[25] Nicolai and Gütt were among those racial planners uniquely positioned to transform what so far had been castles in the sky into the basis for Germany's future development. For them, the race question, seen as a matter of applying natural and divine law in the quest for national salvation, was the central policy area around which all other issues revolved. How could this new axis be firmly inserted into the state apparatus, with its complex mechanics? What counterforces were to be factored in?

III

During the Nazis' "years of struggle" (*Kampfzeit*) before 1933, invoking the party's program and bashing opponents sufficed as proof of ideological commitment. Once Hitler had come to power, more was required to live up to the hazy promise of a racial millennium. Old hobby-horses dragged from the storehouse of anti-Semitic demands, such as excluding *Ostjuden* (Eastern European Jews) or abolishing ritual slaughter, seemed a good start but offered limited political mileage. Bavaria had in fact already introduced a ban on *shechita* in 1930, and the states of Braunschweig, Thuringia, and Oldenburg followed with similar laws of their own before 1933.[26] At the same time, sweeping proposals retrieved from the drawers of long-time race fanatics had to stand the test of the new situation and fit within the wider political context. The regime was hampered by a decentralized system of public administration at the local, state, and national levels that made swift action difficult. But many experienced bureaucrats quickly proved eager to help the Nazis with their efforts to eliminate the political left and to undo the Weimar Republic's transformation of the civil service.[27]

Early efforts toward developing an administrative procedure for racial policy were influenced by both the bureaucratic elite's preferences and the "movement's" dynamics. Not surprisingly, given the party's pre-1933 propaganda, newspaper headlines abroad about massive violence against the Nazis' opponents prompted calls for "defensive action" against "international Jewry," the alleged instigator, that culminated in the nationwide anti-Jewish boycott of April 1, 1933. The response to the boycott initiative stood as evidence that radicals like Julius Streicher, the head of the Hitler-appointed boycott committee, could not mobilize public support and thereby establish a broad social basis for Nazi racial policy.[28] After the eager activists had their day, it was the bureaucrats' turn to show their skill in establishing administrative measures that would produce politically effective and socially acceptable long-term results.

On April 6, 1933, a group of state and party functionaries – among them Rudolf Diels, the head of the Prussian Political Police, and racial expert Johannes von Leers – finished drafting an ambitious piece of anti-Jewish legislation. Defining Jews as "persons whose parents or grandparents were of the Mosaic faith," the proposed law would prohibit Jews from marrying or having extramarital sexual relations with non-Jews, would force Jews to append the letter "J" to their names, and would force them into a Verband der Juden in Deutschland (Association of Jews in Germany) run by a *Judenrat* (Jewish council) under the supervision of an overseer appointed by the Reich chancellor. It would introduce the category of "Jew spouse" (*Judengatte*) and would require them, together with Jews and "half-Jews," to register with the police. Moreover, access to certain professions and business would be restricted for Jews, their spouses, and "half-Jews." As much as this stunning example of early discriminatory planning might seem a precursor to the Nuremberg Laws of September 1935, Uwe Adam has argued that its ties to traditional right-wing radical ideas were stronger than its links to the Nazi program and the broad agenda of racial reformers.[29] As it turned out, the draft proposal remained just that. Its terminology – "Jew," "half-Jew," "Jewish spouse" – reflected the conservative authors' concerns but raised questions regarding definition and applicability. For the time being, Hitler opted for what seemed necessary under the circumstances and for leaving the rest to "comprehensive education" (*umfassende Aufklärung*). It appears he had already decided on a more suitable course of action around the time of the April 1 boycott and used the attempt to purge the civil service of political opponents for the dual purposes of meeting the demand for anti-Jewish legislation and pushing the broader racial political envelope.[30]

Reacting to earlier proposals by ministerial bureaucrats and Nazi party functionaries as well as to the new situation following the April 1 boycott, Frick and his team at the RIM established themselves as the architects of a forward-looking policy and bureaucratic order. By introducing the concept of "non-Aryan descent" (*nicht-arische Abstammung*) as one of the criteria for dismissal, the Civil Service Law (*Berufsbeamtengesetz*, BBG) enacted on April 7, 1933, enshrined a racist category that revoked the principles of Jewish emancipation and transcended the party's hitherto narrow focus on Jews, thus leaving all doors open for future modification or expansion. It all depended on how the question "Who is a non-Aryan?" was to be answered in terms of bureaucratic practice. According to the RIM's implementation order, which took effect on April 11, 1933, all persons "of non-Aryan, especially Jewish descent" were to lose their jobs under the new civil service law; "Jewish descent" was defined as having one parent or grandparent of the Jewish faith.[31] This definition circumvented the problem caused by the absence of clear physiological markers to distinguish between "Aryans" and "non-Aryans," making ancestry the key criterion – a category familiar to racial planners of Helmut Nicolai's ilk but alien to radical anti-Semites like Streicher, who claimed that any intercourse with Jews produced irreparable long-term damage to the *Volk*.[32]

"When in the early days of 1933 the first civil servant wrote the first definition of a 'non-Aryan' into a civil service ordinance," Raul Hilberg claims, "the fate of the European Jews was sealed."[33] Seen from the end point of the process of persecution, this statement indeed rings true. Yet at the time of its enactment, the BBG hardly seemed suited to provide the foundation for a far-reaching, not to mention genocidal, anti-Jewish policy.[34] First, the law had its origins in ministerial bureaucrats' plans for reforming the public service and establishing race, not just the "Jewish question," as a legal concept; second, it included but a fraction of the measures directed against Jews that German anti-Semites had demanded since before World War I; and third, it affected primarily those the regime deemed political opponents and the number of Jews excluded remained comparatively low, partly because of the exemptions granted to World War I veterans.[35] Nevertheless, the "Aryan clause" subsequently assumed key importance as it provided a precedent for anti-Jewish actions enacted in the civil service to be adopted more broadly throughout German society. Organizations from the army to sports clubs and stamp collectors associations were swept by a wave of exclusionary measures driven by a mix of conviction, anticipatory compliance, and opportunism.[36]

In the following weeks and months, the RIM tried to take advantage of the convergence between the regime's planning and the considerable degree of mobilization, especially among elites, to pursue a holistic, step-by-step approach to implementing racial goals. On the day the BBG took effect, Frick informed State Secretary Pfundtner of the imminent appointment of Achim Gercke as the RIM's "expert for racial research" (*Sachverständiger für Rasseforschung*) responsible for checking ancestry and deciding questionable cases. Gercke's credentials included a doctorate in chemistry and two years' experience as head of the NS-Auskunft, a party office set up to investigate the racial background of members.[37] Like Streicher, the twenty-nine-year-old Gercke belonged to a radical group of racists, sometimes labeled "contagionists," whose adherents firmly believed in the indelible negative effects caused by any mixing of the races; both had been members of the party committee charged with organizing the April boycott.[38] In the official *Völkischer Beobachter* in June 1933, Gercke, repeating the party's goal of "separating the Jews from Germany," called for an international initiative to create a "home territory for the Jews" to solve the so-called Jewish problem "not only for

Germany but also for Europe and the world."[39] Gercke's ambition mirrored that of other functionaries in the RIM in his declaration that the "race question" (*Rassenfrage*) provided "the axis around which National Socialist ideology [*Ideenwelt*] turns."[40]

Gercke had strong allies within and outside the RIM in trying to integrate the regime's measures against Jews into a broader policy framework. In May 1933, Frick established an Expert Advisory Board for Population and Race Policy (Sachverständigenbeirat für Bevölkerungs- und Rassenpolitik), headed by Gercke and Gütt. Among its members were the long-time racial activists Rüdin, Plötz, Günther, and Schultze-Naumburg.[41] By the end of the year, Frick had extended the circle of racial policy advisors to include industrial magnate Fritz Thyssen and Reichsführer-SS Heinrich Himmler.[42] On June 28, 1933, addressing the advisory board at its inaugural meeting, Frick provided the government's first programmatic statement on the issue of race. Painting a bleak picture of the situation, Frick spoke of the "threatening increase in hereditary-biological inferiority" within the German population that could be rectified only through "eradication and selection" (*Ausmerze und Auslese*). The state, according to the minister, had the duty to reduce expenditures on "asocial, inferior, and hopelessly hereditarily sick people" and to prevent the procreation of "persons with hereditary conditions" (*erblich belasteten Personen*). Nothing would be worse than acting on the "ill-conceived brotherly love and religious reservations [*kirchliche Bedenken*]" felt by some Catholics and conservatives; instead, Frick espoused the popular slogan of religiously motivated racism as expressed by Hitler, Gercke, and Gütt, claiming that complacency amounted to a "violation of Christian and social compassion."[43] In his speech, Frick echoed Gütt's demand for "hereditary and racial measures of exclusion and support" that would prevent people with hereditary diseases from procreating while supporting the needs of the "hereditarily healthy family with numerous children" (*erbgesunde, kinderreiche Familie*).[44] This was not idle talk; earlier that month, Frick had instructed Gütt to draft a sterilization law for him to present to cabinet in early July before the summer break.[45]

Some of the RIM's ambitious goals turned out to be more realistic than others. On July 4, Pfundtner announced a whole range of new measures, including a law for the sterilization of the "hereditarily ill" (*Erbkranke*), a law for promoting hereditary health, and a "Reich citizenship law" (*Reichsangehörigkeitsgesetz*) that was to differentiate between "Reich citizens of German or foreign blood." The latter followed Nicolai's suggestion discussed above, but it still had no prospect of becoming law. The "Jewish question" seemed to have been temporarily taken care of by way of the BBG; subsequent, more limited anti-Jewish laws; and exclusionary impulses from below. For Frick, the denaturalization law enacted on July 14, 1933 that targeted political opponents and – as anti-Semites had demanded for years – Jews who had acquired German citizenship after 1918 represented a good start on the way to more systematic racial policy.[46] Pushing the anti-Jewish envelope, especially by way of highly visible measures as favored by the National Socialist Handcraft, Commercial, and Business Organization (NS-Hago) and other party interest groups, meant endangering the regime's foreign policy and empowering those who sneered at bureaucratically controlled discrimination. In summer 1933, with the party firmly in power at home but the economic and diplomatic situations still tenuous, Hitler expressed his disinclination to endanger economic recovery and kept open options for the future.[47]

Diplomatic and economic considerations as well as situational contingencies and pressures from below figured prominently in the regime's anti-Jewish policy until September 1935. The attempt to avert outside criticism of the Reich's *Judenpolitik* by introducing the concept of "non-Aryan" into German law created tensions, as various foreign nations – among others Italy, Turkey, and Japan – protested against being labeled as racially inferior. Commenting on Pfundtner's announcement of an exclusionary citizenship law, in early July 1933 State Secretary Bernhard von Bülow of the Foreign Office warned Foreign Minister Constantin von Neurath that such a law would cause a "storm of outrage" and fuel anti-German agitation abroad. Bülow had a keen sense of foreign interests and also perceived the benefits of thinking beyond the limits of legalistic procedures. Instead of passing laws "obviously aimed at persecuting Jews," he advised, the government should "dispose of the Jewish question in practical terms" by fall that year. Frick and his men should learn at last to shift their measures against Jews and others "into the uncontrollable regions of the administration" instead of enacting laws "the domestic propaganda value of which is outweighed by their diplomatic damage."[48] A week later, attempting to prevent further international tensions, the Foreign Office advised German diplomats to refute foreign complaints by stating that the Reich's regulations were not aimed at Jews as Jews but as members of the "ruling class."[49]

The Foreign Office's efforts to avoid diplomatic complications were not helped when a memorandum written in September 1933 by Roland Freisler, then state secretary in the Prussian Ministry of Justice, was leaked.

Freisler, who would later head the Volksgerichtshof, proposed that the BBG's category "non-Aryan" be replaced by the concept of "member of a community of foreign blood" (*Angehöriger fremder Blutsgemeinschaft*) – *fremdrassig* in short form – and called for the outlawing of racial inter-mixture as "race treason" (*Rasseverrat*), a term borrowed from Frick's 1930 Reichstag bill.[50] According to a later report, Freisler's memoran-dum caused a "storm of consternation" abroad, especially in the Middle East, India, and Japan, that the Foreign Office had trouble diffusing.[51] Invoking notions of national sovereignty firmly established as principles of foreign policy since the post – World War I treaties, Neurath and his diplomats tried to label Germany's anti-Jewish move as a purely defensive act.[52] Although determined to proceed, Frick was not oblivious to the need to sweeten the racist pill rhetorically for easier consumption abroad. Addressing members of the diplomatic corps in February 1934, the min-ister declared that Germany had no intention of expelling its Jewish population – in contrast to what Greece and Turkey had done with their Muslim and Greek Orthodox minorities, respectively, after World War I. The Reich, the minister insisted, was a *Rechtsstaat*, a state where the rule of law prevailed; the BBG's "Aryan clause" was not meant to imply a "value judgment against foreign races" but rather marked the starting point of a German system of racial laws demanded by the NSDAP's program.[53]

Concerns about protests by foreign governments and about severe economic blowback, in combination with the lack of unanimity on prac-tical goals and procedures, blocked more radical anti-Jewish measures for the time being. Little stood in the way of implementing other items on the racial agenda, however, especially in regard to hereditary health. Of much greater importance for racial policy in the Third Reich than the denatural-ization law was the GzVeN, passed also on July 14, 1933, but publicly announced only on July 25, after the concordat with the Vatican had been signed, to take effect on January 1, 1934. Race experts and eugenics planners within and beyond Germany widely acknowledged that the nation-state had the right, indeed the duty, to intervene to improve the *Volkskörper* and to determine whom to accept as full-fledged citi-zens and which groups to ostracize as outcasts. Rooted in discussions between public health planners and practitioners of eugenics-oriented cost-cutting measures in view of the world economic crisis, the law showed that Frick was determined to deliver on the promise contained in his June 28 speech. Going beyond his earlier remarks, Frick insisted on the forced, not voluntary, sterilization of persons deemed to be suffering "heredity illnesses," including feeblemindedness, schizophrenia, epilepsy, congenital blindness and deafness, alcoholism, and "severe hereditary physical disfigurement."[54]

Quoting Hitler, who had declared in *Mein Kampf* that preventing "humans with defects" from procreating was "mankind's most humane deed," Gütt and his co-commentators on the law applauded the GzVeN as marking "the beginning of a new era in public health" and as an expression of the government's "firm will to cleanse the body of the *Volk* and to start eradicating malign genetic traits."[55] After the law had taken effect, a network of doctors, public health officials, and jurists ensured the sterilization of those labeled "hereditarily sick." Some even went further than the law by allowing abortions for eugenic reasons.[56] In the following years, especially during the war, the GzVeN proved to be a highly effective tool for a dynamic, process- and ideology-driven racial policy aimed against *Fremdvölkische* as well as members of the racial ingroup who did not conform to the state-determined social or political standards. Even as the GzVeN was being drafted, officials thought a supplementary law targeting "habitual criminals" would be needed to complement eugenic measures.[57] The consequences for those affected were massive and long-term. No further legislative action was required once the matter had moved, to apply Bülow's phrase, "into the uncontrollable regions of the administration." In total, an estimated 400,000 persons were sterilized, including "asocials," "gypsies," and "Rhineland bastards" (the offspring of German women and French soldiers, mainly African colonial subjects, stationed in western Germany after World War I). Gisela Bock estimates the number of deaths among the sterilized at 5–6,000; roughly 90 percent of the total were women. Furthermore, the law triggered roughly 30,000 abortions – about the same number as that of women convicted by courts in Nazi Germany for performing illegal abortions – and moved racial policy in the direction of state-directed mass murder, euphemistically called "euthanasia," under the conditions of war.[58]

It is important to note that the GzVeN, with its focus on "inferiors" within the "Aryan" population, went much further than any of the regulations against Jews enacted before the late 1930s. In the first year of the Third Reich, state and party officials had much clearer ideas on how to revolutionize public health than on how to proceed on the Jewish question. At the same time, and without much guidance from Reich authorities, states and municipalities in Germany increased the control and persecution of Sinti and Roma, advancing arguments of criminal, disorderly, or asocial behavior based on the mix of traditional and racial stereotypes that were to drive German anti-Gypsy policy; in June 1936, this policy was centralized in the Reichszentrale für Bekämpfung der Zigeunerplage (Reich Central Office for Combating the Gypsy Plague) created within the RIM.[59]

IV

The center of gravity in the Nazi state started to shift in 1934, and with it the institutional dynamics of racial policy. After the purge during the so-called Night of the Long Knives (June 30–July 2, 1934), Hitler's takeover of the deceased Reich President Hindenburg's powers, and diplomatic successes that offset the negative impression of Germany's withdrawal from established systems of collective security, the regime was increasingly seen at home and abroad as unpredictable in its policies yet firm in its hold on power. "Individual actions" (*Einzelaktionen*) against Jews became less frequent but remained visible and violent enough to deter German Jews from thinking optimistically about their future in the country.[60] Within the administrative apparatus, new constellations emerged that challenged the RIM's prerogative in racial policy. One competitor was the Nazi party's Racial Policy Office (Rassenpolitisches Amt der NSDAP, or RPA), led by Walter Groß. It was established in April 1934 by Rudolf Hess's office of the Stellvertreter des Führers (StdF) for the purpose of consolidating the party's racial policy and publicly promoting its goals.[61] Reichsärzteführer Gerhard Wagner, who had close contact with Hitler, oversaw the RPA; he remained a vociferous spokesman for expanding sterilizations to "mixed breeds" (*Bastarde*) and for vigorously fighting "Jewish infiltration."[62] Heinrich Himmler's SS, the prime beneficiary of the SA's decapitation, had not yet claimed a stake in this area of national policy, but it was already making sure through the Race and Settlement Main Office (Rasse- und Siedlungs-Hauptamt, or RuSHA) that racial criteria featured prominently in the selection and training of its members.[63]

While growing institutional rivalries increased the pressure to address the disparity between what was regarded as rudimentary anti-Jewish legislation and more evolved hereditary health measures, transforming racial concepts into political practice remained difficult. The scope of the problem came to light during a ten-hour meeting convened by Reich Justice Minister Franz Gürtner on June 5, 1934, in response to Freisler's article of the preceding summer regarding the underlying quandary of how to legally define *fremdrassig*.[64] As was to be expected given the range of participants, opinions on what was to be done to prevent racial intermixture differed, but consensus was achieved on the need to address the whole racial policy agenda, including negative and positive measures, in a broad context. Again, some issues seemed more pressing than others. "Gypsies" remained unmentioned, and "colored races" were deemed to pose a minimal threat at most: Gürtner referred to "mulatto children fathered by the half-dozen by Germans with Negroes domestically [i.e. in Germany]."[65] Jews ranked highest on the list of racial enemies. Diplomatic hindrances continued to stand in the way of action, however. A representative of the Prussian Justice Ministry lamented the diplomatic obstacles to the "true isolation" of racial others in the form of prohibiting marriages and sexual intercourse between members of different races. And then there was the problem of definition. Confronted with the "difficult question of what in fact constitutes a race," Gürtner argued for focusing on the question's practical dimension. Speaking for the RIM, Lösener was all for practicability and long-term consistency, and he criticized those motivated by emotion and the expectation of gain in the short term.[66]

No matter how great the difficulties involved in deciding how to move forward, maintaining the status quo was not an option, as that would have created the impression of systemic inertia and of giving in to outside demands, which would have jeopardized the party program. The path forward seemed blocked, however, by the BBG's concept of "non-Aryan" and the problems inherent in explicitly targeting Jews. When the representatives of several ministries and the StdF met on November 15, 1934, they agreed that something had to be done to reduce the diplomatic fallout. RIM representative Helmut Nicolai proposed that "non-Aryan" be replaced by "Jew" in future legislation, but it remained unclear how such a revision would work out in administrative and diplomatic terms.[67]

As on previous occasions, the meeting produced no decision. Nicolai's suggestion pointed to the future, however. On December 20, 1934, Reichsärzteführer Wagner hosted a gathering of race experts in Munich, including RPA head Groß and other officials from the StdF, Gercke, three representatives of Himmler's RuSHA, and Nazi party judge Walter Buch, to discuss "race policy and the party's general attitude towards a practical legal resolution."[68] The result was a new dual-track approach. To facilitate "the necessary severe measures against the Jews," the experts proposed the enactment of "specific Jewish laws parallel to the general race legislation" in order to separate the Jews from other "non-Aryan" groups. In concrete terms, the participants envisioned two groups of new laws. The first would be aimed at the "final and total exclusion of the Jew from German life" through economic restrictions, social segregation, and the prohibition of sexual intercourse with non-Jews. The second group of laws would regulate the treatment of "mixed breeds" by applying, with a few exceptions, the same restrictions leveled on Jews. The definition of *Jude* followed the key BBG criterion (a person with at least one Jewish grandparent); *Judenmischlinge* were defined as persons with any ancestors who, as of January 1, 1800, had not been baptized at birth. Prohibiting intermixture and the other provisions of the proposed legislation were seen as interim measures; "a final regulation of the Jewish question," the protocol of the meeting noted, would require "the complete spatial separation between the Jewish and the German peoples."[69]

The Munich meeting of December 1934 represents a major caesura in Nazi policy, as it disconnected anti-Jewish measures still to be codified in law from the regime's broader *Rassenpolitik*. At the same time, the meeting marked the beginning of the shift of control over the future course of action in racial policy away from the RIM – a result in part of institutional competition, in part of internal transformations in Frick's realm of influence, and in part of the surge of anti-Jewish agitation in the first half of 1935.[70] The holistic approach nonetheless persisted in both theory and practice. As Cornelia Essner has pointed out, the new anti-Jewish agenda remained tied to legislative efforts in the field of eugenics when, in summer 1935, the Reich Justice and Interior Ministries discussed a revision of the existing marriage laws that, in line with the logic of the GzVeN, would prohibit interracial marriages in general.[71] Clearly, these discussions represented a direct extension of earlier attempts to improve racial health by eliminating influences regarded as detrimental. The fact, however, that the push for a new law for the prevention of "marriages detrimental to the Volk" (*volksschädliche Ehen*) occurred in summer 1935 in the context of intense anti-Jewish unrest confirms the close interrelation between policy-making and public mobilization, between prior planning and ad hoc reaction to contingencies, that had defined the Third Reich from the start.

The year 1935 began with two major demonstrations of the Reich's new confidence vis-à-vis its neighbors: the plebiscite on the future of the Saar region in January and the reintroduction of military conscription in March. The latter, a violation of the Versailles Treaty, was not met by international protest; to the contrary, the Anglo-German naval treaty signed in June essentially legitimated German rearmament and added to the regime's prestige. At the same time, frustration grew among party rank-and-file about the "movement's" loss of momentum, and among the general public as a result of continuing economic problems. These developments helped to generate a new bout of anti-Semitic agitation of unprecedented scale during the first half of 1935.[72] Not surprisingly, Streicher's *Stürmer* spearheaded the increasingly abusive attacks on Jews. By February, physical assaults on people and property had become more widespread. By April, other voices in the Nazi party press had chimed in, agitating not only against Jews, but also against so-called white Jews" (*weisse Juden*) – non-Jews who were suspected of being sympathetic to the racially persecuted – and "women oblivious of their racial identity" (*artvergessene Frauenspersonen*) who associated with Jews. The fuzziness of racial categories made these categories useful tools for a variety of purposes. Economic interests found expression in a new boycott of Jewish-owned business. Although the Reich had not yet abandoned the legal concept of "non-Aryan," towns and villages across the country echoed Nazi rhetoric by greeting visitors with signs proclaiming that Jews were not welcome.[73]

Those within the regime eager to utilize expressions of public discontent to advance state-controlled measures feared diplomatic damage less than losing credibility at home. They feared that calls by state and party leaders for moderation and "order" would be interpreted by the party rank-and-file as verbal concessions to outside pressures rather than as genuine expressions of the regime's readiness to use force against activists who broke existing laws. At the same time, by late July the wave of uncoordinated but no longer isolated "individual actions" had reached proportions beyond the control of any one party agency. Few among the regime's top leaders expressed as clear a sense of this perceptual and functional crisis as Reich Justice Minister Gürtner did during a ministerial conference convened by Reichsbank President Hjalmar Schacht on August 20, 1935. The authority of the state had eroded, Gürtner observed, to the point that authoritative directives from the top were interpreted further down the hierarchy as little more than empty gestures. Everyone, the minister complained, felt justified to interpret the true sense of superior instructions according to his own preference; "there is no order which is believed to represent the true seriousness of a command."[74] During the conference, Gürtner and Schacht called for change, and all participants, including Security Police chief Reinhard Heydrich, agreed on the need to replace disorderly violence with systematic measures. Nevertheless, the phenomenon described by Gürtner and visible out in the streets had already produced a dynamic that supports the interpretation of the Nazi regime as a "consensual dictatorship."[75] For this radicalization to have long-term effects, bureaucrats needed to establish a viable administrative framework.

During the "Party Conference of Freedom" in Nuremberg in September 1935, public discontent dovetailed with already existing plans for revising and expanding racial legislation. Many historians have stressed the importance of heightened anti-Semitic actionism in summer 1935 as a factor behind the enactment of the Nuremberg Laws, thereby questioning the myth of spontaneous and highly improvised yet Hitler-centered decision-making propagated by Bernhard Lösener after the war.[76] As we have seen with the enactment of the BBG, the RIM's initiatives in matters of racial policy had been driven since early 1933 by a mixture of improvisation and determination that reflected the leadership's ideological goals, bureaucratic ambitions, and public expectations. The same was to happen in the course of 1935, but now – stronger than before, yet typical for the overall process – with different agencies favoring different approaches and using the social energies inherent in anti-Jewish actionism to push their own agenda. In late July 1935, Frick picked up on the agitation against "racial mixing" and prohibited state registrars from officiating marriages between "full Aryans" (*Vollarier*) and "full Jews" (*Volljuden*), pointing to a planned law regulating marriage between "Aryans" and "non-Aryans." He was in all likelihood referring to the already mentioned marriage law reform, not to the soon to be enacted measures.[77]

Seen against the background of earlier policy-making and the acute anti-Jewish agitation of 1935, the Nuremberg Laws appear as crisis management, designed by ministerial officials to extend the trajectory of prior legislation and to regain control over party activists. Taking into account earlier discussions between state and party functionaries, it could be argued that they regarded regaining control to be a more urgent need than replacing one racial category with another. As Saul Friedländer puts it, the Nuremberg Laws were part of a political gesture "meant as an homage to the party."[78] Indeed, the Law for the Protection of German Blood and German Honor (*Gesetz zum Schutze des deutschen Blutes und der deutschen Ehre*, BSG) and the Reich Citizenship Law (*Reichsbürgergesetz*) used the terms "German and related blood" (*deutsches und artverwandtes Blut*) and "Jews" but left them, and thus their practical relevance, undefined. The leadership were equally vague: after noting in his diary how he contributed to the "shaping up" of the laws, Goebbels concluded that "this will work out: and give direction to the movement."[79]

Hitler was quoted ten days after the enactment of the Nuremberg Laws as saying that the task at hand was "not to chase after utopias but to look squarely at political reality."[80] The same emphasis on political practicability influenced the lengthy debates about the definitional clauses needed to make the laws work. On September 22, Stuckart sent Wagner drafts of the first and second implementation decrees to the RBG. The proposed regulations would apply to fewer individuals than the BBG's "non-Aryan" clause: first, they pertained only to Jews; second, "German-Jewish mixed breeds," as Stuckart called them, would not be considered Jews if they had less than "75 percent Jewish blood," or in other words fewer than three Jewish grandparents. [81]

Frick and his RIM officials clearly saw the issue of *Mischlinge* as one that could help retain the connection between negative and positive racial policy. "Jews" as defined by the law were to be eliminated from society, the economy, and ultimately the country; *Mischlinge* with fewer than three Jewish grandparents were to be assimilated.[82] A further indication of the attempt to pursue a holistic racial policy was Stuckart's proposal to shift the authority to decide on the racial suitability of marriages from registry officials to public health officers, thus complementing the new law on the "hereditary health" of the German people (*Gesetz zum Schutze der Erbgesundheit des deutschen Volkes*) enacted on October 18, 1935. This law stipulated that a certificate attesting to both partners' "fitness to marry" was mandatory in order to preclude racial intermixture, thus reinforcing the prohibition of sexual relations between Germans and Jews or others of "alien blood" imposed by the First Supplemental Decree to the BSG.[83]

The RIM's initiatives went beyond restricting the citizenship rights of Jews and prohibiting intermarriage. Despite the fact that sweeping anti-Jewish measures discussed in early October were not enacted,[84] Frick's men were eager to eliminate "Jewish influence" from the economy. Furthermore, the RIM planned to prohibit Jews from attending public schools (non-Jewish "mixed breeds," by contrast, were to be fully integrated as students in the public school system). At the same time, "individual actions" against Jews – now defined as measures not based on an explicit order of the Reich government or the party leadership – were to be suppressed by the Gestapo.[85] After the murder of Wilhelm Gustloff in Switzerland in February 1936, and no doubt in view of the Berlin Olympic Games later that year, the RIM instructed all state agencies, including the police, to prevent anti-Jewish "excesses" (*Ausschreitungen*). Frick's subordinates had no trouble complying, as the Jew-bashing wave of the previous summer had ebbed.[86]

V

With the enactment of the Nuremberg Laws, the main momentum of the anti-Jewish movement had been contained and bureaucratic order restored to the process; at the same time, the future course of state action seemed unclear. Characteristically, Hitler sent conflicting messages. In his statement that preceded the proclamation of the laws, he made a token reference to the hope that what he called a "single secular solution" might suffice but also threatened that, in the event of failure, the party would bring about a "definitive solution."[87] Instead of enacting laws regulating the economy, Hitler envisioned that Jewish-owned businesses would be eliminated not through regulations but rather "in a natural way, that is, by letting them die out."[88] But more radical action was also possible. Shortly after the enactment of the Nuremberg Laws, Hitler explained his preference for, as Walter Groß put it, "liquidating the question of mixed breeds through assimilation in the course of a few generations" to those eager to treat all "mixed breeds" like Jews, adding that in a case of all-out war he would be "ready for all consequences."[89]

Once the Führer had set the course for war, his lieutenants pushed forward toward a more sweeping solution of the Jewish question. In a meeting of senior officials from the RIM, the Reich Economics Ministry, and the StdF in September 1936, Stuckart noted the general agreement on the basic goal regarding the Reich's *Judenpolitik*, namely "complete emigration"as demanded in the party program, by force if necessary.[90] The meaning of "need" was redefined by the regime as the war opened up radical new opportunities to pursue its racial agenda. The dual-track approach adopted in December 1934 gave way once again to a more integrated strategy, albeit one very different from the racial policy of the initial phase of Nazi rule. In the process, the dual-track approach adopted in December 1934 merged back into a more integrated strategy, yet one with very different features from the racial policy of the regime's initial phase. First, a growing number of players and their competing courses of action drove the dynamic until Himmler's SS and police apparatus emerged as the winner in early 1942. Second, "positive" racial policy measures had become more violent as they were increasingly directed toward adding to the Volk by "Germanizing" suitable candidates from the occupied territories; at the same time, outright murder had been included among the "negative" measures applied against children and adults deemed "unworthy of life," along with Jews, Gypsies, and members of other groups who seemed to stand in the way of social and ethnic homogeneity. Third, while the Third Reich did not pursue a coherent anti-"non-Aryan" policy during the war, the process of incremental radicalization that developed in the early years of the regime remained of crucial importance. Translating ideology into action, bureaucratic process prepared the path to genocide and linked one type of perpetrator – those who carried out the "Final Solution" on the killing fields of Eastern Europe – with another, namely administrators such as Stuckart and Lösener, who personified the Nazi notion of a "fighting administration" (*kämpfende Verwaltung*). They were part of a genocidal infrastructure that relied more on professional activism than ideological consensus.[91]

The RIM's loss of influence to Himmler's apparatus during the war was significant but far from total and nowhere near the complete sidelining its staff claimed after the war. Equally untenable is the rigid delineation, put forward in many older studies that took an intentionalist perspective, between old-fashioned conservatives and racial anti-Semites, between state bureaucrats and party activists. In reality, the lines separating different camps of race policy reformers were much more fluid. Not only had Frick's men set the stage early on for the implementation of the regime's Janus-faced racial policy, but they also remained committed to their early goals when this policy turned genocidal. Although Frick increasingly withdrew from the political scene, he remained in charge of a sprawling, at its core highly effective apparatus that nominally included even Himmler's police until the Reichsführer himself replaced Frick as interior minister in August 1943.[92] For most of the war, the institutional overlap and synergetic interaction between the RIM and other Reich agencies directly involved in mass murder remained considerable. While some "old fighters" on the racial front, such as Gütt and Gercke, dropped out of the ranks of the RIM before 1939, others joined – most notably Leonardo Conti as State Secretary for Public Health, an advocate of forced sterilizations, abortions, and "euthanasia" killings. Herbert Linden served as a key link between the health administration and the "euthanasia" operation, helping the "Aktion T-4" staff gain expertise in mass killings by gassing that would later be transferred to "Aktion Reinhard" for the annihilation of the Polish Jews.[93] Until after the deportation of German Jews to their death in the East had begun, Bernhard Lösener kept fighting against the loss of "good blood" to the *Volk* by insisting that Jews and *Mischlinge* be separated on the grounds that the latter could be assimilated.[94] And State Secretary Wilhelm Stuckart not only tried to keep the RIM's realm of influence together and working efficiently but, representing the ministry at the Wannsee Conference, also ensured the smooth evolution of German *Judenpolitik* from persecution to annihilation. (His firm beliefs regarding the need to eliminate negative influences on the *Volk* might even have prompted him to deliver his own disabled son to the "euthanasia" killing machine.)[95] Recent scholarship, especially the studies by Cornelia Essner and Hans-Christian Jasch, has debunked the long-held myth of the RIM as a center of anti-Nazi opposition by state bureaucrats determined to "prevent worse" and has deepened our understanding of the complex coalition of race activists during the Third Reich. However, the full story of state bureaucracy's role in determining, enforcing, and radicalizing Nazi Germany's racial policy still remains to be written.

Notes

1 From a growing body of synthetic studies, see Saul Friedländer, *Nazi Germany and the Jews, vol. 1: The Years of Persecution, 1933–1939* (New York, 1997); Peter Longerich, *Holocaust: The Nazi Persecution and Murder of the Jews* (Oxford, 2010) (a revised translation of *Politik der Vernichtung. Eine Gesamtdarstellung der nationalsozialistischen Judenverfolgung* [Munich, 1998]); Mark Roseman, *The Wannsee Conference and the Final Solution: A Reconsideration* (New York, 2002); Christopher R. Browning (with contributions by Jürgen Matthäus), *The Origins of the Final Solution: The Evolution of Nazi Jewish Policy, September 1939–March 1942* (Lincoln, 2004).

2 Raul Hilberg, *The Destruction of the European Jews*, rev. edn. (New Haven, 2003) (first published 1961); Karl A. Schleunes, *The Twisted Road to Auschwitz: Nazi Policy towards German Jews 1933–1939* (Urbana, 1970); Uwe Dietrich Adam, *Judenpolitik im Dritten Reich* (Düsseldorf, 1972); Ernst Klee, *"Euthanasie" im NS-Staat* (Frankfurt am Main, 1983); Benno Müller-Hill, *Murderous Science: Elimination by Scientific Selection of Jews, Gypsies, and Others, Germany 1933–1945* (Oxford, 1988; German edition 1984); Henry Friedlander, *The Origins of Nazi Genocide: From Euthanasia to the Final Solution* (Chapel Hill, 1995); Michael Burleigh, *Death and Deliverance: "Euthanasia" in Germany 1900–1945* (Cambridge, 1994); Gisela Bock, *Zwangssterilisation im Nationalsozialismus. Studien zur Rassenpolitik und Frauenpolitik* (Opladen, 1986); Götz Aly (ed.), *Aktion T4, 1939–1945. Die "Euthanasie"-Zentrale in der Tiergartenstraße 4* (Berlin, 1987); Christian Ganssmüller, *Die Erbgesundheitspolitik des Dritten Reiches. Planung, Durchführung und Durchsetzung* (Cologne, 1987); Michael Zimmermann, *Rassenutopie und Genozid. Die nationalsozialistische "Lösung der Zigeunerfrage"* (Hamburg, 1996).

3 Claudia Koonz, *The Nazi Conscience* (Cambridge, MA, 2003); Friedländer, *Nazi Germany and the Jews, The Years of Persecution*; Michael Wildt, *Hitler's Volksgemeinschaft and the Dynamics of Racial Exclusion: Violence against Jews in Provincial Germany, 1919–1939* (New York, 2012).

4 Ulrich Herbert, "Extermination policy: new answers and questions about the history of the 'Holocaust' in German historiography" in U. Herbert (ed.), *National Socialist Extermination Policies. Contemporary German Perspectives and Controversies* (New York, 2000), 1–52, here 11.

5 Compare, e.g., Müller-Hill, *Murderous Science,* and Friedlander, *Origins,* with Christopher M. Hutton, *Race and the Third Reich: Linguistics, Racial Anthropology and Genetics in the Dialectic of Volk* (Cambridge, 2005) and Eric Ehrenreich, *The Nazi Ancestral Proof: Genealogy, Racial Science, and the Final Solution* (Bloomington, 2007).

6 For a concise overview of key issues in recent Holocaust scholarship see Dan Stone, *Histories of the Holocaust* (Oxford, 2010). Stone stresses the importance of the "return of ideology" as explanatory paradigm; see 125, 129, 142, 144, 158, 243.

7 Of the roughly 360,000 persons sterilized between 1934 and 1945 in Germany proper, only about 16,000 received a one-time compensation payment after 1945: see Paul Weindling, "Entschädigung der Sterilisierungs- und 'Euthanasie'-Opfer nach 1945?" in Klaus-Dietmar Henke (ed.), *Tödliche Medizin im Nationalsozialismus. Von der Rassenhygiene zum Massenmord* (Cologne, 2008), 247–58; Paul Weindling, *Victims and Survivors of Nazi Human Experiments: Science and Suffering in the Holocaust* (London: 2015).

8 Michael Zimmermann, "The National Socialist 'solution of the Gypsy question'" in Herbert, *Extermination Policies,* 186–209, here 205–6.

9 Adam, *Judenpolitik,* 46.

10 Michael Burleigh and Wolfgang Wippermann, *The Racial State: Germany 1933–1945* (Cambridge, 1991), 305.

11 Karl A. Schleunes, *Legislating the Holocaust: The Bernhard Loesener Memoirs and Supporting Documents* (Boulder, 2001), 16.

12 See Stone, *Histories,* 169–78. Michael Mann, *The Dark Side of Democracy: Explaining Ethnic Cleansing* (Cambridge, 2005), 68–9, describes this line of racial thinking as "organicist."

13 Alison Bashford and Philippa Levine (eds.), *The Oxford Handbook of the History of Eugenics* (Oxford, 2010); Regina Wecker, Sabine Braunschweig, Gabriele Imboden, Bernhard Küchenhoff, and Hans Jakob Ritter (eds.), *Wie nationalsozialistisch ist die Eugenik? What Is National Socialist about Eugenics?* (Vienna, 2009), also regarding the interrelation between the concepts of eugenics and modernity as understood by Michel Foucault, Zygmunt Bauman, and others.

14 "Würde Deutschland jährlich eine Million Kinder bekommen und 700 000 bis 800 000 der Schwächsten beseitigen, dann würde am Ende das Ergebnis vielleicht sogar eine Kräftesteigerung sein." Hitler in *Völkischer Beobachter,* August 7, 1929; quoted from Hans-Walter Schmuhl, *Rassenhygiene, Nationalsozialismus, Euthanasie. Von der Verhütung zur Vernichtung "lebensunwerten Lebens" 1890 bis 1945* (Göttingen, 1992), 152.

15 Hitler, *Mein Kampf,* quoted from Schmuhl, *Rassenhygiene,* 151–3.

16 "So glaube ich heute im Sinne des allmächtigen Schöpfers zu handeln: Indem ich mich des Juden erwehre, kämpfe ich für das Werk des Herrn." Hitler, *Mein Kampf* (Munich, 1937 [259/260th printing]), 70.

17 Gisela Bock, "Krankenmord, Judenmord und nationalsozialistische Rassen-
politik. Überlegungen zu einigen neueren Forschungshypothesen" in Frank
Bajohr, Werner Johe, and Uwe Lohalm (eds.), *Zivilisation und Barbarei.
Die widersprüchlichen Potentiale der Moderne. Detlev Peukert zum Gedenken*
(Hamburg, 1991), 285–306, here 302.

18 For a guide through the *"Irrgarten der Rassenlogik"* (labyrinth of racial logic),
see Claudia Essner, *Die "Nürnberger Gesetze" oder die Verwaltung des
Rassenwahns 1933–1945* (Paderborn, 2002), chapter 1.

19 On German public opinion, see Bernward Dörner, *Die Deutschen und der
Holocaust. Was niemand wissen wollte, aber jeder wissen konnte* (Berlin:
Propyläen, 2007); Frank Bajohr and Dieter Pohl, *Der Holocaust als offenes
Geheimnis. Die Deutschen, die NS-Führung und die Alliierten* (Munich,
2006); Peter Longerich, *"Davon haben wir nichts gewußt!" Die Deutschen
und die Judenverfolgung 1933–1945* (Munich, 2006).

20 Though the RIM's role in racial policy-making remains understudied, earlier
analyses by Hilberg, Adam, and others have been significantly broadened by
Essner, *Nürnberger Gesetze*; Günter Neliba, *Wilhelm Frick. Der Legalist des
Unrechtsstaates. Eine politische Biographie* (Paderborn, 1992); and, more
recently, Hans-Christian Jasch, *Staatssekretär Wilhelm Stuckart und die
Judenpolitik. Der Mythos von der sauberen Verwaltung* (Munich, 2012).

21 Reichstag motion by Frick, May 27, 1924; see Neliba, *Frick*, 47.

22 See the biographical sketches in Jasch, *Stuckart*, 462–89.

23 "Die fremden Reichsangehörigen sind aus dem Blutskörper des deutschen
Volkes auszuscheiden und einem besonderen Minderheitenrecht zu unterwer-
fen. Es ist zunächst genau festzustellen, wer nichtdeutscher Staatsangehöriger
ist … Praktisch werden wir vor allem drei Gruppen zu unterscheiden haben:
die Juden, die Polen und die sonstigen Fremden. Für jede dieser Gruppen wird
ein besonderes Gesetz ihre Pflichten und Rechte regeln, zu denen insbesondere
auch die Feststellung einer Autonomie auf kulturellem Gebiet gehören wird.
In einem *Rassenschutzgesetz* werden dann die Eheschliessung und sonstige
Beziehungen zwischen Deutschen und Fremden zu regeln sein, mit dem Ziele,
das Einsickern fremden Blutes in den deutschen Volkskörper fortan unmöglich
zu machen und das deutsche Volk vor weiterer Bastardisierung zu schützen."
Helmut Nicolai, *Grundlagen der kommenden Verfassung. Über den staats-
rechtlichen Aufbau des Dritten Reiches* (Berlin, 1933), 19–23 (emphasis in the
original). On earlier segregation ideas with a strong anti-Semitic bent, see
Adam, *Judenpolitik,* 28–31.

24 Arthur Gütt, *Bevölkerungs- und Rassenpolitik* (Berlin, 1935), 36.

25 "Alles, was die Art- und Rassenerhaltung hindert, muss von der Fortpflanzung
ferngehalten werden, alles, was die Vermehrung der erbgesunden und rassisch
wertvollen Bevölkerung möglich macht, müssen wir fördern! Das ist 'Dienst
an der Rasse'als grösste Aufgabe, die es für den nationalsozialistischen Staat
zu erfüllen gibt!" Ibid., 22.

26 Adam, *Judenpolitik,* 64 fn. 206.

27 Still highly insightful for the Nazi perception of the civil service before 1933 is
Hans Mommsen, *Beamtentum im Dritten Reich. Mit ausgewählten Quellen
zur nationalsozialistischen Beamtenpolitik* (Stuttgart, 1966), 20–38.

28 See Longerich, *Holocaust*, 33–8.
29 Adam, *Judenpolitik*, 33–8; see also Essner, *Nürnberger Gesetze*, 82–6.
30 Adam, *Judenpolitik*, 61; Neliba, *Frick*, 168ff.; Friedländer, *Nazi Germany*, 28.
31 Printed in *Die Verfolgung und Ermordung der europäischen Juden durch das nationalsozialistische Deutschland 1933–1945, Bd. 1 Deutsches Reich 1933–1937 (VEJ)* (Munich, 2008), 130–4, 137–8. On the antecedents of the *Berufsbeamtengesetz* see Adam, *Judenpolitik*, 51–64; Mommsen, *Beamtentum*, 39–61.
32 See Hanns Seel, *Gesetz zur Wiederherstellung des Berufsbeamtentums vom 7. April 1933 in der Fassung vom 23. Juni 1933 und verwandte Gesetze nebst den neuesten Durchführungsverordnungen* (Berlin, 1933). According to RIM state secretary Pfundtner, Seel was the "father" of the BBG (Mommsen, *Beamtentum*, 43).
33 Hilberg, *Destruction*, 1118.
34 Friedländer, *Nazi Germany*, 28 argues that "[A]lthough the scope of the law was general, the anti-Jewish provision represented its very core."
35 Mommsen, *Beamtentum*, 54–7, provides dismissal figures for different parts of the civil service, comprising in total *c.* three million members. Of roughly 5,000 Jewish civil servants in Germany, some 50 percent were exempt from dismissal due to their status as war veterans or children of veterans; a similar ratio applied to lawyers and notaries affected by the Law Concerning Admission to the Legal Professions (Longerich, *Holocaust*, 38–9).
36 Adam, *Judenpolitik*, 64 rightly sees the BBG as *"Anfangspunkt eines neuartigen politischen Verständnisses hinsichtlich der gesetzlichen Behandlung von Minderheitengruppen."*
37 See Neliba, *Frick*, 163–6. Between May and mid-August 1933, Gercke's office – which in 1935 was renamed "Reichsstelle für Sippenforschung," the precursor of the *Reichssippenamt* formed in 1940 – reported it had processed more than 2,500 ancestry cases: Diana Schulle, *Das Reichssippenamt. Eine Institution nationalsozialistischer Rassenpolitik* (Berlin, 2001), 87. For an example of Gercke's role in the removal of public servants due to Jewish ancestry see Eckart Conze, Norbert Frei, Peter Hayes, and Moshe Zimmermann, *Das Amt und die Vergangenheit. Deutsche Diplomaten im Dritten Reich und in der Bundesrepublik* (Munich, 2010), 54.
38 Schulle, *Reichssippenamt*, 79; on the contagionists see Essner, *Nürnberger Gesetze*, 32–40. In the article "Grundsätzliches zur Mischlingsfrage" published in *Nationalsozialistische Monatshefte* 4 (1933), 198–202, Gercke wrote: "Aryan is not anyone who has less than one grandparent of Jewish ancestry; Aryan is anyone who has no Jewish ancestors at all" (quoted from Thomas Pegelow Kaplan, *The Language of Nazi Genocide: Linguistic Violence and the Struggle of Germans of Jewish Ancestry* (New York, 2009), 67–8).
39 Achim Gercke, "Lösung der Judenfrage," *Völkischer Beobachter*, June 25/26, 1933, Rassenhygienisches Beiblatt.
40 Achim Gercke, *Die Rasse im Schrifttum. Ein Wegweiser durch das rassenkundliche Schrifttum*, 2nd edn. (Berlin, 1934 (1st edn. 1933)), 7.
41 Günther, Ploetz, and Lenz had been members of the *Nordischer Ring* founded by Günther in 1911; see Isabel Heinemann, *"Rasse, Siedlung, deutsches Blut"*.

Das Rasse- und Siedlungshauptamt der SS und die rassenpolitische Neuordnung Europas (Göttingen, 2003), 25.

42 Neliba, *Frick*, 178–9.

43 Speech by Frick during the 1st session of the "Sachverständigenbeirat für Bevölkerungs- und Rassenpolitik," June 28, 1933, BA R 53/6.

44 Gütt, *Bevölkerungs- und Rassenpolitik*, 22, interprets Frick's speech as "*nationalsozialistisches Regierungsprogramm.*"

45 Neliba, *Frick*, 176–82.

46 "*Beginn und Ausgangspunkt der deutschen Rassengesetzgebung*"; Frick, quoted from Adam, *Judenpolitik*, 81.

47 Longerich, *Politik der Vernichtung*, 46; Adam, *Judenpolitik*, 82–7.

48 Bernhard von Bülow to Foreign Minister Neurath, July 5, 1933; quoted from Conze et al., *Das Amt*, 56.

49 Leiter Ref. Dtld., Vortr. Leg.rat AA Vicco von Bülow-Schwante, to German representations abroad, July 11, 1933; Politisches Archiv des Auswärtigen Amts Berlin (PAAA) R 78.668, fol.719.

50 Lothar Gruchmann, "Blutschutzgesetz' und Justiz," *VfZ*, 31 (1983), 418–42, here 418.

51 Essner, *Nürnberger Gesetze*, 96–8.

52 Speech by Neurath to press correspondents, September 15, 1933; German delegate von Keller to the League of Nation assembly, June 3–6, 1933; quoted from *Archiv der Gegenwart* 1034, 1064ff.

53 Speech by Frick to members of the diplomatic corps, February 15, 1934; PAAA R. 99.330, fol. 944, 957. On the Nazi concept of "*Volkskörper*" see Boaz Neumann, *Die Weltanschauung der Nazis* (Göttingen, 2011), 129–78.

54 Neliba, *Frick*, 174–83; Bock, *Zwangssterilisation*, 80–100.

55 Arthur Gütt, Ernst Rüdin, and Falk Ruttke, *Gesetz zur Verhütung erbkranken Nachwuchses vom 14. Juli 1933* (Munich, 1934), 5, 55.

56 Neliba, *Frick*, 184–9.

57 Gütt et al., *Gesetz*, 173–4.

58 Friedlander, *Genocide*, 246–7, 254; Bock, *Zwangssterilisation*, 354–67, 381, 388, 462–4.

59 Zimmermann, *Rassenutopie*, 79–80; Martin Luchterhandt, *Der Weg nach Birkenau. Entstehung und Verlauf der nationalsozialistischen Verfolgung der "Zigeuner"* (Lübeck, 2000), 60–2; Guenter Lewy, *The Nazi Persecution of the Gypsies* (Oxford, 2000), 17–23.

60 Jürgen Matthäus and Mark Roseman, *Jewish Responses to Persecution, 1933–1938* (Lanham, 2010), 95–8.

61 Essner, *Nürnberger Gesetze*, 66–8; Koonz, *Nazi Conscience*, 105–25.

62 In mid-September 1934, Wagner informed Frick that Hitler did not want doctors to face legal consequences if they transgressed beyond the letter of the GzVeN by performing eugenically motivated abortions (Neliba, *Frick*, 189; Essner, *Nürnberger Gesetze*, 148).

63 For the history of the RuSHA and its precursor, the "Rasseamt der SS," see Heinemann, *Rasse*.

64 Protocol of a meeting of the Strafrechtskommission, June 5, 1934; Bundesarchiv Berlin (BA) R 22/852, fol. 75–317; partly printed in *VEJ*, 346–9. See also Koonz, *Nazi Conscience*, 172–7.

65 Essner, *Nürnberger Gesetze*, 103. Zimmermann, *Rassenutopie*, 90 points out that German race planners situated Sinti and Roma "in der Schnittmenge von Rassenanthropologie und Rassenhygiene."

66 Essner, *Nürnberger Gesetze*, 99–106.

67 Adam, *Judenpolitik*, 90 fn. 120; Essner, *Nürnberger Gesetze*, 105.

68 Invitation by Wagner re "Besprechung über Rassenpolitik und grundsätzliche Einstellung der Partei zur praktischen gesetzlichen Regelung" to RuSHA (Brandt), December 12, 1934, BA NS 2/143, fol. 16–18; quoted from Heinemann, *Rasse*, 78.

69 File note Groß/Wagner "Ergebnis der Besprechung über Rassenpolitik im Braunen Haus, München, am 20.12.1934," BA R 1509/35, fol. 51–54; printed in *VEJ*, 391–92.

70 In 1935, Achim Gercke and Helmut Nicolai were dismissed from their position in the RIM following allegations of homosexuality, while newly appointed state secretary Wilhelm Stuckart brought more bureaucratic efficiency than ideological vigor into the RIM (Essner, *Nürnberger Gesetze*, 86–90).

71 Essner, *Nürnberger Gesetze*, 106–8.

72 Michael Wildt, "Violence against Jews in Germany, 1933–1939" in David Bankier (ed.), *Probing the Depths of German Antisemitism: German Society and the Persecution of the Jews 1933–1941* (New York, 2000), 181–209; Friedländer, *Nazi Germany*, 137–44; Longerich, *Holocaust*, 52–7; Adam, *Judenpolitik*, 124–4.

73 See Friedländer, *Nazi Germany*, 121–8.

74 "Es gibt keinen Befehl, von dem geglaubt wird, dass hinter ihm der absolute Ernst des Gebotes steht." Gürtner at ministerial conference, August 20, 1935, US Holocaust Memorial Museum Archives (USHMMA) RG.11.001M (SAM 500-1-379, fol. 75–85); printed in *VEJ*, 471–8, here 476.

75 See Koonz, *Nazi Conscience*, 273; also Frank Bajohr, "Vom antijüdischen Konsens zum schlechten Gewissen. Die deutsche Gesellschaft und die Judenverfolgung 1933–1945" in Bajohr and Pohl, *Der Holocaust als offenes Geheimnis*, 15–17.

76 For a detailed evaluation of Lösener's postwar account see Essner, *Nürnberger Gesetze*, 113–34; also Neliba, *Frick*, 203–9; Schleunes, *Legislating*, 3–21; Jasch, *Stuckart*, 396–401.

77 Circular, Frick to state governments and registrars (*Standesbeamte*) in the Reich, July 27, 1935; printed in *VEJ*, 438–9; Essner, *Nürnberger Gesetze*, 106–7.

78 Friedländer, *Nazi Germany*, 147.

79 "... so wird es hinhauen: Und die Bewegung ausrichten": Goebbels diary entry of September 15, 1935; Elke Fröhlich (ed.), *Tagebücher von Joseph Goebbels, Teil I, Bd. 3/I (April 1934–February 1936)* (Munich, 2005), 294.

80 "Report by Dr. Rudolf Schlösser, RuSHA, regarding a meeting at the Rassenpolitisches Amt on the implementation decrees of the Nuremberg Laws," September 25, 1935, BA NS 2/143, fol. 4–8; printed in *VEJ*, 501–7. According to the ambiguously worded report, Hitler's statement was conveyed by RPA-chief Walter Groß.

81 Stuckart to Wagner, September 22, 1935, BA R 1501/5513; quoted from *VEJ*, 494–9.

82 Report by Schlösser, *VEJ*, 501–7.
83 See Burleigh and Wippermann, *Racial State*, 49; Friedländer, *Nazi Germany*,
    153–4. While none of the thirteen subsequent BSG-related regulations men-
    tion "Gypsies," the standard commentary by Stuckart and Hans Globke does
    (Luchterhandt, *Weg*, 66); however, German Sinti and Roma were less affected
    by the Nuremberg Laws than by the *Erbgesundheitsgesetz* and other eugeni-
    cist measures (Zimmermann, *Rassenutopie*, 89).
84 Stuckart to Frick, October 9, 1935, BA R 1501/5513, fol. 135–40; printed in
    VEJ, 512–15.
85 File note Reich education ministry re meeting on December 12, 1935, BA
    R 4901/11787, fol. 30; Gestapa-circular, December 19, 1935; printed in *VEJ*,
    536, 541.
86 Circular RIM, February 5, 1936, BA R 58/276, fol. 36; printed in *VEJ*, 558–9.
    On February 4, 1936, in Davos, the Jewish student David Frankfurter had
    killed the Nazi party head for Switzerland, Wilhelm Gustloff.
87 "Die deutsche Reichsregierung ist dabei beherrscht von dem Gedanken, durch
    eine einmalige säkulare Lösung vielleicht doch eine Ebene schaffen zu können,
    auf der es dem deutschen Volke möglich ist, ein erträgliches Verhältnis zum
    jüdischen Volk finden zu können. Sollte sich diese Hoffnung nicht erfüllen, die
    innerdeutsche und internationale jüdische Hetze ihren Fortgang nehmen, wird
    eine neue Überprüfung der Lage stattfinden ... Das zweite [RBG] ist der
    Versuch der gesetzlichen Regelung eines Problems, das im Falle des abermali-
    gen Scheiterns dann durch Gesetz zur endgültigen Lösung der Nationalsozia-
    listischen Partei übertragen werden müßte. Hinter allen drei Gesetzen steht die
    Nationalsozialistische Partei und mit ihr und hinter ihr die Nation." *Parteitag
    der Freiheit. Reden des Führers und ausgewählte Kongressreden am Parteitag
    der NSDAP 1935* (Munich, 1935), 113–14.
88 File note Gürtner regarding meeting with Hitler, December 12, 1935; BA
    R 3001/8521, fol. 275; printed in *VEJ*, 535; see also Wilhelm Treue, "Hitlers
    Denkschrift zum Vierjahresplan 1936," *VfZ*, 3(1955), 184–210.
89 Report Schlösser re meeting at RPA, September 25, 1935; quoted from
    VEJ, 502.
90 "Letzten Endes müsse in Betracht gezogen werden, die Auswanderung auch
    zwangsweise durchzuführen." (Stuckart in meeting of state secretaries held
    September 29, 1936; BA R 1501/5514, fol. 199–211; quoted from *VEJ*,603).
91 For a highly insightful discussion of the mechanisms of Holocaust perpetra-
    tion see Donald Bloxham, *The Final Solution: A Genocide* (Oxford, 2009),
    261–99.
92 Stephan Lehnstaedt, "Das Reichsministerium des Innern unter Heinrich
    Himmler 1943–1945," *VfZ* 54 (2006), 639–72; Neliba, *Frick*, 353–9; Jasch,
    Stuckart, 155–88.
93 See Browning, *Origins*, 186–91; Friedlander, *Origins*, 63–85.
94 See Essner, *Nürnberger Gesetze*, 113–34; Browning, *Origins*, 404–5.
95 See Roseman, *Wannsee Conference*, 93–140. Jasch, *Stuckart*, 290, bases his
    reference to Stuckart's six-month-old son Gunther falling victim to "child
    euthanasia" in June 1941 on information received from Gunther's younger

brother, Rüdiger Stuckart. In the absence of further evidence, Stuckart's statement to Robert Kempner in an interrogation in April 1947 is revealing: Asked what he said to Frick when learning about the "euthanasia" program, Stuckart claims he told his superior that he found it "unbelievable that these measures were taken without consent by their relatives [Ich habe ihm gesagt, dass ich es unglaublich fände, dass diese Massnahmen ohne Zustimmung der Angehörigen vorgenommen würden]": USHMMA 2001.62 (Robert Kempner collection) box 244, Interrogation April 16, 1947, 11–12.

10

Neither Aryan Nor Semite

Reflections on the Meanings of Race in Nazi Germany

Richard Steigmann-Gall

In July 1945, shortly after his capture, Julius Streicher was interrogated by the Allied authorities. He was asked by his questioner to describe various aspects of his career as Gauleiter of Franken and as a leading racist ideologue of the Nazi movement. At one point, Streicher describes the composition of his Gau: "In Franken about two-thirds of the inhabitants were Protestant. I myself was a Catholic, but I avoided religious controversy." Eager to change the topic, he turned to biology: "Race purity is the important thing ... The pure North German is blonde, blue-eyed and fair, is the highest form of humanity." Streicher's interrogator asked him at this point: "Were you blond?" Streicher answered: "Yes, I, my mother, my sister, and my progenitors for generations." Perhaps in the hope of puncturing the thin veneer of this racial construction, the interrogator knowingly asked: "How was it in regard to the Führer?" Streicher replied: "Well, he wasn't a pure Nordic, about 80 percent. Race is also expressed in character."[1]

Here, in an almost *en passant* fashion, Streicher seemed to concede that race was not a purely scientific category – at least not for the Nazis. This most vituperous and hateful of Nazis, hung at the Nuremberg Trials not for his active participation in the genocide of the Jews but purely for the virulence of his anti-Semitic language, conceded that his own movement did not strictly abide by the alleged logic of "scientific" racial superiority. What might this have meant for the core and seedbed of the Nazis' genocidal beliefs and practices? Is it possible that a conventionally understood racism does not fully explain Nazi ideology? That, in whichever ways and using whichever methods at hand to create a discursive edifice of biological dispassion, something other than scientific racism lay at the core of the Nazi worldview?

Countless scholars have contended that race lay at the very heart of Nazi ideology and practice, both as a movement and in the Third Reich. Yet for all the use to which race as a category of analysis is put in contemporary scholarship, as much as it serves as a foundation upon which our most popular current assumptions about Nazism rest, the precise nature of that racism remains surprisingly under-theorized. At the heart of Nazism seems to lie a paradox between claims that race was fixed, biological, and permanent and the Nazis' recognition of the complexity of culturally constructed "races" that were highly fluid, variable, and nebulous; in other words, between race as immutable and as mutable. This paradox led the Nazis into both contradictory conceptualizations of race and contradictory racial practices. Many historians of the Third Reich have proven unable to distance themselves from the scientistic truth-claims of the Nazis, thereby reifying the Nazis' own categories as well as replicating the conceptual slippage and confusion that comes with those categories. My aim here is to highlight the meanings of these contradictions as a way of understanding one aspect of Nazism that has hitherto remained most elusive: namely, the degree to which race as a scientific truth-claim mattered to them. My ruminations on the deeper conceptual and analytical meanings of race – as the Nazis themselves saw it, and as historians of Nazism see it now – connects to a larger goal as well: to better understand the accepted place of culture in racialist ideologies more broadly, as acknowledged by the historical actors. As Christian Delachampagne has put it, racism "is the reduction of the cultural to the biological, the *attempt* to make the first dependent on the second."[2] What happens when this attempt fails, when the claims to rationality fail not just for historians ex post facto but in the eyes of the historical actors themselves? In this essay, I will attempt to examine some prevailing scholarly tendencies regarding race and Nazi ideology and explain why they are in need of rethinking. This is not the result of years of research in archives: although a few empirical moments will be used to highlight the nature of the current scholarly problem, my larger purpose is to think through and hopefully help to unpack the ways in which scholars have reified the notion of race as they have investigated it in historical contexts, and ultimately to suggest that race, while an important weapon in the Nazis' rhetorical arsenal, was not a motivating factor for the Nazis' anti-Semitic beliefs or practices.

Race has almost completely overtaken a prior generation's focus on class as a category of analysis among historians who study Nazism. For some years now, scholars have taken at face value the Nazi aspiration for a biologically defined racial community whereby workers, craftsmen, professionals, and aristocrats were to be brought together in cross-class harmony.[3] This race community helped to externalize internal dissent and focus the loyalty of the German populace through the creation of *Reichsfeinde* (enemies of the Reich), most importantly (but not solely) Jews, against whom all Germans could supposedly rally. However, although the Nazi *use* of science as a means of defining *Reichsfeinde* is now almost universally agreed upon, this leaves open the question of whether the Nazis themselves believed in race science. This question is complicated further by an older but by no means obsolete view that Nazi racialism was not truly scientific but rather represented a "pseudo-science" that lent spurious legitimacy to the movement's ideology.[4] Opposed to that view are more recent interventions, many of them by culturalist historians informed by postmodernism, who have maintained that the historical contingency of what constitutes science – whereby an alchemist of the Middle Ages was a scientist because he *believed* he was a scientist – means that Nazi racism was indeed science because it was understood in its day to *be* science. One of the most trenchant iterations of this position comes from Peter Fritzsche, who confidently states that "[f]or the Nazis, biology was the key to the destiny of the German people. It offered a completely new understanding of human existence, rearranging what was necessary and possible, what was enduring and ephemeral, what was virtuous and dangerous." Fritzsche claims that this changed the entire political frame of reference: "By thinking in biological terms, the Nazis recast politics in an exceptionally vivid way."[5] That this can be stated so self-assuredly when ten years earlier Alan Beyerchen warned that biology for the Nazis was really a matter of "manipulating the means/ends calculations of instrumental rationality"[6] speaks to the attraction of the "modernity made me do it" paradigm for contemporary scholars. Peter Hutton warns us of the logical conclusion of this scholarly trend: "the idea of Enlightenment modernity as 'Nazi' is the mirror image of the idea of the Enlightenment as 'Jewish', with the Nazis, instead of the Jews, understood as destructive of racio-cultural difference within modernity."[7] That scholars of Nazi science have been able to essentially ignore cautionary interventions such as Beyerchen's and Hutton's (among others) speaks to the elevation of the race paradigm as a kind of new orthodoxy in German historiography. Among the implications of this disagreement is the question of how much we should attribute race and the belief in the biological immutability of the victim as a motivating force in history, especially when the actual belief in immutability on the part of the perpetrators themselves has yet to be established. In other words, if the Nazis knew the science of race was spurious, can we any longer say that their violence was spawned by "racism"? We still, permit me to suggest, lack a general theory of the precise construction of racial categories and identities in the Third Reich.

We need not uncover some heretofore undiscovered trove of denunciations of race science by top Nazis to see that the seemingly immutable category of race as a gauge for belonging to the *Volksgemeinschaft* was in fact highly mutable.[8] The case of the so-called *Mischlinge* brings this out very well. For those of "mixed race," with both Jewish and gentile grandparents, the allegedly watertight racialism of Nazism as signified by the Nuremberg Laws went crashing against the rocks. Without any firm scientific means of dealing with mixed racial composition, the Nazis had to make explicit concessions to the category of culture (read: religion) in order to determine the *Mischling*'s identity. Whereas religious affiliation and practice was deemed irrelevant when the individual in question had three or four Jewish grandparents, for those with one or two, it was the linchpin of their fate. Although the unique situation of the *Mischlinge* has received broader scholarly treatment, of course,[9] the implications of the *Mischling* for the conceptual underpinnings of Nazi racial ideology have yet to be fully interrogated. Nevertheless, a whole stream of scholarship insists that Nazi anti-Semitism was the child of scientific, Enlightenment rationality. But when we remind ourselves that the Nuremberg Laws measured race in the first instance by the *religion* of the grandparents – something we know but do not know what to do with – the need to strip the concept of race of some of its analytical privilege becomes all the greater.

What does this say about Nazism's "mosaic of victims"?[10] A wave of scholarship on eugenics and euthanasia under National Socialism, along with the still-growing literature on Nazi genocide, has greatly expanded our inquiry into racialism beyond the Jews as the driving principle of Nazi ideology.[11] Vast amounts of work on Roma and Sinti, homosexuals, blacks, and Slavs have provided detailed accounts of their fate under Nazi dominance.[12] Work by Doris Bergen and others on the *Volksdeutsche* points to the Nazis' obsession with "rescuing Germanic blood" throughout Europe.[13] This literature points to the many dimensions of Nazi racialism and clearly demonstrates that the Jews were not its only subjects. On the other hand, current scholarship has increasingly unveiled much of the ambiguity of Nazi race theory: we know that in the case of Poles or homosexuals, for instance, some Nazis argued there were physiological criteria for measuring race while others embraced the notion that race was a matter of character. Race could be defined as both tangible and ethereal, biological and cultural. Current scholarly deconstruction of Nazi race science, particularly evident in Saul Fried-länder's study,[14] has helped to unveil some of the many absurdities of logic employed by the movement's theorists. What is particularly revealing about this "mosaic" is that it consisted of outgroups that had all been subjected to various forms of discrimination long before the "shock of the new" brought about by modernity's biological polit-ics. If, per Fritzsche's "rearranging," the Nazis so drastically altered the understanding of human existence, the choice of outgroups resulting from this alleged revolution in thought remained strikingly unchanged. Whether they were homosexuals, Roma, or the physically and mentally handicapped – not just Jews – there had been precedent for their mar-ginalization within German society. Departing from the question of internal ideological consistency, other scholars have rethought the cen-trality of so-called race experts in devising Nazi beliefs and practices. Rejecting the arguments of Henry Friedlander and others that the scien-tists of the race policy apparatus were the primary motor of genocide, Dan Stone succinctly states that "the decision to murder the Jews emerged from the Nazi leadership's interactions with its functionaries on the ground in occupied Europe and not from the dissection tables of anthropologists."[15]

Did the Nazis themselves attempt to reconcile the different and even contradictory methods employed in constructing their racial categories? Were the Nazis aware of the inconsistencies of race theory, or did they simply not care, and thereby acknowledge that they were not truly "racist" in the presumed sense of the word? Telling moments, like the one which began this study, seem to beg these questions. But Streicher was by no means alone. Ernest Krieck, a high-placed party functionary and a leading proponent of educational *Gleichschaltung* in the Third Reich, elaborated rather explicitly on this score:

[T]here are scientists in the world rising to disagree with the possibility of proving the existence of race scientifically ... the verification of the existence of race, and perhaps of existence in general, does not require *artificial* scientific tools. The fact of the existence of race is not doubtful [sic], because man carries it in his heart, his spirit, his soul, or because man wants race to *become* a fact.[16]

Krieck added that this conclusion "is accepted even by outstanding scientists." According to this leading proponent of Nazi race indoctrination, race did not have to exist, let alone be proven – it had merely to be felt. None less than Hitler arrived at almost precisely the same conclusion:

We speak of the Jewish race only as a linguistic convenience, for in the true sense of the word, and from a genetic standpoint, *there is no Jewish race* ... The Jewish race is above all a community of the spirit. Anthropologically the Jews do not exhibit those common characteristics that would identify them as a uniform race ... A *spiritual* race is harder and more lasting than a *natural* race.[17]

Here, with one stroke, Hitler seemed to discard the entire biologistic apparatus used by his followers to justify Nazi anti-Semitic practice. Those race "experts" currently upheld as the true locus of Nazi genocidal belief and practice by the scholarly proponents of the race paradigm could not have been more thoroughly disabused of any pretence of significance for or causal influence on Nazi anti-Semitism.

A brief examination of another type of *Reichsfeind* in the Third Reich, Africans and so-called Afro-Germans, is especially useful in highlighting just how multivalent and perhaps even contradictory Nazi constructions of race could be. The fate of the so-called Rhineland bastards, another variety of *Mischling* in the Nazis' biologistic discourse, typifies their response to racial "defilement" between European and non-European. Lurid propaganda images of black men lasciviously consuming virginal white women abounded in racist imagery long before the Nazis came to power: indeed, racist hysteria about black sexuality existed throughout Europe at this time.[18] Although within Germany this fed racism across the political spectrum,[19] it did not lead to any tangible state action against the "bastards" before 1933. It was only after the Nazi seizure of power that actions were taken against them. The Nazis, aided by the Kaiser Wilhelm Institute, sterilized all Rhineland *Mischlinge* they were able to track down. In this instance, the treatment of this category of racial enemy was somewhat similar to that of Jewish *Mischlinge*. Under the Nuremberg Laws, those defined as half- and quarter-Jews who had abandoned all the signifiers of Jewish belonging, such as membership in a synagogue or marriage to a practicing Jew, received a special status. Although they suffered differing degrees of formal and informal discrimination, like African *Mischlinge* they were not sent to concentration camps or death camps as such. In fact, unlike the African *Mischlinge*, they did not even fall victim to sterilization, even though many Nazis had wanted this (and Heydrich wanted them treated as full Jews).[20]

But what of the status of racially "pure" Africans and Jews? Here, there is an exceptional divergence of paths. A "pure" Jew, of course, was ultimately marked for extermination. The presence of full Jews in the German national body constituted a defilement writ large, while the progeny of the literal "defilement" of Aryan by Jew – the *Mischlinge* – were systematically placed higher in the Nazis' racial hierarchy than those Jews who kept their physical distance from Aryans. Pure Africans, by contrast, apparently met quite a different fate. A very small number of Africans from the former German colonies lived in Nazi Germany. The Nazi leadership, far from seeking their destruction, sterilization, or deportation, found themselves defending the interests of these Africans. For instance, when the party Chancellery discovered that Africans were not receiving gainful employment, it issued them employment authorizations in order to help them find steady work. Actions taken against them were explicitly prohibited.[21] Although this hardly constituted recognition of Africans as full members of the *Volk*, it did demonstrate that the Nazi state apparently considered them worthy of some degree of state paternalism.[22]

Adopting certain cultural practices could not obviate the racial belonging of the half-African as it could the half-Jew. But if full Jews posed a greater danger in the Nazi imagination than half-Jews, the opposite seems to have been the case with Africans. Why was this so? One might point to the negligible number of colonial Africans and suggest that Nazis felt they could be readily absorbed into the *Volkskörper* with little consequence. Their rarity might also have enhanced their allure as colonial "curios," reminders to the Nazis of their nation's brief moment of overseas expansion. Nonetheless, their small numbers and relative social isolation even when compared to Jews should have made them very easy targets for the Nazis' racist fanaticism.

The historiographical tendency to cast Nazi anti-Semitism as a function of a larger racialism has never been stronger. But far too little attention has been paid to the fact that many Nazis did not consider the Jews to be a race. Aside from Hitler's reference to Jewishness as culture rather than biology and Streicher's contention that race was not a matter of appearance, there was also Joseph Goebbels's view that "[t]he Jew is a non-race among the races of the earth."[23] In other words, the problem with the Jew was precisely his *lack* of racial belonging. Africans, while far down the hierarchy of *Völker* from Europeans, nonetheless possessed sufficiently distinct racial qualities to be granted the status of a *Volk*. What would have been the Nazi reaction to Africans had their numbers in

Germany been greater? Almost certainly one of greater alarm. But would they have been fated to a "final solution" of the magnitude meted out to the Jews? The answer, I believe, would have been no. Any act of literal racial defilement was unacceptable, as the case of the "Rhineland bastards" made so clear. But the "racially pure" African – the representative of an unalloyed *Volk* purity, however inferior and primitive – was not regarded as the same threat as the pure Jew, who worked to destroy purity as a "non-race among the races of the earth."

If the Nazis were not scientifically racist, what were they? In his historiographical survey of Nazi race theory, Dan Stone convincingly demonstrates that in their genocidal ambitions, the Nazis were neither motivated in their beliefs by science nor guided in their actions by scientists. While a variety of medical and scientific opportunists within the professions certainly tried to take advantage of a Nazi discourse of race and blood for careerist purposes, Stone shows how the Nazis ultimately had no use for them – if for no other reason than that the promised race science never materialized. As he puts it, by focusing on doctors and race scientists, historians who link Nazi racial science to genocide "overstate the extent to which the Holocaust was conceived as a 'medical' procedure, and thus end by contradicting their own arguments when they admit ... that the origins of the genocidal idea lay more in fantasies of Jewish world power than in scientifically corroborated claims about defective Jewish genes."[24] Stone suggests that, rather than being scientifically racist, the Nazis were "mystically" racist. In other words, race for them was literally a matter of faith, one that preserved their sense of superiority over the Jews and other *Untermenschen* without having to verify those claims empirically. However, given Stone's definition of this race mysticism as primarily a matter of paranoid political conspiracy theory, he does not seek to investigate the most obvious source of mystical anti-Semitism, namely Christianity. Beyond the plain political advantages in doing so, many Nazis simultaneously embraced religious and racialist languages when describing their hatred of Jews. Their prejudices relied not just upon notions of racial inferiority, which they knew could hardly be measured by objective means, but also upon older notions of Jews as religious enemies of Christianity, supposedly responsible for the death of Christ. So-called racial anti-Semitism in theory departed from Christian anti-Semitism by rejecting baptism as a means of "saving" the Jew. This fact alone is often used to explain the unique genocidal brutality of the Nazis. Detlev Peukert, for instance, suggested that Western scientific culture was secularist and amoral in spirit and provided the intellectual means for removing moral barriers against genocide.[25] But what this line of reasoning overlooks is the very possibility that biology was little more than a discursive edifice. In other words, Peukert presumes that Nazi racism was not pseudo-science but science. However, Nazism was not simply the consequence of secular, scientific modernity; indeed, many Nazis saw their movement as a defense of Christian values against secularism. They also showed how their hatred of the Jew was about more than just biology.[26]

One way in which the Nazis attempted to reconcile the inherent contradiction between race, which claimed that Jewishness was an immutable category, and religion, which nominally allows for Jewish mutability, was to insist that race was God's law. In a theological formulation that bears a striking resemblance to the religious arguments of the Ku Klux Klan and the "Christian Identity" movement in the United States as well as the particular Reformed theology underpinning apartheid ideology in South Africa, many leading Nazis – significantly, most of them Protestant – claimed that they were not creating a new race cult but rather preserving pre-existing divine ordinances for racial separation.[27] As David Goldenberg has recently reminded us, the "Curse of Ham" theology has had a long history among racialist societies – a history that extends well beyond the radical fringe or even the slave-holding classes.[28] While the Nazis never relied upon this particular religious construction in their anti-Semitism, the notion that racial separation begat racial subordination was certainly present. For instance, the leader of the Nazi Teachers' League, Hans Schemm, spoke frequently of what he believed was the inherently religious quality of Nazi racialism:

When one puts steel into fire, the steel will glow and shine in its own distinctive way ... When I put the German *Volk* into the fire of Christianity, the German *Volk* will react in its racially distinctive way. It will build German cathedrals and create a German hymn ... We want to preserve, not subvert, what God has created, just as the oak tree and the fir tree retain their difference in a forest. – Why should our concept of race suddenly turn into the Marxist concept of a single type of human? We are accused of wanting to deify the idea of race. But since race is willed by God, we want nothing else but to keep the race pure, in order to fulfill God's law.[29]

Another leading Nazi to synthesize racial and religious tropes was Walter Buch, head of the party's internal supreme court and father-in-law to Martin Bormann. "The Jew," according to Buch, "is not a human being: he is a manifestation of decay." He supposed that the nefarious influence of the Jew was especially notable in the state of German family life.

As he said in a speech from 1932: "Never more than in the last ten years has the truth behind Luther's words been more evident: 'The family is the source of everyone's blessing and misfortune.'" The Jew caused the breakdown of the German family because for him marriage was simply a means to an end, a contract concluded for material benefit. The German, on the other hand, entered into marriage to produce children and imbue them with values such as honor, obedience, and national feeling. For Buch, the antithesis of the Jew was the Christian as well as the German: "The idea of eternal life, of which the Jew knows nothing, is just as characteristic of our Germanic forefathers as it was of Christ."[30] Buch's reference to life after death revealed belief in a supernatural faith rather than a pantheistic religion of nature. Buch insisted that any mixing of Jews and Germans, whether biological or social, was a violation of the "divine world order."[31] Buch blamed this state of affairs very squarely on the secular liberalism of the previous century: "The heresies and entice-ments of the French Revolution allowed the pious German to totally forget that the guest in his house comes from the *Volk* who nailed the Savior to the cross ... In the nineteenth century the lie of the rabbis' sons, that the Holy Scripture made the Savior into a Jew, finally bore fruit." It was under the auspices of Europe's liberal regimes that Jews, according to Buch, were allowed their emancipation, to the detriment of Christian Europe. The nineteenth-century debate over Jesus' Jewishness, exemplified in the debates surrounding biblical criticism, to Buch's mind only facilitated the Jews' hegemony. The truth was that Jesus' "entire character and learning betrayed Germanic blood."[32] In his anti-Semitic cause, Buch was able to appropriate the legacy of Martin Luther: "When Luther turned his attention to the Jews, after he completed his transla-tion of the Bible, he left behind 'On the Jews and their Lies' for posterity."[33]

Hitler himself spoke of the religious underpinning which he believed was intrinsic to his type of racialism: "Peoples that bastardize themselves, or let themselves be bastardized, sin against the will of eternal Provi-dence."[34] Whereas reference to a vague providential force bears little resemblance to belief in the biblical God, elsewhere in *Mein Kampf* Hitler invokes more than a naturalist pantheism devoid of Christian content. Again, it was in the question of race and race purity where Hitler most frequently invoked such a God: it was, in his view, the duty of Germans "to put an end to the constant and continuous original sin of racial poisoning, and to give the Almighty Creator beings such as He Himself created."[35] Even as Hitler elsewhere made reference to an anthropomorphized

"Nature," and the laws of Nature that humanity must follow, he also revealed his belief that these were divine laws ordained by God:

The folkish-minded man, in particular, has the sacred duty, each in his own denomination, of making *people stop just talking superficially of God's will, and actually fulfill God's will, and not let God's word be desecrated.* For God's will gave men their form, their essence and their abilities. Anyone who destroys His work is declaring war on the Lord's creation, the divine will.[36]

The reference to God as the Lord of Creation and the necessity of obeying "His" will reveals a more recognizably Christian conception. Hitler's insistence on another occasion that Jesus was "the true God" and simultaneously "our greatest Aryan leader" only confirms his belief that race was a religious trope.[37] Even as he became increasingly vituperative in the war period against the institutions of Christianity, Hitler always detached Jesus from such criticisms, consistently maintaining that he was upholding Christ's true message in the face of clerical corruption and vanity.[38]

Saul Friedländer points out that the "redemptive" quality of Nazi anti-Semitism was essentially religious, and he uses the eschatological meaning of the Nazi fight against the Jews to explain the fanatical lengths the Nazis went to in pursuit of their genocidal ambitions. In a similar vein, Alon Confino has examined the efforts the Nazis made in physically destroying copies of the Jewish Bible, as a way of arguing that the cultural aspect of negating Judaism was just as vital to them as the physical aspect of murdering Jews.[39] Indeed, that *Mischlinge* under Nazi control were ultimately not designated for extermination because of their *cultural* orientation, despite the presence of their Jewish "blood," would only confirm the argument that culture was more central for the Nazis. Was this eschatological, almost messianic quality evident in Nazi treatment of other racial victims? It would seem that none of them endured the same relentless and unconditional persecution, as a group, that the Jews endured. Could it be that the religious quality that pertained to the Nazis' anti-Semitism explains this?

Another means of resolving the interpretative tension between the universality of Nazi racialism and the particularity of Nazi anti-Semitism might be by gauging the ways in which Nazis categorized those deemed neither Semitic nor Aryan – such as Germans of Southern European, Slavic, Asian, and perhaps even Latin American descent – and how readily a degree of racial accommodation was afforded to these groups. We already know of the almost capricious manner in which members of certain ethnicities, particularly Poles and Czechs, could find themselves becoming racially acceptable in Nazi eyes.[40] Whether it was a combination of physiological features, such as the clichéd blond hair and blue eyes; or the ability to speak German natively; or some other barometer of acculturation such as cleanliness or sexual morality; or, lacking all these, having some distant German ancestor and thereby laying claim to membership in the *Volk* – all groups found that the boundaries of their identity were permeable, save full Jews. This argument has recently been extended to the Roma and Sinti as well, in a controversial monograph that contends distinctions were made between "Aryan" and "mixed Gypsies," between the "nomadic" and the "sedentary."[41]

Our current knowledge seems to suggest that the Jews were distinguished in the Nazi imagination from other racial enemies, for it was only the category of the Jew from which no escape could be found, from which no "passing" was permitted. Even the most Aryan-looking full Jew was to receive one fate and one fate only, regardless of other supposedly scientific criteria like hair- and eye-color, cranial measurements, or any other biological or physiological trait – never mind cultural or linguistic criteria – that could change the racial belonging of other non-Aryans. It is not a question of whether the Nazis realized this for themselves, much as Hitler realized he wasn't blond – there is enough evidence to suggest that they knew Jews defied their own laws of racialism. The question becomes: How did the Nazis reconcile their admission that the Jew was in fact mutable on the one hand, with their exclusive application of the idea of immutability to the Jew on the other? The inevitable answer is that science, as the Nazis themselves realized, does not explain Nazi anti-Semitism – that no scientific inquiries of the day, let alone since, were able to objectively justify after the fact, or create in the first instance, this aspect of Nazi ideology. That the Nazis were not "truly" racist in any dispassionate, scientific manner means that their genocidal anti-Semitism had inspiration elsewhere; namely, in the dark undergrowth of religious Jew-hatred.

Notes

1 "Report of Streicher Interrogation on Afternoon of 19 July 1945": Institut für Zeitgeschichte, ZS 2072.
2 Christian Delachampagne, "Racism and the West: From praxis to logos," in David Theo Goldberg (ed.), *Anatomy of Racism* (Minneapolis, 1990), 83–88, here 87 (emphasis added).
3 See, for instance, Tim Mason, *Social Policy in the Third Reich: The Working Class and the "National Community"* (Oxford, 1993); Detlev Peukert, *Volksgenossen*

und Gemeinschaftsfremde: Anpassung, Ausmerze und Aufbegehren unter dem Nationalsozialismus (Cologne, 1982); David Schoenbaum, *Hitler's Social Revolution: Class and Status in Nazi Germany* (London, 1966); David Welch, "Manufacturing a consensus: Nazi propaganda and the building of a 'national community' (*Volksgemeinschaft*)," *Contemporary European History* 2 (1993), 1–15.

4 See George Mosse, *Toward the Final Solution: A History of European Racism* (New York, 1978); Léon Poliakov, *The Aryan Myth: A History of Racist and Nationalist Ideas in Europe* (New York, 1974).

5 Peter Fritzsche, *Life and Death in the Third Reich* (Cambridge, MA, 2008), 84. Alan Steinweis's work represents the middle ground of a race-centric understanding of Nazism: see his *Studying the Jew: Scholarly Antisemitism in Nazi Germany* (Cambridge, MA, 2006).

6 Alan Beyerchen, "Rational means and irrational ends: thoughts on the technology of racism in the Third Reich," *Central European History* 39(3) (1997), 388.

7 Peter Hutton, *Race and the Third Reich: Linguistics, Racial Anthropology and Genetics in the Dialectic of the Volk* (Cambridge, 2005), 16.

8 In her study of race anthropologists in Weimar Germany and the Third Reich, Rachel Boaz demonstrates how the Nazis were more likely to simply drop racial science than to openly denounce it: Rachel Boaz, *The Search for Aryan Blood: Seroanthropology in Weimar and National Socialist Germany* (Budapest, 2012).

9 The best analytical treatment remains Jeremy Noakes, "The development of Nazi policy towards the German-Jewish 'Mischlinge,' 1933–1945," *Leo Baeck Institute Yearbook* 34 (1989), 291–354. Much of the remaining scholarship, much of it quite good, concerns itself as much with an "untold" dramatic narrative as with historical analysis: see Cynthia Crane, *Divided Lives: The Untold Stories of Jewish-Christian Women in Nazi Germany* (London, 2000); Beate Meyer, *"Juedische Mischlinge": Rassenpolitik Verfolgungserfahrung, 1933–1945* (Hamburg, 1999); Sigrid Lekebusch, *Not und Verfolgung der Christen juedischer Herkunft im Rheinland, 1933–1945: Darstellung und Dokumentation* (Cologne, 1995); Bryan Mark Rigg, *Hitler's Jewish Soldiers: The Untold Story of Nazi Racial Laws and Men of Jewish Descent in the German Military* (Lawrence, 2002); Nathan Stoltzfus, *Resistance of the Heart: Intermarriage and the Rosenstrasse Protest in Nazi Germany* (New York, 1996); James Tent, *In the Shadow of the Holocaust: Nazi Persecution of Jewish-Christian Germans* (Lawrence, 2003).

10 Cf. Michael Barenbaum (ed.), *A Mosaic of Victims: Non-Jews Persecuted and Murdered by the Nazis* (New York, 1990).

11 On eugenics and euthanasia see, *inter alia*: Gisela Bock, *Zwangssterilisation im Nationalsozialismus: Studien zur Rassenpolitik und Frauenpolitik* (Opladen, 1986); Michael Burleigh, *Death and Deliverance: "Euthanasia" in Germany, 1900 to 1945* (Cambridge, 1994); Henry Friedlander, *The Origins of Nazi Genocide: From Euthanasia to the Final Solution* (Chapel Hill, 1995); Ernst Klee, *"Euthanasie" im NS-Staat: die "Vernichtung lebensunwerten Lebens"* (Frankfurt, 1983); Paul Weindling, *Health, Race and*

German Politics between National Unification and Nazism, 1870–1945 (Cambridge, 1989). The literature on the Holocaust is too vast to give a representative sampling here. More recent attempts at synthesis or synopsis include Götz Aly, *"Endlösung": Völkerverschiebung und der Mord an den europäischen Juden* (Frankfurt, 1995); Yehuda Bauer, *Rethinking the Holocaust* (New Haven, 2001); Wolfgang Benz (ed.), *Dimension des Völkermords: Die Zahl der jüdischen Opfer des Nationalsozialismus* (Munich, 1991); Christopher Browning, *Fateful Months: Essays on the Emergence of the Final Solution* (New York, 1985); Saul Friedländer, *Nazi Germany and the Jews,* 2 vols. (New York, 1997–2007).

12 Broader surveys and interpretive analyses include Berenbaum, *A Mosaic of Victims*; Michael Burleigh and Wolfgang Wippermann, *The Racial State: Germany, 1933–1945* (Cambridge, 1991); Walter Grode, *Nationalsozialistische Moderne: rassenideologische Modernisierung durch Abtrennung und Zerstörung gesellschaftlicher Peripherien* (Frankfurt, 1994). On homosexuals, see *inter alia* Günther Grau (ed.), *Homosexualität in der NS-Zeit: Dokumente einer Diskriminierung und Verfolgung* (Frankfurt, 1993); Richard Plant, *The Pink Triangle: The Nazi War against Homosexuals* (New York, 1986). On Sinti and Roma, see Guenther Lewy, *The Nazi Persecution of the Gypsies* (Oxford, 2000); Wolfgang Wippermann, *Wie die Zigeuner: Antisemitismus und Antiziganismus im Vergleich* (Berlin, 1997). On Africans, see Reiner Pommerin, *Sterilisierung der "Rheinlandbastarde": Das Schicksal einer farbigen deutschen Minderheit 1918–1937* (Düsseldorf, 1979); Clarence Lusane, *Hitler's Black Victims* (New York, 2003). On Slavs, see the recent interpretive essay by John Connelly, "Nazis and Slavs: from racial theory to racial practice," *Central European History*, 32 (1999), 1–33; Christoph Klessmann, *Die Selbstbehauptung einer Nation: Nationalsozialistische Kulturpolitik und polnische Widerstandsbewegung im Generalgouvernment 1939–1945* (Düsseldorf, 1971); Manfred Weissbecker, "'Wenn hier Deutsche wohnten ...': Beharrung und Veränderung im Russlandbild Hitlers und der NSDAP" in Hans-Erich Volkmann (ed.), *Das Russlandbild im Dritten Reich* (Cologne, 1994), 9–54.

13 Doris Bergen, "The Nazi concept of 'volksdeutsche' and the exacerbation of anti-Semitism in Eastern Europe, 1939–45," *Journal of Contemporary History* 29 (1994), 569–82; Isabel Heinemann, *"Rasse, Siedlung, deutsches Blut": Das Rasse- und Siedlungshauptamt der SS und die rassenpolitische Neuordnung Europas* (Göttingen, 2003).

14 Friedländer, *Nazi Germany and the Jews*, vol. 1, especially chapter 5, "The spirit of laws."

15 Dan Stone, *Histories of the Holocaust* (New York, 2010), 165.

16 Quoted in Uriel Tal, *Religion, Politics and Ideology in the Third Reich: Selected Essays* (London, 2004), 9 (emphasis added).

17 Adolf Hitler, *Politisches Testament: Die Bormann-Diktate vom Februar und April 1945* (Hamburg, 1981), 64–70 (emphasis added).

18 See Iris Wigger, *Die "Schwartze Schmach am Rhein": Rassistische Diskriminierung zwischen Geschlecht, Klasse, Nation und Rasse* (Münster, 2007).

19 Burleigh and Wippermann, *Racial State*, 128.

20 See Noakes, "The development of Nazi policy towards the German-Jewish 'Mischlinge'."

21 Friedländer, *Nazi Germany*, vol. 1, 208. For a monographic treatment of "Afro-Germans" under Nazism, see Tina Campt, *Other Germans: Black Germans and the Politics of Race, Gender and Memory in the Third Reich* (Ann Arbor, 2004).

22 In the context of Africans, it is also worth noting that Arabs – considered, like Jews, to be "Semitic" by the nineteenth-century philologists who first coined the terms "Semitic" and "Aryan" – were not the targets of Nazi "anti-Semitism." See, *inter alia*, Maurice Olender, *The Languages of Paradise: Race, Religion, and Philology in the Nineteenth Century* (Cambridge, MA, 1992); Gil Anidjar, *Semites: Race, Religion, Literature* (Stanford, 2008). As David Motadel has demonstrated, the Nazis explicitly worked to expunge the words "Semite" or "Semitic" from their publications, "as [they] targeted groups [Muslim Arabs] they did not wish to offend": David Motadel, *Islam and Nazi Germany's War* (Cambridge, MA, 2014), 57–60 (quote 58).

23 Joseph Goebbels, *Michael: A Novel*, trans. Joachim Neugroschel (New York, 1987 [orig. 1929]), 65.

24 Stone, *Histories of the Holocaust*, 191.

25 Detlev Peukert, "The genesis of the 'final solution' from the spirit of science," in Thomas Childers and Jane Caplan (eds.), *Reevaluating the Third Reich* (New York, 1993), 247.

26 Claus-Ekkehard Bärsch, *Die politische Religion des Nationalsozialismus* (Munich, 1997); Richard Steigmann-Gall, *The Holy Reich: Nazi Conceptions of Christianity, 1919–1945* (Cambridge, 2003).

27 For South Africa, see T. Dunbar Moodie, *The Rise of Afrikanerdom: Power, Apartheid, and the Afrikaner Civil Religion* (Berkeley, 1975), and Leonard Thompson, *The Political Mythology of Apartheid* (New Haven, 1985). For the United States, see Kelly J. Baker, *Gospel According to the Klan: The KKK's Appeal to Protestant America, 1915–1930* (Lawrence, 2011); Michael Barkun, *Religion and the Racist Right: The Origins of the Christian Identity Movement* (Chapel Hill, 1994); David Chalmers, *Hooded Americanism: The First Century of the Ku Klux Klan, 1865–1965*, 3rd edn. (Durham, 1987); Leo Ribuffo, *The Old Christian Right: The Protestant Far Right from the Great Depression to the Cold War* (Philadelphia, 1983).

28 David Goldenberg, *The Curse of Ham: Race and Slavery in Early Judaism, Christianity and Islam* (Princeton, 2003).

29 Walter Künneth, Werner Wilm, and Hans Schemm, *Was haben wir als evangelische Christen zum Rufe des Nationalsozialismus zu sagen?* (Dresden, 1931), 19–20.

30 Steigmann-Gall, *The Holy Reich*, 32–3.

31 Donald McKale, *The Nazi Party Courts: Hitler's Management of Conflict in his Movement, 1921–1945* (Lawrence, 1974), 57.

32 Steigmann-Gall, *The Holy Reich*, 33.

33 "On the Jews and Their Lies," Martin Luther's notoriously violent anti-Semitic tract, was well known to the Nazis, and it was frequently to be found among their stated inspirations. Nazis to explicitly refer to it included

Heinrich Himmler. The rising tide of violence in the work finds its climax in the following passages: "If I had power over the Jews, as our princes and cities have, I would deal severely with their lying mouths ... For a usurer is an arch-thief and a robber who should rightly be hanged on the gallows seven times higher than other thieves ... We are at fault in not avenging all this innocent blood of our Lord and of the Christians which they shed for three hundred years after the destruction of Jerusalem, and the blood of the children they have shed since then (which still shines forth from their eyes and their skin). We are at fault in not slaying them": Martin Luther, "On the Jews and Their Lies," *Luther's Works*, trans. Franklin Sherman (Philadelphia, 1971), vol. 47, 289, 267. At one point, Luther anticipates the medical and scientific metaphors used by racialist anti-Semites later: "I wish and I ask that our rulers who have Jewish subjects exercise a sharp mercy towards these wretched people ... They must act like a good physician who, when gangrene has set in, proceeds without mercy to cut, saw, and burn flesh, veins, bone and marrow. Such a procedure must also be followed in this instance" (ibid., 292).

34 Hitler, *Mein Kampf*, trans. Ralph Manheim (Boston, 1962), 214, 327.

35 Ibid., 405.

36 Ibid., 562 (emphasis in the original).

37 Eberhard Jäckel (ed.), *Hitler: Sämtliche Aufzeichnungen 1905–1924* (Stuttgart, 1980), 635. Speech of May 26, 1922, originally reported in the *NSDAP-Mitteilungsblatt*, Nr. 14.

38 Adolf Hitler, *Hitler's Table Talk 1941–1944: His Private Conversations* (London, 1953), 76, 85, 721. Even regarding the institutions of Christianity, Hitler was not consistently anticlerical. For instance, in December 1941 – well into the war period, when his anti-Christian invective was allegedly at its hottest – he stated: "Against a Church that identifies itself with the State, as in England, I have nothing to say" (*Hitler's Table Talk*, 143).

39 Alon Confino, *A World Without Jews: The Nazi Imagination from Persecution to Genocide* (New Haven, 2014).

40 Chad Bryant, *Prague in Black: Nazi Rule and Czech Nationalism* (Cambridge, MA, 2007); Phillip Rutherford, *Prelude to the Final Solution: The Nazi Program for Deporting Ethnic Poles, 1939–1941* (Lawrence, 2007).

41 Guenther Lewy, The Nazi Persecution of the *Gypsies* (Oxford, 2000); Ian Hancock, "Downplaying the Porrajmos: the trend to minimize the Romani Holocaust," *Journal of Genocide Research* 3 (2001), 79–85.

Racializing Historiography

Anti-Jewish Scholarship in the Third Reich

Dirk Rupnow

In recent debates about German scholars' complicity in the Nazi policies of persecution and genocide, only marginal consideration has been given to the work of scholars in the humanities and social sciences who, during the Third Reich, were engaged in studies of Jewish history and culture and the so-called Jewish question.[1] This research has either been perceived as part of the regime's *Ostforschung* (literally, research on the East) – which concerned the Nazi plans for expansion into and restructuring of Eastern Europe – or investigated by means of case studies of individual institutions. The relationship of scholarship to ideology, propaganda, and politics has remained largely unexplored. Instead, a good deal of attention has been paid, more sensationally, to individual scholars whose careers began under Nazism but continued to flourish in the academic elites of postwar Germany.[2]

Judenforschung – an abbreviation of *Erforschung der Judenfrage* (study of the Jewish question) – established itself during the Nazi era as an independent, interdisciplinary field of study, with its own institutions, publications, and events, pursued by non-Jewish scholars in the human-ities and social sciences.[3] The research carried out under the rubric of *Ostforschung* and *Volksgeschichte* (history of the *Volk*) often included anti-Semitic elements, but those fields were by no means focused specific-ally on either Judaism or the Jewish question. Within those disciplines – and, indeed, within the framework of plans for a new social order in Eastern Europe – Jews only ever appeared as a negative element to be

This essay was originally published, in slightly different form, in the journal *Patterns of Prejudice* (2008). It appears here with the permission of Taylor & Francis.

removed.[4] But this obscures the fact that under National Socialism – in contrast to the earlier tradition of mainstream German historiography, which was still in place following the war – Jewish history and culture were in themselves respectable subjects of research. Nazi *Judenforschung* took the Jewish question as its sole object of inquiry and anti-Semitism as its guiding principle.

THE INSTITUTIONALIZATION OF NAZI JEWISH STUDIES

Judenforschung emerged as a field of research soon after the Nazis came to power.[5] Various officials and others sought, whether in cooperation or competition, to establish it as an interdisciplinary, historically based discipline and to make their mark in it. As early as 1935, the Institut zum Studium der Judenfrage (Institute for the Study of the Jewish Question) was founded in Berlin. After 1939, it was known as Antisemitische Aktion (Anti-Semitic Action) and, from 1943, as Antijüdische Aktion (Anti-Jewish Action). It was a division of Goebbels's Propaganda Ministry, but the connection was concealed so that it would appear to be an independent and scholarly body.

The Forschungsabteilung Judenfrage (Department of Research on the Jewish Question) of the Reichsinstitut für Geschichte des neuen Deutschlands (Reich Institute for History of the New Germany) was one of the most important and productive institutes for Nazi Jewish Studies. Established in Munich in 1936, the institute aspired – according to its president, the historian Walter Frank (1905–1945) – to become the center of a new National Socialist historiography. The formal head of the Jewish Studies department was Karl Alexander von Müller (1882–1964), a professor of history at the University of Munich. In practice, though, it was run by his student Wilhelm Grau (1910–2000), who had made his name in 1933 with a dissertation on the demise of the Regensburg Jewish community in 1519. Grau was acknowledged as a pioneer in the (anti-Semitic) German study of Jewish history. He was later dismissed from the Reichsinstitut because of tensions with Frank over the way *Judenforschung* seemed to be overshadowing the institute's other research in the public's perception.

Frank's Reichsinstitut was confronted with a competitor when the Institut zur Erforschung der Judenfrage (Institute for Research on the Jewish Question) was inaugurated in Frankfurt am Main in March 1941 under the direction of none other than Wilhelm Grau. This institute was the first branch of a planned National Socialist university that Alfred

Rosenberg wanted to establish after the war. Its cornerstone was the Hebraica collection of the Frankfurt municipal library. The creation of the institute reflected the convergence of Rosenberg's interests and those of Frankfurt's mayor. Rosenberg, who fancied himself the chief architect of Nazi ideology, was not officially responsible for overseeing research on the Jewish question or racial studies, but he had always taken an interest in these subjects. For his part, the mayor was keen to play down Frankfurt's reputation as a "city of Jews and democrats" by bolstering its Nazi credentials.

The Frankfurt institute, though a latecomer to the field, soon became prominent. Through its connection to Rosenberg's taskforce, the Einsatzstab Reichsleiter Rosenberg, it profited from the large-scale looting of libraries, museums, synagogues, and other cultural institutions throughout occupied Europe during the war. And it was able to give new impetus to Nazi Jewish Studies in circumstances quite different from those that prevailed in 1936, when the Munich branch of Frank's Reichsinstitut was founded. Anti-Jewish policy was more comprehensive and more radical by 1941; the invasion of the Soviet Union and, with it, the systematic mass murder of the European Jews was about to begin. The Institut zur Erforschung der Judenfrage in Frankfurt became the dominant force in *Judenforschung*, a position previously held by the Reichsinstitut.

In 1939, the Institut zur Erforschung und Beseitigung des jüdischen Einflusses auf das deutsche kirchliche Leben (Institute for the Study and Eradication of Jewish Influence on German Church Life) was founded in Eisenach by the Protestant theologian Walter Grundmann (1906–1976). Its task was to bring Christian theology into line with Nazi racial ideology and to rid the New Testament of all references to Jewish sources. Christian theology and biblical exegesis had long been engaged with the history of the Jews, or at least with the history of biblical Judaism. For this reason, theologians and religious scholars played a decisive role in the establishment of Nazi Jewish studies.

Judenforschung became increasingly internationalized during the war as a result of Germany's occupation of or alliances with other European countries. Under Germany's leadership, a Europe-wide network of anti-Semitic agencies and organizations came into being. And it was not only anti-Semitic policies that were exported and implemented in the occupied and allied territories as Germany expanded, but also Nazi Jewish Studies. The Institut für Deutsche Ostarbeit (Institute for German Work in the East) was founded in Cracow in 1940 as a center of German scholarly pursuits in the Government General (Generalgouvernment); its Sektion für Rassen- und Volkstumsforschung (Section for the Study of Races and Ethnicities) included a Jewish Studies department (Referat Judenforschung) that was headed by the historian Josef Sommerfeldt (1914–1992?). In 1941, the Institut d'Études des Questions Juives was founded in occupied Paris under the direction of Réne Gérard, who was succeeded by Paul Sézille and later Georges Montandon (under whom it was renamed the Institut d'Études des Questions Juives et Ethno-Raciales). The French institute's work was influenced by Theodor Dannecker (1913–1945), the head of the Paris office of Eichmann's department in the Reich Security Main Office (Reichssicherheitshauptamt, or RSHA). He was in charge of implementing anti-Jewish policy in occupied France and organizing the deportation of French Jews. Other *Judenforschung* institutions were set up in Milan, Florence, Trieste, Bologna, and Budapest over the course of 1942/1943.

Despite the fact that it was based in research institutions that lay outside the traditional university system, anti-Jewish research in the Third Reich was by no means an isolated branch of scholarship. It was firmly rooted in the contemporary academic landscape. Students submitted contributions to *Judenforschung* to a variety of departments at a number of universities to earn degrees. The universities of Tübingen, Vienna, Berlin, and Frankfurt even planned to create new chairs of anti-Jewish scholarship; however, those plans were never realized.[6]

Scholarly research on Jews and other racial or ideological "enemies" was also pursued within the framework of the security police. Department VII of the RSHA, following plans drawn up by Franz Alfred Six (1909–1975), was responsible for "ideological research and evaluation" *(weltanschauliche Forschung und Auswertung)*; it built on the work of Department II 112 of the SD's head office, among other bodies, and constituted a direct institutional link between the state apparatus of persecution and mass murder and the world of scholarship. In 1941/ 1942, the work of Department VII Bib, which was responsible for Jewish affairs, was characterized as a "scholarly news service" that was "rooted in the present but in certain cases [had] recourse to historical knowledge."[7] Under the Nazis, even the actions of the security police and the implementation of a straightforward scheme for identifying friends and foes apparently required the backing of scholarship and the testimony of historical evidence.

Anti-Jewish scholarship never managed to take definitive shape as a discipline during the twelve years of the Third Reich. The attempt to create a new field of research developed momentum soon after the Nazis came to power under the usual competitive pressures of the system. But because of those pressures, no firm foundations were laid before 1945. In retrospect, it seems that it was precisely the lack of coordination within the political and scholarly spheres that allowed each to develop its own dynamic. Nonetheless, in the end, rivalry and competition were contained by a shared anti-Jewish aim, which guaranteed a common direction.

THE MINDSET OF *JUDENFORSCHUNG*

Unsurprisingly, given the institutional competition, anti-Jewish scholarship in the Third Reich was by no means uniform. The institutions and scholars involved addressed different questions, applied different methods, and were motivated by different interests. The work they produced was very heterogeneous, ranging from historical studies to statistical surveys and drawing on a wide variety of sources and materials. The discipline had no fixed boundaries; it was rather a field of interdisciplinary overlappings and cross-references. Despite the difficulty of generalizing about the substance of *Judenforschung*, certain characteristics do emerge that point to a style of thought that was shared by the Nazi anti-Jewish scholars.

The explicit aim of Nazi Jewish Studies was to de-Judaize research on Jewish history and culture, which had largely been the province of Jewish scholars before 1933. Despite distancing themselves from the German-Jewish tradition of *Wissenschaft des Judentums* (Judaic scholarship), Nazi scholars made no bones about using its results for their own purposes. Nazi *Judenforschung* should be understood as a form of Aryanization, a form of expropriation that was both intellectual and material. Moreover, Aryanization meant not only the transfer of Jewish property to Aryan hands but also the exclusion of Jews from professional and economic life. That was to be the case in the field of Jewish studies as well. Jews were to be the subject, not the authors, of research. The field of German-Jewish history that was allegedly dominated by Jews was to be replaced by a new, non-Jewish, German perspective: a scholarly undertaking that would be supported by the anti-Semitic politics of the Nazi sate. But even in this undertaking, Jews were used as forced labor, hidden from public view, to assist in the plundering and restructuring of libraries as well as in research.

In public, anti-Jewish researchers always sought to distance themselves from politics and propaganda in order to protect the scholarly status of their discipline. Their writings always claimed adherence to a methodology that was "strictly scientific" (*streng wissenschaftlich*). In internal debates, rivals would denounce one another for being unscholarly. But propaganda, politics, and scholarship were almost indistinguishable in the field of Nazi Jewish Studies. Their understanding of historical method did not lead the anti-Jewish scholars – or indeed other practitioners of *Volksgeschichte* – to embrace a model of tolerance and plurality. Rather, they voiced their solidarity with National Socialist ideology and the German *Volk*. This solidarity, anything but concealed, constituted the foundation of their scholarly identity.[8] Academic objectivity was allied to commitment and experience, so that the boundaries between propaganda and politics were blurred even further. The concept of "fighting scholarship" (*kämpfende Wissenschaft*) was invented to bridge the obvious gap between scholarly ideals and propagandistic or political practice. The term was used in various contexts. Walter Frank invoked it in trying to unify the two opposing aspects of the work of his Reichsinstitut as well as in defining its radical character.[9] Fighting scholarship was set against liberal scholarship, which was denounced as "pseudo-science" and "political and moral terrorism."

Nazi researchers were well aware of the paradox at the center of their endeavors: they were working to study and preserve the history of a group deemed to be inferior and an enemy of the German *Volk*. Moreover, they seemed to be neglecting the presumably superior field of German history. So as not to upset these hierarchies, *Judenforschung* was defined as the "history of the Jewish question" and differentiated from Jewish Studies, which dealt generally with Jewish history and Jewish life and customs in the past and the present. In short, Jewish life as experienced by Jews was seen as unnecessary ballast. It was the relationship between Jews and non-Jews that was of principal concern. Accordingly, the Jewish question was considered to be more an aspect of German history than of Jewish history. Thus, Nazi Jewish Studies not only defined an Other; it also made an important contribution to the construction of German identity and history.

The historian Wilhelm Grau went so far as to declare that it was not possible to write a history of Germany or Europe in modern times without taking the Jewish question into account.[10] Volkmar Eichstädt, a librarian and bibliographer at the Reichsinstitut, went even further by suggesting a connection between *Judenforschung* and the elucidation of the German character: "We will be brought much closer to an understanding of our German character [*deutsche Wesen*] by exploring the hard and victorious battle between our German nation and the racially foreign element of Judaism. And, by doing so, we not only increase our knowledge but strengthen our commitment to a volkisch life."[11]

At precisely the moment when the Jews were being removed from German life, the history of anti-Semitism and Jewish history were declared to be essential components of German history and identity. Consequently, the project of Nazi Jewish Studies was perceived outside of Germany to be nothing less than a complete rewriting of "Jewish history from the very beginning": "It was an integral part of the Nazi task of propaganda and politics not only to persecute the Jews and to vilify them for the part they were playing in the world, but to read into past history a reflection of what they considered to be the place of the Jews in the world today."[12]

The Germans had realized "that an assault on the Jewish past [was] an integral part of their assault on the Jewish present."[13] German scholarly interest in Jewish history did not begin with Nazi *Judenforschung,* but it was not until the Nazis came to power that Jewish history was incorporated within the German academic mainstream. The forced introduction of Jewish history into German history was carried out by those who were simultaneously legitimizing and enacting anti-Jewish policies. The institutionalization of Jewish Studies ran parallel and was complementary to the expulsion and murder of German and European Jewry. The "negative symbiosis" that Dan Diner has discerned at work in the post-Auschwitz period had been developed by the perpetrators in conjunction with their crimes.[14] The elimination of the Jews from German society required their inscription in German history: at the same time that they were expelled and murdered, they were historicized and preserved in German scholarship.

This was no mere coincidence. Conventional wisdom has it that Nazi leaders sought the extinction of Jewish history and memory along with the physical annihilation of the Jews. But, in a variety of ways, they selectively preserved the Jewish past and historicized their own anti-Jewish policies.[15] The purpose of Nazi Jewish Studies was not only to legitimate and assist the ongoing marginalization, expulsion, and annihilation of the Jews but also, in the long run, to preserve and perpetuate the image of an enemy that would stand as a perpetual justification for the crimes committed under the Nazis against the Jews of Europe. The denunciation of Jews as "useless" and "superfluous" in Nazi propaganda should not obscure the fact that they were neither useless nor superfluous for the perpetrators. On the contrary, they played the role of the absolutely essential Other within the bipolar ideology of Nazism.

RACE AS SPIRIT AND MIND

In portrayals of the Third Reich as a "racial state," discussion of the relationship between racism and science usually centers on the practice of measuring human bodies and the stereotyped images of the different races that the regime promoted. Clearly, the emphasis in racial classification is on physical characteristics.[16] Racial science had its roots in anthropology, which in the German tradition had *its* roots in medicine: it was physical anthropology, as opposed to the cultural anthropology of the American tradition.[17] Nazi *Judenforschung* was not identical to racial biology or physical anthropology. The field was the preserve of historians, theologians, philologists and literary scholars, jurists, and sociologists who only occasionally pursued interdisciplinary collaboration with natural scientists.

Race, at the time a relatively new concept that was undergoing development within various disciplines, remained a disparate and unstable category throughout the years of the Third Reich. The Nuremburg Laws of 1935, which formed the legal basis for all of the regime's subsequent anti-Jewish measures, show how difficult it was for the perpetrators to find a reliable racial definition of Jewishness that was suited to the practice of discrimination and persecution. The regime had to fall back on the religious affiliation of an individual's grandparents as the criterion for racial categorization. Genealogy rather than physical criteria had been used to identify suspected Jews as early as the fifteenth century under Spain and Portugal's *estatutos de limpieza de sangre*.[18] The emancipation or assimilation of Jews could be revoked only after an investigation of previous affiliation. In the cases of both early modern Iberia and the Third Reich, a historical argument – genealogical descent – was employed rather than one based on physical characteristics. Even at the very moment when National Socialism was using racist ideas about human inequality for unprecedented ends, racial scientists could offer no reliable and definitive method of racial categorization in the absence of direct genetic proof. They turned to the past in order to categorize the present.

In cases in which an individual's racial background was uncertain, the Reichssippenamt (Reich Kinship Office), which checked the racial descent of officials and public employees, would search for more substantial genealogical documentation; in other words, it proceeded historically. These were mainly cases in which the paternity of an individual was in doubt. If genealogical proof continued to elude researchers, the office would resort to evidence of a physical-anthropological nature. A so-called similarity analysis would be carried out that centered on comparison of approximately 120 physical characteristics between the subject, on the one hand, and, on the other, his/her known mother and possible fathers. Even then, it was only possible to determine an individual's racial classification by referring to a specific father, that is, to a genealogical line. The practitioners of the Third Reich's racial science regarded classification based exclusively on "race-typical" physical characteristics as problematic but sometimes unavoidable, as, for instance, in dealing with foundlings.[19] The scientific credibility of these expert opinions grew as public agencies and courts used them as the basis for their actions and conclusions.

Although the theorization of race was based in biology and used the language of the natural sciences, it could not be reduced to a purely scientific project. The racial scientists were attempting to devise a classification system that would naturalize cultural, intellectual, and psychological characteristics as well as physical ones.[20] There was never a clear distinction between bodily and mental attributes in anti-Semitic and racist discourse. All the classic texts of anti-Semitism were much more concerned with what they construed as the "Jewish spirit" or the "Jewish mind" than with biological traits.[21] Even Hitler, shortly before the end of the war, told Martin Bormann that "the Jews" were a "community of intellect" and a "spiritual race."[22] Jewishness transcended heredity and could also be passed on by other means. The natural sciences were thus not sufficient to tackle the Jewish question on their own.

The physicist and Nobel prize-winner Johannes Stark (1874–1957) was a leading advocate of a "German" or "Aryan" physics, distinct from "Jewish physics," and argued for an understanding and modification of the natural sciences based on racist principles. In a contribution to the SS paper *Das schwarze Korps*, Stark referred to a "primitive kind of anti-Semitism" that limited itself to fighting "the Jews *per se.*" He went on in the article to denounce the physicist Werner Heisenberg as "Jewish" for defending Albert Einstein.[23] The triumph of "racial anti-Semitism," he argued, had been no more than a "partial victory": "We must also destroy the Jewish mind, which today can flourish more serenely than ever as long as its hosts can show the most impeccable proof of Aryan ancestry." The term used to characterize those with a "Jewish mind" but no Jewish ancestry was "white Jews." The racialization of natural science was only possible by resorting to the notion of a "Jewish spirit."[24]

The programmatic opening essay in the journal *Archiv für Judenfragen*, published by the Propaganda Ministry in 1943, insisted on the special importance of the humanities in the struggle against Judaism. On their own, the "exact sciences" were incapable of "a root-and-branch solution to the Jewish problem at all levels, politically, ideologically, and intellectually" and required "expanding, supplementing, and deepening":

> If, for example, one considers the Jewish question solely from the standpoint of race, one immediately runs the risk of arbitrarily narrowing and trivializing the problem with no chance of a solution; undoubtedly essential aspects would not be included, for Judaism and Jewry are not only the Jewish people or the Jewish race, but everything that is Jewish and in any way connected with Jewishness.[25]

Concern was also expressed in the RSHA's enemy research program about the relationship between the humanities and race doctrine. The study of race, together with psychology and geography, was seen as a link between the natural sciences and the humanities. It was emphasized that the prevailing "natural science model" of race was not easily accessible to historians or other scholars and that the necessary integration of racial science and historiography had not yet been achieved: "There is something painful about historians measuring skulls, making comparisons between head and limb sizes and then wanting to draw historical conclusions from them."[26] If the study of race were oriented toward the humanities, the "desired collaboration between racial science and history" might be more easily accomplished. The expressed aim was the construction of both a theory and a classification system of all the forms and types of races that had ever existed.

As early as the 1920s, physical anthropology had begun to embrace the methods and theories of the humanities and to develop what would later be racial science by including mental characteristics and social behavior in its research. During the Third Reich, the most prominent representatives of the discipline regularly attended *Judenforschung* meetings and published in *Judenforschung* journals, particularly in the Reichsinstitute's yearbook, *Forschungen zur Judenfrage* (Studies on the Jewish Question). Those outside the disciplines of racial science and anthropology tended to avoid the concept of race because of its biologistic connotations and used the term "Jewish mind" instead. Racial scientists, on the other hand, defined race as a "totality of fixed hereditary characteristics of a physical and mental-spiritual kind." Mental characteristics were thus included among the alleged physical traits of the Jews.[27]

The physician Eugen Fischer (1874–1967) became the first director of the Kaiser-Wilhelm-Institut für Anthropologie, menschliche Erblehre und Eugenik (Kaiser Wilhelm Institute for Anthropology, Human Heredity

and Eugenics) in 1927. Speaking at the annual conference of the Munich
anti-Jewish research department of the Reichsinstitut, Fischer emphasized
that, from a European standpoint, the Jews were "foreign in kind, and
different in body and, above all, in soul."[28] At the same time, even the
racial scientists posited that Jewishness was dependent not only on descent and heredity but also on environmental influences. Consequently,
people who were not racially Jewish could become Jewish: "Jewish identity is certainly not only conditioned by heredity; to some extent it is the
consequence of living in a Jewish milieu. Even non-Jews who mix frequently with Jews acquire a Jewish manner of thinking and behaving."[29]

In 1941, Fritz Lenz (1887–1976), a student of Fischer's who headed
the eugenics department at the Kaiser-Wilhelm-Institut, offered a
defense of Nazi legislation defining Jews by descent rather than physical
characteristics:

It is more important to judge someone by his descent than by his bodily features.
A blond Jew is still a Jew. Indeed, there are Jews who have most of the outward
features of the Nordic race and yet are essentially Jewish. The Nazi law, therefore,
is right to define a Jew by descent rather than physical racial characteristics.[30]

Rejecting an exclusive focus on physical features and anthropological
measurements in racial science, Lenz shifted the center of attention
to mental qualities, which he described as "by far the most difficult to
document." Making reference to the prominent race theorist Hans F. K.
Günther, he proposed a stronger historical component in research on the
races: namely, a comprehensive history of populations that would look at
settlement, migrations, and interbreeding along with living conditions
and their "selection effects."[31]

The dilemma faced by racial biology is most clearly evident in an
article by the physician and geneticist Otmar Freiherr von Verschuer
(1896–1969), Lenz's student and Fischer's successor as director of the
Kaiser-Wilhelm-Institut. After assembling a list of supposedly typical
Jewish physical characteristics, he nevertheless concluded that, given the
possible variations and combinations, there were indeed Jews "who could
not be recognized as such from their outward appearance." But it was "of
little importance whether prominent individuals of mental Jewry [*des
geistigen Judentums*] could be recognized as Jewish from their purely
physical features." Jewry, he argued, was much more unified by its
"spiritual qualities and character traits," which were derived from hereditary dispositions. In this way, the biological argument could be maintained even when the classification methods of the natural sciences were

of little value. Verschuer avoided an exact description of purportedly typical Jewish mental characteristics by referring to research on "outstanding representatives of Jewry."[32] Although the natural sciences provided the basis for a racist view of Judaism, they could not provide a method to determine an individual's race. As in the case of genealogy, they needed the help of the humanities.

Verschuer used the annual meetings of the anti-Jewish research department of the Reichsinstitut as a platform to argue for interdisciplinary collaboration. Touching on an invitation from Wilhelm Grau to participate in one of the annual meetings, he set out in a letter to Eugen Fischer the advantages and disadvantages of collaborating with *Judenforschung*:

It is very important who will address the subject on this occasion. The lectures are widely noticed and highly regarded, and they provide an opportunity to consider these matters in a calmer manner. This opportunity seems to justify a contribution. On the other hand, I believe that we have no need to fear that such a lecture will diminish our scientific standing. International Jewry knows very well what side we are on in any case; as far as that is concerned, it does not matter whether we do or do not take part in such a conference. It is nevertheless important that our racial policy – with regard to the Jewish question as well – acquires an objective, scientific backing that is also acknowledged in wider circles.[33]

Despite the obvious shortcomings of a scientific perspective for the practical application of Nazi racial policy, Verschuer's remarks to his friend and colleague still demonstrate a belief in the superiority of the natural sciences to the humanities and social sciences. It was precisely this superiority that he was willing to mobilize in support of the anti-Jewish policies of the Nazi regime.

LEGITIMIZING RACISM AND PERSECUTION

The humanities were by no means considered outdated or superfluous in the racist discourses of the Nazi era. They were considered to be on an equal footing with the biomedical sciences. Indeed, it was a historical perspective in particular that was needed to make up for the weaknesses and limitations of biomedical research. The perspective of those working in the humanities is evident in a review of a work by Wilhelm Grau that expressed the hope "that through G[rau]'s work the idea of race, which hitherto has enjoyed only a superficial link with historical scholarship, could become an integral part of it."[34] Grau was considered a pioneer of the new German, anti-Semitic approach to Jewish history. In his Munich dissertation, completed in February 1933, he described the expulsion of the Regensburg Jewish community at the beginning of the sixteenth century as paradigmatic of anti-Semitism in the late Middle Ages. Grau later explained the reason for his choice of subject: "I wanted to investigate this example of the timeless hostility towards the Jews thoroughly because the outlawing of anti-Semitism seemed to me a historical impossibility."[35] Reacting to critics who declared that his work was anti-Semitic, Grau sought in his introduction to the revised 1939 edition of his dissertation to underline its objectivity and scholarly character:

The so-called tendency of my book *Antisemitismus im späten Mittelalter* [Anti-Semitism in the late Middle Ages] is in reality no tendency of mine or of the present day but a spiritual trend built into the historical object itself. I have tried to write history as it actually was, not as it should have been. This history was anti-Jewish, and should not be presented as anything other than anti-Jewish, if we are to keep to the historical truth. It was a matter of grasping and understanding late mediaeval anti-Semitism historically and not of condemning it.[36]

This argument rejects the possibility that historians can establish critical distance from their subjects. The historical fact of anti-Semitism has here become its justification. At the same time, it was obviously still necessary and opportune in 1939 to reply to the charge of anti-Semitism by claiming that scholarly methods had been applied rather than by arguing that anti-Semitism was consistent with scholarly and scientific knowledge.

Grau, by implicitly aligning himself with the perspective of medieval anti-Semites, retroactively transforms the perpetrators into victims and vice versa. He relies, in part, on the methodology of *Volksgeschichte.* Grau thereby answers his own demand, made elsewhere, that a historian who wants to tell the truth cannot one-sidedly describe the suffering of the Jews.[37] For him, it was more important to clarify and understand the motives of the anti-Semites than the consequences of their anti-Semitism. The basically religious character of the medieval world, he argued, obscured the racial differences: "The instinct of blood was still buried within the wings of religion."[38] Nevertheless, the principle of race, though theoretically unknown, was already instinctively understood.[39] As in other examples of *Judenforschung,* an attempt was made here to construct a reference point for Nazi policies that pre-dated the Enlightenment. The reference to the Middle Ages and the study of medieval anti-Semitism made it possible to refute the characterization of National Socialism as a "reversion to the Middle Ages." As Grau explained,

If, for example, the National Socialist attempt to solve the Jewish question is branded abroad as a reversion to the Middle Ages, this is a view that corresponds to the Jewish-liberal conception of history that misconstrues the structure both of the new order coming into being as well as that of the Middle Ages. Medieval anti-Semitism is reduced to a narrative of violence and barbarism. However, the historical facts tell a different story.[40]

For Grau and the other anti-Jewish scholars, the political sin of earlier historical writing lay in its lack of attention to the Jewish question. This was the reason why a large number of people in Germany and abroad had found themselves quite unprepared for the "natural solution of the Jewish question according to the principle of clean-cut separation [*reinliche Scheidung*]."[41] The correct historical consciousness would make it unnecessary for "each generation to solve its Jewish problem anew."[42] The narration of the history of anti-Semitism thus became a legitimization for the anti-Jewish policies of National Socialism. This ideologically informed retrospective gaze necessarily ended in a circular argument:

Nothing can teach the world the universal validity of Germany's legislation regarding the Jews [*Judengesetzgebung*] better than a historical view of the Jewish problem. If we make this political statement from the position of scholarship, we do so because the political beliefs of the German people today are confirmed and attested by history itself.[43]

Implicitly, the task of the new *Judenforschung* is here made clear. Claiming that it was objective and that it avoided one-sided condemnation, *Judenforschung* provided justification for both historical and contemporary anti-Semitism.

Historical arguments not only made it possible to legitimize current policies; they also made it possible to identify and denounce "white Jews" in history. In his *Habilitation* thesis on Wilhelm von Humboldt and "the problem of the Jew," Grau discussed how the non-Jewish Prussian scholar and statesman of the Enlightenment "had fallen victim to Jewishness" and how his character had been corrupted by "Jewish ideas."[44] Grau presented a collection of testimonies describing Humboldt's relations with Jews without explaining what he meant by "Jewish ideas." Enlightenment values, individualism, and Judaism all flowed together as one and were scarcely distinguished one from the other conceptually. Although his doctoral dissertation on Regensburg was widely praised, Grau's Humboldt book was heavily criticized by the examiners at the University of Munich, and Grau earned his *Habilitation* by the skin of his teeth.

In most anti-Semitic publications and documents of the Nazi era, no clearly defined or delineated concepts of race or Jewishness are to be found. In a 1981 lecture that surveyed German historiography of the Third Reich, Günther Franz (1902–1992) claimed that Nazi *Juden-forschung* never succeeded in linking racial science and historiography or in developing a racial approach to history.[45] Franz had belonged to the scholarly elite of the Third Reich, serving not only as a professor at Strasburg University but also as a member of the security service of the SS that was involved in the enemy research program of the RSHA. In his 1943 article "Geschichte und Rasse. Bemerkungen zur deutschen Geschichte in der Zeit der Glaubenskämpfe," he argued that, despite methodological and epistemological problems, there were indeed possibilities for a racially oriented view of history.[46] He distinguished between two approaches. The first focused on historical events' effects on the development of races (*Rassegeschichte*). The second dealt with the more difficult question of how far and in what ways race contributed to historical events. One could start, rather arbitrarily, from a predetermined set of individual "racial types," Franz suggested, and ask how these features were manifested in history, or begin empirically with historical facts and ask how they were racially characteristic *(artgemäß)*. In 1981, Franz said this 1943 article had written off the concept of race as meaningless for historical scholarship.

Anti-Jewish scholarship was much less concerned with providing a scholarly or scientific basis for anti-Semitism than with historicizing the Jewish question. This is clear from the subjects examined in Nazi Jewish Studies, which included attempts over the course of history to "solve" the Jewish question, the history of the Jewish question in other countries, and the history of anti-Semitism. Even the Nazi regime's anti-Jewish policies became a research topic. The fourth and fifth editions of Grau's textbook *Die Judenfrage in der deutschen Geschichte* (The Jewish question in German History) ended with a review of the current status of the Jewish question at the time. It noted the founding of Rosenberg's Institut zur Erforschung der Judenfrage and cited the Nuremburg Laws of 1935. History became the leading discipline in the field of Nazi *Judenforschung* because, with the "final solution" on the agenda, a historicization of the Jewish question seemed both possible and necessary. Studies of the history of anti-Semitism could serve Nazi anti-Jewish policies by retroactively constructing a tradition. Analyzing past attempts to solve the Jewish question, in particular the failure of such attempts, could be useful to the Nazi project by constructing supposedly aporetic historical situations that justified ever more radical strategies as a way out of them. The genocide itself constituted the most obvious blind spot of Nazi anti-Jewish scholarship. Although it was frequently present implicitly, it was for the most part never directly addressed or mentioned, apart from a few significant exceptions in which it was publicly named as the only way out of the historically constructed aporias.[47]

LEGITIMIZING MASS MURDER

In the course of implementing anti-Jewish policies in the countries that they occupied, the Germans were confronted with several population groups that either laid claim to special status or whose status was not altogether clear. Given the limited powers of racial biology to categorize racial types, it was entirely logical that, when there were doubts about the racial classification of a particular group, the German authorities would appeal to scholars rather than to race scientists. In such cases, the Foreign Office used its excellent contacts in the *Judenforschung* institutes and consulted the historians, theologians, and genealogists associated with them.

To protect itself, for instance, the Sephardi community in France declared that its members, in contrast to Ashkenazi Jews, were not racially Jewish; they were, rather, "Aryo-Latins of [the] Mosaic faith."[48] Grau dismissed this claim as "utterly untenable" and denounced it as "a remarkable Jewish attempt ... to save the Sephardis from the impending demise of the whole of European Jewry." In his view, "Special treatment for Sephardis would be neither racially acceptable nor historically justifiable and certainly not politically permissible." He noted, moreover, that all the important Jewish historians counted Sephardi history as part of Jewish history.[49] In the occupied Netherlands, the status of Sephardis, known there as "Portuguese Jews," was likewise unclear. Wilfried Euler (1908–1995) of the Reichsinstitut cited the decrees expelling the Jews from Spain (1492) and Portugal (1497) and the Spanish Inquisition's persecution of baptized Jews as arguments against allowing an exception to be made in the case of the Dutch Sephardis.[50] Ultimately, the Sephardis in France and the Netherlands, along with the much larger Sephardi communities in Southeastern Europe, were targeted for extermination by the Nazis without exception.[51]

There was also an attempt to secure exceptional status for so-called Iranians of the Mosaic faith in France. The Iranian consul in Paris declared that "by blood they were not Jews, but of non-Jewish Iranian descent." The fate of this group was linked to that of "Mosaic Georgians and Afghans."[52] Scholars' opinions on these cases differed widely.

The Institut zur Erforschung der Judenfrage found itself unable to give a definitive answer and placed the issue on its research agenda, but it also recommended vigilance against attempts at "Jewish camouflage."[53] Euler proposed that "Caucasian and Georgian adherents of the Mosaic faith" should receive "exceptional treatment." He remained indifferent toward "Persian and Afghan adherents of the Mosaic faith" but did not explicitly ask that they be exempt from persecution. His argument for separating Caucasian Jews from the others was that they were "an agricultural, warlike ... mountain people without an apparent mercantile spirit" and that "Czarist Russia had come to know them as worthy foes and had granted them, unlike the Russian Jews, full civil rights after the conquest of the Caucasus." He also described their anthropological features as "by no means specifically Jewish."[54]

The Institut für Grenz- und Auslandsstudien (Institute for the Study of Border and Foreign Lands) in Berlin, founded and headed by *völkisch* theorist Max Hildebert Boehm (1891–1968), questioned Euler's characterization of the Caucasian Jews as an agricultural and warlike mountain people. It saw them rather as "proper Jews" because they had secured for themselves an influential economic position through trade, because they had "Near Eastern/Oriental" racial characteristics, and because they followed the Talmud.[55] Similarly, Adolf Eichmann's Section IVB4 of the RSHA considered the claim that the members of the French Sephardi community were "Iranians of the Mosaic faith" as "one of the usual ploys used by the Jews to disguise and camouflage themselves." Eichmann pointed out that there had been a Jewish question ever since the heyday of the Persian kingdom. That there had been an improvement in the situation since the nineteenth century and the Jews had acquired equality under the law in the 1920s did not, in his view, constitute a counter-argument because those developments were nothing more than the result of an "intervention by the Alliance Israélite and Russian-Jewish finance capital."[56]

The Protestant theologian Gerhard Kittel (1888–1948) also regarded the arguments supporting an exemption for the Paris "Iranians of the Mosaic faith" as "quite untenable historically," but he did make an exception for the Caucasian Jews, who, he said, needed "separate treatment." His position on the Persian Jews was the same as Eichmann's; he pointed out that their acquiring equal status in 1920–1921 should not be allowed to obscure the "dislike for the Jews" that had been hegemonic in earlier times. In support of the Caucasian Jews, he noted that they had never been the object of anti-Jewish hostility.[57] Walter Gross

(1904–1945), head of the Nazi party's Rassenpolitisches Amt (Racial-Political Office) and a trained physician, attacked Euler's contention that Persian Jews lacked "specific Jewish characteristics" and opposed allowing them "special treatment" (*Sonderbehandlung*). He also rejected Kittel's lenient assessment of the "Afghan Jews," insisting that their adaptation to their environment could not be used as an argument against seeing them as Jews. "The Jews of Germany," he pointed out, "had in part also been very successful in adapting themselves to German ways." As far as the racial status of the "mountain Jews" was concerned, Gross thought clarification was needed and demanded "detailed examinations on the spot." He proposed reversing the usual burden of proof and making a commitment to Judaism decisive: "If we wish to solve the Jewish question, our point of departure must be that those who affirm their adherence to Judaism must also be treated as Jews unless their non-Jewish origin can be proven by documentary evidence."[58]

Biological, historical, and religious arguments were thus closely inter-related. In ambiguous cases like that of the "mountain Jews" or, to cite another example, of so-called first-degree half-breeds (*Mischlinge 1. Grades*), the "mental" dimension was seen as the most decisive. If the individual in question had belonged to the Jewish religious community as of a certain date or had joined it after that date, or if he/she had married a Jew, he/she was to be considered Jewish under the Nuremberg Laws.

These Nazi anti-Jewish scholars were playing with groups of people – Persian/Iranian, Afghan, Caucasian, and Georgian Jews – whom they could only vaguely define and barely distinguish from each other. Lacking anthropological data and relying solely on printed sources, they con-cocted findings that determined who would fall victim to the policy of extermination. In the end, the Foreign Office came to the conclusion that the French "Iranians of the Mosaic faith" would not be exempted from the "general Jewish measures" (*allgemeine Judenmaßnahmen*).[59] The only group to escape persecution was the Djuguts – Persian Jews who had converted to Islam under duress in the nineteenth century and had not been able to adhere openly to Judaism until after their migration to France.[60]

Confronted with great heterogeneity – ethnic, religious, and linguistic – in Central Asia, the Caucasus, and Crimea, the German occupiers needed clear criteria for racial classification to deal with the various Jewish communities in those regions. They had great difficulty, for example, in trying to classify the Karaits, a Jewish sect concentrated in Crimea that rejected the Talmud. When the Nuremberg Laws were enacted, the forerunner of the Reich Kinship Office decided that the community as a whole would be considered non-Jewish and its members would be classified racially, by descent, only on an individual basis. The status of the Karaites came up for discussion again when they were encountered in France and in the Soviet Union.[61] The Protestant theologian and Orientalist Karl Georg Kuhn (1906–1976) remarked after the war that, on commission from the Nazi Party's Racial Policy Office (Rassenpolitische Amt), he had written a report on the Karaites in 1942 and that he had classified them as Tatars, not Jews.[62]

Likewise, the Reich Ministry for the Occupied Eastern Territories (Reichsministerium für die besetzten Ostgebiete) – which had the final say on racial classification in the East – regarded the Karaites as "members of the Jewish religious community" but classed them as a "non-Jewish and Turko-Tatar group." The Karaites' military traditions and agricultural occupations were cited as evidence in favor of their classification as non-Jews. Both of these factors, a ministry official wrote, stood "in contrast to the inclination of the Jews" and their "thoughts and values." Moreover, the Karaites showed none of the "tendency towards the commercial and parasitic that is to be found in the Jews." Therefore they should not be treated as Jews.[63] Political arguments also played a part in this decision. The Germans did not want to disturb the consistently anti-Jewish orientation of the "racially similar" Turkic peoples, even if the "Mosaic faith" was undesirable.[64] Thus, the Karaites, who undoubtedly belonged to the Jewish faith but were deemed to be not of Jewish origin, escaped the "Final Solution." But the Krimchaks, deemed Jewish by blood, were systematically annihilated during the occupation of Crimea.

History was here used as an argument. According to Nazi racial policy, past discrimination and persecution were criteria for classifying a group as Jewish. Persecution in the past, in other words, was the best argument for continuing persecution in the present. The practice of persecution leads to scholarly legitimization rather than the other way around. National Socialist anti-Semitism necessarily required historiographic support. The concept of race, oscillating between spirit and nature, ended in a circular historical argument that perpetuated persecution.

SCHOLARSHIP AND CRIME

Once historians had embraced the concept of race and natural scientists had appropriated the historical method, the way was clear for an ambitious interdisciplinary project that was not to be fully realized during the short existence of the Nazi regime. It marked the intersection of scholarship, racial ideology, and Nazi Jewish policy. As early as 1937, Verschuer chose to make interdisciplinary cooperation a central theme of his lecture at the annual meeting of the anti-Jewish research department of the Reichsinstitut. "What can the historian, the genealogist, and the statistician contribute to research on the biological problem of the Jewish question?" he asked. Verschuer focused, not without reason, on the problem of the "mixing between Jews and non-Jews." This was, he said, not only a "still very poorly researched field within the framework of the biological problem of the Jewish question" but also of vital importance for a society based on racial principles and the concept of "clean-cut separation." This unresolved problem undermined the systematic categorization of Jews and non-Jews, which in turn hobbled the public agencies responsible for implementing National Socialist policies. What was needed, Verschuer went on, was a "detailed analysis of the physical and psychological characteristics of the parents from different racial backgrounds and the children produced by their mixed marriages, as well as their potential future offspring." For Verschuer, the compilation of a comprehensive database was crucial. That was not a task for biologists alone, however: psychologists, historians and genealogists had to be involved as well. "It is not just a question of collecting the documentary evidence that has accumulated in the various archives, but of evaluating it historically and critically."[65]

Biologists could not solve the Jewish question even if it was defined, as it was by Verschuer, as an explicitly biological problem. They had to embrace the historical methodology of the humanities and design an interdisciplinary project. Verschuer's repeated description of the Jewish question as a "biological problem" suggests that he felt the need to assert his claim to expertise in a politically important field that he could not claim as his own. He later took advantage of the possibilities arising from the policy of systematic mass murder to acquire – courtesy of his former student and assistant Josef Mengele – human specimens for his own research. His goal was to design a reliable scientific test to determine race based on biochemical properties – a test that would free racial biology from having to collaborate with the humanities and social sciences.[66]

But if the humanities and social sciences seemed to compensate for the impossibility of conclusively determining "Jewishness" on physiological grounds, scholars in *Judenforschung* found themselves falling back on biological concepts when their own research fell short of the dictates of Nazi ideology. A reference system thus developed in which theories and concepts, despite their obvious inadequacies, were corroborated back and forth across disciplinary borders, leaving blind spots undetected.[67]

Vague concepts such as "Jewish spirit" and "white Jews" might well have sufficed to maintain the dynamic of the Nazis' policies of persecution and extermination, which demanded more and more victims, in the long run. Ever greater numbers of individuals and groups might well have been defined as Jewish and treated as enemies. With the concept of "Judaization" (*Verjudung*), which brought together the biological and the psychological, "the Jew" was finally transformed into "the inner Jew," a category that made it possible to identify a Jewish Other at any given moment. Nazi ideology could not dispense with "the Jews" as an enemy. For that reason, the defining features had to be simultaneously clear (Jewish) and flexible (spirit).

Anti-Semitism and anti-Jewish policies required no further justification from the perspective of the Nazi anti-Jewish scholars. They themselves stressed the primacy of the political and acknowledged that it was not dependent on scholarship. On this, the scholars and scientists were agreed. Their findings could not call into question the basis or the general direction of Nazi racial policy. They could, however, be of assistance to the regime through their work and thereby not only provide scholarly legitimization to official policies but also demonstrate the usefulness of their own work. The project of Nazi *Judenforschung* in the end became less a matter of transforming anti-Semitism into a science than one of pursuing scholarship from a consistently anti-Semitic perspective. Its task was to deliver confirmation and evidence of racial difference.

Judenforschung scholars participated in Nazi crimes in a variety of ways and on several levels. They profited from racial policies that gave them the opportunity to commandeer the entire field of Jewish Studies, including the plundering of libraries, archives, and cultural institutions across Europe. Nazi ideology and Nazi rule, with their focus on race and Jews, spurred a surge of interest in this discipline, making it a scholarly desideratum. Their scholarship legitimized discrimination, persecution, and ultimately mass murder. And, as advisers, they played a direct part in implementing such policies.

Although the direct links between scholarship and genocide have been demonstrated, not least in the case of Nazi *Judenforschung*, there nonetheless remains a curious lack of understanding of the relationship between scholarship, ideology, and politics. Scholarship's complicity with the crimes of Nazism goes beyond its direct and documented participation in specific measures. It extends into the affinity between scholarly discourse and the discourse of Nazi ideology and policy. Were it not for the victims and the gravity of the consequences, the blatant inconsistencies and gross absurdities that mark Nazi *Judenforschung* – and indeed the entire racist and anti-Semitic project of the Third Reich – might occasion an ironic narrative of mad scientists and mindless scholars. For the perpetrators, however, the Nazi *Weltanschauung* was always convincing and coherent enough to provide the basis for plunder, expulsion, persecution, and murder.

Notes

1 For an overview of anti-Jewish scholarship in the Third Reich, see the classic study by Max Weinreich, *Hitler's Professors: The Part of Scholarship in Germany's Crimes against the Jewish People* (New Haven, 1999 [1946]), and the recent study by Alan Steinweis, *Studying the Jew: Scholarly Antisemitism in Nazi Germany* (Cambridge, MA, 2006). Neither author made systematic use of archival material. For an account based on extensive archival research, see Dirk Rupnow, *Judenforschung im Dritten Reich. Wissenschaft zwischen Politik, Propaganda und Ideologie* (Baden-Baden, 2011). On the complex history of the debates on Nazi *Judenforschung* before and after 1945, see Dirk Rupnow, "Antijüdische Wissenschaft im 'Dritten Reich'. Wege, Probleme und Perspektiven der Forschung," *Simon Dubnow Institute Yearbook* 5 (2006), 539–98. That issue of the *Simon Dubnow Institute Yearbook* includes several other essays on Nazi *Judenforschung*.

2 For an overview, see Winfried Schulze and Otto Gerhard Oexle (eds.), *Deutsche Historiker im Nationalsozialismus* (Frankfurt, 1999). See also Peter Schöttler (ed.), *Geschichtsschreibung als Legitimationswissenschaft 1918–1945* (Frankfurt/Main, 1997).

3 The term *Erforschung der Judenfrage* was more common, but *Judenforschung* was also widely used. See the report on the opening of the Frankfurt *Institut zur Erforschung der Judenfrage*, "Zum ersten Mal in der Geschichte. Judenforschung ohne Juden," *Illustrierter Beobachter*, April 30, 1942. The term *Judenforschung* is difficult to translate: it literally means "research on *Jews*." It needs to be distinguished from *Wissenschaft des Judentums*, the term used for research on Jewish history and culture. That field, largely the preserve of Jewish scholars, closely corresponds to what today is known as Jewish Studies.

4 On *Ostforschung*, see Ingo Haar, "'Ostforschung' und 'Lebensraum'-Politik im Nationalsozialismus," in Doris Kaufmann (ed.), *Geschichte der Kaiser-Wilhelm-Gesellschaft im Nationalsozialismus. Bestandsaufnahme und Perspektiven der Forschung* (Göttingen, 2000), vol. 2, 437–67, here 451.

5 On these institutions, see Rupnow, *Judenforschung im Dritten Reich*, 63–153.

6 Humboldt-Universität zu Berlin, Universitätsarchiv (hereafter UA) Phil. Fak. 1453; Universität Wien, UA, Rektorat 1473–1939/40 and Phil. Fak. 734–1941/42; Eberhard-Karls-Universität, UA, 126a/284; letter from Werner von Koeppen to Klaus Schickert, Oct. 31, 1944: BAB, NS 8/266.

7 Memorandum headed "Arbeitsplan VII B 1 b – Judentum" [late 1941 or early 1942]: BAB, R58/7400, 90–6; text reprinted in Jürgen Matthäus, "'Weltanschauliche Forschung und Auswertung.' Aus den Akten des Amtes VII im

Reichssicherheitshauptamt," *Jahrbuch für Antisemitismusforchung* 5 (1996), 287–330; document 4, 301–7, here 301.

8 Important in this respect is Carl Schmitt's formula of a "concrete order" that connects legal normativity with ethnic (*völkisch*) and ideological commitments. See Carl Schmitt, *Über die drei Arten des rechtswissenschaftlichen Denkens* [1934] (Berlin, 1993).

9 The concept of "fighting scholarship" was coined by Walter Frank before the war and was modeled on the ideas of Maurice Barres and Charles Maurras. See Walter Frank, *Nationalismus und Demokratie im Frankreich der dritten Republik (1871 bis 1918)* (Hamburg, 1933). Frank took Heinrich von Treitschke as the exemplar of a specifically German ideal of education and learning (*Bildung*); see Walter Frank, *Kämpfende Wissenschaft. Mit einer Vor-Rede des Reichsjugendführers Baldur von Schirach* (Hamburg, 1934).

10 Wilhelm Grau, "Die Geschichte der Judenfrage und ihre Erforschung," *Blätter für deutsche Landesgeschichte* 83(3) (1937), 163–73, here 167.

11 Volkmar Eichstadt, "Die Judenfrage in den deutschen Bibliotheken," *Forschungen zur Judenfrage* 6 (1941), 253–64, here 264.

12 "Nazis rewrite Jewish history," *Jewish Chronicle*, May 8, 1942.

13 Ibid.

14 Dan Diner, Negative Symbiose – Deutsche und Juden nach Auschwitz, in Dan Diner (ed.), *Ist der Nationalsozialismus Geschichte? Zu Historisierung und Historikerstreit* (Frankfurt a.M. 1987), 185–97.

15 For a detailed discussion, see Dirk Rupnow, *Vernichten und Erinnern. Spuren nationalsozialistischer Gedächtnispolitik* (Göttingen, 2005); Dirk Rupnow, "'Arisierung' jüdischer Geschichte. Zur nationalsozialistischen 'Judenforschung,'" *Leipziger Beitrage zur jüdischen Geschichte und Kultur* 2 (2004), 349–67. See also Dirk Rupnow, "'Ihr müßt sein, auch wenn ihr nicht mehr seid.' The Jewish Central Museum in Prague and historical memory in the Third Reich," *Holocaust and Genocide Studies* 16 (2002), 23–53.

16 On the concept of the "racial state," see Michael Burleigh and Wolfgang Wippermann, *The Racial State: Germany 1933–1945* (Cambridge, 1991). On the concept of "racialization," see Robert Miles, *Rassismus. Eine Einführung in die Geschichte und Theorie eines Begriffs*, trans. Michael Haupt (Hamburg, 1991), 99–103. For an analysis of the Nazi system's tendency to "medicalize" or "biologize" social problems, see Robert N. Proctor, *Racial Hygiene: Medicine under the Nazis* (Cambridge, MA, 2002), 287.

17 On the development of anthropology, human genetics, and racial science in Germany, see Robert N. Proctor, "From 'anthropology' to 'Rassenkunde' in the German anthropological tradition" in George W. Stocking (ed.), *Bones, Bodies, Behaviour: Essays on Biological Anthropology* (Madison, 1988), 138–79.

18 See Cecil Roth, "Marranos and racial antisemitism: a study in parallels," *Jewish Social Studies* 2 (1940), 239–48.

19 On the activities of the *Reichssippenamt*, see Georg Lilienthal, "Arier oder Jude? Die Geschichte des erb- und rassenkundlichen Abstammungsgutachtens" in Peter Propping and Heinz Schott (eds.), *Wissenschaft auf Irrwegen. Biologisierung-Rassenhygiene-Eugenik* (Bonn, 1992), 66–84; Diana Schulle, *Das Reichssippenamt. Eine Institution nationalsozialistischer Rassenpolitik*

(Berlin, 2001); Thomas Pegelow, "Determining people of 'German blood,' 'Jews' and *'Mischlinge'*: The Reich Kinship Office and the competing discourses and powers of Nazism, 1941–1943," *Contemporary European History* 15 (2006), 43–65. For a contemporary description, see Christian Ulrich Freiherr von Ulmenstein, *Der Abstammungsnachweis* (Berlin, 1941).

20 Eric Voegelin had already referred to this in *Rasse und Staat* (Tubingen, 1933), 13. According to Voegelin, the work of anthropologists did not follow scientific methodology but rather adhered to the "conventional methodology of the humanities": "creating types based on historical evidence."

21 See, for example, Houston Stewart Chamberlain, *Die Grundlagen des Neunzehnten Jahrhunderts* (Munich 1899), 457–8, which refers to "the inner Jew" and the "Jewish mind"; and Otto Weininger, *Geschlecht und Charakter. Eine prinzipielle Untersuchung* (Vienna, 1903), 406, 409, 418, which describes Jewishness as a "mental propensity," a "spiritual constitution," and a "platonic idea."

22 Hugh Trevor-Roper (ed.), *Hitlers Politisches Testament. Die Bormann-Diktate vom Februar und April 1945* (Hamburg, 1981), 68–9 (February 3, 1945).

23 Johannes Stark, "'Weiße Juden' in der Wissenschaft," *Das schwarze Korps,* July 15, 1937. On "German" and "Aryan" physics, see Alan D. Beyerchen, *Wissenschaftler unter Hitler. Physiker im Dritten Reich* (Cologne, 1980).

24 This notion was already current in the Third Reich. See Bruno Thüring, "Albert Einsteins Umsturzversuch der Physik und seine inneren Möglichkeiten und Ursachen," *Forschungen zur Judenfrage* 4 (1940), 134–62. Thüring's subject was the difficulty of treating the influence of "the Jewish spirit on the development of the exact sciences" because they supposedly operated according to natural laws that left no room for "purely human accidents, contingencies and irregularities" (134). Thüring also emphasized that Einstein was "not only a Jew in the biological sense" but also "in the whole of his consciousness" (141).

25 Friedrich Löffler, "Weg und Ziel," *Archiv für Judenfragen Schriften zur geistigen Überwindung des Judentums,* Gruppe A 1, no. 1 (1943), 1–5, here 1–2.

26 See Rudolf Levin, "Geisteswissenschaftliche Methodik der Gegnerforschung," in *Grundprobleme der Gegnerforschung. Vorträge, gehalten auf der Oktobertagung 1943 des RSiHA., Amt VII* (n.p. [1943?]), 1–27, here 6.

27 Eugen Fischer, "Rassenentstehung und älteste Rassengeschichte der Hebräer," *Forschungen zur Judenfrage* 3 (1938), 121–36, here 122. See also Otmar Freiherr von Verschuer, "Rassenbiologie der Juden," *Forschungen zur Judenfrage*, 3 (1938), 137–51, here 137, 148; Erwin Baur, Eugen Fischer, and Fritz Lenz, *Menschliche Erblehre und Rassenhygiene, Bd. 1: Menschliche Erblehre* (Munich, 1936 [1921]), 661, and especially the section by Lenz, "Die Erblichkeit der geistigen Eigenschaften," 746–7.

28 Fischer, "Rassenentstehung und älteste Rassengeschichte der Hebräer," 136.

29 Lenz, "Die Erblichkeit der geistigen Eigenschaften," in Baur, Fischer, and Lenz, *Menschliche Erblehre und Rassenhygiene,* 747.

30 Fritz Lenz, "Über Wege und Irrwege rassenkundlicher Untersuchungen," *Zeitschrift für Morphologie und Anthropologie, Erb- und Rassenbiologie* 39(3) (1941), 385–413, here 397.

31 See ibid., 397, 410–12.
32 See Verschuer, "Rassenbiologie der Juden," 143, 148.
33 Letter from Otmar Freiherr von Verschuer to Eugen Fischer, November 5, 1937: Archiv zur Geschichte der Max Planck-Gesellschaft, Berlin, Abt. III, Rep. 86A (NL Otmar Frhr. v. Verschuer), no. 3.
34 Hans Praesent, "Wilhelm Grau: Die Judenfrage als Aufgabe der neuen Geschichtsforschung, Schriften des RI, Hamburg 1935," *Literarisches Zentralblatt für Deutschland* 87(2) (January 31, 1936), 79; first published in *Deutsches Volkstum*, Sept. 1935.
35 Wilhlem Grau, memorandum headed "Zu dem Rundschreiben Walter Franks vom 12.3.1939', n.d.: Bundesarchiv Berlin (hereafter BAB), BDC/OPG-Z Grau, 5–18.
36 Wilhelm Grau, *Antisemitismus im späten Mittelalter. Das Ende der Regensburger Judengemeinde 1450–1519. Mit einem Geleitwort von Karl Alexander von Müller* (Munich, 1934; 2nd revised edn. Berlin, 1939), 12–13.
37 Wilhelm Grau, "Um den jüdischen Anteil am Bolschewismus," *Historische Zeitschrift* 153 (1936), 336–43, here 342.
38 Grau, *Antisemitismus im späten Mittalter*, 205.
39 See also Wilhelm Grau, "Albrecht Altdorfer und das Problem des Juden. Ein Kapitel über Kunst und Politik," *Wille und Macht* 6 (14) (1938), 31–4; Wilhelm Grau, Die Judenfrage als Aufgabe der neuen Geschichtsforschung, 2nd edn. (Hamburg, 1937 [1935]), 24; Wilhelm Grau, "Die geschichtlichen Lösungsversuche der Judenfrage," *Weltkampf* 1/2 (1941), 7–15, here 9–10; Wilhelm Grau, "Die Judenfrage in der deutschen Geschichte," *Vergangenheit und Gegenwart* 26 (1937), 193–209, 249–59.
40 Grau, *Die Judenfrage als Aufgabe der neuen Geschichtsforschung*, 20.
41 Ibid., 19.
42 Grau, "Die Geschichte der Judenfrage und ihre Erforschung," 170.
43 Wilhelm Grau, "Das Judenproblem geschichtlich gesehen," *Der Schlesische Erzieher* 6 (June 1936).
44 Wilhelm Grau, *Wilhelm von Humboldt und das Problem des Juden* (Hamburg, 1935), 56–7.
45 Günther Franz, "Das Geschichtsbild des Nationalsozialismus und die deutsche Geschichtswissenschaft" in Oswald Hauser (ed.), *Geschichte und Geschichtsbewußtsein. 19 Vorträge* (Göttingen, 1981), 91–111, here 107. In his lecture, Franz speaks openly of his involvement in Nazism, though he reduces it to an enthusiasm for *völkisch* ideas and the youth movement rather than for National Socialism itself. He does not mention his work for the RSHA. For a biography of Franz, see Wolfgang Behringer, "Bauern-Franz und Rassen-Günther. Die politische Geschichte des Agrarhistorikers Günther Franz (1902–1992)," in Schulze and Oexle, *Deutsche Historiker im Nationalsozialismus*, 114–41.
46 Günther Franz, "Geschichte und Rasse. Bemerkungen zur deutschen Geschichte in der Zeit der Glaubenskämpfe" in Kurt von Raumer and Theodor Schieder (eds.), *Stufen und Wandlungen der deutschen Einheit*, Festschrift Karl Alexander von Müller (Stuttgart, 1943), 75–96, here 75–8.
47 See Josef Sommerfeldt, "200 Jahre deutscher Abwehrkampf gegen das Ostjudentum," *Deutsche Post aus dem Osten*, 15(2/3) (1943), 8–13, here 12.

48 Letter from the Germany Embassy in Paris to the Foreign Office (Auswärtiges Amt, AA), January 23, 1942: US National Archives and Records Administration, College Park, MD (hereafter NARA), T120 4661; Association Culturelle Sepharadite de Paris, memorandum, January 13, 1941: NARA, T120 4661. The Nazi category "Aryo-Latins" refers to Aryans (non-Jews) of ancient (Latin-speaking) Rome and their (Romance-language-speaking) descendants.

49 Letter from Wilhelm Grau to the Foreign Office, February 7, 1942: NARA, T120 4661.

50 Wilfried Euler, memorandum headed "Zur Frage der genealogischen Einordnung der sogenannten portugiesischen Juden in den Niederlanden," Munich, January 12, 1943: NARA, T120 4666.

51 For an overview of anti-Jewish policies in France, see Juliane Wetzel, "Frankreich und Belgien" in Wolfgang Benz (ed.), *Dimensionen des Völkermords. Die Zahl der jüdischen Opfer des Nationalsozialismus* (Munich, 1996), 105–35. On the fate of Sephardi Jews in the Netherlands, see Jacob Presser, *The Destruction of the Dutch Jews* (New York, 1969), 305–11.

52 Letter from Werner Feldscher to the Foreign Office, Berlin, October 2, 1942: NARA, T120 4668.

53 Letter from Otto Paul to the Foreign Office, Frankfurt am Main, October 27, 1942: NARA, T120 4668.

54 Wilfried Euler, memorandum headed "Die Abstammung der persischen und afghanischen Angehörigen des mosaischen Bekenntnisses," Munich, October 23, 1942: NARA, T120 4668; Wilfried Euler, memorandum headed "Die Abstammung der kaukasischen und georgischen Angehörigen des mosaischen Bekenntnisses," Munich, October 23, 1942: NARA, T120 4668.

55 Letter from Gerhard Teich to Erhard Wetzel, Berlin, January 27, 1943: NARA, T120 4668.

56 Letter from Adolf Eichmann to Karl Klingenfuss, Berlin, December 8, 1942: NARA, T120 4668.

57 Gerhard Kittel, memorandum headed "Über die persischen, afghanischen und kaukasischen Juden," Vienna, February 16, 1943: NARA, T120 4668.

58 Letter from Walter Gross to the Minister of the Interior, Berlin, February 22, 1943: NARA, T120 4668.

59 Klaus von Thadden, memorandum, Berlin, June 2, 1943: NARA, T120 4668.

60 On the fate of some of the Jewish groups in France, see Warner Paul Green, "The fate of Oriental Jews in Vichy France," *Wiener Library Bulletin* 32 (49/50) (1979), 40–50; Asaf Atchildi, "Rescue of Jews of Bukharan, Iranian and Afghan origin in occupied France (1940–1944)," *Yad Vashem Studies* 6 (1967), 257–81.

61 On the fate of the Karaites, see Philip Friedman, "The Karaites under Nazi rule," in Max Beloff (ed.), *On the Track of Tyranny: Essays Presented by the Wiener Library to Leonard G. Montefiore O.B.E. on the Occasion of His Seventieth Birthday* (London, 1960), 97–123; Warren Paul Green, "The Nazi racial policy towards the Karaites," *Soviet Jewish Affairs* 8 (2) (1978), 36–44; Warren Paul Green, "The fate of the Crimean Jewish communities: Ashkenasim, Krimchaks and Karaites," *Jewish Social Studies* 46 (2) (1984), 169–76. On the fate of the Krimchaks, see Rudolf Loewenthal, "The extinction of the

Krimchaks in World War II," *American Slavic and East European Review* 10 (1951), 130–6. On the actions of Einsatzgruppe D, see Andrej Angrick, *Besatzungspolitik und Massenmord. Die Einsatzgruppe D in der südlichen Sowjetunion 1941–1943* (Hamburg, 2003), 326–31, 354.

62 Judgment against Dr Karl Georg Kuhn, Spruchkammer 7, Stuttgart-Feuerbach, Az. 37/9/15161, September 21, 1948: Ruprecht-Karls-Universitat Heidelberg, UA, PA 4714 (Universitäts-Kuratorium Göttingen, Theologische Fakultat, Prof. Dr Kuhn), 11–15; Karl Georg Kuhn, memorandum headed "Wissenschaftliche Entwicklung (mit Angabe aller Veröffentlichungen, Vorlesungen und Ansprachen)," Tübingen, June 17, 1945: Eberhard-Karls-Universitat Tübingen, UA, 162/32 Evangel.-Theol. Fak./Personalakte Karl Georg Kuhn, 21–3. The report itself could not be traced in the relevant archives. Kuhn was considered, along with Grau, to be "one of the few real experts in the field of Jewish studies" inside the Nazi system; in contrast to Grau, he was the lead candidate for the proposed chairs in *Judenforschung* at the universities of Berlin, Vienna, Frankfurt-on-Main, and Tübingen: letter from Walter Gross to the Minister of the Interior, Berlin, February 22, 1943: NARA, T120 4668.

63 Letter from Erhard Wetzel to the Party Chancellery, the Ministry of the Interior, the RSHA and the High Command of the German Army, Berlin, April 1943: BAB, R6/142.

64 Letter from SS-Obergruppenführer Gottlob Berger to SS-Standartenführer Rudolf Brandt, November 24, 1944: Bundesarchiv-Militararchiv, Freiburg, Film SF-01/3971, 886; letter from RFSS/SSHA-Amtsgr. D to Gottlob Berger, Berlin, November 3, 1944: Bundesarchiv-Militärarchiv, Freiburg, Film SF-01/3971, 887.

65 Otmar Freiherr von Verschuer, "Was kann der Historiker, der Genealoge und der Statistik zur Erforschung des biologischen Problems der Judenfrage beitragen?" *Forschungen zur Judenfrage* 2 (1937), 216–22, here 219–20.

66 See Achim Trunk, *Zweihundert Blutproben aus Auschwitz. Ein Forschungsvorhaben zwischen Anthropologie und Biochemie (1943–1945)* (Berlin, 2003), 37–43, 54–61.

67 See, for example, the argument of Karl Georg Kuhn, *Die Judenfrage als weltgeschichtliches Problem*, Schriften des Reichsinstituts für Geschichte des neuen Deutschlands (Hamburg, 1939): "The only explanation of the Jewish character that accounts perfectly for the peculiar role the Jews have played in world history is the explanation that derives from the racial features of the Jewish people, from *its hereditary, biological disposition*" (29: emphasis in the original).

PART IV

RACE AND SOCIETY

12

Volksgemeinschaft

A Controversy

Michael Wildt

Volksgemeinschaft is not a genuinely National Socialist concept. It appears as early as the nineteenth century – in the writings of the theologian Friedrich Schleiermacher, for instance. Ferdinand Tönnies used the concept, as did Theodor Herzl, albeit more in passing and in reference to persistent anti-Semitism, in his book *Der Judenstaat* (The Jewish state). The Jewish people, he writes, have tried conscientiously "to immerse ourselves in the surrounding *Volksgemeinschaft* and to preserve only the beliefs of our fathers. We are not permitted to do so."[1] Hans Ulrich Wehler concluded that the concept of *Volksgemeinschaft* gradually took the place of *Volksnation* during the German Empire.

The first boom in the use of the term *Volksgemeinschaft* occurred at the outset of World War I.[2] Kaiser Wilhelm II's decree in August 1914 that he no longer recognized parties but only Germans resonated widely because it expressed the desire of many Germans for equality and inclusion. The "Spirit of 1914" became a formula for a unified *Volksgemeinschaft* that looked beyond parties and classes, that saw in its unity and solidarity the strength to defy all enemies. The essays, books, brochures, speeches, and treatises by German intellectuals giving testament to their enthusiasm for war were legion. German Jews and Social Democrats in particular hoped their patriotic stance would finally gain them acceptance from the majority of society. Although social divisions soon reappeared during the war, *Volksgemeinschaft* remained a powerful formula that could repeatedly be linked to the myth of German unity in the summer of 1914.

Translated by Andrew F. Erwin.

In what follows, I want first to lay out different conceptions of *Volksgemeinschaft* – the political, social, and racist understandings of *Volksgemeinschaft* – and will then sketch recent historiographical debates about the concept. From this discussion, I will attempt to draw a few conclusions.

POLITICAL *VOLKSGEMEINSCHAFT*

Since the nineteenth century, the concept of *Gemeinschaft* (community) in Germany has stood in opposition to *Gesellschaft* (society) as an expression for the critique of the rapid transformation and pluralization of social relations against the background of industrialization, secularization, the growth of the market economy, and political liberalism. "The longing for *Gemeinschaft* springs always from the reaction to a negatively perceived present. Accordingly, the reality of such communal models is not to be sought in the past to which, as a rule, they refer, but in the present."[3] Calls for *Gemeinschaft* are always a response to *Gesellschaft* and are an authentic reflection of the search for security amid a sense of the crisis of modernity. No one wrote more on this subject than Ferdinand Tönnies, whose book *Gemeinschaft und Gesellschaft* (1887) struck an epochal nerve and determined discourse on society thereafter.[4]

The concept of *Gemeinschaft* encompassed both revolutionary and restorative hopes for the overcoming of alienation. This ambivalence – restoring what was regarded as lost as well as striving toward a better future social order – was inherent to the concept of *Gemeinschaft* from the beginning. We therefore misunderstand the concept if we take it to describe an existing social reality. It was not in the identification of an existing social condition but rather in promise, in mobilization, that the political power of invoking *Volksgemeinschaft* lay.

Wilhelm II's appeal nevertheless contained a significantly altered discursive element. By explicitly not drawing distinctions of class, birth, political belief, or religion and by accepting everyone on an equal footing into the national *Kriegsgemeinschaft* (war community), he constructed a relation between Kaiser and *Volk* that obscured the princes, whose confederation was still the constitutional basis of the German Empire. Thus, the *Volk*, which was to consist of "all Germans," took on an egalitarian shading that, although not able to disguise very real social hierarchies, nevertheless sounded the death knell of the old Wilhelminian social order based on distinctions of class. Just as the belligerents tried during the war to gain allies by promising national self-determination – to the Poles in particular – and thereby had to accept the modern nation-state at least rhetorically, so also did the Kaiser's appeal to *Gemeinschaft* contain a promise to "all Germans" that they would be treated as equals in a future political order.

It was anti-Semitism that broke up this staged but, to some degree, felt *Volksgemeinschaft*. The fact that Walther Rathenau, a Jew, took over an important office in the War Ministry, the Raw Materials Department, roused anger in populist anti-Semitic circles. In March 1915, Rathenau stepped down from the office. Anti-Semitic agitation – "Jewish racketeers" and "war profiteers" were supposedly earning millions while "Germans" were forced to starve – persisted alongside claims that Jewish soldiers were dodging deployment to the front. The infamous "Jewish census" of the German army in 1916, the results of which were never made public (leading to wild speculation and suspicion), was an expression of old anti-Semitic *ressentiment* and showed German Jews just how sharply the boundaries of belonging had been drawn.[5]

The original enthusiasm for war gave way to disillusionment. October 1915 brought the first unrest over food shortages in Berlin. The following year saw short strikes. News of the Russian revolution in the spring of 1917 gave anti-war voices a boost. In January 1918, a wave of strikes grew into the largest protest Germany experienced during the war. When in September the general staff had to admit that the war was lost, the country's artificial confidence collapsed and demands for a rapid end to the hostilities spread like wildfire. When, in an about-face, the admiralty gave the order to keep fighting to preserve "honor" in defeat, sailors took a stand against senseless death. An uprising broke out in Kiel on November 4. In the following days, workers' and soldiers' councils seized power in numerous cities across the country. The power structure of the old regime capitulated without a fight. The revolution reached Berlin on November 9.

The leadership of the Social Democratic Party briefly thought that it could take power under the October Constitution and form a Social Democratic civilian cabinet, but events soon took an unexpected turn. Around midday on November 9, the acting chancellor, Prince Max von Baden, announced – without authorization – the Kaiser's abdication and handed his office over to the Social Democrat Friedrich Ebert. That afternoon, Ebert's party ally Philipp Scheidemann pressed ahead and proclaimed the establishment of the German Republic from the balcony of the Reichstag.

On the following day, the Berlin workers' and soldiers' councils gathered, confirmed the Ebert government, and voted in favor of convening a national constitutional assembly, which was to be selected by a free and equal election. Ebert assigned the liberal constitutional law expert Hugo Preuß the task of preparing a draft constitution. Preuß, born in 1860 to a Jewish family, had been denied a professorship on account of his heritage and liberal political views. During the war, he had taken a stance against the authoritarian state of Wilhelm II in a courageous and widely regarded treatise calling for the creation of a *Volksstaat* that would combine national unity and freedom of the *Volk*.[6] Preuß did not envision a *Volk* constituted from above as a union of subjects, nor did he think homogeneity was a necessary characteristic of a *Volk*. Rather, he envisioned a *Volk* formed from the bottom up, oriented toward the common good, and participating cooperatively in its self-rule. In a programmatic article published on November 14, 1918, in the *Berliner Tageblatt*, Preuß insisted that "Neither classes nor groups, neither parties nor estates in opposing isolation, but rather only the entire German *Volk* – represented by a wholly democratically elected German national assembly – can constitute the German *Volksstaat*."[7]

In a series of articles on "Germany's future form of government" published in the *Frankfurter Zeitung* in November 1918, Max Weber set out a plan for a constitution under which a popularly elected president would share power with a federal assembly (Bundesrat) representing the states. Subordinate functions, including budgetary oversight, would be left to the parliament (Reichstag). Weber had already pressed for the "direct popular election of the highest governing official" in 1917 because he saw it as the only way to guarantee in a modern mass democracy that a leader would be selected by political means.[8]

The historian Friedrich Meinecke spoke in favor of a strong presidency after the American model. Like Preuß, he was concerned that the parliament would be dominated by selfish interests and party factionalism. A popularly elected Reichspräsident, Meinecke argued, would, be "the steward, the tribune of the whole people, the guardian of their collective interests vis-à-vis the degeneracy toward which a many-headed and splintered assembly would always lean, if given the reins without supervision."[9]

In the face of revolutionary and counterrevolutionary violence during the crisis of 1919/1920, which left many thousands dead, appealing to national unity was necessary for those who wanted to help the Republican constitution succeed. From his first day in office as president, Ebert pleaded for the unity of the *Volksgenossen*.[10] Until his death in 1925, he repeatedly invoked the *Volksgemeinschaft* in his speeches as a prerequisite for unity, cohesion, and self-assertion.[11] For Meinecke too, the *Volksgemeinschaft* was a central tenet of rational republicanism. In 1921, he described the *Volksgemeinschaft* as the only idea

capable of reviving the reservoirs of moral strength, the idea of the *Volksgemeinschaft*, so long as it is not treated simply as a superficial slogan and irritant, but is understood and felt in the fullness of its problematics and the depth of its moral history ... Republicanism is the form of government that divides us least today. To strengthen it means now to strengthen the *Volksgemeinschaft*.[12]

SOCIAL *VOLKSGEMEINSCHAFT*

Volksgemeinschaft had a strong social dimension, namely the promise of overcoming the social divisions of class. Of course, the servant might have his own ideas when the master speaks of overcoming social class. But Wilhelm's appeal at the outset of the war is revealing: in raising each of his individual subjects in like measure above social, religious, and cultural inequalities to the status of Germans, he proclaimed equality under the category of the national without having to abolish other inequalities. Master and servant could now feel equal as Germans.

One could also imagine a military order in which social and class inequalities were abolished. In this context, equality was defined as camaraderie. At the very beginning of the war, German professors waxed lyrical about military service, which – according to the Jewish Neo-Kantian Hermann Cohen, for example – was supposed to have "made [the Germans] equal as fighters for the fatherland."[13] Talk of the *Frontgemeinschaft*, which had a solid ideological footing in the political discourse of the Weimar Republic, fed off the old idea that everyone faced death equally in the trenches – the baron, the factory owner, the worker, and the student alike.

According to Hans-Ulrich Thamer, *Volksgemeinschaft* became the "reigning interpretive formula in politics."[14] Liberals used the concept to reclaim the political center. For instance, the left-liberal German Democratic Party (Deutsche Demokratische Partei, or DDP), to which Hugo Preuß and Friedrich Meinecke belonged, entered the 1924 election campaign with the slogan "Democracy means overcoming class warfare through *Volksgemeinschaft*."[15] Indeed, *Volksgemeinschaft* was irrevocably bound up with the DDP's ideas about democracy and the constitutional state.

The right-liberal German People's Party (Deutsche Volkspartei, or DVP) saw itself from the outset as a civilian coalition against the left, as the defender of European culture against "Asiatic Bolshevism." According to the view of party chairman Gustav Stresemann, the DVP was a centrist party that "wished to be neither too far right nor too far left but aimed consciously to balance interests instead."[16] "In our politics, the *Volksgemeinschaft* is neither a political idol nor a catch phrase," Stresemann emphasized to the party's leadership in 1923. "Whoever views it as such has given up believing in Germany's future. If the day finally comes when we have to struggle and fight for the preservation and restoration of the Empire, we will only be able to succeed in this fight if the *Volksgemeinschaft* has been created."[17] Stresemann wrote at one point that the idea of the *Volksgemeinschaft* was the common thread running through his political speeches and "perhaps the essence of his political worldview."[18]

Gemeinschaft was a central concept for social Catholicism as well. The Church understood itself, of course, as an organic community of members, as the body of Christ, as Paul had written in his letter to the Corinthians. What could have been more obvious than to apply the holistic model of *Gemeinschaft* found in the doctrine of the *corpus Christi* to human society, as, for example, the academics Othmar Spann and Max Scheler had? The Volksverein für das Katholische Deutschland (People's Association for Catholic Germany) was an umbrella group for socially engaged Catholic groups. Its longtime general secretary August Pieper and his colleague Anton Heinen worked to make the idea of an "organic" *Gemeinschaft* the anchor of the Catholic social movement.

This organically structured community would of course have a leader. Pieper and Heinen, drawing on a dualism put forward by Tönnies, argued that true leaders (*Führer*), not mere "doers" and "functionaries," were needed – "leaders in life" (*Lebensführer*) rather than "managers" (*Geschäftsführer*).[19] Such a Führer would not be an intellectual or a monarch; he would come, rather, from the *Volk* itself. He would not be "elected arbitrarily [*nach Willkür*] but rather 'chosen' [*gekürt*], 'predestined,' that is to say as the one in whom the idea of *Gemeinschaft* is most embodied and in the highest sense."[20] The Führer, Baumgartner wrote, would come from the *Volk*, would understand the *Volk*, and the *Volk* would understand him.[21]

This Catholic conception of *Volksgemeinschaft* is to be realized through belief and love. True devotion to the *Gemeinschaft* would be possible in the final instance only if one surrendered to the love of God. The power of love to build *Gemeinschaft* would come only from faith in God. Pieper called love the gracious spirit of the *Volksgemeinchaft*. His hope for a revival of the German *Volksgemeinschaft* was based on his confidence that the Christian idea of love was connected both to the notion of loving one's neighbor and to a Germanic spirit of camaraderie.[22] *Volksgemeinschaft* was an order of the heart.

Social Democrats also felt the pressure of *Gemeinschaft*, "the magic word of the Weimar period," as Kurt Sontheimer dubbed it.[23] Friedrich Meinecke was just one of the many who called on the Social Democrats to acknowledge the bankruptcy of Marxism and "reforge the swords of class warfare into sickles of the *Volksgemeinschaft*."[24] At a party conference held in Kassel in October 1920, Adolf Braun made the case for the SPD to position itself as a broad-based *Volkspartei*: "Today we have become a party that also encompasses white collar workers and civil servants, that extends to industry, trade, agriculture, shipping, etc. We are a party of mental and manual laborers of every kind."[25] The party's Görlitzer Program of 1921 had proclaimed that "The Social Democratic Party of Germany is the party of the urban and rural working *Volk*. The party strives to bring together all those physical and mental creators, who depend on their own earnings, and unite them around collective knowledge and goals, around collective struggle [*Kampfgemeinschaft*] for democracy and socialism." As Paul Löbe put it in a speech at the party conference that produced the Görlitzer Program, the SPD wanted to "capture the popular majority [*Volksmehrheit*]" and "win over the entirety of the working *Volk*."[26]

Besides Friedrich Ebert – who invoked the *Volksgemeinschaft* in his speeches in calling for unity, solidarity, and self-assertion – there were many Social Democrats, especially among younger party members and former participants in the youth movement, for whom socialism was in the first instance about lived experience and *Gemeinschaft*: connection to nature, anti-bourgeois habits, play, dance, elite consciousness, and a sense of *Gemeinschaft*.[27]

The main theorist of this vision was Hermann Heller. Born in 1891, he was an SPD member, a Jew, and one of the few democrats among the Weimar Republic's experts on constitutional law. He was appointed to a professorship at the University of Frankfurt am Main in 1932 (and expelled from his position the following year). Heller theorized the state from its basis in social reality rather than seeing it as a metaphysically given entity or as "objective spirit." For Heller, the liberal element of democracy was political freedom, and the socialist component was economic equality.[28] Culture was a key concept in his thought, the goal as well as the precondition of the state. Only when the *Volk* understood itself as a single cultural unit would society reach a level of homogeneity upon which the state – whose goal, in turn, was the self-realization of humanity – could be grounded. *Volksgemeinschaft* was central to Heller's vision of the socialist and democratic nation: "Socialism is in no way the end but rather the perfection of national *Gemeinschaft*, not the elimination of the national *Volksgemeinchaft* through class but the elimination of class through a true national *Volksgemeinchaft*."[29] To be sure, this was not Carl Schmitt. For Heller, the *Volk*'s decision in favor of unity always depended upon its fundamental heterogeneity: "The diverse *Volk* should consciously form itself into the unified *Volk*."[30]

RACIST *VOLKSGEMEINSCHAFT*

Carl Schmitt, on the other hand, had declared that the identity and homogeneity of the political *Volk* was a prerequisite for a democratic constitutional order: "Every true democracy rests not only on the fact that what is equal is handled equally but also, as an inevitable consequence, on the fact that what is not equal is handled as such. What is necessary for democracy is, first, homogeneity and, second, – if need be – the expulsion or elimination of the heterogeneous."[31]

If Schmidt's list of those to be excluded included only "barbarians, the uncivilized, atheists, aristocrats or counterrevolutionaries" in 1923, it was easily expandable and later included "Jews," "foreign races," and "those foreign to the *Gemeinschaft*." In his book *Verfassungslehre* (1928), Schmitt stated coldly that national homogeneity did not exist in the political reality of Europe. There was, of course, the possibility of peaceful assimilation of minorities, but another method was, according to Schmidt, "quicker and more powerful," namely the "removal of the foreign element through repression, resettlement of the heterogeneous part of the population, and similar radical means."[32] The biological definition of the *Volk* allowed neither equal status nor territorial integrity, requiring instead segregation, expulsion, and extermination.

It was above all in this exclusive sense that *völkische* legal theory understood *Volksgemeinschaft*. The central question was less who belonged to the *Volksgemeinschaft* than who could never belong to it under any circumstances. Here, anti-Semitism played the decisive role. The racist, anti-Semitic line of demarcation was irrevocably written into the construction of the *Volk* as a "natural community of blood" (*natürliche Blutgemeinschaft*) seeking to establish a political order other than the bourgeois-liberal nation-state.[33] Anti-Semitism was the basis of the National Socialist *Volksgemeinschaft*. Anti-Semitism fueled the radicalism and destructive power of the *Volksgemeinschaft* and drove it inexhaustibly onward in drawing boundaries and distinctions. *Volksgemeinschaft* thus had always existed but also had still to be created through continuous purification. "Unity through purity," the pan-Germanic anti-Semite Georg von Schönerer – one of Hitler's role models – had demanded. As the Nazi party's 1920 party platform had clearly stated: "One can be a citizen only if one is a *Volksgenosse*. One can be a *Volksgenosse* only if one has German blood, regardless of religious affiliation. Therefore, no Jew can be a *Volksgenosse*."

The concept of *Volksgemeinschaft* was, according to Hans-Ulrich Thamer, of central importance in Hitler's worldview.[34] The NSDAP presented itself as a young "party of the *Volk*," that stretched across class boundaries. Adolf Hitler embodied the charisma of a Führer of the entire people, presenting himself as determined to fulfill the desire for continuity and change, for unity and salvation in a future *Volksgemeinschaft*. In the liberal southwest of Germany, the NSDAP was able to take over the stale culture of local civic clubs. Local party groups oriented their activities toward the local clubs and abolished old restrictions on membership, opening the clubs to all "*Volkgenossinen* and *Volkgenossen*," whether Catholic or Protestant, farmer or craftsman, businessman or laborer, man or woman. The Catholic petit bourgeoisie – which had been on the cultural sidelines since the founding of the Empire and Bismarck's *Kirchenkampf* – took advantage of the opportunity to end its isolation.[35] In other regions, such as Lower Saxony, the NSDAP aligned itself with nationalist groups and was able to profit from the decline of the local bourgeois parties. The Nazis explicitly rejected all social barriers and praised the organizations as small versions of the *Volksgemeinschaft*, to which every man and woman, regardless of their wealth, profession, or social standing, could belong – provided they were not Jewish.[36]

Anti-Semitism was the main difference separating the Nazi conception of *Volksgemeinschaft* from those grounded in the 1914 "August Experience." The *Volksgemeinschaft* of 1914 had expressly encompassed all Germans, including Jews and Social Democrats.[37] Conversely, the inseparability of anti-Semitism and the National Socialist *Volksgemeinschaft* meant that those who saw their own views confirmed in the National Socialist promise of inclusion and who thought the Nazi regime's *Volksgemeinschaft* propaganda spoke to their concerns, particularly after 1933, accepted the exclusion of Jews even if they had not previously been anti-Semitic.

Individuals deemed "lives unworthy of life" by Nazi eugenics were also excluded from the *Volksgemeinschaft*. Under National Socialism, the sick and disabled had no right to become *Volksgenossen*. Following on the heels of laws of April 1933, which drove Jews and the regime's political opponents out of civil service positions, the July Law for the Prevention of Hereditarily Defective Offspring was enacted, which for the first time allowed individuals in Germany to be sterilized against their will. In the three years following the law's enactment, newly formed Courts for Hereditary Health heard nearly 224,000 cases and ruled in favor of sterilization in 199,000 – 90 percent – of them.

Volksgenossen were not citizens with clearly defined rights, and this "comradery" was not based on equality. Rather, the *Volk* – in the organic-biological sense of the *Volkskörper* – formed the core of the *Volksgemeinschaft*. "You are nothing, your *Volk* is everything" was one of the Nazi regime's key slogans. Not egalitarian stasis but racist mobilization was what characterized the National Socialist *Volksgemeinschaft*; not socialism for the nation but increased performance to enhance the development of the German *Volkskörper*.[38]

HISTORIOGRAPHICAL DEBATES

Historians in the past seldom did justice to the complex and multifaceted concept of *Volksgemeinschaft*. For a long time, they regarded the concept as merely a National Socialist propaganda formula, thereby obscuring the diverse meanings of the term *Volksgemeinschaft* that existed prior to 1933. A majority of Germans alive in the 1970s had experienced National Socialism personally, and many had positive recollections of *Volksgemeinschaft*. Social historians used statistical arguments in attempting to unmask these memories as unrealistic propaganda constructs and, in doing so, tried to counter the possible whitewashing of National Socialism. In his meticulously researched *Arbeiterklasse und Volksgemeinschaft* (1975), for instance, Timothy Mason still felt the need to prove that National Socialist rule by no means meant the end of social class in Germany and that social equality did not prevail in the Nazi *Volksgemeinschaft* equality.[39] Heinrich August Winkler asked rhetorically in a review of Mason's book: "Is there any good reason to take the socio-political slogans of National Socialism at face value?"[40] Hans Mommsen and Bernd Weisbrod made similar arguments.[41]

In a 1971 dictionary entry for the word *Volksgemeinschaft*, Mommsen wrote:

Volksgemeinschaft, a political concept introduced in the early 1920s by the youth movement and neo-conservatives, taken up propagandistically by Nazism ... The pseudo-idealistic meaning of the word stands in a certain opposition to *völkisch* ideology, which based the organic unity of the *Volk* upon "equality of kind," i.e. racist homogeneity of blood. At the same time, National Socialist propaganda employed the concept above all in the arena of social politics in order to bust up the unions and justify removing tariff autonomy. The middle class in particular displayed a strong ideological susceptibility to the simulated social integration of this and similar concepts and was able thereby to conceive of Nazism as a positive overcoming of class society.[42]

Mommsen later made the case for avoiding using *Volksgemeinschaft* as an analytical concept because of its propagandistic overtones.[43]

Martin Broszat, by contrast, argued against dismissing the concept as simple propaganda and tried instead to gauge its effectiveness. In a still important 1970 essay on "social motivation and National Socialism's Führer-bond," Broszat maintained that the "inconclusiveness and mendacity of the NSDAP's social promises do not diminish the social dynamic that was actually the basis of the party's mass success and that was kept in motion by the Nazi regime."[44] Broszat has also pointed to the "Nazi movement's appeal to modernity and mobilization"[45] and has stressed:

Seen in this way, the *Volksgemeinschaft* slogan was doubtless the most effective element of Nazi propaganda: not only an unrealistic utopian vision of removing social class conflict, not only an restorative gesture to bygone systems of class order, but also a call to overcome the remnants of pre-bourgeois, pre-industrial social hierarchies and norms, a call for the creation of a modern, mobile bourgeois-nationalist mass society.[46]

According to Broszat, the critique of the status quo and the desire for change expressed in the idea of the *Volksgemeinschaft* unleashed a powerful "social force that redounded to the benefit of the NSDAP and had manifested itself in the enormous industry, sacrifice, and energy of its members and supporters during the *Kampfzeit* [the pre-1933 "time of struggle"]. This explains the extraordinary commitment and readiness for action displayed by large parts of the nation during the Hitler regime."[47]

Broszat's reflections found support in Hans-Ulrich Wehler's work on the social history of the Third Reich. In terms of loyalty to the Nazi regime, the impact of rapid return to full employment cannot be underestimated. The Great Depression had reached its low point in Europe in 1932, and the first signs of recovery were evident by 1933. In Germany, the economic upswing was bolstered by the Nazis' wage freeze, their rapid expansion of public payrolls (which rewarded countless party loyalists with new jobs), and the growing demand for labor in the strongly government-supported armaments industry. Germany was the first industrialized nation to reach full employment after the Great Depression. In 1936, in secret reports to Social Democratic leaders exiled in Prague, party supporters noted with resignation that "large parts of the working class" had exchanged their "freedom" for "security" in the workplace since Hitler took power.[48]

The aircraft industry, for example, attracted workers with its large bonuses, newly constructed housing, and the high social prestige associated with a modern technological industry. Aircraft workers were so proud of themselves, one Social Democratic correspondent reported in 1935, that they were no longer good for political work, which was to say, for union organizing. According to Frank Bajohr, these mainly young workers, individualistically focused on social mobility, were no longer moved by the labor movement's traditional call for working-class solidarity but were unreservedly open to the Nazi regime's offers of integration.[49] Hans-Ulrich Wehler has similarly underscored that the "allure of modernity" (*Modernitätsappeal*) and mobilizing force associated with the *Volksgemeinschaft* unleashed a transformative dynamic that was decisive, particularly among the younger generation, in legitimating the regime.[50]

Norbert Frei gave a decisive turn to the debate on the significance of the *Volksgemeinschaft* when he considered the concept as an element in the "history of experience" (*Erfahrungsgeschichte*) of National Socialism.[51] Consensus and agreement with the regime did not collide with the persistence of social inequality. Rather, participation in mobilization campaigns and membership in one or more of the countless Nazi party organizations – which, as Armin Nolzen notes, had enrolled approximately two-thirds of the German population by the beginning of the war – could induce what Norbert Frei has called "felt equality." That sense of equality, in turn, fostered loyalty to the regime at least during the "good" pre-war years, if not in the "bad" years of the war.[52] "The question of the *Volksgemeinschaft*, Norbert Frei contends, "leads to the heart of the matter."[53]

Contrary to Götz Aly's argument that socialist equality was the defining characteristic of the *Volksgemeinschaft*,[54] the National Socialist *Volksgemeinschaft* was built upon new inequalities, not least as a result of the processes of large-scale exclusion that went along with the inclusion of *Volksgenossen*. Detlev Peukert noted this ambiguity of *Volksgenossen* and *Gemeinschaftsfremde* (outsiders to the community) in the early 1980s: "The utopian National Socialist concept of the *Volksgemeinschaft* was aimed at forming an ideologically homogeneous, socially conformist, achievement-oriented, and hierarchically ordered society through the cultivation of the *gut Gearteten* [those of healthy stock] and the 'elimination' [*Ausmerze*] of the allegedly *Ungearteten* [those of unhealthy stock]."[55]

PERSPECTIVES

Putting the *Volksgemeinschaft* in perspective thus requires keeping the excluded as well as the included in view – both those "alien" to the *Gemeinschaft* and those who belonged. If we think about belonging and exclusion in these terms, we shed new light on *Volksgemeinschaft* and avoid taking the concept on its own terms. Ian Kershaw thus misses the mark, in an intelligent and careful essay, when he argues that the *Volksgemeinschaft* concept presumes that one identity was "completely dominant."[56] This view runs the risk of missing or obscuring rifts in consensus, which is the decisive issue. *Volksgemeinschaft* – even within the framework of the Nazi regime's drive for homogeneity – was not a homogenous, identity-based social unit but rather an imaginary order that had to be continually renegotiated.

Beate Meyer tells the characteristic story of a boy, a "Jewish *Mischling*," who had not been excluded by his classmates during the prewar period. He was excluded, however, when the time came to swear blood brotherhood in imitation of the Karl May characters Winnetou and Old Shatterhand. At that moment, when skin was to be broken and blood mixed, his friends drew the boundary. "That's when they said: that won't fly," he recounted in a 1993 interview. "They explained to me why and were a bit embarrassed, but they stood firm. That much they had already learned."[57] It was in this sense, Kershaw emphasizes, that the concept of the *Volksgemeinschaft* has particular value "as a conceptual device to explore the ways in which ordinary Germans gradually committed themselves to a trajectory of escalating persecution ending in death camps."[58] This boundary between inclusion and exclusion was not a given but was rather drawn by actors through specific practices.

Volksgemeinschaft opened up new realms of behavior in society and, at the same time, structured them as well. *Volksgemeinschaft* was not simply an imagined representation; rather, it formed a new matrix of behavior precisely because it was supposed to become a reality, by means of which desires, expectations, and aspirations could be renegotiated. This did not occur without the conscious knowledge of the actors. To the contrary, it required their willed (inter)action in the everyday – in what Inge Marszolek, with a nod to Norbert Elias, has called *Volksge-meinschaft* as "communicative figuration."[59] The term itself restructured discourse, the boundary between the sayable and the unsayable. It opened up opportunities to say what could not have been said before 1933, but it also excluded participants and demands that had previously figured in German social discourse.

These relations, opportunities for connection as well as differentiation, are only recognizable if one does not think of *Volksgemeinschaft* as a collective singular and takes seriously the plurality of notions and social practices associated with the concept. This also means concretely and precisely analyzing – in the literal epistemological sense of *unpacking* – these notions and practices, or, to use Alf Lüdtke's formulation, examining the "forms in which humans have made the world 'their own' and have thereby always also changed it."[60]

Volksgemeinschaft – as shown in the discussion here of the national, political, social, and racist anti-Semitic conceptions of *Volksgemeinschaft* – encompasses a much wider semantic field than is apparent from National Socialist propaganda. *Volksgemeinschaft* is by no means an exclusively racist or anti-Semitic term. Indeed, it was precisely because *Volksge-meinschaft* had so many different meanings that the Nazis could make use of the term in their propaganda without the racist element being immediately apparent. Those who approved of the party's slogans about *Volksgemeinschaft* before Hitler's appointment to the chancellorship may have believed into 1933 that the slogans were about inclusion, social unity, and overcoming of social divisions. When it soon became evident, once the party took power, that the National Socialist *Volksgemeinschaft* meant terror, persecution, and exclusion, it was too late for many to correct their mistake. How the National Socialists were nevertheless able to dominate the concept of *Volksgemeinschaft* so quickly and with such lasting effect – successfully asserting their conception of it in discourse and practice – remains an open question.

Recent historical research on the concept of *Volksgemeinschaft* thus points toward an epistemological shift in perspective in the study of the history of National Socialism, away from the state – the political structure of the ruling system – and toward society. These studies take up the strand from the project on Bavaria during the Nazi period that was undertaken a number of years ago by the Institut für Zeitgeschichte. But unlike that pioneering project, more recent research is no longer discovering "resistance" to the totalitarian influence of National Socialism. Attention has turned, rather, to the many forms of social behavior that cannot be easily categorized through the approval/rejection dichotomy. What is to be gained by focusing attention on the concept of *Volksgemeinschaft* is an epistemological opening up of Nazi history whereby social praxis, emotions, "modes of appropriation," the "sense of self-ownership" (*Eigen-Sinn*), sharing, and participation become the subject of research. With this opening up will come the possibility of writing a new social history of National Socialism, a history that – although it may eventually outgrow the concept – will have taken *Volksgemeinschaft* as its point of departure.

Notes

1   Theodore Herzel, *Der Judenstaat* (1896), 17.

2   Steffen Bruendel, *Volksgemeinschaft oder Volksstaat. Die "Ideen von 1914" und die Neuordnung Deutschlands im Ersten Weltkrieg* (Berlin, 2003); Jeffrey Verhey, *Der "Geist von 1914" und die Erfindung der Volksgemeinschaft* (Hamburg, 2000).

3   Gérard Raulet, "Die Modernität der 'Gemeinschaft'" in Micha Brumlik and Hauke Brunkhorst (eds.), *Gemeinschaft und Gerechtigkeit* (Frankfurt, 1993), 72–93, here 73.

4   Ferdinand Tönnies, *Community and Civil Society*, ed. Jose Harris (Cambridge, 2001).

5   Jochmann, *Die Ausbreitung des Antisemitismus;* Jacob Rosenthal, *"Die Ehre des jüdischen Soldaten". Die Judenzählung im Ersten Weltkrieg und ihre Folgen* (Frankfurt, 2007). On the radicalization of anti-Semitism during the war, see also Ulrich Sieg, *Jüdische Intellektuelle im Ersten Weltkrieg: Kriegserfahrungen, weltanschauliche Debatten und kulturelle Neuentwürfe* (Berlin, 2001), 174–94.

6   Hugo Preuß, *Das deutsche Volk und die Politik* (Jena, 1915). See also the comprehensive discussion in Marcus Llanque, *Demokratisches Denken im Krieg. Die deutsche Debatte im Ersten Weltkrieg* (Berlin, 2000), 68–102.

7   Hugo Preuß, "Volksstaat oder verkehrter Obrigkeitsstaat," in Hugo Preuß , *Staat, Recht und Freiheit. Aus 40 Jahren deutscher Politik und Geschichte* (Hildesheim, 1964), 365–68, here 367f.

8   Wolfgang Mommsen, *Max Weber und die deutsche Politik 1890–1920*, 2nd ed. (Tübingen, 1974), 364.

9   Ibid., 291; see also Harm Klueting, "'Vernunftrepublikanismus' und 'Vertrauensdiktatur'. Friedrich Meinecke in der Weimarer Republik," *Historische Zeitschrift* 242 (1986), 69–98; Stefan Meineke, "Parteien und Parlamentarismus im Urteil von Friedrich Meinecke" in Gisela Bock and Daniel Schönpflug (eds.), *Friedrich Meinecke in seiner Zeit. Studien zum Leben und Werk* (Stuttgart, 2006), 51–93.

10   Friedrich Ebert, *Schriften Aufzeichnungen, Reden* (Dresden, 1926), vol. 2, 159.

11   In a speech in Hamburg on August 17, 1922, he said: "In the idea of German unity alone, in the comprehensive idea of the German Empire that firmly

encompasses our *Volksgemeinschaft* lie the roots not only of our cultural significance, but also our economic might and the possibility of its unencumbered development." And in Kiel on September 4, 1922: "In this struggle for our self-assertion, we will need the participation of all our German comrades [*Volksgenossen*]. The idea of a steadfast *Volksgemeinschaft* must, therefore, more and more ignore our flesh and blood." Ebert, *Schriften*, vol. 2, 253, 265.

12 Friederich Meinecke, "Volksgemeinschaft," first published in *Der Deutsche. Tageszeitung für die deutsche Volksgemeinschaft*, April 8, 1921; reprinted in Meinecke, *Werke*, vol. 2, *Politische Schriften und Reden* (Darmstadt, 1979), 320–4, here 320f.

13 Hermann Cohen, *Deutschtum und Judentum* (Gießen, 1915), 42; quoted from Bruendel, *Volksgemeinschaft oder Volksstaat*, 117.

14 Hans-Ulrich Thamer, "Volksgemeinschaft: Mensch und Masse" in Richard van Dülmen (ed.), *Erfindung des Menschen. Schöpfungsträume und Körperbilder 1500–2000* (Vienna, 1998), 367–88, here 367.

15 Jürgen C. Heß, *"Das ganze Deutschland soll es sein". Demokratischer Nationalismus in der Weimarer Republik am Beispiel der Deutschen Demokratischen Partei* (Stuttgart, 1978), 332.

16 Stresemann made this remark in December 1918; it is quoted in Wolfgang Hartenstein, *Die Anfänge der Deutschen Volkspartei: 1918–1920* (Düsseldorf, 1962), 53.

17 Quoted in Ludwig Richter, *Die Deutsche Volkspartei 1918–1933* (Düsseldorf, 2002), 270.

18 Henry Bernhard (Gustav Stresemann), "Das Kabinett Stresemann," *Deutsche Stimmen*, 35(24) (Dec. 20, 1923), quoted from Jonathan Wright, *Gustav Stresemann 1878–1929. Weimars größter Staatsmann* (Munich, 2006), 173. See also Karl Heinrich Pohl (ed.), *Politiker und Bürger. Gustav Stresemann und seine Zeit* (Göttingen, 2002).

19 Alois Bamgartner, *Sehnsucht nach Gemeinschaft: Ideen und Strömungen im Sozialkatholisismus der Weimarer Republik* (Munich, 1977), 104.

20 Anton Heinen, "Gemeinsinn, Gemeinschaftsgeist" (1927), quoted from Baumgartner, *Sehnsucht*, 105.

21 Baumgartner, *Sehnsucht*, 105.

22 Ibid., 107.

23 Kurt Sontheimer, *Antidemokratisches Denken in Weimarer Republik* (Munich, 1962), 251.

24 Meinecke, "Volksgemeinschaft," 324.

25 Quoted in Heinrich August Winkler, *Von der Revolution zur Stabilisierung. Arbeiter und Arbeiterbewegung in der Weimarer Republic, 1918 bis 1924* (Berlin, 1984), 436.

26 Quoted in Paul Nolte, *Die Ordnung der deutschen Gesellschaft. Selbstentwurf und Selbstbeschreibung im 20. Jahrhundert* (Berlin, 2000), 101.

27 Ibid.

28 See, e.g., Heller's 1928 essay "Politische Demokratie und soziale Homogenität," in Hermann Heller, *Gesammelte Schriften*, vol. 2, ed. Christoph Müller and Sabine von Levetow (Leiden, 1971), 421–42.

29 Heller, "Sozialismus und Nation" (1925), in *Gesammelte Schriften*, vol. 1, 468.

30 Heller, "Politische Demokratie und soziale Homogenität," 427.
31 Carl Schmitt, *Die geistesgeschichtliche Lage des heutigen Parlamentarismus* (Berlin, 1996 [1923]), 13f.
32 Carl Schmitt, *Verfassungslehre* (Berlin, 1993 [1928]), 232.
33 Avraham Barkai has already drawn attention to this way of construing the *Volk* in his essay "The German Volksgemeinschaft from the persecution of the Jews to the 'Final Solution'" in Michael Burleigh (ed.), *Confronting the Nazi Past: New Debates on Modern German History* (London, 1996), 84–97.
34 Hans-Ulrich Thamer, "Nation als Volksgemeinschaft. Völkische Vorstellungen, Nationalsozialismus und Gemeinschaftsideologie" in Jörg-Dieter Gauger and Klaus Weigelt (eds.), *Soziales Denken in Deutschland zwischen Tradition und Innovation* (Bonn, 1990), 112–28, here 122.
35 See Oded Heilbronner, *"Freiheit, Gleichheit, Brüderlichkeit und Dynamit". Populäre Kultur, populärer Liberalismus und Bürgertum im ländlichen Süddeutschlang von den 1860ern bis zu den 1930ern* (Munich, 2007), 82–92.
36 See Peter Fritzsche, *Rehearsals for Fascism: Populism and Political Mobilization in Weimar Germany* (Oxford, 1990), 198–209.
37 This still resonated with unions in the early part of 1933, when the May 1 appeal urged the German worker to become "a full-fledged member of the German *Volksgemeinschaft*": quoted from Thamer, "Volksgemeinschaft," 384.
38 See Ute Planert, "Der dreifache Körper des Volkes: Sexualität, Biopolitik und die Wissenschaft vom Leben," *Geschichte und Gesellschaft* 26 (2000), 539–76.
39 Timothy W. Mason, *Arbeiterklasse und Volksgemeinschaft. Dokumente und Materialien zur deutschen Arbeiterpolitik 1936–1939* (Opladen, 1975). Parts of this book have been published in English: Timothy W. Mason, *Social Policy in the Third Reich: The Working Class and the "National Community,"* ed. Jane Caplan (Providence, 1993).
40 Heinrich August Winkler, "Vom Mythos der Volksgemeinschaft," *Archiv für Sozialgeschichte* 17 (1977), 484–90, here 485.
41 Hans Mommsen, "Nationalsozialismus als vorgetäuschte Modernisierung" in Walter Pehle (ed.), *Der historische Ort des Nationalsozialismus* (Frankfurt, 1990), 31–46; Bernd Weisbrod, "Der Schein der Modernität. Zur Historisierung der 'Volksgemeinschaft" in Karsten Rudolph and Christl Wickert (eds.), *Geschichte als Möglichkeit. Über die Chancen von Demokratie* (Essen, 1995), 224–42.
42 Hans Mommsen, "Volksgemeinschaft," *Lexikon zur Geschichte und Politik im 20. Jahrhundert*, vol. 2 (L–Z) (Cologne, 1971), p. 830.
43 Hans Mommsen, "Forschungskontroversen zum Nationalsozialismus," *Aus Politik und Zeitgeschichte* 14–15 (2007), 14–21.
44 Martin Broszat, "Soziale Motivation und Führer-Bindung des Nationalsozialismus," *Vierteljahrshefte für Zeitgeschichte* 18 (1970), 392–409, here 393.
45 Martin Broszat, "Zur Struktur der NS-Massenbewegung," *Vierteljahrshefte für Zeitgeschichte* 31 (1983), 52–76, here 66.
46 Ibid.
47 Broszat, "Soziale Motivation," 396.
48 Klaus Behnken (ed.), *Deutschland-Berichte der Sozialdemokratischen Partei Deutschlands (Sopade) 1934–1940*, vol. 3 (1936) (Frankfurt, 1980), 149.

49 Ibid., 84–5.

50 Hans-Ulrich Wehler, *Deutsche Gesellschaftsgeschichte. Vierter Band: Vom Beginn des Ersten Weltkrieges bis zur Gründung der beiden deutschen Staaten 1914–1949* (Munich, 2003), 681.

51 Norbert Frei, "'Volksgemeinschaft'. Erfahrungsgeschichte und Lebenswirklichkeit der Hitler-Zeit" in N. Frei, *1945 und wir. Das Dritte Reich im Bewußtsein der Deutschen* (Munich, 2005), 107–28.

52 Ulrich Herbert, "Die guten und die schlechten Zeiten" in Lutz Niethammer (ed.), *"Die Jahre weiß man nicht, wo man die heute hinsetzen soll". Faschismuserfahrungen im Ruhrgebiet. Lebensgeschichte und Sozialkultur im Ruhrgebiet 1930 bis 1960*, vol. 1 (Berlin, 1983), 67–96.

53 Frei, "Volksgemeinschaft," 128.

54 Götz Aly, *Hitlers Volksstaat. Raub, Rassenkrieg und nationaler Sozialismus* (Frankfurt, 2005).

55 Detlev Peukert, *Volksgenossen und Gemeinschaftsfremde. Anpassung, Ausmerze und Aufbegehren unter dem Nationalsozialismus* (Cologne, 1982), 295.

56 Kershaw, "Volksgemeinschaft: Potential and Limitations of the Concept," in Martina Steber and Berhhard Gotto (eds.), *Visions of Community in Nazi Germany* (Oxford, 2014), 29–42, here 38.

57 Beate Meyer, "Erfühlte und erdachte 'Volksgemeinschaft'. Erfahrungen 'jüdischer Mischlinge' zwischen Integration und Ausgrenzung," in Farnk Bajohr and Michael Wildt (eds.), *Volksgemeinschaft. Neue Forschungen zur Gesellschaft es Nationalsozialismus* (Frankfurt, 2009), 144–64, here 151.

58 Kershaw, "Volksgmeinschaft," 35.

59 Inge Marszolek, "Verhandlungssache: Die 'Volksgemeinschaft' – eine kommunikataive Figuration," in Dietmar von Reeken and Malte Thiessen (eds.), *'Volksgemeinschaft' als soziale Praxis. Neue Forschungen zur NS-Gesellschaft vor Ort* (Paderborn, 2013), 65–77.

60 Alf Lüdtke, "Einleitung: Was ist und wer treibt Alltagsgeschichte?" in A. Lüdtke (ed.), *Alltagsgeschichte. Zur Rekonstruktion historischer Erfahrungen und Lebensweisen* (Frankfurt, 1989), 9–47, here 12.

13

Mothers, Whores, or Sentimental Dupes?

Emotion and Race in Historiographical Debates about Women in the Third Reich

Annette F. Timm

In April 1947, American military police arrested a tall, attractive woman in Bad Tölz, Bavaria, and escorted her to the Palace of Justice in Nuremberg. As a former employee of the SS Lebensborn program, Edith had been summoned as a material witness to alleged crimes against humanity. Her distress at being imprisoned quickly evaporated when she fell in love with a fellow inmate, Horst Wagner, a high-ranking official in Ribbentrop's Foreign Ministry who was standing trial as an accessory to the murder of 356,624 Jews.[1] During the months of their incarceration at Nuremberg and (after Wagner fled prosecution) the seven years of his exile in Italy and South America,[2] the lovers wrote 265 excruciatingly sentimental letters to each other. In page after page of effusive prose, Horst describes Edith as a "woman of absolutely realized [*vollendete*] beauty and perfection" – the angelic epitome of all that is noble and precious (*edel*) in the world.[3] These outpourings represent the dying breaths of the Nazi project of harnessing emotions to the goals of a racial utopia, an impression that is intensified by the lovers' frequent use of the metaphor of blood. After one of their meetings, Horst wrote to Edith:

How indescribably blessed it made me feel to be with you this afternoon – it wasn't only our thoughts and our hearts that conjured one being out of the two of us, but also our hot blood that inescapably strives to bring us near and into each other ... For my blood and my eyes, my lips and hands you are the most perfected and longed for creature [*vollendetste und ersehnteste Geschöpf*] ... Because the

I am very grateful to Michael Thomas Taylor, Scott Anderson, Alon Confino, Paul Steege, Liz Harvey, and the editors and one of the anonymous reviewers of this volume for their thoughtful readings of earlier drafts of this essay.

yearning that dominates my entire being has only you as the goal – in everything. And even in this important matter, the urge toward this fairytale vision that you become for me more each day has become so superhumanly strong that you – my love – will one day live in such an ocean of flowers and fervor that you will have to be happy.[4]

Edith responded with similarly florid references to eternity, perfection, God's gifts, fate, and the need to follow both her heart and the "strong desires" of her "hot," "wild," and "foaming" blood – blood that bore his "likeness" and that "belonged" to him.[5] Written in the ashes of the Third Reich, these letters drip with blood – blood that Horst and Edith viewed as the embodiment of love rather than as a symbol of the crimes for which they were being questioned.[6] In other words, Horst and Edith described their love in terms that melded deep emotion with racialized body imagery.

  Even in their aesthetic banality and hyperbole, these love letters demonstrate the symbiotic relationship between Nazi ideology and individuals' emotional lives and perceptions of gender. When she met Horst, Edith had already had an affair with an SS officer and had given birth to a daughter in one of Himmler's SS Lebensborn homes.[7] She had thus lived up to Himmler's ideal of womanhood by risking social ostracism to bring an "Aryan" baby into the world. And yet, she planned to abandon her child to build a "nest" with Horst in exile. I begin with her story (and will return to it in the conclusion) because it highlights some of the fiercest debates surrounding the relationship between gender and race in Nazi Germany. As both a beneficiary of Nazi largesse toward racially "valuable" citizens and a calculating agent of her own future, Edith embodied a particular mode of female citizenship under Nazi rule. The effusive emotions in these love letters demonstrate that although official rhetoric may have denigrated female *Gefühlsduselei* (unrealistic, irrational sentimentality),[8] propaganda and policies toward both genders depended upon awaking passions and desires.

  A review of some of the most influential general surveys of the period reveals that historians have generally confined their use of the word "emotion" to explorations of how the Nazis tried to appeal to emotions in propaganda and in mass rallies or how they synthesized collective emotions into a form of political religion in support of the racial state.[9] These are rather "cold" emotions, easily conflated with ideology. They are emotions that we can describe with dispassion, relying on the analytical categories of politics and social mobilization, and emphasizing the manipulation of emotions from above rather than their production within interpersonal networks, families, or spiritual communities. They are, in short, emotions that have been spuriously associated with a supposedly exclusively male facility for reason and bodily control since the Enlightenment.[10] But the blood/love imagery in Edith and Horst's letters calls to mind a different kind of emotion, a "hot" emotion, that has tended to be associated with women even in histories that track the emotionally charged devotions of male supporters of totalitarian regimes.[11] I will argue that it is time to move beyond these artificial and gendered distinctions between emotions that are politically operative (cold/male) and those that have previously been considered to be outside the boundaries of useful historical analysis (hot/female). The tendency to label "hot" emotions as female and to ignore their impact on men has had a long-lasting impact on the debates about women's roles in the Third Reich, but, perhaps more importantly, it has hidden important mechanisms of Nazi power from view. Most significantly for this volume, the focus on "cold" emotions has been intertwined with the paradigm of the racial state, which has prioritized conscious, ideological motivations as an explanation for individual decisions and commitments to Nazi policy.[12] This historiographical focus, I suggest, has missed important aspects of the production of feelings of belonging for those who became insiders in the Third Reich; by implicitly categorizing "hot" emotions as female, historians immersed in the racial state model have tended to underplay the communally integrative function of *seemingly* unpolitical emotions like love and lust, and they have failed to acknowledge that these emotions affected men and women equally.

I begin with an exploration of the trajectory of research on women in the Third Reich and the historiographical impact of the *Historikerinnenstreit* – the debate touched off by Claudia Koonz's *Mothers in the Fatherland* (1986).[13] Koonz prompted historians to start exploring how women's emotional work in the home and their welfare work in communities lent critical support to the regime even in the absence of political power. Given what we have since learned about female complicity, the reaction of key feminist historians to Koonz's book and the ensuing debate about whether women should be classified as primarily victims or perpetrators might easily be dismissed as a passing phase of naïve uncertainty. I contend, however, that denying female complicity was central to the paradigm of the racial state and that the resulting picture of a fiercely rationalist, masculine, and medicalized regime implemented only from above depended upon an untenably neat division between male and female experience. That some feminist historians had their own reasons for wishing to maintain this division also meant that the exploration of hot emotions was left to popularizers and sensationalizers, most of whom portrayed female Nazis as lustful vixens led by their passions. Rather than following Koonz's lead to investigate how gendered rhetoric and social roles could contribute to the formation of emotional attachments to the regime – how they could create rewards of belonging that obscured the genocidal consequences of Nazi racial logic from the everyday perceptions of citizens – historians of the Third Reich continued to defend top-down models of social control. We can therefore learn much about the weaknesses of the racial state model by exploring the debates within women's history that have revealed how problematic it was to neatly separate male and female experience. By challenging a description of racial policy that made it seem like a male preserve motivated only by rationalistic, emotionless ideology, historical scholarship on women since the *Historikerinnenstreit* has revealed key weaknesses in the racial state paradigm.

THE *HISTORIKERINNENSTREIT*

A shorthand way of describing early depictions of women in the Third Reich is to call to mind the images of cheering women in the crowds lining the streets of Nuremberg in Leni Riefenstahl's *Triumph of the Will*. This view of female political fanaticism was reinforced by serious commentators on both sides of the Atlantic. In 1939, Hermann Rauschning described "the rapturously rolling, moist, veiled eyes of [Hitler's] female listeners" in his since discredited book about his "conversations" with Hitler.[14] This interpretation was swallowed with little critical reflection by prominent male historians of the 1970s, who wrote of women's responsibility for the "over-excited, distinctly hysterical tone" of Hitler's early rallies (Joachim C. Fest) and the "sexual hysteria" of "spinsters" who projected their "repressed yearnings" onto the Führer (Richard Grunberger).[15] Yet despite the efforts of Richard Evans, Tim Mason, and others to refute this perspective, the political effects of women's supposed irrationality ate up much scholarly energy in the 1970s and 1980s and meant that women were not taken seriously as historical actors in the major historiographical debates of the late Cold War.[16]

Women's historians were not blameless in these developments. Influenced by the themes of New Left feminism in the1960s and 1970s, they tended to emphasize sexual repression and the exclusion of women from political power; men exercised political power, they argued, while women were confined to the sphere of *Kinder, Küche,* and *Kirche.*[17] Both in their descriptions *of* and in their arguments *about* women's experience, these accounts tended to seal off female from male experience; although rich and valuable in their own right, they therefore contributed to the marginalization of women's history from the mainstream of German history.[18] The emphasis in much of this work remained on women as victims of the Nazis.[19] Perhaps as a reaction to the earlier emphasis on hot female emotions in support of Hitler, women's historians virtually ignored any discussion of female contributions to Nazi crimes. It was only after the publication of Koonz's *Mothers in the Fatherland* that the drawbacks of focusing on female victimhood came into focus. Refuting the comfortable assumption that exclusion from political and military roles exculpated women of all guilt, Koonz ignited the *Historikerinnenstreit* by arguing that women had been instrumental in supporting the social order that made Nazism possible.[20] In what began as a direct confrontation with maternalist feminist historians such as Gisela Bock,[21] Koonz opened up a debate about the essentialism of assuming that all women were victims of the Nazis and rejected the idea, put forward by Bock, that women had been able to preserve a space where "humane" values were somehow preserved from the intrusion of genocidal impulses.[22] She emphasized the regime-supporting function of the emotional homes that women helped to build, and she demonstrated that patriarchal systems could empower some women.[23]

Although both Bock and Koonz found support for their positions,[24] the positive reception accorded a 1986 article by Joan Scott in the *American Historical Review* gave the rhetorical advantage in the ensuing debate to Koonz. Insisting upon the utility of gender as a category of historical analysis, Scott called upon women's historians to cease replicating separate-spheres ideologies in their own historical accounts, and she adamantly rejected the existence of any universal female identity or anything that could be easily generalized as women's experience.[25] Her insistence that gender relationships are entirely intertwined and mutually reinforcing of other categories of difference (primarily race and class) has made it difficult to plausibly privilege one category to the exclusion of any other in historical analysis.

Together, Scott's intervention and the *Historikerinnenstreit* transformed the debate about female victimhood/complicity during the Nazi era. This shift inspired an explosion of research that sought to contextualize "women's experience" without universalizing it,[26] and it has focused attention on how gender norms are created through interaction with other categories of difference – particularly race. Historians of Germany who write about women have become much more likely to explore female complicity in Nazi crimes.[27] This did not end, but rather recast, the victim/perpetrator debate.[28] As a result, far more emphasis has been placed on issues of women's own motivations, on their *involvement in* rather than simply *subjection to* the *Volksgemeinschaft*, and on the moral consequences of actions that supported the regime either from within the private sphere (as Koonz had demonstrated) or in female-only but still very public forms of social engagement. Even motherhood itself came under suspicion, as historians such as Irmgard Weyrather insisted that the Nazi "cult of the German mother," with its pseudo-religious rituals and pro-natalist welfare benefits, was a central mechanism for integrating women into the Nazi system of power (*Herrschaftssytem*).[29]

Since the mid-1990s, women's history has progressed beyond universalized notions of feminine motherliness.[30] In the research on Nazi Germany, the result has been new insights about how gender roles intersected with other aspects of Nazi society, including racial categories, to produce spheres of action for both women and men. This, as Susanne Lanwerd and Irene Stoehr note, was a methodological/analytical innovation in the research on perpetrators that preceded the concept of *Handlungsspielräume* (room for maneuver, scope for action) developed by the curators of the revised (2003) version of the Hamburg Institute for Social Research's "Crimes of the Wehrmacht" exhibition.[31] Attention to these mechanisms of empowerment has produced a flurry of research on women who were directly involved in Nazi crimes and the enforcement of racial policy or who were married to powerful men.[32] These accounts reveal the impossibility of neatly distinguishing between perpetrators and bystanders. For example, Dagmar Reese's account of how the forced nature of membership in the Bund Deutscher Mädel did not prevent many women and girls from enjoying their participation in the organization teaches us not only about the Nazi mobilization of women, but about the regime's popular mobilization strategies *tout court*.[33] Similarly, we have a much richer understanding of the Nazi colonization of the East after absorbing Elizabeth Harvey's analyses of the enthusiastic role that women played in the "Germanization" of Poland, where the racial project directly produced empowering social roles for women.[34] As a female recruitment officer put it: "The spaces of the East must be embraced inwardly, only then can this conquered land become homeland [*Heimat*] for Germans."[35] Creating a new racialized *Heimat* thus depended upon female "homeliness" and emotional skills.

Women, we now know, were also active in the military. In her book about the *Wehrmachtshelferinnen* (female military auxiliaries), Franka Maubach has revised perceptions of the non-involvement of women at the front and of the battle front/home front division.[36] Investigations of the wives of soldiers (Birthe Kundrus), female concentration camp guards (Alexandra Przyrembel, Simone Erpel, Insa Eschebach, and Elissa Mailänder), nurses involved in euthanasia (Bronwyn McFarland-Icke), individual Nazi *Führerinnen* (Andrea Böltken), and SS wives (Gudrun Schwarz) have moved us very far beyond victim/perpetrator dichotomies and toward a much more differentiated view of women's involvement in legitimizing the National Socialist regime.[37] Other scholars, such as Elizabeth Heineman, Gabriele Czarnowski, Michelle Mouton, and myself, have eschewed a focus on specific groups of women to investigate the role of marriage, marital status, and the family in the creation of social cohesion and metaphors of racial health.[38] This attention to the ways in which gender dynamics contributed to the emotional landscape of the *Volksgemeinschaft* and thus made dictatorship possible is now finding resonance in broader explanations of Nazism.[39]

By troubling simplistic top-down models of agency – not only challenging them but also pointing out their complex moral dimensions – these new accounts reveal how gendered norms intertwined with ideology to influence how individuals imagined themselves as citizens and Germans.[40] In 1936, one woman responded to an essay contest that asked Germans to answer the question "Why I Became a Nazi" by asserting: "And if you ask me today what brought me to the ranks of Adolf Hitler, I would not be able to dress it up in words and could only say that National Socialism is anchored in the deepest inner being of every German, and expresses the most fundamental [*ureigensten*] sensitivities and emotions."[41] Historically exploring such sentiments helps to break down the neat categories of prevailing historiographical models – the theory of the racial state and the theory of totalitarianism – that in their extreme forms imply that the NSDAP simply imposed its views upon an unwilling public. Attention to gender has, in other words, elucidated the structures of identity and emotional ties to the regime that were part of individuals' self-understanding as citizens and members of the *Volksgemeinschaft* and thus made the imposition of racial policy possible.[42]

In underlining how problematic it was to make synonymous the victim/perpetrator and female/male dichotomies, the *Historikerinnenstreit* made it clear that we must explore the complex ways in which social categories of difference and division interact with each other. As Eve

Sedgwick has argued, categories of gender, sexuality, and race interact with "an entire cultural network of normative definitions" built around dichotomies such as "private/public, masculine/feminine, majority/ minority ... natural/artificial, new/old ... wholeness/decadence ... health/ illness, same/different, active/passive ... utopia/apocalypse, sincerity/senti- mentality."[43] Appreciating how Nazi policy makers instrumentalized such dichotomies to rearrange public and private relationships moves gender analysis into the center of interpretations of the period. The top-down model of the racial state – the government's invasion of the private sphere – is only part of the story. We also need to understand, as Geoff Eley has argued in another context, how notions of difference "generate categories that people then have to inhabit, which interpolate them. Such interpolation is not automatic, not inevitable, not a process over which people can exercise no choice."[44] Social divisions are made real when social and political structures and institutions reinforce them *and* when individual choices and emotional responses make them part of everyday life. This is never simply an imposition from above. Each individual's actions are motivated by subjective responses to the fluid interactions, contradictions, and reinforcements between various forms of difference.

RACE AS QUOTIDIAN PRACTICE

The interconnections of race and gender have, to some extent, always been clear to historians of women and the family in the Third Reich.[45] But race in these accounts often stands as a static and overly medicalized category. Bock provided a model for this form of argument in her widely read article on "Racism and sexism in Nazi Germany" (1983). Her primary goal was to demonstrate that male historians had ignored racial policies because they perceived them as primarily involving the "female sphere" of the family.[46] The argument was extremely influential, helping to ensure that no future general historical account of the Third Reich could leave out specifically female experiences. Michael Burleigh and Wolfgang Wippermann's *The Racial State*, for example, includes a chap- ter on women that rests on Bock's research and arguments. The chapter stands as an example of the kind of consensus that had been reached on the subject of women and the Third Reich by the early 1990s: that women had not voted Hitler into power; that they had suffered a curtailment of reproductive freedom under the Nazis; that Hitler's insistence on trad- itional family forms had prevented the kind of mobilization for the war effort that had occurred in Britain and the US; and that women had been the subject of campaigns that both glorified mothers and stigmatized women who failed to accept racialized norms of sexual behavior.[47]

This was a helpful synthesis, but it also neatly confined the female experience to a narrative of domination from above. Women's lives in the Third Reich, Burleigh and Wippermann implied, were mostly organized by men in white coats who enforced an irrational racial policy upon relatively unwilling individuals through health and welfare policy. Although they observed that "women [like men] were simultaneously victims of and participants in National Socialism, with some of the latter equaling their male colleagues in inhumanity and cruelty,"[48] they said almost nothing about women's involvement in spheres of life outside the family or sexual behavior. Most tellingly, their chapter on "Men in the Third Reich" focuses not on experiences that were actually unique to men (with the exception of brief discussions of membership in the SS and the harsher treatment of male homosexuality than female), but upon political structures, class hierarchies, and conditions of work.[49] We hear nothing about the training of soldiers, about the creation of a uniquely Nazi military ethos, or about the bonds of comradeship created through shared complicity in violence.[50] The overall effect is to confine the story of women to the family and reproduction while allowing the public male to stand as an unchallenged default. Most problematically, this tendency to see biopolitics as female and politics as male elides the fact that it was only in the combination of the two – the cooptation of both male and female reproductive roles for nationalistic and militaristic political goals – that Nazi racial policy was actually instituted at the quotidian level. This is particularly striking in an account of a regime in which not only women's but also *most men's* ability to act politically was almost completely circumscribed. Separating male and female experience from each other, in other words, tends to produce a picture of historical agency that is entirely top-down – it ignores the fact that individuals were not simply the pawns of policies and ideologies but interacted with them, and with each other, in emotional and passionate ways.

Progress has certainly been made since these early attempts to fuse gender analysis with an understanding of Nazi racial policy. Marion Kaplan, for instance, has tackled the extraordinarily sensitive issue of differential survival possibilities for Jewish men and women in the Holocaust.[51] Also exploring the complex connections between gender and race, Elizabeth Heineman has argued that decisions about whether to punish German women for affairs with foreign men depended upon judgments of the man's racial qualities (whether he was a candidate for "Germanization" or not) and the woman's gender qualities (adulterous women were more likely to be sent to a concentration camp).[52] In her account of the sexual violence committed by German soldiers in the Soviet Union, Regina Mühlhäuser argues that illicit sexual relationships between Germans and occupied peoples could not only reinforce but also problematize the racial goals of the Nazi state. In this case, we see a conflict not only between racial goals and traditional structures of gender dominance (the regime wanted to prevent miscegenation but assumed that male sexual urges would need to be satisfied), but also between ideals of masculinity and military strategy (sexual violence threatened military discipline and ideals of honor).[53] In all of these studies, the authors avoid assuming a fixed relationship between race and gender, discussing instead the overlap and shifting balance between them. While Heineman insists that "race was the ideological 'ground zero,'" her analysis operates on the level of interaction at the most intimate, quotidian level and highlights the complexity of women's need to balance interacting identities.[54] Each of these accounts moves beyond the Nazi state's pronouncements on race to explore the messiness of implementing racial policy.

The influence of this gendered approach has moved the discipline toward exploring how racism was practiced not only in medicalized and biologized institutions but also in the emotional and aesthetic lives of everyday citizens.[55] Up until recently, historians of the Third Reich had been so focused upon the carefully planned and bureaucratically administered policies of the racial state that they tended to underplay the quotidian practices and assumptions that made it possible for violence to become part of normal life.[56] Even within the literature on Nazi violence, Alon Confino argues, we have been blind to sentiments, historical resentments, and passions that do not entirely mesh with our picture of industrialized, biological racism. Moving beyond ideology, we need to know more about the culture that produced racial imaginings – "the ways of life and thought, historical memory and representations, that gave meaning and coherence to the Nazi experience and informed collective action."[57] Confino's call for a cultural approach to racism takes individual sensibilities and emotional motivations seriously and asks us to interrogate the deep structures of belief that fostered both violence and intense feelings of national belonging.[58]

When we begin to understand racism as an everyday practice that is not exclusively hatred of the other but also a way of understanding the world and ordering relationships of meaning, we can bring histories of gender and histories of race into close and productive conversation. As Ralph Leck has argued, our previous interpretations of anti-Semitism in the Third Reich have failed to fully appreciate the degree to which racial politics interacted with patriarchal ideologies to construct a "Nazi matrix of empowerment" for women, who often (if certainly not always) bene-fitted from Nazism's racial exclusions and definitions of belonging.[59] Acknowledging that women's political exclusion did not preclude the creation of feelings of empowerment helps us to see that there is no clear distinction between emotions and ideology and that the very notion of "cold" and somehow rational ideologies or emotions is spurious.

The interoperability of categories of difference threatens, of course, to destabilize the analytical category of race itself. Historians of Germany might take inspiration from Paul Gilroy's debates with scholars such as Pierre-André Taguieff, Étienne Balibar, and Immanuel Wallerstein and his argument that renouncing "race" as a critical concept is the "only ethical response to the conspicuous wrongs that raciologies continue to solicit and sanction."[60] The deployment of the category of race (often inflected with gendered undertones) easily distracts historians from the critical task of describing how *positive* racial identifications produced a social landscape in which individuals felt justified in acting out against racial others.[61] Although even Burleigh and Wippermann paid some attention to these positive identifications, we have more work to do to understand how the mechanisms of racial policy intertwined with a *lived* reality of racial thinking and acting – how positive associations with gendered and racialized social categories allowed German citizens to emotionally distance themselves from Nazi crimes. Claudia Koonz, for instance, argues that we need to understand how a new moral universe – a "Nazi conscience" – helped both policy-makers and citizens to justify their murderous actions to themselves.[62] Similarly, Raphael Gross points out that because biological racism could not itself make judgments – "this is done by people who connect alleged biological differences with moral judgments" – we need to understand the moral values and motivations of these individuals.[63] Our growing understanding of the overtly violent moments of the war and the Holocaust (as opposed to calculated, stra-tegic, "industrialized" or "banal" aspects of Nazi decision-making) has made clear that it is not enough to investigate the form and implementa-tion of ideology.[64] More work needs to be done on the relationship between ideology and fears, hatreds, and desires, both transient and enduring. How were intimate relationships influenced by racial thinking and how did new cultural tropes of self-description support a binary

worldview that enabled racial hatreds? Tackling these questions is all the
more pressing because the spheres of intimacy and sexuality in the Third
Reich have been monopolized by popularizers and sensationalizers,
whose apologetic tendencies are masked by implicit arguments about
female irrationality.

SEXUALITY, LUST, AND SENTIMENTALITY

Historians who study women in the Third Reich have always faced the
pressure of a sometimes unspoken undercurrent: the public fascination
with the image of the Nazi whore. From pornographic films about female
concentration camp guards, such as *Ilsa: Shewolf of the SS* (1975), to
supposedly historical yet still highly sexualized documentaries about
famous wives and public figures, such as Guido Knopp's TV series *Hitlers
Frauen* (2001), the basic strategy of popular representations of "Nazi
women" has been to depict them as oversexed creatures enthralled by
the power and sexual pleasure involved in being sorceresses of the racial
state. This "rhetoric of pornographization" (as Silke Wenk puts it),
particularly apparent in film and pulp fiction in the 1970s, rested upon
stereotypes that were already common before World War II and that
gained particular virulence in the social turmoil of the war.[65] Rumors
circulated that the SS Lebensborn maternity homes were actually brothels
serving lustful Nazi officers,[66] and *Blitzmädel* who served the German
military in a variety of functions had to endure being called *Offiziersma-
tratzen* (officers' mattresses).[67] Although literary and social-scientific theories on the seductive power of Nazism (such as those of Klaus Theweleit)
have been influential, we have only recently begun to directly tackle the
sexual politics and the sexual allure of the regime.[68] Sensationalized
images of these Nazi women, it bears emphasizing, have been not only
distinctly pornographic but also – and far too often – apologetic. The
mixture of violence and sexuality used to create interest in Guido Knopp's
"documentaries" is presented as exposing the "secrets" of the regime,
while the sexy bits are simultaneously declaimed and enjoyed.[69] These
popularizations present Nazi women as virtually helpless in the face of
their passions. Whereas actual pornographic films and pulp fiction
novels – extremely common in the 1970s, not only in the English-
speaking world but also in Italy and Israel – are at least honest in their
intent to arouse, popularizations (and too many otherwise serious
accounts) hint at sexual secrets about how the Nazis seduced the population without exploring the gendered assumptions about who was

seducing whom.[70] Both pulp and ostensibly serious forms of "Nazisploitation" rely upon static character tropes, simplistic good vs. evil dichotomies, and the causal factor of sexual perversion.[71] Historians have been quite justifiably dubious of such simplifications and their moral blindnesses. Saul Friedländer, for instance, argues that this "fascination with kitsch and death" arises out of "a kind of malaise in civilization" and is an indication that "modern society and the bourgeois order are perceived both as an accomplishment and as an unbearable yoke. Hence this constant coming and going between the need for submission and the reveries of total destruction, between love and harmony and the phantasms of apocalypse, between the enchantment of Good Friday and the twilight of the gods."[72] For the most part, however, we have ceded to others the task of actually exploring the pleasure that many Germans clearly experienced under Nazism, investigating only the *effects* of lust in the period (the treatment of children born of illicit relationships, prostitution, attitudes toward venereal disease and sex outside of marriage) rather than the emotions themselves.[73]

Historians who focus on sexuality in the Third Reich have tended to grapple with only two aspects of it: reproduction and the repression of "deviant" sexuality.[74] We have extensive research on Nazi attempts to control reproduction, on eugenics, and on the persecution of homosexuals.[75] But as Edward Ross Dickinson and Richard Wetzell have pointed out, this "older literature viewed the Nazi régime's obsession with reproductive heterosexuality and public decency as essentially anti-sex" and did not attend to the various ways in which the regime encouraged opportunities for sex outside of marriage.[76] More recently, historians have begun emphasizing that the relationship between political power and sexuality is never simply top-down – that sexualities are not simply dictated by politicians and scientists – but in the case of Germany, the legacy of the "racial state" argument has complicated this task.[77] It has meant, for one thing, that historians are most likely to *find* sexuality in the record of its legal and medical suppression.[78] But I would argue that if we develop more innovative ways of uncovering the emotional aspects of sexuality – the fears, hopes, dreams, desires for tenderness, longings for love, *and* lust – we will gain new insights into the process through which the interrelation of gender and race produced not only exclusions but also powerfully emotional inclusions.[79]

This is not to say that the stories about the persecution of sexual minorities or those who engaged in interracial sex should no longer figure in our research. Sexual and racial epistemologies are intertwined because racial policies are inseparable from fears of miscegenation and degeneration. But recognizing this is not just a matter of investigating how the state sought to control reproduction, nor is reproduction itself simply a private feminine sphere that needs to be protected from the "colonizing" effects of state intervention.[80] Both traditional liberal and feminist accounts of reproduction that view family policy as primarily about women fail to account for the ways in which subjective desires and objective material realities affecting sexual and reproductive choice are generated not only in the (supposedly feminine) private sphere but within larger economic, political, and cultural systems of exchange and communication. The focus on the racial state has obscured many of these connections because it has reproduced rather than critiqued the public/private, male/female divide. The resulting picture of an uncompromising, ideologically driven state that removes possibilities for love, happiness, and sexual fulfillment, particularly for women, fails to appreciate the real benefits (however unearned and morally reprehensible) that National Socialism provided to the privileged in these spheres while underplaying the role of emotions within racial policy and misinterpreting the role of lust in the Third Reich.

Where do lust and sexual pleasure fit into the Third Reich? For fear of undermining the seriousness of their arguments about the Holocaust, historians did not begin to follow the lead of cultural theorists such as Susan Sontag and explore the erotic aspects of National Socialism and their sensationalization in popular culture until recently.[81] But it is time that we overcame these fears. We need more research into the relationships between sexually charged cultures, anti-Semitism, homophobia, and both repressive and pleasure-obsessed tendencies in the Nazi era and beyond.[82] My argument here builds upon the work of historians such as Dagmar Herzog, Heineman, Dickinson, and Wetzell, who have fearlessly broken the taboos of our profession in placing "sex," "lust," "pleasure," and "Nazis" into uncomfortably close proximity. We need to look beyond sex as a physical act to explore how emotion, perceptions, and political reifications of beauty and purity, along with gendered social configurations outside the biological family, helped transform the social worlds in which Germans thought and *acted* race in the Third Reich. If, following Ute Frevert, we take emotions seriously as subjects of historical investigation, it becomes clear that the Nazis purposely "stag[ed] women as overly enthusiastic and emotional"; they created social codes that valorized fanaticism and sanctioned its specifically gendered forms.[83] In the process, the very definition of citizenship was coded in the terms of racialized heteronormativity.[84]

This was, it must be emphasized, a very specific type of heteronormativity. The National Socialist state also sanctioned and even encouraged sex and reproduction outside of marriage in order to boost the birth rate. *Lebensborn* mothers such as Edith serve as an emblem of this logic. Their extramarital sexual relations, which would earlier have been condemned as indiscretions, were reclassified and ideologically valorized by a state that prized their Aryan babies. The emotional integration of women into the *Volksgemeinschaft* was thus not just another version of *Kinder, Küche, Kirche*; when we understand how the rules of heteronormative behavior were redefined to privilege racial purity above the sanctity of marriage, the inextricability of newly transformed gender norms and the goals of the racial state come into focus. Edith and other female recipients of Nazi largesse were not irrational to see a connection between their own emotional well-being (and even their sexual pleasure) and the fate of the Nazi state. We now know that these emotional connections made it far less likely that these women would worry about the fates of those persecuted by the regime.[85] It is thus critical to understand how racial ideology not only controlled sexual expression but also produced a new moral universe that allowed insider Germans to experience their privileges as not simply ideologically justified but morally valid.[86]

A GENDERED HISTORY OF EMOTIONS IN THE THIRD REICH

Having accepted that gender is a central mechanism of power, historians must now explore how gendered norms produce powerful emotions with political significance. It is only recently that historians such as Frevert, Confino, Frank Biess, and others have taken up Lucien Febvre's call to investigate how "politics itself is not rational, not unemotional."[87] They are supported by work in other disciplines. Philosopher Martha Nussbaum argues, for instance, that understanding emotion is critical to making sense of the political world because emotions are fundamentally "appraisal[s] or value judgment[s], which ascribe to things and persons outside the person's own control great importance for that person's flourishing."[88] Emotions form a bridge between our private selves and the public worlds that we inhabit.[89] Recent attention to the construction of the Nazi *Volksgemeinschaft* has highlighted the importance of emotion to both social cohesion and individual decision-making in the Third Reich. And yet neither Mark Roseman's 1996 call to historians to explore "Germany's emotional inheritance" nor Hannes Heer's insistence that we fail to entirely understand the mobilization of Germans for war if we ignore the emotions of "hate, fear of death, homesickness, megalomania, powerlessness, revenge, desperation, apathy, and ecstasy [*Rausch*]" has found adequate resonance in the discipline.[90] There have been good reasons for reticence. The extent of Nazi crimes demanded careful empirical study, and in the war's aftermath, with its waves of retribution, punishment, forgiveness, and political realignments, historians were wise to remove themselves from the fray by concentrating on the politics and institutionalization of genocide. At a greater temporal distance and drawing on the results of this painstaking empirical research, however, we can now begin to explore how these murderous extremes were justified not only through calculated, rationalized ideology but also through interpersonal passions – even passions like love and lust – that were simultaneously intimate and ideologically legitimated.

And this brings us precisely to the point at which this chapter began. If we take these insights to heart, then the sentimental professions of love and idealizing imagery in Horst and Edith's letters seem less banal than symptomatic of an ideological worldview that we need to understand from new angles. We have access to these love letters because Edith's daughter, Gisela Heidenreich, found and published them after her mother's death. Heidenreich was struck by the contradiction between the effusively romantic goddess she encountered in print and the cold, dishonest woman with whom she had grown up.[91] She concludes that "these proclamations of love eerily blur together with incantations from Nazi propaganda, providing an indication of why such clichés had the power to seduce so many Germans."[92] Just as with any other aspect of the historical record, the operational force of emotions and aesthetics can be historicized. Subjective interpretations of beauty cannot be entirely disentangled from culturally created norms, or, as Susan Sontag put it: "the ascription of beauty is never unmixed with moral values."[93] Horst, invoking the ideals of femininity constructed in/promoted by the Nazi state, considered Edith the "most perfected creature," in contrast to those he had helped sentence to death. Edith's motherliness, which he incessantly praised, had nothing to do with her actual feelings or actions – she was emotionally distant from her daughter and planned to abandon her. Even their sexual relationship, to which we have only rhetorical access, was framed in the racist rhetoric of blood. While it may be convenient for us to read these pronouncements as a perversion of "true" love – as an ideologically tainted delusion – it is more productive to view them as a product of the social world that the Nazis created for true believers.

This view is somewhat heretical. It challenges the arguments of those, like Hannah Arendt, who want to view love as a force that can withstand the political maneuverings of fascism or other ideologies. "Love, by its very nature, is unworldly," Arendt argued in *The Human Condition*, "and it is for that reason, rather than its rarity, that it is not only apolitical but antipolitical, perhaps the most powerful of all antipolitical human forces."[94] But was Horst and Edith's love apolitical? Without the space to delve into a philosophical debate about love and its purity, I will simply disagree with Arendt and insist that professions of love are as contextual as any other human act. They can be historicized, and they can provide insight into the social system in which they are embedded.

CONCLUSION

As our historical methodologies have moved from the level of high policy to the level of the everyday, and as we have found the courage to explain not only the hierarchies of hate within the Third Reich but also the mechanisms of reward that encouraged violent action and obscured its moral consequences, we are increasingly faced with evidence from the intimate lives of the perpetrators and the observers – the *Mittäter* and *Mitläufer* – who made up the majority of the German population under Nazi rule. The historiography on women in the Third Reich has been both path-breaking and somewhat too careful in this regard. While the theoretical insights of anti-essentialism have been more easily incorporated by historians of women than by the mainstream of the profession, the former have, until recently, shared their colleagues' concern about moving into areas of analysis previously occupied by the popularizers and sensationalizers. The paradigm of the racial state, with its rather static imagery of motherhood, female victimhood, and medicalized interpersonal relationships, was a safe haven from the charge of writing moralizing or trivial history. But this charge has been rehearsed so many times as to have lost its threatening power. The vast and critical knowledge that we have gained about women's lives from the work of generations of scholars has helped to demonstrate the mechanisms through which so many Germans found ways of convincing themselves that personal, emotional spaces were somehow immune to and innocent of the larger ideological currents that had engulfed their public lives. It is *this* apologia rather than the threat of our own that should engage future research and debate. To explore the Nazi search for purity at this more quotidian level in no way exculpates those who found that escaping into passionate fantasies was a convenient way of *not* thinking about uncomfortable complicities and their role in supporting violence. Indeed, upon closer inspection these passionate fantasies reveal their politicized origins and function. Horst and Edith's love was less an escape than a justification and personal reconciliation with the society in which it was formed. The façade of beauty that they so excruciatingly articulated in their letters must thus be exposed as what Peter Reichel has called the *schöne Schein* (the deceivingly beautiful appearance) of the Third Reich.[95] This love was not only personal and private. It represented a complex ensemble of strongly felt and socially supported emotions that were inspired under the auspices of the racial state but were sustained in interpersonal relationships.

Notes

1 "Kriegsverbrechen," *Der Spiegel*, No. 42, September 10, 1972, www.spiegel.de/spiegel/print/d-42805134.html.

2 Wagner returned to Italy from Argentina in 1952. He was recognized there and eventually returned willingly to Germany, where trial proceedings began in 1958. Legal delays and Wagner's illnesses drew things out into the 1970s. He died in March 1977 without having faced justice. Ibid.

3 The letters have been partially reproduced in a book by Edith's daughter: Gisela Heidenreich, *Sieben Jahre Ewigkeit: Eine deutsche Liebe* (Munich, 2007). At some risk of trivializing Wagner's crimes, I will use only their first names in this account, because Heidenreich did not publish her mother's last name.

4 Heidenreich, *Sieben Jahre Ewigkeit*, 60. This letter was written while the two were still imprisoned at Nuremberg in the fall of 1947.

5 Ibid., 63, 70, 110, 185, and 199.

6 This invocation of blood was typical of Nazi rhetoric. Hitler, for instance, liked to use the expression *jemanden in Fleisch und Blut übergehen* (to enter into the flesh and blood of another) to emphasize how racial ideas should become second nature to every German. See Uli Linke, *Blood and Nation: The European Aesthetics of Race* (Philadelphia, 1999), 205.

7 I am currently completing work on a book about *Lebensborn* that will underline Georg Lilienthal's conclusion that these homes were not "stud farms," as is so often rumored. See Georg Lilienthal, *Der "Lebensborn e.V.": ein Instrument nationalsozialistischer Rassenpolitik* (Stuttgart, 1985).

8 Gisela Bock, "Nationalsozialistische Geschlechterpolitik und die Geschichte der Frauen" in Georges Duby and Michelle Perrot (eds.), *Geschichte der Frauen*, vol. 5, *20. Jahrhundert* (Frankfurt am Main, 1995), 179.

9 Representative in this regard are Richard J. Evans, *The Third Reich in Power, 1933–1939* (New York, 2005), 123–4, 704, and Michael Burleigh, *The Third Reich: A New History* (New York, 2000), 6, 8, 113, 114, and 187.

10 For an extended discussion of the impact of this gendering of European ideas about rationality, see Annette F. Timm and Joshua A. Sanborn, *Gender, Sex*

and the Shaping of Modern Europe: A History from the French Revolution to the Present Day, 2nd edn. (London, 2016).

11 Myra Marx Ferree and David A. Merrill, "Hot movements, cold cognition: thinking about social movements in gendered frames" in Jeff Goodwin and James M. Jasper (eds.), *Rethinking Social Movements: Structure, Meaning, and Emotion* (Lanham, 2004), 250–1.

12 There are some similarities between how I am using "hot" and "cold" and how Marshall McLuhan defined "hot" and "cool" media. See his *Understanding Media: The Extensions of Man*, rev. edn. (Cambridge, MA, 1994), esp. 22–3. However, McLuhan ignored the gendering of these terms, unconsciously using the "spiritual" ballerina as an example of how "the hot form excludes, and the cool one includes" (23) without explicitly acknowledging that he was gendering agency, rational communal bonds, and contemplative thought as male, and spirituality, visceral emotion, and the uncritical acceptance of the "message" as female.

13 Claudia Koonz, *Mothers in the Fatherland: Woman, the Family, and Nazi Politics* (New York, 1987).

14 Quoted from Hermann Rauschning, *Hitler Speaks: A Series of Political Conversations with Adolf Hitler on His Real Aims* (London, 1939), 259, in R. J. Evans, "German women and the triumph of Hitler," *Journal of Modern History* 48(1) (1976), 123–75. For the debunking of Rauschning, see Martin Broszat, "Enthüllung? Die Rauschning-Kontroverse" in Hermann Graml and Klaus-Dietmar Henke (eds.), *Nach Hitler: Der Schwierige Umgang mit unserer Geschichte* (Munich, 1986), 249ff.

15 Quoted from Joachim C. Fest, *The Face of the Third Reich* (Harmondsworth, 1972), 401 and Richard Grunberger, *A Social History of the Third Reich* (Harmondsworth, 1974), 117 in Evans, "German women," 125–6.

16 Claudia Koonz, "A tributary and a mainstream: gender, public memory, and historiography of Nazi Germany" in Karen Hagemann and Jean H. Quartaert (eds.), *Gendering Modern German History: Rewriting Historiography* (New York, 2007), 147–68, here 150. Koonz is referring to the *Sonderweg* debate, the battle between structuralists and intentionalists, the discussions about the comparability of Nazism and Stalinism, and the heuristic value of terms like totalitarianism and fascism.

17 Women's historians themselves rapidly recognized the weaknesses of these approaches. See Renate Bridenthal and Claudia Koonz's challenge to arguments that women had been forcibly confined to the private sphere in Renate Bridenthal and Claudia Koonz, "Beyond Kinder, Küche, Kirche: Weimar women in politics and work" in Renate Bridenthal, Atina Grossmann, and Marion Kaplan (eds.), *When Biology Became Destiny: Women in Weimar and Nazi Germany* (New York, 1984), 33–65. See also Atina Grossmann's more recent admission that the emphasis on sexual repression was misplaced: "Continuities and ruptures: sexuality in twentieth-century Germany: historiography and its discontents" in Hagemann and Quartaert, *Gendering Modern German History*, 208–27, here 209.

18 I do not have the space here to do justice to this historiography. For an overview see Ute Frevert, Heide Wunder, and Christina Vanja, "Historical

research on women in the Federal Republic of Germany" in Karen Offen, Ruth Roach Pierson, and Jane Rendall (eds.), *Writing Women's History: International Perspectives* (Bloomington, 1991), 291–331, here 293.

19 Frevert et al., "Historical research," 294, and Susanne Lanwerd and Irene Stoehr, "Frauen- und Geschlechterforschung zum Nationalsozialismus seit den 1970er Jahren. Forschungsstand, Veränderungen, Perspektiven" in Johanna Gehmacher and Gabriella Hauch (eds.), *Frauen- und Geschlechtergeschichte des Nationalsozialismus: Fragestellungen, Perspektiven, neue Forschungen* (Vienna, 2007), 36.

20 Koonz, *Mothers in the Fatherland*, 65. Summaries of the debate can be found in Adelheid von Saldern, "Victims or perpetrators? Controversies about the role of women in the Nazi state" in *Nazism and German Society, 1933–1945* (London, 1994), 141–65; Atina Grossmann, "Feminist debates about women and National Socialism," *Gender & History* 3(3) (1991), 350–8; and Ralph M. Leck, "Conservative empowerment and the gender of Nazism: paradigms of power and complicity in German women's history," *Journal of Women's History* 12(2) (2000), 147–69.

21 Bock had recently presented Nazi forced sterilization policies as evidence that women had primarily been victims of the Third Reich. See *Zwangssterilisation im Nationalsozialismus: Studien zur Rassenpolitik und Frauenpolitik* (Opladen, 1986).

22 Leck, "Conservative empowerment," 150–4; Koonz, "A tributary," 151.

23 Leck, "Conservative empowerment," 153 and Claudia Koonz, "Some political implications of separatism: German women between democracy and Nazism, 1928–1934" in Judith Friedländer, Blanche Cook, Alice Kessler-Harris, and Carroll Smith- Rosenberg (eds.), *Women in Culture and Politics: A Century of Change* (Bloomington, 1986), 269–85, here 269.

24 In Germany, those advocating arguments similar to Bock's included Annette Kuhn and Valentine Rothe (*Frauen im Deutschen Faschismus: Eine Quellensammlung mit fachwissenschaftlichen und fachdidaktischen Kommentaren* [Düsseldorf, 1982]), while the most significant support for Koonz came from Christina Thürmer-Rohr ("Aus der Täuschung in die Ent-Täuschung," *Beiträge zur feministische Theorie und Praxis* 8 [1983], 11–26); Karin Windaus-Walser ("Gnade der weiblichen Geburt? Zum Umgang der Frauenforschung mit Nationalsozialismus und Anti-semitismus," *Feministische Studien* 6(1) [1988], 102–15); and Adelheid von Saldern ("Victims or perpetrators?"). Koonz was also critiqued in the US: see Ann Taylor Allen, *Feminism and Motherhood in Germany, 1800–1914* (New Brunswick, 1991), esp. 231–8. In England, Mary Nolan criticized Bock for underemphasizing the difference between sterilization and genocide: see Mary Nolan, "Work, gender and everyday life: reflections on continuity, normality and agency in twentieth-century Germany" in Ian Kershaw and Moshe Lewin (eds.), *Stalinism and Nazism: Dictatorships in Comparison* (Cambridge, 1997), 311–42, here 334.

25 Scott argued that gender was not simply a way of describing the separation between men and women but "a constitutive element of social relationships based on perceived differences between the sexes, and ... a primary way of

signifying relationships of power." See Joan W. Scott, "Gender: a useful category of historical analysis," *American Historical Review* 91(5) (1986), 1067. For a useful summary of this article's impact on the historical discipline as a whole, see Joanne Meyerowitz, "AHA Forum: a history of 'gender,'" *American Historical Review* 113(5) (2008), 1346–56. For a discussion of Scott's impact that focuses on German history, see Eve Rosenhaft, "Zwei Geschlechter – eine Geschichte? Frauengeschichte, Männergeschichte, Geschlechtergeschichte und ihre Folgen für unsere Geschichtswahrnehmung" in Christiane Eifert, Angelika Epple, and Martina Kessel (eds.), *Was sind Frauen? Was sind Männer?: Geschlechterkonstruktionen im historischen Wandel* (Frankfurt am Main, 1996), 257–74.

26 Joan W. Scott, "Experience" in Joan W. Scott and Judith Butler (eds.), *Feminists Theorize the Political* (New York, 1992), 22–40, esp. 31.

27 It should be noted that some historians have strenuously rejected the characterization of pre-1980s women's history as placing exclusive emphasis on women as victims. See Lanwerd and Stoehr, "Frauen- und Geschlechterforschung," 22–6.

28 For an overview up to 1997, see Kirsten Heinsohn, Barbara Vogel, and Ulrike Weckel (eds.), *Zwischen Karriere und Verfolgung. Handlungsräume von Frauen im nationalsozialistischen Deutschland* (Frankfurt am Main, 1997). A more recent recapitulation is available in Christina Herkommer, *Frauen im Nationalsozialismus – Opfer oder Täterinnen?: Eine Kontroverse der Frauenforschung im Spiegel feministischer Theoriebildung und der allgemeinen historischen Aufarbeitung der NS-Vergangenheit* (Munich, 2005).

29 Irmgard Weyrather, *Muttertag und Mutterkreuz: Der Kult um die "deutsche Mutter" im Nationalsozialismus* (Frankfurt am Main, 1993), esp. 8 and 14. See also Elizabeth D. Heineman, "Whose mothers? Generational difference, war, and the Nazi cult of motherhood," *Journal of Women's History* 12(4) (2001), 139–64.

30 For arguments that this focus on women is still necessary and productive, see Karen Hagemann and Jean H. Quartaert, "Gendering modern Germany: comparing historiographies and academic cultures in Germany and the United States through the lens of gender" in Hagemann and Quartaert, *Gendering Modern German History*, 1–38, here 21; Kathleen Canning, "Feminist history after the linguistic turn: historicizing discourse and experience," *Signs*, 19(2) (1994), 368–404; and the contributions in Lynn Abrams and Elizabeth Harvey (eds.), *Gender Relations in German History: Power, Agency and Experience from the Sixteenth Century to the Twentieth* (Durham, 1996).

31 Lanwerd and Stoehr, "Frauen- und Geschlechterforschung," 27–8; Hamburger Institut für Sozialforschung (ed.), *Verbrechen der Wehrmacht. Dimensionen des Vernichtungskrieges, 1941–1944. Begleitbroschüre zur Ausstellung* (Hamburg, 2004), 1. See also Heinsohn, Vogel, and Weckel, *Zwischen Karriere und Verfolgung*.

32 For an overview of popular accounts see Johanna Gehmacher, "Im Umfeld der Macht: Populäre Perspektiven auf Frauen der NS-Elite" in Elke Frietsch and Christina Herkommer (eds.), *Nationalsozialismus und Geschlecht: Zur*

Politisierung und Ästhetisierung von Körper, "Rasse" und Sexualität im "Dritten Reich" und nach 1945 (Bielefeld, 2009), 49–69.

33 Dagmar Reese, *Growing Up Female in Nazi Germany* (Ann Arbor, 2006; originally published in German in 1989). See also Dagmar Reese (ed.), *Die BDM-Generation* (Berlin, 2007).

34 Elizabeth Harvey, *Women and the Nazi East: Agents and Witnesses of Germanization* (New Haven, 2003).

35 Quoted in ibid., 120.

36 Franka Maubach, *Die Stellung halten: Kriegserfahrungen und Lebensgeschichten von Wehrmachthelferinnen* (Göttingen, 2009).

37 Birthe Kundrus, *Kriegerfrauen: Familienpolitik und Geschlechterverhältnisse im Ersten und Zweiten Weltkrieg* (Göttingen, 1995); Alexandra Przyrembel, "Transfixed by an image: Ilse Koch, the 'Kommandeuse of Buchenwald,'" *German History* 19 (2001), 369–99; Ulrike Weckel and Edgar Wolfrum (eds.), *"Bestien" und "Befehlsempfänger": Frauen und Männer in NS-Prozessen nach 1945* (Göttingen, 2003); Simone Erpel, *Im Gefolge der SS: Aufseherinnen des Frauen-KZ Ravensbrück: Begleitband zur Ausstellung* (Berlin, 2007); Insa Eschebach, "SS-Aufseherinnen des Frauenkonzentrationslager Ravensbrück: Erinnerungen ehemaliger Häftlinge," *Werkstatt Geschichte* 5(13) (1996), 39–48; Elissa Mailänder [Koslov], *Gewalt im Dienstalltag: Die SS-Aufseherinnen des Konzentrations- und Vernichtungslagers Majdanek, 1942–1944* (Hamburg, 2009), recently translated as *Female SS Guards and Workaday Violence: The Majdanek Concentration Camp, 1942–1944*, trans. Patricia Szobar (East Lansing, 2015); Bronwyn Rebekah McFarland-Icke, *Nurses in Nazi Germany: Moral Choice in History* (Princeton, 1999); Andrea Böltken, *Führerinnen im "Führerstaat": Gertrud Scholtz-Klink, Trude Mohr, Jutta Rüdiger und Inge Viermetz* (Pfaffenweiler, 1995); Gudrun Schwarz, *Eine Frau an seiner Seite. Ehefrauen in der "SS- Sippengemeinschaft"* (Hamburg, 1997).

38 Elizabeth D. Heineman, *What Difference Does a Husband Make? Women and Marital Status in Nazi and Postwar Germany* (Berkeley, 1999); Gabriele Czarnowski, *Das kontrollierte Paar: Ehe- und Sexualpolitik im Nationalsozialismus, Ergebnisse der Frauenforschung* (Weinheim, 1991); Michelle Mouton, *From Nurturing the Nation to Purifying the Volk: Weimar and Nazi Family Policy, 1918–1945* (Cambridge, 2007); Annette F. Timm, *The Politics of Fertility in Twentieth-Century Berlin* (New York, 2010).

39 See, for example, the following chapters from Michael Geyer and Sheila Fitzpatrick (eds.), *Beyond Totalitarianism: Stalinism and Nazism Compared* (New York, 2008): Christopher R. Browning and Lewis H. Siegelbaum, "Frameworks for social engineering: Stalinist schema of identification and the Nazi *Volksgemeinschaft*," 231–65, esp. 240 and 263; Sheila Fitzpatrick and Alf Lüdtke, "Energizing the everyday: on the breaking and making of social bonds in Nazism and Stalinism," 167–301, esp. 267; Peter Fritzsche and Jochen Hellbeck, "The new man in Stalinist Russia and Nazi Germany," 302–41, esp. 327 and 333; and in particular, David L. Hoffmann and Annette F. Timm, "Utopian biopolitics: reproductive policies, gender roles, and sexuality in Nazi Germany and the Soviet Union," 87–129.

40 On the necessity of "troubling" the historical record by insisting upon the complexity of its moral dimensions, see George Cotkin, "History's moral turn," *Journal of the History of Ideas* 69(2) (2008), 293–315, especially 298, where he insists that "the impetus behind moral history should be to trouble issues, to make palatable the pain and necessity of the moral imagination."

41 Maria Engelhardt, quoted in Koonz, *Mothers in the Fatherland*, 64.

42 Following Kathleen Canning, I define citizenship in its broadest cultural and political sense. See her "Class vs. citizenship: keywords in German gender history," *Central European History* 37(2) (2004), 225–44; *Gender History in Practice: Historical Perspectives on Bodies, Class and Citizenship* (Ithaca, 2006); and "The order of terms: class, citizenship, and welfare state in German gender history" in Hagemann and Quartaert (eds.), *Gendering Modern German History*, 138.

43 Eve Kosofsky Sedgwick, *Epistemology of the Closet* (Berkeley, 1990), 11.

44 Geoff Eley, "The trouble with 'race': migrancy, cultural difference, and the remaking of Europe" in Rita Chin, Heide Fehrenbach, Geoff Eley, and Atina Grossmann (eds.), *After the Nazi Racial State: Difference in Germany and Europe* (Ann Arbor, 2009), 176.

45 See, for example, Atina Grossmann, "Abortion and economic crisis: the 1931 campaign against Paragraph 218," in Bridenthal et al. (eds.), *When Biology Became Destiny*, 66–86; Cornelie Usborne, *The Politics of the Body in the Weimar Republic: Women's Reproductive Rights and Duties* (Basingstoke, 1992); David F. Crew, *Germans on Welfare: From Weimar to Hitler* (New York, 2001); Young-Sun Hong, *Welfare, Modernity, and the Weimar State, 1919–1933* (Princeton, 1998); Seth Koven and Sonya Michel (eds.), *Mothers of the New World: Maternalist Politics and the Origins of Welfare States* (London, 1993).

46 Gisela Bock, "Racism and sexism in Nazi Germany: motherhood, compulsory sterilization, and the state," *Signs* 8(3) (1983), 401.

47 Michael Burleigh and Wolfgang Wippermann, *The Racial State: Germany, 1933–1945* (Cambridge, 1991), 242–66.

48 Ibid., 266.

49 Ibid., 267–303.

50 On this last point, see Thomas Kühne, "The pleasure of terror: belonging through genocide," in Pamela Swett, Corey Ross, and Fabrice D'Almeida (eds.), *Pleasure and Power in Nazi Germany* (Houndmills, 2011), 234–55.

51 Marion Kaplan, *Between Dignity and Despair: Jewish Life in Nazi Germany* (New York, 1998), esp. 7, 235.

52 Heineman, *What Difference*, 58–9.

53 Regina Mühlhäuser, *Eroberungen. Sexuelle Gewalttaten und intime Beziehungen deutscher Soldaten in der Sowjetunion 1941–1945* (Hamburg, 2010). On attitudes towards male sexual urges, see Annette F. Timm, "Sex with a purpose: prostitution, venereal disease and militarized masculinity in the Third Reich," *Journal of the History of Sexuality* 11(1/2) (2002), 223–55. For a discussion of the Wehrmacht's differential concern about the impact of sexual violence on military discipline on the Eastern and Western Fronts,

see Birgit Beck, *Wehrmacht und Sexuelle Gewalt: Sexualverbrechen vor Deutschen Militärgerichten 1939–1945* (Paderborn, 2004).

54 Heineman, *What Difference*, 13.

55 I take inspiration from Rita Chin, Heide Fehrenbach, Geoff Eley, and Atina Grossmann's exploration of how racism remained fiercely present in a post-World War Germany in which the racial state had been dismantled. See Chin et al. (eds.), *After the Nazi Racial State*.

56 There are, of course, exceptions. For a sustained discussion of how even forms of conviviality could help foster forms of dominance and make violence seem normal, see Andrew Stuart Bergerson, *Ordinary Germans in Extraordinary Times: The Nazi Revolution in Hildesheim* (Bloomington, 2004), esp. chapter 4, "A moral community." I thank Paul Steege for helping to me refine my argument here.

57 Alon Confino, "Fantasies about the Jews: cultural reflections on the Holocaust," *History & Memory* 17(1/2) (2005), 296–322, esp. 303–4.

58 Confino argues that a "commingling" of rationalistic ideology and mythical or even religious fantasy produced symbolic meanings that enabled various forms of Nazi violence against Jews. Alon Confino, "Why did the Nazis burn the Hebrew Bible? Nazi Germany, representations of the past, and the Holocaust," *Journal of Modern History*, 84(2) (2012), 369–400, esp. 375–8.

59 Leck, "Conservative empowerment," 163–4.

60 Paul Gilroy, "Race ends here," *Ethnic and Racial Studies*, 21(5) (1998), 838–9. For a summary of the debate, see Alana Lentin, "'Race', racism and anti-racism: challenging contemporary classifications," *Social Identities: Journal for the Study of Race, Nation and Culture* 6(1) (2000), 91–106.

61 Tina Campt has demonstrated how critical it is to be aware of the influence of positive racial associations even among persecuted groups. Tina Marie Campt, *Other Germans: Black Germans and the Politics of Race, Gender, and Memory in the Third Reich* (Ann Arbor, 2004), 5–6.

62 Koonz uses the term "community of moral obligation": Claudia Koonz, *The Nazi Conscience* (Cambridge, MA, 2003), 193. Similar discussions of the need to understand the Nazi moral universe can be found in Zygmunt Bauman, *Modernity and the Holocaust* (Ithaca, 1989); Tzevetan Todorov, *The Morals of History* (Minneapolis, 1995); Tzvetan Todorov, *Facing the Extreme: Moral Life in the Concentration Camps* (New York, 1996); and Raphael Gross, "'Loyalty' in National Socialism: a contribution to the moral history of the National Socialist period," *History of European Ideas* 33(4) (2007), 488–503.

63 Gross, "Loyalty," 489.

64 Mark Edele and Michael Geyer argue, for instance, that cold ideological or military calculations are not enough to explain the brutalization of warfare on the Eastern Front: "Hate propaganda, word of mouth, and experience interacted to incite slaughter and atrocity, a compulsion to destroy, ravage, and kill." See Edele and Geyer, "The Nazi-Soviet war as a system of violence, 1939–1945" in Geyer and Fitzpatrick, *Beyond Totalitarianism*, 345–95. That non-ideological emotions fueled killing in the Holocaust is also demonstrated in Jan T. Gross, *Neighbors: The Destruction of the Jewish*

Community in Jedwabne, Poland* (New York, 2002) and Confino, "Why did the Nazis burn the Hebrew Bible?"

65 Silke Wenk, "Rhetoriken der Pornografisierung: Rahmungen des Blicks auf die NS-Verbrechen" in *Gedächtnis und Geschlecht: Deutungsmuster in Darstellungen des Nationalsozialistischen Genozids* (Frankfurt am Main, 2002), 269–96; Gehmacher, "Im Umfeld."

66 For evidence about pre-1945 rumors of this kind, see Dorothee Schmitz-Köster, *"Deutsche Mutter, bist du bereit": Alltag im Lebensborn* (Berlin, 2003).

67 Jörg Echternkamp, *Die 101 wichtigsten Fragen – der Zweite Weltkrieg* (Munich), 94–5.

68 Klaus Theweleit, *Male Fantasies*, vols. 1 and 2 (Minneapolis, 1987 and 1989). See also Susan Sontag, "Fascinating fascism," *New York Review of Books* 22(1) (1975), 23–30.

69 A good summary is provided in Gehmacher, "Im Umfeld," here 62–4.

70 Wenk, "Rhetoriken der Pornographisierung," 269–73. Wenk discusses the Italian "Sadiconazista" wave. See also Marcus Stiglegger, *Sadiconazista: Faschismus und Sexualität im Film*, 2nd edn. (St. Augustin, 2000). On Holocaust pornography in Israel, see Omer Bartov, "Kitsch and sadism in Ka-Tzetnik's other planet: Israeli youth imagine the Holocaust," *Jewish Social Studies* 3(2) (1997), 42–76.

71 Daniel H. Magilow, "Introduction: Nazisploitation! The Nazi image in low-brow cinema and culture," in Daniel H. Magilow, Elizabeth Bridges, and Kristin T. Vander Lugt (eds.), *Nazisploitation! The Nazi Image in Low-Brow Cinema and Culture* (New York, 2011), 1–20. A prominent example from "high" literature is Jonathan Littell, *The Kindly Ones: A Novel*, trans. Charlotte Mandell (New York, 2010). See Annette F. Timm, "Titillation in the guise of authenticity: myths of Nazi breeding from *Hitler's Children* to *The Kindly Ones*" in Iris Roebling-Grau and Dirk Rupnow (eds.), *Holocaust'-Fiktion. Kunst Jenseits Der Authentizität* (Paderborn, 2014), 271–94.

72 Saul Friedländer, *Reflections of Nazism: An Essay on Kitsch and Death* (New York, 1984), 22, 135. I have explored these connections more thoroughly in my "Titillation in the guise of authenticity."

73 See Birthe Kundrus, "Forbidden company: romantic relationships between Germans and foreigners, 1939–1945," *Journal of the History of Sexuality* 1 (2) (2002), 201–22; Heide Fehrenbach, *Race after Hitler: Black Occupation Children in Postwar Germany and America* (Princeton, 2005); Heineman, *What Difference*; Edward Ross Dickinson, "Policing sex in Germany, 1882–1982: a preliminary statistical analysis," *Journal of the History of Sexuality* 16(2) (2007), 204–50; and Edward Ross Dickinson, "Biopolitics, fascism, democracy: some reflections on our discourse about 'modernity'," *Central European History* 37(1) (2004), 1–48.

74 Elizabeth D. Heineman, "Sexuality and Nazism: the doubly unspeakable?" in Dagmar Herzog (ed.), *Sexuality and German Fascism* (New York, 2005), 27–66, here 24.

75 For a summary of the now extensive literature on homosexuality in the Third Reich, see Edward Ross Dickinson and Richard F. Wetzell, "The

historiography of sexuality in modern Germany," *German History* 23(3) (2005), 291–305, esp. 1–7.

76 Ibid., 297.

77 Franz X. Eder and Sabine Frühstück, "Vorwort," in Eder and Frühstück (eds.), *Neue Geschichten der Sexualität: Beispiele aus Ostasien und Zentraleuropa 1700–2000* (Vienna, 1999), 8. For a similar argument that focuses on the German Democratic Republic, see Josie McLellan, *Love in the Time of Communism: Intimacy and Sexuality in the GDR* (Cambridge, 2011).

78 Even accounts that explicitly frame themselves as "historical anthropology [ies] of sexuality" tend to rely on medical and court records and focus on subjects such as the treatment of hysteria, the persecution of homosexuals, and anti-Semitic sexual stereotypes. See Claudia Bruns and Tilman Walter, "Einleitung. Zur Historischen Anthropologie der Sexualität," in Bruns and Walter (eds.), *Von Lust und Schmerz: Eine Historische Anthropologie der Sexualität* (Cologne, 2004), 4, and the various contributions to that volume.

79 Mark Fenemore makes a similar point in reference to popular fiction, magazines, oral history, biography, and youth culture: "The recent historiography of sexuality in twentieth-century Germany," *The Historical Journal* 52(3) (2009), 763–79.

80 I am purposely using Jürgen Habermas's language here, though in a way that highlights his failure to integrate gender into his account. See Nancy Fraser, *Unruly Practices: Power, Discourse and Gender in Contemporary Social Theory* (Minneapolis, 1989).

81 Sontag, "Fascinating fascism."

82 Dagmar Herzog, "Hubris and hypocrisy, incitement and disavowal: sexuality and German fascism," *Journal of the History of Sexuality* 1(1/2) (2002): 3–21, esp. 3–7; Dagmar Herzog, *Sex after Fascism: Memory and Morality in Twentieth-Century Germany* (Princeton, 2005).

83 Ute Frevert, *Emotions in History: Lost and Found* (Budapest, 2011), 139.

84 On this concept, but in the present-day American context, Lauren Berlant and Michael Warner argue that "a familial model of society displaces the recognition of structural racism and other systemic inequalities." See "Sex in public," in Steven During (ed.), *The Cultural Studies Reader* (New York, 1999), 356.

85 I do not have the space to fully justify this statement here. This assertion rests on extensive research on the *Lebensborn* program housed at the archives of the International Tracing Service in Bad Arolsen.

86 These efforts should integrate the often misunderstood arguments of Herbert Marcuse about the Nazis' mechanisms of "repressive desublimation" – the cooptation of sexual desires in order to produce docile citizens. See Herbert Marcuse, *One Dimensional Man: Studies in the Ideology of Advanced Industrial Society* (London, 1964), chapter 3; Herbert Marcuse, "Repressive tolerance" in Robert P. Wolff and Barrington Moore (eds.), *A Critique of Pure Tolerance* (London, 1969), 95–137.

87 Febvre drew upon his personal experiences in Nazi-occupied France. Quoted in Barbara H. Rosenwein, "Worrying about emotions in history," *American Historical Review* 107(3) (2002), 822. See also Ute Frevert, "Angst vor Gefühlen. Die Geschichtsmächtigkeit von Emotionen im 20. Jahrhundert" in

Paul Nolte, Manfred Hettling, Frank-Michael Kuhlemann, and Hans-Walter Schmuhl (eds.), *Perspektiven der Gesellschaftsgeschichte* (Munich, 2000), 95–111. See also Frevert, Frank Biess, Alon Confino, Uffa Jensen, and Lyndal Roper, "Forum: history of emotions," *German History* 28(1) (2010), 67–80; Frank Biess, "'Everybody has a chance': nuclear angst, civil defence, and the history of emotions in postwar West Germany," *German History* 27 (2) (2009), 215–43, esp. 216–8.

88 Martha Nussbaum, *Upheavals of Thought: The Intelligence of Emotions* (Cambridge, 2003), 4.

89 Biess, "Everybody has a chance," 217.

90 Mark Roseman, "National Socialism and modernization" in Richard Bessel (ed.), *Fascist Italy and Nazi Germany: Comparisons and Contrasts* (Cambridge, 1996), 220, 228; Hannes Heer, *Tote Zonen. Die deutsche Wehrmacht an der Ostfront* (Hamburg, 1999), 310.

91 Heidenreich detailed the painful discovery of the story of her birth in a *Lebensborn* home in Norway and how her mother had lied to her about it. See Gisela Heidenreich, *Das endlose Jahr: Die langsame Entdeckung der eigenen Biographie – ein Lebensborn-Schicksal* (Frankfurt am Main, 2004).

92 Heidenreich, *Sieben Jahre*, 50.

93 Susan Sontag, "An argument about beauty," *Daedalus* 131(4) (2002), 24.

94 Hannah Arendt, *The Human Condition* (Chicago, 1958), 242. Arendt was extremely skeptical about the social value of love. "Love, by reason of its passion destroys the in-between which relates us to and separates us from others," she writes in *The Human Condition*; this situation can only be resolved when a child reconnects the couple to the world (242). Neither love nor fraternity, but only respect, in its Aristotelian sense of *philia politike* – "a kind of 'friendship' without intimacy and without closeness" – can have any role in the public realm, according to Arendt's political philosophy (243). She believed that sexual love has to be confined to the "narrowly circumscribed sphere" of the family, because love means "a loss of the world" – an inability to maintain the "interspace" between humans that alone guarantees freedom. Neither the love between two people nor the love created by fraternity, she argues, can survive exposure to the world. Hannah Arendt, *Men in Dark Times* (San Diego, 1968), 16.

95 Peter Reichel, *Der schöne Schein des Dritten Reiches: Faszination und Gewalt des Faschismus* (Munich, 1991). See also Koonz, "A tributary," 157.

14

Nationalist Mobilization

Foreign Diplomats' Views on the Third Reich, 1933–1945

Frank Bajohr

In the time of National Socialist rule, foreign consuls, envoys, and ambas-
sadors wrote more than 100,000 political reports on the situation in
Germany. Their reports contain noteworthy observations on numerous
developments and events in National Socialist Germany, but they have for
the most part simply gathered dust in the archives since 1945. Only very
recently was a first attempt undertaken to make them accessible for
historical research and to analyze the reports from ten different countries
comparatively.[1] Contrary to what one might expect, the diplomats did
not confine themselves to foreign affairs or the concerns of their fellow
citizens in Germany. Rather, their reports contain numerous noteworthy
analyses of the dictatorial constitution of the Third Reich, internal developments in Germany, and the German population's attitude toward
the National Socialist regime. Their special value for historical research
rests above all on the fact that the diplomats were independent outside
observers who approached the situation in Nazi Germany from a foreign,
sometimes ethnological viewpoint. It would of course be methodologically naïve to presume the objectivity of the diplomatic reports because
they were massively influenced by a number of factors, including the
personal attitudes of the authors and, above all, the relations between
the authors' governments and the National Socialist regime. Unlike the
authors of the regime's internal situation reports, the diplomats were
not National Socialists and were not bound in their reports by regime-
specific rules of communication.[2] Above all, the reports are fascinating

Translated by Chris Chiasson.

as historical snapshots by contemporaries who sought, in often contradictory ways, to capture the many facets of the regime and to describe the dynamics of its constant transformation. They remind today's reader of the openness of the historical process and warn against interpreting the Third Reich and its policies too hermetically and against construing it as a completely conceptual-ideological project coherent in itself. From the outset of Nazi rule, the reports emphasize the hybrid character of the regime. Taken together, they should be seen as an ongoing effort to analyze a system whose most permanent trait was its continuous transformation. The Danish ambassador Herluf Zahle spoke early on of "constant development" and "constant transformation,"[3] for example, and the American consul general George Messersmith referred to "elements of instability in the present government and party."[4]

When one looks over the consular reports as a whole, what strikes one above all is the diversity of interpretations of and opinions about the Third Reich. If nothing else, this diversity reflects the basic difficulty of coming by information in the National Socialist dictatorship. After 1933, many channels of information that diplomats had used to acquire information were sealed off, including a pluralistic press and discussion partners of differing political views. The new regime presented a riddle to many diplomats, who were accustomed to bureaucratic procedures, traditional forms of communication, and the regulations of a liberal constitutional order. Was it the most recent manifestation of the exceptionalism that had characterized German political life since 1870/1871, as British and Swiss diplomats in particular stressed? Or was National Socialism something new and unique? Danish ambassador Herluf Zahle expressed that view, arguing that Hitler's government was "not a government like that in every other country" and the Third Reich was "fundamentally different from the Germany of the past."[5] Was the Third Reich a monocracy and Germany "identical with Adolf Hitler,"[6] as one American report contended? Or was it a polycratic system marked by "personal rivalry for influence" or "competing cliques," as the French ambassador maintained in explaining the Kristallnacht pogrom of November 1938?[7] Were the masses oppressed under National Socialist rule? Or, alternatively, should the Third Reich be defined as "dictatorship of the masses,"[8] as Consul General Messersmith speculated? Did National Socialism gain public approval primarily because it satisfied citizens' everyday interests, such as the desire for a secure job? Or was National Socialism more like a political religion that spoke to and mobilized Germans' hopes and emotional longings? Did German society in the Nazi period constitute a "community of the people" (*Volksgemeinschaft*) or would it be more accurately described as an amalgamation of atomized individuals who dared not speak their minds to even their closest friends? Did the Third Reich reflect the "primitive, brutal, and arrogant mentality" of the Germans, as Swiss consul general Hans Zurlinden thought?[9] Or were they in fact the victims of a dictatorship with whom one must sympathize, as Zurlinden asserted in the very same report?

This rough overview makes clear that almost all of the interpretations and opinions that have ever been expressed about the Third Reich find outlet in the diplomatic reports. Nevertheless, a dominant line of interpretation in recent historical research on the Nazi era is conspicuously absent: none of the diplomats characterized National Socialist Germany as a "racial state."[10] Why?

At first glance, one could adduce that the diplomats, mostly liberals and conservatives, were not used to thinking in racial categories. Racial or racist categories were fundamentally incompatible with the diplomatic culture of mutual esteem and displays of respect. Established hierarchies in the world of diplomats were based primarily on "distinctions," to use Bourdieu's term.[11] Most diplomats posted to Germany were aware of the racism promoted by the Nazi regime precisely because it was at least partially contrary to their own convictions. There are many distanced remarks in the reports about a phenomenon diplomats often deemed crude. "It is hard to see," remarked the Danish ambassador Zahle in May 1933, "why it should actually be finer to come from Inner Asia (like the Aryan race) rather than from Mesopotamia."[12] Even diplomats from Fascist Italy were taken aback when Italians in National Socialist Germany were labeled as members of a "Mediterranean race." That the National Socialists thought in racial and racist categories was readily apparent to diplomats in Germany, but they did not attribute any overarching significance to racism in their analyses of the Third Reich. Interestingly, they did not refer to racism in commenting on the political practices of the National Socialists or even when they examined Nazi ideology.

AN AMERICAN VIEW OF *MEIN KAMPF*

A secret memorandum written by the American consul general in Stuttgart, Leon Dominian, in May 1933 is representative of the diplomats' perspective on National Socialism. Dominian had recently read *Mein Kampf* and saw the Nazi regime's actions during its first months in power as the realization of the vision Hitler had set out in the book.[13] Dominian did not read *Mein Kampf* as a plan for the creation of a racial state but rather as an expression of a violent German nationalism that had its roots in the nineteenth century and was being "revivified" by the Nazis. This violent nationalism was characterized by the "implacable hatred against any form of liberalism or tolerance that impregnates every page of the Chancellor's book," an "intense hatred against all the provisions of the Treaty of Versailles," and "policies of aggression and national aggrandizement ... based on principles denying justice and legality and which advocates arbitrary action resting on the use of force and violence." The new Nazi regime, embodying the "worst features of former Prussian militarism," was clearly making preparations for war even as it pledged itself to preserving peace. The American consul general understood *Mein Kampf*, copies of which he included with his report, as the script for a German bid for world power. The book expresses a "German intention to dominate Europe by violence," which was but the "prelude to plans of world control."

Although Dominian had no doubts that the Nazi regime would use brutal force against its domestic opponents, he did not see the regime as a top-down dictatorship. It aimed, rather, to mobilize the masses. Indeed, he thought the vision presented in *Mein Kampf* was in line with the views of a large part of the German public. "Mr. Hitler's book," he wrote, "betrays and reveals his intimate thoughts and intentions, those of his coworkers and the most cherished ambitions of the millions of Germans whose votes brought the National Socialist Party into power."

Dominian perceived the racism of Hitler and the National Socialists clearly enough, but he interpreted it functionally and in connection with other aspects of the new regime. He read the anti-Semitism in *Mein Kampf* first and foremost as a typical expression of National Socialism's intolerance and violence. Above all, he saw racism as means of national mobilization. Racism nourished feelings of German superiority and was "purely German megalomania based on unwarranted and unscientific belief in the exclusive superiority of Germans over other peoples."

Several of Dominian's colleagues made similar assessments of Nazi racism in their reports. They saw it as a purely external racism directed against other peoples and interpreted it as an aspect of nationalism and nationalistic mobilization. They did not regard it as a *Weltanschauung* that strove for a fundamental biologization of the social or as the paradigm of a racial state.

THE THIRD REICH AS A DICTATORSHIP OF MOBILIZATION

When they used the notion of a paradigm, foreign diplomats connected the Third Reich with the paradigm of a nationalistic dictatorship of mobilization that sought a revision of postwar borders and devoted itself, internally and externally, to preparation for war. When they discussed the foundations of the Third Reich, they referred to terror, force, and violence as the controlling mechanisms of a dictatorship; at the same time, they also stressed elements of public approval that, in their view, contributed to the consolidation of National Socialist dominance and made it unlikely that the regime would collapse on accout of internal tensions. Again and again, they pointed to Hitler's enormous popularity. His image underwent a sea change in early 1933. In the eyes of many Germans, the propagandist and leader of the Nazi party was transformed into a statesman and standard-bearer of the nation's hopes. "Everywhere, in all strata of the population, one meets completely devoted people who look up to him with deep veneration,"[14] the Swiss envoy Paul Dinichert reported to Bern. In the following years, many diplomats reported "a childlike faith in the Führer,"[15] who was "almost deified." Germans voiced many complaints and grievances throughout the duration of the Third Reich, but they generally did not include Hitler in their criticisms of the regime. It was not until the final years of the war that his reputation declined.

Diplomats noticed a growing public satisfaction with conditions in the Third Reich. Ever more Germans considered the Nazis' policies to be successful. The diplomats found the broadest public approval of the regime's actions in the area of foreign policy. Most Germans, they believed, firmly supported revision of the Treaty of Versailles. The British consul general in Hamburg noted in 1936, for instance, that there was "a wide measure of unanimity on the foreign issue."[16] His American colleague in Stuttgart, Samuel Honacker, had reported a year earlier that the reintroduction of military conscription had been "enthusiastically received by the overwhelming part of the population."[17] Even if there was no "bellicose spirit" hiding behind this feeling, many Germans supported the foreign policy of the Nazi regime even if at the same time they showed a marked fear of war.

The consuls also devoted considerable attention to the regime's presentation of itself before the German public. This staging, they believed, satisfied important emotional needs and had a role to play in community-building. The regime's rituals and propaganda were directed in particular at younger Germans. Although many young people were receptive, a British counsel, in a long report on "the general attitude of the younger generation," maintainted that young Germans were not fully in sync with the regime.[18] Early on, the French ambassador, André François-Poncet, pointed to the emotional bonding fostered by the regime's public events, which had, he suggested, a mystical and quasi-religious dimension.

The diplomats of larger countries initially boycotted the NSDAP party rallies in Nuremberg, but in later years they usually attended. Their reports were sometimes saturated by a lyrical pathos that conveyed the authors' fascination, their distance from the regime notwithstanding. A French report on the 1935 party rally, which goes on for forty-three pages, comes dangerously close to echoing the bombastic language of Nazi propaganda. It speaks of a "grandiose spectacle" that led "countless masses to the sacred place" where they "wait[ed] longing" to see an "extraordinary man."[19] If foreign observers predisposed by their positions to be critical of the Third Reich were carried away by the dynamism of the staging, one can well imagine that the same happened to the other attendees and participants.

A third area of focus in the consular reports was Germany's economic recovery. Many Germans credited the Nazi regime with the rapid decline in unemployment after 1933. An employee of the American embassy wrote in 1936 that most Germans "find the present conditions of employment satisfactory and prefer to retain the present political system."[20] Nonetheless, stagnant wages, shortages of some foodstuffs, the poor quality of many products, and the curtailment of production of consumer goods depressed the public's mood. The Third Reich was still a long way from being a consumer society. Although many Germans had a modest standard of living, they were doing well compared to other Europeans. An employee at the British consulate in Hamburg reported in 1936, for example, "It is quite certain that the workmen of the distressed city of Hamburg look incomparably more clean, healthy and prosperous than those of the distressed city of Newcastle."[21]

For many Germans, the reference point in judging the state of the economy was not earlier periods of prosperity but rather the low point of the international economic crisis in 1932. American chargé d'affaires Prentiss Gilbert observed in late 1938:

Above all it must not be forgotten that every German has a job and that every German has enough to eat and drink and is relatively very well housed. He does not want the chaos in his country which a blind revolution would presumably bring. Nor does he wish to return to 1932. From his past experience he values as a greater good his present sense of internal and external security derived from his country's unity and strength.[22]

Five years after the Nazi accession to power, even critical observers grudgingly conceded that the Nazi dictatorship had achieved "unity" and "strength." They allowed the other facets of the regime, including its racism, to recede into the background.

GAPS IN PERCEPTIONS OF NAZI SOCIAL POLICY

With two major exceptions, racism barely figures in diplomatic reports from the Third Reich. In discussing social policy, diplomatic observers focused more on mobilization and popular support for the regime than on its policies of discrimination and ostracism. The biologization of social policy consequently went largely unnoticed. The ostracization of so-called asocials, the preventive arrests of "career criminals" on biological and criminological grounds, and the persecution of the Sinti and the Roma almost never come up in the reports.[23]

Foreign diplomats took note of other Nazi racial policy measures of the regime, such as the Law for the Prevention of Offspring with Hereditary Defects (July 1933), but did not express alarm. As a rule, they only reacted when their own citizens were affected. A report that American vice consul in Hamburg, Malcolm C. Burke, submitted in October 1934 on the "Sterilization of the Unfit" was typical in this respect.[24] It was based on a conversation that Burke had had with a doctor at the Hamburg Health Office. Emphatically conciliatory, the American Burke pointed to the "conservative spirit" behind the law, noting that it prohibited the sterilization of healthy patients, and explained that the law was "necessary for the protection of the patient's own health." Patients would not have to bear the cost of the procedure: "In no case are ordinary and necessary expenses unloaded upon the individual, even though he is a person of no wealth, unable to pay." The only aspect of the law Burke criticized was the provision that if a "mentally incapable" patient could not understand the measure, the "idiot's guardian" could decide whether the patient was to be sterilized. Burke's conclusion was reassuring: "The purpose and effect of the German sterilization law should be clearly understood. It provides for two specific operations, one each for the male and the female subject, the sole result of which is to prevent the birth of offspring. In no case is the sexual nature of the person operated upon either injured or destroyed."

Given that approxmiately 6,000 of the 400,000 individuals subjected to forced sterilization died as a result of the procedure, Burke's assessment of the policy now seems excessively optimistic. He did not interpret the Law for the Prevention of Offspring with Hereditary Defects, and the practice of sterilization, as a measure of National Socialist racial policy; rather, he saw it as a preventative health policy that took into account the interests of those affected. Implicitly, one could even read the report as proposing that a similar measure be considered in the US, as Burke took care to note that "about one per cent of the population in a modern civilized community are tainted with a serious hereditary defect."

That comment serves as a reminder that National Socialist racial policy should not be viewed as an isolated phenomenon and must be set in the international context of the time. The eugenic-racist discourse was not limited to Germany.[25] Diplomats sometimes regarded certain of the Nazis' racist measures as potential models for regulations in their home countries. More frequently, however, they did not find matters touching on race worth mentioning. In other words: it was generally only those aspects of Nazi racial policy that radically differed from international standards of the time that were highlighted in diplomatic reports. There was thus little mention of many racist domestic policies. Discussion of racial policy in diplomatic reports focused almost exclusively on two clearly delineated issues: the persecution of Jews and the so-called euthanasia policy.

THE "UNLIMITED PERSECUTION OF A RACE"

Many diplomats realized surprisingly early on that the enactment of a handful of laws targeting Germany's Jewish minority and assigning Jews a lower legal status would not satisfy the Nazis' anti-Semitism. They pointed to the radical quality of anti-Jewish measures and of an anti-Semitism that did not remain within the usual bounds of prejudice. Violent attacks upon Jews by Storm Troopers and other Nazi activists played a decisive role in sharpening foreign diplomats' perception of the persecution of the Jews under the new regime. Many consuls saw such attacks as breaches of the standards of civilization that were unworthy of a modern society, and did not hide their aversion in their reports. One day before the start of the boycott of Jewish shops on March 31, 1933, George Messersmith, the American consul general in Berlin, was already speaking of "instances of a brutality and a directness of action which have not been excelled in the history of modern times."[26] In practice, he

reported, the National Socialists were aiming for the "practically unre-
stricted persecution of a race." Messersmith used the concept "race" quite
consciously in this context. It was clear to him and the other diplomats
that the anti-Semitism of the National Socialists was racially-biologically
charged: it was not rooted in Christian anti-Judaism, nor was it merely an
expression of socio-cultural reservations about Jews that some diplomats
shared. The Danish envoy Herluf Zahle, for instance, admitted that he
would have understood certain constraining regulations on the Jewish
minority to limit its "economic and political influence" in Germany.
Nevertheless, he went on to say, the labeling of the Jews as an "inferior
race" and the Nazi regime's measures aimed at them were "worse than
Medieval."[27] For Ambassador André François-Poncet of France, anti-
Semitism constituted the essential core of National Socialism. Other labels
applied to the National Socialist *Weltanschauung*, such as *völkisch* or
"racial," were nothing more than gilded code words for anti-Semitism,
he argued: "The word 'völkisch,' i.e. 'racist,' means nothing other than
'non-Jewish,' 'hostile to Jews.'"[28] François-Poncet believed the National
Socialist *Weltanschauung* was merely conceptual hocus-pocus, lacking
any inner logic or coherence, and nothing more than a cover for hate
and prejudices. He commented on anti-Jewish policies with a mixture of
contempt and biting derision. Remarking on the 1935 Nuremberg Laws,
he wrote,

In the end, the law to protect German blood and German honor, in which
comedy mixes so wonderfully with baseness as tragedy, is nothing other than
the simple expression of hate, prejudices, rancor, and above all the low-
mindedness which animates the editors and readers of the notorious anti-Jewish
organ "Der Stürmer." It helps the coarse czar of the Franks, this Julius Streicher,
in whose company anti-Semitism takes on the most vulgar and grotesque forms,
to authority.[29]

Many diplomats agreed with the general tenor of this assessment. In
their view, National Socialist racial theory was nothing more than anti-
Semitism – in other words, nothing more than crude hate and hubris. It
did not constitute a coherent *Weltanschauung*, or certainly not one that
the diplomats shared. One of the few exceptions was the Argentine consul
in Munich, Ernesto Sarmiento, who sent his ambassador a commentary
on the Nuremberg Laws in the hope "that this work [could be] of some
use for our fatherland on the burning question of race."[30]

Only a handful of foreign diplomats argued that the National Socialists' political ideas were part of a larger ideological project. One who did
was Henri Jourdan. As the head of Maison Académique Francaise in

Berlin, he wrote a study of "Hitler's ideology" in May 1933. Although Ambassador François-Poncet was not in agreement with Jourdan's assessment, the embassy forwarded the report to Paris.

Jourdan remarked:

The French public is inclined to see only a foolhardy undertaking in the National Socialist revolution, whose character, aided by unemployment and misery, is political in its essence and is driven on by mere adventurers. The public neglects or refuses to take the theories on which these adventurers allegedly build seriously. The "racism," the return to "Germanness," the renewal of the world through "Aryans of pure blood" appear to them as assertions so ridiculous that they see no occasion to waste time on them. If one wants to, one can consider this romantic pseudo-science as completely porous and silly. But we should know that Hitler's followers believe in it. We should be clear that for a majority of them it is the new Gospel.[31]

The main contours of later lines of interpretation of National Socialism are evident in the differing assessments François-Poncet and Jourdain put forwardin the regime's early years. Jourdan's "programmatic" interpretation stands in marked contrast to François-Poncet's political-functional reading of Nazism. The two ultimately agreed, however, in identifying racism as an element in the Nazis' political religion. The majority of the diplomats tended toward a more political-functional view. In their eyes, there was nothing particularly programmatic about Nazi anti-Semitism. They saw it as an inchoate sentiment that repeatedly erupted into action, and for that reason they thought it difficult, if not impossible, to offer prognoses on the future course of persecution. The diplomats therefore did not see any given anti-Jewish measure as the endpoint of the regime's persecutory efforts. However, none of them predicted the Holocaust.

Insofar as the diplomats occupied themselves with the driving forces of Jewish persecution in the Third Reich instead of merely reporting on it, they usually distinguished between the National Socialist movement and the German population. The latter appear in many of the reports as passive observers rather than active participants. Some of the diplomats did, however, also mention a growing anti-Jewish consensus. Many Germans, they observed, no longer considered Jews as members of the *Volksgemeinschaft*.

Foreign diplomats identified the Nazi party and its associated organizations as the central actors in the persecution of the Jews. Anti-Semitism was "deep-rooted in the National-Socialist Party,"[32] asserted the American consul general Douglas Jenkins in November 1935. Only days later, his colleague in Berlin, Raymond Geist, laid out the most brilliant analysis of National Socialist anti-Semitism penned by a consul. Geist wrote:

In the Party itself anti-Semitism is the common tie which unites the various groups and factions which manifest otherwise entirely different political tendencies, and binds them strongly because they all know that on this point Adolf Hitler will not compromise. Anti-Semitism provides a channel for all the explosive forces in the Party – an exhaust which continues to function successfully ... The Party as the determining living factor must be in a constant state of aggression and must endeavor to maintain the offensive and consequently must have an ever present object of attack.[33]

Geist's analysis was noteworthy in three respects. First, he did not see the National Socialist movement as a monolith. Rather, he portrayed it as a collection of networks and wings in competition for influence but held together by their shared animosity toward the Jewish enemy. Second, he pointed to the dynamic of inclusion and, above all, exclusion as a central element of the National Socialist movement. It was this dynamic that drove the process of constant social transformation. Third, he saw in Hitler not only the central integrating force for the National Socialist movement but also the representative of a hard line on the "Jewish question." This observation was all the more noteworthy because quite a few Germans, indulging in wishful thinking that had nothing to do with what was happening around them, ascribed a moderate position on this matter to the Führer. Geist understood the persecution of the Jews in its totality as a dynamic process that, although sometimes contradictory, was continuously becoming more radical.

This development was registered attentively by the diplomats of all countries, particularly as it was unparalleled on the international scene. Nonetheless, the threat and, as of 1939, reality of war tended to push anti-Semitic persecution and the gradual development of the Holocaust into the background. The deaths of millions of soldiers and civilians overshadowed the mass murder of Europe's Jews in the perception of the diplomats still left in Germany, even when they were well-informed about what was happening. For example, the Swiss consul general in Cologne, Franz-Rudolf von Weiss, reported in 1942 on a deportation transport out of the city to Eastern Europe: "My informant, who represents the German agency in this Jewish question, assumes that this transport has in the meantime been gassed, as since then no reports have reached Cologne concerning its whereabouts," he wrote.[34] The word "gassed" was apparently already so common by the summer of 1942 that the consul did not have to offer further explanation. Weiss also sent photos leaked to him on to Bern that showed the corpses of Jews being unloaded from freight cars. In October 1943, he reported, "On the handling of the Jewish question, it more and more leaks out that the evacuated Jews have been completely exterminated."[35] The diplomatic reports confirm that there were widespread informal information networks in which the Holocaust was an open secret. [36]

THE MASS MURDER OF THE SICK AND THE DISABLED

Diplomats were even more fully and accurately informed about the practice of "euthanasia" in Nazi Germany.[37] Outraged Germans leaked detailed information to foreign consuls. That these murders, unlike the mass murder of Jews, did not happen "somewhere in the east" but rather in Germany, that the perpetrators were exclusively Germans, and that a multitude of German families were affected certainly played a role in the dissemination of information. The families involved received mysterious death notices from clinics, and in many cases they undertook their own investigations. Moreover, the protest against the euthanasia program found an institutional catalyst in the Catholic clergy.[38]

The Swiss consul general in Munich, Hans Gremminger, and his colleague in Cologne sent transcripts of the sermons by Bishop Clemens August Graf von Galen to the Swiss embassy. Gremminger called the sermons "dreadful accusations," and he also sent along detailed information about the extent of the killings:

The fact is that months ago at this consulate, trustworthy testimony was taken, according to which not hundreds but rather thousands of unlucky ill people have been "released from their sufferings as ordered" ... Such occurrences are also spoken of among the people, although with the greatest reticence and a certain timidity. Such transgressions injure the feeling of the German people deeply and they are harshly condemned.[39]

The Swiss envoy and minister Hans Frölicher referred this report on to Bern, although with the conciliatory formulation: "It cannot, however, be supposed that the inner peace could somehow be disturbed because of this measure, for which rational grounds can be given in war time."[40]

Frölicher's text is one of the few diplomatic reports that, between the lines, expressed a certain understanding for the euthanasia killings. Most diplomats were no less outraged than the German public. Paul Dutko, the American deputy consul in Leipzig, noted in October 1940: "The inhabitants of Leipzig are not only shocked beyond description, but are genuinely perturbed and stricken with a fear of the far-reaching consequence of this horrible affair. A feeling of horror and complete insecurity of life has begun to set in."[41] Few Germans shared the National Socialist view of the ill and disabled as "burdens" (*Ballastexistenzen*) and "useless eaters" (*unnütze Esser*). To the contrary, they saw the murders as an attack on the *Volksgemeinschaft* that could threaten to include other unwelcome groups. Dutko pointed directly to such fears: "It is this knowledge that makes many people shudder with fear at the fate the future holds on them. They feel that if Germany wins the war they will be at the mercy of this unprincipled, ruthless and lawless body of men."[42] The consulates' files hold letters from outraged Germans who hoped that the representatives of foreign governments might intervene. A nurse who had to work in a euthanasia clinic, for example, explained at the close of her letter to the American embassy in Berlin that she had written "in the expectation that you will do what lies in your power to bring the murderers to justice."[43] The diplomats recorded such protests at length because they expected popular oppostion to National Socialism to grow, and eagerly searched for any sign of resistance to the regime. Of course, some diplomats relayed information about the euthansia killings and the Holocaust simply because the Nazis overstepped all limits of tolerable conduct and all international standards of legitimate governmental action.

CONCLUSION

Foreign diplomats posted to Germany usually described the Third Reich as a nationalist dictatorship of mobilization. Some diplomats classified the new regime as a break with the German past, while others saw problematic German national traditions at work in National Socialism and argued for a fundamental continuity between the Nazi regime and its predecessors.

The paradigm of the racial state played an astonishingly small role in the diplomatic reports. As a rule, diplomatic observers generally took notice of Nazi racism only when it deviated seriously from international standards of the time, as in the case of the persecution of the Jews and the euthanasia killings. Many examples of racist policies were registered with little comment or little show of concern. Many diplomats regarded Nazi racism as identical to hatred of the Jews and anti-Semitism and did not recognize a coherent ideology in Nazi political ideas. Only a few argued that the Nazi party's description of itself as a *Weltanschauungspartei* should be taken seriously. Many of the reports implicitly gave priority to foreign policy and to the interests of the diplomats' governments. With that point in mind, we cannot take the diplomatic reports as evidence repudiating the racial state paradigm. Nonetheless, the diplomats should be taken seriously as contemporary observers. They constantly tried to analyze afresh a hybrid, self-transforming regime. From their perspective, the Third Reich was characterized by continuous change and unpredictability. They did not see the regime carefully attempting to implement a preset program.

To the question of the direction of National Socialist policy, the American consul general George Messersmith gave the telling answer that he could predict the future course of Germany only insofar as "the keeper of a madhouse is able to tell what his inmates will do in the next hour,"[44] a comparison as remarkable as it is revealing. The explicit reluctance of many diplomats to see a coherent whole in the regime's policies should give us pause about attempting to find such coherence in retrospect.

In closing, it should be noted that there is an interesting tension between the observations of contemporaries and retrospective interpretations of National Socialism, particularly with respect to racism. This becomes clear in the example of the French ambassador, André François-Poncet. In his reports, he presented Nazi ideology as a pretext for base motives and muffled feelings of hatred; at best, he thought, Nazism belonged to the realm of mysticism. But in the memoir he published immediately after the war, François-Poncet devoted an entire chapter to Nazi racism, calling it the "foundation ... on which the edifice of Hitler's world of ideas was constructed."[45] As this example suggests, it was only after the fact that race and the racial state paradigm were taken up as a means to impose order on and make sense of the various policies enacted after 1933. Contemporaries, by contrast, were not yet willing to ascribe such a function to racism.

Notes

1 See Frank Bajohr and Christoph Strupp (eds.), *Fremde Blicke auf das "Dritte Reich." Berichte ausländischer Diplomaten über Herrschaft und Gesellschaft in Deutschland 1933–1945* (Göttingen, 2011). The project investigated the reports filed by diplomats from the following countries: the United States, Great Britain, France, Poland, Denmark, Switzerland, Italy, Japan, Argentina, and Costa Rica. This essay would not have been possible without the preliminary spadework of the colleagues who dealt with the records of the various countries: Cristoph Strupp (US), Eckard Michels (UK), Jean-Marc Dreyfus (France), Jerzy Tomaszewski (Poland), Karl Christian Lammers and Therkel Straede (Denmark), Gregor Spuhler (Switzerland), Ruth Nattermann (Italy), Tatsushi

Hirano (Japan), Holger Meding (Argentina), Christiane Berth and Dennis Arias (Costa Rica).

2 On the internal reports, see, for example, Heinz Boberach (ed.), *Meldungen aus dem Reich 1938–1945. Die geheimen Lageberichte des Sicherheitsdienstes der SS* (Herrsching, 1984); Eberhard Jäckel and Otto Dov Kulka (eds.), *Die Juden in den geheimen NS-Stimmungsberichten 1933–1945* (Düsseldorf, 2004). On the reports of the socialist opposition, see *Deutschland-Berichte der Sozialdemokratischen Partei Deutschlands (Sopade) 1934–1940* (Frankfurt am Main, 1980).

3 Imperial Archives Copenhagen, Ministry of Foreign Affairs 1900–1945, H 52, No. IX, Dispatch of Ambassador Zahle, February 3, 1938. Quotations from American and British reports are given in the original English. Quotations from other countries' diplomatic reports are translated from German.

4 US Consul General George S. Messersmith, With Reference to the Campaign Against So-Called "Muckertum" or Middle Class Bigotry, Berlin, November 17, 1933, National Archives, College Park, MD, Record Group 59. United States Department of State, Central Decimal File 1930–1939, 862.401/2./611.

5 Imperial Archives Copenhagen, Ministry of Foreign Affairs 1900–1945, H 52, No. IX, Dispatch of Ambassador Zahle, February 3, 1938.

6 US Consul General Raymond H. Geist, The German Economic Situation with Particular Reference to the Political Outlook, Berlin, November 12, 1935, National Archives, College Park, MD, Record Group 59. United States Department of State, Central Decimal File 1930–1939, 862.50/913.

7 Diplomatic Archives Center, Nantes (CADN), Berlin, Series A, Dispatch of Alphonse Barton de Montbas from the French Embassy in Berlin, November 15, 1938, B 220, No. 1234.

8 US Consul General George S. Messersmith in Berlin, Uncertainty as to the Developments in the Economic and Financial Situation in Germany, May 9, 1933, National Archives, College Park, MD, Record Group 59. United States Department of State, Central Decimal File 1930–1939, 862.51/3605.

9 Hans Zurlinden, Swiss Consul General in Munich, to Minister Pierre Bonna, Berne, on Mentalität der Deutschen, Rottach-Egern (Tegernsee), March 24, 1944, Swiss Federal Archives Berne, E 2300, Munich, Vol. 295, No. 615.

10 Michael Burleigh and Wolfgang Wippermann, *The Racial State: Germany 1933–1945* (Cambridge, 1991).

11 Pierre Bourdieu, *Distinction: A Social Critique of the Judgement of Taste* (Cambridge, 1987).

12 Imperial Archives Copenhagen, Ministry of Foreign Affairs 1900–1945, H 52, No. XXXVI, Dispatch of Ambassador Zahle, May 17, 1933.

13 Leon Dominian, Confidential Memorandum, Stuttgart, May 19, 1933, National Archives, College Park, MD, Record Group 59, United States Department of State, Central Decimal File 1930–1939, 862.20/611. All quotations in this paragraph and the two that follow are taken from this memorandum.

14 Minister Paul Dinichert, Swiss Ambassador in Berlin, to Bundesrat Giuseppe Motta, Head of the Swiss Political Department, November 17, 1933, Swiss Federal Archives Berne, E 2300, Berlin, Vol. 63, No. 118.

15 Quotation from a memo from the British Consulate General in Munich on the pogrom of November 9/10, 1938, in Bavaria, Munich, November 24, 1938, National Archives Kew/Surrey, FO 371/21638.

16 D. F. S. Filliter, British Consulate General in Hamburg, Report on the Election Campaign 1936, March 31, 1936, National Archives Kew/Surrey, FO 371/19923.

17 Samuel W. Honaker, US Consul General in Stuttgart, General Reactions in the Stuttgart District Concerning Compulsory Military Service and Armament Activities, May 3, 1935, National Archives, College Park, MD, Record Group 59, United States Department of State, Central Decimal File 1930–1939, 862.20/1001.

18 British Consulate General in Hamburg to Nevile M. Henderson, Memorandum on the General Attitude of the Young Generation, 1939, National Archives Kew/Surrey, FO 371/23009.

19 Diplomatic Archives Center, Nantes (CADN), Embassy Berlin, Series A, A 437, Dispatch No. 1344, September 13, 1935.

20 Wright, US Embassy in Berlin, on The German Mining Industries Under the Nazi Government, Berlin, August 17, 1936, National Archives, College Park, MD, Record Group 59, United States Department of State, Central Decimal File 1930–1939, 862.63/54.

21 British Consulate General in Hamburg, Memo on "Some Observations on the Working Classes in Hamburg," June 24, 1936, National Archives Kew/Surrey, FO 371/19933.

22 Prentiss Gilbert, US Chargé d'Affaires in Berlin, Comment on the German Political Situation, December 5, 1938, National Archives, College Park, MD, Record Group 59, United States Department of State, Central Decimal File 1930–1939, 862.00/3806.

23 See Susan Bachrach and Dieter Kunz (eds.), *Deadly Medicine: Creating the Master Race* (Washington, DC, 2004); Wolfgang Ayass, *"Asoziale" im Nationalsozialismus* (Stuttgart, 1995); Dietmar Sedlaczek et al. (eds.), *"Minderwertig" und "Asozial." Stationen der Verfolgung gesellschaftlicher Außenseiter* (Zurich, 2005); Robert Gellately and Nathan Stotzfus (eds.), *Social Outsiders in Nazi Germany* (Princeton, 2001); Patrick Wagner, *Volksgemeinschaft ohne Verbrecher. Konzeptionen und Praxis der Kriminalpolizei in der Zeit der Weimarer Republik und des Nationalsozialismus* (Hamburg, 1996); Michael Zimmermann, *Rassenutopie und Genozid. Die nationalsozialistische "Lösung der Zigeunerfrage"* (Hamburg, 1996).

24 Malcolm C. Burke, Vice Consul in Hamburg, on "Sterilization of the Unfit," October 11, 1934, National Archives, College Park, MD, Record Group 59, United States Department of State, Central Decimal File 1930–1939, 862.1241. All quotations in this paragraph and the one that follows are taken from this report.

25 See, e.g., Nancy Ordover, *American Eugenics: Race, Queer Anatomy and the Science of Nationalism* (Minneapolis, 2003); Harry Bruinius, *Better for the World: The Secret History of Forced Sterilization and America's Quest for Racial Purity* (New York, 2006); Michael Schwartz, "Eugenik und 'Euthanasie.' Die internationale Debatte und Praxis bis 1933/1945" in Klaus-Dietmar Henke (ed.), *Tödliche Medizin im Nationalsozialismus* (Cologne, 2008), 65–83.

26 George S. Messersmith, US Consul General in Berlin, With Further Reference to the Manifold Aspects of the Anti-Jewish Movement in Germany, March 31, 1933, National Archives, College Park, MD, Record Group 59, United States Department of State, Central Decimal File 1930–1939, 862.4016/568.

27 Imperial Archives Copenhagen, Ministry of Foreign Affairs 1900–1945, H 52, No. 36, Dispatch from Ambassador Zahle, May 17, 1933.

28 Report of the Ambassador André Francois-Poncet in Berlin, March 30,1933, Diplomatic Archives Center, Nantes (CADN), Berlin, Series A, No. 423.

29 Report of the Ambassador André Francois-Poncet in Berlin, September 13, 1935, Diplomatic Archives Center, Nantes (CADN), Berlin, Series A, A 437, Dispatch No. 1344.

30 Ernesto Sarmiento, Argentinian Consul in Munich, to Ambassador Ricardo Olivera, Munich, February 18, 1941, published in DAIA/Centro de Estudios Sociales (eds.), *Proyecto Testimonio. Relaciones de los Archivos Argentinos sobre la Politica Oficial e la Era Nazi-Fascista* (Buenos Aires, 1998), Vol. 1, 153–9.

31 Memorandum by Henri Jourdain, Head of the Maison Académique Francaise in Berlin, on Hitler's Ideology, June 30, 1933, Diplomatic Archives Center, Nantes (CADN), Berlin, Series A, A 424, Dispatch No. 660.

32 Douglas Jenkins, US Consul General, Political and Economic Trends in Germany During the Past Twelve Months, Berlin, November 4, 1935, National Archives, College Park, MD, Record Group 59, United States Department of State, Central Decimal File 1930–1939, 862.00/3552.

33 Raymond Geist, US Consul, The German Economic Situation with Particular Reference to the Political Outlook, Berlin, November 12, 1935, National Archives, College Park, MD, Record Group 59, United States Department of State, Central Decimal File 1930–1939, 862.50/913.

34 Markus Schmitz and Bernd Haunfelder, *Humanität und Diplomatie. Die Schweiz in Köln 1940–1949* (Münster, 2001), 179; report of June 24, 1942.

35 Ibid., 208, report of October 5, 1943.

36 Frank Bajohr and Dieter Pohl, *Der Holocaust als offenes Geheimnis. Die NS-Führung, die Deutschen und die Alliierten* (Munich, 2006); Bernward Dörner, *Die Deutschen und der Holocaust. Was niemand wissen wollte, aber jeder wissen konnte* (Berlin, 2007); Peter Longerich, *"Davon haben wir nichts gewusst" Die Deutschen und die Judenverfolgung 1933–1945* (Munich, 2006).

37 Hundreds of books and articles have been published on this topic. See Jana Wolf, "Auswahlbibliographie zu Eugenik, Rassenhygiene, Zwangssterilisation, NS-"Euthanasie" und deren Strafverfolgung nach 1945," in Henke (ed.), *Tödliche Medizin*, 291–338.

38 On the protest movement against euthanasia, see Winfried Süß, "'Dann ist keiner von uns seines Lebens mehr sicher.' Bischof von Galen, der katholische Protest gegen die 'Euthanasie' und der Stopp der 'Aktion T4'" in Martin Sabrow (ed.), *Skandal und Öffentlichkeit in der Diktatur* (Göttingen, 2004), 102–29.

39 Hans Gremminger, Swiss Consul General in Munich, to Ambassador Frölicher in Berlin, September 6, 1941, Swiss Federal Archives Berne, E 2300, Munich, Vol. 295.

40 Swiss Ambassador Frölicher, Berlin, to Bundesrat Pilet-Golaz, Berne, September 15, 1941, Swiss Federal Archives Berne, E 2300, Munich, Vol. 295.

41 Paul Dutko, American Deputy Consul in Leipzig, on "Mysterious Deaths of Mental Patients from Leipzig Consular District and the Connection therewith of the Black Guard (SS)," October 16, 1940, National Archives, College Park, MD, Record Group 59, United States Department of State, Central Decimal File 1930–1939, 862.143/12.

42 Ibid.

43 Leland Morris, Chargé d'Affaires at the American Embassy, Berlin, March 13, 1941, Supplementary Information in Respect of the Killing of Mentally Diseased Persons by the State, with enclosed letter of a German nurse, National Archives, College Park, MD, Record Group 59, United States Department of State, Central Decimal File 1930–1939, 862.1241/15.

44 Quotation from a letter by Messersmith to the Under Secretary of State, William Phillips: Jesse H. Stiller, *George S. Messersmith: Diplomat of Democracy* (Chapel Hill, 1987), 46.

45 André François-Poncet, *Als Botschafter in Berlin 1931–1938* (Mainz, 1947; first published in French, 1946), 75.

15

Race and Humor in Nazi Germany

Martina Kessel

Humor in Nazi Germany was many things except, for the most part, funny. This essay will trace some of the meanings conveyed by practices considered at the time to be entertaining. I would like to argue that humor can be understood as a form of communicative contract among non-Jews, who used it to act out exclusion and inclusion. Moreover, anecdotes can and did work as an "everyday historiography"[1] in that they actualized (hi)stories that contemporaries told themselves and others to render plausible their understanding of social order. Here, I would like to concentrate on the imaginary, long present in German culture, that non-Jewish Germans had been victims of a history writ large, perpetrated by foreigners and/or Jews. Historians have emphasized that during the National Socialist era non-Jews attacked Jews ever more aggressively as alleged enemies and acted out violence against them in public to create an emotional community that was not only talked about but felt.[2] In the eyes of the perpetrators, the accusation that Jews were the enemy justified violence. I would like to broaden that argument and analyze joking as a form of behavior that non-Jews used to turn themselves from imagined victims into victors within their new social order but that, by continuing to frame Jews as perpetrators, allowed non-Jews to act as perpetrators without having to consider themselves as such.

The jokes I am discussing in this essay often circled around race. However, my argument starts from the assumption that the formation of self and other during National Socialism did not rely on the notion of race as a scientific category. Rather, contemporaries constructed their understanding of "Germanness" through intertwining cultural projections and practices, drawing on categories that had been familiar in German history for a long time. Jokes about race can thus be understood as one among many practices used to enforce a boundary between those who should be considered German and those who should not. They formed part of a social imaginary that could become crucial during National Socialism because it had been familiar before and therefore helped to render legitimate and plausible the processes of exclusion.[3] By "elements of the social imaginary," I mean ways of making sense of the world and forms of construing meaning that contemporaries used not only to interpret historical situations but also to organize their world in specific ways. The best known of these imaginaries is probably the widespread desire for a Führer who would cut across social, cultural, and political differences, no matter how differently that figure might have been conceptualized by various groups and individuals.

In this essay, I would like to highlight the equally deep-seated self-conception of non-Jewish Germans through which they saw themselves as victims and Jewish Germans as perpetrators. Nazi activists not only told jokes that rested upon that self-conception but also made it come alive in practices deemed humorous. Instead of following the fantasy, deeply entrenched in German cultural memory after 1945, that joking during Nazism had signaled non-Jewish opposition,[4] I read jokes about race by those who were not persecuted as narratives of empowerment. The humor I am searching for did not project a belief in biological difference. Rather, it was racist as a cultural practice in that it discursively established a distinction between Germans and Jews as absolute, among other ways by repetition but also by physically embodying the enemy. And humor could and did turn into an important performance of "being German" during the Nazi era because it had been used as an interpretative framework to identify belonging or non-belonging long before the Weimar Republic collapsed. Therefore, before turning to analyze in greater detail what humor as a communicative contract and humor as an everyday historiography meant during National Socialism, I would like to flesh out briefly how Germans since the nineteenth century had connected a particular notion of humor with a specific understanding of German history and identity.

HUMOR AS A FAMILIAR CULTURAL TROPE

Intellectuals occupied with defining what it meant to be German used the notion of humor since at least the early nineteenth century as a narrative about German history.[5] Philosophers such as Fichte opted to frame German history since the Middle Ages within what Hayden White termed the "tragic emplotment" because it supposedly lacked unity.[6] In this historiography, Germans appeared as victims of history. Their attempts at unity had supposedly been impeded in modern times by various Others, both foreign (e.g., the French) and internal (Catholics, Jews).[7] Humor was understood to imply the desire and the willingness to end that tragic fate and achieve unity, if need be by fighting. The establishment of the empire through the war against France did not, however, put an end to such a reading of the German past. Instead, its proponents developed what Michael Geyer has called "catastrophic nationalism," namely the understanding that true German unity still had to be and would only be borne by war.[8] For example, Arthur Moeller van den Bruck, a well-known representative of the so-called conservative revolution, insisted in his 1910 *Die lachenden Deutschen* (Laughing Germans) on an intrinsic connection between German culture and combat. He defined the real task of art, and thus of humor as well, as not only to entertain but to fulfill a higher function, namely the realization of a German unity that, in his eyes, was still being tragically thwarted by various enemies.[9] For those who saw the participation revolution of the 1900s and the growing power of parliament as threats to their vision of a paternalistic social and political order in which everyone accepted their place in society humor was the most appropriate form of behavior in the struggle for genuine unity and an end to Germany's tragic fate. Thus, the notion of humor served as a cultural concept to integrate the idea of war, or at least of fighting, as essentially German into German culture.[10]

The idea of thwarted unity worked, however, only if culpability could be attributed to others. In other words, the desire to project an image of oneself as having been victimized needed the projection of a perpetrator in order to work as a cultural logic. Humor, as an everyday historiography, served to tell that story. Accordingly, whoever figured as other in this construct appeared not only as other but also as enemy. That enemy might be identified through the polar opposite of humor, namely irony. For those who understood humor to be a signifier of the desire and willingness to work for German unity, if need be through war, irony was a form of behavior dedicated to preventing unity. Irony, understood as a reflexive analysis of what it meant to be modern, was criticized as non-German[11] and, although attributed to any other classified as an enemy, identified as typically Jewish.[12] Regardless of its actual content, irony was said to hurt and to prolong the *Zerrissenheit* (inner conflict and disunity) of German history. Humor, by contrast, was supposed to heal and to integrate. The inclusionary/exclusionary character of both terms intensified during the Vormärz era and the Revolution of 1848 as humorous media in Germany became a tool to convey and comment upon political programs. To take just one example: Protestant intellectuals condemned Heinrich Heine as non-German on account of his use of irony, thereby discrediting both his political ideas and his aesthetic approach.[13] The binary construction humor vs. irony was therefore not intended to explain how these two modes functioned aesthetically; rather, it helped to classify historical phenomena as either belonging or not belonging to what was deemed to be German.

Certainly, the assertion that German and Jewish were inherently different was acted out through any number of binary categories. The most prominent were probably work vs. non-work and purity vs. non-purity.[14] Humor gave such categories additional pungency through the overarching idea that history could be considered as German only if Jews were excluded from it.[15] I should emphasize that this framing did not necessarily arise; claiming to be acting or speaking humorously did not automatically imply a specific political position. Still, the narrative called humor could convey the image of an individual and collective self as German that inherently excluded the possibility of a Jewish-German self without having to mention exclusion as a constitutive element in the formation of the self. Saying that does not imply the existence of a widespread "eliminationist anti-Semitism" before the Nazi era,[16] but it does emphasize the desire to define being German through juxtaposition with a Jewish-German self. That juxtaposition was argued all the more forcefully as it became all the more difficult to distinguish Jewish and non-Jewish members of the culturally influential middle classes.[17]

I do not buy into the notion of a special German humor (as a cultural variant of the *Sonderweg*), but instead would like to emphasize that studying Germans' understandings of humor and irony illuminates how intensely some of them insisted that German history had taken a special path. And finally, this essay is not intended as a study of anti-Semitism in German culture; rather, I am asking how Germans defined Germanness through categories of difference, constituting "being German" by juxtaposing it with a number of Others whose meaning and relevance may have varied according to context.

That political groups like the Alldeutscher Verband or, at other times, a majority of the German population described themselves as having been victimized has been highlighted as a prominent storyline in modern German history but emphasized primarily in studies of Imperial Germany, the Weimar Republic, and postwar West Germany.[18] However, the imaginary of self-victimization also played a crucial role for non-Jewish Germans during the Nazi era because, I would argue, it allowed them to avoid having to explain their acceptance of violence as the basis of social order. That form of self-fashioning had been fostered earlier by the wartime understanding of World War I as a defensive war and, in turn, by interpretations after 1918 of Germany's defeat. The anti-Jewish impulse sharpened markedly during World War I.[19] Sarcastic caricatures excluded Jewish Germans from both the "community of sufferers" at home and "the community of fighters" at the front, which, taken together, represented the fantasy of achieving unity through the experience of war.[20] Defeat in 1918 worsened the situation for Jewish Germans. It also made the self-description of non-Jewish Germans as victims ever more popular because in this situation too, I would argue, it allowed them to evade complicated questions about the causes of the war and of Germany's defeat. But, again, the "victim" self-projection could be successful only if a perpetrator could be identified. Although recent research on the Weimar Republic has pointed out its successes on the level of symbolic politics,[21] German society still managed to achieve only a negative consensus that was based on rejecting the Versailles agreements and holding Jewish Germans responsible for defeat and the hated treaty.[22] Peter Jelavich has shown the ramifications of this imaginary for the arena of humor, tracing how the discursive possibilities for Jewish-German comedians had already begun to narrow during the Weimar Republic. In Imperial Germany, Jewish entertainers had used ironic quips about supposedly Jewish character traits to position themselves as Germans *and* Jews, in much the same way that Saxons or Bavarians had integrated their sense of regional *and* national belonging. During the Weimar Republic, however, the state turned a blind eye to anti-Jewish violence so often that the Centralverein deutscher Staatsbürger jüdischen Glaubens (Central Association of German Citizens of the Jewish Faith) wanted to forbid some of the best known Jewish-German entertainers from indulging in self-irony, fearing that anti-Semites would misrepresent such joking as truths told by Jews about their own race.[23] Jews' ability to comment on political and social issues was thus sharply circumscribed long before exclusion became official governmental policy.

HUMOR AS A COMMUNICATIVE CONTRACT

It was this longstanding tension that helps explain why humor could turn into a communicative contract and a practice of the self as German during the Nazi era that posited an absolute divide between Germans and Jews. Reading humor as a communicative understanding has bearing on the way we interpret the Nazi regime. I agree with the characterization of Nazi Germany as an authoritarian society in which the government ruled with the consent of the many. Citizens could negotiate to attain many of their desires and could criticize some aspects of the regime so long as they generally complied with its demands; in return for popular compliance, the regime was expected to provide security and to be sensitive to its supporters' concerns.[24] In communicative terms, this agreement meant that all sides expected the other to talk in a certain fashion in order to create an inclusionary/exclusionary society. Scorn and derision were among the means used to turn Jewish Germans into a supposedly homogeneous group of enemies.[25] In turn, many of those who classified themselves as German demanded that they be addressed not with arguments but in a humorous, entertaining manner, which, paradoxically, assured them that they were taken seriously as members of the society they were helping to create.

Finding the right note in humor thus entailed establishing boundaries and achieving the positioning expected by all involved. However, as the difference between humor and irony was as impossible to define as race was, the slippery character of humor could also threaten engaged Nazis. After 1933, German society engaged in a wild goose chase for "white Jews," that is, non-Jews who allegedly displayed a Jewish mentality or engaged in "Jewish" behavior.[26] The pursuit of "white Jews" again underscores that the formation of self and other was cultural, not biological. The debate about humor functioned in similar terms. The awareness that a lack of particular cultural virtues signaled a problematic deficiency worried the leaders of all National Socialist organizations. The Gestapo, the SS, and those who trained party members in "political correctness" all urged their listeners to distinguish carefully between entertainment for tough men and "dirty jokes."[27] The reference to "dirt" served as a typical cultural classification of exclusion: The implication of sexual immorality and depravity played on stereotypes to define Jews and Jewishness as culturally inferior. But the sheer impossibility of defining exactly what made a joke "dirty" forced editors of joke collections to emphasize that they were not offering "dirty jokes" but rather entertainment for "real men."[28] Nor were the elites spared in the constant negotiation of what constituted acceptable humor, i.e. the correct form of communication between rulers and ruled. When politicians or the media turned their sarcasm against ordinary non-Jewish Germans, instead of jovially reminding them of the right path to the new future, the latter showed their anger. In 1934, readers criticized the producers of the satirical journal *Brennessel* as "Jews," "pimps," and "perverts"[29] for mocking non-Jewish Germans, thus using categories of supposed deviance to describe their leadership. When Goebbels ridiculed German teachers in 1942 for not being up to date, listeners complained that this was like the "Jewish disparagement of the German order of living" that had supposedly happened during the Weimar Republic. Teachers, so they fumed, could still be caricatured "maliciously," as "in the liberal times."[30]

As one of the regime's most frequently heard voices, Goebbels was probably the Nazi leader most commonly targeted in jokes for failing the racial test. Such jokes were perhaps a criticism less of what he said than of how he said it. It was precisely the impossibility of defining Jewishness scientifically that necessitated an endless stream of advice about the behavior that would prove one's Germanness. And because they were trained to think about internal enemies who supposedly deviated from the norm, non-Jews threatened one another with the reminder that inclusion could prove to be only temporary and depended on appropriate conduct. Accusing someone of "going Jewish" could be and was used as a means of defense and as a disciplinary device in working out power relations among those who thought they belonged among "the Germans."

Joking about leading politicians failing racial standards was standard procedure for non-Jews, but to avoid risky misunderstandings, those who made such jokes explicitly referred to humor as a communicative practice shared by rulers and ruled. On Christmas 1939, a little booklet was given as a gift. It carried the dedication "From M. for P., Christmas 1939." The booklet resembled a *Poesiealbum*, those popular autograph books in which children asked friends and family to enter a few sentences as a token of friendship. In this case, the pages were already filled with handwritten entries offering, as the title given in large letters on the first page proclaimed, "Humor nach 1933" (Humor after 1933). One of the jokes made fun of Robert Ley, leader of the Deutsche Arbeitsfront (German Labor Front), who was known for heavy drinking. The "Matchstick Game" challenged the reader to "make an Aryan out of a Jew" by moving only one match ("Legespiel mit Streichhölzern: Durch Verlegen eines Streichholzes mach aus einem Juden einen Arier"). The joke implied that Ley was Jewish and had become non-Jewish simply by combining the "V" and the "I" in "LEVI" into the "Y" in "LEY."[31] Written down in 1939, the joke worked as an integral part of an interactive communication about the social "victory" that had been achieved under the Nazis. It was considered an appropriate present on such a festive occasion, rendered personal by writing jokes down for somebody close enough to merit such affective effort, and constructed as an invitation to play along. The booklet's second page, in turn, emphasized the presenter's allegiance to the regime's leadership: it was garnished with the smiling faces of Hitler, Goebbels, Goering, and Heß, cut out carefully from print media and pasted into the book right after the title page.[32] The gift booklet, offered as a testament to the cheerfulness of German society under the tutelage of its Nazi leaders, rested on the assumption that the population and the political elite spoke the same language. To put it differently: presenting joker and listener as smiling people who were simply doing as Hitler did would eliminate any dangerous misunderstanding that joking about politicians might produce. Far from implying resistance to racial policy, a joke about racial belonging could confirm the teller's status as a member of German society in good standing.

In the publishing industry, producers and censors negotiated what constituted the most acceptable way of presenting contemporary society. After 1933, newcomers to the scene of print media and theatre took advantage of its exclusionary re-formation and flooded the market to such an extent that censors became wary of the often mediocre humor publications being produced in ever greater numbers.[33] Established authors and editors also produced humor books by the dozen. The anthologies *Lachendes Volk* (A laughing people) and *Lustiges Leben* (Happy life) compiled by Johannes Banzhaf were among the top twenty bestselling books in Germany. The 1943 collection of soldiers' humor assembled by the *Völkischer Beobachter, Darüber lache ich noch heute. Soldaten erzählen heitere Erlebnisse* (I'm still laughing about it today: soldiers recount amusing experiences), sold 2.6 million copies.[34] Of course, the book market was not free, but to explain the vast number of humorous publications as merely propaganda would miss their meanings. Such offerings were certainly ideologically framed, but researchers have pointed out that propaganda can be successful only if it ties in with people's expectations and desires.[35] Propaganda should therefore not be understood as a solely *top-down* phenomenon, just as the media did not simply produce or manipulate the audience's wishes; instead, producers and consumers together regulated discursively which interpretation of the world would be predominant and which would be marginalized or excluded.[36] Again, successful publications activated not racial theories but cultural stereotypes to distinguish between German and non-German, usually in the form of binary framings such as purity or work. Also, producers and censors alike preferred narratives in which German society had already conquered all of its enemies, narratives in which all others had been eradicated. Such entertainment offered a vision of society without indicating how it was to be achieved – a vision of the society the Nazi regime was trying to create without mentioning the means it was employing.[37] At the same time, however, abusive caricatures and derisive comments about Jews or the Allies never disappeared.[38] I argue instead that consumers had a choice between different ways of representing German society.

All in all, the number of jokes circulating in German society was so immense, and the degree of active participation in communicating them so high, that early emigrants hoped they might foreshadow serious political opposition. That hope was voiced, for example, by the Social Democrat Franz Osterroth, who fled to Czechoslovakia in 1933 and published a collection of jokes from Germany – *Deutsche Flüsterwitze. Das Dritte Reich unterm Brennglas* (German whispered jokes: the Third Reich under the magnifying glass) – in 1935 under the pseudonym of Jörg Willenbacher.[39] Indeed, sarcastic semantics could allow criticism or self-distancing without entering the realm of censored speech. Jokes were not always expressions of political opposition, however. I would argue that Germans also used jokes to live their "victory" under Nazi rule, communicating not only with each other but also with their political elite through jocular performance, as Hitler himself continuously made derisive fun of opponents and Jews.[40]

In communicating through jokes, all sides involved betrayed the desire for non-argumentative forms of politics. According to the SD, the security police of the SS, non-Jewish Germans were fond of humorous radio broadcasts and short films that told them, through a variety of folksy figures, how to deal with shortages or foreign workers. Listeners and viewers pointed out explicitly that it was so much nicer to be educated with a little German humor instead of outright propaganda.[41] In turn, they answered with jokes about leading politicians that were, in a form of continuous meta-commentary, explained as a sign of affection or attachment. The many jokes about Göring, for example, were widely told and constantly commented upon, and the butt of the jokes himself was said to be so keen on this display of interest that he sent out his driver every day to collect the latest witticisms. In 1936, Walter Hofmann, star caricaturist of the SS journal *Das Schwarze Korps*, published a cartoon showing a paternalistic Göring complaining to a stunned man whom he had caught telling jokes on the street that he was getting a bit bored, so would the man please come up with some new ones.[42] The joke book *Landser lachen* (Infantrymen laugh), which was reprinted repeatedly between 1941 and 1944, carried a lengthy story about the "Wehrmacht-Witz-Zentrale," the army's headquarters for jokes, straining under the burden of having to come up with batches of fifty new Göring jokes on a regular basis.[43] Loyal soldiers in turn mentioned them in letters from the front. Peter G., a deeply anti-Semitic officer in a rifle battalion, wrote home in 1940 that his unit had cheered Göring's appointment as Reichsmarschall with "the usual folksy jokes." The Siegessäule (victory column) in Berlin, he wrote, would now be taken down so that Hermann could carry it as a scepter.[44]

Jokes about political figures can be a sign of grudging respect or even admiration. That appears to have been the case, for instance, in the German Democratic Republic. Historians seem reluctant to accept that possibility in the case of Nazi Germany and maintain instead that the constant joking stands as confirmation of the party's grip on a reluctant populace.[45] I would argue that joking constituted one side of an ongoing conversation between the German public and the Nazi political elite. Joking allowed non-Jewish Germans to talk among themselves without having to argue explicitly about politics and society. It allowed them – both at the time and after 1945 – to present themselves as bystanders unable to do anything more than make jokes about what was going on even though in fact their joking was a form of political commentary and a way of participating in the reorganization of German society. Understanding humor in Nazi Germany as a communicative agreement between the Nazi leadership and those recognized as full members of German society helps us to see how it allowed the rulers and the ruled to voice their political understanding and consensus on basic ideas that did not need to be spelled out explicitly.

Needless to say, Jewish Germans ran the risk of immediate danger by telling any kind of joke. Their liability to arrest for making quips otherwise considered harmless confirmed the everyday historiography I mentioned earlier: it reaffirmed the stereotypical association of irony with the "perpetrators" responsible for Germany's sufferings. Dr. Nathan Hirsch, a German Jewish doctor in Baden, was denounced and imprisoned in August 1934 for having told "a mean joke about Reichsminister Göring."[46] Even more tellingly, the Gestapo in Osnabrück took a Jewish-German woman into so-called protective custody (*Schutzhaft*) in January 1936 for "endangering public order and security" by telling a joke about an Aryan cow that was brown like Hitler, fat like Göring, and broad-mouthed like Goebbels,[47] a quip that circulated in many variations. In 1935, the Gestapo in Breslau claimed that Jewish Germans had provoked riots by their "*mocking laughter* and cheeky comments" and that residents could not rest before these "criminals" had been rounded up.[48] Jewish emigrants picked up on references to the harmful laughter of Jews that regularly appeared on the eve of anti-Jewish rioting. Alfred Wiener's Library in London, monitoring the press in Germany, noted the headline "Juden lachen in Berlin" (Jews laugh in Berlin) in the *Deutsche Wochenschau* on August 1, 1935. The article rebutted British reports of anti-Semitic violence with the argument that all was as it always had been: "the Jews under the protection of the German Reich" were continuing to "act against Germans."[49] The author of the article thereby underlined the emotionally framed juxtaposition of mocking Jews and mocked Germans, continuing the projection of German victimization at a time when Jewish Germans were being stripped of all rights. The article, which appeared about a month before the announcement of the Nuremberg Laws, might have helped whip up aggressive emotions in support of the move toward more radical action against German Jews.

HUMOR AS THE EMBODIMENT OF POWER

The storyline of non-Jewish victims endangered by Jewish perpetrators not only figured in humor and discourse about humor but was also acted out in derisive practices that I understand as performances of Germanness. In doing so, non-Jews toyed with the notion of race in various ways, again not as a scientific issue but as a way of implementing the Jewish vs. German distinction as an absolute divide that only the non-Jewish self was allowed to play with. They not only questioned the possibility of the non-Jewish self's racial purity, as in the homemade joke book discussed above, but also raised the issue either by assuming a stereotyped Jewish identity for a limited time or by jokingly paralleling the fates of Jews and non-Jews. Although some jokes might have indicated the desire to distance oneself, I think that most of these moments did not serve to create a third space or to allow for any form of hybrid identity. Rather, the practices themselves, and the emotions they might have expressed or engendered, lived off the ability to draw a supposedly clear dividing line that could not be undone by the Other, except with the victor's permission. Such practices of boundary-making highlighted and symbolized the non-Jewish self as the master of difference, enacting the gratification of belonging through the ability to play with the danger of exclusion momentarily but then take comfort in the security of being a member of German society again.

Particularly striking were situations of entertainment where non-Jews bodily re-enacted a Jewish identity. Humorous print media often described a society without German Jews and thereby allowed readers to ignore violence on a representational level. Photographs from Lenten carnival processions between 1933 and 1939, however, show that non-Jews ritually performed the progression of exclusion as a success. Each year, newly enacted measures against the Jews were celebrated. At least in the Rhineland and southern Germany, carnival, the "fifth season" of the year, was and is a highly important annual event in which countless individuals and organizations participate. During the Nazi era, the non-Jewish German population ritually replayed, for example, the forced emigration of German Jews or their loss of property by dressing up as stereotypical Jews and wearing costume "Jewish noses." Their behavior could convey multiple meanings. Dressing up in this particular form could create feelings of community by portraying emigration as an accomplished fact. By turning anti-Semitic sign systems into live tableaux, the actors could arouse feelings of anger, resentment, and hatred. But by mocking their former neighbors' helplessness, the performers also celebrated their own position as winners and as participants in a history in the making.

Carnival floats can be compared to the compulsory parading of Jewish Germans through the streets.[50] But the difference between the two practices was that non-Jewish carnival participants embodied the subjects of exclusion themselves. For example, in Singen, a town in Baden-Wurttemberg, the local association of innkeepers and the gun club created a carnival float in 1934 on which non-Jewish Germans replayed Jewish migration from Germany. The float resembled a railroad passenger car. A sign on the side read "From Berlin to Palestine" (misspelled in German as "von Berlin nach Palestina"). Two men and a woman sat inside, looking out the windows and laughing. The laughter of the float's "Jews" ambiguously united their pleasure in their own joke – that is, in their new position of power – with an allusion to the sardonic smile typically ascribed to the Jewish perpetrator.[51] A similar float in the Nuremberg festivity the year before had drawn spontaneous applause on the street, noted Elisabeth Schmitz, a member of the Bekennende Kirche (Confessing Church) and an outspoken critic of anti-Semitic persecution.[52]

Carnival actors also mocked other forms of deprivation forced upon German Jews, such as the loss of property. A carnival float in the Bavarian town of Schwabach in 1936 reminded onlookers that the shops of Moritz Rosenstein and David Bleicher had changed ownership the year before: the announcement "Firmenwechsel" (loosely, "under new management") was painted above the window of the mock-up shop. On a pulled-down window-blind, in large lettering, the former owners' names were combined into "David Bleichstein." Semantically, this implied that Jews should not be seen as individuals with their own identities but as "Jews," representatives of an inherent "Jewish identity." As such, their names were interchangeable.[53]

The most prominent feature was the embodiment of those who had lost their shops. A photograph shows three men on the float. One, standing apart, is clad in a long black coat suggestive of those often worn by Eastern European Jews; lest anybody miss the meaning, he also has on an artificial "Jewish nose." The other two men crouch on the other side of the float. One wears a white shirt with wide sleeves under a long vest, the other rather drab workers' clothing, implying that the business had been neither successful nor "German." Their posture suggests that, as Jews, they are cowering or trying to hide; but as "Germans," they can communicate easily with onlookers.

Reliving the expropriation of Jews' property was not an abstract phenomenon. When actors named the businesses lost by Jewish owners, they symbolically signaled that they had turned a neighbor into an outcast – an outcast who had no chance of entering into the conversation, let alone of undoing the disadvantageous commercial transaction. These enactments were not in the carnival tradition of the "world turned upside down," where ordinary people can mock the high and mighty during a few days of levity. These actors were, rather, playing their real world and its power structures. They mocked those who had in fact been cast out from the community, using a regularly performed rite of power to highlight and bolster the act of exclusion. Scorn and derision worked as a cultural performance of control, without hurting the self as an economic boycott might do. The repetitive performance of the various stages of exclusion turned into a ritualized assertion of the non-Jewish self gaining ever greater control.

Furthermore, impersonating the Jewish enemy provided an outlet for yet another anti-Jewish fantasy of long standing. It had been a staple of the anti-Judaic impulse in German culture to accuse German Jews of misguidedly trying – and ultimately failing – to imitate "real" Germans. Jews' attempts to live as both Jews and Germans were framed as inauthentic, illegitimate, and deliberately harmful to the nation. During

National Socialist rule, non-Jewish stage actors demonstrated their ability to unmask Jews, much as researchers on race and photographers claimed to do.[54] In 1937, Wilhelm Stapel, a well-known literary scholar, added to the Jews' alleged offenses in his infamous *Die literarische Vorherrschaft der Juden in Deutschland 1918 bis 1933* (The literary predominance of Jews in Germany, 1918–1933). Embracing the historical narrative of recurring German victimhood at the hands of outside aggressors, he wrote that German culture, thanks to its superiority, had been able to repel Roman and French "attacks." But against the Jews, he continued, culture alone would not suffice. Jews lived within German culture and had appropriated its language. Consequently, political power would be needed to counter their subversion from within. Stapel attributed yet another dangerous meaning to Jewish assimilation. He insisted that it had aimed not only at turning Jews into Germans but also at "demeaning" the "true Germans" by turning them into "Jews."[55] Theatrical impersonation could imply that Jewish Germans had been unsuccessful in their attempts to pose as German and to subvert real German identity. In impersonating Jews, non-Jewish actors first brought the threat of continued German victimization to life, but then, stepping out of role, they reveled in the despised other's failure.

Actors in ostensibly humorous performances evoked difference that did not need to be defined, relying instead on stereotypes as they reenacted the disempowering of Jewish Germans. It was the reenactment, I would argue, that served a crucial purpose. Staging their own empowerment in this way reversed the fantasy of the non-Jew as victim of history, allowing actors and audience to feel that they were now history's victors. At the same time, enacting the other in its guise as perpetrator made it possible to perpetuate the fantasy that Germans might once again become victims, an imaginary that in itself could serve as an impulse to more radical action. The non-Jewish self was not explained in scientific terms but rather demonstrated and performed by having actors step across identity boundaries that had been decreed as insurmountable for the other. Allowing such performances underlined the new rulers' ability to adopt identities and discard them again, whereas attempts by the persecuted to survive by adopting a supposedly non-Jewish demeanor were interpreted in the anti-Semitic reading as cunning.

Acting out the roles of victor and vanquished remained a favorite pastime during the war. Reinhard Gröper was an enthusiastic member of the Hitler Youth; in May 1945, he voiced regret only that joining the SS was no longer a possibility. In his diary and his letters to his mother, he described the "jolly evening" (*Bunter Abend*) of amateur theater that his Hitler Youth unit staged on July 20, 1944. Proud of his talent, Gröper described the various sketches performed and the roles he played. In one sketch, he played a Jewish boy who, in his words, "cheated others in a Jewish way and made a fool of them" and then offered "the weirdest goods." These scenes always drew the greatest applause, he told his mother.[56] Pointedly, the message was not only that Jews would harm non-Jews but also that they wanted to make fools of them, thereby wounding their feelings or their honor. When Gröper stepped out of his role and bowed to his audience, he reminded them that their society had "overcome" such "dangers" but that Germans must remain vigilant against the Jewish threat. That message had been delivered in similar fashion in the 1942 radio comedy *Rothstein und Co.* This series of "political short stories" (*politische Kurzscenen*) presented the Jewish banker Rothstein dealing with all of the countries waging war on Germany and trying to cheat them all as well. Rothstein was portrayed, moreover, as the driving force of the war of all against Germany. According to the SD, listeners cheered the series in general and applauded the actor who played Rothstein in particular; their only recommendation was that the ideological message should not be made too explicit because that would render the series less effective.[57] As politicians and media outlets blamed the Jews ever more aggressively for the war,[58] such commentators walked a fine line. They wanted Jews to be depicted as cheaters, liars, and warmongers to justify their society's violence against them, but they did not want to hear about that violence too explicitly. Rather, they applauded actors who crossed boundaries of identity for signaling that the non-Jewish self could do so without sacrificing its identity and for confirming its power.

Humorous anecdotes were likewise used to legitimize genocidal violence during the war. Wartime jokes about the disappearance of Jews were not only as blunt as the prewar carnival floats, but their punchlines also rested on the pretense of defining identities. Systematic deportation of Jews from Germany started in October 1941. Soldiers training at the military camp at Döberitz entered a "missing person report" in their camp journal:

Attention! Attention! Missing since December 3, 1941, the local instructor of the Fourth Division, Isidor Kettler. Missing Person Notice! The missing individual is 1.7 meters tall, blond, thin, married. Distinguishing characteristics: blue eyes, flat feet. The missing individual presumably brought his very eventful life to an end. Should anyone see the missing individual, it is only his ghost. May his ashes rest in peace![59]

Blond hair and blue eyes were ironically associated with flat feet and the name Isidor: bodily and cultural indicators served as semantic codes to send the message "Jew trying to pass as German." The opposition of the hapless Jew and the resolute German soldier, and the insinuation that someone ineligible for military service was trying to pass himself off as an army instructor, likewise rested upon stereotypes and hinted not so subtly that Jews would always give themselves away – and that they were destined to end up as ashes.

Other jocular practices during the war support my argument that non-Jewish Germans continued throughout the Nazi era to link German identity to victimization. While casting the persecuted as perpetrators, non-Jewish Germans derisively dramatized their own position as just as hopeless as that of the Jews. Some soldiers, for example, located themselves in the same position as Jewish Germans, namely at the bottom of a hierarchy. In German popular culture, it was common for small groups to create so-called *Bierzeitungen*, informal humorous publications typically produced to mark a special occasion; contingents of conscripts, for example, often issued such publications at the end of their military training as they celebrated their new soldierly prowess. In September 1942, one group of conscripts complained that it had been impossible to relax during their training because the camp had been too far away from any place of entertainment. Furthermore, they had been forbidden to take the bus to the train station because "Jews and soldiers walk."[60] German Jews had been banned from public transportation in April 1942; soldiers, on the other hand, were the most esteemed group in German society, no matter how much they might have been at the mercy of their commanders.[61] In this instance, inverting the positions of victims and perpetrators was a humorous appropriation of the wartime terminology that cast *Volksdeutsche* as the victims of the crimes that Germans were committing against Jews, Poles, and other persecuted groups.[62] Racial convictions, not in a scientific or biological sense but as the awareness of one's own self being able to install a racially argued totalizing hierarchy, resonated throughout the group when its members renewed the difference by sarcastically comparing and thereby actually setting off the soldier from the excluded.

MAKING FUN, MARKING BOUNDARIES

Humor was attractive in Nazi times because it provided a way to avoid argument. It served as a non-argumentative way not only of debating or supporting an exclusionary society, but of acting out and symbolizing new power structures. While SS concentration camp guards performed a violent "theatre of terror" by spitefully making fun of inmates in the 1930s, recommending themselves for higher positions by demonstrating their absolute relentlessness,[63] participants in various theatrical performances used public space as an arena for shaming Jewish Germans through laughter. When exclusion turned to extermination, neither the practice nor its public character changed, as onlookers confirmed their acceptance of violence through laughter. The theologian Aimé Bonifas, a French resistance fighter deported to Buchenwald in 1943, described how the Weimar population had mocked his group of prisoners "with malicious laughter" when they were marched through town to the camp, while one of them had been even more explicit: "A Gretchen on her bicycle yelled: 'Why don't you just bump them all off?'"[64]

By acting out (hi)stories about the self and its boundaries, non-Jewish Germans used humor as a narrative of empowerment during the Nazi era. Joking about race did not necessarily imply a belief in a scientific conception of race. The notion of race was performed rather than debated, and whenever it came up, cultural categories served as parameters to bolster a notion of difference that people might yet deal with differently. At the same time, laughter signified not only non-Jewish feelings of superiority but also their ability to play with identities. Re-enactments of their coercive power functioned as rituals confirming the boundaries of the self and the group. In carnival processions and lay theatre, acting "Jewish" while communicating only with one's own added spice to the fun, possibly intensifying the feeling of belonging. Audiences applauded entertainment that attempted to please with portrayals of the stereotypical Jew and implications that a cohesive German society had overcome the Jewish threat. Assuming the role of the outcast did not mean tolerating the ambiguity of identity. Safely crossing back and forth over the boundaries of projected identity served rather as a constant reminder of what members of this society were allowed to do, bringing the Other in temporarily without running the risk of opening a social space that was not tightly controlled.

Spurred by the desire to turn an imagined history into violent reality, humorous performance provided a means to avoid argument, between the included and the excluded as well as among the included. As narrative or performance, humor brought to life the historical trope of non-Jews being victimized or threatened by Jews. By enacting anti-Semitic stereotyping, non-Jews made the supposed threat as real as their sense of victory, as the act of performance itself symbolized their power to insist on a difference that they had the sole authority to define. Showing off their ability to toy with a boundary deemed immovable and conjuring up the presence of the persecuted through momentary mimicry ensured their own security of belonging and their growing sense of control. And by continuing to present the persecuted as perpetrators, they were able to participate in mass murder without calling it by name.

Notes

1 Joel Fineman, "The history of the anecdote: fiction and fiction" in Harold A. Veeser (ed.), *The New Historicism* (New York, 1989), 49–76; Fineman defines anecdotes as the "smallest minimal unit of the historiographic fact" (57).

2 Most recently, and in compelling fashion, Alon Confino, *A World without Jews: The Nazi Imagination from Persecution to Genocide* (New Haven, 2014).

3 In addition to Confino, *A World without Jews*, see Dan Stone, "Holocaust historiography and cultural history" in Dan Stone (ed.), *The Holocaust and Historical Methodology* (New York, 2012), 44–60, esp. 46.

4 For a nuanced assessment see Meike Wöhlert, *Der politische Witz in der NS-Zeit am Beispiel ausgesuchter SD-Berichte und Gestapo-Akten* (Frankfurt, 1997).

5 Karl Heinz Bohrer (ed.), *Sprachen der Ironie, Sprachen des Ernstes* (Frankfurt, 2000); Martina Kessel, "Gelächter, Männlichkeit und soziale Ordnung. 'Deutscher Humor' und Krieg 1870–1918" in Christina Lutter, Margit Szöllözi-Janze, and Heidemarie Uhl (eds.), *Kulturgeschichte. Fragestellungen, Konzepte, Annäherungen* (Innsbruck, 2004), 97–116.

6 Hayden V. White, *Metahistory: The Historical Imagination in Nineteenth-Century Europe* (Baltimore, 1973).

7 Defining identity through binary opposition seems a regular feature of modern societies. See Linda Colley, *Britons: Forging the Nation 1707–1837*, 2nd edn. (New Haven, 2005); Michael Jeismann, *Das Vaterland der Feinde. Studien zum nationalen Feindbegriff und Selbstverständnis in Deutschland und Frankreich 1792–1918* (Stuttgart, 1992). The framing in terms of victimization seems to be particular to Germany.

8 Michael Geyer, "The stigma of violence: nationalism and war in twentieth-century Germany," *German Studies Review* 15 (1992), 75–110. See also Martina Kessel, "Laughing about death? 'German humor' in the two world wars" in Alon Confino, Paul Betts, and Dirk Schumann (eds.), *Between Mass Death and Individual Loss: The Place of the Dead in Twentieth-Century Germany* (New York, 2008), 197–218, here 199–201.

9 Arthur Moeller van den Bruck, *Lachende Deutsche* (Minden, 1910), 5.

10 Geyer, "The stigma of violence," raises the question of how this fusion developed.

11 Bohrer, *Sprachen der Ironie*.

12 For the projection of "Jewish" as a key trope in Christian thinking, see David
    Nirenberg, *Anti-Judaism: The Western Tradition* (New York, 2013).

13 Jefferson C. Chase, *Inciting Laughter: The Development of "Jewish Humour"
    in Nineteenth Century German Culture* (Berlin, 2000).

14 Examples in Peter K. Klein, "Alltags-Antisemitismus im Kaiserreich. Das
    Beispiel der 'Judenspottkarten'" in Andrea Hoffmann et al. (eds.), *Die kul-
    turelle Seite des Antisemitismus zwischen Aufklärung und Shoah* (Tübingen,
    2006), 125–70.

15 On this point with regard to memory construction, see Confino, *A World
    without Jews*.

16 The argument that such an anti-Semitism long prevailed in German culture is
    put forward in Daniel Goldhagen, *Hitler's Willing Executioners: Ordinary
    Germans and the Holocaust* (New York, 1996).

17 Uffa Jensen, *Gebildete Doppelgänger. Bürgerliche Juden und Protestanten im
    19. Jahrhundert* (Göttingen, 2005); Klaus Holz, *Nationaler Antisemitismus.
    Wissenssoziologie einer Weltanschauung* (Hamburg, 2001).

18 Roger Chickering, *We Men Who Feel Most German: A Cultural Study of
    the Pan-German League, 1886–1914* (Boston, 1984); Robert Moeller, *War
    Stories: The Search for a Usable Past in the Federal Republic of Germany*
    (Berkeley, 2001).

19 Saul Friedländer, "Die politischen Veränderungen der Kriegszeit und ihre
    Auswirkungen auf die Judenfrage" in Werner E. Mosse, *Deutsches Judentum
    in Krieg und Revolution 1916–1923* (Tübingen, 1971), 27–65; Elke Kimmel,
    *Methoden antisemitischer Propaganda im Ersten Weltkrieg. Die Presse des
    Bundes der Landwirte* (Berlin, 2001). On the plurality of positions among
    Jewish Germans, see Elisabeth Albanis, *German-Jewish Cultural Identity from
    1900 to the Aftermath of the First World War* (Tübingen, 2002); Sharon
    Gillerman, *Germans into Jews: Remaking the Jewish Social Body in the
    Weimar Republic* (Stanford, 2009).

20 Martina Kessel, "Talking war, debating unity: conflict and exclusion in
    German humour during the First World War" in Martina Kessel and Patrick
    Merziger (eds.), *The Politics of Humour: Laughter, Inclusion, and Exclusion
    in the Twentieth Century* (Toronto, 2012), 82–107.

21 See, for example, Kristina Kratz-Kessemeier, *Kunst für die Republik. Die
    Kunstpolitik des preußischen Kultusministeriums 1918 bis 1932* (Berlin, 2008).

22 Cornelia Hecht, *Deutsche Juden und Antisemitismus in der Weimarer Repub-
    lik* (Bonn, 2000).

23 Peter Jelavich, "When are Jewish jokes no longer funny?" in Kessel and
    Merziger, *Politics of Humour*, 22–51.

24 Michael Geyer and Konrad Jarausch, *Zerbrochener Spiegel. Deutsche
    Geschichten im 20.Jahrhundert* (Munich, 2005), 187. On social bonding
    through violence, see Michael Wildt, *Volksgemeinschaft als Selbstermächti-
    gung. Gewalt gegen Juden in der deutschen Provinz 1919 bis 1939* (Hamburg,
    2007).

25 On the 1930s, see Kim Wünschmann,"Cementing the enemy category: arrest
    and imprisonment of German Jews in Nazi concentration camps, 1933–8/9,"
    Journal of Contemporary History 45 (2010), 576–600.

26 Claudia Koontz, *The Nazi Conscience* (Cambridge, MA, 2005), 207–12.

27 Philipp Wegehaupt, *"Wir grüssen den Hass!" Die ideologische Schulung und Ausrichtung der NSDAP-Funktionäre im Dritten Reich* (Berlin, 2012), 47f.; Otto Kulka and Eberhard Jäckel (eds.), *Die Juden in den geheimen Stimmungsberichten 1933–1945*, CD-ROM (Düsseldorf, 2004), Doc. No. 1435.

28 Friedrich Richter and Friedrich Ebeling (eds.), *Humor in Feldgrau. Erlebtes – Erzähltes aus den Kriegsjahren 1939/41* (Berlin, 1942), 4.

29 Quoted in Patrick Merziger, "Humour in the *Volksgemeinschaft*: the disappearance of destructive satire in National Socialist Germany" in Kessel and Merziger, *Politics of Humour*, 132.

30 Heinz Boberach (ed.), *Meldungen aus dem Reich 1938–1945. Die Geheimen Lageberichtes des Sicherheitsdienstes der SS* (Herrsching, 1984), vol. 9, Jan. 19, 1942, 3180–85, quotations 3180.

31 Anon, "Humor nach 1933." I am very grateful to Mr. S. for showing me the manuscript booklet. The initials "M." and "P." were used in the original.

32 Ibid.

33 Martina Kessel, "Gewalt schreiben. 'Deutscher Humor' in der Epoche der Weltkriege" in Wolfgang Hardtwig (ed.), *Ordnungen in der Krise. Zur politischen Kulturgeschichte Deutschlands 1900–1933* (Munich, 2007), 229–8, 250f.

34 Dietrich Adam, *Lesen unter Hitler. Autoren, Bestseller, Leser im Dritten Reich* (Berlin, 2010), 159–74, 162, 323. See also Patrick Merziger, *Nationalsozialistische Satire und "Deutscher Humor." Politische Bedeutung und Öffentlichkeit populärer Unterhaltung 1931–1945* (Stuttgart, 2010), 301ff.

35 Harold D. Lasswell, *Propaganda Technique in World War I* (Cambridge, MA, 1971; first published 1927).

36 Stephen Lowry, "Ideology and excess in Nazi melodrama: the golden city," *New German Critique* 74 (1998), 125–49, here 129–31. See also Scott Spector, "Was the Third Reich movie-made? Interdisciplinarity and the 'reframing' of Ideology," *American Historical Review* 106 (2001), 460–84.

37 Wilhelm Utermann (ed.), *Im Angriff und im Biwak: Soldaten erzählen Soldatengeschichten* (Berlin, 1943) (=VB-Feldpost), 81–7. Wilhelm Hape, *"Husarenstreiche." Humoristisches aus Krieg und Frieden* (Rathenow, 1935), introduction, 34. See also Kessel, "Gewalt schreiben."

38 See the drawings in Landesbibliothek Stuttgart, ZF 205, Der Durchbruch. Soldatenzeitung der Ostfront, Folge 464, Aug. 20, 1944, 7. On this point, I disagree with Merziger, *Nationalsozialistische Satire*, who argues that satire disappeared.

39 Jörg Willenbacher (Franz Osterroth), *Deutsche Flüsterwitze. Das Dritte Reich unterm Brennglas* (Karlsbad, 1935).

40 For a summary of the arguments of Ian Kershaw and others, see Donald Bloxham and Tony Kushner, *The Holocaust: Critical Historical Approaches* (Manchester, 2005), 127.

41 Gerhard Stahr, *Volksgemeinschaft vor der Leinwand. Der nationalsozialistische Film und sein Publikum* (Berlin, 2001), 179.

42 *Lacht ihn tot! Ein tendenziöses Bilderbuch von Waldl*, Nationalsozialistischer Verlag für den Gau Sachsen (Dresden, 1936), unpaginated.

43 Werner Lass and Hans Adolf Weber (eds.), *Landser lachen. Fronthumor dieses Krieges* (= VB-Feldpost, 4. Folge) (Berlin, 1944), 46–50.

44 Bibliothek für Zeitgeschichte Stuttgart, Sammlung Sterz, O'Jäger (O.A.) Peter G., 2. Kp./ Inf.Ers.Btl. 2, z.Zt. Döberitz, July 19, 1940.

45 Michael Geyer and Konrad Jarausch, *Shattered Past: Reconstructing German Histories* (Princeton, 2003), 160, 166.

46 Kulka and Jäckel, *Juden in den geheimen Stimmungsberichten*, Doc. No. 238.

47 Ibid., Doc. No. 1617.

48 Quoted in Alexandra Przyrembel, *"Rassenschande." Reinheitsmythos und Vernichtungslegitimation im Nationalsozialismus* (Göttingen, 2003), 74 (emphasis in the original).

49 Wiener Library, 055-WL-1624, Various Reports from the Jewish Central Information Office, 3.

50 Michael Wildt, "Gewalt als Partizipation. Der Nationalsozialismus als Ermächtigungsregime" in Alf Lüdtke and Michael Wildt (eds.), *Staats-Gewalt: Ausnahmezustand und Sicherheitsregimes. Historische Perspektiven* (Göttingen, 2008), 217–40, esp. 235ff. On cheerful community-producing practices, see also Pamela E. Swett, Corey Ross, and Fabrice d'Almeida (eds.), *Pleasure and Power in Nazi Germany* (Basingstoke, 2011).

51 Printed in Klaus Hesse and Philipp Springer (eds.), *Vor aller Augen. Fotodokumente des nationalsozialistischen Terrors in der Provinz* (Essen, 2002), 85.

52 Elisabeth Schmitz, "Zur Lage der Nichtarier, 1933" in Hannelore Erhart et al., *Katharina Staritz 1903–1953*, vol. 1 (Neukirchen, 1999), 5–6.

53 Printed in Hesse and Springer, *Vor aller Augen*, 91.

54 Hanno Loewy, "'... ohne Masken'. Juden im Visier der 'Deutschen Fotografie' 1933–1945" in Kunst- und Ausstellungshalle der Bundesrepublik Deutschland (ed.), *Deutsche Fotografie. Macht eines Mediums 1879–1970* (Cologne, 1997), 135–49.

55 Wilhelm Stapel, *Die literarische Vorherrschaft der Juden in Deutschland 1918 bis 1933* (Hamburg, 1937), 40–3.

56 Reinhard Gröper, *Erhoffter Jubel über den Endsieg. Tagebuch eines Hitlerjungen 1943–1945* (Sigmaringen, 1996), 184: "Außerdem 'beschummelte' ich noch einige auf jüdisch, 'foppte' einige so und pries die seltsamsten Waren an."

57 *Meldungen aus dem Reich*, vol. 10, 3810, (June 11, 1942). Rudolf Stache, *Rothstein & Co. (Filiale London): Satirische Hörszenen aus dem deutschen Rundfunk um Agitatoren und Börsenjobber* (Erfurt, 1943).

58 Saul Friedländer, *The Years of Extermination: Nazi Germany and the Jews, 1939–1945* (New York, 2008); Jeffrey Herf, *The Jewish Enemy: Nazi Propaganda during World War II and the Holocaust* (Cambridge, MA, 2008).

59 "Achtung! Achtung! Vermisst wird seit dem 3.12.1941 der einheimische Ausbilder der 4. Abteilung, Isidor Kettler. Vermisstenmeldung! Der Vermisste ist 1,70 groß, blond, schlank, verheiratet. Besondere Merkmale: blaue Augen, Plattfüße. Der Vermisste hat vermutlich seinem sehr bewegten Leben ein Ende gemacht. Sollte jemand den Vermissten sehen, so ist das nur sein Geist. Friede seiner Asche!" Bundesarchiv, Militärarchiv Freiburg, Militärgeschichtliche Sammlung, MSG 2/1829, Bierzeitung der Kriegsschule Döberitz, 02.1941, 16.

60 Bundesarchiv, Militärarchiv Freiburg, Militärgeschichtliche Sammlung, MSG 2 / 2094, Wolfgang Karow, Berlin, Bierzeitung der 2. Abteilung, 20.6.-26.9.1942.

61 Frank Werner, "'Hart müssen wir hier draußen sein.' Soldatische Männlichkeit im Vernichtungskrieg 1941–1944," *Geschichte und Gesellschaft* 34 (2008), 5–40.

62 Doris Bergen, "Instrumenalization of *Volksdeutschen* in German propaganda in 1939: replacing/erasing Poles, Jews, and other victims," *German Studies Review*, 31 (2008), 447–70.

63 Christopher Dillon, *Dachau and the SS: A Schooling in Violence* (Oxford, 2015), esp. 119–33, quote 133.

64 Quoted in Karola Fings, "The public face of the camps" in Jane Caplan (ed.), *Concentration Camps in Nazi Germany: The New Histories* (New York, 2010), 108–26, 119.

16

Legitimacy Through War?

Nicholas Stargardt

Conceptualizing Nazi Germany as a racial state came out of a realization that separate research projects into the persecution of Jews, Roma and Sinti, homosexuals, vagrants, patients in psychiatric asylums, and recidivist petty criminals could be understood not just as discrete activities but as part of the central agenda of the Third Reich.[1] This synthesizing effort drew some of its intellectual and moral energy from the profound change in significance accorded to the Holocaust in the 1980s and 1990s, a shift which Alon Confino has compared to the "foundational" status formerly accorded to the French Revolution among historians more widely. Although many of these areas of research have continued to be conducted largely independently of one another and although historians have continued to discuss how unified the many Nazi projects of racial "cleansing" ever were, they effected a paradigm change from the history writing of the 1970s and early 1980s in which race scarcely featured beyond the margins.[2]

One of the accidental consequences of this shift in research energy has been a retreat from any broadly conceived attempt to write the social history of the period. As the focus has shifted to policy formation and implementation, so professional elites have largely supplanted social class as the key German actors in this history. It has become startlingly clear that there was a huge gulf between the principal targets of persecution and annihilation and the majority of Germans, with only the murder of German psychiatric patients sparking any wider sense of social disquiet and opposition. And yet the clearer this divide has become, the less obvious it is how we should now set about understanding the unpersecuted German majority. Terms such as *milieu* or *class*, to say nothing of *Resistenz* or collective action, have been retired from active service along with any residual optimism that large sections of German society escaped the Third Reich morally unscathed. Indeed, in so far as historians have remained interested in German society, it has been to show the ways in which it colluded in, participated in, benefitted from, and became morally tainted by the racial projects of the regime, culminating in a war of colonial conquest and genocide. In place of interpretations that emphasized difference and conflicts within society and with the regime, the second wave of scholarship on racial persecution looks at the nation as defined by exclusion, redeploying the once programmatic slogan of a *Volksgemeinschaft* as an analytical historical construct.[3]

The notion that Nazi Germany is best understood as a *Volksgemeinschaft* finds its ultimate test in World War II. On the face of it, the "national community" withstood the war better than anyone might have expected at its outset. Germany carried on until it was completely defeated and occupied in May 1945. As Michael Geyer, Richard Bessel, and Ian Kershaw have all noted, such "holding out" was unmatched even by Imperial Japan in World War II.[4] But in what sense does the concept of a *Volksgemeinschaft* explain this outcome? Was social solidarity strengthened in the face of an external threat? Broadly, there are three different ways in which the *Volksgemeinschaft* has been extended to the war. The first is in terms of social mobilization; the second is in terms of socio-economic benefit; and the third concerns shared participation in genocide.

That mass mobilization occurred during wartime and that it made a significant contribution to civil defense cannot be doubted. Research by Dietmar Süß and Nicole Kramer, in particular, suggests that participation in the Reichluftschutzbund, the National Socialist People's Welfare, and the women's organizations, to name only the principal ones, was one of the major reasons why civil defense coped with the mass air raids on German cities at the height of Allied "strategic bombing" in 1943–1944. The commonsense of civil defense, rescue, salvage, assistance, and evacuation provided strong and positive reasons for seeing emergency measures and ad hoc initiatives as a positive contribution to the *Volksgemeinschaft*, even engendering forms of "antagonistic cooperation" between the churches and the party for the common cause. This does not mean, of course, that the bombing increased the sense of social solidarity overall or that participation in practical initiatives necessarily or automatically involved buying into more specific Nazi objectives, such as anti-Catholicism or medical killing. Yet even cultural performances – like mouthing *völkisch* formulations in an instrumental fashion in order to secure particular advantages, such as evacuation supplements or war widows' pensions – still leave their traces: people were both molded by their constraints and remained the authors of themselves.[5]

The two other ways of thinking about the *Volksgemeinschaft* try to locate reasons for a more active buy-in to the Nazi war of colonial conquest and genocide. By insisting on the socio-economic benefits of *Raubmord* (murder for purpose of robbery), Götz Aly extended and radicalized a more traditional explanation for growing social consensus in the later 1930s: where historians had traditionally argued that an end to the dire poverty and insecurity of the Great Depression provided secondary reasons for making Nazism popular before the war, which had little to do with the appeal of its core values and beliefs, Aly has pushed back against this depoliticizing claim, contending that the emergence of a Nazi welfare state during the war effectively aligned German society with genocide. Aly points out that plunder, loot, colonial conquest, and social welfare all went hand-in-hand to create a "national community" defined by race and sealed by blood.[6] Some of Aly's insights are clearly demonstrable, such as a widespread awareness that German rationing entitlements – both widely resented and widely broken through "hamstering" in the countryside – were dependent on massive transfers of food from Ukraine and France. Equally, reequipping bombed-out households with Jewish furniture, clothing, and other domestic items did spread a kind of knowledge and collusion, an insight Aly derived from the work of Frank Bajohr.[7] But these were also "gains" that were often tinged by loss, nostalgia, and discontent. It is unconvincing that the war was ever regarded primarily in socio-economic terms. And it remains debatable too whether those economic terms were considered favorable for much of the war's duration; whether the economic gains of war came close to offsetting its economic costs in terms of taxation, regulation, extended working hours and compulsory labor deployment, let alone a monotonous diet, the growing shortages in clothing and consumer goods, not to mention the destruction of property and housing stock through bombing. By this point, it should be clear that such an accounting is ultimately inadequate for measuring the sheer disruption to family life or the meanings people sought for the unprecedented numbers of German dead.[8] Viewed from this perspective, it becomes less surprising that the war was probably only ever truly popular for relatively brief periods in its very long duration: times, such as the summer and autumn of 1940 and, with less certainty, again in the summers of 1941 and 1942, when a German victory – and peace – looked imminent.[9]

The third of these contributions to thinking about how war created a German *Volksgemeinschaft* turns from the economic to the symbolic character of genocide. Thomas Kühne has argued that it was the mass murder itself which served to bind the German *Volksgemeinschaft* together. In making this argument, he reaches back to Michael Wildt's work on the way that the public rituals of humiliation visited on Jews in the prewar years represented an exercise in "self-empowerment," creating a congruence of values and a theatre of public involvement of "ordinary" Germans with Nazi racial violence. While Kühne is able to offer a detailed and convincing account of the dynamics within small groups of mobile killing units on the eastern front, he has greater trouble translating his findings back to German society at large: the rituals of degradation and the killing were not directly experienced on the home front.[10] Rather, they were mediated by – largely private – accounts that spread after the event, so that there was no affective moment in which these "rites of violence" (to borrow Natalie Zemon Davis's term) could directly refashion social attitudes through the kinds of mass participation that Wildt found in parts of prewar Germany.[11]

As with so much of the historiography of the Third Reich, the terms of the *Volksgemeinschaft* debate have a strongly moralizing undertow. Kühne and Aly place the murder of the Jews at the center not only of Hitler's war but also of German society's in order to insist on the wider social responsibility for the Holocaust, which the older historiography of Nazi Germany in the Federal Republic had tried to fend off so obstinately. Martin Broszat attempted to rescue German society from contamination with mass murder by depicting the period "from Stalingrad to the [West German] currency reform" as a period of silent self-denazification and "defeatism." For Broszat, postwar liberal democracy was born from the silent, "inner" resources of German society, rather than being imposed from without by the Allies, in exactly the period in which the war was being fought ever more ruthlessly.[12] In this respect, the efforts to try to make sense of how German society benefitted from, colluded in, and absorbed the facts of the Holocaust are a timely corrective.[13]

Despite the huge differences of approach between the older, Broszatian view and the newer focus on the *Volksgemeinschaft*, both nonetheless often seem to fall back on a similar kind of functional behavioralism in explaining how society dealt with the war. The regime's successes are automatically identified with consent and, by a parallel symmetry, its failures are equally inevitably identified with defeatism. The two sides differ, of course, in what counts as success or failure. But what I would want to question is any automatic functionality of success and dysfunctionality of failure. What both sides have left out of consideration here is a more complex range of possible social responses that might breach any tidy symmetry between success and failure: that the war might have been both unpopular and legitimate; that defeats and crises might have been destabilizing – destroying existing hopes and confidence in the regime – *and* also failed to undermine a basic commitment to the war effort itself, resulting in a radicalization of social attitudes. It is these more complex, more dynamic, and more disturbing elements in German social responses to war that I want to explore in this essay.

* * *

It seems fitting to start by addressing the question of how the murder of the Jews became a subject of conversation and discussion in public. During the summer and early autumn of 1943, reports came in that just such talk was taking place across the Reich – and in public places among relative strangers. On August 15, 1943, the cultivated patrician Lothar de la Camp wrote a circular letter to his siblings, friends, and acquaintances. It was not a personal, family letter but set out to offer a detailed private report of the fire-bombing of Hamburg and to make as expert and sober as possible an estimate of the destruction it had caused. Quoting well-placed sources, he thought that there were 200,000 to 240,000 dead, but even if he had known that this was five to six times the actual number, he was not wrong in seeing the devastation and loss of civilian life as unprecedented. Then he turned to what people were saying about the raids:

Whatever the rage against the English and Americans for their inhuman way of waging war, one has to say quite objectively that the common people, the middle classes, and the rest of the population make repeated remarks in intimate circles and also in larger gatherings that the attacks count as retaliation for our treatment of the Jews.[14]

Over the summer and autumn of 1943, as the "area bombing" raids continued and evacuees from all over northern and western Germany brought their tales to the south and east of the country, similar sentiments were amplified across the Reich. Locals might doubt many of the evacuees' personal testimonies about their own suffering and losses, but the one thing that was taken seriously was something about which no one had direct knowledge: who was behind the bombing. Under the immediate impact of the Hamburg air raids, the inhabitants of Ochsenfurt were wondering whether Würzburg would be next. While some claimed it was being spared because "in Würzburg no synagogues were burned," others warned "that now the airmen would come to Würzburg too, given that the last Jew recently left Würzburg." For good measure, this "last Jew" was even reported to have "declared before his deportation that now Würzburg would also receive air raids."[15] After the second daylight raid by the USAAF on Schweinfurt in October 1943, the local Nazi party noted that "One frequently hears the opinion among national comrades that the terror attacks are a consequence of the measures taken against the Jews."[16]

Talk about "Jewish retaliation" surfaced when people felt particularly vulnerable, most often in the wake of heavy air raids. It provided the most frequent occasions of Germans talking about the genocide of the Jews as an accomplished fact, and yet such comments were not a direct commentary on the murder of the Jews. Instead, they came only when people felt that they were being held to account for it by an external power that would retaliate on the victims' behalf. So, when the Jewish star was introduced in September 1941, a rumor began to circulate that Germans in the United States were being made to wear a badge marked with a "G" or a swastika on their clothes in retaliation. In so far as one can judge from the surviving reports on public opinion, after this first flurry of anxiety, there were very few rumors of this kind when the genocide was at its height in 1942.[17] Instead, talk of "retaliation for what we did to the Jews" returned like a talisman of destruction in 1943, in response to the Allied strategic bombing of the Ruhr, Hamburg, and Berlin. What both the timing and content of these public conversations reveal is that their principal referent was not the fate of the Jews. Germans' prime concern was the Allied bombing campaign and the Red Army, not the "final solution" itself.

This nationally self-centered reference point creates an important gap in time as well as empathies, for in 1941 or 1942, when the greatest number of eyewitnesses brought back news of the mass shootings in the east, and when consent or opposition to the killing might have mattered, people had spoken about it differently. At that time, the murder of the Jews was almost always discussed in relation to the specific circumstances of particular killings. It was as if the narrators had not yet grasped or were trying to insulate themselves from acknowledging the full genocidal dimensions, even though this was a period in which the Nazi press and

party organizations were encouraging a knowing collusion in the genocide among the public. Most likely, the fact that the German armies were
once more advancing rapidly on the eastern front during the summer and
autumn of 1942 spread a renewed confidence that Germany would win
the war and, in the absence of external prompting, there was no immediate reason to discuss the murder of the Jews in public.[18] By the summer
and autumn of 1943, when these conversations about "what we did to the
Jews" occurred, the key events of deportation and murder already lay in
the past, providing an acknowledgement that had mostly been withheld at
the time. It was their own predicament, not that of the Jews, that precipi-
tated such an admission.

Here lies a key asymmetry between Jewish and German responses. For
the Jews, their own persecution and impending murder framed their
understanding of the war; for Germans, the war shaped their understanding and response to the murder of the Jews. This means that we cannot
read these SD and Nazi party reports as if they offered a direct commentary on the "Final Solution." Rather, the "measures carried out against
the Jews," as the report writers euphemistically tended to call them,
appear as one step in a cycle of what Germans saw as mutually destructive escalation.

To German Jews such as Rudolf Schottländer and Victor Klemperer,
forcibly deassimilated but still working alongside their fellow Germans,
this talk of "Jewish bombing" was a frightening sign of just how far the
Nazis had succeeded in shaping commonsense axioms about the war,
the enemy, and the Jews.[19] To Goebbels, talk of "Jewish retaliation" was
ominously frustrating for quite different reasons. It reversed the terms of
two major propaganda campaigns of 1943. The first had revolved around
re-establishing the Jews as Germany's unitary and implacable enemy, bent
on its annihilation: Jewish "terror bombing" and footage of the mass
grave of Polish officers executed by the NKVD in the Katyn forest
furnished the evidence of the Jews' implacable resolve to annihilate the
German people. It was, of course, a theme that had been deployed before,
most notably in the autumn of 1941, but it had gone relatively quiet in
1942 (the media tracked here by the parallel quiet in public conversations), only to burst out in a still more shrill and heavily saturated
campaign of fear and hatred in the spring and summer of 1943.[20] It
was a campaign in which the press occasionally alluded directly to the
"extermination of the Jews" as a timely form of German self-defense, and
so it is not hard to see how a few months later, in changed circumstances,
people might draw upon this publicly established equivalence between the

bombing and the murder of the Jews in order to criticize the Nazi regime. The topic itself appeared to be a legitimate one because the German media had itself devoted so much space to it.

A second propaganda campaign was being recycled into public discourse here too, and it also worked against the regime's promises; specifically, the promise, which Goebbels had been making since spring 1943, of massive "retaliation" against Britain for the bombing of German cities.[21] Here too, pessimism after the bombing of Hamburg led people to invert the "correct" relationship and talk not of German but of Jewish retaliation; not for the bombing, but for the genocide. All the elements of this discussion had been provided by German propaganda and yet were being combined in order to produce the "wrong" result. By September 2, 1943, the *Stuttgarter NS-Kurier* felt it had to publicly rebut the argument that world Jewry would not have fought Germany had it not so radically solved the Jewish question. The following day, the Gau paper in Baden, *Der Führer*, chided its readers in a similar vein: "It is said, if National Socialist Germany had not solved the Jewish Question so radically, international World Jewry would not be fighting us today." Only a "senile fool" could believe such stuff, the paper derided, pointing out that the Jews had caused both world wars, with the present one being "no more than a continuation of the first."[22]

These sources are not new. Following the example set by David Bankier and Ian Kershaw, scholars have examined them in order to weigh up whether or not Germans approved of the genocide.[23] But both chronology and the internal reference points suggest a different logic. In a quite profound sense, these conversations could never serve as a commentary – let alone a surrogate opinion poll – on the murder of the Jews. They came too late for that. And the fate of the Jews emerged only as an explanatory backdrop, an irreversible – if also oft regretted – fact that illuminated Allied intentions toward the Germans. It was German rather than Jewish vulnerabilities that sparked this outpouring, so unwelcome to the Nazi leadership because of its mixture of defeatism and regret, and yet, from the point of view of the small number of surviving Jews in Germany, so frighteningly steeped in *völkisch* and racist evaluations of the war itself.

In this external sense, of facing a "ring of enemies" in an all-out war, Germans did undoubtedly possess a very lively sense of being a *Volk*. Was the feeling of being under siege strong enough to bind German society internally together through a deepened sense of national community into a *Volksgemeinschaft*? This question goes to the heart of the problem, and the answer is not immediately obvious because the evidence cuts both

ways. What is so striking and surprising about the strategic bombing of
1943 and 1944 is the dramatic mobilization of resources and people,
which saved the local state authorities from being completely over-
whelmed. Soldiers, firemen, concentration camp prisoners, the largely
female air raid auxiliaries of the Reichsluftschutzbund, local authority
social workers, the National Socialist People's Welfare, stormtroopers,
youth, and women's organizations were all drafted in, amalgamating
civilians and military, prisoners, and civilian volunteers. Special trains
brought refugees out and food, clothing, real coffee, and schnapps in,
followed later by the furniture and households of deported Jews. Ralf
Blank, Malthe Thiessen, Nicole Kramer, and Dietmar Süss have drawn
attention to the regime's capacity to survive the bombing of German cities
both by these measures of emergency mobilization but also, crucially, by
offering a moral frame of explanation that shared key overlaps with those
of the Christian churches in its emphasis on withstanding the trials and
tests of war, as well as in cultivating a spirit of sacrifice.[24]

This was a full-scale social mobilization, but it was also one which
focused on local communities, cities, and regions, and even at this level it
frequently went hand in hand with new kinds of conflicts. Despite a major
construction program between 1940 and 1942 in the cities that became
targets in 1943/1944, there were too few air raid bunkers to shelter
everyone. Regulations excluding Jews, "gypsies," and "eastern workers"
were put in place early either on local initiative or by central fiat. More
privileged allied or "western" workers were to be admitted only after
Germans had been accommodated. In June 1943, Hermann Göring
tackled the thornier problem of who should be given priority for scarce
bunker places among German "national comrades" (*Volksgenossen*).
Sticking by a chivalrous code of protecting women, children, the infirm,
and the elderly, he ordained that men aged 16–60 and especially military
personnel, including soldiers on leave, should generally be refused entry
until a bombardment was actually underway on the grounds that they
were needed for civil defense. As competition for places increased, in
1944 the age was raised to 70 in Essen and other heavily bombed cities.[25]

After the mass evacuations of autumn 1943, this system for rationing
bunker places was the target of much popular criticism. Working women
in particular, the Security Service noticed in February 1944, were speaking out against such privileged treatment of women with small children:
they should not be in the cities, let alone the bunkers, at all. By now, men
were writing to Goebbels to make much the same point: they had to
remain in the city as key workers and therefore should take precedence

over the non-working population, who ought to have left already. Goebbels had some sympathy with their point of view, although the existing regulations remained in force and hundreds of prams parked in front of the bunkers continued to provide a familiar sign of air raid alerts.

What do such disputes mean? Are they evidence of social atomization, as Neil Gregor has argued, or of the self-mobilizing and self-destructive potential of the *Volksgemeinschaft*, as Dietmar Süss proposes?[26] Perhaps they are evidence of both. Much of the evidence does point toward a deepening of ethnonationalist exclusion. In the wake of heavy air raids, foreign workers were the target of retaliatory violence, especially in the final phase of the war. Executions and lynchings became more frequent in Ruhr towns from the autumn of 1944 onwards. That this could happen in cities, which had had strong labor movement subcultures and where the looting of Jewish shops and burning of synagogues in November 1938 had not produced the kind of popular participation in a pogrom witnessed in small-town Franconia, tells us that something profound had changed during the war years.[27] Even so, a willingness to exclude others – and to wreak vengeance upon them – may tell us a great deal about the external boundaries of the national community without revealing very much about its internal integrity. Such violence could result as easily from a sense of panic and crisis as from any sense of collective cohesion.

As both gender roles and concepts of entitlement came under question and were argued out among national comrades, the government appeared not as the cause of the problem, having built insufficient bunkers, but as the source of legitimate authority needed to regulate this new social conflict. Joachim Szodrynski has argued that the socio-political impact of the Hamburg firestorm was gradual rather than sudden: his emphasis is less on the destruction of half of the city and the deaths of 34,000 people than on the failure of the government's promises of reconstruction and full compensation for lost homes and possessions. As the bulk of the population returned to Hamburg over the following three months, the woefully inadequate rehousing and the rather basic replacement of furniture – much of it confiscated from Jewish households – revealed an unbridgeable material and rhetorical gap which spelled a crisis of confidence in the Nazi regime.[28] But these failures remained partial. Compared to the Italian case, where people resorted to the black market and looted cities such as Naples in the wake of Allied air raids, the failure of the state in Germany was far more limited: family networks certainly came into play, and many people did make their own arrangements, using private connections to procure clothes and household goods in other parts of the

Reich, but they generally continued to cover the purchases with ration stamps and currency. With the exception of meat and dairy products, the black market remained relatively small until the end of the war. And it was in the immediate postwar years that the black market eclipsed the official system of rationing in Germany. Nor, despite police fears, did looting take on major proportions in the wake of air raids.[29]

Evacuation to the countryside both insulated society from the full effects of the bombing of the cities and engendered new social conflicts, which the local representatives of the party and its mass organizations, especially the National Socialist People's Welfare and the Frauenschaft, were all called in to mediate. Amid burgeoning complaints over lodgings, the provision of bedding, heating, and the lack of cooking facilities, the party organizations tried to conciliate evacuees and their hosts and to find practical solutions, such as establishing communal cooking facilities for evacuees in villages and small towns. The whole system of state pensions, family payments, evacuation supplements, and rationing also contributed to mitigating the economic and financial hardship of evacuation as well as making housing evacuees more attractive to their hosts during the war. Swabian farmers' wives might resent having to cater for working-class women from the Ruhr and scoff at their refusal to work and "lady-like airs," but they could at least pay their way, reviving prewar tourist hotels and locales in southern Germany, the Czech lands, and Austria. Indeed, a glance at the far more bitter discrimination experienced by post-1945 German refugees, when the state no longer paid out, illuminates how much the system did to lessen conflicts in the period 1942–1945.[30]

In Mussolini's Italy, Pétain's France, and Hitler's Germany, it was assumed that air attack could be met through acts of social solidarity, through a national rallying of effort and resources. In France, the Vichy regime encouraged unbombed cities to twin with those which had been bombed. But, just as in Germany, such authoritarian communitarian models of solidarity proved inadequate, and the state had to fill the widening gap in provision. In Italy, the Allied bombing campaign rapidly led to a crisis of the state itself. The near absence of public shelters provoked riots in Genoa, giving a quite different focus to the privileges of private provision. In October 1941, women threw stones and forced their way into the private shelters of the wealthy. A month later, whole sections of the city were in revolt and the police were attacked by crowds. Just over a year later, these events were repeated when tunnels in the city center were flooded during an air raid alarm: women marched on the prefecture and the headquarters of the Fascist Party demanding an end to the war. Still more violent riots broke out in Turin in June and July 1943, amid a clamor for justice against landlords and the rich. Unlike in Germany, there were no fighter squadrons and very little anti-aircraft artillery, and their absence made people feel undefended, however ineffective their protection in many other cases. The abdication of action by a state that had claimed to be "everything" prompted many Italians to turn to the Church. They gathered in churches or in crypts and sanctuaries, and religious explanations abounded for both the destruction and what was spared. As the Fascist state failed to organize adequate evacuation measures, the extended family, the black market, and the Church became alternate sources of food, shelter, and security. In Italy, the bombing played a direct part in the fall of the Fascist regime. In the wake of heavy raids on Turin, Milan, Genova, and Rome, there were spontaneous demonstrations against the prefects and the Fascist Party, with demands for peace and liberty.[31]

In Germany, by contrast, talk of "rights" was not aimed at securing freedom from dictatorship or peace from war but often drew the state into mediating new kinds of social conflicts. German society was clearly deeply divided when it came to claims on scarce resources, whether it was one's right to a place in a bunker, to a war widow's pension, to a special family supplement for evacuees, to replacement furniture and clothing, or simply to a ticket for the cinema. In that sense, it certainly did not approximate to a united *Volksgemeinschaft*, except – and, of course, this is a crucial sense – when it came to enforcing the daily subjugation of "outsiders" within their midst. To foreign workers and the small number of Jews protected by Aryan marriages from deportation but visibly marked as they moved around German cities, there was no doubt where the lines of belonging and entitlement were drawn. Although "self-evacuation" rose in the chaos of the final phase of the bombing war, from 1944 onwards, in fact official channels continued to account for most evacuees. After he had shed his yellow star, Victor Klemper and his wife Eva were helped at each step of their journey through Bavaria in April 1945 by the National Socialist People's Welfare and its network of volunteers doling out soup and looking for villages with room. Finally, the benign *Ortsbauernführer* (local farmers' leader) – and old-time Nazi – in the village of Unterbernbach put them up in his house until he found them a billet.[32]

What this points to is that the German state, at both local and national levels, did continue to play a major role. In 1942, in 1943, and for most of 1944, the German state could still respond to major air raids by mobilizing the party's mass ancillary organizations and the resources of surrounding regions. The significance of the state, especially at the local level of the *Kommunalverwaltung* (municipal administration), grew to fill part of the gap left by the relative failure of the *Volk* to act as a *Gemeinschaft* and provide organic social solidarity across social classes and regional divides. With it, the family emerged as the principal recipient of public good and financial aid. This was not individuated, egalitarian, or social democratic welfare; as Nazi policy quietly abandoned the party's own communitarian promises, it returned to a model of unequal and family-oriented measures that left class differentials intact. This had its Weimar origins in the policies of the Centre Party and would be continued by postwar Christian Democracy.

If the Nazi regime was itself generally disappointed by the failure of German wartime society to display the solidarity, communal spirit, and generosity ascribed to the ideal of the *Volksgemeinschaft*, a more puzzling problem remains for historians. What did it mean to Germans to continue with this war at all? Unlike Mussolini's Italy, German society did not collapse, and, unlike Pétain's France, it was faced with the far greater challenge that it was supporting a war effort in which up to a quarter of the entire population was under arms. Here the problem may simply be that historians have tended, like the regime itself, to see the war as a kind of plebiscite on Nazi ideology. But Nazism, of course, possessed no monopoly over German nationalism, and so it is worth looking more broadly than at the rise or fall of Nazi propaganda themes. If it is society that primarily interests us, we would do better to look, instead, at those currents of German nationalism which had existed during World War I and continued to offer reservoirs for self-mobilization throughout the second.

The first and most significant continuity lies in the notion of national defense. Despite criticism from the radical left during and after World War I, self-defense against Russian attack remained axiomatic to the wartime *Burgfrieden* (the "truce" among the political parties) and continued to shape the nationalist consensus about why that war had been fought – in the case of West Germany, right down to the Fischer debate of 1961. According to the official calendar, World War II broke out not on September 1, 1939, when the Wehrmacht "returned Polish fire," but on September 3, when Britain and France declared war on Germany. The occupation of Norway pre-empted a British plan to do so; the attack on the Soviet Union forestalled Stalin's plans to invade the Reich; the declaration of war against the United States merely clarified a situation in which

Roosevelt had been supporting the British war effort since the summer of 1940 and working to encircle Germany. There was a broad element of consensus in Nazi Germany, but it was a national rather than a social or political one: it was not primarily bound up with the social program of the *Volksgemeinschaft* or even the domestic elements of the Hitler myth so much as with an older theme that had much in common with the cross-party support for the previous war, namely national defense. In World War II, this bedrock of belief in the fundamental legitimacy of the war often appeared in the guise of ostensibly "apolitical" writing and a kind of familial patriotism.

Here, the work of Klaus Latzel and Sven Oliver Müller on war correspondence and military censors' reports has been highly suggestive too: Latzel's in emphasizing the common currency of positive patriotic notions of national defense which held good in World War I (at least up to 1916–1917) as well as World War II (at least until early 1945 for many of his letter-writers); Müller's for showing how the negative side of this pre-Nazi patriotic coin, the image of Germany's encirclement by a ring of enemies, was in many respects nazified during the course of World War II, with the Jews and the Bolsheviks emerging as the epitome of absolute enmity and inhumanity.[33] One of the great advantages of this kind of discursive or semantic analysis is that it discloses the common reference points and antitheses in popular circulation and, with them, a common bedrock of axioms about why the war was being fought, which, as the military censors realized and noted, were often so obvious to the letter-writers and their readers that they were often present as a stable, implicit sub-stratum, rather than a matter of explicit commentary.

This kind of work can give us vital clues about where to start looking, but what discourse analysis cannot do is to explain belief and change, relationships and action. It can tell us that a set of attitudes existed but not what strains they came under or how they were nurtured and sustained in private against the news of destruction of home, dislocation, and death. This brings us back to the family, for it was parents and children, husbands and wives, lovers and siblings who wrote to each other most often. The regime might issue guidance on how to write; it might encourage work colleagues to send letters between the factory and the front and sanction young men and women writing to each other out of the blue, becoming pen-pals and eventually going on blind dates as a means of strengthening soldiers' ties to the home front; but the authorities knew that the most important affective bonds were the ones that already existed.[34]

Most of the letters that connected these apparently so divided realms of experience – the military and the civilian worlds – were family correspondence. With mass evacuation from the cities, compulsory labor service for teenage boys and girls, pre-military training and service as air force and naval auxiliaries, families were so scattered that the front was only one of their dislocated points of temporary residence. Correspondence was the one way to keep increasingly virtual families together, with soldiers at the front and their mothers and wives at home serving as key relay stations for the news of scattered siblings, cousins, children, and parents. While military historians have tended to focus most of their attention on the real or imagined cult of comradeship within the much-vaunted "primary groups" of the Wehrmacht, much of the evidence for how men felt about their units in fact derives from letters they wrote home.[35] Deaths, births, and, above all, the tantalizing prospect of leave reminded many letter-writers that their attachments to family still held them, too: Indeed, one of the longest-lasting illusions sustained by couples was the hope that the war could be treated as lost time to be bracketed out of the married life as a wasted interlude. These oft-repeated sentiments of course also underlined one of the primary purposes in writing – to reassure their spouses that the relationship was intact, that the war had changed nothing that was fundamental to their relationships – and this emotional imperative often cramped what could be said in war letters.

Here, I can only probe the subjective response to the crises of the war by looking at the private ruminations of one man in order to see how he coped with the shock of military defeat and disillusionment. The advantage of this approach is that it offers a micro-test. As Leutnant Peter Stölten ransacked the liberal, Protestant, and romantic traditions in which he had been educated in order to re-invigorate his sense of patriotic commitment, so his individual choices suggest one way of responding within the cultural resources available to him. During the first weeks of the Normandy invasion, his Panzer-Lehr-Division was in the thick of the fighting and, in successive June battles, the young officer saw all three of his closest friends burn to death in their tanks. By the time his battalion was withdrawn from the front line on July 3, he was the only surviving officer – and within days he was in medical care for a head wound and suspected loss of an eye after he crashed a motorbike. Thrown back on his inner resources as he recuperated at Verdun, Peter Stölten tried to ward off recurring bouts of depression and to make sense of what he was fighting for. Writing feverishly into the night, he penned a dialogue between three young men – all soldiers – and two young women. Giving two of the men the names of his dead friends, Theo and Karl, and one of the women the characteristic vitality and love of life of his fiancée Dorothee, he let his characters argue his dilemmas out among themselves. Karl got the best lines, claiming that there was neither God nor purpose in a lost war, in men crawling toward their own death in masses, like flies toward a gigantic swatter. Theo took the opposite, religious position, in which men fall back in awe of the infinity of the divine which lies beyond their comprehension:

"My ways are not your ways, for as high as the heavens are above the earth, so are my thoughts above your thoughts." All that we find and say bears the imprint of the limitations of man. But religious awe is the first step beyond the painful experience of man's boundaries: to want to know the infinite – but only to be able to know the finite.[36]

But the author gave the final word to the quietest and most contained of the three, Michael, who offered an entirely private reason to go on: "Love! It is the longing for a union with the better und the will to melt into the beautiful. In this feeling and will we want to learn to overcome the world like Empedocles," as in Hölderlin's drama.[37]

Like so many of his class and generation, Peter Stölten had gone to war regarding military service as a personal test of his moral qualities of courage and commitment. In this, Hölderlin's *Hyperion* provided the key formulation: "You are now put to the test, and must show who you are."[38] His had been an education in the patriotic virtues of *Hingabe, Tapferkeit, Einsatzbereitschaft, Opfermut,* and *Treue* (dedication, bravery, willingness to serve, self-sacrifice, and loyalty). In Normandy, his answer was straightforward: action and command could provide a clarity and sense of purpose that reflection no longer offered. By late 1944, having participated in crushing the Warsaw uprising, Peter Stölten had become far more critical of the way Germany had fought the war and treated the nations it had conquered; he was also losing his confidence in his own private postwar hopes. When he returned to Berlin for leave in December, everything in his atelier at the top of his parents' house now seemed alien, and his confidence in his own personal future as a painter was seeping away. Like so many men, his fears of loss and separation surfaced in his dreams: he dreamt that he was losing his fiancée Dorothee.

Peter Stölten's personal development reminds us that the way in which Germans experienced World War II was steeped in the cultural values of their own education and formation: it tested them and offered what to us must often seem poor answers to their doubts, their grief, their fear, and their sense of disorientation. But we also need to take their values and formation seriously. Peter Stölten privately admired the spirit of patriotic self-sacrifice displayed by the Polish fighters in the Warsaw uprising, but he nonetheless went on fighting against them alongside the SS's Dirlewanger brigade, whose brutality he so loathed. Not to have done so would, in his eyes, have been an even greater betrayal of the liberal patriotic tradition in which he had been raised. Stölten is interesting in this regard, not because his sympathies with the Polish insurgents against whom he fought in the Warsaw uprising were somehow typical, but because his cultural resources bring us back to the bourgeois mainstream, and remind us that this type of well-meaning, broadly liberal, Protestant nationalism was sufficient to see many people through moments of crisis and despair.[39]

From his father and his father's father, Stölten had acquired a Protestantism and set of theologian friends who had, by this time, mostly joined the Confessing Church and remained involved in liberal educational initiatives. And even in Peter's most raucous period of drinking, dancing all night, and stealing fruit from the orchards in Eisenach during his training with Tiger and Goliath tanks in 1943, his father had comforted himself with the thought that under the surface, which was so "loud, stormy, almost too military [*zackig*], more strongly imbued with his duty to lead than we had thought possible before," nonetheless "in secret all the good spirits like Hölderlin and Rilke, whom he is so touched by, are already working away."[40] When the news came of the attempt to assassinate Hitler on July 20, 1944, Stölten *père* immediately decried it as a betrayal of the soldiers at the front, writing to his son, "how can they endanger the front so?"[41]

Such letter-writing was important, not because it rendered an accurate account of correspondents' increasingly divergent lives – too much was omitted for that – but because it perpetuated their relationships. The letters themselves became the promise of a better future, and through their own regular rhythms of writing and repetitive themes laid down a structure of how to deal with the present. Even later, the father still urged his son to go on trusting: "to set his personal fate even in defeat in God's will, in the deep knowledge that we belong to the Lord whether we live or die."[42] And the "we" was not accidental: whereas the Wihlemine fathers had had no inkling of the conditions endured by their sons in World War I, Dr. Wilhelm Stölten had served in that conflict – even if a heart condition had kept him in the Landsturm – and he routinely adopted a comradely, fraternal "we" to temper the paternal advice he offered his son. Despite their differences over religiosity, father and son were bound more closely together than had been the case for the previous generation of fathers and sons in the previous war.

What makes Peter Stölten's *oeuvre* significant is that there are no specifically Nazi utterances in it. His, like many others', was a patriotism that could have been expressed – and often was – in terms wrought by Romantic poets and tempered in the previous war. And it worked. Stölten's last letter home was written on January 14, 1945, as he awaited the Russian attack he knew was coming: he closed with the assurance that "we're sitting on our warm vehicles and packed clothes and spinning our theories and whiling away the hours that remain to us and we are waiting – for, yes, he is coming to *us* ... And now there's a pretty big rumpus which we're awaiting smiling and completely calm."[43] Ten days later, his tank was hit by an artillery shell and burned out. He was just 22 years old.

There may have been no Nazi references in Stölten's reading of Hölderlin, but the reservoirs of "apolitical" familial patriotism meant that there would be no niche society, no inner, private spaces untainted by the German war. Hölderlin was the least militaristic and most lyrical and mystical of the German Romantic poets. *The Death of Empedokles*, which so influenced Stölten as he recovered from the Normandy battles, had been rescued from near obscurity and republished in 1942 in the small, pocket-sized Reclam edition, just the right size for weight-limited parcels for soldiers.[44] It was precisely Hölderlin's appeal to an "inner" quality that had prompted the George-Kreis to begin publishing his work in its entirety for the first time on the eve of World War I. German readers found a union of the Christianity Hölderlin had rejected and the classicism he had embraced. They found a Eucharistic sense of sacrifice combined with a dithyrambic evocation of Orpheus and Dionysius, an energizing tension between the world of the senses, of fate and divination. In Hyperion's short "Song of Fate," the contrast could not have been starker or more telling. The first stanza, establishing the harmony of the divine world where "Fateless, like sleeping/ infants, the divine beings breathe," served to seal it off from the fate-bound mortals down below. The second stanza reads:

> Doch uns ist gegeben,
> Auf keiner Stätte zu ruhn;
> Es schwinden, es fallen
> Die leidenden Menschen
> Blindlings von einer

Stunde [zur] andern,
Wie Wasser von Klippe
Zu Klippe geworfen,
Jahrlang ins Ungewisse hinab.

Yet we are granted
no place to rest;
we vanish, we fall –
suffering humans –
blind from one
hour to another,
like water thrown from cliff
to cliff,
for years into the unknown depths.[45]

In his famous setting of the song, Brahms ended the music with a recapitulation of the opening elegy, but the final words, which he repeated four times, were the fateful plunge into the abyss: "ins Ungewisse hinab." On Sunday June 6, 1943, the centenary of Hölderlin's death was commemorated with readings and concerts across the Reich. In his hometown of Tübingen, a sharp-tongued history graduate, Hellmuth Günther Dahms, observed the Nazi epigones' efforts to kidnap the poet and "declare Hölderlin the first SS man" during the crass official lectures. But he found the final concert itself "deeply moving," with its "sublime" readings of the poetry. It closed with the Brahms setting of the "Song of Fate," leaving Dahms "quietly convinced that the effect of this hour was so powerful that nothing contemporary can compare with it, that this one true figure can say more than all the stupid clap-trap of our days, that morally speaking Hölderlin's centenary is on the same level as Katyn."[46]

Dahms' heartfelt parallel is as jarring as it is revealing. By June 1943, the Katyn forest had occupied the media for the previous two months. Blanket coverage was given to disinterring the mass grave of Polish officers shot by the NKVD, forensic examination of their skulls furnishing the most vivid evidence of the "Jewish-Bolshevik" threat that Goebbels could find.[47] To place Brahms and Hölderlin alongside Katyn may sound like a jarring juxtaposition to us, but for this very reason it reveals something profound about the nationalist, symbolic world of Germany's "apolitical" educated middle classes at this stage of the war that otherwise might remain obscure. The mere word "Katyn" came to sum up the shot in the back of the neck and the abstract threat of Jewish-Bolshevik annihilation that faced Germany. It also involuntarily reminded many Germans of what they had already heard tell about the murder of the Jews and, as we have seen, contributed its own element to the talk which would start later that summer about the bombing as Allied retaliation for the murder of the Jews. By contrast, Hölderlin's poetry was read less for the relatively few verses which simply validated heroic death on the battlefield – for many other poets had done that. What mattered more was his capacity to speak to a sense of individual authenticity: this allowed educated young Germans to transport not only themselves but also the war they were fighting into an elegiac and mystical realm.

Theirs was not a choice between a mystical poetics and a crude materiality: in calculating the course of the war on the basis of genocide while treasuring the culture for which they were fighting, people were actively enlisting both.

***

All this reminds us of a complex of emotional associations that identified patriotism not with the state or Nazi propaganda but with intimate thoughts and conversations with loved ones. Above all, if we look at the affective ties to the family, we can begin to see how a brutal war of colonial conquest could appear to so many Germans as a war of national defense. The war, which had been so unpopular in prospect during the late 1930s and so unpopular for most of its duration, became the ultimate source of legitimacy, even of meaning. It was in relation to its conduct of the war that the regime's own popularity rose and fell. Indeed, the gradual narrowing of support from the representatives of the regime to the figure of the Führer traces the fact that, when each of the crises of the middle years of the war had subsided, popular support for the regime did not fully recover. Yet in the face of the military defeats and human disasters of Germany's long war, one striking feature emerges. The ultimate legitimacy of the war itself went unquestioned by all but a tiny minority even among committed opponents of the regime. And it was in relation to the war that German responses to the murder of the Jews were formed. Neither "terror" nor "consent" captures the internal, emotional dynamics of this "total war," with its crises, recoveries, unstable oscillations, and escalations. Hope and fear are a more relevant pairing here.

In the translation tussle over whether the *Volksgemeinschaft* approximates more to race or nation, it does not help us to understand these as stable social identities or even as programmatic visions of society. Rather, what mattered was the ways in which they were operationalized in an on-off fashion by powerful but heterogeneous factors. These ranged from the opportunity to stake a claim on scarce resources within the prevailing rhetoric, to the psychological need to understand and give meaning to the existential crises of the air war. As the regime quietly recognized that spontaneous social solidarity would not do as much to shore up the home front as family-oriented social subsidies paid out by the state, it tacitly accepted that the *Volksgemeinschaft* was not the glue binding German society together. Instead, the language of the *Volksgemeinschaft* emerged more as the symbolic terms of exchange, a way of obtaining goods and services or, as citizens jealously eyed each other's conduct, taking them away from others. *Gemeinschaft* remained a staple of domestic propaganda, but the regime had trouble settling on a persuasive prefix, invoking the World War I sense of a *Kampfgemeinschaft* and, later, a *Schicksalsgemeinschaft* as well as the *Volksgemeinschaft*. But they all proved problematic. German society never approximated to the romantic unity of a *Gemeinschaft*. And yet there was no getting away from the demands of war, and, in the privacy of diaries and family letters, Germans of all backgrounds readily spoke of themselves as the *Volk*. It is for this reason that subjectivity came to matter ever more as the war extended into its fourth, fifth, and sixth years. Far from serving as a safe, apolitical space to withdraw and wait out the collapse of National Socialism, as Broszat contended, German *Innerlichkeit* itself became a means not just of self-reflection, but also of self-mobilization. The Nazi leadership could not control the cultural resources of the nation they were leading through war, but they did dictate the way the war was fought. And as each fresh crisis forced German society to update its expectations, so not even the least militarist of the Romantic poets could emerge uncontaminated or unscathed from a war whose genocidal character had become prosaic.

Notes

1 The term gained real currency with Michael Burleigh and Wolfgang Wippermann, *The Racial State: Germany 1933–1945* (Cambridge, 1991). Their work drew on a range of separate literatures, illustrated here on sterilization and gender by Gisela Bock, *Zwangssterilisation im Nationalsozialismus: Studien zur Rassenpolitik und Frauenpolitik* (Opladen, 1986). There is a huge literature on medical killing, including pioneering works by Klaus Dörner such as "Nationalsozialismus und Lebensvernichtung," *Vierteljahreshefte für Zeitgeschichte,* 15 (1967), 121–52 and his edited collection, *Der Krieg gegen die psychisch Kranken* (Frankfurt, 1989); Ernst Klee (ed.), *Dokumente zur "Euthanasie"* (Frankfurt, 1986) and his *"Euthanasie" im NS-Staat: die "Vernichtung lebensunwerten Lebens"* (Frankfurt, 1983); Götz Aly (ed.), *Aktion T-4 1939–1945: die "Euthanasie"-Zentrale in der Tiergartenstrasse* (Berlin, 1987); Kurt

Nowak, *"Euthanasie" und Sterilisierung im "Dritten Reich": die Konfrontation der evangelischen und katholischen Kirche mit dem Gesetz zur Verhütung erbkranken Nachwuchses und der "Euthanasie"-Aktion*, 3rd edn. (Göttingen, 1984). On the treatment of asocials, see Wolfgang Ayass, *"Es darf in Deutschland keine Landstreicher mehr geben": Die Verfolgung von Bettlern und Vagabunden im Faschismus* (Kassel, 1980). Research on the treatment of asocials gave rise to further work on criminality: Patrick Wagner, *Volksgemeinschaft ohne Verbrecher: Konzeption und Praxis der Kriminalpolizei in der Zeit der Weimarer Republik und des Nationalsozialismus* (Hamburg, 1996); Nikolaus Wachsmann, *Hitler's Prisons: Legal Terror in Nazi Germany* (London, 2004).

2 Despite huge differences over political positioning and intellectual approach, this near complete absence characterized all sides: Timothy Mason, "Open questions on Nazism" in Raphael Samuel (ed.), *People's History and Socialist Theory* (London, 1981), 205–10; "Whatever happened to fascism" in Jane Caplan (ed.), *Nazism, Fascism and the Working Class: Essays by Tim Mason* (Cambridge, 1995), 323–31; and "Ends and beginnings," *History Workshop Journal*, 30 (Autumn 1990), 133–50; Hans Mommsen, *Beamtentum im Dritten Reich: mit ausgewählten Quellen zur nationalsozialistischen Beamtenpolitik* (Stuttgart, 1966); Karl Dietrich Bracher, *The German Dictatorship: The Origins, Structure, and Effects of National Socialism* (Harmondsworth, 1973); Alf Lüdtke, *Eigen-Sinn: Fabrikalltag, Arbeitererfahrungen und Politik vom Kaiserreich bis in den Faschismus* (Hamburg, 1993); Detlev Peukert, *Inside Nazi Germany: Conformity, Opposition and Racism in Everyday Life* (London, 1987).

3 Frank Bajohr and Michael Wildt (eds.), *Volksgemeinschaft. Neue Forschungen zur Gesellschaft des Nationalsozialismus* (Frankfurt, 2009); Michael Wildt, "'Volksgemeinschaft'. Eine Antwort auf Ian Kershaw," *Zeithistorische Forschungen/Studies in Contemporary History*, online edn., 8 (2011), www.zeithistorische-forschungen.de/16126041-Wildt-1-2011; Frank Bajohr, "Von der 'Täterforschung' zur Debatte um die 'Volksgemeinschaft'" in Forschungsstelle für Zeitgeschichte in Hamburg (ed.), *Zeitgeschichte in Hamburg. 1960–2010. 50 Jahre Forschungsstelle* (Hamburg, 2011), 55–68.

4 Michael Geyer, "Endkampf 1918 and 1945: German nationalism, annihilation and self-destruction" in Alf Lüdtke and Bernd Weisbrod (eds.), *No Man's Land of Violence: Extreme Wars in the 20th Century* (Göttingen, 2006), 35–7; Richard Bessel, "The shock of violence in 1945 and its aftermath in Germany" in Lüdtke and Weisbrod, *No Man's Land of Violence*, 69–99; R. Bessel, *Germany in 1945: From War to Peace* (London, 2009); Ian Kershaw, *The End: Hitler's Germany, 1944–45* (London, 2011).

5 Olaf Groehler, *Bombenkrieg gegen Deutschland* (Berlin, 1990); Ralf Blank, "Kriegsalltag und Luftkrieg an der "Heimatfront"" in Militärgeschichtliches Forschungsamt (ed.), *Das Deutsche Reich und der Zweite Weltkrieg*, vol. 9, part 1 (Munich, 2004),. 382–411; Michael Foedrowitz, *Bunkerwelten. Luftschutzanlagen in Norddeutschland* (Berlin, 1998), 117; Dietmar Süß, *Tod aus der Luft: Kriegsgesellschaft und Luftkrieg in Deutschland und England* (Munich, 2011); Nicole Kramer, *Volksgenossinnen an der Heimatfront. Mobilisierung, Verhalten, Erinnerung* (Göttingen, 2011); Franka Maubach, "Expansion

weiblicher Hilfe: zur Erfahrungsgeschicht von Frauen im Kriegsdienst" in Sybille Steinbacher (ed.), *Volksgenossinnen: Frauen in der NS-Volksgemeinschaft* (Göttingen, 2007), 93–111; Malte Thiessen, *Eingebrannt ins Gedächtnis: Hamburgs Gedenken an Luftkrieg und Kriegsende 1943 bis 2005* (Hamburg, 2007).

6 Götz Aly, *Hitlers Volksstaat: Raub, Rassenkrieg und nationaler Sozialismus*, (Frankfurt, 2005).

7 Frank Bajohr, *"Aryanisation" in Hamburg: The Economic Exclusion of the Jews and the Confiscation of Their Property in Nazi Germany* (Oxford, 2002), 277–82 and 284, n34.

8 Adam Tooze, *The Wages of Destruction: The Making and Breaking of the Nazi Economy* (London, 2007); see also Tooze's critical review of Aly's *Hitlers Raubstaat* in TAZ, Mar. 12, 2005, www.taz.de/1/archiv/archiv/?dig= 2005/03/12/a0289. Also Joachim Szodrzynski, "Die 'Heimatfront'" in Forschungsstelle für Zeitgeschichte in Hamburg (ed.), *Hamburg im "Dritten Reich"* (Göttingen, 2005), 633–85.

9 Marlis Steinert, *Hitlers Krieg und die Deutschen: Stimmung und Haltung der deutschen Bevölkerung im Zweiten Weltkrieg* (Düsseldorf, 1970).

10 Thomas Kühne, *Belonging and Genocide: Hitler's Community, 1918–1945* (New Haven, 2010); see also the review by Mark Roseman, *Social History*, 36 (2011), 372–4; see also the erratum to Roseman's review, 548.

11 Natalie Zemon Davis, *Society and Culture in Early Modern France: Eight Essays* (Stanford, 1975). On discussion of the Holocaust among Germans, see Nicholas Stargardt, "Speaking in public about the murder of the Jews: what did the Holocaust mean to the Germans?" in Christian Wiese and Paul Betts (eds.), *Years of Persecution, Years of Extermination: Saul Friedländer and the Future of Holocaust Studies* (London, 2010), 133–55.

12 Martin Broszat, "Einleitung" in Martin Broszat, Klaus-Dietmar Henke, and Hans Woller (eds.), *Von Stalingrad zur Währungsreform: zur Sozialgeschichte des Umbruchs in Deutschland* (Munich, 1988), xxv–xlix.

13 Dietmar Süß and Winfried Süß, "'Volksgemeinschaft' und Vernichtungskrieg: Gesellschaft im nationalsozialistischen Deutschland" in D. Süß and W. Süß (eds.), *Das "Dritte Reich": Eine Einführung* (Munich, 2008), 79–100; Bajohr and Wildt, *Volksgemeinschaft*; Hans-Ulrich Thamer and Simone Erpel (eds.), *Hitler und die Deutschen: Volksgemeinschaft und Verbrechen. Eine Ausstellung der Stiftung Deutsches Historisches Museum, Berlin, 15. Oktober 2010 bis 6. Februar 2011* (Berlin, 2010); Martina Steber, *Ethnische Gewissheiten: Die Ordnung des Regionalen im bayerischen Schwaben vom Kaiserreich bis zum NS-Regime* (Göttingen, 2010); and M. Steber, "Region and National Socialist ideology: reflections on contained plurality" in Claus-Christian W. Szejnmann and Maiken Umbach (eds.), *Heimat, Region and Empire: New Approaches to Spatial Identities in National Socialist Germany* (Houndmills, 2012), 25–42.

14 Lothar de la Camp, circular letter to "Geschwister, Freunde und Bekannte, 15.8.1943," printed in R. Hauschild-Thiessen (ed.), *Die Hamburger Katastrophe vom Sommer 1943 in Augenzeugenberichten* (Hamburg, 1993), 228–31, here 230.

15 Otto Dov Kulka and Eberhard Jäckel (eds.), *Die Juden in den geheimen NS-Stimmungsberichten, 1933–1945* (Düsseldorf, 2004), reports 3628, SD Außenstelle Würzburg, Aug. 3, 1943; 3718, SD Außenstelle Lohr, May 15, 1944.

16 Kulka and Jäckel, *Die Juden in den geheimen NS-Stimmungsberichten*, reports 3571, SD Außenstelle Bad Brückenau, Apr. 22, 1943; 3647, SD Außenstelle Schweinfurt, Sept. 6, 1943; 3661, NSDAP Kreisschulungsamt Rothenburg/T., Oct. 22, 1943.

17 Kulka and Jäckel, *Die Juden in den geheimen NS-Stimmungsberichten*, report 3388, SD Außenstelle Minden, Bericht, Minden, Dec. 12, 1941; Telegram from Leland Morris, the US Consul General in Berlin, to Secretary of State, Sept. 30, 1941, in John Mendelsohn and Donald S. Detwiler (eds.), *The Holocaust: Selected Documents in Eighteen Volumes* (New York, 1982), vol. 2, 280.

18 David Bankier, *The Germans and the Final Solution: Public Opinion under Nazism* (Oxford, 1992); Frank Bajohr and Dieter Pohl, *Der Holocaust als offenes Geheimnis / Die Deutschen, die NS-Führung und die Alliierten* (Munich, 2006); Peter Longerich, *"Davon haben wir nichts gewußt!" Die Deutschen und die Judenverfolgung 1933–1945* (Munich, 2006); Nicholas Stargardt, "Rumors of revenge in the Second World War," in Belinda Davis, Thomas Lindenberger, and Michael Wildt (eds.), *Alltag, Erfahrung, Eigensinn. Historisch-anthropologische Erkundungen* (Frankfurt, 2008), 373–88.

19 See Victor Klemperer, *To the Bitter End: The Diaries of Victor Klemperer 1942–45* (London, 1999), 289 and 291 (entries for March 12 and 19, 1944), and his *The Language of the Third Reich: LTI – Lingua Tertii Imperii: A Philologist's Notebook* (London, 2000), 172–81; Frank Stern, "Antagonistic memories" in Luisa Passerini (ed.), *Memory and Totalitarianism, International Yearbook of Oral History* (Oxford, 1992), 26; Rudolf Schottländer, *Trotz allem ein Deutscher* (Freiburg, 1986), 48ff.

20 Longerich, *"Davon haben wir nichts gewußt!"* is particularly good on the changing tenor of the press.

21 Jeffrey Herf, *The Jewish Enemy: Nazi Propaganda during World War II and the Holocaust* (Cambridge, MA, 2006).

22 Hermann Hirsch in *Stuttgarter NS-Kurier*, Sept. 2, 1943; *Der Führer*, Sept. 3, 1943.

23 First attempt to use them: Lawrence Stokes, "The German people and the destruction of the European Jews," *Central European History*, 6 (1973), 167–91; for interpretations, reading these sources as expressing moral indifference, see Ian Kershaw, *Popular Opinion and Political Dissent in the Third Reich: Bavaria, 1933–1945* (Oxford, 1984), 369, and Ian Kershaw, "German public opinion during the 'Final Solution': information, comprehension, reactions" in Asher Cohen, Joav Gelber, and Charlotte Wardi (eds.), *Comprehending the Holocaust* (Frankfurt, 1989), 145–58; echoed by Longerich, *"Davon haben wir nichts gewußt!"*, 284–7; read as evidence of popular approval of the murder of the Jews, Friedländer, *The Years of Extermination*, 211–12; 293–6; 399–400; 510–20; 634–6; 643–4.

24 Blank, "Kriegsalltag," 382–5; D. Süß, *Tod aus der Luft*; Kramer, *Volksgenossinnen an der Heimatfront*; Thiessen, *Eingebrannt ins Gedächtnis*, 61–6.

25 Blank, "Kriegsalltag," 399–400, 409–11; Roger Moorhouse, *Berlin at War: Life and Death in Hitler's Capital* (London, 2010), 327; Michael Foedrowitz, *Bunkerwelten. Luftschutzanlagen in Norddeutschland* (Berlin, 1998), 117; Dietmar Süß, "Der Kampf um die Moral im Bunker: Deutschland, Großbritannien und der Luftkrieg" in Frank Bajohr and Michael Wildt (eds.), *Volksgemeinschaft: Neue Forschungen zur Gesellschaft des Nationalsozialismus* (Frankfurt, 2009), 130.

26 Neil Gregor, "A Schicksalsgemeinschaft? Allied bombing, civilian morale, and social dissolution in Nuremberg, 1942–1945," *Historical Journal* 43(4) (2000), 1051–70; Dietmar Süß (ed.), *Deutschland im Luftkrieg. Geschichte und Erinnerung* (Munich, 2007), 99-100.

27 On the lynching of foreign workers in the Ruhr, Ulrich Herbert, *Hitler's Foreign Workers: Enforced Foreign Labor in Germany under the Third Reich* (Cambridge, 1997), 362–3; on Franconian towns in 1938, Michael Wildt, "Gewalt gegen Juden in Deutschland 1933 bis 1939," *Werkstattgeschichte* 18 (1997), 59–80.

28 Szodrzynski, "Die 'Heimatfront' zwischen Stalingrad und Kriegsende."

29 On looting in Naples, see Gabriella Gribaudi, *Guerra totale: Tra bombe alleate e violenze naziste. Napoli e il fronte meridionale 1940–1944* (Turin, 2005); on the black market in Germany, Gustavo Corni and Horst Gies, *Brot – Butter – Kanonen. Die Ernährungswirtschaft in Deutschland under der Diktatur Hitlers* (Berlin, 1997); examples of urban and rural trading, Malte Zierenberg, *Stadt der Schieber: der Berliner Schwarzmarkt 1939–1950* (Göttingen, 2008); Jill Stephenson, *Hitler's Home Front: Württemberg under the Nazis* (London, 2006), 204–20.

30 Michael Krause, *Flucht vor dem Bombenkrieg: "Umquartierungen" im Zweiten Weltkrieg und die Wiedereingliederung der Evakuierten in Deutschland 1943–1963* (Düsseldorf, 1997); Kramer, *Volksgenossinnen*, 247–99; Jill Stephenson, "'Emancipation' and its problems: war and society in Württemberg, 1939–45," *European History Quarterly* 17 (1987), 358–60; Birthe Kundrus, *Kriegerfrauen: Familienpolitik und Geschlechterverhältnisse im Ersten und Zweiten Weltkrieg* (Hamburg, 1995), 261, 271; Nicholas Stargardt, *Witnesses of War: Children's Lives under the Nazis* (London, 2005), 256–60, 329–37.

31 Gribaudi, *Guerra totale*; Claudia Baldoli, "Spring 1943: the Fiat strikes and the collapse of the Italian Home Front," *History Workshop Journal* 72 (2011), 181–9; also Claudia Baldoli and Marco Fincardi, "Italian society under Anglo-American bombs: propaganda, experience and legend, 1940–1945," *The Historical Journal* 52 (2009), 1017–38; Richard Overy (ed.), *Bombing, States and Peoples in Western Europe 1940–1945* (London, 2011); Claudia Baldoli and Andrew Knapp, *Forgotten Blitzes: France and Italy under Allied Bombs, 1940–1945* (London, 2012); Michael Schmiedel, "'Sous cette pluie de fer': Frankreich im Luftkrieg: Die allierten Luftangriffe im zweiten Weltkrieg und die französische Gesellschaft," Ph.D. dissertation, University of Leipzig (2010).

32 Klemperer, *To the Bitter End*, 421–38 (April 2–15, 1945).

33 Klaus Latzel, *Deutsche Soldaten – nationalsozialistischer Krieg? Kriegserlebnis – Kriegserfahrung 1939–1945* (Paderborn, 1998); Sven Oliver Müller, *Deutsche Soldaten und ihre Feinde: Nationalismus an Front und Heimatfront im Zweiten Weltkrieg* (Frankfurt, 2007).

34 On Austria in World War I, see Christa Hämmerle, "'Zur Liebesarbeit sind wir hier, Soldatenstrümpfe stricken wir...': Zu Formen weiblicher Kriegsfürsorge im ersten Weltkrieg," Ph.D. dissertation, University of Vienna (1996), and her "'Habt Dank, Ihr Wiener Mägdelein ...' Soldaten und weibliche Liebesgaben im Ersten Weltkrieg," *L' Homme*, 8(1) (1997), 132–54; "Liebes unbekanntes Fräulein Giesela!" in Ingrid Hammer and Susanne zur Niedern (eds.), *Sehr selten habe ich geweint: Briefe und Tagebücher aus dem Zweiten Weltkrieg von Menschen aus Berlin* (Zurich, 1992), 203–22; on the predominance of family correspondence, Ortwin Buchbender and Reinhold Sterz (eds.), *Das Andere Gesicht des Krieges: deutsche Feldpostbriefe, 1939–1945* (Munich, 1982); Stargardt, *Witnesses of War*; Hester Vaizey, *Surviving Hitler's War: Family Life in Germany, 1939–1948* (London, 2010).

35 The sociology of the Wehrmacht, pointing to its privileging of small units drawn from the same localities, was pioneered by E. A. Shils and M. Janowitz, "Cohesion and disintegration in the Wehrmacht in World War II," *Public Opinion Quarterly* 12 (1948), 280–315; also Martin van Creveld, *Fighting Power: German and U.S. Army Performance, 1939–1945* (Westport, 1982). For a critique based on the high rate of attrition suffered on the Eastern Front, see Omer Bartov, *Hitler's Army: Soldiers, Nazis and War in the Third Reich* (Oxford, 1991) and *The Eastern Front 1941–1945: German Troops and the Barbarisation of Warfare* (Oxford, 1985); on comradeship as a binding myth, see Thomas Kühne, *Kameradschaft: Die Soldaten des nationalsozialistischen Krieges und das 20. Jahrhundert* (Göttingen, 2006).

36 Astrid Julia Irrgang, *Leutnant der Wehrmacht: Peter Stölten in seinen Feldpostbriefen: Vom richtigen Leben im falschen* (Freiburg im Breisgau, 2007), 188: "'Meine Wege sind nicht eure Wege, denn so hoch der Himmel über der Erde ist, so hoch sind meine Gedanken über euren Gedanken.' Alles, was wir finden und sagen, trägt den Stempel der Beschränkung, ist vom Menschen her gesagt. Das heilige Staunen aber ist der erste Schritt über die schmerzlich empfundene Grenze des Menschen: das Unendliche erkennen zu wollen – aber nur das Endliche erkennen zu können."

37 Irrgang, *Leutnant der Wehrmacht*, 189: "*... die Liebe! Sie ist die Sehnsucht nach einer Vereinigung mit dem Besseren und der Wille zum Verschmelzen mit dem Schönen. In diesem Gefühl und Willen wollen wir die Welt überwinden lernen wie Empedokles.*"

38 Irrgang, *Leutnant der Wehrmacht*, 190–1: "Du bist nun auf der Probe, und es muß sich zeigen, wer du bist."

39 Irrgang, *Leutnant der Wehrmacht*, 193–221; 229–41.

40 Irrgang, *Leutnant der Wehrmacht*, 162: Wilhelm Stölten to Dr Victor Meyer-Eckhardt, June 27, 1943: "laut, stürmisch, fast zu zackig, von seiner Führeraufgabe stärker geprägt, als wir das je für möglich gehalten hatten"; "Im Geheimen arbeiten schon alle guten Geister wie Hölderlin und Rilke, denen er sehr zugetan ist, an dieser Aufgabe."

41 Irrgang, *Leutnant der Wehrmacht*, 82: Wilhelm to Peter Stölten, July 21, 1944: "Wie kann man die Front so gefährden?"

42 Irrgang, *Leutnant der Wehrmacht*, 79–80: Wilhelm to Peter Stölten, Sept. 5, 1944: "sein persönliches Schicksal auch noch im Untergehen gläubig in

Gottes Willen zu stellen, im tiefen Wissen, ob wir leben oder sterben, so sind
wir des Herrn."

43 Irrgang, *Leutnant der Wehrmacht*, 237: Peter Stölten to parents, Jan. 14,
1945: "Liebe Familie, Täglich beginnt nun der Russe an einer Stelle einen
Angriff ... Nun kommt langsam Klarheit in den Laden und wir erwarten an
einem der Brückenköpfe nun die Schwerpunktbildung, sitzen auf den warmen
Karren und gepackten Klamotten und wälzen unsere Theorien und verwetten
die Stunden, die uns noch bleiben und warten, – er kommt ja zu uns ... Und
nun kommt davon ein ganz großes Gekrakel, auf das wir lächelnd und in aller
Ruhe warten ... So bleibt Euch mein alter Wunsch: Laßt es Euch gut gehen ...
Viele, viele Grüße Euch allen, Euer Peter."

44 Claudia Albert, "Hölderlin" in C. Albert (ed.), *Deutsche Klassiker im Nationalsozialismus. Schiller – Kleist – Hölderlin* (Stuttgart, 1994). 189–Y248;
Bernhard Zeller (ed.), *Klassiker in Finsteren Zeiten 1933–45: Eine Austellung
des Deutschen Literaturarchivs im Schiller-Nationalmuseum Marbach am
Neckar* (Marbarch, 1983), 2, 76–134; 300–35.

45 Friedrich Hölderlin, 1798, set to music by Johannes Brahms, "Hyperions
Schicksalslied," op. 54 (1868), published 1871; trans. Emily Ezust, "Hyperion's Song of Fate," copyright © 1995, (re)printed with kind permission from
the website www.lieder.net/lieder/get_text.html?TextId=8134.

46 Brahms, "Hyperions Schicksalslied," op. 54; *Klassiker in finsteren Zeiten*, 2,
99: Hellmuth Günther Dahms to Wolfgang Hermann, June 10, 1943.

47 On Katyn propaganda and discussion of the murder of the Jews, see Kulka
and Jäckel, *Die Juden in den geheimen NS-Stimmungsberichten*, report 3652,
SD Außenstelle Bad Neustadt, Bericht ("I-Bericht - Allgemeine Stimmung und
Lage"), 15.10.1943; Willi A. Boelcke (ed.), *Wollt Ihr den totalen Krieg? Die
geheimen Goebbels-Konferenzen 1939–1943* (Munich, 1969), 409–13; David
Bankier, "German public awareness of the Final Solution" in David Cesarani
(ed.), *The Final Solution: Origins and Implementation* (London, 1994),
219–21; Herf, *Jewish Enemy*.

PART V

RACE WAR? GERMANS AND NON-GERMANS IN WARTIME

17

Volk Trumps Race

The Deutsche Volksliste *in Annexed Poland*

Gerhard Wolf

THE RACIAL TURN AND ITS PITFALLS

Research on National Socialism has certainly not been immune to paradigmatic shifts. The linguistic, cultural, postcolonial, and spatial turns have all left their mark. It seems to me, however, that this field has been most strongly shaped in the past twenty-five years by what I would call the racial turn. A conference organized by Jane Caplan and Thomas Childers at the University of Pennsylvania in 1988 was one of the first attempts to test the explanatory powers of this new approach. The papers presented at that conference, later published under the apt title *Reevaluating the Third Reich*, all placed Nazi racial ideologies and practices at the center of their analyses. Sped up by the collapse of the Eastern bloc, which helped to delegitimize Marxist and structural approaches in general, and after the last ounce of intellectual surplus value had been squeezed out of the intentionalist/functionalist debate, the new approach seemed to offer a way forward. In the more sophisticated accounts, this "return of ideology" did not, however, reinstate ideology as an explanatory factor per se but rather saw it as a feature of the modernization process. That ideology called for the division of the German population between those with and without "value," for example, and justified using the unprecedented powers of a modern state to enforce the Nazi social program.[1] Nazi crimes such as the mass killing of Jews, Soviet prisoners of war, inmates of mental asylums, and so-called asocials, and more generally the targeting

The author would like to thank Hester Barron, Paul Betts, Donald Bloxham, and Dirk Moses for their helpful comments.

of all those who for whatever reason did not fit into the Nazi dystopia could now be understood as discrete but interconnected aspects of a policy aiming at the "establishment of a racist utopia in which the social question would be 'finally solved.'"[2] The vast number of studies published since the 1990s testify to just how quickly historians adopted the phrase "racial state" – the title of Michael Burleigh and Wolfgang Wippermann's influential 1991 study – to describe Nazi Germany.[3]

In this essay, I do not want to deny that race was of paramount importance in Nazi ideology and practice. Rather, I want to highlight some of the shortcomings of the racial state paradigm. Its strongest point – its integration of the Nazis' multiple mass crimes into a single coherent narrative – comes at a high cost. It threatens to underplay the role of anti-Semitism in Nazism and, consequently, to obscure the question why the regime opted for genocide in its policy toward the Jews while taking more flexible approaches to other designated enemy groups. Moreover, the focus on race also ignores more traditional elements of Nazi ideology that were not only more important for bringing Hitler to power but also arguably pivotal in shaping the regime's policies and actions. In this context, the ideologically charged notion of *Volksgemeinschaft* is of particular importance.[4] *Volk*, to take just one crucial example, was not defined primarily in racial terms either in popular perception or in the many ways party officials used it; rather, it preserved and evoked more traditional, often cultural understandings of belonging going back to Herder and Fichte.

Although Burleigh and Wipperman, following the trend of the historiography in the West, focused exclusively on the German Reich, the racial state paradigm soon transformed research on Nazi occupation policies, which expanded quickly in the 1990s.[5] Few of those studies passed up the opportunity to explore Nazi ideology in detail and to trace the regime's actions back to its beliefs. Hitler is of particular importance here because, in contrast to most of the other Nazi leaders, he left behind an extensive corpus of letters and speeches, along with, of course, the expansive *Mein Kampf* and its unpublished sequel. Whatever value one might attach to Hitler's rambling and often self-contradictory writings, it is difficult to maintain that they have much to offer on the *Lebensraum* dystopia, which was, together with the final solution to the "Jewish question," the Nazi movement's raison d'être. What contemporaries could gather from listening to Hitler's speeches was how important the notion of *Raum* was in his thinking.[6] But his comments on this point were rarely more concrete than his insistence in *Mein Kampf* that the "*foreign policy of a folkish State is charged with guaranteeing the existence ... of the race ... by establishing between the number and growth of the population, on the one hand, and the size and value of the soil and territory, on the other hand, a viable, natural relationship.*[7] In Hitler's vision, this "war for space" (*Raumkrieg*) was, as Frank-Lothar Kroll notes, "the archetype of political action."[8]

This crude understanding of politics was all the more explosive as it drove Hitler far beyond the call for an annulment of the Versailles settlement. He sneered at the Weimar political establishment for demanding a return to the borders of 1914. For Hitler, this was "*political nonsense*," a "*crime*,"[9] as even a possible success "would still be so miserable that it would not pay ... to invest the blood of our nation for *that* again."[10] Hitler's vision was on a grander scale. The National Socialists would "terminate the endless German drive to the south and west of Europe, and direct our gaze towards the lands in the east. We finally terminate the colonial and trade policy of the pre-War period, and proceed to the territorial policy of the future."[11] Hitler left no doubt as to where this future lay: "if we talk about new soil and territory in Europe today, we can think primarily only of *Russia*."[12]

What about the population living there? Here, too, Hitler stylized himself as a politician overturning all political norms, calling for an unequivocal break with the past. Referring to the anti-Polish policies of Prussia and, later, the German Empire, Hitler insisted that "Germanization" should no longer be misunderstood as an "enforced outward acceptance of the German language": it could "only be carried out with the *soil* and never with *men*."[13] In his unpublished second book, Hitler was more explicit:

The folkish state, conversely, must under no conditions annex Poles with the intention of wanting to make Germans out of them some day. On the contrary it must muster the determination either to seal off these alien racial elements, so that the blood of its own people will not be corrupted again, or it must without further ado remove them and hand over the vacated territory to its own national comrades.[14]

It would be all too easy to point out that "Germanization of the soil" did in fact become a ubiquitous slogan during the war and was heard everywhere between Gotenhafen and Hegewald. How, one might ask, could *Mein Kampf* not have been the blueprint for the subsequent policy of forced population exchange and mass murder?

On an epistemological level, scouring the writings of Nazi leaders for programmatic content is problematic if it becomes part of a simplified

model in which the relationship between individual belief and social
practice is imagined as a hierarchical and unilinear nexus, as in belief →
planning → action.[15] I would not go as far as Franz Neumann and insist
that taking National Socialist ideology seriously makes no sense at
all, given that with the Nazis "[e]very pronouncement springs from
the immediate situation and is abandoned as soon as the situation
changes."[16] Nor would I follow Theodor Adorno in dismissing the relevance of Nazi ideology with the argument that the Nazis, able to rely on
force, did not need to win the public's endorsement for their program:
"Power was referred to with a wink; listen to reason and you will
see where you end up."[17] Although I share this skepticism toward
approaches that mistake ideology as a blueprint for action, I do not think
that this justifies dismissing ideology as such; to the contrary, it makes
clear the need for a more sophisticated understanding of the relationship
between ideology and power.[18] A promising approach, it seems to me,
is an understanding of ideology informed by the work of structuralists
such as Louis Althusser. Defining ideology as the "'lived' relationship
between men and their world," Althusser argued that "ideology has a
material existence."[19] For Althusser, ideology is no longer mainly a
theoretical enterprise pressing for worldly expression; rather, it describes
a set of *dispositifs*, rituals, and practices in which the production of
theoretical knowledge about the world is inextricably linked with its
performative affirmation. It was in this context that Althusser pointed
to Blaise Pascal: "Kneel down, move your lips in prayer, and you will
believe."[20]

   If, in short, ideology does not precede action but emerges in and
through it, historians should not separate what the Nazis called *Weltanschauung* from the regime's policies and conduct. Rather, we have to
explain which of the various strands in Nazi ideology become dominant
over time and why by linking this internal ideological struggle to the
political situation confronting the regime. Ideology, in this sense, has to
be understood as having provided a vocabulary to articulate these
challenges and to frame solutions while at the same time securing and
perpetuating the regime's existence. Ideology, in other words, has to be
linked to power. Even hardcore Nazis had no qualms about ignoring
Hitler's writings if some aspect of Nazi ideology proved to be dysfunctional and threatened the perpetuation of the political system. When,
for example, racial ideology proved an obstruction to an occupation
policy intended to minimize the need for occupation troops and to
maximize economic exploitation, actors on the scene quickly became

ideological entrepreneurs who contributed to the incoherent corpus of Nazi ideology by reinterpreting it.

It is exactly this process that I will focus on in my analysis of the Nazi *Lebensraum* dystopia. Obviously, population policy was not the only aspect of Germanizing the conquered lands, and annexed Poland formed only a very small part of the quickly expanding Nazi empire. Nonetheless, I think that the analysis of the biggest Germanization project ever undertaken during the war in occupied Europe, the so-called *Deutsche Volksliste* in annexed Poland, offers an exemplary insight into German policies in Eastern Europe as a whole. For the Nazis, annexed Poland was a "testing ground" (*Experimentierfeld*) for new policies that might then be applied in other occupied areas or even the German Reich.[21] What better case study for looking into how racial politics worked in Nazi Germany?

COMPETING TRADITIONS: GERMANIZING POLES

In analyzing National Socialist Germanization policy in Poland, one should not take Nazi claims of breaking decisively with the past at face value. Doing so would mean ignoring continuities with Prussian policies from before 1918. Prussian Germanization policy in the eastern provinces had rested in large part on the belief that the Polish-speaking inhabitants could and had to be assimilated into the German *Volk*. The largescale denationalization campaigns expanded considerably with the establishment of the German Empire as a nation-state. If Poles were seen as an irritant before 1871, they were now increasingly perceived as a threat to national unity. Such perceptions eventually led to largescale settlement programs, expropriations, and deportations. There were even plans to replace Poles residing in eastern Germany with ethnic Germans from Russia. Such policies culminated in discussion of expelling all Poles from a proposed "border strip" during World War I.[22]

These visions of violence might help to fill the gap left by Hitler's sketchy outlines of a National Socialist Germanization policy. Hitler's call for a "Germanization of the soil" appears to be less a clear-cut break with the past than a radicalization of earlier policies when compared to measures that had been taken around the turn of the century or some of the plans that government ministries drafted during World War I. The radicalizing element was the notion of race. Whereas the Imperial governments had sought to assimilate or displace an ethnic Other, the Nazis aimed for the total exclusion of racial inferiors. And they showed none of the qualms or hesitations that had prevented the Imperial governments from turning their fantasies into reality.[23]

Reflecting on the course of National Socialist Germanization policy in Poland, it is hard not to be astonished by its chaotic start, its turbulent progress, and the fact that it remained contested until the very end of the war. One reason for the chaotic start, of course, was that Poland had initially played no role in Nazi leaders' fantasies of *Lebensraum*. This changed abruptly not for ideological but rather for pragmatic reasons. After blackmailing Prague into surrendering its western territories, the German government tried the same with Warsaw. During a diplomatic visit to Warsaw in January 1939, Foreign Minister Joachim von Ribbentrop proposed a quid pro quo: Germany would finally recognize the Polish-German border if Poland agreed to accept Danzig becoming part of the German Reich, to allow an extraterritorial link between Danzig and the rest of the Reich, and to join the Anti-Comintern Pact. In other words, the Polish government had to decide whether it was willing to become Germany's junior partner in a future conflict with the Soviet Union. Much to Germany's surprise, the Polish government resisted, prompting Hitler to prepare for *Fall Weiß*, that is, for the invasion of Poland. Thus the war launched in September was not a joint Polish-German strike against the Soviet Union intended to solve Germany's supposed need for *Lebensraum* once and for all but rather an attack on Poland by a Germany aligned with the Soviet Union through the Molotov-Ribbentrop Pact.

This context is necessary, I think, to make sense of the lack of planning and downright confusion in Germany regarding Poland. The military had been quick in putting together an invasion scenario, but political post-invasion planning lagged seriously behind. True, Hitler moved quickly to transfer power from the military to new civilian authorities under the control of Nazi party "old fighters." German-occupied Poland was divided in two, with the Government General in central Poland handed over to Hans Frank and the west incorporated into the German Reich. The annexed territory was divided into three provinces: Danzig-West Prussia in the north under Albert Forster, the Wartheland under Arthur Greiser, and Upper Silesia in the south under Josef Wagner and, later, Fritz Bracht. Strengthening party control, however, did not in itself guarantee a unified policy, as soon became clear. Even after the decision was taken in early October 1939 to turn the Government General into what the Germans called a "dumping ground" for the population ejected from the western parts of Poland that had been incorporated into the German Reich and Germanized, the institutions and power blocs ruling Poland had very conflicting visions of how to accomplish this aim.

The key question was how the native population in the annexed territories was to be treated – a question not entirely unfamiliar to German ethnocrats. After the annexation of Austria, the Sudetenland, and Memel, the local populations had been granted German citizenship, with the exception in the latter two cases of individuals who had moved to the areas after a given date.[24] The Interior Ministry took a similar approach in Poland after Hitler signed a decree on the "Structure and Organization of the Eastern Territories" (October 8, 1939). Inhabitants "of German or related [*artverwandten*] blood," the ministry announced, would provisionally become "German state citizens" (*deutsche Staatsangehörige*). "Ethnic Germans" (*Volksdeutsche*), by contrast, would become "Reich citizens" (*Reichsbürger*) and receive full political rights.[25] In other words, inhabitants of German ancestry who were judged no longer to be members of the German minority on account of their social practices stood in a less advantageous position than the *Volksdeutsche* who had demonstrated their "Germanness" by, for example, joining German organizations. Only one group was to be categorically excluded from the annexed territories: the *artfremde* (alien) Polish Jews. Everybody else was put in line for German citizenship, not just the *Volksdeutsche* but also the supposedly *artverwandte* Christian Poles. Official racial terminology notwithstanding, the Interior Ministry opted for a very inclusive selection process that aimed to integrate the majority of the population. This is, of course, the exact opposite of what Hitler had in mind when he ruled out the Germanization of Poles in his second book.

The transfer of German citizenship to the native population was planned as a two-phase process. First, the *Volksdeutsche* who were to be granted Reich citizenship were to be registered; registration of the *artverwandte* population slated for state citizenship would follow. To start the first phase, the Interior Ministry issued a decree on November 25, 1939, that linked Reich citizenship solely to *völkisch* identity. The decree explained:

He who declares himself a member of the German Volk [will be deemed to be] of German ethnicity [*deutscher Volkszugehörigkeit*] if this declaration is backed up by certain facts like *language, education, culture,* etc. Under the given circumstances a clearer definition of the term German ethnicity is not possible. However, it will generally pose no difficulty to decide whether somebody is of German ethnicity or not. [26]

Interestingly, German ethnicity did not necessarily require "German" ancestors. In fact, a declaration (*Bekenntnis*) that one belonged to the German people trumped descent (*Abstammung*) in the Interior Ministry's criteria for Reich citizenship:

Since the declaration of belonging to the German *Volk* is crucial, it is in fact possible to accept as German someone who is partially or fully of alien stock. Conversely, it is possible in particular circumstances that, due to his statement, a person has to be seen as belonging to an alien people even he is of partial or full German stock.[27]

If in doubt, officials had to establish whether "according to his overall behavior [the applicant] constitutes a desired addition to the population. If this is the case, the decision ... has to be considered generously."[28]

The Interior Ministry was not the only institution that established a selection process for the native population. On October 28, 1939, only three days after the civilian administration had taken over from the military, the Reichsstatthalter and Gauleiter in the Wartheland, Arthur Greiser, issued the *Deutsche Volksliste*, which proclaimed: "Who is listed in the deutsche *Volksliste* is German."[29] Drawn up by Karl Albert Coulon, the head of the ethnicity desk (*Volkstumreferent*) in Greiser's administration, with support from the local SD branch, the selection procedure in the Wartheland differed in three key aspects from the one decreed by the Interior Ministry. First, Greiser objected to the timetable contemplated in Berlin, which postponed the registration of *artverwandte* Poles until after the registration of *Volksdeutsche*. The population should be screened immediately and in its totality, Greiser insisted. Second, Greiser vehemently rejected the inclusive selection criteria aimed at the assimilation of Poles. The *Deutsche Volksliste* was to register "Germans" only. Third, in January 1940 Coulon provided German bureaucrats in the Wartheland with very detailed instructions that stood in sharp contrast to the deliberately vague selection criteria issued by the Interior Ministry. Instead of talking about a "desirable addition to the population," Greiser declared that the "[b]asic precondition for belonging to the German Volk [is]: Having declared oneself to be part of the German Volk in the time of ethnic alien rule." The *Deutsche Volksliste* was divided into two groups, A and B. The former consisted of individuals who had declared their allegiance to the German cause in the interwar period (*Bekenntnisdeutsche*), the latter of individuals who could prove that they were of German ancestry (*Stammesdeutsche*). But ancestry alone was not sufficient for admittance to group B: even applicants who could produce the requisite two German grandparents (who, interestingly, were not a precondition for admittance to group A) still had to demonstrate that they had "preserved [their] Germanness." For example, families who did not speak German at home or who had chosen to send their children to a Polish-speaking school or given their children Polish names were to be treated as Poles – no matter how many German grandparents they could claim.[30] As Coulon put it: "In a *völkisch* embattled territory there is no room for *völkisch* dubious elements."[31]

Greiser's initiative found little support in Berlin. Given the inextricable link between ethnicity (*Volkszugehörigkeit*) and citizenship (*Staatsangehörigkeit*) in Germany, the Interior Ministry feared that the Wartheland regulations would undermine German citizenship law by effectively deciding applicants' citizenship status in advance. The differences between the Interior Ministry's more inclusive and the Wartheland's more exclusive approaches notwithstanding, it is crucial not to overlook that both cloaked their selection criteria in the language of *Volk*. In Berlin as well as in Posen, the selection processes aimed at establishing applicants' *Volkszugehörigkeit* as the precondition for deciding admission to the German *Volksgemeinschaft*. Given the focus of much of the recent scholarship on the racial underpinnings of Nazi policies, one might wonder where race was in all this. Is it conceivable that two key Nazi institutions tasked with defining Germanness chose to simply ignore race? That, in a sense, is exactly what happened. The Interior Ministry did not mention race at all and only implicitly referred to a racial rationale when excluding Jews and others of "wholly alien blood" (*voll Fremdblütige*), which expressly did not include Poles. The ethnocrats in the Wartheland did mention race but then only to explicitly reject it as a selection criterion:

Certain racial criteria are indeed often evidence that some of the applicants' ancestors were German. Still, given the situation in the province, racial criteria are not a sound basis on which to decide whether the [applicant belongs] to the German people.[32]

THE STRUGGLE FOR A UNIFIED SELECTION PROCESS

If the selection procedures were contested right from the start, the conflicts only became more bitter during the following months. After the scuffles between the Interior Ministry and Gauleiter Greiser, the SS intervened. On October 7, 1939, Hitler entrusted Himmler with the task of

bringing ethnic Germans from Eastern Europe "home to the Reich" by
settling them in the annexed territories and with "eliminating the harmful
influence of . . . *völkisch* alien elements."[33] Adding "Reich Commissar for
the Strengthening of Germandom" (Reichskommissar für die Festigung
deutschen Volkstums, or RKF) to his list of titles, Himmler realized that
these two new tasks had to be combined, as housing and jobs for the ever-
increasing number of incoming "Germans" could best be supplied by
deporting Poles.[34] Himmler's criticism of the selection procedure established by the Interior Ministry has to be understood against the backdrop
of these developments. He demanded a speedy selection process that
would identify not only future *Reichsbürger* but everybody who was
eventually to be integrated into the German *Volksgemeinschaft*, thus
facilitating the planning of deportations. He also pressed for much more
exclusive selection criteria, demanding that more Poles be deported to
free up housing for the increasing number of ethnic Germans being
resettled in the annexed territories. Racial discourse proved compatible
here with the political aims of the SS. As Himmler wrote to the Interior
Ministry on January 13, 1940, the decision to recognize an applicant as
German could not be made on the basis of "purely outward declar-
ations of belonging to the German people (language, education, culture, etc.)": rather, "racial belonging" had to be taken as the "most
important criterion for belonging to the German people."[35] Obviously,
this protest was anything but altruistic, given that the only German
institution with the necessary expertise and manpower for such an
undertaking was Himmler's SS Race and Settlement Head Office
(Rasse- und Siedlungshauptamt, RuSHA). Handing the selection process to the RuSHA would have increased the SS influence and ensured
that the more inclusive selection criteria used by the civilian administration in Danzig-West Prussia and Upper Silesia would not derail the
SS resettlement program.

Himmler's intentions were quickly frustrated by the resistance of the
Gauleiter, however, forcing the SS to refocus its efforts on overcoming
the resistance of the other decisive opponent to racial screening, the
Interior Ministry. On May 24, 1940, the SS Reich Security Head Office
(Reichssicherheitshauptamt, RSHA) presented Himmler with a memorandum. Drawn up by Dr. Hans Joachim Beyer of the SD, an organization
already heavily involved in population policies in the annexed territories,
the memorandum complained that the Interior Ministry's guidelines were
being interpreted in very different ways in the annexed territories, making
the selection processes "greatly incompatible."[36] Even more problematic

were the guidelines themselves, the memorandum charged, because they "aim solely at establishing the declaration of belonging [to the German people] while neglecting racial criteria." The RSHA therefore demanded a total overhaul of the selection process, ideally by introducing a *Deutsche Volksliste*, not dissimilar to the one in use in the Wartheland, in all of western Poland. In the meantime, Greiser had come to the realization that the criteria in use in the Wartheland were not producing the numbers of new Reich and state citizens needed to stabilize German rule and thus issued an order that lowered – but did not abolish – the conduct requirements for admission to the *Deutsche Volksliste*. Beyer, following suit, proposed that the new and unified *Deutsche Volksliste* consist of four groups (A-D), including, in addition to *Volksdeutsche*, "passively" and "actively Polonised individuals of German descent" (groups C and D, respectively). Furthermore, he demanded that "the criteria in force in the Wartheland should be applied in all Reich German Eastern territories." There was one significant difference, however: racial screening was to be introduced for those selected for group C.[37]

The memorandum exacerbated the dispute. The climax came when Himmler refused to accept an alternative draft presented by the Interior Ministry.[38] It was only during a meeting between Himmler and Wilhelm Stuckart, the permanent secretary in the Interior Ministry, that the two parties somehow settled their differences – or, more accurately, the ministry accepted defeat. Stuckart apparently gave in to the demands of the SS, clearing the path for Himmler to sign the decree on "Screening and Selecting the Population in the Annexed Territories" the following day (September 12, 1940). Following Beyer's recommendations, Himmler instructed the Reichsstatthalter in annexed Poland to create the *Deutsche Volksliste* based on the four-group (A–D) classification.

The selection criteria were more or less identical to those used in the Wartheland. Indeed, Greiser's guidelines were often simply copied. There was, however, one important difference: following the Wartheland's newly expanded *Deutsche Volksliste*, Himmler expanded group C so as to include applicants who had "links to Polishdom ... but because of their conduct possess the necessary qualities to become full members of the German *Volksgemeinschaft*." But given that they had not been loyal *Volksdeutsche* before the invasion, it would not be enough to declare their loyalty now. Instead, they had to prove that their application was backed up by "facts like descent, race, upbringing, and culture." Particular importance was placed on the requirement that they represent "a valuable addition to the population in racial terms."[39] For the first time, race had become a decisive selection criterion, even if that stipulation applied only to persons assigned to group C.

It took another six months to resolve all the differences and the *Deutsche Volksliste* was finally introduced in all the three provinces in annexed Poland. The delay is indicative of the many differences that remained unresolved – not only between the SS and the Interior Ministry but also among other actors such as the party and the civilian administrations in the annexed territories. Although the ethnocrats in the Wartheland had closely cooperated with the SS to block the Interior Ministry's more inclusive approach, for instance, they continued to oppose the use of race as a selection criterion. Having rejected race as a criterion outright only the year before, they now felt the need for a more sophisticated reasoning more in line with Himmler's racial discourse. So instead of simply repeating his old argument, Coulon suddenly claimed that the importance given to applicants' behavior was in fact a form of racial screening:

Times of fighting are always also times during which a selection takes place. A selection with regard to character qualifications, however, is always simultaneously a process of racial selection.[40]

Minister of the Interior Wilhelm Frick signed the order creating the *Deutsche Volksliste* on March 4, 1941. One week later, Frick proved himself no less adept than Himmler in exploiting racial discourse for his own ends. He employed the racial terminology introduced by the SS, but to widen, not tighten, the selection criteria. Frick maintained: "An indifferent or even a bad German remains a German and pushing him against his will into the non-German camp, thus supplying it with German blood, must be averted. No German in the eastern territories must be refused access to the German *Volksgemeinschaft*."[41]

Whereas Himmler demanded that borderline cases in group C would be added to the list only if they would be "a valuable addition to the population in racial terms," the Interior Ministry was less choosy and said simply that questionable group C applicants would be accepted provided that they were not "racially unsuitable."[42]

The citizenship of inhabitants of the annexed Polish territories was determined by their grouping on the *Deutsche Volksliste*. Members of group 1 and 2 (formerly A and B) became full Reich citizens; members of group 3 (formerly C) were eligible only for the lower status of state citizens.[43]

FUTILE ATTEMPTS

Although it watered down Himmler's demands, Frick's implementation order represented a defeat for the Interior Ministry. Frick was forced to recognize race as a criterion for the *Deutsche Volksliste*, and in doing so he presented the SS with an ideal opportunity to gain direct influence over the selection process. In contrast to earlier confrontations with the Gauleiter, the SS could now point to the new regulations and demand that the RuSHA be involved. RuSHA screening personnel were already active in the annexed territories, conducting racial screening of the hundreds of thousands of incoming ethnic Germans and selecting many fewer Poles for inclusion into the Regermanization Program (*Wiedereindeutschungsprogramm*).[44]

In line with the ad hoc character of Germanization policy and, indeed, with the internal contradictions of the entire project, the RuSHA had no clear-cut criteria to define Germanness racially. Incoming Germans from Eastern Europe and the Soviet Union were deemed racially suitable even if they had been assigned to the third (of four) racial groups in a biometric racial-screening process. The requirements for the native population were more stringent, however. Only individuals classified as racial group I or II were deemed fit for admission to the German *Volksgemeinschaft*. Because the SS tended to see members of group 3 as Poles rather than as *Volksdeutsche*, Fritz Schwalm, head of the RuSHA branch office in Litzmannstadt, initially demanded that everybody not assigned to the upper two racial groups be rejected. As a result, sixteen out of twenty families were turned down in a first test run. This caused great turmoil in the regional office of the *Deutsche Volksliste*. Officials feared that retroactively expelling tens of thousands of residents from the *Deutsche Volksliste* would provoke a backlash; they also thought such a step would be counterproductive, as, after all, group 3 had been created to help bolster the number of Germans in the province. Greiser was certainly not prepared to let a racial argument get in his way. In the end, the RuSHA realized that it could either stick with its restrictive interpretation and see the entire process shelved or take a more accommodating stance. Schwalm chose the latter option and acknowledged that "accepting into the *Deutsche Volksliste* only individuals classed in racial groups I and II would deliver too small a result." Ever adept at finding an ideological justification for the second-best option, Schwalm now argued that because most of the members of group 3 probably had "German" ancestors, they could also be treated like the incoming ethnic Germans from Eastern Europe and

accepted even if classed in racial group III.[45] After reaching a compromise
with the ethnocrats in Litzmannstadt, the RKF head office in Berlin
prepared for the racial screening of all members of group 3. The
first protests came from Posen. Coulon, the architect of the *Deutsche
Volksliste*, argued:

> integrating racial screening into the procedure of the *Deutsche Volksliste* ...
> contradicts ... its fundamental principle. The list is a summary registration of
> those of German descent based on a declaration of belonging to the German
> people for groups 1 and 2 and of descent for groups 3 and 4 ... Therefore,
> questions of ethnicity [*Volkstumsfragen*] and questions of race [*Rassefragen*] have
> to be kept separate in principle.

In Coulon's view, the Germanization policy in the Wartheland and
beyond had to establish once and for all a "truly united ethnic front
[*Volkstumsfront*] against Polishdom." It was crucial not to lose the necessary support of the native *Volksdeutschen* by retrospectively expelling
some of them from the *Volksliste*.[46]

The ongoing arguments between the SS and the civilian administration
were resolved only after Himmler promised the authorities in Posen that,
to maintain political stability, members of group C would be expelled
only if they could be deported from the Wartheland.[47] The agreement
with at least one Gauleiter allowed Himmler to press ahead and sign the
decree on the "Racial Screening of Members of Group 3 of the Deutsche
Volksliste" on September 30, 1941. The RuSHA was entrusted with the
screening process. The decree stipulated that "[a] negative result during
the racial screening will necessarily lead to the rejection of the application
to or to removal from the *Deutsche Volksliste*."[48]

In the other two provinces, Himmler's advance was met with even
greater hostility. The biggest defeat awaited Himmler in Danzig-West
Prussia. Gauleiter Albert Forster was neither willing to change his inclusive selection practice nor prepared to accept any procedure that would
increase the power of the SS in his province. After learning about the plan
to introduce racial screening, Forster made sure to exclude all SS institutions from the selection process and instructed his subordinates that if
the RuSHA tried to influence the process by submitting results of racial
screening, the results were "to be treated as not binding for the decision
of the ... *Deutsche Volksliste*."[49]

The SS fared only slightly better in Upper Silesia. When the RuSHA
informed Gauleiter Bracht in February 1942 that racial screening would
soon commence in his province and asked him to ensure that the DVL
offices cooperated fully with the screening personnel, Bracht flatly refused.

Like the ethnocrats in the Wartheland, Bracht stated that given the present political situation in his province, he would "absolutely reject" any plans for subjecting members of group 3 to racial screening.[50] Instead, he proposed screening only the roughly 50,000 members of group 4.

If RuSHA officials thought that agreeing to the terms set out by Bracht would ensure smooth cooperation with state authorities, they were mistaken. Shortly before the RuSHA dispatched its men to the province, the president of the district of Kattowitz, Walther Springorum, raised new doubts in a meeting on January 6, 1943. The differences were hard to overcome. While the head of the RuSHA's Rassenamt (Racial Office), Bruno Kurt Schultz, insisted on carrying out Himmler's order, Springorum and his county officials remained skeptical. They claimed that the racial screening of members of the *Deutsche Volksliste* would damage their authority, as they had repeatedly promised members of group 3 that it was their conduct alone that would decide their future. In the end, Schultz and Springorum agreed to disagree.[51] Bracht informed the men on the selection committees by secret courier that "[m]y view was and is: The registration of individuals belonging to the German people with the *Deutsche Volksliste* cannot in principle be made dependent on the result of a racial screening."[52] The racial screening process, it thus appears, was simply ignored at the local level. As Walrab von Wangenheim, a county official for Beuthen Tarnowitz, reported, he had received the names of 321 members of group 4 who were allegedly racially unfit to remain on the *Deutsche Volksliste*. He had, however, decided that they "will not be processed for the time being as they are not relevant for the war effort."[53]

But even in the Wartheland the success of the SS was more apparent than real. Because of Himmler's good relations with Greiser and the promise to link the rejection of an applicant to his/her expulsion from the province, the RuSHA was allowed to commence with racial screening. But given the widespread opposition within the civilian administration, it comes as no surprise that the disagreement started afresh as soon as the first round of screenings was completed in spring 1942. The first argument erupted when Greiser refused to exclude individuals already on the *Volksliste* who had either relatives in groups 1 or 2 or four German grandparents – regardless of the racial group to which they were assigned. That would have ripped families apart and caused exactly the sort of unrest Greiser was anxious to avoid. This line was supported by the local SD and RKF offices as well as by the RSHA in Berlin, which casts an interesting light on the differences among the various SS head offices. The RuSHA had to back down.[54]

A second argument revolved around members of group 3 fit for military service. After the Wehrmacht was presented with the results of the first round of racial screenings, the commander of the Warthegau military district wrote a letter to Greiser complaining that the RuSHA had asked him not to draft 748 men deemed racially unsuitable. For the military, this was a highly unwelcome development: only a few months earlier the DVL guidelines had been changed to grant members of group 3 provisional citizenship, thereby making them liable for compulsory military service. The commander asked Greiser to help him at least with those fifty-three who had already been drafted.[55] Greiser concurred, instructing his ethnocrats that "nothing must be done which might dampen a soldier's enthusiasm."[56] In addition to the exceptions already forced upon the RuSHA, Greiser now decreed that soldiers could be expelled from the *Volksliste* only if they were classed in racial group IVf, a subgroup of group IV indicating a Jewish or "extra-European" bloodline. The other soldiers in racial class IV would just have to be "digested."[57] The same apparently happened to a further eighty-one soldiers reported to the Wehrmacht after the second and final round of screening in spring 1943. As Rolf-Heinz Höppner, Coulon's successor and concurrently head of the SD in the Wartheland, informed the RuSHA shortly after the Sixth Army was wiped out at Stalingrad, expelling soldiers was unthinkable given the "current problems with replenishing the ranks of the Wehrmacht."[58]

Although historians have recently claimed that "[t]he Nazi state relied primarily on racial categories ... to determine whether a person was a German" or that "the population policy in the National Socialist racial state followed the principles of racial selection," these events suggest otherwise.[59] It was only in the Wartheland that the RuSHA was able to carry out racial screening on individuals included on the *Deutsche Volksliste* – and then only because of Himmler's good relations with Greiser and, crucially, his promise not to expel anybody from the *Deutsche Volksliste* until provision could be made for their deportation. In Upper Silesia, by contrast, the RuSHA Eignungsprüfer (suitability examiners) were allowed to screen only the members of the much smaller group 4, and in Danzig-West Prussia they were barred from screening anyone on the *Deutsche Volksliste*. It was only in the Wartheland that Himmler's instructions were not countered by open refusal, and about 75,000 people there were screened. Although it is hard to assess how many people were racially screened, Isabel Heinemann's assumption that "a large part" of the more than two million members of groups 3 and 4 were affected is clearly overstated.[60] The number of people screened in

Upper Silesia was probably in the low tens of thousands, and the figure for Danzig-West Prussia was undoubtedly much lower still. Any estimate of the total for the three provinces above 130,000 – less than 10 percent of the figure Himmler envisaged – is likely too high.

Even harder to assess is how many people – if any – had to suffer negative consequences as a result of racial screening. I was unable to find any indication that anybody was removed from the *Volksliste* in Danzig-West Prussia or Upper Silesia; in the Wartheland, the Eignungsprüfer wanted to exclude 6,227 individuals after the first round of screening in the spring of 1942. As mentioned earlier, that was allowed only when the SS could guarantee their subsequent deportation. Since deportations from the annexed territories had been canceled in the wake of the invasion of the Soviet Union in March 1941 and never resumed, it is most likely that this demand was simply ignored. Ironically, the only consequence for men deemed racially unfit and not already in uniform was that they were spared conscription into the German army and thus escaped the carnage of the final years of the war.

CONCLUSION

Given that the decision for war had already been taken in spring 1939 and that the question of how the population in territories annexed to the German Reich was to be treated was not a novel one, it seems surprising that no coherent plan existed about what to do with the population in the annexed Polish territories. Arguably even more astonishing is that the plans concerning the non-Jewish population in Poland that emerged in October/November 1939 were anything but informed by the racial ideas set out, for example, by Hitler in *Mein Kampf*.

In keeping with the often uncoordinated, contradictory, and ad hoc policy-making process in Nazi Germany, the first steps taken by the Interior Ministry and the civilian administration in the Wartheland were guided by very different ideas about the future *Deutscher Osten*. Whereas the Interior Ministry opted for a very inclusive selection process in which the majority of the native population eventually would have become part of the German *Volksgemeinschaft*, Greiser's *Deutsche Volksliste* did the opposite. This conflict notwithstanding, in both cases the granting of full German citizenship was linked to establishing the applicant's *Volkszugehörigkeit*, his or her belonging to the German people, as evidenced by his or her conduct in the time before the German invasion – not to the applicant's racial suitability. This assumption was questioned only after the selection procedure had already begun. Himmler's protest forcefully brought race into play, widening the discursive parameters and calling the hitherto hegemonic *völkisch* argument into question. After Himmler faced down the Interior Ministry, his plan to turn race into the decisive criterion of Germanness was struck down by the powerful Gauleiter. One would be forgiven for assuming that racial arguments would prevail in disputes in a racial state. The disagreement over the local population of the annexed Polish territories ended, however, in Himmler's defeat.

Historians have too often cast such conflicts in Nazi Germany as contests pitting pragmatists against ideologues. Obviously, Himmler and his subordinates pushed a racial agenda because they were racists. But surely Stuckart, Forster, and Coulon were not simply pragmatists guided by practical concerns rather than by ideology.[61] In assessing the role of ideology, I think we would be well advised to avoid two temptations: to confuse perpetrators' ideological utterances for their motives or, at the other extreme, to belittle ideology simply as a smokescreen covering the "real" rationale behind an action or policy. Instead, I would suggest that we try to understand ideology as a *Weltanschauung* in the true sense of the word; that is, not a veil blurring the outlook of historical actors that prevented them from advancing their own interests but rather a mental framework that provided actors with grammar and language, forms of thought and terminology, with which to calculate and articulate those interests. The conflict over the direction of Germanization policy in Poland was not a contest between pragmatists in the Interior Ministry and the provinces on the one hand, and SS fanatics on the other. It was a conflict between *völkisch* and racial ideologues, in which deeply felt (ideological) convictions did not impede (rational) political calculations, but rather framed them. For the Interior Ministry and, especially, the civilian administrators entrusted with securing German rule and economic exploitation of the annexed territories, a *völkisch* selection process made sense: firmly rooted in Nazi ideology, it provided a flexible framework for granting German citizenship primarily to those who could be counted on for support. For the SS, confronted with a procedure that affected Himmler's new responsibility as Reich Commissioner for the Strengthening of Germandom but was beyond his control, demanding the introduction of race as a selection criterion was no less logical, however: it was not only in line with Himmler's racial thinking but also, with the RuHSA at his disposal, the most effective way for him to gain de facto control over Germanization policy. Racial screening certainly was a highly ideological undertaking; that did not make it any less functional from Himmler's point of view.

Unlike their predecessors during World War I, the Nazis were uninhibited by any moral or legal restraints, and they subjected the native population in the annexed Polish territories to a genocidal policy. They killed the social elites and everybody deemed a threat to the occupation regime. Many more were deported to the Government General, and the territories' Jewish residents were annihilated. As an analysis of the *Deutsche Volksliste* shows, however, this is not all there is to say about German population policies – at least, not when looking at the annexed Polish territories. National Socialist population policy was not solely a policy of exclusion. Out of more than eight million people living in the annexed territories, roughly three million were registered on the *Deutsche Volksliste* – more than one third of the entire population. The degree to which National Socialist Germanization policy was indebted to its Prussian precursors becomes even more apparent when looking at the territories with particularly high numbers of people accepted for the *Deutsche Volksliste*. In Danzig-West Prussia and Upper Silesia – provinces established on territory that, for the most part, had belonged to Germany until 1919 – roughly two-thirds of the population was registered on the *Volksliste*. That stood in stark contrast to the 14 percent registered in the Wartheland, a province comprising mainly territories that had belonged to czarist Russia before 1919. Similar differences occurred within the provinces. The two counties in Danzig-West Prussia in which less than 20 percent of the population was registered on the *Deutsche Volksliste* were both on the eastern border and were the only counties that had formerly belonged to Russian Poland. Local variations were even more conspicuous in Upper Silesia, even though the implementation of the screening process was in general more inclusive there than in other provinces. Officials there, even more so than their counterparts in Danzig-West Prussia, made a clear distinction between formerly German and formerly Russian areas, registering a record 89 percent of the population in former German territory on the *Deutsche Volksliste* and merely 2 percent in former Russian territory. Administrators in those two provinces were clearly more inspired by their Prussian forerunners than by whatever Hitler might have meant by the "Germanization of the soil."

Obviously, an assessment of National Socialist *Lebensraum* policies cannot be reduced to the *Deutsche Volksliste* in the annexed Polish territories. A quick glance over the borders suffices to make clear that although the Germanization discourse in the territories that were predominantly

German before 1919 was dominated by *völkisch*, not racial terminology, that was not necessarily true for the occupied areas of Czechoslovakia and the Soviet Union. Still, terminological differences must not obscure underlying similarities in reasoning. The ideological basis for Forster's *Deutsche Volksliste* might have been miles away from Heydrich's racial assessment of the Czech population or the equally racially informed versions of the General Plan East. But as the war dragged on, these three approaches to Germanization converged in policies that, despite the ideological differences among their proponents, targeted substantial portions of the local populations for acceptance into the German *Volksgemeinschaft*: two-thirds of the population of Danzig-West Prussia, roughly half the inhabitants of Bohemia and Moravia, and as much as 50 percent of the population in the occupied Soviet territories, varying greatly from one republic to another.[62] It would certainly be misleading to take the results of my research to mean that population policies based on *völkisch* terminology were per se more inclusive than policies deriving from a racial discourse. That a more inclusive policy was pursued in western Poland had little to do with the innate qualities of the terminology used and much to do with the specific power matrix of the institutions involved. In other words, analysis of Germanization policy in the annexed Polish territories requires not an exegesis of, say, *Mein Kampf* but rather a reconstruction of the interests driving the actors involved. Whatever Hitler or other radical Nazi leaders might have meant by the catchphrase "Germanization of the soil," a guide for population policies in the annexed territories it was not.

Notes

1 Dan Stone, "Beyond the 'Auschwitz Syndrome': Holocaust historiography after the Cold War," *Patterns of Prejudice* 44(5) (2010), 454–68, here 454. On the new importance of ideology, see also Geoff Eley, "Hitler's silent majority? Conformity and resistance under the Third Reich" (part one), *Michigan Quarterly Review* 42(2) (2003), 389–425.

2 Detlev J. K. Peukert, "The genesis of the 'Final Solution' from the spirit of science" in Jane Caplan and Thomas Childers (eds.), *Reevaluating the Third Reich* (New York, 1993), 234–52, here 235.

3 Michael Burleigh and Wolfgang Wippermann, *The Racial State: Germany 1933–1945* (Cambridge, 1991).

4 See for example Stefan Breuer, *Die Völkischen in Deutschland. Kaiserreich und Weimarer Republik* (Darmstadt, 2008), and Manfred Hettling, "Volk und Volksgeschichten in Europa" in M. Hettling (ed.), *Volksgeschichten im Europa der Zwischenkriegszeit* (Göttingen, 2003), 7–37.

5 This is true of the relevant chapters in general overviews on the Third Reich, such as Richard J. Evans, *The Third Reich at War* (London, 2008) and, even more markedly, Shelley Baranowski, *Nazi Empire: German Colonialism and Imperialism from Bismarck to Hitler* (Cambridge, 2010), where the racial state morphs into a racial empire. The same is true for more specialized studies looking directly at Nazi population policies in occupied Europe, for example Isabel Heinemann, *Rasse, Siedlung, deutsches Blut. Das Rasse- und Siedlungshauptamt der SS und die rassenpolitische Neuordnung Europas* (Göttingen, 2003).

6 See, for example, the speech Hitler gave in Ingolstadt in 1928, discussed in Frank-Lothar Kroll, *Utopie als Ideologie: Geschichtsdenken und politisches Handeln im Dritten Reich: Hitler – Rosenberg – Darré – Himmler – Goebbels* (Paderborn, 1998), 62.

7 Adolf Hitler, *Mein Kampf* (New York, 1941), 935 (emphasis in the original).

8 Kroll, *Utopie als Ideologie*, 63, quoting Hitler from *Monologe im Führerhauptquartier*, ed. Werner Jochman (Hamburg, 1980), 76.

9 Hitler, *Mein Kampf*, 944 (emphasis in the original).

10 Ibid., 946 (emphasis in the original).

11 Ibid., 950.

12 Ibid., 950–1 (emphasis in the original).

13 Ibid., 588 (emphasis in the original). The potential of violence encapsulated in this notion was already recognized by Raphael Lemkin as he was developing the concept of genocide; see his *Axis Rule in Occupied Europe: Laws of Occupation – Analysis of Government – Proposals for Redress* (Washington, 1944).

14 Adolf Hitler, *Hitler's Secret Book* (New York, 1962), 47–8.

15 Ulrich Herbert puts forward a similar argument less explicitly; see his essay "Arbeit und Vernichtung. Ökonomisches Interesse und Primat der 'Weltanschauung' im Nationalsozialismus," in U. Herbert (ed.), *Europa und der 'Reichseinsatz'. Ausländische Zivilarbeiter, Kriegsgefangene und KZ-Häftlinge in Deutschland 1938–1945* (Essen, 1991), 384–426, 385.

16 Franz Neumann, *Behemoth, The Structure and Practice of National Socialism, 1933–1944* (Toronto, 1944), 37.

17 Theodor W. Adorno, "Beitrag zur Ideologienlehre" in Adorno, *Soziologische Schriften I, Gesammelte Schriften* (Darmstadt, 1998), vol. 8, 457–77, 466.

18 Jan Rehmann, *Einführung in die Ideologietheorie* (Hamburg, 2008), 71–5.

19 Louis Althusser, "Ideology and ideological state apparatuses," in L. Althusser, *On Ideology* (London, 2008), 1–60, here 38.

20 Ibid., 42. Of course, this must not be seen, as Slavoj Žižek has remarked, as a "reductionist assertion of the dependence of inner belief on external behaviour," but rather as an "intricate reflective mechanism of retroactive 'autopoetic' foundation": Slavoj Žižek, "Introduction: the spectre of ideology," in S. Žižek (ed.), *Mapping Ideology* (London, 1994), 1–33, here 12.

21 On the importance of the annexed territories in the Nazis' planning for the future, see, for example, Werner Röhr, "Reichsgau Wartheland 1939–1945. Vom Exerzierplatz des praktischen Nationalsozialismus zum 'Mustergau'?" *Bulletin für Faschismus- und Weltkriegsforschung* 18 (2002), 28–54. Schemes similar to the *Deutsche Volksliste* were tried out in the other annexed

territories in western and southern Germany as well as in occupied areas in France, Poland, and Ukraine.

22 Immanuel Geiss, *Der polnische Grenzstreifen, 1914–1918. Ein Beitrag zur deutschen Kriegespolitik im Ersten Weltkrieg* (Lübeck, 1960).

23 Interestingly, the Nazi slogan "Germanisierung des Bodens" was coined during the 1880s. See, for example, Ernst Hasse, *Das Deutsche Reich als Nationalstaat* (Munich, 1905), 56–8.

24 Alexander Ernst, "Das Staatsangehörigkeitsrecht im Deutschen Reich unter der Herrschaft der Nationalsozialisten und seine Auswirkungen auf das Recht der Bundesrepublik Deutschland," Ph.D. dissertation, University of Münster (1999), 73–8.

25 RGBl. 1939, Part 1, 2042–043.

26 Decree of the Reich Interior Ministry, March 26, 1939, RMBliV Reichsministerialblatt der inneren Verwaltung (1939), 783 (emphasis in the original).

27 Frick's decree on citizenship in the incorporated territories (November 25, 1939) was reprinted in Karol M. Pospieszalski (ed.), *Hitlerowskie "prawo" okupacyjne w Polsce. Wybór documentów i próba syntezy: Ziemie "wcielone"* (Poznań, 1952), 108–14.

28 Decree of the Reich Interior Ministry, March 29, 1939, RMBliV 1939, 783 (emphasis in the original). This decree was promulgated after the invasion of Czechoslovakia and incorporated into the decree of November 1939.

29 Decree issued by Greiser, October 28, 1939, State Archive Poznan, 406/1105, 1.

30 Guidelines for the registration of ethnic Germans by the *Deutsche Volksliste*, probably end of January 1940, State Archive Poznań, 406/1106 (emphasis in the original).

31 Note by Coulon, February 5, 1941, State Archive Poznań, 406/1109, 320–32.

32 Guidelines for the registration of ethnic Germans by the *Deutsche Volksliste*, probably end of January 1940, State Archive Poznań, 406/1106.

33 Decree by Hitler on the Strengthening of Germandom, October 7, 1939, Bundesarchiv Berlin R43 II/1412, Bl. 575–577; reprinted in Pospieszalski, *Hitlerowskie "prawo" okupacyjne*, 176–8, and in Martin Moll (ed.), *"Führer-Erlasse"* (Stuttgart, 1997), 100–2.

34 On the RKF, see Robert L. Koehl, *RKFDV: German Resettlement and Population Policy 1939–1945* (Cambridge, 1957) and more recently Alexa Stiller, "Reichskommissar für die Festigung deutschen Volkstums" in Ingo Haar and Michael Fahlbusch (eds.), *Handbuch der völkischen Wissenschaften* (Munich, 2008), 531–40.

35 Note by Dr. Walter, May 20, 1940, Bundesarchiv Berlin, R 49/61, 47–8.

36 The institution set up to screen the incoming ethnic Germans from Eastern Europe, the Central Immigration Office, and the institution set up to deport the native population, the Central Resettlement Office, were put under the supervision of Hans Ehlich, the head of Department II ES of the SD, and Adolf Eichmann, head of Department IV R.

37 Ohlendorf to Himmler, May 24, 1940, Bundesarchiv Berlin, R 49/61, 70–7.

38 Reich Interior Ministry, draft on the acquisition of German citizenship by residents of the incorporated eastern territories, July 3, 1940, Bundesarchiv Berlin, R 49/61, 8–41.

39 Decree issued by Himmler, September 12, 1940, Bundesarchiv Berlin, NS 19/ 3979, 29–33; reprinted in Pospieszalski, *Hitlerowskie "prawo" okupacyjne* (DO V), 114–18.

40 Coulon, comment on the draft of the new implementing order of the *Deutsche Volksliste*, November 13, 1940, State Archive Poznań, 406/1109, 143–5.

41 Frick's decree on the acquisition of German citizenship by former Polish and Danzig citizens, March 13, 1941, State Archive Poznań, 406/1105, 9–28.

42 Ibid.

43 The regulations regarding the members of group 3 were changed on January 31, 1942. In order to increase German troop strength, members of group 3 were awarded provisional German citizenship that could be revoked within ten years. See the second decree regarding the *Deutsche Volksliste* and German citizenship in the incorporated eastern territories, signed by Frick, Bormann, Himmler, RGBl. 1, 1942, 51–2.

44 As Götz Aly and Susanne Heim have pointed out, the screening personnel were revealingly called "suitability examiners" (*Eignungsprüfer*), not racial examiners: Götz Aly and Susanne Heim, *Vordenker der Vernichtung. Auschwitz und die deutschen Pläne für eine neue europäische Ordnung* (Frankfurt, 1997), 135.

45 Note by Fritz Schwalm, May 24, 1941, Main Commission for the Investigation of Crimes Against the Polish Nation 167/39, 3–5.

46 Note by Coulon, September 10, 1941, State Archive Poznań, 406/1131, 41–5.

47 Jäger to Reich Ministry of the Interior, September 11, 1941, State Archive Poznań, 406/1131, 46–8.

48 Decree issued by Himmler, September 30, 1941, State Archive Poznań, 406/ 1114, 5–6; reprinted in Pospieszalski, *Hitlerowskie "prawo" okupacyjne* (DO V), 144–5.

49 Forster to DVL offices, February 9, 1943, State Archive Bydgoszcz, 9/380, 243.

50 Bracht to Schultz, March 1, 1942, Bundesarchiv Berlin, NS 2/80, 68–70.

51 Minutes by Hohlfeld, January 6, 1943, January 8, 1943, State Archive Kattowice, 117/140, 113–15.

52 Note by Bracht, most probably January 25, 1943, State Archive Kattowice, 117/140, 116.

53 Wangenheim to Springorum, August 19, 1943, Special Archive in the Military Archive of Russia, 1232/37, 34–5.

54 Höppner to Ehlich, June 19, 1942, State Archive Poznań, 406/1130, 63; note by Höppner, June 22, 1942, State Archive Poznań, 406/1131, 417–18.

55 Commander of Military District XXI to Greiser, July 17, 1942, State Archive Poznań, 406/1117, 89.

56 Greiser to Jäger, July 24, 1942, State Archive Poznań 406/1117, 94.

57 Note by Höppner, July 31, 1942, State Archive Poznań, 406/1117, 103–5.

58 Höppner to RuSHA office in Litzmannstadt, February 15, 1943, State Archive Poznań, 406/1117, 157–8.

59 Eli Nathans, *The Politics of Citizenship in Germany* (Oxford, 2004), 228; Oliver Trevisiol, *Die Einbürgerungspraxis im Deutschen Reich 1871–1945* (Göttingen, 2006), 206. See also Isabel Heinemann, *Rasse, Siedlung, deutsches Blut. Das Rasse- und Siedlungshauptamt der SS und die rassenpolitische Neuordnung Europas* (Göttingen, 2003).

60 Heinemann, *Rasse, Siedlung, deutsches Blut*, 260.
61 See, for example, the discussion of Aly and Heim's Vordenker der Vernichtung in Wolfgang Schneider (ed.), *"Vernichtungspolitik." Eine Debatte über den Zusammenhang von Sozialpolitik und Genozid im nationalsozialistischen Deutschland* (Hamburg, 1991).
62 On Germanization policies in Bohemia and Moravia, see Chad Bryant, *Prague in Black: Nazi Rule and Czech Nationalism* (Cambridge, MA, 2007). On the General Plan East, see Czesław Madajczyk (ed.), *Vom Generalplan Ost zum Generalsiedlungsplan* (Munich, 1994).

18

Sex, Race, Violence, *Volksgemeinschaft*

German Soldiers' Sexual Encounters with Local Women and Men during the War and the Occupation in the Soviet Union, 1941–1945

Regina Mühlhäuser

The German war of annihilation in the Soviet Union is one of the best researched examples of wartime violence and genocide. Since the beginning of the 1990s, the actions and motives of the "ordinary men" who participated in mass murder during World War II have been the subject of extensive research and debate.[1] Until recently, however, the role of sexuality and, more specifically, the sexual activities of German soldiers during the attack on and occupation of the Soviet Union have remained largely absent from work in this field. Historians have touched upon individual cases of sexual violence or prostitution but have not analyzed such instances in detail. As Gaby Zipfel has argued, the connection between sexuality and violence that becomes manifest in wartime is ultimately regarded as natural, as an inevitable fact that does not seem to need investigation except in cases of particular brutality or if sexual violence was explicitly encouraged by military commanders.[2]

Moreover, it was – and often still is – widely assumed that German men who were committed to Nazi ideology exercised "racially aware" self-restraint and, in turn, that Wehrmacht and SS troops who violated the Nazi racial laws were harshly punished. A closer look reveals, however, that those assumptions apply to the German campaign in the Soviet Union only to a very limited extent. Indeed, a large number of men acted on the assumption that they were entitled to almost unlimited access to

I would like to thank the members of the International Research Group *Sexual Violence in Armed Conflict* (SVAC; www.warandgender.net) as well as Richard Wetzell, Ulf Heidel, and Therese Roth for their inspiring and critical comments.

women's bodies. Furthermore, German soldiers and SS men occasionally engaged in intimate contact with other men.

Contemporary and postwar eyewitness accounts as well as military documents indicate that sexual violence by German troops was widespread. It included coerced disrobement, sexual torture, sexual assault, sexual blackmail, rape, gang rape, and sexual enslavement. German soldiers also took advantage of "secret prostitution" and military brothels, and they engaged in relations with women who traded sex for protection or food. Some German men were involved in consensual relationships with local women that sometimes led, especially in Estonia and Latvia, to applications for permission to marry. Under the circumstances, however, "consensual" did not mean that these encounters were based on mutual understanding or affection. Women became involved in such relationships largely on account of specific needs, pragmatic choices, and fears caused by the war. The boundaries between consensual and forced, non-violent and violent, non-commercial and commercial sex were fluid. On occasion, sexual violence, sexual barter, and consensual relations merged.[3] Although heterosexual encounters have become a subject of research in the past two decades, German soldiers' sexual involvement with other men – whether consensual or forced – is still largely unexplored.[4]

The Wehrmacht command and the SS issued regulations to prevent violations of the laws on sexual assault (Paragraph 5a of the Wartime Penal Code), "racial defilement" through sexual relations between "Aryans" and Jews (Paragraph 2 of the Law for the Protection of German Blood and German Honor), and sexual contact between men (Paragraphs 175 and 175a of the Reich Criminal Code). They also tried to keep troops from engaging in "undesirable intercourse" with women regarded as "ethnically alien" (*fremdvölkisch*). These regulations, however, were not enforced consistently. Field Marshall Walther von Brauchitsch, the commander in chief of the Army (Oberkommando des Heeres, OKH), even expressed sympathy for men who experienced sexual tension. On September 6, 1941, his rules on "self-discipline" were disseminated among troop leaders on the eastern front:

Since the predispositions of men differ, it is . . . inevitable that tensions and distress [*Spannungen und Nöte*] in the sexual realm will arise here and there that we cannot and should not close our eyes to.

This problem can by no means be solved with a ban on sexual activity. Besides other negative consequences, such a ban would increase the number of sexual crimes [*Notzuchtverbrechen*] and the risk of offenses against §175.[5]

Brauchitsch's view that soldiers were not autonomous subjects and were governed by biological impulses was widely shared in the German military. To keep soldiers under control, Brauchitsch advised the establishment of military brothels.

Furthermore, Brauchitsch instructed military judges to exempt from serious punishment men found guilty of sexual assault unless they were repeat offenders or had acted with extreme brutality.[6] Homosexual offenses, in contrast, were to be rigorously prosecuted. Wehrmacht and SS officials assumed, however, that many offenders were "normal" heterosexuals who had merely been led astray in the exceptional situation of war. Wehrmacht courts varied widely in the sentences they handed down for sexual assault and "indecent" behavior. Many men were granted parole after only a few weeks or months; the rationale for early release was that, rather than enjoying the relative safety of penitentiary or prison, they should once again contribute to the war effort. And although the threat of punishment in cases of homosexual offenses was even higher in the SS, the sources indicate that there, too, the regulations were not applied consistently.[7]

In this essay, I will look at various forms of sexual encounters – forced and consensual, violent and non-violent, commercial and non-commercial – and examine ambivalences and contradictions between: (i) soldiers' sexual practices, (ii) military regulations, (iii) Nazi racial ideology, and (iv) the idea of the *Volksgemeinschaft.* I will argue that the Nazi concepts of race and ethnicity (*Volkstumszugehörigkeit*) were ambiguous and were applied inconsistently when it came to the sexual activities of Wehrmacht soldiers and SS men. That was due in part to concerns about military efficiency and manpower. However, the military authorities – and individual soldiers as well – also harbored contradictory ideas about the racial and ethnic "value" of the local populations in the Soviet Union. And last but not least, the understanding of soldierly sexuality played a crucial role.

HETEROSEXUAL VIOLENCE

Naum Epelfeld was 13 years old when the German army invaded Berdychev, Ukraine, on July 5, 1941. Fleeing from air raids, he and his family found shelter in a nearby hospital.

After a while, two soldiers entered the cellar where we were hiding. They lit their way with flashlights, said something, nobody understood them. Then they started to approach the people sitting on the floor and to shine their light on their faces.

Eventually they stopped in front of a girl and a woman, led them into an empty room, and raped them. The girl – she was our neighbour's daughter – was named Guste. Guste Glosman was fourteen or fifteen years old. Soon afterward, she was shot together with her parents.[8]

Epelfeld describes the situation immediately after the invasion of the city. In his depiction (as well as in numerous other testimonies and, in fact, soldiers' firsthand accounts), the Germans appear to have felt a sense of entitlement that presumed the (sexual) availability of women and girls. Ruth Seifert has pointed out that it is one of the unwritten rules of war that victors are allowed to perpetrate violence against women in the short, unsettled period directly after combat.[9] In the middle of the twentieth century, sexual violence was still considered a quasi-normal byproduct of war. Even though international law included provisions that allowed the prosecution of sexual violence, for example, such acts were not made part of the indictment during the Nuremberg Trials or other postwar tribunals (rather, the documentation of acts of rape and other forms of sexual violence during the taking of evidence was a means to illustrate the ruthless, sadistic brutality of German soldiers). Only since the 1970s have feminists started to develop a more nuanced understanding of conflict-related sexual violence, and since the 1990s lawyers have been developing strategies to prosecute perpetrators.[10]

This kind of "sexual conquest" was directed against all women indiscriminately. Still, in the case described by Epelfeld, the occurrence of sexual violence might come as a surprise. Nazi racial ideology defined sexual contact between men regarded as Aryan and women categorized as Jewish as "racial defilement," which was strictly forbidden and a punishable offense. Recent research has demonstrated that anti-Semitism and the threat of punishment did indeed restrict the sexual behavior of German men within the borders of the German Reich and, in particular, within the confined spaces of concentration and death camps.[11] In the vast territory of the Soviet Union, however, the situation seems to have been different, as a conversation between the 23-year-old naval petty officer Helmut Hartelt and the 21-year-old sailor Horst Minnieur demonstrates. In 1943, Hartelt and Minnieur were prisoners in a British POW camp. Unaware that their captors had installed listening devices to monitor their conversations, Minnieur recounted a killing operation that he had witnessed while serving with the Reich Labor Service in Lithuania. His narrative focused on "a beautiful broad." When he and his comrades asked where she was going, she replied: "to my execution." The men thought at first that she was joking; only later did they learn that she had indeed been killed. Minnieur explained that the woman had been cleaning barracks for the Germans before she was shot. The conversation went on:

HARTELT: So she certainly let herself get banged [*sich hacken lassen*], didn't she?

MINNIEUR: She let herself get banged, but you had to be careful that you didn't get caught. That's not new, of course, they got laid, the Jewish broads, in a way that it was not nice anymore.

HARTELT: So what did she say, that she...?

MINNIEUR: Nothing. Oh, we chatted ... she was at the university in Göttingen.

HARTELT: And she let them turn her into a whore!

MINNIEUR: Yes, they didn't realize she was a Jewess, she was quite decent and such, too. Just bad luck that she had to bite the dust! Seventy-five thousand Jews were shot there.[12]

The young submariners addressed each other in formal German; they were obviously not well acquainted, but that did not stop them from talking about mass shooting and sexual violence, topics that were clearly neither taboo nor particularly unusual. Young men in particular could interpret blunt talk about violence as a demonstration of their ability to overcome scruples and an affirmation of their virility.[13] The expression *sich hacken lassen* indicates that the merging of sexuality and violence seemed natural to them. They even blamed the woman for her fate; in their interpretation, she had permitted sexual intercourse and in doing so became "a whore."

The conversation also demonstrates that Nazi ideas about racial defilement did not necessarily restrict the behavior of German men in the Soviet Union, even though official ideology clearly held sexual contact between Aryans and Jews to be harmful to the Aryan race and to the *Volksgemeinschaft*.[14] In Minnieur's account, the soldiers' main concern seems to have been to avoid being caught. One way to cover up the trespassing of racial boundaries was to kill the victims. In his study of Einsatzgruppe D, an SS mobile killing squad, Andre Angrick documents a particularly insidious practice. SS men sometimes promised Jewish women that their lives would be spared in exchange for sexual favors. As soon as the SS men had had enough of the women or were in danger of being caught, however, the women were killed.[15] The sources indicate that this kind of behavior was widely tolerated within the male communities of the Wehrmacht and SS.

The fear of punishment could lead to specific forms of sexual violence. Some women have recounted that their tormentors tortured them sexually while complaining that they were not allowed to "have" them.[16]

Indeed, acts that did not involve genital intercourse – such as forced disrobement, sexual humiliation, sexual torture, rape with fingers and hands, rape with non-bodily objects – were likely to be interpreted as not violating the racial laws, at least in occupied Soviet territory.[17] The testimonies of a number of victims indicate that such acts were often accompanied by additional violence, for example beatings on the genitalia with whips or sticks.

Especially in the first months after the German invasion, sexual violence seems to have been a practice that soldiers and SS men used when they searched houses or conducted interrogations. Women and, sometimes, men, Jews and non-Jews, were subject to sexual violence. Military regulations instructed soldiers to body-search people for firearms or secret messages. The instructions did not specify, however, that soldiers touch women's breasts, squeeze their nipples, finger their vaginas, or commit other sexual violations while conducting searches, as some soldiers did. Testimony regarding such incidents shows that the men sometimes interpreted regulations according to their own inclination (displaying a willful disregard of rules much like the *Eigen-Sinn* Alf Lüdke has documented among industrial workers).[18] For the (often very young) soldiers – for whom the day-to-day military operations were largely characterized by boredom and fear – sexual violence in its myriad forms offered an opportunity to affirm their superiority and power vis-à-vis enemy peoples as well as to relieve their boredom or stress. For the victims, such acts could mean not only humiliation but also violation of their sexual integrity and severe bodily injury.

Sexual violence was a form of violence that could structure everyday life during the occupation. Numerous reports document that women constantly anticipated falling victim to rape. Sometimes, the perpetrators selected the objects of their desire by chance; in other instances, a man would target a specific woman. A number of reports suggest that Germans involved the local population in finding and providing women. Voluntarily or under duress, local men participated in rounding up women for German troops on occasion.[19]

The Nazi authorities were well aware of such practices of sexual violence and, indeed, the violations of military law. On August 10, 1941, less than two months after the German invasion of the Soviet Union began, the command of the Ninth Army reported that the number of sexual crimes in the combat zone had risen significantly.[20] Three months later, on November 10, 1941, the OKH issued guidelines in which soldiers were urged to exercise "restraint with respect to the other sex." Only in cases in

which German soldiers were "growing wild/ morally decadent [*verwildern*] and lacked discipline," however, was "rigorous action" to be taken.[21]
What was meant by "rigorous action" remained vague. In November and December 1941, the officer of the Commissariat IIb at the 55 Army Corps in Charkov documented cases of gang rape in his diary and noted that the commanding general had ordered that men who committed acts of sexual violence were not to be tried in court; at most, they were to be subject to disciplinary action.[22] Only in exceptional cases were heterosexual offenses prosecuted in front of Wehrmacht courts. In general, the Wehrmacht did not consider sexual violence – in contrast to desertion, unauthorized leave, self-mutilation, or acts that undermined military morale – to be a "major crime."[23]

As Birgit Beck has demonstrated, Wehrmacht judges in the occupied territories of the Soviet Union, in contrast to those on the western front, imposed comparatively light sentences when soldiers were found guilty of rape. This difference was due mainly to the military strategies of racial warfare on the eastern front. The Barbarossa Decree of May 13, 1941 stipulated that criminal offenses committed by German soldiers against Soviet civilians were not to be punished. Exceptions were to be made only when the security of the troops required it, as, for instance, in the case of "grave actions that result from a lack of self-restraint."[24] Consequently, heterosexual sexual offenses were punished only when they were seen as a threat to military discipline, health, or the credibility of the troops; that is, as counterproductive with regard to military aims.

That German men chose women considered to be ethnically alien or "of alien race" (*artfremd*, that is, Jewish) as the objects of their desire seldom drew special attention. The verdicts in rape cases usually ignored the question of race and focused instead on how the defendant had harmed the discipline or reputation of the Wehrmacht.[25] We know of only one court case that explicitly dealt with racial defilement in the Soviet Union. The defendant maintained that he had not been aware of the fact that the woman involved was Jewish. He was acquitted of the charge.[26]

Leaders of the SS and the police also dealt with sexual activities, including sexual violence, by members of the SS and the police. "Undesirable sexual intercourse" was the topic discussed at greatest length during a meeting of senior judges of the SS and police courts in Poland and the "occupied Eastern territories" held in May 1943. According to the minutes of the meeting, SS-Sturmbannführer Heinz of the SS and Police Court in Kiev assumed that at least 50 percent of the members of the SS and the police violated the "ban on undesirable sexual intercourse with ethnically alien women." Because judges had no interest in punishing upwards of half of the SS men and police officers in the occupied territories, the participants in the meeting agreed to recommend to Himmler that the order be revoked.[27]

HETEROSEXUAL TRADE

Herbert Maeger joined the Adolf Hitler Lifeguard Regiment (Leibstandarte Adolf Hitler) at the age of 16. In December 1941, his unit marched into the Soviet Union. In a memoir published in 2000 based upon the diary he had kept at the time, he describes the weeks after a plundering operation in spring 1942 while his unit was in the vicinity of Charkiw, Ukraine:

> In our living quarters, there were often pretty but completely unwilling girls and young women. Of course, we were all quite interested, but I don't know of a single case in which one of us scored. Babucke [the non-commissioned officer responsible for organizing the provisioning of food], on the other hand, sought and found, with somnambulistic self-assurance, plump, mature, female partners who were appropriately realistic and approachable, matched his tastes, and knew how to take advantage of his food-related responsibilities.[28]

In many areas under German occupation, the food supply situation for local residents was disastrous and became increasingly precarious as a result of German military requisitioning and random plundering by German troops. In some places, dozens of people died daily of malnutrition.[29] As a consequence, some women decided to engage in sexual barter in order to ensure survival. Women who carried out jobs for the German authorities, for example, had the opportunity to initiate contact with the occupation soldiers. Furthermore, women met German men at the places where they lodged.[30]

The boundaries between sexual barter and commercial prostitution sometimes blurred. Prostitution had been officially prohibited since the establishment of the Soviet Union in 1922. When the first German troops marched into Estonia in June 1941, women had to offer their services in secret. To visit a prostitute, a German man either had to be approached by the woman herself (or by her partners) or had to ask for the help of a third party who knew the local services. In this virtually private sphere, the women faced the potential brutality of the German men as well as the measures enacted by the German occupation authorities and local police to prevent prostitution. This was indeed potentially a threat to all women, as the Nazi authorities sometimes considered it suspicious when a woman simply wore lipstick.[31]

The Wehrmacht command feared the spread of sexually transmitted diseases, the betrayal of military secrets, the birth of "unwanted children," and the development of personal contacts that would blur boundaries between military personnel and the enemy population. In trying to keep the sexual activities of its soldiers under control, Wehrmacht medical personnel were instructed to educate the men about the risks of sexual activity and the symptoms of venereal disease. In larger cities, the Wehrmacht also established "hygiene facilities" (*Sanierstuben*) where men could disinfect their genitals after sexual intercourse. Men who contracted a venereal disease were to have easy access to medical treatment. The Wehrmacht leadership eventually came to the conclusion that disciplinary measures in the wake of sexual encounters were counterproductive: a man who feared punishment would probably not come forward to receive proper treatment. Nevertheless, soldiers sometimes faced investigation by the Security Service (Sicherheitsdienst, SD) aimed at locating the "source of infection."[32]

The most radical measure the Wehrmacht took to control and channel the sexual activities of its men was the establishment of military brothels. On March 20, 1942, the chief medical officer of the Army High Command issued a directive ordering the establishment of medically supervised brothels for the exclusive use of Wehrmacht soldiers.[33] The Wehrmacht pursued a similar policy as had been in operation in occupied France and Poland since 1939.[34] The organization of military brothels varied from region to region, however, reflecting differences in German occupation policies and in the extent of collaboration with local authorities. The Wehrmacht hoped that the military atmosphere and the supervision of the brothels would prevent soldiers from abusing alcohol or becoming emotionally intimate with the women. The women were required to undergo weekly medical examinations. To date, we still know very little about how women were recruited for Wehrmacht brothels. Some women appear to have been forced into sexual slavery; others seem to have agreed to work in the brothels in exchange for money and protection. None of the women, however, were free to reject a customer or to quit. Moreover, they were subject to forced medical examinations. In short, all of the them lived in a situation characterized by force and violence.

The idea that the soldiers needed to find release for their sexual urges was disputed. Some officials envisioned the strong soldier as being in control of his sexual urges. In a letter written in August 1944, one officer maintained that "brothels have no right to exist. They are feeble concessions to impulse-driven human beings and typical of the rear echelon spirit [*Etappengeist*]."[35] In this view, images of "racially aware" men, which were shaped by conceptions of superior manliness and focused on willpower and sexual self-restraint, contradicted the dominant idea of the masculine, sexually active soldier. Ultimately, however, this view remained marginalized.

The SS leadership did not organize official brothels, arguing that they would harm the reputation of Germany's "racial elite." There is evidence suggesting, however, that SS members visited Wehrmacht brothels. Furthermore, SS units organized their own form of sexual trade. When Einsatzgruppe D was stationed in Taganrog, Russia, for a longer period of time, some members of the command established a theater group. The members of this group were mostly "pretty Russian women and girls, who supplemented their food rations." After the show, there was "dancing, drinking and the girls then somehow came to an agreement." Secret meeting points outside of the city were arranged for members of the command. Houses were seized and "building superintendents" (*Hausmeister*) were appointed to "protect" the women.[36]

CONSENSUAL HETEROSEXUAL RELATIONS

German men serving in the occupied territories behind the front often stayed in the same region for extended periods of time. They lodged in private houses and performed their tasks in the immediate vicinity of the local population, which the Wehrmacht employed in various service functions. Against the background of everyday life during the occupation, German men and local women developed friendly contacts and intimate relationships. Such encounters are sometimes interpreted today as cases of young people falling in love, with the war and the occupation playing little part. The notion of love developing outside of or in opposition to the structures of political power fails, however, to grasp the ways in which love and power are mediated. To paraphrase Foucault's analysis of modern sexual discourse, sexuality is not opposed to power, nor does it subvert it. On the contrary, sexuality is "a dense transfer point of power, charged with instrumentality."[37] Correspondingly, love cannot exist outside of or in opposition to power relations. Consensual encounters in the occupied territories of the Soviet Union developed not in spite of but, indeed, due to the circumstances of war and occupation and were structured by its specific conditions. When I use the term "consensual" I thus do not mean to suggest that such relationships were mutually agreed on by partners who had similar scopes of interpretation and action. Rather, these relationships developed due to specific needs, pragmatic choices, particular fears, and other emotions in the situation of war and occupation.

In an interview with filmmaker Hartmut Kaminski, Zita Vidrinskiene emphasized that her family in Latvia had had contacts among the Germans for a long time, as her grandfather had fought on the German side in World War I:

When the Germans visited grandfather, mother appreciated that they looked very nice, neat, that they had dressed elegantly, and perfumed themselves. And they always had chocolate and gave it to the girls as a present. So the women liked these men very much, and maybe those were reasons why our Lithuanian women loved the Germans so much.[38]

In Vidrinskiene's narrative, German men personified a world beyond the harsh conditions of everyday life during war and occupation. They carried the promise of security, prosperity, and modernity – especially in the eyes of women in areas like the Baltic States, where political instability had a long history and admiration for Germany ran deep. Latvia, Estonia, and Lithuania had been annexed by the Soviet Union in the spring of 1940. When the Germans invaded the region, many locals saw them as liberators. Within weeks, however, it became clear that the foreign soldiers were pursuing brutal policies that were not beneficial to the local population.

The situation during the occupation was made even more complicated by the fact that a large part of the male population had left home to participate in the war – as Red Army soldiers, as partisans, or, in the case of almost one million men, as foreign volunteers in the Wehrmacht.[39] Women often did not know if their partners, male relatives, or friends were still alive. In this situation, a relationship with a German soldier could offer local women comparative security. For some women, moreover, such liaisons might also have presented an opportunity to emancipate themselves from their families. The decision to take up with a German man, however, meant a woman became involved with the occupying power. Depending on the political climate, a woman might be supported by her neighbors for allying herself with a liberator, or despised for collaborating with the enemy.[40]

The Wehrmacht High Command (Oberkommando der Wehrmacht, OKW) regarded these relationships with suspicion. On September 15, 1942, Field Marshal Wilhelm Keitel outlined the military leadership's concerns.[41] Keitel feared that consensual relationships – just like sexual violence or "secret prostitution" – would increase cases of sexually transmitted diseases, facilitate enemy espionage, undermine German claims of racial superiority, harm the reputation of the Wehrmacht, and result in the proliferation of "racially mixed bastards." In addition, long-term relations with local women carried an implicit risk of emotional distress to German soldiers. Military commanders dreaded the thought of soldiers distracted by stressful liaisons in the occupied territories or by the complications such liaisons might cause for their relationships with women at home. Several German soldiers in Norway, for example, committed suicide because they felt unable to handle both their families in Germany and their girlfriends and children in Norway.[42] The OKW tried to solve the problem of "fraternization" by dissuading the soldiers from seeking solace with the local people, especially women, and ordering the eviction of all inhabitants from houses used to accommodate soldiers.

The German civil occupation authorities feared, meanwhile, that a complete ban on relationships between German men and local women would offend the local population and minimize their willingness to collaborate. On July 27, 1941, the Reich Commissioner for the Ostland, the head of the civilian occupation administration in the Baltic States, observed that the ban on marriages between "Reich German men" and local women would destroy the opportunity "to lead these peoples towards the German *Volk*." Moreover, he found it problematic to award the Iron Cross to local men who had volunteered for the Wehrmacht and risked their lives for Germany while discriminating against their sisters by deeming them unworthy to marry German men.[43] The administration in Berlin dismissed these objections, however. The Decree on the Implementation of German Law on German Citizens in the Occupied Eastern Territories (April 27, 1942) affirmed the ban on marriages between "Reich Germans and the local population." Exceptions would be made only on a case-by-case basis and only after both parties had been thoroughly investigated.[44]

The situation in the field was more ambiguous. The Wehrmacht, not wanting to alienate soldiers who applied for marriage permits, generally did not object to the legalization of existing relationships. Security Division 207 in Dorpat, Estonia, even issued a daily order that facilitated application procedures for their men who sought permission to marry local women.[45] Himmler conceded that there could – after a positive "racial inspection" of a woman – be individual exceptions to the marriage ban in Estonia and Latvia.[46] In this situation of legal ambiguity, some marriages were allowed and others prohibited. In fact, a crucial factor in these decisions was the rationale of the doctor responsible for determining the racial and ethnic value of the woman in question.[47]

With the aim of establishing fixed procedures for dealing with marriage applications, the civil occupation authorities soon began planning a marriage law. The Reich Ministry for the Occupied Eastern Territories in Berlin argued that the prospective brides needed to undergo a thorough "racial inspection." Deputy General Commissioner Wilhelm Burmeister of the RKO, by contrast, emphasized that the evaluation of a woman should focus on ethnic belonging (*Volkstumszugehörigkeit*) rather than race:

Marriages between East Frisians and Tyroleans, that is, between Germans, will usually be marriages between people who are farther apart from one another in racial terms than, for instance, marriages between Saxons and Latvians. Nevertheless, the former are undoubtedly to be approved of, whereas the latter are to be accepted with the utmost caution, not because of racial differences but because of ethnic differences [*Volkstumverschiedenheiten*], and ethnicity [*Volkstum*], not race, is decisive in the life of nations [*Völkerleben*].[48]

Burmeister maintained that races would never exist in their pure forms; that had not been the case even in prehistoric times. The will, the character, and the actions of an individual would be shaped less by his/her racial origins than by his/her environment, that is, by language, religion, and cultural traditions. In Burmeister's view, ethnicity – a historically rooted identity – was the most important factor in determining an individual's value for marriage. That view found both supporters and critics among the civil occupation authorities. Nothing came of the discussion, however, and the parties involved waited for Hitler's pronouncement on the matter.[49]

At the end of 1942, the Nazi authorities began expressing a special interest in the children of German men stationed in the East. Amid extensive discussion of the "racial value" of the children, authorities began registering soldiers' offspring and planning for their education. By the spring of 1944, however, merely 350 children had been registered. Himmler expected that no more than 150 of them would be deemed "racially valuable." The subject turned out to be of negligible importance.[50]

SEXUAL ENCOUNTERS BETWEEN MEN

Historical studies indicate that man-to-man sexual encounters on the part of Wehrmacht soldiers and SS men can be roughly grouped into the categories of sexual violence and consensual contact. The question whether German men resorted to homosexual activity in exchange for money or goods has yet to be investigated.[51] Historians have focused thus far on the question of how the Wehrmacht and the SS dealt with homosexual activity within their units. There has been little research on actual sexual encounters between German soldiers and local men in the occupied territories – a subject that poses problems not only of evidence but also of conceptual approach.

As noted in the first section of this essay, the understanding of sexual violence has changed since World War II. Indeed, what is perceived as sexual or sexualized can vary from culture to culture and can change over time.[52] Whereas rape was rarely considered to be a crime worthy of prosecution after the end of World War II, the feminist discussion of conflict-related sexual violence in the 1970s as well as the heightened focus on the subject since the 1990s has generated a substantive transformation in the acknowledgment of sexual violence in armed conflict as a crime. Today, acts of sexual violence can be prosecuted as crimes against humanity, war crimes, or acts of genocide, depending on the circumstances.

With this new consciousness that sexual violence is a crime has come an awareness that men can be not only perpetrators but also victims of sexual violence – or, more precisely, victims of actions that would immediately be seen as sexual if directed against a woman. In her book *Country of My Skull*, Antije Krog notes that male witnesses who testified before the Truth and Reconciliation Committee in South Africa used the term "rape" exclusively to describe the sexual subjugation of women. When talking about their own experiences, the men spoke about "being sodomized, or about iron rods being inserted into them." According to Krog, the men thus marked rape as a "women's issue" and ultimately bonded with the perpetrators.[53] In today's understanding of gendered and sexed bodies and the symbolic order of heteronormative gender relations in Western societies, male bodies and male subjects are associated with the power to inflict sexual harm; men's sexual vulnerability is seldom part of the script.[54] Accordingly, it seems to be almost impossible for adult men to perceive themselves as victims of sexual violence by enemy soldiers. The moment they admit to having been involuntarily subjected to the desire of someone else, they appear effeminized and cease to be "real" men.[55]

Investigating the positions of the (mostly male) perpetrators of sexual violence against men also raises questions about sexual attributions. In the majority of cases, they appear as heterosexual men who subordinate to their will a body that is denied masculinity and thus signified as feminine. Questions about sexual sensations and sexual effects are taboo (arguably the possible ascription of homoerotic experiences and homosexual desire is one factor at play in this repression).[56]

At any rate, we can safely assume that there are cases in which victims, perpetrators, or witnesses do not perceive certain acts of violence between men as sexual – directly or indirectly, mainly or partly – even though they carry meanings and effects connected to bodily self-perception, sexual integrity, and sexual values and norms as well as to their sexual practices. I would thus suggest taking into consideration incidents of violence that are not easily classified as sexual/sexualized, such as, for example, the forcible examination of a man's penis to check whether he had been circumcised. Eyewitness accounts attest that boys and men were ordered, sometimes at gunpoint, to drop their pants and underwear and display their glans to uniformed Germans and local collaborators. Historian Emanuel Ringelblum recorded the pervasiveness of this practice in a diary written while he was hiding in a Warsaw cellar:

The investigators and the police made great progress in the detection of Jews. If men were involved, this matter posed no trouble at all: Pants down and there's the evidence. And orders are given to let your pants down without further ado and prudery [*Zimperlichkeit*] at every possible opportunity; Aryans who are suspected to be of Jewish descent are also checked frequently in this way.[57]

Ringelblum's narrative makes clear that the mere possibility of being subject to genital examination was deemed threatening. Sometimes a soldier would use a stick to hold the victim's genitals up or to prod the victim to display his genitals more openly. Such inspections might take place in in private settings (e.g., houses or apartments) or in public, possibly in front of other soldiers. For many Wehrmacht soldiers and SS men, genital inspections were nothing unusual. During military training, recruits occasionally had to show their penises to their superior officer for hygiene checks – a procedure that entailed embarrassment and gendered subjugation. We know from the accounts of former Wehrmacht soldiers and SS men that officers occasionally made comments about the size and shape of men's penises during these inspections.[58] It thus does not seem far-fetched to assume that men who had to endure an inspection by German soldiers to establish whether they were circumcised were likewise subject to taunts and jokes about their masculinity.

Circumcision was a sign that a man was Jewish. In the eyes of German soldiers, it also confirmed his status as an imperfect, effeminate man. The humiliating act of being subject to inspection, a violation of one's privacy and bodily integrity, was a manifestation of the feminization and racialization of Jewish boys and men – a manifestation that carried the threat of violence, deportation, or being killed.[59]

Other acts of violence against men were more explicitly marked as sexual. In a camp in Koldichevo, Belorussian guards forced a male prisoner at gunpoint to perform sexual acts with female prisoners while the guards watched. Survivor accounts tell of German guards making similar demands of prisoners in camps in Poland.[60] These acts constituted sexual violence against female and male prisoners. The guards attempted to instrumentalize the libidinal reaction of the male prisoners for their own interests. As we have seen in other theaters of war, in some instances men can display physical arousal against their will. In Bosnia, for example, a father was forced to rape his daughter. Gaby Zipfel has used the term "libidinal coercion" in order to describe this exploitation of sexual arousal.[61]

It is not always easy to draw a line between violent and consensual contacts. David Raub Snyder briefly mentions four cases in which Wehrmacht soldiers engaged in sex with local male minors and were tried in Wehrmacht courts.[62] In judging whether German men committed acts of sexual violence when they engaged in sexual relations with underage male civilians, it is necessary to address the question of what constituted consent. For one thing, age is an important factor – that is, the age of the civilian boys, but also the age of the soldiers, because especially toward the end of the war, many German soldiers were underage. In addition, a definition of consent must take considerations such as an individual's cultural and religious background into account.

Peter Steinkamp suggests that there might have been homosexual contact between German soldiers and local men who worked for the German occupation authorities. On July 14, 1944, for example, 40-year-old Corporal Erich D. killed the 17-year-old Russian kitchen helper Waldemar R. and then shot himself. The Wehrmacht records indicate that Erich D. acted under the influence of alcohol, but the motives behind the murder-suicide remain unclear. The fact that the two were found in Waldemar R.'s room – the young Russian dead on the floor, the German barely alive on the kitchen helper's bed – leads Steinkamp to assume that the two might have had an intimate relationship.[63] Regardless of the validity of that hypothesis, this example suggests that men did seek secluded spaces in military buildings or in the immediate vicinity of military facilities where they could engage in sexual activity.

The risks were particularly high for men who sought partners for same-sex sexual relations in their immediate surroundings. If the men they addressed did not respond positively to their advances or the encounter was overheard or observed by a third party, they could easily be denounced and put under investigation. In a number of cases before military courts, soldiers stood accused of having sought intimate encounters with other members of their units. Usually, these cases concerned non-violent encounters. In some cases, officers were tried for allegedly having used their positions to pressure their subordinates into having sexual relations with them.

The Wehrmacht regarded such encounters as "offenses against morality" (*Sittlichkeitsverbrechen*) and tried them according to Paragraph 175 of the civil code, which had been added to the Reich Criminal Code in 1871 and revised by the Nazis in 1935. Before the revision, only men who had initiated sexual encounters with other men were liable to imprisonment. Under the Nazi regime, any man who "allowed himself to be abused indecently" was also to be punished with prison. The law furthermore came to include a broader definition of homosexual contact. Whereas Paragraph 175 had formerly criminalized only acts that imitated heterosexual intercourse, the Nazis' revision broadly criminalized "indecent behavior" – a rather vague term that could include a variety of acts, such as touching, mutual masturbation, etc.[64]

The Wehrmacht faced a fundamental conflict in dealing with the question of homosexuality. During times of war and in combat, soldiers are extremely dependent on each other, and the Wehrmacht relied on the camaraderie and trust among its men. This form of homosocial bonding was regarded not only as important in the front units but also as a symbol of national strength.[65] At the same time, however, the Wehrmacht feared that the intimacy of the tightly knit male society would be conducive to the development of erotically charged physical bonds and sexual relations between the men. Because the Wehrmacht high command regarded a certain amount of homosexual activity among the troops as inevitable, labeling such activity as "degenerate" when it occurred outside the context of military life was all the more important. The cliché of the effeminate homosexual man stood as the antithesis of the Nazi ideal of the strong, masculine soldier.[66]

On the eve of the invasion of the Soviet Union, Brauchitsch complained that the number of homosexual incidents was on the rise. He attributed the increase to the abuse of alcohol and urged military commanders to control their men.[67] During the first years of the war, the Wehrmacht differentiated between "true" homosexuals (*Hangtäter*), who were believed to be biologically predisposed to homosexuality, and "opportunity offenders" (*Gelegenheitstäter*), who were considered to be heterosexuals by nature but had either been seduced or succumbed to temptation under the trying conditions of war. Ultimately, however, the Wehrmacht had no criteria for determining whether a man was a homosexual or had merely engaged in homosexual sexual activity.[68] Most of the cases that came to the attention of the military authorities were classified as the latter. They were, as Geoffrey Giles concludes, not prosecuted "with much vigor, except where an abuse of rank had occurred."[69]

In 1943, the OKW issued new "Guidelines for the Treatment of Criminal Cases concerning Indecent Behavior" that introduced more serious punishment for soldiers who violated Paragraph 175. "True homosexuals" were now to be punished with long penitentiary sentences or even the death penalty. Even men who were suspected of being one-time offenders were to be subjected to rigorous investigation: a suspect's family members, for instance, could be questioned to determine his sexual orientation. Should the investigation determine that a suspect was heterosexual but had indeed engaged in homosexual activity, he was to serve a prison term before being sent back to the front to "prove" himself. Offenders whose affinities were unclear were to be held in military detention camps (*Feldstraflager*) for further surveillance.[70]

Medical and psychological evidence played an increasingly important part in Wehrmacht trials conducted after the new guidelines were issued. To establish the sexual orientation of the accused, his sexual history was examined by the court. As Monika Flaschka has emphasized, courts considered defendants' appearance as well as their behavior: "It was not necessarily the kind of sexual contact that was engaged in that mattered to the court," she argues, "but the degree to which the soldiers acted in ways perceived to be feminine."[71] Men who were perceived as acting in an unmanly fashion were likely to be regarded as "true homosexuals." No matter how long the sentence they received, many soldiers convicted of violating Paragraph 175 were granted parole after a short time. Especially from 1943 onward, manpower considerations led the army to decide not to keep men convicted as homosexual offenders in the relative safety of imprisonment.[72]

Whereas the Wehrmacht tried to educate and warn its men, the SS took another position. On November 15, 1941, Hitler issued an edict that aimed at keeping the SS and police "free from vermin with a predisposition towards the same sex." It decreed that "a member of the SS or police who commits indecent acts with another man or allows himself to be abused in an indecent manner will be punished with death." Only in "less serious cases" involving first-time offenders under the age of 21 could the punishment could be reduced to imprisonment for a minimum of six months.[73] Hitler did not want the edict to be published in the *Reichsgesetzblatt* for fear that it would draw unwanted attention and lead to the suspicion that homosexuality was widespread in the ranks of the SS. Nearly four months later, on March 7, 1942, Himmler issued a confidential memo in which he ordered that instructions be given to "all members of the SS and police verbally." SS members were required to sign a formal statement confirming that the problem of homosexual activity in the ranks had been explained to them and they knew how to deal with it. It is clear from the surviving documentation, however, that these procedures were not put into practice systematically. Giles's analysis of case files has demonstrated that the SS did in fact carry out death sentences in some cases; in general, however, "the new ruling was applied rarely and inconsistently."[74]

CONCLUDING REMARKS

Since the 1960s, historians have demonstrated that sexuality was an element of the Nazis' racial, ethnic, and national policies. The control of reproduction to advance racial goals was one of the regime's central objectives. As Dagmar Herzog, Elisabeth Heineman, and others have pointed out, however, Nazi sexual politics were not directed solely at controlling the "racial quality" of the population. They were also aimed at controlling sexual choices and practices – even, indeed, sexual desire.[75] Who should be allowed to have sex with whom? Which sexual practices were considered to be normal and healthy, and which regarded as deviant or perverted? What sort of sexual encounters were to be forbidden? Which should be tolerated, welcomed, or even encouraged? Questions such as these were the subject of much debate within the Nazi regime, and the answers varied depending on whom they came from and when and where they were given. Ultimately, the regulation of sexual behavior was a crucial factor in the process of establishing ideas of exclusion/inclusion – in giving meaning to the Nazis' racial hierarchies.

Men at the fronts and in the occupied territories, in particular soldiers, were subject to particular ideas about functions, practices, and meanings of sexuality. Ulrich Bröckling has noted that the transformation of men destined for deployment in combat zones includes unleashing their "individual potential for violence" while at the same time keeping that potential under control through disciplinary measures.[76] To compensate the men for the extreme demands placed upon them and the subjugation they are expected to endure, the army makes concessions to them.[77] One is to allow, tolerate, or encourage sexual activity. In the case described here, German men serving at the front and in the occupied territories in Eastern Europe and the Soviet Union were granted the liberty of heterosexual activity, including sexual violence, and, to some extent, homosexual contact.

Only in cases in which military discipline, soldiers' health, or the credibility of the troops was thought to be at stake could rape or other sexual transgressions become the subject of disciplinary action or judicial persecution. The question whether soldiers violated Nazi racial ideology and laws was of little importance on the eastern front or in the occupied territories. The Wehrmacht and the SS issued a variety of bans to curb sexual violence and/or sexual contact with women deemed racially inferior but did not enforce them vigorously or consistently. The regulations on sexual activity appear to have been issued largely as a deterrent – as a means to discourage sexual activities deemed undesirable by holding out the possibility of punishment.

The Wehrmacht and the SS faced a dilemma. On the one hand, sexual contact with local women in the occupied territories was considered undesirable because it jeopardized military discipline as well as the health and the reputation of the troops. Moreover, such activity could violate the principles of Nazi racial ideology. But on the other, heterosexual activity was considered a sign of virility and masculine strength, and thus ultimately of benefit to the war effort. The conquest of "enemy women" furthermore symbolized the victory over foreign territory. As Annette Timm has argued, "the expression of male sexuality was not a matter of individual pleasure but of the nation's military strength."[78] Nazi authorities thus widely accepted German soldiers' heterosexual activity as a natural, virtually unavoidable part of warfare.

The Wehrmacht and SS leaderships followed similar paths in regulating and channeling rather than repressing heterosexual activities. They actively created opportunities for their men to seek comparatively uncomplicated and inexpensive heterosexual contact with limited risks, for example by educating their men about STD symptoms, passing out condoms, arranging hygiene stations, and, in the case of the Wehrmacht, even establishing military-controlled brothels. Overall, the Wehrmacht placed more emphasis on moral arguments about soldiers' military and "racial" duties. The SS adopted a more pragmatic stance by focusing on avoiding the dangers of disease.

German men in uniform took advantage of the opportunities for sexual activity according to their individual preferences as well as to the habitual practices within their units. Their degree of commitment to Nazi ideology did not necessarily have a direct influence on their sexual choices. Even soldiers and SS men who were enthusiastic Nazis could breach the racial laws by engaging in sexual liaisons with non-Aryans without assuming that their actions contradicted the German military aims. In the male-dominated front society, specifically male warrior standards were created that emphasized the capacity to overstep rules and overcome doubts as a masculine strength. Still, the men's awareness that they were violating Nazi ideas and laws and could be punished for their actions appears to have heightened the likelihood of their treating victims with additional violence and cruelty.

The military authorities regarded a certain amount of sexual disobedience as beneficial to the spirits of the men and the cohesion of the troops. Moreover, the often inconsistent ways in which the Nazi authorities dealt with sexual violence, prostitution, and consensual encounters (heterosexual as well as homosexual) are an indication that the categories used to evaluate race and ethnicity were highly ambiguous and contested. Commanders in the field had to deal with the contradictions between the ideals of Nazi racial policy and the practical problems entailed in trying to abide by those ideals. For example, Nazi authorities took increasing interest in the offspring of German troops and local women in the Baltic States, Ukraine, Belarus, and Russia after mid-1942 as it became impossible to ignore the fact that even an extremely large increase in the German birthrate would not provide the population needed to dominate the recently conquered territories. In the process, they changed their thinking about the racial and ethnic classification of those children and their mothers.

What becomes clear is that the criteria for racial and ethnic categorization were permeable and open to discussion. In a vast gray area, in which the criteria for the exclusion or inclusion of a person were ambiguous, each case was supposed to be handled individually. On September 16, 1942, Himmler himself conceded that the Nazi categories for assessing the "racial value" of non-German woman were vague, and he voiced concern that "it is pure chance [*reiner Zufall*] whether the girl a soldier gets attached to is purebred or unfit."[79]

The Nazis tried to realize their violent, megalomaniac vision of a racially reordered Europe, but the racial and ethnic categories they used in deciding the fates of millions of people remained unstable and were subject to continuous redefinition. The complex combination of strict regulations, leeway in deciding how those regulations were to be applied, and pragmatic changes in policy allowed the regime to proclaim its notions of "racial purity" and, at the same time, to respond flexibly in the field and to assure the individual German solider in the East that he had its support. The ambiguity of this system helped secure the loyalty of the men serving on the eastern front and in the occupied territories.

Notes

1 Christopher Browning, *Ordinary Men: Reserve Police Battalion 101 and the Final Solution in Poland* (New York, 1993). For an overview of research, see Gerhard Paul, "Von Psychopathen, Technokraten des Terrors und 'ganz gewöhnlichen' Deutschen. Die Täter der Shoah im Spiegel der Forschung" in Gerhard Paul (ed.), *Die Täter der Shoah. Fanatische Nationalsozialisten oder ganz normale Deutsche?* (Göttingen, 2002), 13–90.

2 Gaby Zipfel, "Ausnahmezustand Krieg? Anmerkungen zu soldatischer Männlichkeit, sexueller Gewalt und militärischer Einhegung" in Insa Eschebach and Regina Mühlhäuser (eds.), *Krieg und Geschlecht. Sexuelle Gewalt im Krieg und Sex-Zwangsarbeit in NS-Konzentrationslagern* (Berlin, 2008), 55–74, here 55.

3 On sexual violence, see Birgit Beck, *Wehrmacht und sexuelle Gewalt. Sexualverbrechen vor deutschen Militärgerichten 1939–1945* (Paderborn, 2004); Wendy Jo Gertjejanssen, "Victims, heroes, survivors: sexual violence on the Eastern Front during World War II," Ph.D. dissertation, University of Minnesota (2004); Birgit Beck, "Sexual violence and its prosecution by courts martial of the Wehrmacht" in Roger Chickering, Stig Förster, and Bernd Greiner (eds.), *A World at Total War: Global Conflict and the Politics of Destruction, 1937–1945* (Cambridge, 2005), 317–31; David Raub Snyder, *Sex Crimes under the Wehrmacht* (Lincoln, 2007), 135ff.; Doris F. Bergen, "Sexual violence in the Holocaust: unique or typical?" in Dagmar Herzog (ed.), *Lessons and Legacies VII: The Holocaust in International Perspective* (Evanston, 2008), 179–202; Monika Flaschka, "Race, rape and gender in Nazi occupied territories," Ph.D. dissertation, Kent State University (2009); Sönke Neitzel and Harald Welzer, *Soldaten. Protokolle vom Kämpfen, Töten und Sterben* (Frankfurt, 2011), 217–28. On prostitution: Gertjejanssen, "Victims, heroes, survivors"; Franz W. Seidler, *Prostitution, Homosexualität, Selbstverstümmelung. Probleme der deutschen Sanitätsführung 1939–1945* (Neckargemünd, 1977). On consensual relations: Hartmut Kaminski, "Liebe im Vernichtungskrieg" (film, 2002); Rolf-Dieter Müller, "Liebe im Vernichtungskrieg. Geschlechtergeschichtliche Aspekte des Einsatzes deutscher Soldaten im Rußlandkrieg 1941–1944" in F. Becker, T. Großbölting, A. Owzar, and R. Schlögl (eds.), *Politische Gewalt in der Moderne. Festschrift für Hans-Ulrich Thamer* (Münster, 2003), 239–67.

This chapter also draws on the author's book *Eroberungen. Sexuelle Gewalttaten und intime Beziehungen deutscher Soldaten in der Sowjetunion 1941–1945* (Hamburg, 2010).

4 Geoffrey J. Giles, "The denial of homosexuality: same sex incidents in Himmler's SS and police," *Journal of the History of Sexuality* 11 (2002), 256–90; Geoffrey J. Giles, "A gray zone among the field gray men: Confusion in the discrimination against homosexuals in the Wehrmacht" in Jonathan Petropoulos and John K. Roth (eds.), *Gray Zones: Ambiguity and Compromise in the Holocaust and Its Aftermath* (New York, 2005), 127–46; Snyder, *Sex Crimes under the Wehrmacht*, 102–32; Flaschka, "Race, rape and gender," 137–76.

5 "OKH, von Brauchitsch, Schreiben an den Generalquartiermeister, betr.: Selbstzucht, 31.7.1940," Bundesarchiv-Militärarchiv Freiburg (hereafter BA-MA), RH 53–7/v. 233a/167. Brauchitsch issued this order in the context of the German occupation of France but explicitly renewed and disseminated it at the beginning of the war in the Soviet Union.

6 "OKH, von Brauchitsch, Betr.: Notzuchtverbrechen, 05.07.1940," BA-MA RH 14/v. 30.

7 Snyder, *Sex Crimes under the Wehrmacht*, 102, 109ff.; Giles, "The denial of homosexuality."

8 Naum Epelfeld, "Möge mein Gedächtnis das Vergessen verhindern …" in Boris Zabarko (ed.), *"Nur wir haben überlebt." Holocaust in der Ukraine. Zeugnisse und Dokumente* (Berlin, 2004), 110–29, 111.

9 Ruth Seifert, "Krieg und Vergewaltigung. Ansätze zu einer Analyse" in Alexandra Stiglmayer (ed.), *Massenvergewaltigung. Krieg gegen die Frauen* (Freiburg, 1993), 85–108.

10 In 2002, the International Criminal Court codified a variety of acts of sexual violence as war crimes, crimes against humanity, or genocide. The procedures for collecting and utilizing evidence are complicated, however, and prosecutors have often decided against indicting suspects even if there are witnesses who are willing to testify. See Carsten Gericke and Regina Mühlhäuser, "Vergebung und Aussöhnung nach sexuellen Gewaltverbrechen in bewaffneten Konflikten. Zur Funktion und Bedeutung internationaler Strafprozesse" in Susanne Buckley-Zistel and Thomas Kater (eds.), *Nach Krieg, Gewalt und Repression. Vom schwierigen Umgang mit der Vergangenheit* (Baden-Baden, 2011),. 91–111.

11 See, e.g., Na'ama Shik, "Sexual abuse of Jewish women in Auschwitz-Birkenau" in Dagmar Herzog (ed.), *Brutality and Desire, War and Sexuality in Europe's Twentieth Century* (Basingstoke, 2009), 221–46.

12 Cited in Neitzel and Welzer, *Soldaten*, 164f.

13 Frank Werner, "Soldatische Männlichkeit im Vernichtungskrieg. Geschlechtsspezifische Dimensionen der Gewalt in Feldpostbriefen 1941–1944" in Veit Didczuneit, Jens Ebert, and Thomas Jander (eds.), *Schreiben im Krieg. Schreiben vom Krieg. Feldpost im Zeitalter der Weltkriege* (Essen, 2011), 283–94, here 286.

14 Cornelia Essner, *Die "Nürnberger Gesetze" oder Die Verwaltung des Rassenwahns 1933–1945* (Paderborn, 2002).

15 Andre Angrick, *Besatzungspolitik und Massenmord. Die Einsatzgruppe D in der südlichen Sowjetunion 1941–1943* (Hamburg, 2003), 449f.

16 Sala Pawlowicz, *I Will Survive*, recorded by Kevin Close (New York, 1962).

17 Within the borders of the Reich, the courts did not focus exclusively on reproduction; sexual desire could also be an issue. That is illustrated in a case in which the judge convicted a couple of "racial defilement" even though he was convinced their sexual activity had been limited to mutual masturbation. See Alexandra Przyrembel, *"Rassenschande." Reinheitsmythos und Vernichtungslegitimation im Nationalsozialismus* (Göttingen, 2003).

18 On the concept of *Eigen-Sinn*, see Alf Lüdtke, *Eigen-Sinn. Fabrikalltag, Arbeitererfahrungen und Politik vom Kaiserreich bis in den Faschismus* (Hamburg, 1993), 377.

19 Mühlhäuser, *Eroberungen* 84–139.

20 "AOK 9, Anweisung, Betr.: Überwachung der Disziplin, 10.08.1941," National Archives and Record Administration, College Park, MD [hereafter NARA] RG 242/314/679, 649.

21 "AOK 11, Abt. Ic, AO Nr. 2379/41 geh., gez. von Manstein, 10.11.1941," printed in Iternational Military Tribunal, *Der Prozess gegen die Hauptkriegsverbrecher vor dem Internationalen Militärgerichtshof. Nürnberg 14. November 1945–1. Oktober 1946* (Munich, 1989), vol. 3/4, Doc. 4064-PS, 129–32.

22 See, for example, Hamburger Institut für Sozialforschung (ed.), *Vernichtungskrieg. Verbrechen der Wehrmacht 1941–1944* (Hamburg, 1996), 100.

23 Beck, *Wehrmacht und sexuelle Gewalt*, 327.

24 Cited in Beck, "Sexual violence and its prosecution," 326ff. David Raub Snyder has tried to challenge Beck's hypothesis by demonstrating that some Wehrmacht judges on the Eastern Front did in fact impose harsh sentences on occasion (Snyder, *Sex Crimes under the Wehrmacht*). Ultimately, however, that does not refute Beck's line of argument.

25 Beck, *Wehrmacht und sexuelle Gewalt*, 277–8; 247ff.; Snyder, *Sex Crimes under the Wehrmacht*, xii, 138ff.

26 Snyder *Sex Crimes under the Wehrmacht*, 192f.

27 "Richtertagung in München am 07.05.1943, Bericht und Vermerk zu diversen Besprechungspunkten," Bundesarchiv Berlin Lichterfelde [hereafter BArch] NS 7/13, 1–21, 7–9.

28 Herbert Maeger, *Verlorene Ehre, verratene Treue. Zeitzeugenbericht eines Soldaten* (Rosenheim, 2008), 169.

29 See, for example, Manfred Oldenburg, *Ideologie und Militärisches Kalkül. Die Besatzungspolitik der Wehrmacht in der Sowjetunion 1942* (Cologne, 2004), 68ff., 87.

30 Gertjejanssen, "Victims, heroes, survivors," 92f.

31 "Bormann, Schreiben an Koch, 23.7.1942," NARA, RG-242 454/92, Bl. 000894–000897.

32 Mühlhäuser, *Eroberungen*, 168–206.

33 "Heeresarzt im OKH, gez. Dr. Hanloser, Prostitution und Bordellwesen im besetzten Gebiet in Sowjetrußland, 20.03.1942," BA-MA H 20/825.

34 Insa Meinen, *Wehrmacht und Prostitution im besetzten Frankreich* (Bremen, 2002), 17ff.

35 "Partei und Wehrmacht im Generalgouvernement und ihre Führungsaufgaben, 24.08.1944," BArch NS 55/26, 1499–1506.

36 Angrick, *Besatzungspolitik und Massenmord,* 447.

37 Michel Foucault, *The History of Sexuality* (New York, 1985), 103.

38 Kaminski, "Liebe im Vernichtungskrieg"; also cited in Müller, "Liebe im Vernichtungskrieg."

39 On foreign volunteers in the Wehrmacht and the SS, see Rolf-Dieter Müller, *An der Seite der Wehrmacht. Hitlers ausländische Helfer beim "Kreuzzug gegen den Bolschewismus" 1941–1945* (Berlin, 2007).

40 Anette Warring, "War, cultural loyalty, and gender: Danish women's intimate fraternization" in Kjersti Ericsson and Eva Simonsen (eds.), *Children of World War II: The Hidden Enemy Legacy* (Oxford, 2005), 35–52.

41 "OKW, gez. Keitel, Erlass, Betr.: Unerwünschter Verkehr deutscher Soldaten mit Einwohnern in den besetzten Ostgebieten, 15.09.1942," copy, BArch NS 19/1691, 1.

42 Kare Olsen, *Vater: Deutscher. Das Schicksal der norwegischen Lebensbornkinder und ihrer Mütter von 1940 bis heute* (Frankfurt, 2002), 25–26, 123.

43 Müller, "Liebe im Vernichtungskrieg," 250.

44 *Reichsgesetzblatt,* 1942, vol. 1, 255.

45 "Sicherungsdivision 207 Abt. 2a, Tagesbefehl Nr. 47, 18.08.1942," copy, BArch, R 90/460, 207.

46 "Brief RFSS, Himmler, an SS-Obergruppenführer Gottlob Berger, Betr: Zu Ihren Aktennotizen, Reval, 28.07.1942," BArch NS 19/1772, 5.

47 Mühlhäuser, *Eroberungen,* 275–99.

48 "RKO, Hauptabteilungsleiter II, Burmeister, Stellungnahme zum Vermerk des Abteilungsleiters I Politik, Regierungsrat Trampedach, vom 15. Februar 1943, und des rassepolitischen Referenten Regierungsrat Dr. Steininger vom 15. März 1943 zur Frage der Eheschließung zwischen Deutschen und Angehörigen der ehemals baltishen Staaten, 19.03.1943," BArch R 90/136, unpaginated. The author of the memorandum draws on Karl C. von Loesch, *Völker im Wandel der Zeiten,* no date [1943], BARch R 90/460, 239–43.

49 Mühlhäuser, *Eroberungen,* 287ff.

50 Regina Mühlhäuser, "Between extermination and Germanization: children of German men in the 'occupied Eastern territories,' 1942–1945" in Kjersti Ericsson and Eva Simonsen (eds.), *Children of World War II. The Hidden Enemy Legacy* (Oxford, 2005), 167–89.

51 A soldier on the Western Front was convicted for allowing another man "to take advantage of [him] like a male whore [*männliche Dirne*]" in exchange for money in June 1940: Flaschka, "Race, rape and gender," 157. Further research is needed to determine whether similar cases occurred on the eastern front as well.

52 Joanna Bourke, *Rape: Sex, Violence, History* (Berkeley, 2007), 10ff.

53 Antjie Krog, *Country of My Skull* (Johannesburg, 1998), 181. See also Louise du Toit, "Feminism and the ethics of reconciliation," www.eurozine.com/articles/2007-03-16-dutoit-en.html.

54 Miranda Alison, Debra Bergoffen, Pascale Bos, Louise du Toit, Regina Mühl-häuser, and Gaby Zipfel, "'My plight is not unique.' Sexual violence in conflict zones: a roundtable discussion," www.eurozine.com/articles/2009-09-02-zipfel-en.html.

55 This degradation can be intensified when the perpetrator is female, as has been suggested in the case of sexualized torture in Abu Ghraib. The fact that one of the torturers, Private Lynndie England, was a woman was deemed especially shameful for the male victims. See Regina F. Titunik, "Are we all torturers now? A reconsideration of women's violence at Abu Ghraib," *Cambridge Review of International Affairs* 22(2) (2009), 257–77, here 267.

56 Joshua Goldstein, *War and Gender: How Gender Shapes the War System and Vice Versa* (Cambridge, 2001).

57 Emanuel Ringelblum, *Ghetto Warschau. Tagebücher aus dem Chaos* (Stutt-gart, 1967), 119. Some men, as Ringelblum notes, tried to "undo" their circumcision by undergoing complicated surgery that involved numerous risks. See also Gerhard Henschel, *Neidgeschrei. Antisemitismus und Sexualität* (Hamburg, 2008), 252ff.

58 Mühlhäuser, *Eroberungen*, 210f

59 The same occurred during the Bangladesh Liberation War of 1971. The Pakistani army confirmed that men were Muslims by inspecting whether they were circumcised; men found to be uncircumcised were deemed to be Hindus and thus enemies. These inspections usually occurred at checkpoints, which became sites of anticipated (sexual) violence. Suspected Hindus were some-times killed on the spot. See Nayanika Mookherjee, "Héroïnes de guerre" et hommes oubliés de la guerre de libération du Bangladesh" in Raphaelle Branche and Fabrice Virgili (eds.), *Viols en temps de guerre* (Paris, 2011), 71–82.

60 KGB RB, record 19592–9, N.A.K., 55, 57, 62, cited in Bernhard Chiari, *Alltag hinter der Front. Besatzung, Kollaboration und Widerstand in Weißrußland 1941–1944* (Düsseldorf, 1998), 192f.; Pawlowicz, *I Will Survive*, 109; Henschel, *Neidgeschrei*, 75.

61 Zipfel, "Ausnahmezustand Krieg?" 70ff.

62 Snyder, *Sex Crimes under the Wehrmacht*, 119.

63 Peter Steinkamp, "Zur Devianz-Problematik in der Wehrmacht: Alkohol- und Rauschmittelmissbrauch bei der Truppe," PhD dissertation, University of Freiburg im Breisgau (2008), 289f.

64 Geoffrey G. Giles, "Legislating Nazi homophobia: the radicalization of pros-ecution against homosexuality by the legal profession in the Third Reich," *German History* 23 (2005), 339–54.

65 Thomas Kühne, *Kameradschaft. Die Soldaten des nationalsozialistischen Krieges und das 20. Jahrhundert* (Göttingen, 2006).

66 Stefan Micheler, "Homophobic propaganda and the denunciation of same-sex-desiring men under National Socialism," *Journal of the History of Sexuality* 11 (2002), 95–130, here 96.

67 "Von Brauchitsch, Rundschreiben, Betreff: Alkoholmißbrauch, 06.06.1941," BA-MA RH 54/95.

68 Flaschka, "Race, rape and gender," 145.

69 Giles, "Legislating Nazi homophobia," 128.

70 "Chef OKW, Keitel, Richtlinien für die Behandlung von Strafsachen wegen widernatürlicher Unzucht, 19.05.1943," BA MA H 20/479. On the political pressure that led to these changes, see Giles, "Legislating Nazi homophobia," 130ff.

71 Flaschka, "Race, rape and gender," 145.

72 Snyder, *Sex Crimes under the Wehrmacht,* 103ff.

73 "Erlaß des Führers zur Reinhaltung von SS und Polizei. Vom 15. November 1941, Abschrift durch den Chef der Ordnungspolizei, zur Kenntnis an sämtliche Angehörige der Deutschen Ordnungspolizei, Berlin, 23.01.1942," United States Holocaust Memorial Museum, RG-18.002M, Reel 11, Fond R 83, Opis 1, Folder 80.

74 Giles, "The denial of homosexuality," 266, 269f.

75 Elisabeth Heineman, "Sexuality and Nazism. The doubly unspeakable?" *Journal of the History of Sexuality* 11 (2002), 22–66; Dagmar Herzog, *Sex after Fascism: Memory and Morality in Europe's Twentieth Century* (Princeton, 2005).

76 Ulrich Bröckling, *Disziplin. Soziologie und Geschichte militärischer Gehorsamsproduktion* (Munich, 1997), 10.

77 Jan-Philipp Reemtsma, "Die Wiederkehr der Hobbesschen Frage. Dialektik der Zivilisation," *Mittelweg 36* 3(6) (1995), 47–56, here 51.

78 Anette Timm, "Sex with a purpose: prostitution, venereal disease, and militarized masculinity in the Third Reich," *Journal of the History of Sexuality* 11 (2002), 253f.

79 "Rede Heinrich Himmlers auf der SS- und Polizeiführertagung in der Feldkommandostelle in Hegewald bei Shitomir, 16.09.1942," BArch NS 19/4009, 78–127, 124.

19

The Disintegration of the Racial Basis of the Concentration Camp System

Stefan Hördler

To avoid unnecessarily burdening the facility with bodily deficient human material and the accumulation thereby of those incapable of working, a correspondingly rigorous selection of prisoners (medical inspection) before assignment to work is unconditionally recommended.[1]

Following a visit to Dora concentration camp in late 1943, SS hygiene expert Karl Groß outlined the ideal working methods and spatial arrangements to maximize the exploitation of the prisoner labor force while maintaining sanitary conditions and the camp's functional capacity. His central concern was to stabilize the camp and to shield SS personnel and the prisoners from epidemic diseases. "It is proposed," Groß continued, "to provide at least the valuable skilled workers among the prisoners with warm clothing ... and also to separate them in terms of accommodation from the other prisoners."[2] Prisoners' value was determined not by their race but rather by their ability to contribute to the manufacture of V1 and V2 rockets.

Groß's proposal, put forward in December 1943, can be read as a general plan for all of the concentration camps. It is one of the few surviving SS administrative records that allow us to draw conclusions about planning for the concentration camp system. A few months earlier, the so-called euthanasia killings (Operation 14 f 13) and executions of Soviet prisoners of war (Operation 14 f 14) were officially halted in favor of making greater use of prisoner labor.[3] In May 1944, the ban on Jews in the Reich began to be lifted with Himmler's announcement of the transfer of 200,000 Jewish concentration camp prisoners to worksites in the Reich.[4] According to instructions issued in August 1944, Jews incapable of working were to be sent to Auschwitz.[5] In late November 1944, the systematic murder of Europe's Jews was halted and new guidelines on the treatment of Jewish prisoners were issued.

The racist structures of the concentration camp system were dismantled during the second half of the war as the camps were reorganized on utilitarian lines. During this period, the SS had to reconcile two demands on the camp system. First, beginning in March 1944, the SS came under pressure from outside – notably from Reich Armaments Minister Albert Speer – to increase the economic utility of the camps. Second, there were calls from within the SS itself for the stabilization of the camp system. Grappling with shortages of resources and space on all fronts, the camp system could not handle the rapidly growing number of prisoners. Economic utilization and stabilization made the rationalization of the camp system unavoidable in the short term. Rationalization led to the abandonment of racial criteria in two key areas in the operation of the camps: the "selection" of prisoners – that is, the decisions as to which prisoners were to be deployed as laborers and which were to be killed – and the recruitment and deployment of camp guards.

THE RATIONALIZATION OF THE CAMP SYSTEM

Along with tens of thousands of forced labor camps, labor education camps, youth detention camps, prisoner-of-war camps, transit camps, ghettos, and other confinement sites, the approximately 1,000 main camps and subcamps under the jurisdiction of the Inspectorate of Concentration Camps (Inspektion der Konzentrationslager) and, later, Amtsgruppe D of the SS Economic Administration Main Office (SS-Wirtschafts-Verwaltungshauptamt, SS-WVHA) were a central fixture of the National Socialist camp system. A federally organized network of concentration camps was established in 1933/1934. The system was made uniform and put under the control of Theodor Eicke, Inspector of Concentration Camps and Leader of the SS Guard Units (Inspekteur der Konzentrationslager und Führer der SS-Wachverbände, IKL/FWV) in 1934/5. At that point, only five camps remained: Dachau, Lichtenburg, Sachsenburg, Esterwegen, and Columbia.[6] The system was overhauled in 1936/1937 with the beginning of the construction of "modern" barracks camps.[7] By 1939, all of the old camps but Dachau had been closed and replaced by five new major barracks camps: Sachsenhausen (July 1936), Buchenwald (July 1937), Flossenbürg (May 1938), Mauthausen (August 1938), and Ravensbrück (May 1939).[8] Between September 1939 and April 1944, the number of main camps grew to twenty-two (with 165 sub-camps); fifteen were located within the territory of the Reich, three in the Government General, three in the Reich Commissariat Ostland, and one in the Netherlands.[9]

A major administrative turning point came in March 1942 when the IKL was reorganized as Amtsgruppe D in the newly established SS-WVHA. The first year of the SS-WVHA's control of the camps saw the most comprehensive effort on the part of the SS to improve conditions and to reduce prisoner mortality rates in order to increase the supply of prisoner labor for the armaments industry.[10] Numerous external work sites and sub-camps were established, initially close to the main camps and later at armaments plants. The number of sub-camps grew tremendously following the intensification of Allied bombing raids on industrial facilities in early 1944 and the establishment of a special interministerial staff to oversee the relocation of the armaments industry. The main camps became steadily less important. The second-to-last camp with the status of an independent concentration camp was the Concentration Camp Mittelbau, an underground facility for rocket production in the Harz Mountains. A sub-camp of Buchenwald, the Mittelbau camp was given the same status as the main camps in October 1944. Only ten main camps were still in existence in April/May 1945.

The German retreat in both East and West in the summer of 1944 resulted in the closing or evacuation of a number of camps: Kauen, Riga, and Vaivara in the Baltic States; Lublin, Warsaw, and Heidelager/Dębica in Poland; Herzogenbusch in the Netherlands; and Natzweiler in Alsace. At the same time, the remaining camps were reorganized and adapted to serve a new function in response to changing conditions and requirements. One of the first changes was the designation of the Stutthof concentration camp as the receiving camp for prisoners from the closed camps in the East. Stutthof became the testing ground for the regrouping of prisoners and SS personnel and for measures to grapple with the rising numbers of prisoners and the shortage of food. A crucial part of the "solution" to that problem at Stutthof was the murder of sick prisoners starting in the summer of 1944. The experience gained there was to influence practices at other camps in the months that followed, particularly once the remaining main camps had become receiving camps for prisoners evacuated from camps further east in late 1944 and early 1945. The systematic killing of sick and incapacitated prisoners was supplemented by a policy of deliberate neglect. The holding camp Bergen-Belsen became synonymous with the hellish conditions at the camps during this period.

From the perspective of the SS, the mass killings during the final year of the war, especially the killing of sick prisoners, were a stabilizing measure. The thinking of the SS was dominated by the need to maintain order, and the preservation of the camp system became an end in itself. The horrific conditions endured by the prisoners were the price to be paid for maintaining the camp world's functioning. Killing seriously ill prisoners, prisoners suffering infectious diseases, and prisoners incapable of working was, in the view of the SS, necessary to avert the looming collapse of the camps. Selective murder perpetuated the state of emergency that began with the dissolution of the camps in the Baltic states in 1944. The highest priority was maintaining control of the camps against the background of the tension between the forced expansion of the camp system and the dwindling availability of resources.

The murder of sick prisoners was justified as mercy killing and as a measure to prevent the spread of epidemic diseases; the conditions at Stutthof and Ravensbrück might have lent a certain measure of credibility to that argument in the eyes of those responsible. Racial considerations played a marginal role. Beginning in 1944, three categories were used in prisoner selections at all camps: fit (*tauglich*), partially fit (*bedingt tauglich*), and unfit (*ungeeignet*).[11]

Overcrowding, lack of space, and disease created a state of emergency above all in concentration camps in northern Germany. Remote from industrial sites and underground production facilities, northern camps such as Ravensbrück, Stutthof, and Bergen-Belsen did not play an important role in armaments production,[12] and increasingly became transit and receiving camps for prisoners unable to work. A north-south divide in the concentration camp system thus arose as a result of the increased use of prisoner labor, in connection with the relocation of armaments factories to underground facilities and the establishment of new regional and supraregional administrative structures such as the SS executive staff (*Führungsstab*) and special inspectorate (*Sonderinspektion*).

The suspension of mass killings of Jews and other victims at Auschwitz in November 1944 contributed to the escalation in the systematic killing of sick prisoners. The demolition of the crematoria and the end of extermination transports to Auschwitz created serious problems for the other camps. In August 1944, on the order of SS Major General Richard Glücks, the leader of Amtsgruppe D, all sick Jewish prisoners were transferred to Birkenau.[13] When that option disappeared, the SS looked for alternatives to prevent the camps system from collapsing.[14] The establishment of death zones was only a short-term expedient. The arrival of transports from closed camps and the return of prisoners from sub-camps intensified the problem of overcrowding. As a result, targeted killing actions were undertaken in 1944 (Stutthof, Ravensbrück, and Mauthausen) and 1945 (Sachsenhausen and Buchenwald). At least 18,700 prisoners, most of them sick or unable to work, were killed in these operations, with little regard to their religion, nationality, ethnicity, or gender.

THE LIFTING OF RACIAL SELECTION CRITERIA IN THE CAMPS

"The majority of these prisoners can no longer be considered for work duty," concluded Gerhard Schiedlausky, the head SS camp doctor in the Buchenwald camp, after inspecting approximately 1,600 Jewish prisoners who had been transferred there in September 1944 from the sub-camps "Wille" (Tröglitz and Rehmsdorf bei Zeitz) and "Magda" (Magdeburg-Rothensee) that were part of the Brabag synthetic fuel plant.[15] More than 5,000 prisoners from Wille had been housed in tents in Tröglitz from June through December 1944 before being transferred to a new barracks camp in Rehmdorf in early 1945. Among them was the young Imre Kertész, whose autobiographical novel *Fateless* (*Sorstalanság*) is based in part on his experiences in Tröglitz.[16] The rates of sickness and death were very high. In January 1945, despite the transfers to Buchenwald, roughly 57 percent of 3,411 Wille prisoners were deemed unfit to work (31 percent temporarily and 26 percent permanently).[17] Prisoners sent back from sub-camps were usually transferred to Auschwitz and murdered there. Of the 8,572 prisoners recorded as having been transferred from Buchenwald to Wille between June 1944 and March 1945, the SS sent 3,434 back as unfit to work. In all, 5,871 prisoners at the Wille sub-camp died, including the sick and unfit prisoners transferred to Auschwitz and other camps.[18]

On August 24, 1944, Glücks issued the order to concentration camp commandants that Jewish prisoners unfit for work were to be deported to Auschwitz. Responsibility for conveying the order to SS doctors responsible for carrying out prisoner selections fell to the head of the SS-WVHA's department for sanitation (Amt D III), Enno Lolling.[19] Among those affected by this order, which amounted to a death sentence, were the above mentioned prisoners transferred from the Magda sub-camp to Buchenwald on September 27, 1944.[20] SS medical personnel in Buchenwald selected 388 of the 525 ill and incapacitated prisoners for transfer to Auschwitz. They were sent in a transport of a total of 1,188 prisoners deemed unfit for work; most were murdered shortly after their arrival in

Auschwitz on October 5, 1944. It was the largest transport of prisoners from Buchenwald for annihilation.[21] At least another 550 of the 2,172 Jewish prisoners held at the Magda sub-camp died in Magdeburg. In the three months following the September 27 transfer, the SS transported another 1,151 prisoners deemed unfit for work from Magda back to Buchenwald, Auschwitz, or Bergen-Belsen. On December 29, for example, 401 prisoners unfit for work were sent from Magda to Bergen-Belsen. More than 800 of the 1,151 transferred prisoners died.[22]

The process of selecting prisoners too sick or too unfit to work for transfer was systematic and routinized to a certain extent. It was directly connected to the mass killings in the final year of the war; indeed, the transferred prisoners were among the main victims, whether they were killed or murdered by deliberate neglect. Consideration must be given to those who participated in the selection process by applying the criteria for the "discharge of prisoners" (*Ausmusterung von Häftlinge*).[23] One group involved in the selection process has been largely ignored by scholars, namely the representatives of private companies that made use of prisoner labor. Whereas the SS focused on sick and unfit prisoners, who, from the SS perspective, "heavily burdened the prisoner infirmary,"[24] private companies gave priority to prisoners' technical skills and ability to carry out production tasks. In this regard, we can speak of "negative" and "positive" selection. There were considerable differences in the organization and methods of the two forms of selection, even if for prisoners the results were much the same.

NEGATIVE SELECTION

Selections were carried out collaboratively by the medical and labor departments. In the main camps, the selections were usually overseen by the SS camp doctor, the labor detail supervisor (*Arbeitseinsatzführer*), or their representatives. In sub-camps, SS medics (*Sanitätsdienstgrad*) and labor detail leaders (*Kommandoführer*) carried out the selections. SS doctors conducted inspection tours of sub-camps to check medical and sanitary conditions; together with medical or sanitation personnel at the sub-camps, they also selected unfit prisoners for transfer back to a main camp. In November 1944, for example, Flossenbürg camp doctor Heinrich Schmitz[25] visited a sub-camp in Nossen[26] during an inspection tour that, Schmitz later testified, took him to at least ten sub-camps.[27] Following Schmitz's visit, the leader of the labor detail in Nossen, SS Master Sergeant Wetterau, reported to the commandant in Flossenbürg,

"The detail [*Kommando*] requests permission to transfer the following prisoners because they are not fit for work for the time being. Certification from the camp doctor is attached; also, Dr. Schmitz already arranged for the transfer [*Abstellung*] during his inspection of the camp on Sunday."[28]

For the SS, a prisoner unable to work for an extended period of time was, as previously noted, "bodily deficient human material" that "unnecessarily burdened" a camp and had to be dealt with as quickly as possible.[29] Three factors lay behind this outlook. The first was economic: the labor department and camp administration earned nothing from prisoners who could not work.[30] Sick and severely weakened prisoners needed costly and time-consuming care, and resources were in extremely short supply. A prisoner unable to work was no longer of interest to the SS. Second, the firms that used prisoner labor refused to pay for prisoners who could not work. The SS was eager to avoid conflicts with companies and the administrative burden of adjusting billing to deduct for unfit prisoners.[31] Third, the camps lacked the medical and sanitary resources to deal with infectious diseases. Proper medical treatment of the ill and unfit was not an option open to SS doctors, but selective murder was. According to Friedrich Entress, a former head camp doctor in Mauthausen, efforts to treat ill prisoners would have been useless. An exception was made for those who might recover quickly and be able to return to work without a long convalescence.[32] The Auschwitz commandant Rudolf Höß, the head of Amt DI of the SS-WHHA since November 1943, allowed medicine and extra food to be given to ill prisoners "who can be made healthy and fit for work within six weeks."[33] Entress testified that, in carrying out selections, he focused on seriously ill prisoners; those whom he selected would then be killed in Mauthausen's gas chamber.

Amtsgruppe D's efforts to improve conditions for prisoners were limited to healthy prisoners, above all those who were skilled workers, which served to widen the gap between the fit and the unfit. In an October 1944 circular on "Preservation of Prisoners' Capacity for Work" (*Erhaltung der Arbeitskraft der Häftlinge*) – just one of many issued on the subject – Glücks repeated the orders of his superior, Oswald Pohl, the head of the SS-WVHA: "You are to give your attention with particular care to all of these points [allowing prisoners adequate sleep, housing them in dry quarters, and giving them adequate clothing] to ensure the health of the prisoners and their deployment in arms production."[34] Actual practice fell far short of such instructions as a result of catastrophic supply shortages and the indifference of the SS guards, but the instructions nonetheless convey an impression of the goals the SS leadership sought to pursue.

The SS and private companies pushed for the elimination of sick prisoners in order to avoid "burdening" the camps with the unfit and to contain the risk of infecting prisoners able to work. Rudolf Höß set out the thinking behind this policy in his memoirs:

If, in line with my repeatedly expressed view, we had selected only the healthiest and fittest Jews, we would, it is true, have been able to register fewer [prisoners] able to work but then we would have had truly useful [prisoners] for a long time. So we had high numbers on paper, in reality we could subtract a large percentage of them. They only burdened the camp, took space and food away from those able to work, accomplished nothing – indeed, by their presence, they made many of those able to work unfit for work. You didn't need a slide rule to calculate the results.[35]

By Höß's logic, murdering the unfit was a form of mercy killing: "If the prisoners in Auschwitz had been taken directly to the gas chambers, they would have been spared much suffering."[36]

In all the camps, negative selection rested on dividing prisoners into three groups.[37] Gerhard Schiedlausky, the head SS camp doctor in Buchenwald, defined the three groups:

1st Group: strong, suitable for deployment in the work detail.

2nd Group: prisoners physically not suitable for the work detail but who can certainly be used in industrial production

3rd Group: prisoners unsuitable on account of sickness or general bodily weakness.[38]

During a selection at the Wille sub-camp in late January 1945, Schiedlausky categorized 1,472 of 2,132 prisoners as Group 1, 340 as Group 2, and 320 as Group 3. In addition, another 1,279 prisoners were listed as "under care" (*in Schonung*), of whom he categorized 353 as Group 1 ("mainly sick [prisoners] who will be fully fit for work in the foreseeable future but are in the infirmary at present"), 358 as Group 2, and 568 as Group 3, "of whom 200–300 prisoners should die in the next days or weeks."[39] Of the 3,411 prisoners he categorized in total, 56 percent were deemed either temporarily or permanently unfit for work. In the listing by name of the prisoners in the first two groups, notice was made of their trade or occupation; the SS did not bother to note that information for prisoners in the third group. The camp administration decided on death for them.

In similar fashion, Percival Treite, a young SS doctor who had earned his *Habilitation* in gynecology at the University of Berlin, divided the women imprisoned in the Ravensbrück concentration camp into three groups: (1) fully able to work, (2) able to work with limitations, (3) incapacitated or unfit for work.[40] It was above all Jewish women transferred from Auschwitz whom Treite assigned to the third group. "These prisoners were fully broken down physically and mentally [*seelisch*]. About 50 percent of them died in the course of time, mainly from general exhaustion [*allgemeine Körperschwäche*]."[41]

POSITIVE SELECTION

While negative selection was oriented toward Group 3, positive selection focused on Group 1, healthy prisoners fully fit to work. A decisive factor in positive selection – and for a prisoner's chances of survival – was the prisoner's trade or occupation. After the establishment of the SS-WVHA in March 1942, Amtsgruppe D, the camps, and private companies engaged in detailed correspondence on the deployment of individual prisoners.[42] Letters asking for prisoners with particular skills were routinely circulated.[43] In connection with the large-scale relocation of industrial facilities in 1944, all concentration camps were asked to prepare lists of prisoners with urgently needed skills. SS First Lieutenant Vinzenz Schöttl, the head of the protective detention camp within the Auschwitz III camp (Monowitz), informed all the sub-camps within his jurisdiction in June 1944 of an upcoming transfer of skilled Polish prisoners. In preparation, the labor detail leaders were to put together lists of skilled workers and possible assignments. The central criterion was occupation.[44] In October 1944, Schöttl ordered that lists of indispensible skilled workers be prepared. "In order to avoid premature disclosure, the lists may *not* be prepared by prisoners."[45] The Groß-Rosen concentration camp transferred 400 prisoners with needed skills for labor deployment in Buchenwald in November 1944.[46] Such prisoners not only received better accommodation, clothing, medical care, and food than others but were also better treated by the camp's SS personnel.

Another difference between positive and negative selection lay in the actors involved. Prisoners deployed at private companies were generally selected by representatives of the companies, not by SS doctors or labor detail leaders. The well-documented case of the Berlin-based firm OSRAM is typical of private sector use of prisoner labor. OSRAM maintained a production facility for aircraft parts in an underground tunnel in Leitmeritz, the largest of the Flossenbürg sub-camps. The facility was referred to in documents as "Richard II" (R II). According to an internal company memorandum dated January 29, 1945, SS First Lieutenant

Wilhelm Biermann[47] "recommended that the next 140 prisoners in Groß-Rosen now be chosen because a selection is available at the moment and there are numerous skilled laborers [*Handwerker*] among them. The selected prisoners could remain at Groß-Rosen until our call."[48] Skilled workers were to be housed apart from *Bauhäftlinge*, prisoners employed in low-skilled manual labor on construction projects. The mortality rate for *Bauhäftlinge* was substantially higher than that for *Fertigungshäftlinge* (prisoners engaged in industrial production) as a result of the difference in the treatment they received. The terms *Bauhäftlinge* and *Fertigungshäftlinge* came to figure as selection criteria.[49] OSRAM repeatedly insisted on separate accommodations for "our prisoners" to maintain their fitness for work and was backed by the SS-WVHA.[50]

OSRAM also ran a light bulb factory at a Flossenbürg sub-camp in Plauen. When the camp was established in the summer of 1944, the SS provided prisoners suitable for employment in the factory. In preparation, in mid-August 1944 Flossenbürg camp commandant Max Koegel and his head administrator, Hermann Kirsammer, met with representatives of OSRAM in Plauen to discuss how 500 prisoner laborers were to be selected from a transport of Hungarian Jews and subsequently accommodated. OSRAM representatives had made several visits to Plauen the previous month to check on the state of preparations for the prisoners' arrival.[51] At an agreed-upon point in time, OSRAM was to receive notice "in which camp the prisoners designated for us are. Our men can then travel there shortly before the transfer date and select workers suited to our work."[52] OSRAM engaged the necessary female guards and arranged for their travel to a training program for guards at the Holleischen sub-camp.

Following the negotiations between OSRAM and Amtsgruppe D, a company employee traveled to Auschwitz in August 1944 to choose 250 female prisoners for deployment in the Plauen sub-camp. The women arrived in Plauen the following month.[53] In early October, however, OSRAM informed Amtsgruppe D that it had reservations about the women – Jewish prisoners who, from the company's perspective, were not suited for the work they were to perform. Wilhelm Biemann, an SS officer with Amt DII of the SS-WVHA, promised, in response, to make female prisoners aged 17 or 18 available to the company. OSRAM noted that, as in Auschwitz, it would choose the prisoners it deemed suitable.[54]

At this time, selection was carried out in Groß-Rosen to choose prisoners for deployment at a sub-camp in Leitmeritz. "There are at present [i.e., November 1944] once again 1,200 men available in Groß-Rosen,

Hungarian Jews, of whom knowledge of the German language can probably be presumed."[55] On December 29, 1944, an OSRAM employee was in Flossenbürg to choose 180 prisoners from a transport from Groß-Rosen. He was accompanied by the head of the labor supply, SS Sergeant Friedrich Becker. OSRAM's report stated:

The prisoners put at our disposal were Hungarian Jews, almost all of whom were between the ages of 20 and 40 and who appeared to be in good physical condition. The camp doctor examined all of them beforehand and divided them into groups according to health, which made it easier for me to reject ill and sickly [*anfällig*] prisoners. I succeeded in pressing our demand for skilled labor to the extent that, for example, we will receive all the skilled metalworkers in the transport.[56]

Representatives of OSRAM visited the offices of Amtsgruppe D and the SS-WVHA in Oranienburg and Berlin several times while negotiations were underway to discuss the numbers of prisoners to be deployed in Leitmeritz and Plauen and the terms of their deployment. During one meeting, Biemann explained that the SS had set aside its reservations about using foreign prisoners in arms production "under the pressure of circumstances."[57] There had, however, been problems in mixed deployments of male and female prisoners, in training prisoners, and in the deployment of Jewish prisoners. But although a large number of prisoners, mainly Jews, with useful skills were available for labor deployment, some high-ranking Nazi officials such as Reichsstatthalter and Gauleiter Martin Mutschmann of Saxony opposed the deployment of Jews within their jurisdictions. It was stated that "an attempt must be made as quickly as possible to have this prohibition lifted" because Amtsgruppe D was not able to "place Aryans at the disposal" of the company.[58] OSRAM and its employees used what room for maneuver they had to secure as many prisoners as possible for use as laborers. The company looked for support within the SS even though requests for prisoner laborers were handled by the Reich Ministry of Armaments and War Production.[59] In a letter dated October 9, 1944, Reich Armaments Minister Albert Speer informed OSRAM that, in his view, all of the company's applications for prisoner workers had been granted, with the exception of the one then under review. OSRAM thereupon turned to the SS. After discussion with Amt D II in mid-November, a company employee noted with relief that "directly dealing with the SS in our case, which can be considered in progress, can be viewed as absolutely permitted."[60]

OSRAM was by no means the only company whose employees were involved in selecting concentration camp prisoners for use as workers in its factories. Private firms sought prisoner workers in all of the concentration camps. That occurred with the approval of Amtsgruppe D, camp commandants, and department heads within the camp administrations. Buchenwald camp commandant Hermann Pister informed the commandant of the Bergen-Belsen holding camp in December 1944, for example, that two employees of the firm Heerbrandt AG would carry out a selection of 500 female prisoners. The firm requested that its two employees be accommodated near the camp.[61] The 500 women and girls, most of whom were Jewish, arrived at the Raguhn sub-camp on February 7, 1945, for deployment in an aircraft factory owned by Junkers, Heerbrandt's corporate parent. Raguhn was the second-to-last sub-camp of Buchenwald to be established. Because of shortages of raw materials and supplies, the factory was never able to begin production.[62]

In another instance, an employee of BMW visited the Stutthof concentration camp to select a small number of *Fertigungshäftlinge*. Commandant Paul Werner Hoppe informed his staff of the transfer of prisoners: "In line with the orders of Amtsgruppe D of the SS-WVHA, 72 prisoners will be transferred to the Dachau concentration camp. The selection of prisoners by a representative of the BMW Works has already taken place."[63] Not only the guards provided by the Dachau SS Death's Head Battalion but also the prisoners to be transported were provided with three days' worth of warm food and supplies for the march – another indication of the improved treatment "production prisoners" received.

That was confirmed by Ravensbrück commandant Fritz Suhren in his 1946 testimony regarding negotiations with private companies on the use of prisoner labor in production facilities at sub-camps. The heads of several of the factories in which Ravensbrück prisoners were deployed had visited the main camp at least once "to discuss questions about labor deployment" with Hans Pflaum, who was in charge of the labor supply in Ravensbrück.[64] Suhren provided a list featuring the names of senior staff members of a diverse array of companies, including Siemens & Halske, Polte, Dornier, and Heinkel.

In selecting prisoners, private companies generally looked for a healthy constitution and qualification in a skilled trade, typically in metalworking. The ability to speak German was also a consideration, particularly when it came to Jewish prisoners from Eastern Europe. Knowledge of German, together with physical fitness, increased the chances that a prisoner without a particular skill might be chosen by a private company. In the fall of 1944, for example, representatives of Daimler-Benz selected a large number of female Hungarian Jews at Ravensbrück for deployment at an airplane engine factory at the Sachsenhausen sub-camp in Genshagen.[65] The main criteria for Daimler-Benz in this instance were fitness for work and the ability to speak German.[66]

Given the differing interests of the various parties involved, conflicts were unavoidable. After the Reich Ministry of Armaments and War Production and the various special staffs for weapons production had increased their influence on the camp empire, Amtsgruppe D's jurisdiction was further eroded by private companies' ability to exploit their room for maneuver in negotiations over prisoner workers. In response to an order issued by the Organisation Todt for a transfer of prisoners, for example, the head of the Amt II, Gerhard Maurer, issued a reminder that the authority to assign prisoners for labor deployment lay solely with Amtsgruppe D:

It recently happened that, at a sub-camp of a concentration camp, the head of an OT worksite ... wanted on his own authority to persuade the camp leader to transfer several hundred prisoners from that population [*Bestand*] to another work camp within the jurisdiction [*Bereich*] of another concentration camp. In so doing, this OT leader attempted to assume authority he did not possess.[67]

In another case, the Adlerwerke of Frankfurt am Main complained about a mistake in the assignment of prisoners after the company's "labor deployment engineer" (*Arbeitseinsatzingenieur*) had personally taken charge of selecting 1,000 prisoners at the Natzweiler concentration camp. The company refused to pay for the prisoners it had not selected.[68]

Jurisdictional disputes and clashes of interest notwithstanding, private employers, the SS, and other official agencies were disregarding racial criteria in prisoner selections by 1944. Race was subordinated to bodily fitness, professional skills, and language abilities in deciding which prisoners were to be deployed as laborers and which were to be murdered. The most important criterion was a prisoner's ability – or inability – to work.[69] The selection process was carried out according to centrally issued orders; although they might have been implemented differently from camp to camp, those orders reflected a conscious change of policy at the leadership level. Among the changes in policy was the deployment of Jewish prisoners at worksites within the Reich despite the opposition of influential figures such as Kaltenbrunner, Sauckel, and Mutschmann. The use of Jewish prisoners in armaments production was allowed in the Reich, initially with the exception of Berlin, starting in May/June 1944, and distinctions between Jews and other prisoner laborers steadily disappeared.[70] The use of the yellow star to stigmatize Jewish prisoners, for instance, ended in November 1944.[71]

Being Jewish was thus no longer grounds in itself for negative selection. Jewish and non-Jewish prisoners alike were categorized as unfit to work and systematically shot, poisoned, or asphyxiated. Between January and April 1945, for instance, 5,000–6,000 prisoners were murdered in Ravensbrück, approximately half of them by asphyxiation in the gas chamber. The victims were registered as having been transferred to the fictitious Mittwerda "recuperation camp" (*Schonungslager*) in Silesia. A list of Ravensbrück prisoners to be killed or transferred to Mittwerda dated April 6, 1945, and signed by camp commandant Fritz Suhren has survived (the dates given on such lists are not necessarily the dates when the prisoners were killed).[72] Of the 493 women on the list, 156 were Jewish.[73] Poles constituted the largest group of the remaining victims. The selection focused above all on the health of the prisoners.

Having suffered long periods of persecution and privation, Jewish prisoners often fell victim to negative selection.[74] Non-Jewish Germans, on the other hand, ranked among the "old" and experienced prisoners and often received privileged treatment in the concentration camps. In contrast to new arrivals transferred from camps in the East, German prisoners were generally healthy and fit for work. Many of them had long been entrusted with positions of authority and contributed to the stability the SS considered so important.

Still, as is clear from the lists of murdered prisoners, even non-Jewish Germans were sent to their deaths through negative selection.[75] An SS order for the mustering of the entire Ravensbrück camp is a representative instance of the separation of the fit from the unfit. On September 1, 1944, the overseer of the labor supply (*Arbeitsdienst*) ordered that "after the work formation ... a) all prisoners over 50 years-old [and] b) all prisoners with the red card [are] to remain standing on the camp street! The block elders are responsible for [ensuring that] the aforementioned prisoners actually stand."[76] Since 1944, the prisoners' infirmary had issued red and pink cards to prisoners unable to work so that they could be transferred to a "recuperation camp."[77] The selections carried out in the final year of the war thus were not a part of the "final solution of the Jewish question," but rather a de facto resumption of euthanasia killings.

THE ABANDONMENT OF RACIAL CRITERIA IN RECRUITING CAMP GUARDS

As a result of personnel transfers, administrative changes, and the changing military situation, very few SS concentration camp guards served in that capacity for the entire duration of the war.[78] By 1944, a multi-ethnic prisoner population was under the surveillance of a multi-ethnic guard corps that did not correspond to the racial criteria of the SS. Those guards were not indoctrinated in Nazi racial ideology, and many of them did not meet the racial criteria previously required for service in the SS. The constantly changing multi-ethnic guard corps was plagued by tensions arising from xenophobia, language barriers, discipline problems, the lack of *esprit de corps*, poor morale, and differing conceptions of the workings of hierarchy. A variety of measures were taken to strengthen obedience and *esprit de corps* among the guards, to prevent desertions, and to address distrust within the multinational, multi-ethnic, and multi-generational guard troops. To avoid endangering "the willingness to serve [*Dienstfreudigkeit*], morale, and discipline of Ukrainian guards," for example, the SS leadership went so far as to enforce the public execution of Soviet prisoners.[79]

The SS began recruiting *Volksdeutsche* – ethnic Germans mainly from Eastern Europe – for the Waffen-SS in 1941.[80] By October 1943, roughly 7,000 *Volksdeutsche* were serving in the SS as concentration camp guards,[81] and they constituted nearly half of the 15,000-strong guard troops.[82] *Volksdeutsche* continued to make up about half of the guard corps even as the number of guards more than doubled in the last year and a half of the war. The majority of the ethnic Germans came from Romania and Hungary. Of the 7,000 ethnic Germans serving in the SS in October 1943, 3,100 were from Romania. The majority of them were assigned to one of four camps: Lublin (850); Mauthausen (510); Sachsenhausen (400); and Buchenwald (350).[83] Forging a sense of unity among the Reich Germans, the ethnic Germans, and the non-German auxiliaries (*fremdvölkische Hilfswillige*) was not considered feasible and was not attempted: Ensuring the day-to-day functioning of the concentration camps was a higher priority than promoting a sense of shared identity among the guards. SS-WVHA head Oswald Pohl stressed that, on racial grounds, *Volksdeutsche* did not "fully meet the conditions for acceptance into the SS."[84]

The group furthest from the SS racial ideal was the so-called Trawniki men, who were transferred to the concentration camp system in large numbers in 1943 with the end of "Operation Reinhard," i.e. the mass murder of Jews in the Government General and Bialystok.[85] Their deployment was an indication that the SS leadership had set aside racial criteria in the recruitment of guards in its efforts to rationalize the concentration camp system. In early 1944, 1,000 Ukrainians and 200 Estonians and

Latvians were serving as guards in concentration camps, representing approximately 6 percent of the guard force.[86] The Trawniki men were not members of the Waffen-SS, and their service in the camps was not recognized as active military service. They were nonetheless considered part of the retinue of the Waffen-SS – like the female camp guards – and were under SS jurisdiction.[87] They were used solely to guard the perimeter of camps and were not posted inside the protective detention camps. In contrast to Reich Germans and ethnic Germans from Croatia, Romania, Slovakia, and Hungary, they were allowed to take leave in the Reich but not in their home countries.[88] Unlike other camp personnel, they were allowed to visit the bordellos staffed by prisoners because they were non-German (*fremdvölkisch*).[89] In addition to the Trawniki men, other Ukrainian, Lithuanian, and Latvian soldiers and policemen were taken into the concentration camp guard corps as of 1944.

Responsibility for the integration of ethnic German SS volunteers, non-German auxiliaries, and Wehrmacht soldiers assigned to the camps fell to the welfare and ideological training (*Fürsorge und Weltanschauliche Schulung*) departments that were established in every camp after 1941. In 1943, Amtgruppe D's troop training department began a targeted program for ethnic German recruits, above all those from Romania, who were the largest group of *Volksdeutsche* serving as camp personnel until the end of 1943. An ethnic German was to be assigned to each camp's welfare and ideological training department to oversee the integration of ethnic Germans serving in the SS. Separate training for ethnic Germans and troops transferred from the Wehrmacht after 1944 remained standard practice in the camps through the end of the war.[90] That included the training of expert instructors for ethnic German SS volunteers from Southeastern Europe.[91] Oversight and ideological training was made flexible to accommodate the increasingly multi-ethnic guard corps and to ensure the functioning and discipline of multi-ethnic SS Death's Head units.[92]

Given the far-reaching transformation of the SS guard corps, the guards' adherence to Nazi ideology probably varied tremendously during the final year of the war. Nonetheless, new guards unhesitatingly participated alongside long-serving SS men in the killing of prisoners. No group within the guard corps was notably over- or underrepresented among the participants in murder.[93] That might seem surprising given the numerous survivor accounts of the cruelty of long-serving SS men and Ukrainian camp guards. It is also surprising in light of the different levels of ideological-racist indoctrination received by the various groups of guards.

THE COLLAPSE OF THE CAMP SYSTEM AND THE
"DEATH MARCHES"

Despite the burdens caused by the Allied advance on both the eastern and western fronts, the concentration camp system was still functioning at the close of 1944. But if exploiting prisoner labor for arms production had been the highest priority of the SS during 1944, holding off the collapse of the camp system became an end in itself in the final months of the war. It is against this background of shifting priorities that the evacuation of concentration camps and the question whether these transports or "death marches" should be seen as the final chapter of the Holocaust need to be considered.

Daniel Blatman, for example, draws parallels between the evacuation of the Baltic camps Kauen, Riga, and Vaivara in the summer of 1944 and the evacuations from Auschwitz that began in November 1944, on the one hand, and the uncoordinated and often chaotic evacuations of the camps still in existence in April and May 1945, on the other. However, he disregards crucial differences in the functions these evacuations served, in how they were carried out, and in the state of the concentration camp system at the time they occurred. Crucially, he fails to mention that the closing of the Baltic camps coincided with the opening of numerous new sub-camps at arms production sites further west and that many prisoners from the Baltic camps were ultimately transferred to sub-camps.[94]

The main receiving camp for prisoners from the evacuated Baltic camps was Stutthof. Danuta Drywa has argued that Stutthof took over Auschwitz's function as the central site for the systematic murder of Jews and that the large-scale killings carried out there beginning in 1944 should be regarded as the last stage of the Nazis' "final solution to the Jewish question."[95] There is, however, little evidence to support this argument. Drywa relies in part on contradictory statements from the postwar testimony of the Stutthof camp commandant Paul Werner Hoppe. During his trial, Hoppe repeatedly claimed that he had received an order from Richard Glücks for the extermination of Jewish prisoners and, through that order, had become aware of "Hitler's fundamental order for the final solution of the Jewish question." Hoppe's testimony notwithstanding, there is no evidence of such an order from Glücks, or of the targeted killing of Jewish prisoners at Stutthof, in the surviving documentation.[96] It was first and foremost sick prisoners and those who could not work who fell victim to the systematic killings carried out at Stutthof between the evacuation of the Baltic camps in the summer of 1944 and the camp's own evacuation in early 1945. Jewish women made up a large portion of those murdered at Stutthof in the second half of 1944. That is to be explained by the high number of Jewish prisoners that had been previously evacuated, the conditions they had previously endured in hierarchically organized camps, and the long, often harsh persecution many of them had suffered. Jeanette Wolf, a Jewish Social Democrat who was imprisoned in Stutthof from August 1944 to January 1945, stressed that point: "These [Jewish] Hungarian women arrived from Auschwitz already in extremely poor mental condition ... Diarrhea lasting weeks or months had reduced their bodies to skeletons, they were overrun by lice, and often their entire bodies were covered with the vermin ... Very many of them had gone insane so that every effort one took with them was in vain."[97]

The camp closings and evacuation marches of the final months of the war in 1945 stand as a distinct phase in the history of the Nazi concentration camp system. This phase was characterized by the abandonment of clearly defined spaces of confinement and spaces for the exercise of power. The opening and expansion of the geographic space in which prisoners and guards interacted meant the loss of established power structures. With the dissolution of the camps in the territory of the Reich, the concentration camp system and, with it, any semblance of planning and organization ceased to exist.

* * *

The imposition of a racial hierarchy among concentration camp prisoners was abandoned during the final year of the war. Under pressure to increase armaments production, governmental and party officials set aside racial categories and ideological considerations in favor of a flexible approach to managing the deepening crisis. In May 1944, against the opposition of senior SS and party officials, Heinrich Himmler ordered the deployment of 200,000 Jews imprisoned in concentration camps on "militarily important tasks" in the Reich. The demands of the situation gave a new value to prisoners and spurred a shift in priorities and, at least on paper, in the treatment of prisoners. In late November and early December 1944, Richard Glücks issued new guidelines on improving the treatment of Jewish prisoners, and from that point Jewish prisoners were no longer stigmatized by having to wear the yellow star. Prisoners' health and ability to work, not their race, became the decisive criterion in selections and mass killings. Being Jewish was in itself no longer grounds for "negative selection." Analysis of the lists of prisoners killed makes clear that race was not a priority in the final year of the war and that Jews were not singled out for murder. The SS gave priority, rather, to economic utility and to maintaining the concentration camp system as the pressures on it mounted. The spatial reorganization of camp complexes and the murder of prisoners who were ill or unable to work were intended to stabilize the camp system and to maximize its economic utility. Contrary to Saul Friedländer's argument that the last year of the war saw "the final drive toward the complete extermination of the European Jews," the situation during this phase of the war was more complex and not dominated by an eliminationist anti-Semitism.[98]

Similarly, race was largely abandoned as a criterion in the selection and training of concentration camp guards during the last years of the war. Ideology ceased to be a factor in the duty of guards in the concentration camps as emphasis shifted to the practical problem of maintaining order and the functioning of the camps. National Socialist ideology also played little part as an integrative force or as a factor shaping guards' willingness to engage in violence against prisoners. By 1944, ethnic German SS volunteers, non-German auxiliaries, and Wehrmacht soldiers serving as guards were as likely to engage in violence and commit atrocities as long-serving members of the SS. As its importance in defining hierarchy waned in the final year of the war, the concept of race lost much of its importance in the concentration camp system.

Notes

1 Report by Karl Groß to SS-WVHA Amt D III, Dec. 23, 1943, Archive of the Directie-generaal Oorlogsslachtoffers, Archief- en documentatiedienst, Brussels, 1546/Ding-Schuler.
2 Ibid.
3 Circular from Richard Glücks to camp commanders, Apr. 27, 1943, Nuremberg Document NO-1007.
4 Order from Heinrich Himmler to Gottlob Berger and Oswald Pohl, May 11, 1944, Bundesarchiv Berlin (hereafter BArchB), NS 19/1922. Initially, Jews were not to be deployed in Berlin: report of the Jägerstab, June 9, 1944, BArchB, R 3/1756, 47. Ernst Kaltenbrunner, the head of the Reich Security Main Office (Reichssicherheitshauptamt, or RSHA), and Gauleiter Fritz Sauckel and Martin Mutschmann were adamantly opposed to the use of Jewish prisoners as laborers within Germany's prewar borders and were able to block the transfer of Jewish prisoners into the "old Reich" in part until the autumn of 1944.
5 Circular from Enno Lolling, head of Amt DIII of the SS-WVHA, to SS camp doctors, Aug. 25, Thüringisches Hauptstaatsarchiv Weimar (hereafter ThHStAW), KZ und Haftanstalten Buchenwald, No. 9, 28.
6 List compiled by Günther Tamaschke, Nov. 27, 1935, BArchB, NS 31/256.

7 Sachsenhausen in particular corresponded to Himmler's vision of the "completely new, immediately expandable, modern and up-to-date concentration camp" that should serve as the model in planning for the camp system. Letter from Heinrich Himmler to the Reich Ministry of Justice, Feb. 8, 1937, BArchB, R 2/24006.

8 Stefan Hördler, "Before the Holocaust: Concentration Camp Lichtenburg and the evolution of the Nazi camp system," *Holocaust and Genocide Studies* 25 (2011), 100–26; Stefan Hördler, "SS-Kaderschmiede Lichtenburg. Zur Bedeutung des KZ Lichtenburg in der Vorkriegszeit" in Stefan Hördler and Sigrid Jacobeit (eds.), *Lichtenburg. Ein deutsches Konzentrationslager* (Berlin, 2009), 75–129.

9 Letter from Oswald Pohl to Heinrich Himmler, Apr. 5, 1944, BArchB, NS 19/1921.

10 A quota was established whereby no more than 10 percent of all prisoners could be excused from work on account of illness: secret letter from Oswald Pohl to the camp commandants, Oct. 26, 1943, Archiwum Muzeum Stutthof/Archiv des Museums Stutthof (hereafter AMSt), I-IB-8. On the prisoner mortality rate, see the letter by Oswald Pohl to Heinrich Himmler, Sept. 30, 1943, which cites figures compiled by Amt D III on mortality rates in the concentration camps during 1942/1943 (Sept. 22, 1943), BArchB, NS 19/1542, 98–103 (= Nuremberg Document PS-1469). The figures were demonstrably falsified.

11 Letter from Gerhard Schiedlausky to Hermann Pister, commandant of the Buchenwald concentration camp, Jan. 31, 1945, ThHStAW, NS 4/Bu-54, 138.

12 The sole exception was the comparatively small Neuengamme camp, which, on account of its favorable location, supplied labor for shipbuilding and arms production. See Marc Buggeln, *Arbeit & Gewalt. Das Außenlagersystem des KZ Neuengamme* (Göttingen, 2009).

13 Letter from Enno Lolling to SS doctors, Aug. 25, 1944, ThHStAW, KZ und Haftanstalten Buchenwald, No. 9, 28.

14 The outbreak of typhus and the SS officials' indifference to the high rate of prisoner mortality were indications of the breakdown in control in the camp and the deteriorating conditions in which the prisoners lived. Stutthof was placed under quarantine on account of typhus in late 1944, and Ravensbrück was likewise quarantined in early 1945. See the special orders for Stutthoff, Dec. 29, 1944, Jan. 9, 1945, and Jan. 21, 1945, AMSt, I-IB-3; Encrypted radio message from the Kripoleitstelle Cologne to the RKPA Fürstenberg/Mecklenburg, Feb. 10, 1945: The National Archives/Public Record Office, Kew (TNA/PRO), HW 16/43, msg 143.

15 Monthly hygiene report on the Buchenwald concentration camp by Gerhard Schiedlausky, Sept. 30, 1944, ThHStAW, KZ und Haftanstalten Buchenwald, No. 10, 85f.

16 Imre Kertész, *Roman eines Schicksallosen* (Berlin, 1996), 143ff.

17 Letter from Gerhard Schiedlausky to Hermann Pister, Jan. 31, 1945, ThHStAW, NS 4/Bu-54, 138.

18 Lothar Czoßek, "Tröglitz/Rehmsdorf ('Wille')" in Wolfgang Benz and Barbara Distel (eds.), *Der Ort des Terrors. Geschichte der nationalsozialistischen Konzentrationslager* (Munich, 2006), vol. 3 (Sachsenhausen, Buchenwald), 593–6.

19 Letter from Enno Lolling to SS doctors, Aug. 25, 1944, ThHStAW, KZ und Haftanstalten Buchenwald, No. 9, 28.

20 Transfer list, Sept. 27, 1944, BArchB, NS 4/Bu-136a, 121; 525 people are listed.

21 Danuta Czech, *Kalendarium der Ereignisse im Konzentrationslager Auschwitz-Birkenau 1939–1945* (Hamburg, 1989), 895–7; Harry Stein, *Konzentrationslager Buchenwald 1937–1945. Begleitband zur historischen Ausstellung,* ed. Gedenkstätte Buchenwald (Göttingen, 2000), 221.

22 Franka Bindernagel and Tobias Bütow, "Magdeburg-Rothensee" in Benz and Distel, *Der Ort des Terrors,* vol. 3, 512–15; Tobias Bütow and Franka Bindernagel, *Ein KZ in der Nachbarschaft. Das Magdeburger Außenlager der Brabag und der "Freundeskreis Himmler"* (Cologne, 2004).

23 Letter from Gerhard Schiedlausky to Hermann Pister, Jan. 31,1945, ThHStAW, NS 4/Bu-54, 138.

24 Monthly hygiene report on the Buchenwald concentration camp by Gerhard Schiedlausky, Sept. 30, 1944, ThHStAW, KZ und Haftanstalten Buchenwald, No. 10, 85f.

25 Schmitz was an exception among the camp doctors. He was a member of the NSDAP from 1932 to 1937 but was never a member of the SS. In 1943, he was sterilized and released from military service after a hereditary illness court found him to be manic-depressive. Reichsarzt SS Ernst-Robert Grawitz arranged for Schmitz to serve as a civilian in Flossenbürg concentration camp, where he was chief of surgery from May 1944 to May 1945. Heinrich Schmitz, affidavit, Aug. 25, 1947, NARA, RG 549, US Army Europe, Executee Files, Box 12, file on Heinrich Schmitz. On Dec. 12, 1947, a US military tribunal sentenced Schmitz to death; he was executed on November 26, 1948. The SS doctor in Flossenbürg from October 1944 to March 1945 was SS-Obersturmbannführer Hermann Fischer. BArchB (ehem. BDC), SSO, Fischer, Hermann, 22.03.1883.

26 Nossen was administratively subordinate to Leitmeritz. Approximately 650 prisoners were transferred to Nossen between November 1944 and April 1945. Ulrich Fritz, "Nossen," in Benz and Distel, *Der Ort des Terrors,* vol. 4 (Flossenbürg, Mauthausen, Ravensbrück), 210–13.

27 The sub-camps he visited in November 1944 were Lengenfeld, Zwickau, Chemnitz, Nossen, Mittweida, Dresden, Zschachwitz, Rabstein, Leitmeritz, and Holleischen. Heinrich Schmitz, affidavit, Jan. 3, 1946. NARA, RG 549, US Army Europe, Executee Files, Box 12, file on Heinrich Schmitz.

28 Letter from SS NCO Wetterau to the Kommandatur Flossenbürg, Nov. 25, 1944, Centre d'Études et de Documentation Guerre et Société Contemporaines, Brussels (CEGESOMA), microfilm 14368+.

29 Report by Karl Groß to SS-WVHA Amt D III, Dec. 23, 1943, Archive of the Directie-generaal Oorlogsslachtoffers, Archief- en documentatiedienst, Brussels, 1546/Ding-Schuler.

30 See, e.g., the report on ill and recuperating prisoners prepared by Albert Schwartz, supervisor of the labor detail in Buchenwald, for Rudolf Höß, March 20, 1945, ThHStAW, KZ und Haftanstalten Buchenwald, No. 10, 393.

31 Letter from Robert Nitsch, supervisor of the labor detail in the Natzweiler camp, to the camp commandant, Nov. 4, 1944, International Tracing Service Bad Arolsen (ITS), HIST/SACH, Natzweiler, Folder 7, 243.

32 Testimony of Friedrich Entress, Jan. 29, 1946, NARA, RG 549, US Army Europe, Cases tried, Case 000-50-5 (Mauthausen), Box 345, Folder No. 3, Prosecution Exhibit No. P-83.

33 Rudolf Höß, *Kommandant in Auschwitz. Autobiographische Aufzeichnungen*, ed. Martin Broszat (Munich, 2000), 250.

34 Letter from Richard Glücks to the commandant of Auschwitz III (Monowitz), Heinrich Schwarz, Oct. 26, 1944, NARA, RG 549, US Army Europe, Cases not tried, Case 000-50-011 (Ravensbrück), Box 523, Folder No. 5.

35 Höß, *Kommandant*, 205f.

36 Ibid.

37 This holds for the selection of registered concentration camp prisoners and does not apply to new arrivals. The Hungarian Jews deported to Auschwitz, for example, were classified upon arrival either as capable of working, in which case they were registered as prisoners and assigned a number, or as incapable of working, in which case they were sent to the gas chamber.

38 Letter from Gerhard Schiedlausky to Hermann Pister, Jan. 31, 1945, ThHStAW, NS 4/Bu-54, 138.

39 Ibid.

40 Testimony of Percival Treite, Oct. 3, 1946, TNA/PRO, WO 235/309, Exhibit No. 8.

41 Testimony of Percival Treite, May 5, 1945, ibid. On the mortality rate in Ravensbrück, see also the testimony of the former prisoner Danuta Tulmacka, May 13, 1945, NARA, RG 549, US Army Europe, Cases not tried, Case 000-50-011 (Ravensbrück), Box 522, Folder No. 3.

42 In July 1942, for example, the head of Amt D II, Gerhard Maurer, ordered the transfer of Josef Menzel, an imprisoned stone polisher, from Buchenwald to Mauthausen because Deutschen Erd- und Steinwerke GmbH had urgent need of his skills. Camp officials in Buchenwald thus arranged a transport for a single prisoner. Radio message from Gerhard Maurer to the Buchenwald concentration camp, July 6, 1942, and letter from the head of the Political Department of the Buchenwald Concentration Camp, SS-Hauptscharführer Fritz Stollberg, to Abteilung III, July 13, 1942, NARA, RG 549, US Army Europe, Cases tried, Case 000-50-9 (Buchenwald), Box 436, Folder No. 3. In another instance, Amtsgruppe D arranged for two porcelain workers to be transferred from Ravensbrück to Buchenwald: letter from Arthur Liebehenschel to the commandants of the Ravensbrück and Buchenwald Concentration Camps, Dec. 11, 1942, NARA, RG 549, US Army Europe, Cases tried, Case 000-50-9 (Buchenwald), Box 443, Folder No. 1.

43 For example, message regarding skilled workers between the head of Amt DII and the Buchenwald camp commandant, Oct. 1, 1942; response from Hermann Pister and Philip Grim to Amt DII of the SS-WVHA, Oct. 13, 1942. NARA, RG 549, US Army Europe, Cases tried; Case 000-50-9 (Buchenwald), Box 443, Folder No. 1.

44 Order from Vinzenz Schöttl to the sub-camps of Concentration Camp Auschwitz III, June 14, 1944, NARA, RG 549, US Army Europe, Cases not tried, Case 000-50-11 (Ravensbrück), Box 523, Folder 5.

45 Letter from Vinzenz Schöttl to the Golleschau sub-camp, Oct. 22, 1944, ibid.

46 List of more than 400 prisoners ("political Poles/Jews") received at the Buchenwald Concentration Camp from the Groß-Rosen Concentration Camp, Nov. 4, 1944, ITS, List Material, Groß-Rosen, Ordner 11, 20-26.

47 Biemann was, beside Karl Sommer, the most important staff member serving under the head of Amt D II, Gerhard Maurer and, from Jan. 1945 on, Hans Moser. BArchB (ehem. BDC), SSO, Biemann, Wilhelm, 09.12.1900.

48 OSRAM company record of "a telephone conversation with O.St.F. Biemann on Jan. 29, 1945 regarding prisoners," Landesarchiv Berlin (LAB), A Rep. 231, No. 0482, 179.

49 The SS used the terms *Bauhäftlinge* and *Fertigungshäftlinge*. Letter from Friedrich Hartjenstein, commandant of the Natzweiler Concentration Camp, to commando leader of the Thil-Longwy sub-camp, Eugen Büttner, July 11, 1944, ITS, HIST/SACH, Natzweiler, Folder 19, 42.

50 OSRAM company record on a phone conversation with Obersturmführer Biemann, Jan. 24, 1945, LAB, A Rep. 231, No. 0500, 197.

51 OSRAM company report on visits to Plauen (July 21-25, July 29, Aug. 1, 1944), Aug. 8, 1944, LAB, A Rep. 231, No. 0490, 133.

52 OSRAM company report on a visit to Plauen (Aug. 14–15, 1944), Aug. 21, 1944, LAB, A Rep. 231, No. 0490, 129.

53 OSRAM telegram regarding the transport of 250 prisoners from Auschwitz to Plauen, Sept. 13, 1944, LAB, A Rep. 231, No. 0489, 18.

54 OSRAM report on a meeting with the SS-WVHA Oranienburg (Oct. 3 1944), Oct. 4, 1944, LAB, A Rep. 231, No. 0502, 15.

55 OSRAM report on a meeting with the SS-WVHA (Nov. 13, 1944), Nov. 14, 1944, LAB, A Rep. 231, No. 0500, 210.

56 OSRAM report on "visit to the Flossenbürg concentration camp for the purpose of the discharge of prisoners," Jan. 3, 1945, LAB, A Rep. 231, No. 0500, 330.

57 OSRAM report on a meeting with the SS-WVHA (Nov. 13, 1944), Nov. 14, 1944, LAB, A Rep. 231, No. 0500, 210.

58 OSRAM, "Aktennotiz Richard II Nr. 47," Oct. 19, 1944, LAB, A Rep. 231, No. 0502, 121.

59 In mid-1944, Hitler gave Speer oversight of arms production and sweeping authority over the war economy. See the "Decree on the Concentration of Arms and War Production," June 6, 1944, BArchB, R 3/3286.

60 OSRAM report on a meeting with the SS-WVHA (Nov. 13, 1944), Nov. 14 1944, LAB, A Rep. 231, No. 0500, 210.

61 Letter from Hermann Pister to the commandant of the Bergen-Belsen concentration camp, Josef Kramer, Dec. 21, ITS, HIST/SACH, Buchenwald, Folder 48, 151.

62 Irmgard Seidel, "Raguhn" in Benz and Distel, *Der Ort des Terrors*, vol. 3, 551f.

63 Order Nr. 15, Stutthof Concentration Camp, Feb. 21, 1944, AMSt, I-IB-3.

64 Affidavit of Fritz Suhren, June 17, 1946, Nuremberg Document NI-091.

65 List, "Special Transport" 123 to the Ravensbrück Concentration Camp from Budapest (Nov. 22, 1944), Institut Pamięci Narodowej/Archiwum Głównej Komisji Badania Zbrodni przeciwko Narodowi Polskiemu/Archiv der Hauptkommission zur Erforschung der Verbrechen am polnischen Volk, Warschau (IPN/AGK), KL Ravensbrück, sygn. 75, k. 13-31. The transport consisted of 753 Hungarian Jewish women.

66 Eva Féjer, account of her experiences as a prisoner (Jan. 1956), Sammlungen Mahn- und Gedenkstätte Ravensbrück/Stiftung Brandenburgische Gedenkstätten (MGR/SBG), NL 28, 8.

67 Letter from Heinrich Schwarz, to the commanders of the Auschwitz III subcamps, Aug. 14, 1944, NARA, RG 549, US Army Europe, Cases not tried, Case 000-50-011 (Ravensbrück), Box 523, Folder No. 5.

68 Letter from Adlerwerke AG to the commandant of the Natzweiler Concentration Camp, Nov. 18, 1944, ITS, HIST/SACH, Natzweiler, Folder 19, 114.

69 See the "Overview of the Number and Deployment of Female Prisoners of the Bergen-Belsen Camp," March 15, 1945, signed by camp commandant Josef Kramer, TNA/PRO, WO 235/21, British Military Court War Crimes Trial, Bergen-Belsen & Auschwitz Concentration Camps Case, JAG No. 12, Vol. X, Exhibit No. 122. The listing of the work detail gives no information about the categorization of prisoners and does not distinguish between Jewish and non-Jewish prisoners. That was not a particularity of the final phase of the war. See, e.g., the mustering of a work detail of prisoners in the Mauthausen Concentration Camp, Nov. 11–17, 1941, ITS, HIST/SACH, Dokumente/Schriftwechsel zu Verfolgung/Haftstätten, Folder 11, 121.

70 Report of the Jägerstab, June 9, 1944, BArchB, R 3/1756, 47.

71 Letter from Richard Glücks to the commandant of Auschwitz III, Nov. 11, 1944 (copy), NARA, RG 549, US Army Europe, Cases not tried, Case 000-50-011 (Ravensbrück), Box 523, Folder No. 6.

72 Prisoner transfer from the Ravensbrück Concentration Camp to the "Schonungslager Mittwerda," Apr. 6, 1945, IPN/AGK, KL Ravensbrück, sygn. 15.

73 Mahn- und Gedenkstätte Ravensbrück (ed.), *Gedenkbuch für die Opfer des Konzentrationslagers Ravensbrück 1939–1945*, compiled by Bärbel Schindler-Saefkow and Monika Schnell (Berlin, 2005), 49.

74 Testimony of Percival Treite, May 5, 1945, TNA/PRO, WO 235/309, Exhibit No. 8; Linde Apel, *Jüdische Frauen im Konzentrationslager Ravensbrück 1939–1945* (Berlin, 2003), 336f., 352f.

75 Stefan Hördler, "Die Schlussphase des Konzentrationslagers Ravensbrück. Personalpolitik und Vernichtung," *Zeitschrift für die Geschichtswissenschaft* 56 (2008), 222–48, here 239f.

76 Order from the Arbeitsdienst of the Ravensbrück Concentration Camp to the block elders, Sept. 1 1944, IPN/AGK, KL Ravensbrück, sygn. 1, 4.

77 Germaine Tillion, *Frauenkonzentrationslager Ravensbrück* (Frankfurt, 2001; first published in French, 1973), 258–78.

78 Card index of SS camp guards, 1933-1939/41, BArchB, NS 3/1566-1569. Data on camp guards compiled by the author, Oct. 28, 2012.

79 Execution petition from Walter Ernstberger, head of protective detention camp within the Groß-Rosen camp, July 6, 1944, Nuremberg Document PS-1234.

80 Circular from Gottlob Berger to the Waffen-SS, June 25, 1941, BArchB, NS 4/Hi-21, 792f.

81 Letter from the Training Department (D I/5) of the SS-WVHA to the Volksbund für das Deutschtum im Ausland, Oct. 2, 1943; memo on a meeting of Sept. 13, 1943, BArchB, NS 3/395, 100f.

82 On the staffing of the concentration camps, see the letter from Richard Glücks to the Department for Care of the Troops (Truppenbetreuung), Reich Ministry for Popular Enlightenment and Propaganda, Oct. 29, 1943, BArchB, NS 3/409, 136.

83 Letter from the Training Department (D I/5), SS-WVHA to SS headquarters, Sept. 9, 1943, BArchB, NS 3/395, Bl. 102.

84 Letter from Oswald Pohl to Heinrich Himmler, June 5, 1944, BArchB, NS 19/1922.

85 The Trawniki men were "foreign volunteers" (*fremdvölkische Hilfswillige*), mainly former Soviet POWs, Ukrainians, ethnic Germans (*Volksdeutsche*), and Balts. See Peter Black, "Foot soldiers of the Final Solution: The Trawniki training camp and Operation Reinhard," *Holocaust and Genocide Studies*, 25 (2011), 1–99.

86 Letter from Rudolf Höß to the Reich Ministry for Popular Enlightenment and Propaganda, March 28, 19444, BArchB, NS 3/395, Bl. 83.

87 Letter from Walter Unger, adjutant at the Stutthof Concentration Camp, Jan. 22, 1944, AMSt, I-ID-13.

88 Attachment to the special order on wartime leave for members of the Waffen-SS serving abroad, Jan. 7, 1944, AMSt, I-IB-3.

89 See the invoice for bordello visits "for Ukrainian guards" in the letter from Richard Glücks to concentration camp commandants, Dec. 15, 1943, BArchB, NS 3/426, 170.

90 Training of volkdeutsche SS-Freiwillige Stutthof: Order No. 81 (Nov. 11, 1943), AMSt, I-IB-2; training of Wehrmacht troops at Stuttfhoff: Order No. 46 (July 1944), AMSt, I-IB-3. Information service for the Stutthof subcamps (series 1-7), Oct. 17, 1944 - Jan.15, 1945, AMSt, I-IB-9.

91 Training for "Southeastern Specialists" (*Sachbearbeiter Südost*) took place from May 6 to May 11, 1944, in Vienna on order from Richard Glücks: Commandant's Order Nr. 28, Stutthof Concentration Camp, Apr. 24, 1944, AMSt, I-IB-3.

92 On ideological training and the integration of the new guards, see Stefan Hördler, *Ordnung und Inferno. Das KZ-System im letzten Kriegsjahr* (Göttingen, 2015), 182-7, 203-18.

93 Ibid., 218-30.

94 Daniel Blatman, *Die Todesmärsche 1944/45. Das letzte Kapitel des nationalsozialistischen Massenmords* (Reinbeck, 2011).

95 Danuta Drywa, *The Extermination of Jews in Stutthof Concentration Camp 1939–1945*, trans. Tomasz Gałązka (Gdańsk, 2004).

96 On Hoppe's defense strategy, see Karin Orth, *Die Konzentrationslager-SS. Sozialstrukturelle Analysen und biographische Studien* (Göttingen, 2000), 223f.

97 Hans Lamm (ed.), *Jeanette Wolf, Mit Bibel und Bebel. Ein Gedenkbuch* (Bonn, 1981), 49–67. Wolf's account of her concentration camp experiences were first published in 1947 under the title *Sadismus oder Wahnsinn* (Sadism or Insanity); excerpts reprinted in Hermann Kuhn (ed.), *Stutthof. Ein Konzentrationslager vor den Toren Danzigs* (Bremen, 2004; previously published Gdańsk, 1999), 133–7.

98 Saul Friedländer, *The Years of Extermination: Nazi Germany and the Jews, 1939–1945* (New York, 2008), 602.

Index

36775997R00318

Printed in Great Britain
by Amazon